THE ALMANAC OF HIGHER EDUCATION
1993

THE ALMANAC OF HIGHER EDUCATION
1993

The Editors of
The Chronicle of Higher Education

The University of Chicago Press
Chicago and London

The University of Chicago Press, Chicago 60637
The University of Chicago Press, Ltd., London

© 1993 by The Chronicle of Higher Education, Inc.
All rights reserved. Published 1993
Printed in the United States of America

International Standard Serial Number 1044-3096
International Standard Book Number 0-226-18458-7

∞The paper used in this publication meets the minimum requirements of the American National Standard for Information Sciences–Permanence of Paper for Printed Library Materials, ANSI Z39.48-1984.

CONTENTS

The Nation

INTRODUCTION 1-5

SUMMARY STATISTICS 6-14

MAPS

    Proportion of Adults With a Bachelor's Degree or Higher 15
    Projected Change in the Number of Public High-School Graduates 15
    High-School Dropout Rates 16
    Number of Colleges and Universities 16
    Proportion of College Students Who Are Minority-Group Members 17
    Proportion of College Students Who Are Enrolled Full Time 17
    Proportion of First-Time College Freshmen Enrolled
      on Campuses in Their Home States 18
    States' Share of Total U.S. College Enrollment 18
    Percentage Change in College Enrollment 19
    Percentage Change in State Appropriations for Higher Education 19

9 ISSUES AFFECTING COLLEGES 20-21

STUDENTS

    Average SAT Scores by Sex and Racial and Ethnic Group 22
    Average ACT Scores by Sex and Racial and Ethnic Group 22
    Student Financial Aid 23
    College Enrollment by Racial and Ethnic Group 24-25
    College Enrollment by Age of Students 26
    Administrators' Views on Changes in Enrollment
      and Student Characteristics 27
    Attitudes and Characteristics of Freshmen 28-31
    Proportion of Full-Time Students Receiving Financial Aid 32
    Colleges With the Most Freshman National Merit Scholars 33
    Earned Degrees Conferred 34-35
    Professional Degrees Conferred 34
    Degrees Conferred by Racial and Ethnic Group 36
    Number of Institutions Conferring Degrees 36
    Universities Awarding the Most Earned Doctorates 37
    Characteristics of Recipients of Doctorates 38-39
    Foreign Students' Countries of Origin 40
    Educational Attainment of the U.S. Population 40
    Institutions Enrolling the Most Foreign Students 41
    Campuses With the Largest Enrollments 42
    Educational Attainment of 1980 High-School Seniors by 1986 43

STUDENTS continued

    Projections of College Enrollment, High-School Graduates,
       and Degrees Conferred **44-47**
    Proportion of 18-to-24-Year-Olds Enrolled in College **46**
    Number of Colleges by Enrollment **48**

FACULTY AND STAFF

    Median Salaries of Administrators **49-51**
    Average Faculty Salaries **52-53**
    Average Faculty Salaries by Rank in Selected Fields **54-55**
    Characteristics of Full-Time College Professors **56-57**
    Faculty Attitudes and Activities **58-61**
    Changes in the Size of the Full-Time Faculty
       in the Next 5 Years **62**
    Employment Status of Faculty Members **63**
    Faculty Workloads **63**
    Full-Time Employees in Colleges and Universities **64**
    Median Salaries of Chief Executive and Academic Officers **64**
    Employment Policies and Perquisites for College Presidents **65**

RESOURCES

    Total Return on College Endowments **66**
    Top Fund Raisers **66**
    College and University Endowments Over $80-Million **67-69**
    Largest Endowments per Student **70**
    Voluntary Support for Higher Education **70**
    Revenues and Expenditures of Colleges and Universities **71**
    Average College Costs **72**
    Non-Profit Institutions Receiving the Largest Contracts
       From the Defense Department **72**
    Range of Tuition at Four-Year Institutions **73**
    Top Institutions in Total Research-and-Development Spending **74**

INSTITUTIONS

    Administrators' Views of Most-Important Campus Issues **75**
    Changes in Campus Operating Budgets **75**
    Campus Responses to Financial Pressures **76**
    Holdings of University Research Libraries **77-79**

The States

Alabama 81	Kentucky 154	North Dakota 227
Alaska 85	Louisiana 159	Ohio 231
Arizona 89	Maine 163	Oklahoma 236
Arkansas 93	Maryland 167	Oregon 240
California 98	Massachusetts 171	Pennsylvania 244
Colorado 104	Michigan 176	Rhode Island 249
Connecticut 108	Minnesota 180	South Carolina 253
Delaware 112	Mississippi 184	South Dakota 257
D.C. 116	Missouri 189	Tennessee 261
Florida 120	Montana 193	Texas 265
Georgia 125	Nebraska 197	Utah 270
Hawaii 130	Nevada 201	Vermont 274
Idaho 133	New Hampshire 205	Virginia 278
Illinois 137	New Jersey 209	Washington 282
Indiana 142	New Mexico 213	West Virginia 287
Iowa 146	New York 217	Wisconsin 291
Kansas 150	North Carolina 223	Wyoming 295

SOURCES AND NOTES 300-304

Enrollment by Race 305-367

The Nation

CONCERNS ABOUT money—where to find more and how to spend what's available—dominate higher education's agenda in academic 1992-93.

After months of bad news about budget shortfalls, layoffs, and program cuts, the nation's 3,500 colleges and universities approached the year warily.

Many institutions hope the worst financial pressures in nearly half a century are behind them. Others, such as the public institutions in economically troubled California, fear the worst is yet to come.

A dose of optimism was injected into this otherwise sobering picture with the election of Bill Clinton as President. Many college officials believe Mr. Clinton will make education a centerpiece of his economic strategy. They expect him to overhaul the student-loan program and put a stop to federal efforts to bar minority scholarships. Still, some officials say the tight budget will make it difficult for Mr. Clinton to find money for new programs.

On college campuses, the challenge that educators now face is how to insure student access and academic quality at a time when state appropriations, tuition revenues, and student aid are not likely to grow significantly.

"We're in for some very tough times for a fair number of years ahead," says Robert H. Atwell, president of the American Council on Education. "State fiscal problems will continue. To the extent that the states address those problems through tax increases, the line of competitors for those dollars is very long—and we're not necessarily at the front of it."

Such fiscal realities are driving what may be the most profound review of institutional priorities that many colleges have seen in a long time. Some are looking inward, considering how they can become better by becoming smaller. They will continue to review basic questions about their campuses: How many students can we afford to educate? How many doctoral and undergraduate programs can we afford to offer?

Some critics, however, say institutions are not going far enough in their efforts to cut costs and restructure their operations. These observers are calling for fundamental changes and are challenging such sacred cows as how faculty workloads are determined.

Many in academe say the problem is not faculty productivity but a rigid faculty-reward system that values research over teaching and service. On individual campuses the debate is intensifying over ways to reform the system of hiring and promoting faculty members.

Academics are reassessing the way they do business on a variety of fronts.

Accreditation is under close scrutiny: More and more people, from the U.S. Education Department to the campuses, are raising questions about its value.

Concerns about the quality of undergraduate education are receiving renewed attention. Reformers have called for smaller classes and more contact between tenured professors and students. Some campuses have announced plans to improve undergraduate education, but whether such efforts will be gutted by budget problems remains to be seen.

In this era of economic uncertainty, community colleges are taking on an increasingly important role in higher education. State cutbacks will bring lower enrollments at many four-year public institutions. Two-year colleges, which are already under stress as they deal with large numbers of "underprepared" and non–English-speaking students, will be the only option available to many people.

The outlook for significant increases in the federal government's student-aid programs is bleak. In reauthorizing the Higher Education Act, Congress agreed to increase the maximum Pell Grant that students can receive in 1993-94—if more funds become available. However, an education-appropriations bill signed by President Bush cut the maximum Pell Grant for 1993-94 to $2,300—a $100 decrease from current levels.

A lack of money is the common thread running through other issues affecting higher education at the federal level. Competition for scarce government dollars will continue to heat up this year among scientists. Despite some intense opposition, the $8.25-billion Superconducting Supercollider survived in the federal budget for 1992-93, but will probably face a tough fight again when the next budget is considered. Critics fear that spending billions of dollars on "big science" projects like the supercollider will siphon away money from smaller science programs.

TWO RECENT Supreme Court decisions are affecting college campuses in 1992-93.

The court set the stage for renewed political and judicial battles over desegregation in 19 Southern and border states when it ruled that Mississippi's public colleges were still illegally segregated. Educators and civil-rights leaders say the decision may force predominantly white institutions to take more steps to attract black students and faculty members. As for public black colleges, legal experts differ on whether the language in the decision will lead states to close some of these institutions or give them more financial support.

In Mississippi, a new desegregation plan proposed by the state would merge some colleges, close two professional schools, move academic programs to different institutions, and shift most graduate programs to the four largest universities. The plan is being hotly contested by almost everyone.

Meanwhile, a decision by the Supreme Court on "fighting words" will give rise to new debates about whether limits can and should be set on what people may say on college campuses. The Court ruled that it was unconstitutional for public entities to ban specific kinds of fighting words, defined as forms of speech that inflict injury or incite immediate violence. Many colleges adopted "hate speech" codes in recent years, following racial incidents on their campuses. Some colleges are drafting new speech codes to comply with the Court's decision, while others have concluded that their hate-speech policies would be upheld if challenged.

College sports programs face a different set of legal issues: how to comply with a law requiring them to provide equitable treatment for female athletes. In the last half of 1992, female students at several colleges filed lawsuits against their institutions, seeking reinstatement of women's sports teams that were cut. At least one of the lawsuits was successful in a federal district court. The National Collegiate Athletic Association created a special panel to determine what the NCAA and its member institutions should do to improve sports opportunities for women.

The dim financial outlook across academe will continue to put pressure on campus fund-raising staffs. At many colleges, the recession has affected the participation of alumni in their annual funds: Gifts have grown little, if at all. No similar drop-off has been seen in major gifts from wealthy donors.

The 1990's have proved to be a dynamic time for curricular and scholarly innovations. Multiculturalism will continue to influence scholars in the humanities and social sciences. The academic and publishing worlds are also seeing a surge of interest in gay and lesbian studies.

Among scientists, debate is raging over genetic research that makes connections between biology and aspects of human behavior, such as intelligence.

Despite some intriguing debates in both the humanities and the sciences, many administrators fear that sustaining faculty interest and vitality at a time of retrenchment will be a major challenge in 1992-93.

"Even if we've reached the trough nationally, there's no indication there's going to be any significant upswing," says Robert M. Rosenzweig, president of the Association of American Universities, "unless there are some large resources hidden somewhere that nobody knows about."

DEMOGRAPHICS

Population: 252,177,000

Age distribution:
Up to 17 .... 25.8%
18 to 24 .... 10.5%
25 to 44 .... 32.6%
45 and older 31.1%

Racial and ethnic distribution:
American Indian 0.8%
Asian 2.9%
Black 12.1%
White 80.3%
Other and unknown 3.9%
Hispanic (may be any race) .. 9.0%

Educational attainment of adults (highest level):
9th grade or less 10.4%
Some high school, no diploma 14.4%
High-school diploma 30.0%
Some college, no degree 18.7%
Associate degree 6.2%
Bachelor's degree 13.1%
Graduate or professional
  degree 7.2%

Proportion who speak a language other than English at home: 13.8%

Per-capita personal income: $19,092

Poverty rate:
All 13.1%
Under age 18 .... 18.3%
Age 18 and older 11.3%

New public high-school graduates in:
1992-93 (estimate) 2,215,070
2001-02 (estimate) 2,583,990

New GED diploma recipients: 461,849

High-school dropout rate: 11.2%

POLITICAL LEADERSHIP
President:
Bill Clinton (D), term ends 1997

Vice-President:
Al Gore (D), term ends 1997

COLLEGES AND UNIVERSITIES
Higher education:
Public 4-year institutions 595
Public 2-year institutions 972
Private 4-year institutions 1,546
Private 2-year institutions 446
Total 3,559

Vocational institutions: 6,455

FACULTY MEMBERS
Full-time faculty members by rank:
Professor 114,315
Associate professor 90,593
Assistant professor 90,841
Instructor 22,739
Lecturer 7,790
No rank 53,095
Total 379,373

Full-time faculty members with tenure:
Men 161,765
Women 50,207
Total 211,972

Average pay of full-time professors
Public 4-year institutions:
Professor $56,658
Associate professor $42,732
Assistant professor $35,511
Instructor $26,129
No rank $32,307
All $44,497

Public 2-year institutions:
Professor $45,412
Associate professor $38,040
Assistant professor $32,671
Instructor $28,637
No rank $37,086
All $37,064

Private 4-year institutions:
Professor $56,107
Associate professor $40,064
Assistant professor $33,208
Instructor $25,095
No rank $31,140
All $42,183

STUDENTS
Enrollment:
At public 4-year
  institutions 5,802,877
At public 2-year
  institutions 4,937,663
At private 4-year
  institutions 2,726,255
At private 2-year institutions 243,355
Undergraduate 11,862,910
Graduate 1,573,637
Professional 273,603
American Indian 102,618
Asian 554,803
Black 1,223,303
Hispanic 758,054
White 10,674,784
Foreign 396,588
Total 13,710,150

Enrollment highlights:
Women 54.4%
Full-time 56.7%

Minority 19.8%
Foreign 2.9%
10-year change in total
  enrollment .... Up 13.3%

Proportion of enrollment made up of minority students:
At public 4-year institutions . 17.3%
At public 2-year institutions . 22.5%
At private 4-year institutions   15.4%
At private 2-year institutions   26.6%

Degrees awarded:
Associate 454,679
Bachelor's 1,049,657
Master's 323,844
Doctorate 38,238
Professional 70,980

Residence of new students: 81% of all freshmen attended colleges in their home states.

Test scores: Students averaged 20.6 on the A.C.T. and 899 on the S.A.T.

Graduation rates at NCAA Division I institutions: 53%

MONEY

Average tuition and fees:
At public 4-year institutions . $1,888
At public 2-year institutions .. $824
At private 4-year institutions $9,083
At private 2-year institutions $5,570

Expenditures:
Public institutions . $85,770,530,000
Private institutions $48,885,041,000

State funds for higher-education operating expenses: $39,394,108,000
Two-year change: Down 1%

State spending on student aid:
Need-based: $1,773,990,000
Non–need-based: $219,954,000
Other: $341,195,000

Total spending on research and development by doctorate-granting universities: $16,057,003,000
Sources:
Federal government 58.9%
State and local governments .. 8.1%
Industry 6.9%
The institution itself 18.6%
Other 7.5%

Total federal spending on college- and university-based research and development: $9,031,047,000
Selected programs:
Department of Health and
  Human Services . $4,774,514,000
National Science
  Foundation $1,304,613,000
Department
  of Defense $1,196,888,000
Department
  of Agriculture $349,121,000
Department of Energy $512,376,000

The Nation: SUMMARY STATISTICS

	1991 population	Rank	1991 per-capita income	1990 poverty rate	1992-93 public high-school graduates	High-school dropout rate in 1990
Alabama	4,089,000	22	$15,518	18.3%	38,940	12.6%
Alaska	570,000	49	$21,067	9.0%	5,260	10.9%
Arizona	3,750,000	23	$16,579	15.7%	29,690	14.4%
Arkansas	2,372,000	33	$14,629	19.1%	25,500	11.4%
California	30,380,000	1	$20,847	12.5%	243,550	14.2%
Colorado	3,377,000	26	$19,358	11.7%	31,400	9.8%
Connecticut	3,291,000	27	$26,022	6.8%	25,670	9.0%
Delaware	680,000	46	$20,816	8.7%	5,440	10.4%
D.C.	598,000	48	$24,063	16.9%	2,790	13.9%
Florida	13,277,000	4	$18,992	12.7%	78,640	14.3%
Georgia	6,623,000	11	$17,436	14.7%	58,580	14.1%
Hawaii	1,135,000	40	$21,190	8.3%	9,490	7.5%
Idaho	1,039,000	42	$15,333	13.3%	12,280	10.4%
Illinois	11,543,000	6	$20,731	11.9%	102,330	10.6%
Indiana	5,610,000	14	$17,179	10.7%	56,790	11.4%
Iowa	2,795,000	30	$17,296	11.5%	30,890	6.6%
Kansas	2,495,000	32	$18,322	11.5%	25,160	8.7%
Kentucky	3,713,000	24	$15,626	19.0%	34,080	13.3%
Louisiana	4,252,000	21	$15,046	23.6%	33,600	12.5%
Maine	1,235,000	39	$17,454	10.8%	12,280	8.3%
Maryland	4,860,000	19	$22,189	8.3%	38,690	10.9%
Massachusetts	5,996,000	13	$23,003	8.9%	46,260	8.5%
Michigan	9,368,000	8	$18,655	13.1%	85,960	10.0%
Minnesota	4,432,000	20	$19,125	10.2%	48,530	6.4%
Mississippi	2,592,000	31	$13,328	25.2%	23,180	11.8%
Missouri	5,158,000	15	$17,928	13.3%	46,930	11.4%
Montana	808,000	44	$15,675	16.1%	9,220	8.1%
Nebraska	1,593,000	36	$17,718	11.1%	17,390	7.0%
Nevada	1,284,000	38	$19,783	10.2%	9,890	15.2%
New Hampshire	1,105,000	41	$21,760	6.4%	9,440	9.4%
New Jersey	7,760,000	9	$25,666	7.6%	62,070	9.6%
New Mexico	1,548,000	37	$14,644	20.6%	15,400	11.7%
New York	18,058,000	2	$22,471	13.0%	131,610	9.9%
North Carolina	6,737,000	10	$16,853	13.0%	60,720	12.5%
North Dakota	635,000	47	$15,605	14.4%	7,470	4.6%
Ohio	10,939,000	7	$17,770	12.5%	107,060	8.9%
Oklahoma	3,175,000	28	$15,541	16.7%	30,300	10.4%
Oregon	2,922,000	29	$17,575	12.4%	25,530	11.8%
Pennsylvania	11,961,000	5	$19,306	11.1%	101,700	9.1%
Rhode Island	1,004,000	43	$19,207	9.6%	7,280	11.1%
South Carolina	3,560,000	25	$15,467	15.4%	33,130	11.7%
South Dakota	703,000	45	$16,071	15.9%	7,700	7.7%
Tennessee	4,953,000	18	$16,486	15.7%	43,710	13.4%
Texas	17,349,000	3	$17,230	18.1%	174,660	12.9%
Utah	1,770,000	35	$14,625	11.4%	24,860	8.7%
Vermont	567,000	50	$17,997	9.9%	5,180	8.0%
Virginia	6,286,000	12	$20,082	10.2%	56,520	10.0%
Washington	5,018,000	16	$19,484	10.9%	46,340	10.6%
West Virginia	1,801,000	34	$14,301	19.7%	20,340	10.9%
Wisconsin	4,955,000	17	$17,939	10.7%	49,970	7.1%
Wyoming	460,000	51	$16,937	11.9%	5,670	6.9%
U.S.	252,177,000		$19,092	13.1%	2,215,070	11.2%

Note: U.S. figures may include data for service schools and outlying areas not shown separately. Sources and additional notes begin on Page 300.

Educational attainment of adults in 1990 (highest level)

	9th grade or less	Some high school no diploma	High-school diploma	Some college no degree	Associate degree	Bachelor's degree	Graduate degree
Alabama	13.7%	19.4%	29.4%	16.8%	5.0%	10.1%	5.5%
Alaska	5.1%	8.2%	28.7%	27.6%	7.2%	15.0%	8.0%
Arizona	9.0%	12.3%	26.1%	25.4%	6.8%	13.3%	7.0%
Arkansas	15.2%	18.4%	32.7%	16.6%	3.7%	8.9%	4.5%
California	11.2%	12.6%	22.3%	22.6%	7.9%	15.3%	8.1%
Colorado	5.6%	10.0%	26.5%	24.0%	6.9%	18.0%	9.0%
Connecticut	8.4%	12.4%	29.5%	15.9%	6.6%	16.2%	11.0%
Delaware	7.2%	15.3%	32.7%	16.9%	6.5%	13.7%	7.7%
D.C.	9.6%	17.3%	21.2%	15.6%	3.1%	16.1%	17.2%
Florida	9.5%	16.1%	30.1%	19.4%	6.6%	12.0%	6.3%
Georgia	12.0%	17.1%	29.6%	17.0%	5.0%	12.9%	6.4%
Hawaii	10.1%	9.8%	28.7%	20.1%	8.3%	15.8%	7.1%
Idaho	7.4%	12.9%	30.4%	24.2%	7.5%	12.4%	5.3%
Illinois	10.3%	13.5%	30.0%	19.4%	5.8%	13.6%	7.5%
Indiana	8.5%	15.8%	38.2%	16.6%	5.3%	9.2%	6.4%
Iowa	9.2%	10.7%	38.5%	17.0%	7.7%	11.7%	5.2%
Kansas	7.7%	11.0%	32.8%	21.9%	5.4%	14.1%	7.0%
Kentucky	19.0%	16.4%	31.8%	15.2%	4.1%	8.1%	5.5%
Louisiana	14.7%	17.0%	31.7%	17.2%	3.3%	10.5%	5.6%
Maine	8.8%	12.4%	37.1%	16.1%	6.9%	12.7%	6.1%
Maryland	7.9%	13.7%	28.1%	18.6%	5.2%	15.6%	10.9%
Massachusetts	8.0%	12.0%	29.7%	15.8%	7.2%	16.6%	10.6%
Michigan	7.8%	15.5%	32.3%	20.4%	6.7%	10.9%	6.4%
Minnesota	8.6%	9.0%	33.0%	19.0%	8.6%	15.6%	6.3%
Mississippi	15.6%	20.1%	27.5%	16.9%	5.2%	9.7%	5.1%
Missouri	11.6%	14.5%	33.1%	18.4%	4.5%	11.7%	6.1%
Montana	8.1%	10.9%	33.5%	22.1%	5.6%	14.1%	5.7%
Nebraska	8.0%	10.2%	34.7%	21.1%	7.1%	13.1%	5.9%
Nevada	6.0%	15.2%	31.5%	25.8%	6.2%	10.1%	5.2%
New Hampshire	6.7%	11.2%	31.7%	18.0%	8.1%	16.4%	7.9%
New Jersey	9.4%	13.9%	31.1%	15.5%	5.2%	16.0%	8.8%
New Mexico	11.4%	13.5%	28.7%	20.9%	5.0%	12.1%	8.3%
New York	10.2%	15.0%	29.5%	15.7%	6.5%	13.2%	9.9%
North Carolina	12.7%	17.3%	29.0%	16.8%	6.8%	12.0%	5.4%
North Dakota	15.0%	8.3%	28.0%	20.5%	10.0%	13.5%	4.5%
Ohio	7.9%	16.4%	36.3%	17.0%	5.3%	11.1%	5.9%
Oklahoma	9.8%	15.6%	30.5%	21.3%	5.0%	11.8%	6.0%
Oregon	6.2%	12.3%	28.9%	25.0%	6.9%	13.6%	7.0%
Pennsylvania	9.4%	15.9%	38.6%	12.9%	5.2%	11.3%	6.6%
Rhode Island	11.1%	16.9%	29.5%	15.0%	6.3%	13.5%	7.8%
South Carolina	13.6%	18.1%	29.5%	15.8%	6.3%	11.2%	5.4%
South Dakota	13.4%	9.5%	33.7%	18.8%	7.4%	12.3%	4.9%
Tennessee	16.0%	17.0%	30.0%	16.9%	4.2%	10.5%	5.4%
Texas	13.5%	14.4%	25.6%	21.1%	5.2%	13.9%	6.5%
Utah	3.4%	11.5%	27.2%	27.9%	7.8%	15.4%	6.8%
Vermont	8.7%	10.6%	34.6%	14.7%	7.2%	15.4%	8.9%
Virginia	11.2%	13.7%	26.6%	18.5%	5.5%	15.4%	9.1%
Washington	5.5%	10.7%	27.9%	25.0%	7.9%	15.9%	7.0%
West Virginia	16.8%	17.3%	36.6%	13.2%	3.8%	7.5%	4.8%
Wisconsin	9.5%	11.9%	37.1%	16.7%	7.1%	12.1%	5.6%
Wyoming	5.7%	11.2%	33.2%	24.2%	6.9%	13.1%	5.7%
U.S.	**10.4%**	**14.4%**	**30.0%**	**18.7%**	**6.2%**	**13.1%**	**7.2%**

The Nation: SUMMARY STATISTICS

	Number of institutions, 1990-91					Average pay of full-time faculty members, 1990-91		
	Public 4-year	Public 2-year	Private 4-year	Private 2-year	Total	Public 4-year	Public 2-year	Private 4-year
Alabama	18	37	18	14	87	$38,481	$33,240	$30,947
Alaska	3	0	3	1	7	$44,567	n/a	$29,948
Arizona	3	17	14	4	38	$45,918	$40,478	$32,438
Arkansas	10	10	10	5	35	$34,960	$26,811	$31,410
California	31	107	142	30	310	$55,380	$47,122	$48,804
Colorado	13	15	20	9	57	$43,262	$29,606	$42,974
Connecticut	7	17	20	3	47	$51,222	$43,335	$49,717
Delaware	2	3	5	0	10	$44,231	$37,175	$40,069
D.C.	2	0	15	0	17	$45,057	n/a	$48,393
Florida	9	28	47	17	101	$43,855	$32,294	$35,881
Georgia	20	29	30	16	95	$39,909	$31,709	$36,501
Hawaii	3	6	6	0	15	$47,053	$38,436	$26,068
Idaho	4	2	3	2	11	$36,649	$30,532	$27,890
Illinois	12	47	93	18	170	$42,447	$40,239	$44,388
Indiana	14	14	41	11	80	$41,975	$27,169	$40,268
Iowa	3	15	35	5	58	$47,944	$30,745	$34,196
Kansas	8	21	21	3	53	$39,869	$31,337	$25,263
Kentucky	8	14	25	15	62	$38,818	$28,463	$30,086
Louisiana	14	6	12	4	36	$36,705	$29,878	$41,362
Maine	8	6	12	5	31	$40,122	$31,775	$39,463
Maryland	14	19	21	3	57	$46,028	$40,313	$42,484
Massachusetts	14	17	71	14	116	$46,965	$35,873	$51,004
Michigan	15	29	50	3	97	$46,407	$32,793	$34,078
Minnesota	10	26	34	8	78	$44,975	$39,536	$37,351
Mississippi	9	20	12	5	46	$33,717	$28,195	$34,888
Missouri	13	14	55	11	93	$39,031	$34,915	$36,860
Montana	6	8	3	2	19	$34,404	$24,641	$26,680
Nebraska	7	11	15	1	34	$41,233	$27,393	$32,879
Nevada	2	4	1	2	9	$43,777	$36,434	$31,445
New Hampshire	5	7	12	4	28	$41,977	$30,582	$42,839
New Jersey	14	19	22	4	59	$50,329	$42,030	$47,557
New Mexico	6	16	5	1	28	$39,437	$27,768	$30,949
New York	42	48	186	48	324	$50,914	$43,373	$46,120
North Carolina	16	58	37	14	125	$43,035	$26,141	$35,798
North Dakota	6	9	4	1	20	$34,391	$29,438	$26,250
Ohio	25	36	65	28	154	$47,142	$34,951	$36,832
Oklahoma	14	15	13	6	48	$37,921	$30,342	$37,535
Oregon	8	13	24	1	46	$37,147	$33,724	$35,983
Pennsylvania	43	20	101	56	220	$44,618	$38,392	$43,805
Rhode Island	2	1	9	0	12	$46,351	$37,706	$49,161
South Carolina	12	21	20	11	64	$40,541	$27,649	$31,510
South Dakota	7	1	10	1	19	$33,607	$18,628	$27,442
Tennessee	10	14	42	21	87	$41,089	$30,509	$35,883
Texas	40	65	57	10	172	$41,351	$33,439	$40,273
Utah	4	5	2	4	15	$38,483	$28,606	$41,157
Vermont	4	2	13	3	22	$42,272	$27,546	$36,154
Virginia	15	24	33	11	83	$47,650	$35,361	$36,269
Washington	6	27	20	4	57	$43,780	$33,156	$36,647
West Virginia	12	4	9	3	28	$35,610	$27,610	$28,904
Wisconsin	13	17	28	3	61	$43,894	$37,699	$36,320
Wyoming	1	7	0	1	9	$42,133	$28,930	n/a
U.S.	595	972	1,546	446	3,559	$44,497	$37,064	$42,183

	Full-time faculty members, 1990-91	Degrees awarded, 1989-90			
		Associate	Bachelor's	Master's	Doctorate	Professional
Alabama	5,942	6,254	17,059	4,510	354	832
Alaska	757	603	1,043	324	8	0
Arizona	4,823	6,361	14,265	5,178	545	408
Arkansas	2,957	2,606	7,475	1,691	135	324
California	37,763	48,353	98,157	34,529	4,747	7,814
Colorado	5,391	6,144	16,435	5,099	718	794
Connecticut	5,594	4,721	14,179	6,285	572	956
Delaware	1,288	1,288	3,539	791	114	329
D.C.	3,352	403	7,449	5,122	535	2,467
Florida	13,038	33,718	35,494	10,802	1,251	2,138
Georgia	7,648	7,389	21,402	6,427	800	1,835
Hawaii	1,829	2,103	3,720	1,007	114	113
Idaho	1,517	2,979	3,169	790	90	124
Illinois	17,811	23,327	49,757	19,288	2,409	4,412
Indiana	8,985	8,947	27,625	7,407	1,040	1,443
Iowa	5,255	7,888	16,129	3,006	604	1,427
Kansas	4,659	5,547	12,428	3,309	346	566
Kentucky	5,249	5,387	12,225	3,681	320	1,127
Louisiana	6,006	2,642	15,905	3,993	405	1,459
Maine	1,923	1,859	4,944	731	34	162
Maryland	6,613	7,429	18,493	6,469	824	1,122
Massachusetts	15,571	13,316	43,559	17,827	2,122	3,657
Michigan	14,193	21,156	42,428	13,297	1,313	2,418
Minnesota	7,286	7,674	22,881	4,366	750	1,561
Mississippi	3,920	4,995	8,808	2,370	293	477
Missouri	7,215	6,909	24,628	8,607	619	2,283
Montana	1,342	782	3,862	709	71	71
Nebraska	2,767	2,678	8,677	1,713	230	658
Nevada	1,128	949	2,235	543	38	49
New Hampshire	1,918	2,512	6,745	1,944	83	165
New Jersey	8,485	9,935	22,859	7,246	855	1,763
New Mexico	2,222	2,455	5,022	1,838	223	179
New York	34,459	48,814	89,067	37,150	3,805	7,145
North Carolina	9,675	10,647	27,288	6,015	861	1,597
North Dakota	1,381	1,875	4,202	620	71	109
Ohio	15,569	17,547	47,017	13,051	1,696	3,071
Oklahoma	4,460	6,204	13,601	3,943	408	923
Oregon	4,652	4,769	12,586	3,276	452	928
Pennsylvania	20,665	17,760	60,495	14,821	2,036	3,462
Rhode Island	2,697	3,495	8,789	1,795	190	82
South Carolina	5,520	5,202	13,215	3,828	342	587
South Dakota	1,135	791	3,617	769	44	102
Tennessee	7,270	5,642	17,577	4,839	626	1,289
Texas	22,095	22,828	60,472	18,047	2,268	4,109
Utah	3,337	3,750	10,907	2,479	361	380
Vermont	1,504	1,262	4,517	1,002	59	87
Virginia	9,974	8,378	27,119	7,159	839	1,732
Washington	6,847	14,319	18,359	5,284	632	852
West Virginia	2,552	2,841	7,414	1,740	128	302
Wisconsin	10,112	8,549	25,888	5,599	784	1,023
Wyoming	1,022	1,629	1,646	361	58	67
U.S.	379,373	454,679	1,049,657	323,844	38,238	70,980

The Nation: SUMMARY STATISTICS

Enrollment, fall 1990

	Public 4-year	Public 2-year	Private 4-year	Private 2-year	Under-graduate	Graduate	Pro-fessional
Alabama	123,848	72,091	17,799	3,812	194,269	20,225	3,056
Alaska	27,792	0	1,647	394	28,593	1,240	0
Arizona	95,657	153,143	13,980	1,955	236,505	26,792	1,438
Arkansas	61,408	17,237	9,799	1,981	82,506	6,364	1,555
California	496,757	1,057,921	203,820	11,499	1,569,383	169,074	31,540
Colorado	128,616	72,037	21,719	4,759	191,300	32,806	3,025
Connecticut	64,920	44,562	57,470	1,578	133,442	31,878	3,210
Delaware	23,424	10,828	7,752	0	36,822	3,309	1,873
D.C.	12,595	0	68,074	0	49,860	22,525	8,284
Florida	176,989	262,829	91,939	6,632	478,315	52,508	7,566
Georgia	141,106	55,307	46,368	9,029	214,413	29,605	7,792
Hawaii	23,085	19,979	10,708	0	46,920	6,408	444
Idaho	35,709	5,606	2,338	8,228	44,683	6,692	506
Illinois	198,464	352,869	168,953	8,960	623,525	88,688	17,033
Indiana	186,318	36,611	56,441	3,645	246,902	30,770	5,343
Iowa	67,957	49,877	50,352	2,329	144,984	19,452	6,079
Kansas	90,164	58,953	13,280	978	142,003	19,209	2,163
Kentucky	106,421	40,674	24,982	5,775	155,271	18,093	4,488
Louisiana	136,635	21,655	26,067	2,242	160,555	20,271	5,773
Maine	34,616	6,884	14,262	1,424	51,787	4,771	628
Maryland	110,830	109,953	38,174	743	219,707	36,207	3,786
Massachusetts	110,031	74,641	220,711	13,491	333,956	72,005	12,913
Michigan	259,879	227,480	79,599	2,845	500,739	58,624	10,440
Minnesota	133,622	65,589	50,224	4,354	222,683	25,361	5,745
Mississippi	58,781	50,257	10,640	3,205	110,333	10,415	2,135
Missouri	125,270	74,823	85,310	4,004	245,658	34,368	9,381
Montana	28,015	3,850	3,046	965	32,187	3,479	210
Nebraska	60,692	33,922	17,885	332	97,878	12,210	2,743
Nevada	29,424	31,818	313	173	56,215	5,333	180
New Hampshire	23,799	8,364	24,546	2,801	50,942	7,885	683
New Jersey	137,691	123,910	58,672	3,674	276,320	41,464	6,163
New Mexico	48,013	35,486	1,917	180	74,853	10,133	610
New York	359,381	248,392	399,282	28,268	842,045	167,024	26,254
North Carolina	148,698	136,559	61,522	5,211	316,240	29,686	6,064
North Dakota	27,277	7,413	2,980	208	35,214	2,169	495
Ohio	288,809	136,787	111,493	17,698	480,616	62,155	12,016
Oklahoma	92,945	58,128	17,758	4,390	149,148	20,741	3,332
Oregon	68,500	76,827	21,080	234	146,982	15,970	3,689
Pennsylvania	235,271	108,207	214,417	46,165	514,387	75,979	13,694
Rhode Island	25,730	16,620	35,923	0	68,499	9,467	307
South Carolina	81,303	49,831	23,787	4,381	139,982	16,829	2,491
South Dakota	26,451	145	7,363	249	30,197	3,564	447
Tennessee	109,944	65,105	46,032	5,157	198,709	22,285	5,244
Texas	417,777	384,537	94,305	4,818	788,613	96,926	15,898
Utah	57,529	28,579	33,687	1,508	110,637	9,464	1,202
Vermont	16,075	4,835	13,462	2,026	31,646	4,137	615
Virginia	160,200	131,086	57,899	4,257	302,072	45,177	6,193
Washington	81,433	146,199	33,503	2,143	240,208	19,922	3,148
West Virginia	63,362	10,746	7,880	2,802	74,660	8,839	1,291
Wisconsin	152,691	100,838	45,095	1,150	266,775	29,452	3,547
Wyoming	12,517	18,106	0	703	28,212	2,894	220
U.S.	5,802,877	4,937,663	2,726,255	243,355	11,862,910	1,573,637	273,603

	Enrollment, fall 1990		Minority enrollment, fall 1990			Enrollment highlights, fall 1990		
	Total	Public 4-year	Public 2-year	Private 4-year	Private 2-year	Woman students	Full-time students	Foreign students
Alabama	217,550	18.6%	19.9%	45.5%	46.7%	54.6%	68.3%	2.1%
Alaska	29,833	16.9%	n/a	20.7%	39.1%	59.8%	36.5%	1.6%
Arizona	264,735	15.1%	23.1%	21.5%	28.7%	53.6%	43.8%	2.6%
Arkansas	90,425	15.6%	14.4%	12.5%	37.3%	57.2%	71.9%	1.6%
California	1,769,997	34.5%	34.7%	25.0%	46.9%	54.0%	44.3%	3.7%
Colorado	227,131	12.4%	16.9%	12.4%	22.3%	53.2%	53.1%	2.0%
Connecticut	168,530	9.4%	16.7%	12.3%	12.5%	56.6%	50.5%	2.9%
Delaware	42,004	13.9%	18.6%	11.8%	n/a	56.7%	60.4%	1.9%
D.C.	80,669	91.6%	n/a	33.4%	n/a	53.3%	62.2%	11.2%
Florida	538,389	23.0%	23.3%	26.1%	35.0%	55.0%	49.5%	3.0%
Georgia	251,810	18.4%	22.1%	36.7%	32.1%	54.4%	66.3%	2.3%
Hawaii	53,772	71.0%	74.3%	46.0%	n/a	53.3%	58.3%	6.8%
Idaho	51,881	5.4%	4.1%	5.0%	3.2%	54.2%	66.9%	2.6%
Illinois	729,246	20.3%	28.1%	19.3%	44.4%	54.6%	50.1%	2.1%
Indiana	283,015	8.6%	9.7%	8.8%	12.2%	52.7%	64.6%	2.6%
Iowa	170,515	5.9%	4.2%	5.3%	4.8%	53.4%	70.4%	4.0%
Kansas	163,375	8.4%	10.4%	10.7%	37.5%	55.1%	57.3%	3.3%
Kentucky	177,852	7.7%	7.4%	4.7%	15.0%	58.1%	64.0%	1.3%
Louisiana	186,599	27.3%	30.9%	31.6%	34.9%	56.7%	71.7%	2.4%
Maine	57,186	1.7%	2.7%	3.7%	0.8%	57.9%	56.8%	0.7%
Maryland	259,700	27.9%	24.2%	14.4%	16.3%	56.6%	46.3%	2.9%
Massachusetts	418,874	8.0%	13.4%	13.4%	17.4%	55.1%	62.6%	5.0%
Michigan	569,803	13.0%	14.6%	18.2%	18.9%	55.1%	50.8%	2.5%
Minnesota	253,789	5.0%	5.6%	5.3%	6.9%	54.9%	60.1%	2.2%
Mississippi	122,883	30.8%	25.8%	31.4%	44.7%	56.4%	75.9%	1.6%
Missouri	289,407	9.6%	13.2%	11.7%	24.2%	54.8%	56.3%	2.3%
Montana	35,876	4.4%	22.2%	5.7%	74.9%	52.9%	73.2%	2.0%
Nebraska	112,831	4.9%	6.0%	7.1%	11.8%	54.9%	55.7%	1.8%
Nevada	61,728	13.4%	19.2%	1.0%	15.8%	56.3%	29.9%	1.4%
New Hampshire	59,510	1.9%	2.1%	5.7%	5.2%	54.5%	62.9%	1.4%
New Jersey	323,947	22.7%	23.7%	18.1%	35.3%	55.1%	50.2%	3.8%
New Mexico	85,596	33.2%	43.6%	29.4%	44.7%	55.6%	52.8%	1.7%
New York	1,035,323	30.0%	21.8%	19.2%	41.5%	55.8%	62.3%	4.6%
North Carolina	351,990	21.4%	20.1%	21.2%	35.1%	56.0%	63.4%	1.4%
North Dakota	37,878	3.5%	14.2%	5.5%	100.0%	49.4%	79.8%	3.1%
Ohio	554,787	10.0%	11.8%	11.1%	19.7%	53.2%	61.0%	2.5%
Oklahoma	173,221	15.9%	15.9%	14.4%	28.1%	53.8%	59.4%	3.1%
Oregon	166,641	9.0%	7.6%	8.5%	6.8%	52.9%	56.8%	4.6%
Pennsylvania	604,060	10.1%	13.2%	8.5%	24.7%	54.0%	63.0%	2.4%
Rhode Island	78,273	5.7%	9.9%	9.3%	n/a	54.6%	63.4%	2.6%
South Carolina	159,302	17.6%	24.4%	25.3%	43.9%	56.5%	68.5%	1.5%
South Dakota	34,208	5.6%	85.5%	12.0%	0.4%	56.0%	71.4%	1.9%
Tennessee	226,238	15.1%	15.4%	17.4%	26.4%	54.4%	65.1%	1.9%
Texas	901,437	27.7%	33.1%	22.6%	42.5%	53.3%	54.5%	2.7%
Utah	121,303	5.9%	8.8%	2.0%	9.7%	48.8%	64.0%	3.9%
Vermont	36,398	3.8%	1.1%	6.2%	1.6%	56.8%	68.0%	2.0%
Virginia	353,442	19.4%	18.0%	19.3%	42.7%	55.3%	55.4%	1.7%
Washington	263,278	13.9%	12.3%	11.4%	15.4%	55.9%	57.0%	2.0%
West Virginia	84,790	5.4%	3.6%	5.7%	7.3%	55.4%	68.5%	1.9%
Wisconsin	299,774	6.1%	9.6%	8.4%	2.3%	54.7%	63.6%	2.1%
Wyoming	31,326	5.5%	6.1%	n/a	6.6%	56.3%	54.0%	1.8%
U.S.	**13,710,150**	**17.3%**	**22.5%**	**15.4%**	**26.6%**	**54.4%**	**56.7%**	**2.9%**

The Nation: SUMMARY STATISTICS

	Test scores 1991 A.C.T. 1992 S.A.T.	Score	Public 4-year	Public 2-year	Private 4-year	Private 2-year
Alabama	A.C.T.	19.8	$1,593	$689	$5,942	$4,148
Alaska	S.A.T.	908	$1,382	n/a	$5,842	$10,400
Arizona	A.C.T.	20.9	$1,478	$579	$4,660	$8,977
Arkansas	A.C.T.	19.9	$1,418	$648	$4,464	$2,482
California	S.A.T.	900	$1,220	$114	$10,863	$7,942
Colorado	A.C.T.	21.3	$1,919	$943	$9,516	$6,731
Connecticut	S.A.T.	900	$2,313	$972	$12,315	$8,586
Delaware	S.A.T.	895	$2,910	$936	$5,831	n/a
D.C.	S.A.T.	842	$664	n/a	$11,939	n/a
Florida	S.A.T.	884	$1,337	$788	$7,992	$4,751
Georgia	S.A.T.	842	$1,680	$946	$7,542	$4,457
Hawaii	S.A.T.	878	$1,290	$413	$4,448	n/a
Idaho	A.C.T.	21.1	$1,189	$802	$7,203	$1,609
Illinois	A.C.T.	20.8	$2,465	$906	$8,853	$5,279
Indiana	S.A.T.	868	$2,067	$1,423	$8,451	$6,756
Iowa	A.C.T.	21.7	$1,880	$1,298	$8,703	$5,119
Kansas	A.C.T.	21.1	$1,569	$748	$5,997	$4,135
Kentucky	A.C.T.	20.0	$1,444	$771	$5,200	$4,662
Louisiana	A.C.T.	19.4	$1,791	$852	$9,783	$5,671
Maine	S.A.T.	882	$2,263	$1,497	$10,928	$3,899
Maryland	S.A.T.	907	$2,287	$1,244	$10,698	$6,101
Massachusetts	S.A.T.	902	$2,580	$1,528	$12,446	$7,750
Michigan	A.C.T.	n/a	$2,635	$1,124	$6,885	$4,749
Minnesota	A.C.T.	21.4	$2,216	$1,578	$9,507	$7,664
Mississippi	A.C.T.	18.6	$1,927	$722	$5,238	$3,721
Missouri	A.C.T.	21.0	$1,733	$891	$7,487	$5,208
Montana	A.C.T.	21.6	$1,553	$964	$5,565	$1,140
Nebraska	A.C.T.	21.2	$1,592	$990	$6,893	n/a
Nevada	A.C.T.	20.9	$1,275	$651	$6,200	n/a
New Hampshire	S.A.T.	923	$3,110	$1,899	$11,154	$5,547
New Jersey	S.A.T.	891	$2,860	$1,235	$10,281	$5,874
New Mexico	A.C.T.	20.1	$1,409	$536	$8,187	$3,594
New York	S.A.T.	882	$1,587	$1,419	$10,340	$5,926
North Carolina	S.A.T.	855	$1,112	$334	$7,826	$4,964
North Dakota	A.C.T.	20.7	$1,930	$1,584	$5,389	n/a
Ohio	A.C.T.	20.9	$2,622	$1,768	$8,729	$6,093
Oklahoma	A.C.T.	20.1	$1,340	$864	$5,852	$5,732
Oregon	S.A.T.	925	$1,906	$794	$9,606	$7,570
Pennsylvania	S.A.T.	877	$3,401	$1,505	$9,848	$6,314
Rhode Island	S.A.T.	881	$2,311	$1,100	$10,885	n/a
South Carolina	S.A.T.	831	$2,317	$813	$6,434	$5,110
South Dakota	A.C.T.	21.0	$1,854	$1,920	$6,346	$4,515
Tennessee	A.C.T.	20.1	$1,518	$848	$6,889	$4,203
Texas	S.A.T.	876	$986	$495	$6,497	$4,394
Utah	A.C.T.	21.0	$1,524	$1,173	$2,182	$4,319
Vermont	S.A.T.	897	$4,092	$2,424	$10,649	$6,768
Virginia	S.A.T.	893	$2,691	$867	$7,621	$4,852
Washington	S.A.T.	916	$1,823	$844	$9,463	$6,743
West Virginia	A.C.T.	19.8	$1,543	$930	$8,751	$2,767
Wisconsin	A.C.T.	21.7	$1,951	$1,234	$8,237	$4,768
Wyoming	A.C.T.	21.2	$1,148	$662	n/a	$7,500
U.S.	**A.C.T./S.A.T.**	**20.6/899**	**$1,888**	**$824**	**$9,083**	**$5,570**

	Expenditures, 1989-90		State appropriations, 1992-93	
	Public institutions	Private institutions	Total	2-year change
Alabama	$1,831,657,000	$229,369,000	$824,000,000	+1%
Alaska	$268,057,000	$20,050,000	$174,118,000	−7%
Arizona	$1,446,388,000	$90,409,000	$605,267,000	+1%
Arkansas	$751,336,000	$108,888,000	$411,827,000	+25%
California	$11,230,941,000	$5,077,597,000	$4,841,606,000	−12%
Colorado	$1,374,188,000	$250,811,000	$529,158,000	+4%
Connecticut	$811,282,000	$1,193,877,000	$486,239,000	−7%
Delaware	$342,119,000	$43,184,000	$122,469,000	+4%
D.C.	$111,468,000	$1,873,297,000	n/a	n/a
Florida	$2,766,267,000	$1,162,843,000	$1,415,262,000	−9%
Georgia	$1,769,744,000	$1,099,658,000	$951,726,000	−1%
Hawaii	$424,473,000	$35,223,000	$341,693,000	+9%
Idaho	$314,398,000	$69,032,000	$192,609,000	+5%
Illinois	$3,310,763,000	$3,544,542,000	$1,718,849,000	−1%
Indiana	$2,186,604,000	$773,866,000	$894,242,000	+2%
Iowa	$1,617,626,000	$490,214,000	$601,983,000	+3%
Kansas	$1,131,558,000	$135,958,000	$465,860,000	+3%
Kentucky	$1,236,680,000	$251,329,000	$621,794,000	+2%
Louisiana	$1,286,648,000	$531,135,000	$620,791,000	+6%
Maine	$334,435,000	$186,175,000	$172,985,000	−7%
Maryland	$1,576,934,000	$1,356,011,000	$788,159,000	−3%
Massachusetts	$1,357,588,000	$4,922,923,000	$625,380,000	−10%
Michigan	$4,076,519,000	$637,849,000	$1,539,460,000	+4%
Minnesota	$1,802,133,000	$753,255,000	$965,288,000	−4%
Mississippi	$922,574,000	$93,959,000	$437,215,000	+3%
Missouri	$1,349,451,000	$1,340,923,000	$590,483,000	0%
Montana	$218,231,000	$27,990,000	$125,863,000	+8%
Nebraska	$762,480,000	$226,173,000	$358,591,000	+9%
Nevada	$281,018,000	$3,893,000	$207,572,000	+27%
New Hampshire	$259,157,000	$363,330,000	$74,026,000	+1%
New Jersey	$2,165,562,000	$944,968,000	$1,177,880,000	+10%
New Mexico	$828,157,000	$28,022,000	$364,895,000	+9%
New York	$5,058,750,000	$7,640,442,000	$2,689,086,000	−5%
North Carolina	$2,420,825,000	$1,599,803,000	$1,541,926,000	+4%
North Dakota	$357,832,000	$25,646,000	$145,535,000	+12%
Ohio	$3,726,135,000	$1,402,876,000	$1,376,490,000	−7%
Oklahoma	$973,213,000	$262,526,000	$557,532,000	+12%
Oregon	$1,219,341,000	$256,067,000	$485,482,000	+16%
Pennsylvania	$3,390,869,000	$4,437,071,000	$1,388,920,000	0%
Rhode Island	$287,194,000	$486,764,000	$118,911,000	−7%
South Carolina	$1,324,647,000	$297,112,000	$633,379,000	−1%
South Dakota	$184,153,000	$79,252,000	$104,472,000	+16%
Tennessee	$1,519,680,000	$1,005,210,000	$747,525,000	+5%
Texas	$5,604,164,000	$1,397,222,000	$2,802,348,000	+9%
Utah	$914,771,000	$252,753,000	$345,888,000	+13%
Vermont	$260,371,000	$245,813,000	$54,912,000	−3%
Virginia	$2,682,902,000	$609,665,000	$934,776,000	−13%
Washington	$1,922,673,000	$330,200,000	$909,892,000	+6%
West Virginia	$493,825,000	$96,910,000	$284,606,000	+3%
Wisconsin	$2,307,325,000	$588,850,000	$902,988,000	+7%
Wyoming	$227,131,000	$4,104,000	$122,152,000	−2%
U.S.	$85,770,530,000	$48,885,041,000	$39,394,108,000	−1%

The Nation: SUMMARY STATISTICS

	State spending on student aid, 1991-92	Research spending by universities fiscal 1990	Federal funds for college- and university-based research, fiscal 1990
Alabama	$13,191,000	$239,556,000	$129,701,000
Alaska	$2,630,000	$65,571,000	$25,060,000
Arizona	$3,328,000	$260,187,000	$115,683,000
Arkansas	$8,031,000	$48,861,000	$23,586,000
California	$221,368,000	$2,007,361,000	$1,317,370,000
Colorado	$26,294,000	$249,958,000	$168,905,000
Connecticut	$35,842,000	$298,076,000	$189,462,000
Delaware	$1,669,000	$40,119,000	$17,922,000
D.C.	$1,010,000	$112,146,000	$78,658,000
Florida	$72,674,000	$433,413,000	$181,474,000
Georgia	$21,913,000	$445,011,000	$175,024,000
Hawaii	$661,000	$76,525,000	$48,276,000
Idaho	$759,000	$36,570,000	$10,381,000
Illinois	$209,489,000	$647,863,000	$351,598,000
Indiana	$50,963,000	$240,696,000	$138,349,000
Iowa	$61,877,000	$232,147,000	$106,735,000
Kansas	$6,613,000	$114,651,000	$44,005,000
Kentucky	$27,519,000	$90,880,000	$38,185,000
Louisiana	$15,214,000	$207,038,000	$69,265,000
Maine	$5,044,000	$23,605,000	$10,197,000
Maryland	$22,236,000	$977,593,000	$589,856,000
Massachusetts	$39,989,000	$898,808,000	$635,891,000
Michigan	$83,477,000	$527,070,000	$274,276,000
Minnesota	$79,273,000	$292,046,000	$141,748,000
Mississippi	$1,246,000	$85,229,000	$36,277,000
Missouri	$19,900,000	$281,133,000	$169,883,000
Montana	$395,000	$34,980,000	$13,041,000
Nebraska	$2,352,000	$105,373,000	$29,379,000
Nevada	$377,000	$38,301,000	$23,111,000
New Hampshire	$1,544,000	$69,731,000	$52,386,000
New Jersey	$119,505,000	$319,797,000	$139,264,000
New Mexico	$13,841,000	$151,927,000	$69,397,000
New York	$463,543,000	$1,410,700,000	$851,970,000
North Carolina	$65,325,000	$441,860,000	$305,255,000
North Dakota	$1,924,000	$29,966,000	$22,429,000
Ohio	$85,668,000	$457,189,000	$252,157,000
Oklahoma	$38,828,000	$130,650,000	$35,866,000
Oregon	$11,852,000	$171,550,000	$95,772,000
Pennsylvania	$159,181,000	$829,518,000	$536,674,000
Rhode Island	$9,561,000	$82,634,000	$51,828,000
South Carolina	$18,224,000	$137,269,000	$42,705,000
South Dakota	$570,000	$14,342,000	$5,791,000
Tennessee	$19,291,000	$232,121,000	$133,724,000
Texas	$135,966,000	$1,123,816,000	$469,460,000
Utah	$11,838,000	$187,076,000	$122,880,000
Vermont	$11,302,000	$45,162,000	$31,687,000
Virginia	$26,620,000	$321,547,000	$166,017,000
Washington	$24,359,000	$312,169,000	$240,010,000
West Virginia	$14,723,000	$46,946,000	$22,240,000
Wisconsin	$45,722,000	$363,364,000	$198,712,000
Wyoming	$220,000	$22,831,000	$9,731,000
U. S.	$2,335,139,000	$16,057,003,000	$9,031,047,000

The Nation

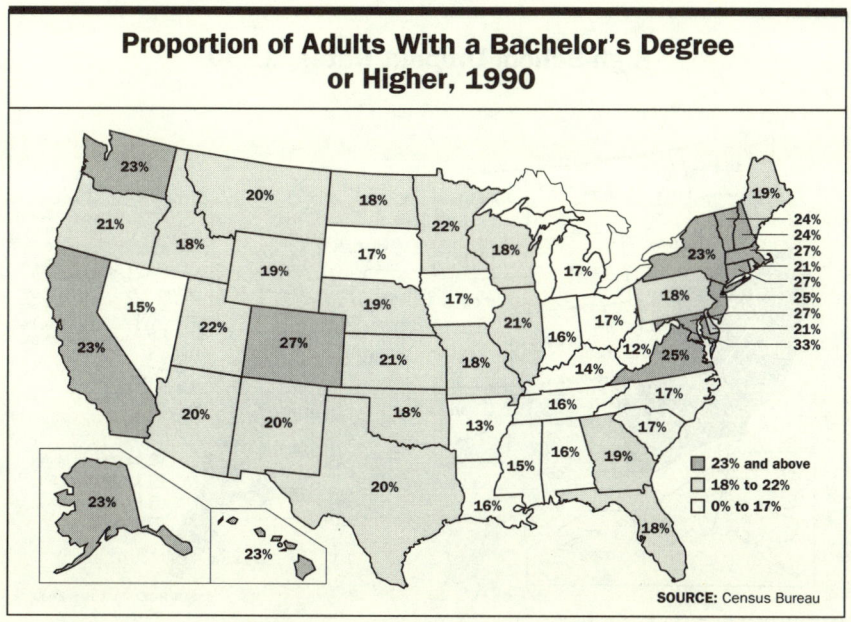

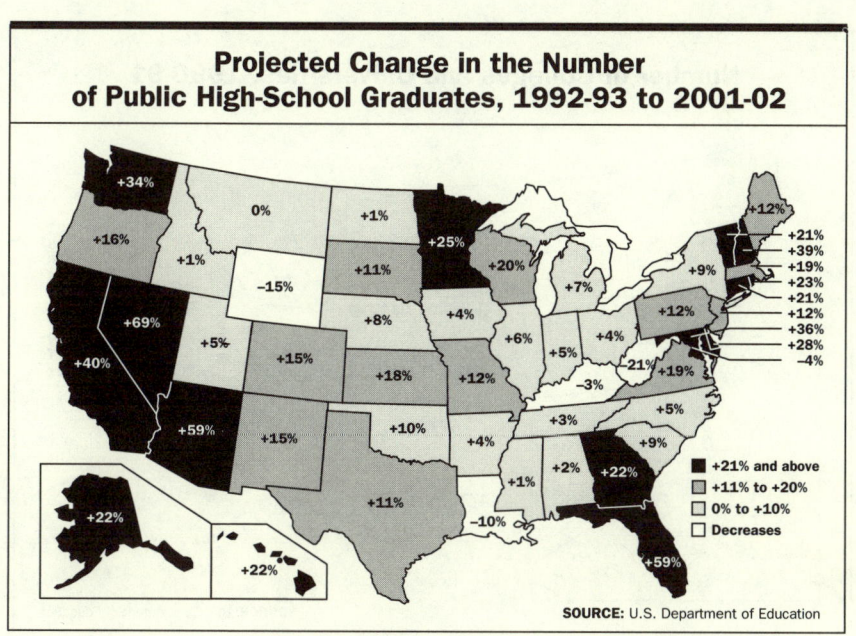

THE ALMANAC OF HIGHER EDUCATION • THE NATION

The Nation

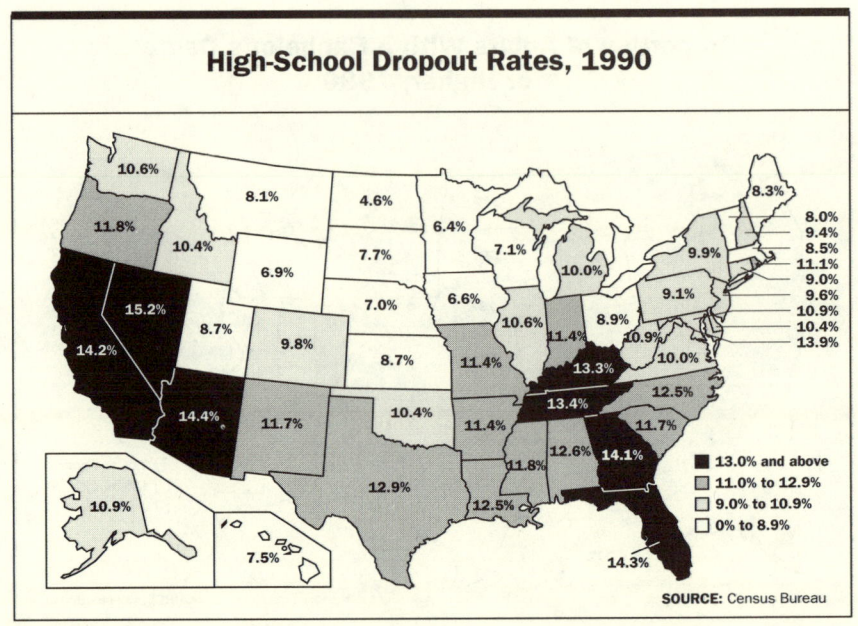

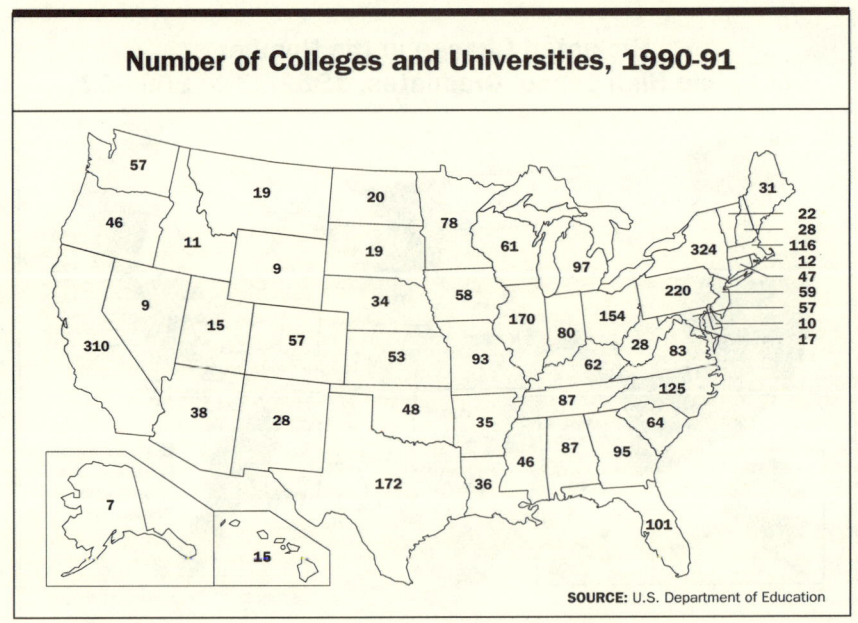

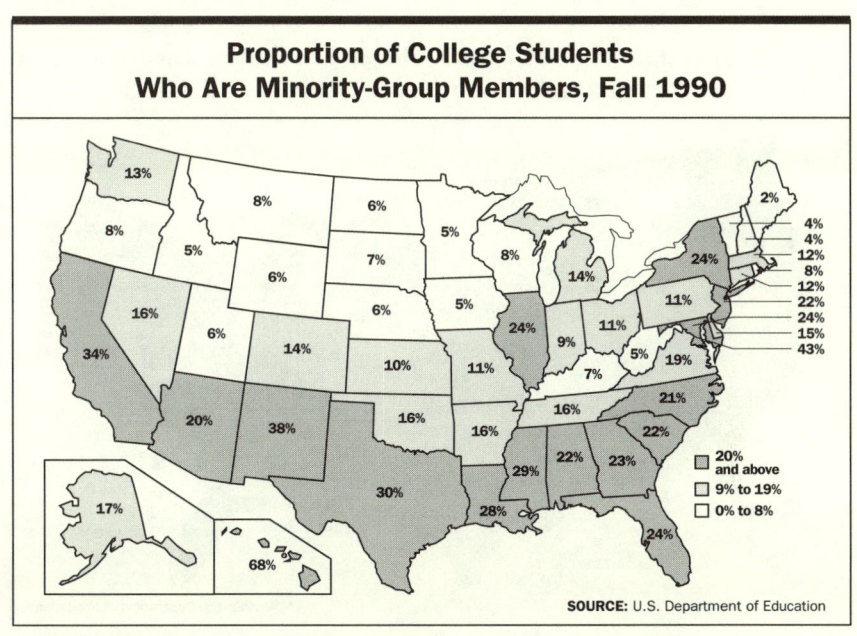

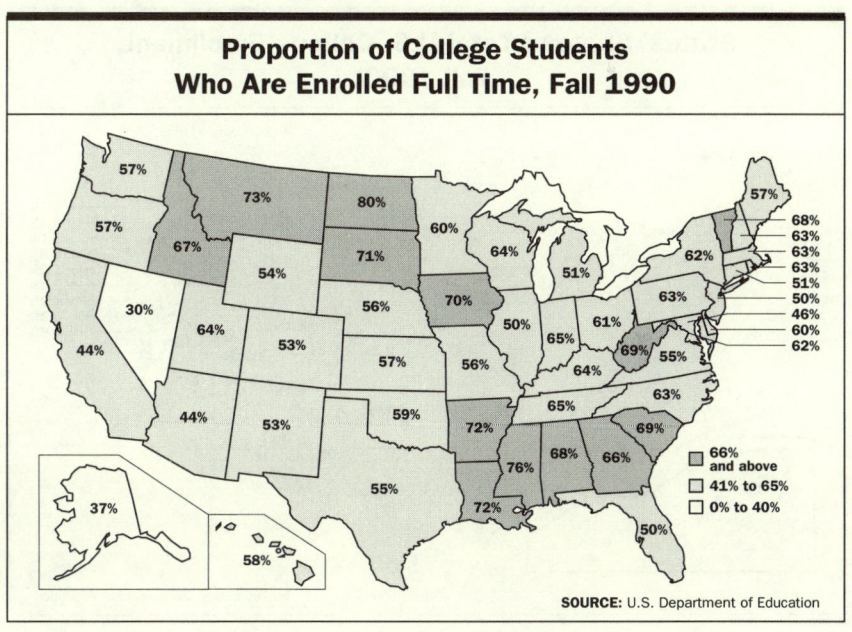

The Nation

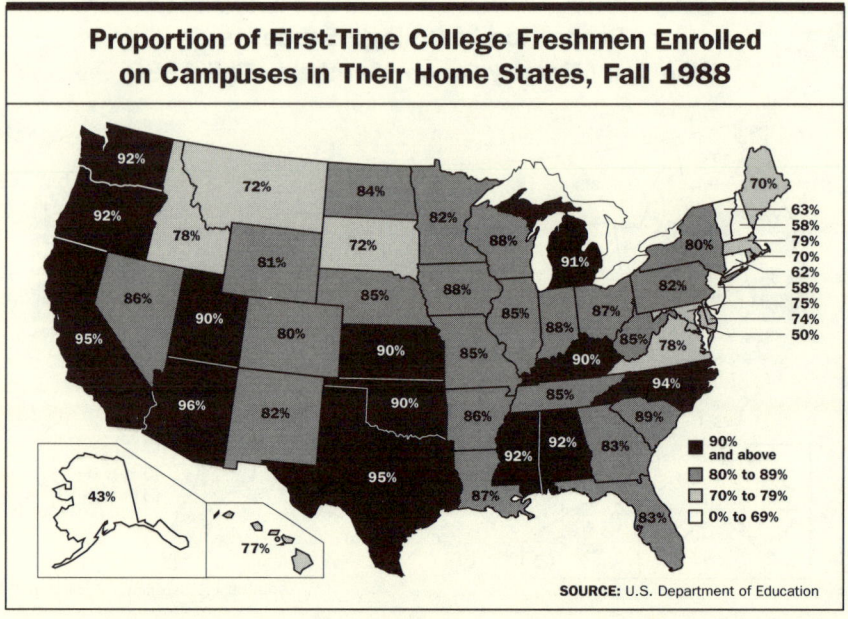

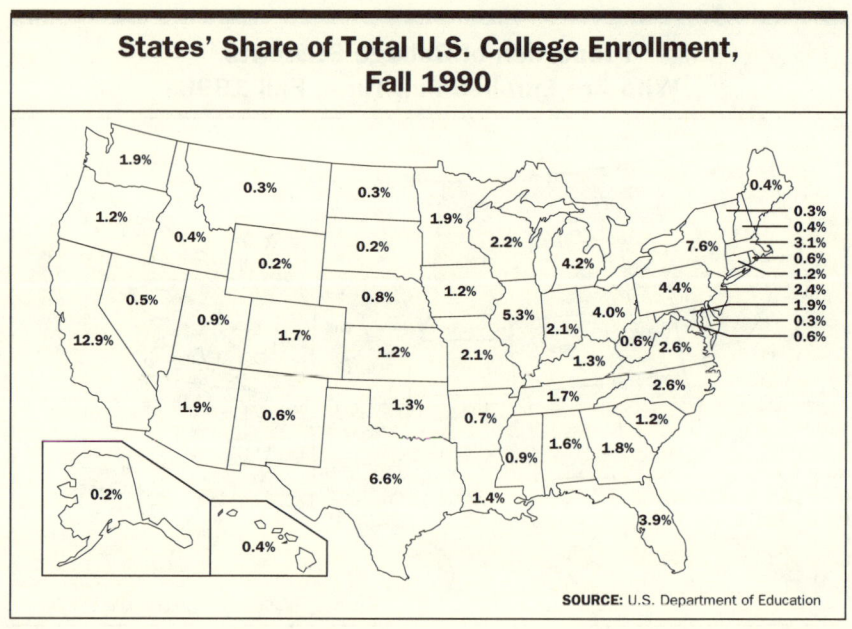

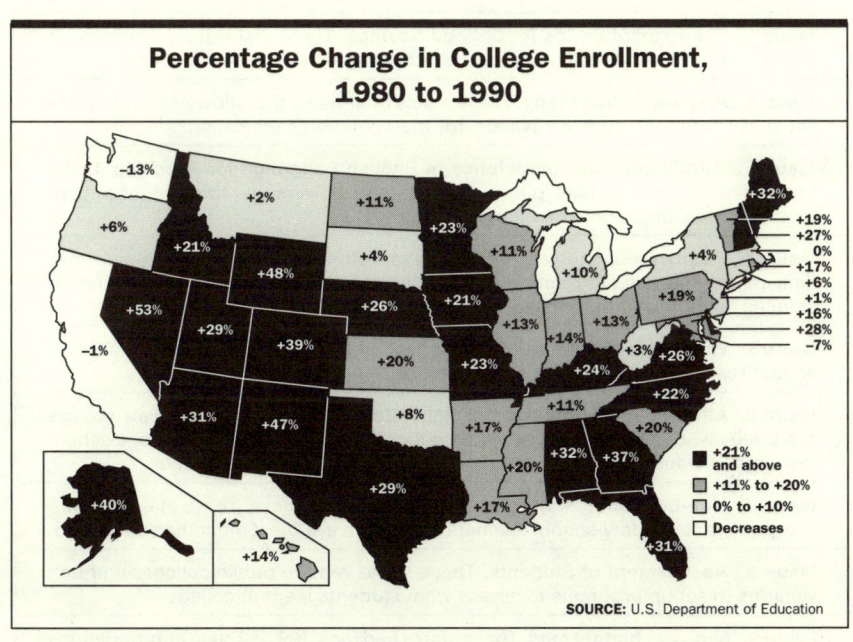

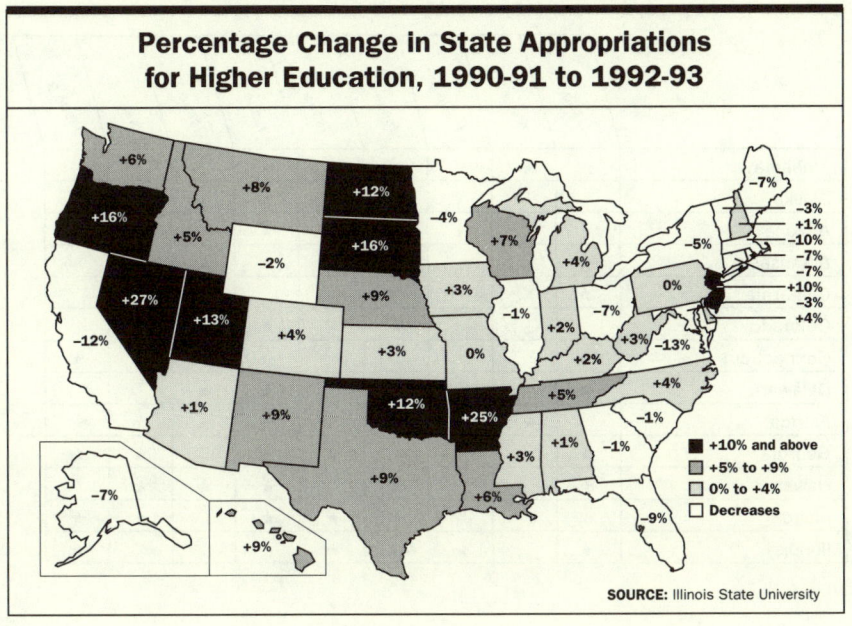

9 Issues Affecting Colleges: Roll Call of the States

Issue 1. Tax-Exempt Bonds for College Savings. These states have programs to sell tax-exempt bonds to families to help them finance college education.

Issue 2. Prepaid Tuition Plans. These states offer plans that allow parents to pay a set sum of money, years in advance, for their children's education.

Issue 3. Certification of Competence in English Language for Teaching Assistants. These states require public colleges and universities to certify that their teaching assistants are competent in English.

Issue 4. Restrictions or Taxes on Business Activities of Colleges. These states limit or tax the business activities of colleges and universities (or, in some instances, all non-profit groups).

Issue 5. Vandalism of Animal-Research Facilities. These states treat vandalism of animal-research facilities as a specific crime.

Issue 6. Alternative Certification for Schoolteachers. These states allow college graduates who have not completed an education major to become public-school teachers without completing a traditional course of study in education.

Issue 7. Non-Education Majors for High-School Teachers. These states require prospective secondary-school teachers to major in a subject other than education.

Issue 8. Assessment of Students. These states require public colleges and universities to set up programs to assess what students learn in college.

Issue 9. Mid-year budget cuts. These states had their 1991-92 state appropriations cut at some time during the fiscal year.

	Issue 1	Issue 2	Issue 3	Issue 4	Issue 5	Issue 6	Issue 7	Issue 8	Issue 9
Alabama		★				★			
Alaska		★				★			
Arizona			★	★	★	★			★
Arkansas	★			★	★	★	★	★	
California	★							★	
Colorado				★		★	★		
Connecticut	★					★	★		★
Delaware	★					★	★		
Florida		★	★			★	★	★	★
Georgia	★	★			★	★		★	★
Hawaii	★			★		★	★	★	
Idaho				★	★	★		★	★
Illinois	★		★	★	★				★

	Issue 1	Issue 2	Issue 3	Issue 4	Issue 5	Issue 6	Issue 7	Issue 8	Issue 9
Indiana	★				★				
Iowa			★		★			★	★
Kansas			★	★	★				★
Kentucky			★		★	★	★		★
Louisiana	★		★	★	★	★			★
Maine	★				★		★		★
Maryland						★		★	★
Massachusetts	★				★	★	★		
Michigan		★					★		
Minnesota					★	★	★		★
Mississippi						★			★
Missouri			★	★		★			★
Montana					★		★		★
Nebraska						★			★
Nevada							★	★	★
New Hampshire	★			★		★	★		★
New Jersey	★					★	★	★	
New Mexico				★		★			
New York					★	★	★		
North Carolina	★			★	★	★	★		
North Dakota	★		★		★		★		★
Ohio	★	★	★			★	★		★
Oklahoma	★	★	★		★	★	★	★	
Oregon	★				★				★
Pennsylvania	★	★	★			★	★		★
Rhode Island	★					★			
South Carolina			★			★		★	★
South Dakota	★			★			★		
Tennessee	★			★	★	★	★	★	★
Texas	★		★		★	★	★		
Utah					★	★	★	★	
Vermont									★
Virginia					★	★	★	★	★
Washington	★			★	★	★	★	★	★
West Virginia	★					★		★	★
Wisconsin	★		★	★	★		★		
Wyoming		★							

A STAR INDICATES AN ACTION EITHER BY A STATE LEGISLATURE OR BY A STATEWIDE COORDINATING BOARD OR GOVERNING BOARD, AS OF NOVEMBER 1, 1992. SOURCE: CHRONICLE REPORTING

Average SAT Scores by Sex and Racial and Ethnic Group, 1992

	Verbal section		Mathematical section	
	Score	1-year change	Score	1-year change
Men	428	+ 2	499	+ 2
Women	419	+ 1	456	+ 3
American Indian	395	+ 2	442	+ 5
Asian	413	+ 2	532	+ 2
Black	352	+ 1	385	0
Mexican-American	372	− 5	425	− 2
Puerto Rican	366	+ 5	406	0
Other Hispanic	383	+ 1	433	+ 2
White	442	+ 1	491	+ 2
Other	417	+ 6	473	+ 7
All	423	+ 1	476	+ 2

Note: Each section of the Scholastic Aptitude Test is scored on a scale from 200 to 800.

SOURCE: THE COLLEGE BOARD

Average ACT Scores by Sex and Racial and Ethnic Group, 1992

	Score	1-year change
Men	20.9	0.0
Women	20.5	+0.1
American Indian	18.1	−0.1
Asian	21.6	0.0
Black	17.0	0.0
Mexican-American	18.4	0.0
Other Hispanic	19.3	0.0
White	21.3	0.0
All	20.6	0.0

Note: The American College Testing Program's ACT Assessment is scored on a scale from 1 to 36.

SOURCE: AMERICAN COLLEGE TESTING PROGRAM

Student Financial Aid, 1991-92

Total spending, by source

Federal programs
Generally available aid
Pell Grants	$5,242,000,000
Supplemental Educational Opportunity Grants	415,000,000
State Student Incentive Grants	63,000,000
College Work-Study	791,000,000
Perkins Loans	824,000,000
Income Contingent Loans	5,000,000
Stafford Student Loans	10,639,000,000
Supplemental Loans for Students	1,952,000,000
Parent Loans for Undergraduate Students	1,125,000,000
Subtotal	21,055,000,000

Specially directed aid
Veterans	908,000,000
Military	376,000,000
Other grants	161,000,000
Other loans	350,000,000
Subtotal	1,794,000,000
Total federal aid	22,849,000,000
State grant programs	1,931,000,000
Institutional and other grants	5,991,000,000
Total federal, state, and institutional aid	$30,771,000,000

Number of recipients and amount of aid per recipient, selected programs

Program	Recipients	Amount
Pell Grants	4,027,000	$1,302
Supplemental Educational Opportunity Grants	728,000	570
College Work-Study	841,000	940
Perkins Loans	660,000	1,248
Stafford Student Loans	3,854,000	2,761
Supplemental Loans for Students	670,000	2,915
Parent Loans for Undergraduate Students	348,000	3,234
State Grants and State Student Incentive Grants	1,648,000	1,210

Note: Figures are estimates and include assistance to undergraduate and graduate students.
  Several of the federal programs include small amounts of money from sources other than the federal government. For example, College Work-Study includes some contributions by institutions, although most of the funds in the program are federal.
  Federal spending for State Student Incentive Grants is reported under federal programs; state spending for those grants is reported in the "state grants" category.
  Funds for Stafford Student Loans, Supplemental Loans for Students, and Parent Loans for Undergraduate Students come mostly from private sources. The federal government subsidizes interest payments and repays defaults. Amounts reported represent loan commitments rather than amounts loaned, but the difference between the two is insignificant.
  Veterans' benefits are payments for postsecondary education and training to veterans and their dependents.
  Military aid covers the Armed Forces Health Professions Scholarship program; Reserve Officers Training Corps programs for the Air Force, Army, and Navy; and tuition assistance for military personnel on active duty.
  Because of rounding, details may not add to totals.

SOURCE: THE COLLEGE BOARD

College Enrollment by Racial and Ethnic Group, Selected Years

American Indian	1980	1982	1984	1986	1988	1990
All	84,000	88,000	84,000	90,000	93,000	103,000
Men	38,000	40,000	38,000	39,000	39,000	43,000
Women	46,000	48,000	46,000	51,000	53,000	60,000
Public	74,000	77,000	72,000	79,000	81,000	90,000
Private	10,000	10,000	11,000	11,000	11,000	12,000
4-year	37,000	39,000	38,000	40,000	42,000	48,000
2-year	47,000	49,000	46,000	51,000	50,000	54,000
Undergraduate	79,000	82,000	78,000	83,000	86,000	95,000
Graduate	4,000	5,000	5,000	5,000	6,000	6,000
Professional	1,000	1,000	1,000	1,000	1,000	1,000
Asian						
All	286,000	351,000	390,000	448,000	497,000	555,000
Men	151,000	189,000	210,000	239,000	259,000	287,000
Women	135,000	162,000	180,000	209,000	237,000	268,000
Public	240,000	296,000	323,000	371,000	406,000	445,000
Private	47,000	55,000	67,000	77,000	91,000	109,000
4-year	162,000	193,000	223,000	262,000	297,000	343,000
2-year	124,000	158,000	167,000	186,000	199,000	212,000
Undergraduate	253,000	313,000	343,000	393,000	437,000	485,000
Graduate	28,000	30,000	37,000	43,000	46,000	52,000
Professional	6,000	8,000	9,000	11,000	14,000	18,000
Black						
All	1,107,000	1,101,000	1,076,000	1,082,000	1,130,000	1,223,000
Men	464,000	458,000	437,000	436,000	443,000	476,000
Women	643,000	644,000	639,000	646,000	687,000	747,000
Public	876,000	873,000	844,000	854,000	881,000	952,000
Private	231,000	228,000	232,000	228,000	248,000	271,000
4-year	634,000	612,000	617,000	615,000	656,000	715,000
2-year	472,000	489,000	459,000	467,000	473,000	509,000
Undergraduate	1,028,000	1,028,000	995,000	996,000	1,039,000	1,124,000
Graduate	66,000	61,000	67,000	72,000	76,000	84,000
Professional	13,000	13,000	13,000	14,000	14,000	16,000
Hispanic						
All	472,000	519,000	535,000	618,000	680,000	758,000
Men	232,000	252,000	254,000	290,000	310,000	344,000
Women	240,000	267,000	281,000	328,000	370,000	414,000
Public	406,000	446,000	456,000	532,000	587,000	648,000
Private	66,000	74,000	79,000	86,000	93,000	110,000
4-year	217,000	229,000	246,000	278,000	296,000	344,000
2-year	255,000	291,000	289,000	340,000	384,000	414,000
Undergraduate	438,000	485,000	495,000	563,000	631,000	702,000
Graduate	27,000	27,000	32,000	46,000	39,000	46,000
Professional	7,000	7,000	8,000	9,000	9,000	10,000

Note: Because of rounding, details may not add to totals.

White	1980	1982	1984	1986	1988	1990
All	9,833,000	9,997,000	9,815,000	9,921,000	10,283,000	10,675,000
Men	4,773,000	4,830,000	4,690,000	4,647,000	4,712,000	4,841,000
Women	5,060,000	5,167,000	5,125,000	5,273,000	5,572,000	5,834,000
Public	7,656,000	7,785,000	7,543,000	7,654,000	7,964,000	8,340,000
Private	2,177,000	2,212,000	2,272,000	2,267,000	2,319,000	2,335,000
4-year	6,275,000	6,306,000	6,301,000	6,337,000	6,582,000	6,757,000
2-year	3,558,000	3,692,000	3,514,000	3,584,000	3,702,000	3,918,000
Undergraduate	8,556,000	8,749,000	8,484,000	8,558,000	8,907,000	9,231,000
Graduate	1,030,000	1,002,000	1,087,000	1,133,000	1,153,000	1,221,000
Professional	248,000	246,000	243,000	231,000	223,000	222,000
Foreign						
All	305,000	331,000	335,000	345,000	361,000	397,000
Men	211,000	230,000	231,000	233,000	235,000	248,000
Women	94,000	101,000	104,000	112,000	126,000	149,000
Public	204,000	219,000	219,000	224,000	238,000	265,000
Private	101,000	113,000	116,000	120,000	123,000	132,000
4-year	241,000	270,000	282,000	292,000	302,000	322,000
2-year	64,000	61,000	53,000	53,000	60,000	75,000
Undergraduate	208,000	220,000	216,000	205,000	205,000	226,000
Graduate	94,000	108,000	115,000	136,000	151,000	165,000
Professional	3,000	3,000	3,000	4,000	5,000	5,000
All						
Total	12,087,000	12,388,000	12,235,000	12,504,000	13,043,000	13,710,000
Men	5,868,000	5,999,000	5,859,000	5,885,000	5,998,000	6,239,000
Women	6,219,000	6,389,000	6,376,000	6,619,000	7,045,000	7,472,000
Public	9,456,000	9,695,000	9,458,000	9,714,000	10,156,000	10,741,000
Private	2,630,000	2,693,000	2,777,000	2,790,000	2,887,000	2,970,000
4-year	7,565,000	7,648,000	7,708,000	7,824,000	8,175,000	8,529,000
2-year	4,521,000	4,740,000	4,527,000	4,680,000	4,868,000	5,181,000
Undergraduate	10,560,000	10,875,000	10,610,000	10,798,000	11,304,000	11,863,000
Graduate	1,250,000	1,235,000	1,344,000	1,435,000	1,472,000	1,574,000
Professional	277,000	278,000	278,000	270,000	267,000	274,000

SOURCE: U. S. DEPARTMENT OF EDUCATION

College Enrollment by Age of Students, Fall 1990

	All	Undergraduate 2-year Full-time	2-year Part-time	4-year Full-time	4-year Part-time	Graduate Full-time	Graduate Part-time
All students							
15 to 17	1.3%	2.4%	0.8%	1.9%	0.3%	0.0%	0.0%
18 and 19	22.2	41.0	9.7	34.7	4.3	0.2	0.0
20 and 21	20.3	20.9	14.0	34.1	8.5	2.3	0.1
22 to 24	16.0	11.6	12.3	16.6	17.9	34.2	8.6
25 to 29	14.1	9.7	17.7	6.4	23.6	31.1	23.0
30 to 34	9.1	6.2	15.0	2.7	15.5	16.0	17.8
35 to 39	7.1	3.8	13.1	1.8	12.3	8.0	18.4
40 to 44	4.9	2.0	8.4	1.2	8.3	4.7	15.3
45 to 49	2.6	1.2	3.7	0.4	6.0	1.9	8.2
50 to 54	1.2	0.5	2.9	0.1	2.0	1.3	3.3
55 to 59	0.5	0.5	0.6	0.1	0.2	0.5	2.8
60 to 64	0.2	0.0	0.8	0.0	0.4	0.0	0.8
65 and older	0.4	0.2	1.0	0.0	0.7	0.0	1.8
Number of students	13,621,000	1,953,000	2,012,000	5,644,000	1,499,000	1,100,000	1,413,000
Men							
15 to 17	1.4%	2.4%	0.9%	2.0%	0.5%	0.0%	0.0%
18 and 19	23.3	48.4	11.1	32.6	5.9	0.4	0.0
20 and 21	22.0	21.9	18.3	34.7	9.6	2.1	0.0
22 to 24	18.0	11.8	14.3	19.8	19.6	32.3	7.9
25 to 29	14.7	7.5	19.2	6.9	24.2	35.1	25.6
30 to 34	8.1	3.2	14.1	2.0	14.4	16.7	21.1
35 to 39	5.9	3.1	10.1	1.2	12.3	6.0	20.1
40 to 44	3.3	0.7	5.9	0.5	7.3	4.0	11.6
45 to 49	1.7	0.9	2.1	0.2	4.1	1.6	6.9
50 to 54	0.7	0.2	1.4	0.0	1.8	1.1	2.0
55 to 59	0.3	0.0	0.5	0.0	0.0	0.5	1.7
60 to 64	0.2	0.0	0.9	0.0	0.0	0.0	1.3
65 and older	0.4	0.0	1.2	0.0	0.3	0.0	1.7
Number of students	6,192,000	849,000	775,000	2,779,000	627,000	569,000	593,000
Women							
15 to 17	1.2%	2.4%	0.7%	1.9%	0.2%	0.0%	0.0%
18 and 19	21.2	35.3	9.0	36.6	3.3	0.0	0.0
20 and 21	18.9	20.1	11.2	33.6	7.7	2.4	0.2
22 to 24	14.3	11.6	11.0	13.5	16.6	36.0	9.0
25 to 29	13.7	11.3	16.7	5.9	23.2	26.7	21.1
30 to 34	9.9	8.5	15.5	3.4	16.4	15.3	15.5
35 to 39	8.1	4.4	15.0	2.4	12.3	10.2	17.2
40 to 44	6.3	3.1	10.0	1.9	9.1	5.3	17.9
45 to 49	3.3	1.4	4.8	0.6	7.2	2.4	9.1
50 to 54	1.6	0.7	3.9	0.2	2.3	1.5	4.1
55 to 59	0.7	0.8	0.6	0.1	0.3	0.4	3.5
60 to 64	0.2	0.0	0.7	0.0	0.7	0.0	0.4
65 and older	0.5	0.4	1.0	0.0	0.9	0.0	1.8
Number of students	7,429,000	1,103,000	1,237,000	2,864,000	872,000	531,000	820,000

Note: The figures are based on a Census Bureau survey of 60,000 households conducted in October 1990. The statistics may differ from enrollment data compiled by the U.S. Department of Education because of differences in survey methodology. Figures may not add to 100 per cent because of rounding.

SOURCE: CENSUS BUREAU

Administrators' Views on Changes in Enrollment and Student Characteristics from 1990-91 to 1991-92

	Total Increase	Total Decrease	Public 2-year Increase	Public 2-year Decrease	Public 4-year Increase	Public 4-year Decrease	All private Increase	All private Decrease
Proportion reporting change in number of:								
All students	68%	21%	79%	11%	68%	23%	54%	31%
First-time freshmen	53	31	68	17	45	39	40	42
Full-time students	62	24	69	17	64	25	52	33
Part-time students	66	17	75	13	56	28	61	16
American Indian students	24	9	26	7	33	18	17	7
Asian-American students	48	8	42	10	56	6	50	6
Black students	53	9	56	8	55	16	49	7
Hispanic students	45	8	45	11	53	9	40	5
Foreign students	40	12	20	13	50	13	55	10
Transfer students	56	17	55	11	60	19	55	21
Proportion reporting change in number of students who:								
Are from low-income backgrounds	42	4	57	2	26	4	35	6
Are returning adults	68	3	76	3	56	4	67	4
Are out of work	56	2	82	0	49	1	30	4
Require remedial courses	47	5	73	1	32	14	25	5
Require full financial support	61	0	67	0	52	2	59	0
Take a semester off for financial reasons	40	0	37	0	29	3	49	0
Attend part-time for financial reasons	47	3	51	4	38	2	45	3
Take longer to earn degree because of finances	53	1	58	2	49	2	51	0
Graduate and cannot find jobs	33	2	25	4	41	2	37	0

Note: The figures are based on responses to a survey sent to senior administrators at 510 colleges and universities in the winter of 1992. The response rate was 81 per cent. The percentages of those reporting "No change" are omitted.

SOURCE: AMERICAN COUNCIL ON EDUCATION

Attitudes and Characteristics of Freshmen, Fall 1991

	Total	Men	Women
Racial and ethnic background:			
American Indian	1.5%	1.5%	1.6%
Asian-American	3.1	3.3	2.8
Black	9.2	8.0	10.3
White	83.4	84.5	82.4
Mexican-American	2.7	2.4	3.0
Puerto Rican-American	0.6	0.6	0.6
Other	1.9	1.9	1.8
Estimated parental income:			
Less than $6,000	3.3	2.6	3.8
$6,000-$9,999	3.3	2.7	3.8
$10,000-$14,999	5.3	4.3	6.3
$15,000-$19,999	5.3	4.5	6.0
$20,000-$24,999	6.7	6.2	7.1
$25,000-$29,999	7.2	6.7	7.7
$30,000-$39,999	14.0	14.2	13.9
$40,000-$49,999	13.7	13.9	13.4
$50,000-$59,999	11.9	12.4	11.4
$60,000-$74,999	11.4	12.1	10.8
$75,000-$99,999	8.0	9.2	6.9
$100,000-$149,999	5.0	5.9	4.2
$150,000-$199,999	2.1	2.3	1.9
$200,000 or more	2.8	3.0	2.6
Number of other colleges applied to for admission this year:			
None	37.6	35.7	39.2
One	14.7	14.3	15.2
Two	15.8	15.9	15.8
Three	13.7	14.5	13.0
Four	7.8	8.3	7.4
Five	4.7	5.1	4.3
Six or more	5.6	6.1	5.0
College attended is student's:			
First choice	73.7	73.1	74.2
Second choice	19.6	19.6	19.5
Third choice	4.3	4.4	4.2
Other	2.4	2.8	2.1
Highest degree planned:			
None	1.4	1.6	1.2
Vocational certificate	1.8	2.2	1.5
Associate (or equivalent)	7.3	6.5	8.0
Bachelor's	28.2	29.4	27.2
Master's	35.5	35.1	35.7
Ph.D. or Ed.D.	12.5	12.7	12.3
M.D., D.O., D.D.S., or D.V.M.	6.9	6.2	7.4
LL.B. or J.D.	4.4	4.1	4.6
B.D. or M.Div.	0.3	0.4	0.2
Other	1.8	1.7	1.9

Note: The statistics are based on survey responses of 210,739 freshmen entering 431 two-year and four-year institutions in the fall of 1991. The figures were statistically adjusted to represent the total population of 1.6 million first-time, full-time freshmen. Because of rounding or multiple responses, figures may add to more than 100 per cent.

* Frequently only; all other activities frequently or occasionally.

	Total	Men	Women
Political views:			
Far left	2.1%	2.4%	1.7%
Liberal	23.6	21.2	25.8
Middle of the road	54.0	51.4	56.3
Conservative	19.1	23.1	15.6
Far right	1.2	1.8	0.6
Reasons noted as very important in deciding to go to college:			
Parents wanted me to go	33.7	31.9	35.2
Could not find job	7.3	6.7	7.9
To get away from home	15.6	15.5	15.7
To be able to get a better job	78.6	77.7	79.4
To gain a general education and appreciation of ideas	60.7	53.5	66.9
To improve reading and study skills	37.4	32.6	41.6
Nothing better to do	2.8	3.4	2.3
To become a more cultured person	37.2	30.5	43.0
To be able to make more money	74.7	77.1	72.6
To learn more about things that interest me	73.2	69.4	76.4
To prepare for graduate or professional school	54.2	48.8	58.9
Reasons noted as very important in selecting college attended:			
Relatives' wishes	9.1	8.4	9.8
Teachers' advice	4.3	4.5	4.1
Good academic reputation	51.6	48.9	53.8
Good social reputation	22.1	22.3	21.9
Offered financial assistance	27.8	23.8	31.3
Offered special education programs	22.2	18.6	25.4
Low tuition	27.7	25.1	30.0
Advice of guidance counselor	8.5	8.1	8.8
Wanted to live near home	21.3	16.3	25.6
Friend's suggestion	9.5	9.0	9.9
Recruited by college	3.9	4.6	3.4
Recruited by athletic department	5.0	7.5	2.8
Graduates go to top graduate schools	22.2	20.5	23.5
Graduates get good jobs	43.5	42.4	44.4
Religious affiliation of college	4.5	3.9	5.0
Size of college	35.0	28.3	40.8
Racial or ethnic makeup of student body	7.4	6.2	8.4
Not accepted anywhere else	2.2	2.7	1.7
Students estimate chances are very good that they will:			
Change major field	11.7	11.2	12.2
Change career choice	11.1	10.0	12.0
Fail one or more courses	1.5	1.9	1.2
Graduate with honors	13.6	14.2	13.2
Be elected to student office	3.0	2.9	3.0
Get a job to pay college expenses	37.5	34.2	40.3
Work full-time while attending college	4.8	4.7	4.9
Join a social fraternity or sorority	16.3	14.2	18.0
Play varsity athletics	14.4	19.9	9.7
Be elected to an honor society	7.7	7.5	7.9
Make at least a B average	42.0	41.4	42.5
Need extra time to complete degree	8.5	7.7	9.2
Get tutoring in some courses	14.7	12.3	16.8

Continued on Following Page

Attitudes and Characteristics of Freshmen, continued

	Total	Men	Women
Students estimate chances are very good that they will:			
Work at outside job	23.2%	19.7%	26.3%
Seek vocational counseling	4.6	4.0	5.0
Seek individual counseling on personal problems	3.7	3.1	4.2
Get bachelor's degree	64.0	62.2	65.6
Participate in student protests or demonstrations	5.9	4.9	6.7
Transfer to another college	13.0	12.7	13.3
Drop out permanently	0.8	1.0	0.6
Drop out temporarily	1.0	1.2	0.8
Be satisfied with college	51.1	45.3	56.0
Find job in preferred field	70.8	66.8	74.2
Marry while in college	6.6	4.5	8.5
Participate in volunteer or community-service work	14.6	10.0	18.6
Activities in the past year:			
Attended a religious service	82.7	78.9	86.1
Was bored in class *	30.0	30.8	29.3
Participated in organized demonstrations	39.0	36.8	40.8
Failed to complete homework on time	65.6	70.9	61.0
Tutored another student	44.7	43.6	45.6
Did extra work or reading for a class *	10.6	8.8	12.1
Studied with other students	84.1	83.0	85.1
Was a guest in teacher's home	27.9	28.1	27.7
Smoked cigarettes *	11.3	10.4	12.1
Drank beer	57.3	63.8	51.6
Drank wine or liquor	56.8	54.8	58.6
Stayed up all night	78.8	79.9	77.9
Felt overwhelmed by all I had to do *	20.2	13.3	26.2
Felt depressed *	8.9	6.1	11.3
Performed volunteer work	64.7	62.1	66.8
Asked a teacher for advice after class *	18.6	16.3	20.6
Voted in a student election	78.0	77.6	78.4
Used a personal computer *	37.5	38.9	36.2
Discussed politics *	20.5	23.9	17.6
Discussed sex *	31.5	35.8	27.9
Demonstrated for change in some military policy	9.2	10.2	8.3
Agree strongly or somewhat that:			
Government is not doing enough to protect the consumer from faulty goods and services	69.1	65.1	72.6
Government is not doing enough to control pollution	85.5	84.4	86.5
Taxes should be raised to reduce the federal deficit	25.5	29.3	22.2
There is too much concern in the courts for the rights of criminals	65.3	67.6	63.4
Military spending should be increased	26.0	28.1	24.1
Abortion should be legal	63.0	63.0	63.0
The death penalty should be abolished	21.1	18.8	23.2
It is all right for two people who really like each other to have sex even if they've known each other for a very short time	50.1	65.0	37.2
Married women's activities are best confined to home and family	26.0	31.9	20.8
Marijuana should be legalized	20.9	24.2	18.0

	Total	Men	Women
Agree strongly or somewhat that:			
Busing to achieve racial balance in schools is all right	54.7%	54.7%	54.8%
It is important to have laws prohibiting homosexual relationships	42.2	53.4	32.5
The chief benefit of college is that it increases one's earning power	71.0	75.2	67.3
Employers should be allowed to require employees or job applicants to take drug tests	80.8	79.1	82.3
The best way to control AIDS is through widespread, mandatory testing	66.4	66.3	66.5
Just because a man thinks that a woman has "led him on" does not entitle him to have sex with her	87.1	80.4	92.8
The government should do more to control the sale of handguns	78.1	66.8	87.8
A national health-care plan is needed to cover everybody's medical costs	75.8	72.1	79.0
Nuclear disarmament is attainable	63.7	64.8	62.7
Racial discrimination is no longer a major problem in America	20.3	22.8	18.0
The federal government should do more to discourage energy consumption	78.5	78.2	78.8
Realistically, an individual can do little to bring about changes in our society	31.3	35.0	28.0
Objectives considered essential or very important:			
Becoming accomplished in a performing art	10.1	9.7	10.5
Becoming an authority in own field	67.6	69.4	66.1
Obtaining recognition from colleagues for contributions to field	53.2	53.9	52.6
Influencing the political structure	17.9	19.5	16.5
Influencing social values	39.6	33.6	44.7
Raising a family	67.7	66.4	68.9
Having administrative responsibility for the work of others	41.2	41.9	40.6
Being very well-off financially	73.7	77.3	70.5
Helping others who are in difficulty	60.3	50.2	68.9
Making a theoretical contribution to science	15.8	18.5	13.5
Writing original works	12.0	12.0	12.1
Creating artistic work	11.3	11.4	11.2
Becoming successful in own business	42.0	47.3	37.5
Becoming involved in programs to clean up environment	31.3	30.4	32.0
Developing a meaningful philosophy of life	43.2	41.6	44.6
Participating in a community-action program	23.5	19.9	26.6
Helping to promote racial understanding	33.7	29.9	36.8
Keeping up to date with political affairs	37.1	39.9	34.7

SOURCE: "THE AMERICAN FRESHMAN: NATIONAL NORMS FOR FALL 1991," BY ALEXANDER W. ASTIN, PUBLISHED BY AMERICAN COUNCIL ON EDUCATION AND UNIVERSITY OF CALIFORNIA AT LOS ANGELES

Proportion of Full-Time Students Receiving Financial Aid, Fall 1989

	Any aid	Federal	State	Institutional	Other
Undergraduate students					
Total	56.4%	41.9%	21.1%	23.6%	9.9%
Public					
All	48.3	34.8	19.1	15.9	9.0
4-year	49.9	36.0	19.7	17.3	9.3
2-year	44.5	32.2	18.4	13.5	8.1
Less-than-2-year	56.3	37.5	10.2	10.2	12.1
Private, non-profit					
All	70.4	49.4	30.6	49.7	14.7
4-year	70.5	49.1	31.0	51.3	14.7
2-year	66.9	49.4	26.9	32.6	16.5
Less-than-2-year	79.3	69.2	21.0	17.6	7.1
Private, for-profit					
All	87.0	82.1	12.2	18.2	5.0
2-year and above	87.2	81.7	19.3	15.2	7.2
Less-than-2-year	86.9	82.4	6.4	20.7	3.3
Graduate students					
Total	66.9%	36.8%	6.2%	43.0%	13.5%
Master's					
All	60.7	27.9	4.9	40.1	12.3
Public	58.9	24.9	6.1	41.9	9.3
Private	63.5	32.7	2.8	37.1	17.2
Doctoral					
All	77.6	18.8	6.1	69.6	17.2
Public	76.1	16.7	7.9	68.5	19.4
Private	80.0	22.4	3.2	71.4	13.7
Professional					
All	73.4	62.5	8.8	34.9	14.6
Public	72.9	62.8	11.8	35.2	11.1
Private	73.8	62.3	6.7	34.7	17.0

Note: Figures are based on a survey of 61,000 students enrolled at 1,130 colleges, universities, and proprietary institutions in 1989-90. Information on graduate students includes those enrolled at both non-profit and for-profit institutions.

SOURCE: U. S. DEPARTMENT OF EDUCATION

Colleges With the Most Freshman National Merit Scholars, 1991

	Number of scholars	Number sponsored by institution
Harvard and Radcliffe Colleges	292	0
Rice University	246	162
University of Texas at Austin	210	163
Stanford University	159	0
Texas A&M University	154	118
Yale University	144	0
Princeton University	107	0
Northwestern University	105	71
Ohio State University	102	74
Massachusetts Institute of Technology	100	0
Duke University	100	10
Brigham Young University	100	74
University of Florida	96	79
University of Chicago	96	72
Georgia Institute of Technology	90	72
University of California at Los Angeles	90	70
Carleton College	86	64
University of New Orleans	75	63
Virginia Polytechnic Institute and State University	74	61
University of Oklahoma	73	53
University of Houston	70	61
Michigan State University	67	52
Cornell University	67	0
Brown University	60	0
University of California at Berkeley	58	0
Johns Hopkins University	56	45
University of Michigan	55	0
University of Arizona	54	41
Dartmouth College	53	0
Harvey Mudd College	50	39
University of Kansas	48	40
Iowa State University	48	37
University of Kentucky	48	35
University of Minnesota–Twin Cities	48	33
Baylor University	47	35
University of Illinois at Urbana-Champaign	47	0
Washington University (Mo.)	46	31
University of Pennsylvania	46	0
University of California at San Diego	46	39
George Washington University	46	22
Vanderbilt University	45	30
Macalester College	44	37
University of Alabama at Tuscaloosa	43	30
University of North Carolina at Chapel Hill	42	0

Note: The table shows the total number of Merit Scholarship winners and the number whose scholarships were paid for by the institution, not by the National Merit Scholarship Corporation or other corporate sponsors. The rankings were determined by The Chronicle from an alphabetical listing appearing in the 1990-91 annual report of the National Merit Scholarship Corporation.

SOURCE: NATIONAL MERIT SCHOLARSHIP CORPORATION

Earned Degrees Conferred, 1989-90

	Associate degrees		
	Total	Men	Women
Agriculture, natural resources	4,832	3,230	1,602
Architecture, environmental design	2,011	268	1,743
Area and ethnic studies	68	12	56
Business and management	106,980	32,751	74,229
Communications	1,658	746	912
Communications technologies	2,014	1,347	667
Computer, information sciences	7,604	3,820	3,784
Education	8,018	2,311	5,707
Engineering	2,380	2,098	282
Engineering technologies	51,751	46,872	4,879
Foreign languages	329	78	251
Health sciences	64,128	7,969	56,159
Home economics	10,230	2,746	7,484
Law	4,547	583	3,964
Letters	567	185	382
Liberal / general studies	128,721	53,007	75,714
Library and archival sciences	112	13	99
Life sciences	1,034	439	595
Mathematics	760	489	271
Military sciences	129	114	15
Multi / interdisciplinary studies	11,803	5,228	6,575
Parks and recreation	461	279	182
Philosophy and religion	93	59	34
Physical sciences	2,135	1,317	818
Protective services	12,848	9,441	3,407
Psychology	1,110	285	825
Public affairs and social work	5,228	2,771	2,457
Social sciences	2,870	1,272	1,598
Theology	653	389	264
Visual and performing arts	13,923	8,041	5,882
Not classified by field of study	5,682	2,912	2,770
All fields	454,679	191,072	263,607

Professional Degrees Conferred, 1989-90

	Total	Men	Women
Chiropractic	2,581	1,906	675
Dentistry	4,093	2,830	1,263
Law	36,437	21,059	15,378
Medicine	15,115	9,977	5,138
Optometry	1,072	646	426
Osteopathic medicine	1,561	1,119	442
Pharmacy	1,191	482	709
Podiatry, podiatric medicine	675	493	182
Theological professions	5,851	4,406	1,445
Veterinary medicine	2,160	901	1,259
Other	244	183	61
All fields	70,980	44,002	26,978

SOURCE: U.S. DEPARTMENT OF EDUCATION

| Bachelor's degrees ||| Master's degrees ||| Doctoral degrees |||
Total	Men	Women	Total	Men	Women	Total	Men	Women
13,070	8,955	4,115	3,373	2,245	1,128	1,272	1,029	243
9,261	5,637	3,624	3,492	2,221	1,271	97	69	28
4,399	1,760	2,639	1,198	656	542	128	68	60
249,081	132,704	116,377	77,203	50,983	26,220	1,142	863	279
50,063	19,536	30,527	4,070	1,562	2,508	263	141	122
1,220	655	565	299	150	149	6	3	3
27,434	19,178	8,256	9,643	6,968	2,675	623	533	90
104,715	22,980	81,735	86,057	20,834	65,223	6,922	2,931	3,991
64,077	54,249	9,828	23,953	20,691	3,262	4,953	4,519	434
18,033	16,558	1,475	895	738	157	12	12	0
11,326	3,010	8,316	1,995	627	1,368	512	210	302
58,816	9,235	49,581	20,354	4,534	15,820	1,543	697	846
14,987	1,480	13,507	2,153	310	1,843	303	89	214
1,582	510	*1,072	1,869	1,311	558	113	90	23
48,075	15,874	32,201	7,223	2,458	4,765	1,266	566	700
24,956	10,416	14,540	1,594	554	1,040	31	13	18
84	16	68	4,349	960	3,389	41	12	29
37,170	18,325	18,845	4,861	2,377	2,484	3,844	2,395	1,449
14,597	7,812	6,785	3,677	2,205	1,472	915	746	169
417	384	33	0	0	0	0	0	0
19,188	8,753	10,435	3,505	2,023	1,482	311	203	108
4,404	1,941	2,463	430	179	251	35	18	17
6,848	4,374	2,474	1,326	839	487	432	324	108
16,131	11,091	5,040	5,447	4,008	1,439	4,168	3,364	804
15,387	9,575	5,812	1,151	796	355	37	24	13
53,586	15,291	38,295	9,231	2,992	6,239	3,353	1,414	1,939
16,241	5,310	10,931	17,993	6,181	11,812	495	229	266
116,925	65,248	51,677	11,419	6,758	4,661	3,023	2,037	986
5,162	3,919	1,243	4,686	2,998	1,688	1,298	1,147	151
39,695	15,325	24,370	8,546	3,749	4,797	842	472	370
2,727	1,387	1,340	1,852	736	1,116	258	153	105
1,049,657	491,488	558,169	323,844	153,643	170,201	38,238	24,371	13,867

SOURCE: U.S. DEPARTMENT OF EDUCATION

Degrees Conferred by Racial and Ethnic Group, 1989-90

	U.S citizens and resident aliens					Non-resident aliens	Race unknown
	American Indian	Asian	Black	Hispanic	White		
Associate							
Men ...	1,436	6,470	13,171	9,810	154,301	2,972	2,912
Women	2,089	6,956	22,107	12,252	214,228	3,205	2,770
Total ..	3,525	13,426	35,278	22,062	368,529	6,177	5,682
Bachelor's							
Men ...	1,828	19,617	23,276	14,871	413,469	17,040	1,387
Women	2,510	19,442	37,798	17,815	469,527	9,737	1,340
Total ..	4,338	39,059	61,074	32,686	882,996	26,777	2,727
Master's							
Men ...	465	6,070	5,492	3,566	112,976	24,338	736
Women	643	4,576	9,839	4,339	138,542	11,146	1,116
Total ..	1,108	10,646	15,331	7,905	251,518	35,484	1,852
Doctorate							
Men ...	52	910	533	417	15,102	7,204	153
Women	50	372	612	366	10,691	1,671	105
Total ..	102	1,282	1,145	783	25,793	8,875	258
Professional							
Men ...	138	1,966	1,650	1,454	37,909	702	183
Women	119	1,370	1,739	973	22,382	334	61
Total ..	257	3,336	3,389	2,427	60,291	1,036	244

SOURCE: U.S. DEPARTMENT OF EDUCATION

Number of Institutions Conferring Degrees, 1989-90

	Number conferring degrees	Number of degrees conferred
Associate		
Public	1,213	375,420
Private	920	79,259
Bachelor's		
Public	546	698,786
Private	1,262	350,871
Master's		
Public	478	185,681
Private	783	138,163
Doctorate		
Public	206	24,529
Private	251	13,709
Professional		
Public	n/a	28,867
Private	n/a	42,113

SOURCE: U.S. DEPARTMENT OF EDUCATION

Universities Awarding the Most Earned Doctorates, 1991

University of California at Berkeley	778
University of Illinois at Urbana-Champaign	738
University of Texas at Austin	710
University of Wisconsin at Madison	706
University of Minnesota–Twin Cities	704
University of Michigan at Ann Arbor	659
Ohio State University	639
University of California at Los Angeles	572
Stanford University	556
Harvard University	534
Cornell University	500
Massachusetts Institute of Technology	497
Pennsylvania State University	473
University of Washington	459
University of Maryland at College Park	453
University of Pennsylvania	449
Texas A&M University	445
Purdue University	430
New York University	427
University of Southern California	422
University of Massachusetts at Amherst	400
Columbia University	398
Michigan State University	390
University of Arizona	384
University of Florida	368
Indiana University at Bloomington	360
University of Iowa	359
University of California at Davis	347
Yale University	344
University of Pittsburgh	341
University of North Carolina at Chapel Hill	336
Virginia Polytechnic Institute and State University	336
University of Georgia	332
City University of New York Graduate School and University Center	326
University of Chicago	317
Northwestern University	316
Rutgers University at New Brunswick	304
University of Colorado	298
Iowa State University	297
University of Virginia	292

SOURCE: NATIONAL RESEARCH COUNCIL

Characteristics of Recipients of Doctorates, 1991

	All fields [1]	Arts and humanities	Business and management
Doctoral degrees conferred	37,451	4,094	1,164
Median age at conferral	33.9	35.8	35.4
Median number of years from bachelor's degree to doctorate	10.4	12.3	12.0
Median number of years registered as a graduate student	7.0	8.4	7.0
Proportion with bachelor's degree in same field as doctorate	56.4%	57.7%	35.1%
Sex			
Male	63.2%	53.5%	74.9%
Female	36.8	46.5	25.1
Citizenship			
United States	66.0	77.0	57.5
Non-U.S., permanent visa	4.8	5.8	6.7
Non-U.S., temporary visa	23.6	12.5	28.3
Unknown	5.5	4.7	7.6
Racial and ethnic group [3]			
American Indian	0.5	0.3	0.3
Asian	5.6	2.5	8.0
Black	4.1	3.0	2.9
Hispanic	3.2	4.2	1.3
White	85.2	88.2	86.2
Other, unknown	1.4	1.7	1.2
Planned postdoctoral study			
Fellowship	12.6%	4.6%	1.2%
Research associateship	10.2	1.1	0.6
Traineeship	1.1	0.6	0.4
Other	1.5	1.3	0.2
Planned postdoctoral employment			
Educational institution	39.7	69.8	75.7
Industry or business	13.6	4.3	7.7
Government	5.8	1.9	1.9
Non-profit organization	3.9	4.1	0.7
Other or unknown	3.6	4.1	1.1
Postdoctoral status unknown	8.1	8.1	10.5
Primary postdoctoral employment activity			
Research and development	28.5%	8.4%	32.3%
Teaching	32.4	63.0	48.3
Administration	10.9	4.0	2.6
Professional services	12.1	4.5	2.1
Other	2.3	3.4	1.3
Unknown	13.9	16.7	13.3

[1] Includes degree categories not listed separately
[2] Excludes business, which is listed separately
[3] Figures cover only U.S. citizens and those with permanent visas

Education	Engineering	Life sciences	Physical sciences	Social sciences	Professional fields [2]
6,397	5,212	6,928	6,276	6,127	1,172
42.1	31.4	32.4	30.5	34.1	38.3
18.4	8.5	9.1	7.8	10.5	15.0
8.1	6.1	6.7	6.3	7.5	8.0
39.3%	79.0%	54.1%	69.1%	54.2%	26.5%
41.9%	91.3%	61.4%	81.6%	50.6%	56.9%
58.1	8.7	38.6	18.4	49.4	43.1
84.8	37.9	66.8	55.0	73.4	74.4
2.6	7.3	4.8	5.1	4.1	3.1
7.6	47.4	24.3	35.2	15.7	15.8
5.0	7.3	4.0	4.7	6.8	6.7
0.9	0.3	0.4	0.4	0.4	0.4
2.2	17.0	6.5	8.1	3.2	3.9
7.8	2.3	2.3	1.4	4.9	6.8
3.3	2.5	2.5	2.6	4.1	2.3
84.9	75.8	86.6	85.6	86.0	85.3
0.8	2.1	1.6	1.8	1.3	1.2
1.7%	6.5%	31.4%	19.3%	10.8%	1.7%
1.5	13.0	18.6	23.6	3.3	1.2
0.7	1.4	1.7	0.8	1.5	0.4
1.1	0.6	4.2	0.9	0.9	0.7
68.2	21.4	18.5	19.6	39.4	57.6
5.0	34.9	8.3	21.0	11.5	6.9
5.7	7.2	6.2	4.4	8.9	4.6
4.6	1.2	2.0	1.0	8.5	14.4
4.1	3.3	2.7	2.2	5.9	4.0
7.4	10.5	6.2	7.3	9.2	8.4
6.1%	64.4%	43.9%	57.7%	22.7%	10.9%
32.7	16.0	23.7	23.6	25.7	43.6
31.9	1.5	7.4	1.5	4.6	11.5
10.4	6.2	10.8	4.6	31.2	14.5
1.5	2.3	2.4	2.1	2.4	4.2
17.5	9.6	12.0	10.5	13.5	15.4

SOURCE: NATIONAL RESEARCH COUNCIL

Foreign Students' Countries of Origin, 1991-92

Country or territory	Students	Country or territory	Students
China	42,940	Peru	2,670
Japan	40,700	Jamaica	2,640
Taiwan	35,550	Italy	2,490
India	32,530	Kenya	2,410
Republic of Korea	25,720	Norway	2,410
Canada	19,190	Sri Lanka	2,380
Hong Kong	13,190	Sweden	2,270
Malaysia	12,650	Trinidad & Tobago	2,170
Indonesia	10,250	Netherlands	2,100
Pakistan	8,120	Argentina	2,050
Thailand	7,690	Australia	2,020
Germany	7,570	U.S.S.R.	2,020
United Kingdom	7,470	South Africa	2,010
Mexico	6,650	Bahamas	1,930
France	5,580	Kuwait	1,830
Iran	4,930	Cyprus	1,810
Singapore	4,760	Panama	1,720
Spain	4,590	Egypt	1,580
Turkey	4,560	Ethiopia	1,550
Greece	4,490	United Arab Emirates	1,460
Brazil	4,260	Yugoslavia	1,430
Philippines	3,950	Switzerland	1,410
Jordan	3,700	Poland	1,260
Saudi Arabia	3,550	Ireland	1,250
Nigeria	3,160	Ecuador	1,220
Israel	3,130	Syria	1,120
Venezuela	3,130	Honduras	1,090
Lebanon	3,080	Morocco	1,060
Colombia	2,930	Ghana	1,010
Bangladesh	2,780		

Note: Includes only countries with over 1,000 students in U.S. institutions.

SOURCE: INSTITUTE OF INTERNATIONAL EDUCATION

Educational Attainment of the U.S. Population by Racial and Ethnic Group, 1990

Highest level reached	All	American Indian	Asian	Black	Hispanic	White
9th grade or less	10.4%	14.0%	12.9%	13.8%	30.7%	8.9%
Some high school, no diploma	14.4	20.4	9.5	23.2	19.5	13.1
High-school diploma	30.0	29.1	18.5	27.9	21.6	31.0
Some college, no degree	18.7	20.8	14.7	18.5	14.3	19.1
Associate degree	6.2	6.4	7.7	5.3	4.8	6.3
Bachelor's degree	13.1	6.1	22.7	7.5	5.9	13.9
Graduate or professional degree	7.2	3.2	13.9	3.8	3.3	7.7

Note: The figures are based on the 1990 census and cover adults age 25 and older. The total includes those whose racial or ethnic group is not known. Hispanics may be of any race. The figures may not add to 100 per cent because of rounding.

SOURCE: CENSUS BUREAU

Institutions Enrolling the Most Foreign Students, 1991-92

University of Texas at Austin	4,119
University of Southern California	4,063
Boston University	3,925
University of Wisconsin at Madison	3,834
New York University	3,384
Ohio State University main campus	3,354
Columbia University	3,090
University of Pennsylvania	2,962
University of Illinois at Urbana-Champaign	2,928
Texas A&M University main campus	2,785
Southern Illinois University at Carbondale	2,718
University of Minnesota–Twin Cities	2,680
George Washington University	2,669
Harvard University	2,583
University of Houston at University Park	2,567
University of Maryland at College Park	2,564
Purdue University main campus	2,389
University of Michigan at Ann Arbor	2,367
Northeastern University	2,367
Michigan State University	2,361
Temple University	2,308
Arizona State University	2,289
Cornell University	2,289
Rutgers University at New Brunswick	2,280
Iowa State University	2,261
University of Florida	2,188
Indiana University at Bloomington	2,144
Massachusetts Institute of Technology	2,133
University of Hawaii at Manoa	2,130
Stanford University	2,114
University of California at Berkeley	2,097
State University of New York at Buffalo	2,071
University of Iowa	2,051
University of Arizona	2,045
Pennsylvania State University main campus	1,988
University of Washington	1,930
Miami-Dade Community College	1,924
University of Missouri at Columbia	1,922
University of Kansas	1,920
University of California at Los Angeles	1,860
University of Illinois at Chicago	1,844
Wayne State University	1,829
City University of New York City College	1,818
University of Miami	1,786
University of Massachusetts at Amherst	1,779
Louisiana State University	1,685
Santa Monica College	1,671
Oklahoma State University main campus	1,670
California State University at Los Angeles	1,649
State University of New York at Stony Brook	1,604

Note: Beginning with the 1991-92 survey, institutions were asked to exclude refugees from the count of foreign students. This change accounts for the large drop in foreign enrollment at Miami-Dade Community College.

SOURCE: INSTITUTE OF INTERNATIONAL EDUCATION

Campuses With the Largest Enrollments, Fall 1990

University of Minnesota–Twin Cities	57,168
Ohio State University main campus	54,087
University of Texas at Austin	49,617
Michigan State University	44,307
Miami-Dade Community College	43,880
University of Wisconsin at Madison	43,209
Arizona State University	42,936
Texas A&M University	41,171
Pennsylvania State University main campus	38,864
University of Illinois at Urbana-Champaign	38,163
Purdue University main campus	37,588
Houston Community College	36,437
University of California at Los Angeles	36,420
University of Michigan at Ann Arbor	36,391
University of Arizona	35,729
University of Florida	35,477
Indiana University at Bloomington	35,451
Northern Virginia Community College	35,194
University of Maryland at College Park	34,829
San Diego State University	34,155
Wayne State University	33,872
University of Washington	33,854
California State University at Long Beach	33,179
University of Houston–University Park	33,115
Rutgers University at New Brunswick	33,016
St. Louis Community College	32,347
University of South Florida	32,326
Brigham Young University main campus	31,662
Macomb Community College	31,538
University of Cincinnati main campus	31,013
New York University	30,750
University of California at Berkeley	30,634
Northeastern University	30,510
Temple University	29,714
University of Southern California	29,657
Community College of the Air Force	29,567
California State University at Northridge	29,401
College of Du Page	29,185
University of Iowa	28,785
Pima Community College	28,766
University of Colorado at Boulder	28,600
University of Georgia	28,395
Florida State University	28,170
Tarrant County Junior College District	28,161
University of Pittsburgh main campus	28,120
Oakland Community College	28,069
Boston University	27,996
University of Akron main campus	27,818
State University of New York at Buffalo	27,638
Indiana University–Purdue University at Indianapolis	27,517

SOURCE: U.S. DEPARTMENT OF EDUCATION

Educational Attainment of 1980 High-School Seniors by 1986

	No high-school diploma	High-school diploma	License	Associate degree	Bachelor's degree	Professional/ graduate degree
Sex						
Men	1.0%	64.0%	10.5%	5.9%	17.6%	0.9%
Women	0.8	59.6	13.3	7.0	18.8	0.6
Racial and ethnic group						
American Indian	—	61.3	18.6	9.3	10.8	—
Asian	—	49.6	12.6	8.7	27.3	1.7
Black, non-Hispanic	1.2	69.4	13.9	5.3	9.9	0.2
Hispanic	1.7	70.2	13.8	7.3	6.8	0.1
White, non-Hispanic	0.8	60.0	11.5	6.6	20.2	0.9
Socioeconomic status						
Low	1.2	74.1	12.3	5.5	6.6	0.2
Low-middle	0.5	66.7	13.6	8.0	11.1	0.2
High-middle	0.1	58.4	12.9	7.7	20.4	0.6
High	—	45.7	8.7	6.3	37.1	2.2
High-school program						
General	0.8	69.7	12.6	6.5	10.2	0.2
Academic	0.1	45.6	8.8	7.2	36.6	1.8
Vocational	0.6	72.8	16.2	6.9	3.6	0.0
Type of high school						
Public	1.0	63.2	12.1	6.6	16.4	0.7
Catholic	—	47.4	11.9	6.4	32.8	1.6
Other private	—	52.3	7.0	3.9	36.7	0.1
Postsecondary education plans						
No plans	1.4	83.5	12.7	2.1	0.2	—
Attend voc/tech school	0.3	72.5	17.7	8.4	1.1	—
Attend college less than 4 years	0.2	65.5	14.4	13.1	6.8	—
Earn bachelor's degree	—	48.3	8.2	6.9	35.8	0.7
Earn advanced degree	0.1	43.5	7.9	4.9	40.6	3.0
1980 enrollment status						
Part-time 2-year public college	0.7	66.4	17.7	8.8	6.5	—
Part-time 4-year public college	2.7	57.1	15.4	1.6	22.6	0.6
Full-time 2-year public college	—	49.5	11.7	20.7	17.6	0.5
Full-time 4-year public college	—	41.7	7.6	4.5	44.9	1.3
Full-time 4-year private college	—	31.1	8.8	5.1	51.9	3.0
Not a student	1.8	78.2	12.8	3.6	3.5	0.2
Total	0.9%	61.8%	11.9%	6.5%	18.2%	0.7%

Note: Figures are based on data from "High School and Beyond," a longitudinal study of more than 10,500 students who were high-school seniors in 1980. They show students' highest level of education achieved by the spring of 1986.
Because of rounding, figures may not add to 100 per cent. A dash indicates less than 0.1 per cent.
Socioeconomic status was determined by parental education, family income, father's occupation, and household characteristics in 1980.

SOURCE: U. S. DEPARTMENT OF EDUCATION

Projections of College Enrollment, High-School Graduates, and Degrees Conferred, 1992-2002

	1992	1993	1994	1995	1996
College enrollment					
Total	14,235,000	14,366,000	14,512,000	14,621,000	14,803,000
Men					
Total	6,516,000	6,531,000	6,549,000	6,575,000	6,647,000
Full-time	3,868,000	3,855,000	3,854,000	3,852,000	3,893,000
Part-time	2,648,000	2,676,000	2,695,000	2,723,000	2,754,000
Women					
Total	7,719,000	7,835,000	7,963,000	8,046,000	8,156,000
Full-time	4,003,000	4,040,000	4,095,000	4,136,000	4,202,000
Part-time	3,716,000	3,795,000	3,868,000	3,910,000	3,954,000
Public institutions	11,083,000	11,187,000	11,305,000	11,393,000	11,537,000
Private institutions	3,152,000	3,179,000	3,207,000	3,228,000	3,266,000
Full-time students	7,871,000	7,895,000	7,949,000	7,988,000	8,095,000
Part-time students	6,364,000	6,471,000	6,563,000	6,633,000	6,708,000
Full-time-equivalent *					
Total	10,171,000	10,232,000	10,321,000	10,385,000	10,519,000
Public	7,628,000	7,675,000	7,743,000	7,794,000	7,897,000
Private	2,543,000	2,558,000	2,578,000	2,592,000	2,622,000
Four-year institutions					
Total	8,923,000	8,990,000	9,066,000	9,120,000	9,227,000
Public	6,045,000	6,088,000	6,139,000	6,175,000	6,247,000
Private	2,878,000	2,902,000	2,927,000	2,945,000	2,980,000
Two-year institutions					
Total	5,312,000	5,376,000	5,446,000	5,501,000	5,576,000
Public	5,038,000	5,099,000	5,166,000	5,218,000	5,290,000
Private	274,000	277,000	280,000	283,000	286,000
Undergraduate					
Total	12,165,000	12,247,000	12,356,000	12,449,000	12,610,000
Public	9,818,000	9,892,000	9,987,000	10,065,000	10,196,000
Private	2,347,000	2,355,000	2,369,000	2,384,000	2,414,000
Graduate					
Total	1,752,000	1,793,000	1,826,000	1,842,000	1,859,000
Public	1,134,000	1,160,000	1,182,000	1,192,000	1,204,000
Private	618,000	633,000	644,000	650,000	655,000
Professional					
Total	318,000	326,000	330,000	330,000	334,000
Public	131,000	135,000	136,000	136,000	137,000
Private	187,000	191,000	194,000	194,000	197,000
High-school graduates					
Total	2,446,000	2,470,000	2,464,000	2,563,000	2,615,000
Public	2,193,000	2,215,000	2,209,000	2,298,000	2,345,000
Private	253,000	255,000	255,000	265,000	270,000

1997	1998	1999	2000	2001	2002
14,978,000	15,227,000	15,462,000	15,692,000	15,865,000	16,030,000
6,691,000	6,774,000	6,853,000	6,922,000	6,991,000	7,052,000
3,924,000	3,995,000	4,061,000	4,122,000	4,183,000	4,234,000
2,767,000	2,779,000	2,792,000	2,800,000	2,808,000	2,818,000
8,287,000	8,453,000	8,609,000	8,770,000	8,874,000	8,978,000
4,288,000	4,413,000	4,527,000	4,648,000	4,723,000	4,801,000
3,999,000	4,040,000	4,082,000	4,122,000	4,151,000	4,177,000
11,673,000	11,864,000	12,043,000	12,220,000	12,355,000	12,478,000
3,305,000	3,363,000	3,419,000	3,472,000	3,510,000	3,552,000
8,212,000	8,408,000	8,588,000	8,770,000	8,906,000	9,035,000
6,766,000	6,819,000	6,874,000	6,922,000	6,959,000	6,995,000
10,656,000	10,871,000	11,070,000	11,270,000	11,418,000	11,561,000
7,999,000	8,161,000	8,308,000	8,456,000	8,569,000	8,672,000
2,656,000	2,712,000	2,763,000	2,813,000	2,850,000	2,889,000
9,334,000	9,500,000	9,655,000	9,810,000	9,927,000	10,041,000
6,320,000	6,434,000	6,539,000	6,646,000	6,727,000	6,803,000
3,014,000	3,066,000	3,116,000	3,164,000	3,200,000	3,238,000
5,644,000	5,727,000	5,807,000	5,882,000	5,938,000	5,989,000
5,353,000	5,430,000	5,504,000	5,574,000	5,628,000	5,675,000
291,000	297,000	303,000	308,000	310,000	314,000
12,768,000	12,998,000	13,216,000	13,436,000	13,598,000	13,748,000
10,322,000	10,501,000	10,670,000	10,841,000	10,969,000	11,084,000
2,446,000	2,497,000	2,546,000	2,595,000	2,629,000	2,664,000
1,872,000	1,888,000	1,901,000	1,908,000	1,915,000	1,926,000
1,212,000	1,223,000	1,231,000	1,236,000	1,241,000	1,248,000
660,000	665,000	670,000	672,000	674,000	678,000
338,000	341,000	345,000	348,000	352,000	356,000
139,000	140,000	142,000	143,000	145,000	146,000
199,000	201,000	203,000	205,000	207,000	210,000
2,719,000	2,831,000	2,885,000	2,932,000	2,943,000	2,882,000
2,438,000	2,538,000	2,587,000	2,629,000	2,639,000	2,584,000
281,000	293,000	298,000	303,000	304,000	298,000

Continued on Following Page

Projections of College Enrollment, High-School Graduates, and Degrees Conferred, continued

	1992	1993	1994	1995	1996
Degrees					
Associate					
Total	477,000	476,000	478,000	480,000	487,000
Men	205,000	204,000	204,000	203,000	204,000
Women	272,000	272,000	274,000	277,000	283,000
Bachelor's					
Total	1,081,000	1,101,000	1,100,000	1,100,000	1,098,000
Men	495,000	514,000	511,000	510,000	507,000
Women	586,000	587,000	589,000	590,000	591,000
Master's					
Total	338,000	343,000	350,000	354,000	354,000
Men	157,000	159,000	162,000	165,000	164,000
Women	181,000	184,000	188,000	189,000	190,000
Doctoral					
Total	39,300	39,800	40,000	40,200	40,400
Men	24,300	24,400	24,100	23,800	23,600
Women	15,000	15,400	15,900	16,400	16,800
Professional					
Total	80,100	82,600	85,500	87,800	88,100
Men	49,000	50,400	51,500	52,500	52,800
Women	31,100	32,200	34,000	35,300	35,300

Note: Details may not add to totals because of rounding.
* Estimate based on full-time enrollment plus the full-time equivalent of part-time enrollment as reported by institutions

Proportion of 18-to-24-Year-Olds Enrolled in College, by High-School-Graduation Status and Race

	White All	White High-school graduates	Black All	Black High-school graduates	Hispanic All	Hispanic High-school graduates
1980	26.2%	31.8%	19.2%	27.6%	16.1%	29.8%
1981	26.7	32.5	19.9	28.0	16.7	29.9
1982	27.2	33.1	19.8	28.0	16.8	29.2
1983	27.0	32.9	19.2	27.0	17.2	31.4
1984	28.0	33.7	20.4	27.2	17.9	29.9
1985	28.7	34.4	19.8	26.1	16.9	26.9
1986	28.6	34.5	22.2	29.1	18.2	30.4
1987	30.2	36.6	22.8	30.0	17.6	28.5
1988	31.3	38.1	21.1	28.1	17.0	30.9
1989	31.8	38.8	23.5	30.8	16.1	28.7
1990	32.5	39.4	25.4	33.0	15.8	29.0

Note: The figures are based on annual Census Bureau surveys of 60,000 households. The survey defined high-school graduates as those who had completed four years of high school or more. Hispanics may be of any race.

SOURCE: CENSUS BUREAU

1997	1998	1999	2000	2001	2002
491,000	500,000	507,000	519,000	529,000	539,000
205,000	208,000	209,000	213,000	216,000	219,000
286,000	292,000	298,000	306,000	313,000	320,000
1,100,000	1,102,000	1,114,000	1,129,000	1,164,000	1,189,000
505,000	503,000	507,000	509,000	523,000	528,000
595,000	599,000	607,000	620,000	641,000	661,000
355,000	357,000	362,000	368,000	376,000	383,000
164,000	165,000	168,000	173,000	179,000	184,000
191,000	192,000	194,000	195,000	197,000	199,000
40,600	40,900	41,100	41,200	41,400	41,400
23,400	23,300	23,200	22,900	22,700	22,400
17,200	17,600	17,900	18,300	18,700	19,000
88,100	89,100	90,900	92,200	92,900	94,400
52,800	53,500	54,600	55,300	56,000	57,000
35,300	35,600	36,300	36,900	36,900	37,400

SOURCE: U. S. DEPARTMENT OF EDUCATION

Number of Colleges by Enrollment, Fall 1990

	All institutions	Universities	Other 4-year institutions	2-year institutions
Public institutions				
Under 200	11	0	1	10
200 to 499	34	0	11	23
500 to 999	108	0	21	87
1,000 to 2,499	376	0	98	278
2,500 to 4,999	336	0	106	230
5,000 to 9,999	340	6	135	199
10,000 to 19,999	231	27	101	103
20,000 to 29,999	82	39	20	23
30,000 or more	30	22	3	5
All	1,548	94	496	958
Private institutions				
Under 200	402	0	279	123
200 to 499	398	0	232	166
500 to 999	369	0	280	89
1,000 to 2,499	504	0	466	38
2,500 to 4,999	162	5	152	5
5,000 to 9,999	77	25	51	1
10,000 to 19,999	32	24	7	1
20,000 to 29,999	6	5	0	1
30,000 or more	3	3	0	0
All	1,953	62	1,467	424
All institutions				
Under 200	413	0	280	133
200 to 499	432	0	243	189
500 to 999	477	0	301	176
1,000 to 2,499	880	0	564	316
2,500 to 4,999	498	5	258	235
5,000 to 9,999	417	31	186	200
10,000 to 19,999	263	51	108	104
20,000 to 29,999	88	44	20	24
30,000 or more	33	25	3	5
All	3,501	156	1,963	1,382

Note: Figures exclude approximately 50 institutions that did not report enrollment.

SOURCE: U.S. DEPARTMENT OF EDUCATION

Median Salaries of Administrators, 1991-92

Executive

Chief executive of a system	$99,452
Assistant to chief executive of a system	62,676
Chief executive of a single institution	95,500
Assistant to chief executive of a single institution	46,723
Executive vice-president	75,743

Academic

Chief academic officer	$72,676
Chief health-professions officer	105,000
Director, library services	47,064
Circulation librarian	29,165
Acquisitions librarian	33,611
Technical-services librarian	33,817
Public-services librarian	36,000
Reference librarian	31,328
Director, institutional research	48,980
Associate director, institutional research	38,474
Director, educational-media services	35,931
Director, learning-resources center	38,742
Director, international studies	47,947
Director, academic computer center	47,800
Administrator, grants and contracts	47,874
Dean, architecture	90,441
Dean, agriculture	90,168
Dean, arts and letters	61,944
Dean, arts and sciences	72,363
Dean, business	71,658
Dean, communications	56,127
Dean, continuing education	54,471
Dean, dentistry	120,000
Dean, education	70,000
Dean, engineering	90,400
Dean, extension	62,899
Dean, fine arts	65,050
Dean, graduate programs	70,784
Dean, health-related professions	65,000
Dean, home economics	82,000
Dean, humanities	50,992
Dean, instruction	57,854
Dean, law	124,965
Dean, library and information sciences	69,607
Dean, mathematics	51,453
Dean, medicine	173,287
Dean, music	61,542
Dean, nursing	65,000
Dean, pharmacy	99,300
Dean, public health	128,250
Dean, sciences	60,001
Dean, social sciences	51,714
Dean, social work	84,043
Dean, special programs	48,469
Dean, undergraduate programs	59,500
Dean, veterinary medicine	110,250
Dean, vocational education	54,065

Continued on Following Page

Median Salaries of Administrators, continued

Administrative

Chief business officer	$68,500
Chief administration officer	68,712
Chief financial officer	63,268
Director, environmental health and safety	46,897
Director, telecommunications	46,736
Chief planning officer	62,797
Chief budget officer	55,030
Chief planning and budget officer	70,200
General counsel	73,826
Staff attorney	55,461
Chief personnel and human resources officer	50,637
Manager, benefits	33,570
Manager, training and development	36,193
Manager, employee relations	40,803
Manager, labor relations	49,662
Manager, employment	33,413
Manager, wage and salary	37,147
Manager, personnel information systems	36,130
Director, affirmative action and equal employment	51,315
Director, personnel and affirmative action	39,557
Chief information systems officer	57,872
Data base administrator	43,700
Systems analyst, highest level	38,892
Systems analyst, lowest level	32,064
Programmer analyst, highest level	32,684
Programmer analyst, lowest level	26,832
Director, administrative computer center	47,230
Chief physical-plant officer	49,410
Manager, landscape and grounds	31,723
Manager, building maintenance trades	35,097
Manager, technical trades	37,588
Manager, custodial services	30,120
Manager, power plant	39,460
Comptroller	50,000
Manager, payroll	30,531
Director, accounting	41,508
Staff accountant, highest level	30,000
Staff accountant, lowest level	24,228
Bursar	36,630
Director, purchasing	38,976
Director, bookstore	29,088
Director, internal audit	47,706
Director, auxiliary services	51,180
Manager, mail services	23,213
Director, campus security	37,382
Director, risk management and insurance	51,266
Administrator, hospital medical center	136,667

External affairs

Chief development officer	$64,000
Director, annual giving	36,130

Note: The figures are based on a survey sent to 3,400 colleges and universities in the fall of 1991. The response rate was 42 per cent. The figures are meant to provide a broad overview of salaries in higher education.

Director, corporate and foundation relations	$43,343
Coordinator, resource development	30,725
Director, estate planning	48,900
Chief public-relations officer	43,048
Director, governmental relations	65,840
Chief development and public-relations officer	71,000
Director, alumni affairs	36,490
Director, development and alumni affairs	45,000
Director, special and deferred gifts	45,856
Director, church relations	36,000
Director, community services	42,761
Director, publications	36,915
Manager, printing services	30,990
Director, information office	37,745
Director, news bureau	33,168

Student services

Chief student-affairs officer	$60,662
Dean, students	49,945
Chief admissions officer	45,621
Associate director, admissions	32,568
Admissions counselor	21,889
Academic adviser	27,420
Director, admissions and registrar	46,989
Registrar	40,000
Associate registrar	33,790
Director, admissions and financial aid	48,550
Director, student financial aid	39,264
Associate director, student financial aid	29,203
Director, food services	40,728
Director, residence halls	36,000
Associate director, student housing	31,860
Housing officer, administrative operations	32,320
Housing officer, residential life	26,702
Director, foreign students	33,643
Director, student union and student activities	38,070
Director, student union	41,004
Director, student activities	30,500
Director, student placement	36,875
Director, student counseling	42,750
Director, student health services, physician	79,615
Director, student health services, nurse	29,510
Director, campus ministries	32,000
Director, athletics	50,500
Men's	49,100
Women's	40,543
Director, sports information	28,000
Director, campus recreation	32,911
Chief, enrollment management	54,372
Director, minority affairs	37,000
Director, conferences	36,225

SOURCE: COLLEGE AND UNIVERSITY PERSONNEL ASSOCIATION

Average Faculty Salaries, 1991-92

	All Salary	All 1-year increase	Public Salary	Public 1-year increase
Doctoral institutions				
Professor	$65,190	3.1%	$61,950	2.5%
Associate professor	46,290	3.0	45,090	2.4
Assistant professor	39,120	3.3	38,030	2.8
Instructor	27,670	3.2	26,610	2.7
Lecturer	32,510	—	32,250	—
All	51,080	3.1	48,930	2.6
Comprehensive institutions				
Professor	53,880	3.6	53,750	3.2
Associate professor	43,010	4.0	43,020	3.6
Assistant professor	35,720	4.4	35,730	3.9
Instructor	27,310	4.6	27,210	4.5
Lecturer	27,410	—	26,990	—
All	43,440	3.9	43,490	3.5
Baccalaureate institutions				
Professor	46,860	4.3	47,480	2.8
Associate professor	37,680	4.4	39,150	2.8
Assistant professor	31,500	4.8	32,580	3.1
Instructor	25,830	4.2	26,390	2.8
Lecturer	28,250	—	27,300	—
All	37,260	4.5	37,890	2.9
2-year institutions with academic ranks				
Professor	47,300	3.8	47,700	3.8
Associate professor	38,860	3.2	39,300	3.2
Assistant professor	33,150	3.4	33,550	3.4
Instructor	27,610	4.2	27,950	4.1
Lecturer	23,710	—	23,820	—
All	37,760	3.6	38,210	3.6
2-year institutions without academic ranks				
All	38,060	3.0	38,220	3.0
All institutions except those without academic ranks				
Professor	58,220	3.4	57,370	2.8
Associate professor	43,260	3.5	43,420	2.8
Assistant professor	36,060	3.8	36,330	3.2
Instructor	27,170	3.9	27,180	3.6
Lecturer	30,470	—	29,990	—
All	45,360	3.5	45,260	2.9

— No data reported

Note: Figures cover full-time members of the instructional staff except those in medical schools. The salaries are adjusted to a standard nine-month work year. The salary figures are based on 2,072 institutions; percentage increases are based on 1,944 institutions.

Private, independent		Church-related	
Salary	1-year increase	Salary	1-year increase
$76,890	4.8%	$68,140	5.3%
51,700	4.8	48,720	5.7
43,630	4.6	40,630	4.9
33,220	4.0	34,710	6.5
34,090	—	29,280	—
60,260	4.7	51,820	5.4
54,980	4.3	53,350	5.8
43,330	4.7	42,620	5.8
35,700	5.0	35,690	6.4
27,250	4.5	27,890	5.7
28,890	—	35,460	—
43,670	4.6	42,790	5.9
52,230	4.5	41,980	5.1
40,220	4.6	34,910	5.2
33,370	5.1	29,580	5.5
27,510	5.4	24,680	4.7
34,620	—	22,390	—
40,920	4.7	34,090	5.2
37,180	4.9	32,140	4.5
29,880	4.3	27,740	5.4
26,520	4.3	24,010	3.9
21,100	4.6	22,360	6.1
—	—	—	—
28,400	4.5	26,610	4.8
29,210	5.9	26,150	8.7
66,060	4.6	49,480	5.3
45,570	4.7	39,300	5.5
37,820	4.8	32,620	5.6
28,470	4.6	25,940	5.5
33,260	—	28,180	—
50,030	4.7	39,020	5.5

SOURCE: AMERICAN ASSOCIATION OF UNIVERSITY PROFESSORS

Average Faculty Salaries by Rank in Selected Fields at 4-Year Institutions, 1991-92

	Professor	Associate professor	Assistant professor*	New assistant professor	Instructor	All ranks
Accounting						
Public	$62,262	$51,784	$46,097	$51,749	$30,024	$50,714
Private	59,767	39,880	40,457	41,843	32,280	42,009
Agribusiness and agricultural production						
Public	51,116	39,480	33,416	34,067	22,844	43,035
Private	—	—	31,830	—	—	36,921
Anthropology						
Public	53,304	40,661	31,907	30,666	28,834	43,665
Private	53,514	40,869	33,333	—	—	43,590
Architecture and environmental design						
Public	54,920	42,434	34,595	32,563	—	44,769
Private	60,423	44,673	36,090	33,376	31,762	45,713
Business						
Public	60,741	50,470	46,399	49,607	30,133	50,443
Private	71,688	50,635	43,324	41,264	29,948	51,647
Chemistry, general						
Public	53,452	40,489	33,232	32,471	25,611	45,073
Private	52,600	38,905	32,352	30,168	26,502	43,910
Communications						
Public	51,019	40,221	32,285	31,466	26,471	38,084
Private	46,698	38,540	31,171	30,772	24,603	35,380
Computer and information science						
Public	59,466	48,590	42,045	44,263	28,037	47,345
Private	58,410	44,378	38,470	36,887	30,814	43,504
Economics						
Public	57,682	45,192	38,535	38,950	30,267	47,491
Private	66,262	43,305	38,158	36,851	32,003	48,905
Education						
Public	50,666	40,561	33,186	32,802	24,836	41,207
Private	48,776	37,969	31,623	31,390	24,399	37,986
Engineering						
Public	60,028	48,658	42,343	43,261	31,236	50,158
Private	71,292	52,577	45,989	43,244	28,792	59,027
Foreign languages						
Public	51,637	39,705	31,447	30,276	24,692	38,889
Private	49,480	39,301	31,729	29,884	25,737	38,412
Geography						
Public	52,146	40,707	33,170	32,644	27,959	43,015
Private	49,668	39,133	32,502	—	—	41,236
History						
Public	51,432	39,904	31,350	30,265	27,429	43,619
Private	50,016	39,308	31,501	29,613	26,395	41,724
Letters						
Public	50,198	39,167	31,224	30,504	23,866	38,550
Private	48,819	37,809	30,630	29,100	25,493	38,672

Note: The figures are based on reports from 290 public institutions that are members of the American Association of State Colleges and Universities and from 517 private colleges and universities.

* Includes data for new assistant professors

— Indicates fewer than 10 positions in a rank

	Professor	Associate professor	Assistant professor*	New assistant professor	Instructor	All ranks
Library sciences						
Public	$52,285	$41,266	$33,882	—	$27,064	$39,903
Private	48,574	37,571	31,024	—	25,946	34,463
Life sciences						
Public	51,051	41,058	33,287	31,209	24,802	43,364
Private	49,412	38,068	31,887	30,309	23,411	41,266
Mathematics						
Public	53,438	41,304	34,271	33,562	25,219	41,163
Private	53,789	40,429	33,043	31,759	25,269	41,184
Nursing, general						
Public	51,127	40,774	33,179	32,027	27,972	36,029
Private	44,914	36,591	31,518	29,611	28,021	33,489
Philosophy and religion						
Public	52,590	40,221	31,927	30,496	27,608	43,281
Private	47,154	38,162	31,009	29,682	24,798	39,640
Physical sciences						
Public	53,627	40,002	33,636	33,322	26,230	43,647
Private	51,347	38,164	32,541	29,242	—	41,363
Physics, general						
Public	55,088	42,070	34,862	33,406	24,872	47,095
Private	58,620	42,311	35,138	31,232	26,197	48,466
Political science and government						
Public	53,069	40,642	32,203	31,563	27,102	43,009
Private	53,967	40,445	32,503	30,882	29,060	42,961
Psychology						
Public	53,207	41,221	33,838	31,318	27,544	44,147
Private	50,840	39,006	32,063	31,186	24,192	41,238
Social sciences						
Public	50,997	39,359	30,688	30,621	26,475	40,135
Private	51,780	37,934	31,488	29,905	24,468	40,740
Social work, general						
Public	53,235	42,694	33,845	32,589	29,924	41,326
Private	47,137	38,768	31,676	31,020	26,940	36,438
Sociology						
Public	51,692	40,819	32,786	31,530	27,347	42,638
Private	48,766	38,416	31,936	30,240	26,953	39,805
Special education, general						
Public	51,712	40,844	33,362	32,002	28,458	42,287
Private	49,219	40,641	30,330	—	—	39,382
Teacher education, general programs						
Public	49,893	41,114	33,333	32,651	27,963	40,525
Private	42,838	35,744	30,153	29,485	24,209	34,758
Visual and performing arts						
Public	48,456	38,109	30,593	29,290	26,567	38,491
Private	46,636	37,503	30,664	29,313	25,900	37,006

SOURCE: COLLEGE AND UNIVERSITY PERSONNEL ASSOCIATION

Characteristics of Full-Time College Professors by Type of Institution, 1987

	All	Research Public	Research Private	Doctoral Public	Doctoral Private
Total	489,000	96,000	39,000	36,000	15,000
Sex					
Men	72.7%	79.3%	80.5%	74.5%	77.3%
Women	27.3	20.7	19.5	25.5	22.7
Racial and ethnic group					
American Indian	0.7	0.7	—	0.6	0.5
Asian	4.2	4.8	3.5	4.5	5.9
Black, non-Hispanic	3.2	1.6	6.1	1.8	0.1
Hispanic	2.3	2.4	5.0	1.1	2.2
White, non-Hispanic	89.5	90.4	85.4	92.0	91.3
Age					
Under 30	1.6	1.1	0.6	1.8	1.3
30 to 34	8.3	7.1	11.5	10.2	4.5
35 to 39	14.7	16.5	21.4	14.8	17.9
40 to 44	16.7	15.2	17.6	14.0	11.4
45 to 49	18.9	18.5	15.1	18.7	17.3
50 to 54	15.1	14.8	12.3	15.9	18.4
55 to 59	12.0	12.1	8.6	13.2	10.7
60 and older	12.7	14.7	12.8	11.5	18.5
Highest academic degree					
Doctorate	54.7	72.1	69.1	73.0	74.4
Professional	12.7	18.3	23.9	5.4	14.9
Master's	27.9	8.5	6.2	19.2	10.7
Graduate work, no degree	1.5	0.2	0.7	1.0	—
Bachelor's	2.2	0.9	0.2	0.9	—
Less than bachelor's	0.9	—	—	0.5	—
Academic rank					
Professor	33.1	45.3	39.2	35.6	35.4
Associate professor	23.7	28.1	25.3	30.1	34.3
Assistant professor	22.8	21.2	29.1	25.9	28.3
Instructor	11.5	2.7	3.1	6.7	2.0
Lecturer	1.6	2.7	2.4	1.4	—
Other	0.9	0.1	0.8	0.3	—
No rank	6.5	—	0.1	—	0.1

Note: The figures are based on a 1988 survey of 11,013 faculty members at 480 colleges and universities. The response rate was 76 per cent. The category of "Other" institutions includes such specialized institutions as theological seminaries. Because of rounding, figures may not add to 100 per cent. A dash indicates less than 0.1 per cent.

Comprehensive		Liberal arts	2-year			
Public	Private	All	Public	Private	Medical	Other
93,000	35,000	39,000	91,000	4,000	25,000	15,000
71.1%	72.5%	70.9%	62.1%	64.2%	75.7%	78.7%
28.9	27.5	29.1	37.9	35.8	24.3	21.3
0.6	1.1	1.2	0.9	—	1.4	—
5.8	4.4	2.7	1.6	0.5	10.3	1.0
3.5	1.7	8.0	3.0	3.1	3.0	2.3
2.1	1.6	1.2	3.5	2.3	—	1.6
88.0	91.2	86.9	91.0	94.1	85.3	95.1
1.6	2.1	2.2	1.9	9.5	0.7	1.2
7.9	6.2	8.5	5.6	6.7	22.1	5.7
12.5	16.3	14.4	12.2	4.6	10.7	17.0
15.7	18.4	19.8	18.1	36.3	16.9	17.0
21.2	18.0	19.9	21.2	3.3	13.5	18.2
15.3	16.9	9.9	18.2	19.8	10.5	15.6
13.2	10.2	13.6	13.5	12.8	8.6	9.1
12.6	11.9	11.7	9.3	6.8	17.0	16.3
62.7	64.0	60.3	17.5	13.8	25.9	40.6
6.2	8.1	1.8	1.5	3.2	62.7	27.8
29.9	24.3	34.6	64.9	58.1	9.8	26.5
0.6	1.2	2.0	4.8	6.1	—	1.8
0.6	1.8	1.3	7.7	10.9	—	2.9
—	0.6	—	3.7	8.0	1.5	0.5
37.2	30.8	29.4	15.6	12.5	31.6	34.3
26.5	29.5	23.0	9.5	4.6	26.9	22.4
23.4	32.7	31.2	10.9	21.9	29.0	16.3
8.7	6.1	9.3	33.3	25.0	11.8	9.1
3.0	0.4	0.5	0.7	0.5	—	—
1.2	0.3	0.6	1.7	0.6	0.7	3.2
—	0.2	5.9	28.3	34.9	—	14.6

SOURCE: U.S. DEPARTMENT OF EDUCATION

Faculty Attitudes and Activities, 1989-90

Political orientation:
Far left
Liberal
Moderate
Conservative
Far right

Professional writings accepted for publication or published in last two years:
None
1-2
3-4
5-10
11-20
21-50
50 or more

Professional goals noted as essential or very important:
Engage in research
Engage in outside activities
Provide services to the community
Participate in committee or other administrative work
Be a good colleague
Be a good teacher

Aspects of job noted as very satisfactory or satisfactory:
Salary and fringe benefits
Opportunity for scholarly pursuits
Teaching load
Quality of students
Working conditions
Autonomy and independence
Relationships with other faculty
Competency of colleagues
Visibility for jobs at other institutions and organizations
Job security
Undergraduate course assignments
Graduate course assignments
Relationship with administration
Overall job satisfaction

Attributes noted as being very descriptive of own institution:
It is easy for students to see faculty outside of regular office hours
There is a great deal of conformity among students
Most students are very bright
The administration is open about its policies
There is keen competition among most students for high grades
Faculty are rewarded for their advising skills
The faculty are typically at odds with the campus administration
Intercollegiate sports are overemphasized
Faculty here respect each other
Most students are treated like "numbers in a book"

	All institutions			Universities		Other 4-year colleges		2-year colleges
	Total	Men	Women	Public	Private	Public	Private	Public
	4.9%	4.9%	5.1%	6.5%	8.2%	4.3%	5.3%	2.3%
	36.8	35.6	39.7	42.1	48.0	35.7	37.0	27.1
	40.2	39,8	40.9	37.9	30.8	42.1	39.2	45.0
	17.8	19.2	14.2	13.1	12.5	17.5	18.3	25.2
	0.4	0.5	0.1	0.3	0.5	0.4	0.2	0.4
	45.3%	40.9%	56.3%	21.6%	15.8%	42.8%	51.9%	81.9%
	25.7	26.1	24.5	27.6	26.1	31.2	29.5	13.9
	15.8	17.4	11.7	25.1	28.4	15.8	12.1	2.8
	10.8	12.4	6.7	21.0	23.9	8.5	5.4	0.9
	1.9	2.4	0.6	3.8	4.4	1.4	0.7	0.2
	0.4	0.6	0.2	0.9	1.3	0.2	0.2	0.1
	0.1	0.1	0.1	0.1	0.1	0.1	0.1	0.1
	58.5%	61.1%	52.3%	78.6%	85.2%	61.0%	54.2%	25.1%
	52.5	49.8	59.1	48.7	48.3	54.4	53.9	54.9
	43.4	39.9	52.0	35.8	33.6	45.7	44.8	52.4
	29.2	25.7	37.9	23.0	19.3	30.7	32.1	36.3
	80.0	77.4	86.4	75.9	74.8	79.7	83.4	84.5
	98.2	98.1	98.4	97.6	95.5	98.3	99.0	99.2
	44.5%	44.3%	44.9%	44.3%	51.3%	39.0%	40.2%	52.1%
	45.4	48.4	37.8	53.3	62.4	38.1	38.8	43.6
	50.3	51.3	47.7	58.3	63.5	42.2	45.2	49.3
	37.5	35.5	42.5	38.0	58.6	32.2	43.3	30.2
	64.6	65.7	62.0	66.4	74.8	58.9	66.2	63.9
	82.9	83.3	81.9	85.0	89.1	80.0	83.8	80.6
	75.1	74.5	76.5	69.0	74.3	73.9	79.7	80.0
	68.4	68.1	69.0	64.6	75.0	63.3	74.4	71.2
	43.1	43.7	41.7	45.5	58.8	38.3	39.5	42.0
	74.6	77.7	66.9	73.5	73.8	75.4	69.9	79.4
	77.5	77.8	76.8	76.8	79.5	75.4	79.7	78.2
	72.3	73.9	66.0	75.1	78.0	71.0	68.2	41.3
	51.8	50.7	54.4	48.4	53.1	49.0	58.2	52.8
	69.2	69.0	69.8	65.6	74.8	64.9	71.4	74.4
	33.6%	33.6%	33.7%	20.6%	27.6%	30.5%	53.6%	38.2%
	24.6	25.1	23.3	26.2	24.9	22.7	35.7	15.8
	8.9	9.0	8.6	7.0	35.5	4.0	13.6	2.3
	11.9	11.5	13.0	7.9	8.8	10.1	17.3	15.8
	20.1	20.5	19.0	25.4	48.9	13.9	20.6	9.4
	2.0	1.9	2.2	1.3	2.0	1.6	4.1	1.4
	18.6	19.1	17.5	19.8	14.9	21.0	14.7	19.1
	16.1	17.1	13.5	33.0	6.8	15.6	10.0	5.5
	31.7	30.1	35.7	23.3	35.0	24.4	44.1	38.2
	5.9	6.3	4.8	12.1	4.5	6.2	1.5	2.8

Continued on Following Page

Faculty Attitudes and Activities, continued

Attributes noted as being very descriptive of own institution, continued:
There is little or no contact between students and faculty
The student body is apathetic and has little "school spirit"
Faculty are rewarded for being good teachers
Student services are well supported

Agree strongly or somewhat that at own institution:
Faculty here are interested in students' personal problems
Most faculty are sensitive to the issues of minorities
The curriculum has suffered from faculty overspecialization
Faculty are committed to the welfare of institution
Many courses include minority-group perspectives

Administrators consider student concerns when making policy
Faculty here are strongly interested in the academic problems of undergraduates
There is a lot of campus racial conflict
Students of different racial or ethnic origins communicate well with one another
Campus administrators care little about what happens to students

There is little trust between minority-student groups and campus administrators
Many courses include feminist perspectives
There are many opportunities for faculty and students to socialize with one another
Administrators consider faculty concerns when making policy
Faculty feel that students are well prepared academically
Institutional demands for doing research interfere with my effectiveness as a teacher

Issues noted as being of highest or high priority at own institution:
Promoting the intellectual development of students
Helping students examine and understand their personal values
Increasing the representation of minorities in the faculty and administration
Developing a sense of community among students and faculty
Developing leadership ability among students

Conducting basic and applied research
Raising money for the institution
Developing leadership ability among faculty
Increasing the representation of women in the faculty and administration
Facilitating student involvement in community-service projects

Helping students learn how to bring about change in American society
Helping solve major social and environmental problems
Maintaining a campus climate where differences of opinion can be aired openly
Increasing or maintaining institutional prestige
Developing among students and faculty an appreciation for a multicultural society

Hiring faculty "stars"
Economizing and cutting costs
Recruiting more minority students
Enhancing the institution's national image
Creating a positive undergraduate experience
Creating a diverse multicultural environment on campus

Note: The figures are based on survey responses of 35,478 faculty members at 392 colleges and universities. The survey was conducted in the fall and winter of 1989-90 and was limited to full-time professors who spent at least part of their time teaching undergraduates. The response rate was 55 per cent. The figures were statistically adjusted to represent the total population of full-time faculty members. Because of rounding or multiple responses, figures may add to more than 100 per cent. The total includes figures for private two-year colleges, which are not shown separately.

	All institutions		Universities		Other 4-year colleges		2-year colleges
Total	Men	Women	Public	Private	Public	Private	Public
5.1%	5.5%	4.3%	7.5%	5.9%	5.9%	2.0%	3.9%
17.0	18.3	13.7	12.9	7.6	21.4	8.6	27.3
9.8	9.6	10.2	6.2	10.8	8.1	19.2	8.0
18.8	18.6	19.4	15.9	18.1	15.4	25.9	20.5
73.8%	71.9%	78.5%	58.4%	60.8%	72.7%	89.3%	84.9%
69.1	69.5	68.0	64.8	67.0	67.6	73.4	73.0
28.3	29.8	24.5	42.3	37.4	27.2	21.0	16.1
76.1	75.2	78.2	67.5	76.3	71.9	87.1	81.5
36.0	34.6	39.6	33.2	29.7	37.3	37.3	40.0
59.7	59.3	61.0	51.7	55.9	58.2	71.2	62.6
76.4	75.3	79.0	61.6	67.6	77.2	90.4	84.2
11.8	11.0	13.8	20.8	11.1	10.4	9.4	5.4
59.0	59.3	58.4	50.2	51.4	58.4	62.2	69.7
23.8	24.8	21.4	30.8	21.2	26.5	13.2	22.5
27.5	28.2	25.7	41.0	34.7	26.6	19.3	17.5
28.8	29.8	26.3	28.4	30.1	25.0	32.4	31.1
38.4	39.3	36.1	28.0	39.6	34.7	58.6	36.8
50.0	50.3	49.1	45.9	52.7	45.7	61.5	49.5
27.4	26.6	29.5	23.7	50.5	22.1	37.7	20.3
26.7	26.9	26.2	44.4	34.7	31.9	15.7	6.1
76.1%	75.5%	77.6%	70.6%	83.7%	72.4%	85.5%	75.8%
47.4	45.6	51.7	32.3	47.2	43.0	71.9	48.8
46.9	46.1	49.0	52.3	40.5	52.2	39.0	44.4
41.0	38.7	46.5	25.5	34.8	38.4	60.6	47.9
37.6	35.5	43.0	25.8	32.0	37.6	53.9	39.7
44.5	47.0	38.4	80.5	74.0	41.9	24.4	10.9
58.3	57.2	61.2	63.7	77.7	53.1	71.5	39.1
24.0	22.0	28.9	20.2	20.6	23.1	25.9	29.0
39.2	40.9	34.8	45.2	36.7	42.1	35.2	33.6
23.3	21.2	28.4	13.3	25.1	21.6	40.0	22.6
21.1	19.4	25.3	14.7	15.7	21.5	31.0	22.2
26.3	25.9	27.2	26.4	25.8	25.1	31.1	24.2
52.0	53.4	48.5	53.0	54.9	48.1	56.5	51.1
75.3	75.0	76.2	80.4	87.0	71.0	77.9	67.6
46.5	44.5	51.5	45.6	40.0	46.6	54.3	44.2
26.8	26.9	26.4	49.8	47.4	20.5	12.7	10.8
54.5	53.0	58.3	58.9	57.4	53.9	50.1	52.4
46.9	45.8	49.7	50.7	44.0	52.1	43.7	40.5
61.7	62.6	59.6	78.0	84.9	56.7	64.3	37.2
69.2	68.0	72.1	52.3	71.8	69.1	85.7	73.9
40.0	38.2	44.3	38.9	35.0	42.4	43.4	37.9

SOURCE: "THE AMERICAN COLLEGE TEACHER: NATIONAL NORMS FOR THE 1989-90 H.E.R.I. FACULTY SURVEY," PUBLISHED BY UNIVERSITY OF CALIFORNIA AT LOS ANGELES HIGHER EDUCATION RESEARCH INSTITUTE

Changes in the Size of the Full-Time Faculty in the Next 5 Years

	Total	2-year	Bacca-laureate	Compre-hensive	Doctoral
Proportion of institutions expecting to increase faculty hiring	53%	67%	45%	48%	30%
Expected increase:					
1% to 4%	11	8	13	14	30
5% to 9%	19	17	21	20	27
10% to 14%	29	27	46	19	15
15% or more	41	48	21	47	29
Proportion of institutions expecting to decrease the size of their faculty	20	14	15	28	34
Expected decrease:					
1% to 4%	20	29	0	15	34
5% to 9%	43	38	66	38	44
10% to 14%	28	19	17	46	14
15% or more	9	14	17	2	8
Proportion of institutions expecting an increased pace of retirements	69	82	54	71	48
Proportion of faculty expected to retire:					
1% to 4%	6	6	0	11	6
5% to 9%	24	16	53	17	20
10% to 14%	31	27	36	34	37
15% or more	38	50	11	38	37

Note: The figures are based on responses to a survey sent to senior administrators at 510 colleges and universities in the winter of 1992. The response rate was 81 per cent. Because of rounding, figures may not add to 100 per cent.

SOURCE: AMERICAN COUNCIL ON EDUCATION

Employment Status of Faculty Members, 1987

	All	Public 4-year	Private 4-year	Public 2-year	Other
Number of faculty members	825,000	319,000	218,000	218,000	70,000
Regular full-time	60%	72%	58%	41%	63%
Regular part-time	22	14	21	35	20
Temporary full-time	3	4	3	1	1
Temporary part-time	16	9	19	23	16

Note: The figures are based on a 1988 survey of administrators at 480 colleges and universities. The response rate was 88 per cent. The figures are adjusted to represent the distribution of all professors whose regular assignment includes instruction. The category of "Other" institutions includes private two-year colleges and specialized institutions. "Temporary" faculty members include visiting, acting, and adjunct professors. Because of rounding, figures may not add to 100 per cent.

SOURCE: U.S. DEPARTMENT OF EDUCATION

Faculty Workloads, 1989-90

	\multicolumn{9}{c}{Proportion reporting number of hours per week}
	0	1-4	5-8	9-12	13-16	17-20	21-34	35-44	45+
Teaching	0.3%	7.2%	26.2%	32.0%	17.6%	10.1%	5.9%	0.5%	0.1%
Preparing for teaching	0.3	8.4	22.9	25.2	17.3	13.8	9.4	2.0	0.7
Research and scholarly writing	20.2	27.9	16.4	12.4	7.3	6.7	6.3	1.8	1.0
Advising or counseling students	2.6	56.6	29.5	8.0	2.0	0.9	0.4	0.1	0.0
Committee work / meetings	4.6	68.8	20.6	4.3	1.1	0.3	0.1	0.0	0.0
Other administration	36.5	38.6	11.5	5.8	3.0	2.3	1.7	0.4	0.2
Consultation with clients or patients	68.8	20.7	6.3	2.2	0.8	0.6	0.4	0.1	0.1

Note: The figures are based on survey responses of 35,478 faculty members at 392 colleges and universities. The survey was conducted in the fall and winter of 1989-90 and was limited to full-time professors who spent at least part of their time teaching undergraduates. The response rate was 55 per cent. The figures were statistically adjusted to represent the total population of full-time faculty members. Because of rounding, figures may not add to 100 per cent.

SOURCE: "THE AMERICAN COLLEGE TEACHER: NATIONAL NORMS FOR THE 1989-90 H.E.R.I. FACULTY SURVEY," PUBLISHED BY UNIVERSITY OF CALIFORNIA AT LOS ANGELES HIGHER EDUCATION RESEARCH INSTITUTE

Full-Time Employees in Colleges and Universities by Racial and Ethnic Group, 1989-90

	Total	American Indian	Asian	Black	Hispanic	White
Professional						
Faculty	514,662	1,498	24,252	23,225	10,087	455,600
Executive, administrative, managerial	137,561	491	1,980	11,796	3,183	120,111
Other professionals	343,699	1,398	17,193	29,045	9,510	286,553
Non-professional						
Clerical, secretarial	370,336	1,969	8,928	58,966	18,798	281,675
Technical, paraprofessional	147,569	735	6,657	23,126	7,484	109,567
Skilled crafts	63,728	441	702	7,094	3,410	52,081
Service, maintenance	201,973	1,317	4,348	67,025	16,766	112,517
Total	1,779,528	7,849	64,060	220,277	69,238	1,418,104

Note: The figures are based on reports of 3,156 colleges.

SOURCE: U. S. EQUAL EMPLOYMENT OPPORTUNITY COMMISSION

Median Salaries of Chief Executive and Academic Officers, 1991-92

Type of institution by full-time-equivalent enrollment	Chief executive officer	Chief academic officer
Public		
Up to 2,012	$78,960	$58,227
2,013 to 4,498	89,444	70,103
4,499 to 10,743	98,000	82,272
10,744 or more	121,850	103,000
All	93,547	76,425
Private, independent		
Up to 653	$87,365	$57,963
654 to 1,316	98,950	69,833
1,317 to 2,784	122,500	84,254
2,785 or more	150,206	107,646
All	114,114	78,440
Private, religious		
Up to 648	$62,601	$46,800
649 to 1,106	80,000	55,740
1,107 to 1,933	94,580	62,672
1,934 or more	117,353	82,888
All	88,391	60,000

Note: The figures are based on reports of 1,438 colleges and universities.

SOURCE: COLLEGE AND UNIVERSITY PERSONNEL ASSOCIATION

Employment Policies and Perquisites for College Presidents, 1990-91

Housing
Residence provided on campus	47.7%
Allowances for housing provided by institution:	
Maintenance	91.5
Utilities	91.0
Household staff	70.0
Remodeling	54.8
Assistance where residence not provided:	
Home-purchase allowance	59.8
Mortgage-interest subsidy	24.5
Property-tax allowance	8.8
Rental allowance	33.3
Rent paid in full	5.9

Relocation
Household moving expenses:	
Paid in full	79.9%
Paid in part	12.0
Travel expenses for family:	
Paid in full	50.1
Paid in part	10.7

Car
Personal car provided	67.4%
Pool car:	
Assigned to chief executive	18.6
Available as needed	6.9
Operating expenses:	
Paid	65.3
Allowance provided	12.1
Option to purchase car	3.0
Driver provided as needed	11.3
No provision	14.8

Business travel, entertainment
Reimbursement	89.4%
Per-diem allowance	25.9
Unrestricted expense account	10.6
Reimbursement for spouse's expenses	27.1
Airline V.I.P. club	8.3
First-class air travel	4.8
Use of institution-owned aircraft	3.5

Local entertainment
Reimbursement	76.1%
Fixed allowance	23.8
Unrestricted expense account	13.3
Use of campus facilities	57.3
Use of institution staff	53.8
No provision	15.0

Tuition assistance for children
Full tuition at own institution	77.8%
Full tuition at other institution	48.0
50% or more at own institution	19.9
50% or more at other institution	29.5
Up to 50% at own institution	2.3
Up to 50% at other institution	11.6

Assistance to spouse
Staff and facilities for entertaining	17.5%
Secretarial staff	8.8
Remuneration for involvement at institution	3.4
No provision	78.8

Employment contracts
Provided	76.9%
Formal written contract	57.6
Letter of agreement	33.8
Oral agreement	5.4
Term of agreement specified	63.4
Time period:	
One year	31.3
Two years	10.4
Three years	31.8
Four years	10.4
Five years	11.6
Six or more years	2.7

Performance review
Formal performance review	77.9%
Frequency of review:	
End of contract term	5.1
Annually	69.1
Every two years	5.0
Every three years	5.8
Other	12.7
Responsibility for review:	
Chairman of the board	12.7
Committee of the board	28.2
Entire governing board	37.8
Special review committee	7.2
Other	14.1

Involuntary departure
Involuntary departure policy	25.8%
Departure pay	76.0
Amount:	
Less than 6 months' pay	23.3
6-12 months' pay	35.0
Over 12 months' pay	11.6
Negotiable at time of departure	30.1

Note: The figures are based on the reports of chief executive officers at 874 colleges and universities.

SOURCES: AMERICAN COUNCIL ON EDUCATION
ASSOCIATION OF GOVERNING BOARDS OF UNIVERSITIES AND COLLEGES
COLLEGE AND UNIVERSITY PERSONNEL ASSOCIATION

Total Return on College Endowments

	Average annual returns for periods ending June 30, 1991			
	1 year	3 years	5 years	10 years
All investment pools	+7.2%	+10.2%	+9.0%	+12.7%
By size				
$25-million and under	+7.8%	+9.6%	+8.4%	+12.2%
$25-million to $100-million	+7.2	+10.1	+8.8	+12.3
$100-million to $400-million	+7.0	+10.7	+9.3	+13.2
$400-million or more	+6.0	+10.7	+9.6	+13.3
By type of institution				
Public	+7.9%	+10.0%	+8.7%	+12.6%
Private	+7.0	+10.3	+9.1	+12.8
Comparative measurements				
Standard & Poor's 500 Index	+7.4%	+14.7%	+11.9%	+15.5%
Lehman Brothers Government Corporate Bond Index	+10.2	+9.9	+8.3	+13.2
Lehman Brothers Government Bond Index	+10.1	+9.7	+8.1	+12.7
Consumer Price Index	+4.6	+4.8	+4.3	+3.9

Note: The figures represent total-return rates, including changes in market value plus dividends and interest, for the periods ending June 30, 1991, based on data for 395 college and university investment pools.

SOURCE: NATIONAL ASSOCIATION OF COLLEGE AND UNIVERSITY BUSINESS OFFICERS

Top Fund Raisers, 1990-91

Institution	Amount	Amount per student
Harvard University	$195,582,616	$7,937
Stanford University	180,922,249	12,662
Cornell University	177,075,032	8,850
University of Pennsylvania	143,384,123	6,546
Yale University	132,416,904	12,213
University of Wisconsin at Madison	128,394,787	2,980
Columbia University	128,241,788	7,030
University of California at Berkeley	117,656,562	3,840
Duke University	113,693,144	10,391
Massachusetts Institute of Technology	110,307,644	11,457
University of Minnesota	109,131,731	1,493
University of Washington	102,831,966	3,066
Johns Hopkins University	100,437,183	7,157
University of Michigan	94,789,039	1,869
University of Southern California	94,303,629	3,324
Indiana University	90,901,034	985
University of Illinois	89,589,324	1,419
Princeton University	88,288,317	13,901
New York University	87,555,158	1,844
University of Chicago	82,185,081	7,405

SOURCE: COUNCIL FOR AID TO EDUCATION

College and University Endowments Over $80-Million, 1991

	Market value June 30, 1991
Harvard University	$4,669,683,000
University of Texas System	3,374,301,000
Princeton University	2,624,082,000
Yale University	2,566,680,000
Stanford University	2,043,000,000
Columbia University	1,525,904,000
Washington University	1,442,616,000
Massachusetts Institute of Technology	1,442,526,000
Texas A&M University System	1,395,454,000
Emory University	1,289,630,000
Rice University	1,140,044,000
University of Chicago	1,080,462,000
Northwestern University	1,046,905,000
Cornell University	953,600,000
University of Pennsylvania	825,601,000
University of Notre Dame	637,234,000
Vanderbilt University	613,207,000
Dartmouth College	594,582,000
New York University	581,921,000
University of Rochester	578,358,000
Johns Hopkins University	561,433,000
Rockefeller University	535,865,000
California Institute of Technology	534,085,000
Duke University	527,635,000
University of Southern California	522,931,000
University of Virginia	507,002,000
University of Michigan	500,430,000
Case Western Reserve University	442,722,000
Brown University	431,444,000
Macalester College	390,024,000
University of Delaware	389,523,000
Wellesley College	388,186,000
Southern Methodist University	366,566,000
Ohio State University	351,238,000
Smith College	343,133,000
Swarthmore College	342,453,000
Loyola University of Chicago	338,382,000
Wake Forest University	336,361,000
University of Cincinnati	329,176,000
Texas Christian University [1]	328,624,000
University of Tulsa [1]	319,492,000
Pomona College	316,196,000
Williams College	315,056,000
Carnegie Mellon University	313,331,000
Boston College [1]	312,000,000
Trinity University [1]	307,195,000
George Washington University	305,047,000
University of Richmond	297,478,000
University of Pittsburgh	296,515,000
Grinnell College	292,928,000
University of Minnesota	291,218,000

Continued on Following Page

College and University Endowments Over $80-Million, continued

	Market value June 30, 1991
Berea College	$286,279,000
Wesleyan University	271,903,000
Amherst College	268,411,000
Georgetown University	265,763,000
Baylor University [1]	264,163,000
Lehigh University	261,534,000
Vassar College	243,166,000
Rensselaer Polytechnic Institute	240,458,000
Kansas University Endowment Association	235,107,000
Tulane University	234,066,000
University of Florida Foundation	224,854,000
Oberlin College	224,294,000
Georgia Institute of Technology	223,153,000
Middlebury College	209,182,000
Pennsylvania State University	207,825,000
Saint Louis University	206,389,000
Lafayette College	206,382,000
University of Nebraska	201,153,000
University of Minnesota Foundation	200,803,000
University of Washington	198,343,000
University of Miami [1]	196,112,000
Purdue University	181,659,000
Mount Holyoke College	180,974,000
University of North Carolina at Chapel Hill	180,568,000
Washington State University	179,067,000
Thomas Jefferson University	176,665,000
Syracuse University	175,840,000
University of Alabama System [2]	175,000,000
Carleton College	174,132,000
Northeastern University	171,978,000
Tufts University	167,571,000
Boston University	167,097,000
Rochester Institute of Technology	165,659,000
Bryn Mawr College	163,802,000
Bowdoin College	161,556,000
Brandeis University	161,112,000
University of Missouri	160,193,000
Agnes Scott College	158,688,000
Rush University	156,549,000
University of Illinois Foundation	153,353,000
State University of New York at Buffalo and Foundation	151,017,000
Colgate University	146,555,000
University of Wisconsin Foundation	144,780,000
Trinity College (Conn.)	144,321,000
University of Oklahoma	143,966,000

Note: Table includes institutions participating in the comparative-performance study by the National Association of College and University Business Officers.

[1] As of May 31   [2] As of September 30

	Market value June 30, 1991
Academy of the New Church	$143,825,000
Colorado College	143,622,000
Occidental College	140,391,000
Southwestern University	136,462,000
Wabash College	135,934,000
Virginia Tech Foundation	130,200,000
Earlham College	129,634,000
Rutgers University	125,643,000
Claremont McKenna College	119,728,000
Hamilton College	118,447,000
University of Tennessee System	117,790,000
Santa Clara University	115,366,000
Washington and Lee University	113,638,000
Cranbrook Educational Community	112,322,000
Loyola Marymount University	112,279,000
Samford University [1]	111,778,000
University of Houston System	109,948,000
Bucknell University	109,470,000
University of Wisconsin System	108,842,000
Cooper Union	108,580,000
Radcliffe College	106,817,000
Worcester Polytechnic Institute	105,819,000
Union College (N.Y.)	105,806,000
Whitman College	104,877,000
University of Louisville Foundation	103,016,000
University of Georgia and Foundation	102,658,000
Mercer University	102,103,000
De Pauw University	98,838,000
University of the South	98,558,000
Reed College	97,802,000
University of California at Los Angeles Foundation	95,967,000
Marquette University	95,062,000
College of William and Mary	93,712,000
University of Iowa Foundation	92,724,000
Davidson College	92,568,000
Auburn University and Foundation	92,402,000
Franklin and Marshall College	90,357,000
Haverford College	89,059,000
College of the Holy Cross	88,344,000
University of Saint Thomas	87,986,000
Furman University [1]	87,867,000
Denison University	85,894,000
St. Lawrence University	85,718,000
Wheaton College (Ill.)	84,937,000
University of Kentucky	84,790,000
Drew University	84,497,000
Rhodes College	84,444,000
Pepperdine University	80,295,000
University of Colorado Foundation	80,081,000

SOURCE: NATIONAL ASSOCIATION OF COLLEGE AND UNIVERSITY BUSINESS OFFICERS

Largest Endowments per Student, 1991

	Endowment	Enrollment	Amount per student
Private institutions			
Academy of the New Church	$143,825,000	330	$435,833
Princeton University	2,624,082,000	6,349	413,306
Agnes Scott College	158,688,000	547	290,106
California Institute of Technology	534,085,000	1,861	286,988
Rice University	1,140,044,000	4,074	279,834
Harvard University	4,669,683,000	17,057	273,769
Swarthmore College	342,453,000	1,319	259,631
Yale University	2,566,680,000	10,702	239,823
Grinnell College	292,928,000	1,269	230,834
Pomona College	316,196,000	1,390	227,479
Public institutions			
Oregon Health Sciences University Foundation	$54,332,000	1,343	$40,456
University of Virginia	507,002,000	18,036	28,111
University of Delaware	389,523,000	17,192	22,657
Texas A&M University System	1,395,454,000	66,653	20,936
Georgia Institute of Technology	223,153,000	13,558	16,459
University of Medicine and Dentistry of New Jersey	46,017,000	3,215	14,313
College of William and Mary	93,712,000	6,935	13,513
University of Cincinnati	329,176,000	26,707	12,325
University of Michigan	500,430,000	43,599	11,478
Washington State University	179,067,000	17,503	10,231

Note: Based on market values of endowments as of June 30, 1991, and full-time-equivalent enrollment for fall 1990.

SOURCE: NATIONAL ASSOCIATION OF COLLEGE AND UNIVERSITY BUSINESS OFFICERS

Voluntary Support for Higher Education, 1990-91

Sources	Amount	Per cent	Percentage change 1-year	Percentage change 5-year
Alumni	$2,680,000,000	26%	+6%	+47%
Other individuals	2,310,000,000	23	+4	+30
Corporations	2,230,000,000	22	+3	+31
Foundations	2,030,000,000	20	+6	+49
Religious organizations	240,000,000	2	0	+14
Other organizations	710,000,000	7	+1	+37
Total	$10,200,000,000	100%	+4%	+38%

SOURCE: COUNCIL FOR AID TO EDUCATION

Revenues and Expenditures of Colleges and Universities, 1989-90

	Public institutions		Private institutions	
	Amount	Per cent of total	Amount	Per cent of total
Revenues				
Tuition and fees	$13,820,240,000	15.5%	$20,105,820,000	39.6%
Federal government				
Appropriations	1,636,047,000	1.8	254,000,000	0.5
Grants and contracts	7,320,948,000	8.3	4,805,437,000	9.4
Research-and-development centers	214,493,000	0.2	3,023,949,000	6.0
State governments				
Appropriations	34,858,904,000	39.2	364,270,000	0.7
Grants and contracts	2,193,403,000	2.4	932,663,000	1.8
Local governments				
Appropriations	2,910,444,000	3.3	9,003,000	—
Grants and contracts	353,858,000	0.4	366,597,000	0.7
Private gifts, grants, and contracts	3,368,635,000	3.8	4,412,787,000	8.7
Endowment income	461,701,000	0.5	2,681,995,000	5.3
Sales and services				
Educational activities	2,423,779,000	2.7	1,208,322,000	2.4
Auxiliary enterprises	8,473,282,000	9.5	5,465,187,000	10.8
Hospitals	8,433,369,000	9.5	4,783,295,000	9.4
Other	2,442,330,000	2.7	2,310,720,000	4.6
Total current-fund revenues	$88,911,433,000	100.0%	$50,724,044,000	100.0%
Expenditures				
Instruction	$29,257,209,000	34.1%	$12,888,779,000	26.4%
Research	8,542,235,000	10.0	3,963,726,000	8.1
Public service	3,688,664,000	4.3	1,001,094,000	2.0
Academic support	6,535,076,000	7.6	2,902,568,000	5.9
Student services	4,021,328,000	4.7	2,366,819,000	4.8
Institutional support	7,490,137,000	8.7	5,183,893,000	10.6
Plant operation and maintenance	6,333,582,000	7.4	3,124,680,000	6.4
Scholarships and fellowships	2,386,493,000	2.8	4,269,051,000	8.7
Mandatory transfers	909,234,000	1.1	720,508,000	1.5
Auxiliary enterprises	8,282,332,000	9.7	4,921,653,000	10.1
Hospitals	8,113,989,000	9.5	4,565,297,000	9.3
Federally financed research-and-development centers	210,252,000	0.2	2,976,973,000	6.1
Total current-fund expenditures	$85,770,530,000	100.0%	$48,885,041,000	100.0%

Note: A dash indicates less than 0.1 per cent. Because of rounding, details may not add to totals.

SOURCE: U.S. DEPARTMENT OF EDUCATION

Average College Costs, 1992-93

	Public colleges		Private colleges	
	Resident	Commuter	Resident	Commuter
4-year colleges				
Tuition and fees	$2,315	$2,315	$10,498	$10,498
Books and supplies	528	528	531	531
Room and board*	3,526	1,549	4,575	1,762
Transportation	497	843	487	794
Other	1,205	1,238	936	1,036
Total	$8,071	$6,473	$17,027	$14,621
2-year colleges				
Tuition and fees	$1,292	$1,292	$5,621	$5,621
Books and supplies	502	502	512	512
Room and board*	—	1,592	3,750	1,558
Transportation	—	926	517	812
Other	—	970	866	941
Total	—	$5,282	$11,266	$9,444

Note: The figures are weighted by enrollment to reflect the charges incurred by the average undergraduate enrolled at each type of institution.
* Room not included for commuter students
— Insufficient data

SOURCE: THE COLLEGE BOARD

Non-Profit Institutions Receiving the Largest Contracts From the Defense Department, Fiscal Year 1991

Johns Hopkins University	$403,931,000
Massachusetts Institute of Technology	400,182,000
Aerospace Corporation	395,136,000
Mitre Corporation	247,857,000
Rand Corporation	76,122,000
Institute for Defense Analyses	73,468,000
Charles S. Draper Laboratory	59,615,000
Pennsylvania State University	56,360,000
University of Texas System	55,296,000
IIT Research Institute	51,421,000
South Carolina Research Authority	50,658,000
Carnegie Mellon University	47,656,000
Analytic Services	42,733,000
Utah State University	42,197,000
SRI International	37,125,000
Battelle Memorial Institute	35,169,000
University of Southern California	34,560,000
University of California	31,175,000
Logistics Management Institute	26,696,000
Georgia Tech Research Corporation	26,278,000

Note: The list includes those colleges, universities, and other non-profit organizations that received a total of $25-million or more in contracts from the Department of Defense. The figures cover only contracts of more than $25,000 for research, development, testing, and evaluation for military projects and for civilian water-resource projects. Other types of funding are not included in this table.

SOURCE: U.S. DEPARTMENT OF DEFENSE

Range of 1992-93 Tuition at 4-Year Colleges

	Number of colleges	Average tuition and fees	Proportion of total enrollment
Private institutions			
$15,000 or more	100	$16,661	15.6%
14,000 — 14,999	29	14,533	3.1
13,000 — 13,999	34	13,444	3.3
12,000 — 12,999	61	12,447	6.0
11,000 — 11,999	82	11,492	8.0
10,000 — 10,999	104	10,442	10.6
9,000 — 9,999	110	9,529	10.5
8,000 — 8,999	138	8,483	10.0
7,000 — 7,999	118	7,466	7.7
6,000 — 6,999	97	6,480	6.7
5,000 — 5,999	84	5,498	4.7
4,000 — 4,999	84	4,477	5.2
3,000 — 3,999	66	3,576	2.0
2,000 — 2,999	45	2,556	5.5
1,000 — 1,999	7	1,621	0.1
Less than $1,000	10	457	1.0
Total	1,169	—	100.0%
Public institutions			
$3,000 or more	96	$3,689	17.8%
2,500 — 2,999	107	2,745	20.9
2,000 — 2,499	84	2,236	15.6
1,500 — 1,999	150	1,718	25.5
1,000 — 1,499	100	1,344	18.8
Less than $1,000	17	873	1.4
Total	554	—	100.0%

Note: Includes only those institutions that provided final or estimated 1992-93 tuition and fees by September 10, 1992.

SOURCE: THE COLLEGE BOARD

Top Institutions in Total Research-and-Development Spending, Fiscal 1990

Johns Hopkins University *	$668,915,000
Massachusetts Institute of Technology	311,767,000
University of Michigan	310,578,000
University of Wisconsin at Madison	309,841,000
Stanford University	305,700,000
Cornell University	300,144,000
University of Minnesota	292,046,000
Texas A&M University	272,800,000
Pennsylvania State University	256,926,000
University of California at Los Angeles	246,795,000
University of Washington	245,313,000
University of California at San Francisco	238,278,000
University of California at San Diego	237,032,000
University of California at Berkeley	231,061,000
University of Texas at Austin	228,203,000
University of Illinois at Urbana-Champaign	227,742,000
Harvard University	220,812,000
University of California at Davis	198,075,000
University of Arizona	195,633,000
University of Pennsylvania	189,390,000
Columbia University	182,769,000
Yale University	180,706,000
Ohio State University	178,569,000
University of Southern California	169,102,000
Georgia Institute of Technology	168,193,000
University of Maryland at College Park	166,022,000
University of Georgia	156,742,000
Baylor College of Medicine	155,122,000
University of Colorado	154,723,000
Washington University	151,249,000
Duke University	140,708,000
University of Florida	139,678,000
Rutgers University	137,985,000
Louisiana State University	135,849,000
Northwestern University	131,979,000
North Carolina State University	131,133,000
Purdue University	130,379,000
University of Rochester	129,011,000
Michigan State University	126,987,000
University of Tennessee System	126,790,000
University of North Carolina at Chapel Hill	123,113,000
Virginia Polytechnic Institute and State University	121,423,000
University of Chicago	117,955,000
University of Pittsburgh	117,716,000
Iowa State University	115,945,000

Note: Figures cover only research-and-development expenditures in science and engineering, and exclude spending in such disciplines as the arts, education, the humanities, law, and physical education.

* Includes the Applied Physics Laboratory with $416-million in total research-and-development expenditures.

SOURCE: NATIONAL SCIENCE FOUNDATION

Administrators' Views of Most-Important Campus Issues, 1991-92

	Total	2-year	Bacca-laureate	Compre-hensive	Doctoral
Financial issues					
Budget cuts, reduced revenue	39%	54%	23%	29%	46%
Enrollment growth without budget increases	23	21	32	18	16
Capital improvements	19	17	23	21	11
Faculty issues					
Salaries, benefits	34	33	24	44	37
Budget cuts	17	17	12	16	26
Workloads, class size	15	17	17	11	10
Curriculum issues					
General-education requirements	36	22	37	53	46
Multiculturalism	14	13	21	9	18
Assessment	12	23	4	8	2

Note: The figures are based on responses to a survey sent to senior administrators at 510 colleges and universities in the winter of 1992. The response rate was 81 per cent. The table lists the top three issues cited by administrators in each category.

SOURCE: AMERICAN COUNCIL ON EDUCATION

Changes in Campus Operating Budgets, 1990-91 to 1991-92

	Total	2-year	Bacca-laureate	Compre-hensive	Doctoral
Proportion reporting each change:					
Increase of 11% or more	11%	10%	12%	11%	17%
Increase of 7% to 10%	19	12	38	13	15
Increase of 5% to 6%	20	15	25	25	12
Increase of 1% to 4%	17	20	10	15	25
No change	9	6	14	10	11
Decrease of 11% or more	2	3	0	3	1
Decrease of 7% to 10%	5	9	0	5	4
Decrease of 5% to 6%	7	14	0	4	6
Decrease of 1% to 4%	9	11	2	13	9

Note: The figures are based on responses to a survey sent to senior administrators at 510 colleges and universities in the winter of 1992. The response rate was 81 per cent. Because of rounding, figures may not add to 100 per cent.

SOURCE: AMERICAN COUNCIL ON EDUCATION

Campus Responses to Financial Pressures, 1991-92

	Total	2-year	Bacca-laureate	Compre-hensive	Doctoral
Short-term impact					
Most frequently cited responses:					
Increased student fees	65%	67%	61%	65%	69%
Achieved greater efficiency in some operations	58	55	65	55	62
Postponed spending for buildings and equipment	57	61	45	58	65
Reallocated resources productively	46	48	47	40	51
Reduced library acquisitions	40	36	39	41	56
Increased class size in introductory courses	37	45	24	37	42
Imposed a freeze on hiring in regular faculty positions	35	45	20	32	38
Reduced administrative staff	35	29	35	34	62
Reduced number of courses or sections	33	33	28	37	41
Delayed or reduced salary increases	32	32	31	30	44
Held off on introducing new programs	32	46	10	29	33
Possible long-term impact					
Most frequently cited responses:					
Increased reliance on tuition revenue	50	62	39	42	42
Reallocation of resources among departments	48	57	29	44	61
Labs and equipment will be more dated	47	60	27	43	41
More maintenance will be deferred	46	59	18	49	47
Slower expansion of new technology	44	53	34	39	34
More programs will be revenue-generating	37	39	43	28	39
Slower growth than planned	35	46	27	23	40

Note: The figures are based on responses to a survey sent to senior administrators at 510 colleges and universities in the winter of 1992. The response rate was 81 per cent.

SOURCE: AMERICAN COUNCIL ON EDUCATION

Holdings of University Research Libraries in U.S. and Canada, 1990-91

	Rank[1]	Volumes in library	Volumes added	Current serials	Total staff	Total expenditures[2]
Harvard University	1	12,169,049	402,984	96,704	1,134	$50,249,192
University of California at Berkeley	2	7,697,027	188,270	87,530	776	32,723,415
Yale University	3	9,013,561	166,244	52,210	689	30,151,200
University of California at Los Angeles	4	6,179,973	179,309	96,723	662	31,926,086
University of Toronto	5	6,091,828	188,691	39,016	692	28,430,815
University of Illinois at Urbana-Champaign	6	7,918,951	170,493	91,017	502	19,482,434
University of Michigan	7	6,579,152	128,783	70,157	619	25,759,418
University of Texas	8	6,505,219	215,341	52,182	596	19,447,403
Stanford University[3]	9	5,987,592	142,689	50,157	536	31,697,862
Columbia University	10	6,142,293	122,219	60,764	633	25,396,688
Cornell University[3]	11	5,344,481	145,157	59,928	570	22,872,682
University of Washington	12	5,065,669	153,014	53,408	511	22,379,841
University of Wisconsin	13	5,133,457	111,900	49,626	521	23,020,227
University of Minnesota	14	4,761,630	117,678	42,304	526	24,386,140
Indiana University	15	5,099,250	156,020	38,782	475	19,931,037
University of Chicago	16	5,328,849	140,573	46,976	389	16,083,176
Princeton University	17	4,839,356	135,239	32,950	390	18,748,412
Pennsylvania State University[3]	18	3,191,245	112,240	33,460	479	18,505,042
Duke University	19	4,016,036	167,705	35,554	331	14,919,597
Rutgers University[3]	20	3,302,416	97,601	28,161	512	22,592,499
Ohio State University	21	4,517,095	99,734	32,151	474	17,020,796
University of North Carolina	22	3,856,378	112,134	39,223	391	15,435,157
University of Arizona	23	3,817,361	128,928	31,919	376	14,708,494
University of Pennsylvania	24	3,756,762	95,568	32,118	388	17,640,959
University of British Columbia	25	3,019,879	108,398	22,729	406	18,607,619
Arizona State University[3]	26	2,712,934	114,349	33,899	415	15,548,558
New York University	27	3,151,486	74,899	28,817	438	19,129,172
University of Florida	28	2,966,891	110,496	27,831	439	15,028,682
University of California at Davis	29	2,441,855	80,495	52,042	327	16,307,264
University of Georgia	30	2,968,339	79,535	54,851	360	12,310,976
Northwestern University	31	3,550,250	85,912	37,054	353	14,262,619
University of Alberta[3]	32	3,179,572	88,920	23,096	377	15,655,603
University of Virginia	33	3,266,649	93,717	25,365	340	15,185,994
University of California at San Diego	34	2,055,113	123,304	23,784	373	16,286,677
Johns Hopkins University	35	2,902,881	75,729	20,677	339	17,866,060
University of Southern California	36	2,685,444	67,119	36,844	358	15,231,319
Wayne State University	37	2,578,970	205,836	24,658	238	11,990,794
University of Pittsburgh	38	2,962,991	94,481	23,045	354	13,483,938
University of Kansas[3]	39	2,960,765	79,583	28,902	330	12,132,493
Michigan State University	40	2,811,363	81,083	28,142	314	12,931,442
McGill University	41	2,570,377	70,614	17,812	324	14,684,399
University of Maryland	42	2,119,523	71,330	22,825	348	15,667,442
University of Iowa	43	3,174,269	77,204	18,514	283	12,653,125

Continued on Following Page

Holdings of University Research Libraries in U.S. and Canada, continued

	Rank[1]	Volumes in library	Volumes added	Current serials	Total staff	Total expenditures[2]
University of Hawaii	44	2,573,224	73,902	38,363	235	$10,346,925
State University of New York at Buffalo	45	2,654,744	69,519	23,292	289	12,306,444
University of Connecticut	46	2,323,672	83,526	22,337	231	13,651,521
Vanderbilt University	47	1,981,132	88,821	19,092	301	11,901,787
Washington University	48	2,642,917	70,316	18,931	266	12,316,487
Texas A&M University	49	1,962,346	71,944	25,428	308	11,531,165
Emory University	50	2,101,967	64,039	22,287	263	13,545,980
University of California at Santa Barbara	51	2,043,462	54,576	30,181	250	12,451,601
Georgetown University	52	1,855,343	60,718	23,842	296	12,489,462
University of Western Ontario	53	2,011,123	68,608	17,033	287	12,226,627
University of Colorado	54	2,349,410	64,816	26,563	229	11,372,486
Boston University	55	1,809,437	54,835	29,437	273	10,784,047
University of Laval	56	1,855,291	64,424	15,841	264	12,223,185
University of Notre Dame	57	2,094,598	107,735	20,231	198	9,039,620
Florida State University	58	1,936,507	116,660	18,751	244	8,891,332
University of Kentucky	59	2,212,083	56,597	27,902	271	9,646,307
University of New Mexico	60	1,760,646	61,238	18,230	347	12,160,872
Massachusetts Institute of Technology	61	2,223,822	55,015	21,577	245	10,513,389
University of Cincinnati	62	1,791,905	56,874	20,554	310	12,475,557
York University (Ontario)[3]	63	1,901,562	59,262	19,917	257	11,953,108
Howard University	64	1,832,793	49,934	26,149	233	10,695,404
Louisiana State University	65	2,874,571	57,360	19,815	251	8,756,965
University of Illinois at Chicago	66	1,695,329	46,695	17,593	294	11,806,890
University of Delaware	67	2,014,431	63,597	23,471	214	9,492,250
Purdue University	68	1,968,656	50,619	18,238	271	10,165,748
Brown University	69	2,503,827	45,798	14,792	274	11,144,301
University of Tennessee	70	1,914,674	46,101	22,972	258	9,113,296
Brigham Young University	71	2,132,747	72,848	18,358	360	10,160,063
University of Missouri	72	2,528,304	47,159	17,395	232	9,100,508
University of Miami	73	1,739,855	51,526	18,349	239	10,478,437
University of California at Irvine	74	1,500,867	52,251	19,522	234	12,074,992
University of South Carolina	75	2,476,527	48,443	20,552	208	8,484,026
University of Nebraska	76	2,059,989	49,193	20,776	211	8,854,221
University of Rochester	77	2,734,373	52,816	13,199	230	8,839,303
State University of New York at Stony Brook	78	1,752,232	52,243	20,841	222	9,542,641
Iowa State University	79	1,914,946	44,848	21,467	227	9,882,345
Syracuse University	80	2,352,547	32,829	16,733	255	9,717,897
Dartmouth College	81	1,873,324	52,880	21,083	185	8,973,917
Temple University[3]	82	2,107,910	48,862	15,414	220	9,794,213
Queen's University (Ontario)	83	1,838,616	44,270	15,866	206	10,155,316
Southern Illinois University	84	2,144,277	50,092	17,831	234	8,472,995

	Rank[1]	Volumes in library	Volumes added	Current serials	Total staff	Total expenditures[2]
Virginia Polytechnic Institute and State University	85	1,754,830	54,735	16,265	230	$9,149,801
McMaster University	86	1,596,911	46,214	15,291	207	9,972,287
Kent State University[3]	87	2,428,223	47,639	14,038	252	8,191,726
University of Oregon	88	1,931,789	48,250	18,776	217	8,948,119
University of Waterloo[3]	89	1,625,111	44,707	15,364	199	9,361,047
Tulane University[3]	90	1,851,203	50,735	17,236	185	8,243,450
Washington State University	91	1,644,342	39,714	23,017	209	8,619,267
University of Saskatchewan	92	1,459,334	65,368	13,700	181	8,631,855
University of Massachusetts	93	2,445,150	47,969	13,807	186	8,053,151
University of Manitoba	94	1,552,507	41,785	12,465	228	9,826,152
University of Alabama	95	1,863,474	53,318	17,945	182	7,759,687
University of Utah	96	1,870,457	58,970	12,144	217	7,833,002
University of Oklahoma	97	2,335,957	44,814	17,440	189	7,558,792
Colorado State University	98	1,372,670	153,978	11,730	137	6,707,827
University of Guelph	99	1,964,118	63,702	13,473	160	6,703,676
Oklahoma State University[3]	100	1,595,257	67,480	18,276	186	7,079,749
North Carolina State University	101	1,407,875	42,710	16,860	219	8,647,259
University of California at Riverside	102	1,916,286	48,897	12,483	170	7,562,642
State University of New York at Albany[3]	103	1,310,993	43,164	17,218	177	8,454,102
Case Western Reserve University	104	1,732,430	36,320	15,311	168	7,481,451
Georgia Institute of Technology	105	1,697,021	49,940	22,227	110	5,520,979
University of Houston	106	1,648,921	27,927	14,862	197	6,914,297
Rice University	107	1,501,162	39,884	12,340	128	6,407,061

Note: Institutions are asked to report figures for their main campuses only, unless a branch campus is indicated. The amounts listed under "volumes in library," "volumes added," and "current serials" may include materials not counted in previous years because of a 1990-91 revision in the method of reporting government documents.

[1] Based on an index developed by the Association of Research Libraries to measure the relative size of university libraries. The index takes into account the number of volumes held, number of volumes added during the previous fiscal year, number of current serials, total operating expenditures, and size of staff, excluding student assistants. It does not measure a library's services, the quality of its collections, or its success in meeting the needs of users.

[2] Figures for Canadian libraries are expressed in U.S. dollars.

[3] Includes branches as well as the main institution.

SOURCE: ASSOCIATION OF RESEARCH LIBRARIES

The States

ALABAMA

In the last days of 1991, a federal district judge ruled that Alabama's higher-education system was illegally segregated. His decision closed a chapter in a 10-year-old case that began when the U.S. Justice Department sued Alabama for not providing a desegregation plan.

Judge Harold Murphy, who normally hears cases in U.S. Federal District Court in the Northern District of Georgia, ordered Alabama's predominantly white colleges to hire additional black administrators and faculty members and called for an increase in "other race" students at all institutions.

Judge Murphy also ordered the Alabama Commission on Higher Education—the state coordinating board—to change its financing formula to provide more money to the historically black public four-year institutions, Alabama A&M and Alabama State Universities. Those institutions also are to receive $10-million for capital improvements.

The U.S. Supreme Court's ruling in June 1992 that Mississippi had not done enough to desegregate its formerly segregated higher-education system makes it more likely that Judge Murphy's decision will stand.

Many of Judge Murphy's orders will require spending money, and some politicians and educators wonder where the state will find it, given its regressive tax structure. Tax reform has been debated in Alabama for several years, and in late 1991 Republican Gov. Guy Hunt created a special committee to make suggestions for changing the system.

The Governor's Tax Reform Task Force proposed a tax package that would generate nearly $500-million a year in additional revenue. The package was linked with a dozen accountability measures for elementary, secondary, and postsecondary education, including a provision to make it easier for students to transfer between colleges and a requirement that students pass standardized tests before being permitted to take junior-level courses.

Another measure would give the higher-education commission authority to close degree programs in which enrollments and graduation rates are low. Alabama has more colleges and universities per person—and the lowest enrollment per institution—among Southern states, according to the Southern Regional Education Board.

Although the reform package was greeted with enthusiasm by many legislators, it did not win the backing of enough lawmakers to pass. Tax re-

ALABAMA
Continued

form is expected to come up again when legislators convene in February 1993.

Legislators did pass a measure that would pay public- or private-college tuition for poor and middle-class students who make good grades. The Legislature's vote allows the commission to design the program, but appropriates no money for the 1992-93 academic year.

Alabama's fiscal year started on October 1, 1992, and the Legislature approved $824-million for public colleges and universities. That amount restored some of the money that was cut in the course of two budget reductions since 1990, but it fell short of the commission's request for nearly $1-billion.

Alabama's two largest public institutions are the University of Alabama and Auburn University. Alabama also is home to several private colleges, including seven historically black institutions, such as Tuskegee University and Stillman College.

In this state where football is king, Auburn has been racked by a former football player's allegations that coaches and boosters broke National Collegiate Athletic Association rules by giving him cash and other assistance. The controversy renewed faculty concerns about interference by trustees in the university's day-to-day governance, and about what many viewed as the failure of the retiring president, James E. Martin, to stand up to the board.

The university's new president, William V. Muse, immediately separated the jobs of athletics director and football coach and forced Pat Dye, the man who had held them both, to relinquish his duties as director. The trustees promised to give Mr. Muse more control over athletics, but the charges against the football program are likely to keep Auburn's program in the public eye.

DEMOGRAPHICS

Population: 4,089,000 (Rank: 22)

Age distribution:
Up to 17 .... 26.2%
18 to 24 .... 10.9%
25 to 44 .... 30.7%
45 and older 32.2%

Racial and ethnic distribution:
American Indian 0.4%
Asian 0.5%
Black 25.3%
White 73.6%
Other and unknown 0.1%
Hispanic (may be any race) .. 0.6%

Educational attainment of adults (highest level):
9th grade or less 13.7%
Some high school, no diploma 19.4%
High-school diploma 29.4%
Some college, no degree 16.8%
Associate degree 5.0%
Bachelor's degree 10.1%
Graduate or professional
 degree 5.5%

Proportion who speak a language other than English at home: 2.9%

Per-capita personal income: $15,518

Poverty rate:
All 18.3%
Under age 18 .... 24.2%
Age 18 and older 16.2%

New public high-school graduates in:
1992-93 (estimate) 38,940
2001-02 (estimate) 39,540

New GED diploma recipients: 8,022

High-school dropout rate: 12.6%

POLITICAL LEADERSHIP

Governor: Guy Hunt (R), term ends 1995

Governor's higher-education aide:
Henry J. Hector, One Court Square, Suite 221, Montgomery 36104; (205) 269-2700

U.S. Senators: Howell Heflin (D), term ends 1997; Richard C. Shelby (D), term ends 1999

U.S. Representatives:
4 Democrats, 3 Republicans
Spencer Bachus (R), Tom Bevill (D), Glen Browder (D), Sonny Callahan (R), Bud Cramer (D), Terry Everett (R), Earl F. Hilliard (D)

Legislature: Senate, 28 Democrats, 7 Republicans; House, 82 Democrats, 23 Republicans

COLLEGES AND UNIVERSITIES

Higher education:
Public 4-year institutions 18
Public 2-year institutions 37
Private 4-year institutions 18
Private 2-year institutions 14
Total 87

Vocational institutions: 74

Statewide coordinating board:
Commission on Higher Education

One Court Square, Suite 221
Montgomery 36104
(205) 269-2700
Henry J. Hector, executive director

Private-college association:
Council for the Advancement
   of Private Colleges in Alabama
6 Office Park Circle, Suite 112
Birmingham 35223
(205) 879-1673
James D. Harvey, president

Institutions censured by the AAUP:
Alabama State University, Auburn University, Talladega College

Institution under NCAA sanctions:
Auburn University

FACULTY MEMBERS

Full-time faculty members by rank:
Professor 1,146
Associate professor 1,226
Assistant professor 1,582
Instructor 561
Lecturer 42
No rank 1,385
Total 5,942

Full-time faculty members with tenure:
Men 2,392
Women 1,135
Total 3,527

Average pay of full-time professors
Public 4-year institutions:
Professor $51,324
Associate professor $39,317
Assistant professor $33,467
Instructor $25,699
No rank .... n/a
All $38,481

Public 2-year institutions:
Professor .... n/a

ALABAMA
Continued

Associate professor .... n/a
Assistant professor .... n/a
Instructor .... n/a
No rank $33,240
All $33,240

Private 4-year institutions:
Professor $40,648
Associate professor $31,624
Assistant professor $27,007
Instructor $20,126
No rank .... n/a
All $30,947

STUDENTS

Enrollment:
At public 4-year institutions   123,848
At public 2-year institutions . 72,091
At private 4-year institutions   17,799
At private 2-year institutions . 3,812
Undergraduate 194,269
Graduate 20,225
Professional 3,056
American Indian 591
Asian 1,699
Black 42,916
Hispanic 1,138
White 166,617
Foreign 4,589
Total 217,550

Enrollment highlights:
Women 54.6%
Full-time 68.3%
Minority 21.8%
Foreign 2.1%
10-year change in total
    enrollment .... Up 32.4%

Proportion of enrollment made up of minority students:
At public 4-year institutions . 18.6%
At public 2-year institutions . 19.9%
At private 4-year institutions   45.5%
At private 2-year institutions   46.7%

Degrees awarded:
Associate 6,254
Bachelor's 17,059
Master's 4,510
Doctorate 354
Professional 832

Residence of new students: State residents made up 79% of all freshmen enrolled in Alabama; 92% of all Alabama residents who were freshmen attended college in their home state.

Test scores: Students averaged 19.8 on the A.C.T., which was taken by an estimated 60% of Alabama's high-school seniors.

Graduation rates at NCAA Division I institutions:
Alabama State University 18%
Auburn University 64%
Samford University .... n/a
University of Alabama
    at Tuscaloosa 51%
University of Alabama
    at Birmingham 36%
University of South Alabama .. 26%

MONEY

Average tuition and fees:
At public 4-year institutions . $1,593
At public 2-year institutions .. $689
At private 4-year institutions $5,942
At private 2-year institutions $4,148

Expenditures:
Public institutions .. $1,831,657,000
Private institutions ... $229,369,000

State funds for higher-education operating expenses: $824,000,000
Two-year change: Up 1%

State spending on student aid:
Need-based: $2,887,000
Non–need-based: $5,413,000
Other: $4,891,000

Salary of chief executive of largest public 4-year campus:
William V. Muse, Auburn University main campus: $157,000

Total spending on research and development by doctorate-granting universities: $239,556,000
Sources:
Federal government 52.0%
State and local governments . 10.7%
Industry 7.8%
The institution itself 21.2%
Other 8.2%

Total federal spending on college- and university-based research and development: $129,701,000
Selected programs:
Department of Health
  and Human Services $72,442,000
National Science
  Foundation $6,833,000
Department of Defense $12,926,000
Department
  of Agriculture $9,244,000
Department of Energy .. $2,772,000

Largest endowment:
University of Alabama
  System $175,000,000

Top fund raisers:
Samford University ... $66,414,000
University of Alabama
  at Tuscaloosa $20,158,000
Auburn University $15,287,000

MISCELLANY

■ The Alabama Legislature in 1992 passed a law barring groups that support homosexuality from meeting on public-college campuses. The law came after the Auburn University Student Government Association's denial of recognition to the campus Gay and Lesbian Association was overturned by the university's Board of Trustees.

■ Harvey F. Kline, a professor of political science at the University of Alabama, in 1992 raised more than $800 for his department by obtaining sponsors for a 100-mile bike ride.

■ Auburn University students hold the world's record for a two-day blood drive. They donated 4,812 pints in 1967 to support American troops in Vietnam.

■ Some dispute exists as to which college in Alabama is the oldest. The state's first constitution, in 1819, required the establishment of the University of Alabama; its doors opened in 1831. It had been beaten to the punch, however, by Athens Academy (now Athens State College), whose first class was held in 1822.

ALASKA

ALASKA's legacy of oil wealth could soon become the bane of the University of Alaska System.

With the revenues from its seemingly limitless oil supplies, Alaska created many programs and services in the late 1970's and early 1980's, including generous student-aid and loan programs, a far-flung network of college campuses that touched the most rural "bush" communities of the vast state, and a trust fund that now pays out nearly $1,000 a year to each resident.

ALASKA
Continued

The state even abolished its income tax in 1980.

But Alaska's dependence on petroleum—85 per cent of its budget comes from oil royalties—leaves the state vulnerable to fluctuations in the market. In 1987, a sharp drop in oil prices drove the University of Alaska to absorb its community colleges into the system as a money-saving move—one that caused great controversy.

Further declines in prices in 1992 prompted more fears of upheaval, because such popular and expensive programs as the trust-fund dividend have become politically inviolate.

The university system was ultimately spared cutbacks in 1992. It received a $250,000 increase while most other state agencies saw their state appropriations reduced by 2 per cent. But the small increase forced the university to raise tuition by 16 per cent, to about $1,500 a year, provoking student protests.

The fear of cuts also brought some rivalries among campuses to the surface. At one point in the 1992 legislative session, members of the Chambers of Commerce from Fairbanks and Anchorage could be found at the Capitol in Juneau belittling the needs of the campus in each other's city. Such tensions are likely to continue. Although the Fairbanks campus is the oldest and is often considered the flagship of the system, university officials predict most of the enrollment growth will occur at Anchorage and at other campuses in south-central Alaska.

Enrollment has increased by about 6 per cent in each of the last three or four years, in part because Alaska still attracts newcomers from other states.

The university system has been less successful in attracting and graduating Alaska Natives. That has been the source of continued criticism from Eskimo and other native leaders. Legislators and community leaders have also pressed the campus in Anchorage to provide more services to meet the needs of its increasing population of black students.

To improve its services to Alaska Natives in bush communities, the university's president, Jerome Komisar, has reorganized the system's College of Rural Alaska. University officials say the change will give the five campuses in that college greater flexibility to devise programs that meet their communities' needs, such as courses in small-boat repair, without interference from Fairbanks.

A boat-repair course would not be out of place in this system. Since it absorbed the community colleges, the university has carried out an expansive academic mission that ranges from vocational classes in airplane mechanics to doctoral studies in geology.

DEMOGRAPHICS

Population: 570,000   (Rank: 49)

Age distribution:
Up to 17	31.6%
18 to 24	9.8%
25 to 44	38.9%
45 and older	19.6%

Racial and ethnic distribution:
American Indian	15.6%
Asian	3.6%
Black	4.1%
White	75.5%
Other and unknown	1.2%
Hispanic (may be any race)	3.2%

Educational attainment of adults (highest level):
9th grade or less 5.1%
Some high school, no degree . 8.2%
High-school diploma 28.7%
Some college, no diploma ... 27.6%
Associate degree 7.2%
Bachelor's degree 15.0%
Graduate or professional
  degree 8.0%

Proportion who speak a language other than English at home: 12.1%

Per-capita personal income: $21,067

Poverty rate:
All 9.0%
Under age 18 .... 11.4%
Age 18 and older 7.9%

New public high-school graduates in:
1992-93 (estimate) 5,260
2001-02 (estimate) 6,410

New GED diploma recipients: 1,623

High-school dropout rate: 10.9%

POLITICAL LEADERSHIP

Governor: Walter J. Hickel (Ind), term ends 1994

Governor's higher-education aide:
Jerry Covey, Department of Education, 801 West 10th Street, Suite 200, Juneau 99801; (907) 465-2800

U.S. Senators: Frank H. Murkowski (R), term ends 1999; Ted Stevens (R), term ends 1997

U.S. Representative:
1 Republican
Don Young (R)

Legislature: Senate, 9 Democrats, 10 Republicans, 1 Independent; House, 20 Democrats, 18 Republicans, 2 Independents

COLLEGES AND UNIVERSITIES

Higher education:
Public 4-year institutions 3
Public 2-year institutions 0
Private 4-year institutions 3
Private 2-year institutions 1
Total 7

Vocational institutions: 34

Statewide coordinating board:
Alaska Commission on
  Postsecondary Education
400 Willoughby Avenue
P.O. Box 110505
Juneau 99811
(907) 465-2854
Allan Barnes, executive director

Private-college association:
None

Institutions censured by the AAUP:
None

Institutions under NCAA sanctions:
None

FACULTY MEMBERS

Full-time faculty members by rank:
Professor 139
Associate professor 231
Assistant professor 231
Instructor 95
Lecturer 0
No rank 61
Total 757

Full-time faculty members with tenure:
Men 247

ALASKA
Continued

Women 87
Total 334

Average pay of full-time professors
Public 4-year institutions:
Professor $57,519
Associate professor $48,895
Assistant professor $38,606
Instructor $31,831
No rank $33,754
All $44,567

Public 2-year institutions: n/a

Private 4-year institutions:
Professor .... n/a
Associate professor $30,950
Assistant professor $27,994
Instructor $27,340
No rank $30,431
All $29,948

STUDENTS

Enrollment:
At public 4-year institutions . 27,792
At public 2-year institutions 0
At private 4-year institutions . 1,647
At private 2-year institutions .. 394
Undergraduate 28,593
Graduate 1,240
Professional 0
American Indian 2,648
Asian 740
Black 1,079
Hispanic 634
White 24,264
Foreign 468
Total 29,833

Enrollment highlights:
Women 59.8%
Full-time 36.5%
Minority 17.4%
Foreign 1.6%
10-year change in total
  enrollment .... Up 40.1%

Proportion of enrollment made up of minority students:
At public 4-year institutions . 16.9%
At public 2-year institutions .... n/a
At private 4-year institutions 20.7%
At private 2-year institutions 39.1%

Degrees awarded:
Associate 603
Bachelor's 1,043
Master's 324
Doctorate 8
Professional 0

Residence of new students: State residents made up 78% of all freshmen enrolled in Alaska; 43% of all Alaska residents who were freshmen attended college in their home state.

Test scores: Students averaged 908 on the S.A.T., which was taken by an estimated 42% of Alaska's high-school seniors.

Graduation rates at NCAA Division I institutions: n/a

MONEY

Average tuition and fees:
At public 4-year institutions . $1,382
At public 2-year institutions .... n/a
At private 4-year institutions $5,842
At private 2-year institutions $10,400

Expenditures:
Public institutions $268,057,000
Private institutions $20,050,000

State funds for higher-education operating expenses: $174,118,000
Two-year change: Down 7%

State spending on student aid:
Need-based: $471,000
Non–need-based: $2,159,000
Other: None

Salary of chief executive of largest public 4-year campus:
Donald F. Behrend, University of Alaska at Anchorage: $111,940

Total spending on research and development by doctorate-granting universities: $65,571,000
Sources:
Federal government 48.6%
State and local governments .. 3.4%
Industry 6.3%
The institution itself 36.0%
Other 5.7%

Total federal spending on college- and university-based research and development: $25,060,000
Selected programs:
Department of Health
 and Human Services ... $424,000
National Science
 Foundation $9,781,000
Department of Defense ... $256,000
Department
 of Agriculture $1,315,000
Department of Energy .. $1,092,000

Largest endowment:
University of Alaska .. $16,009,000

Top fund raisers:
data not reported

MISCELLANY

■ To expose students to native Arctic cultures, Sheldon Jackson College offers a three-credit course called "Culture of the Kayak." Students learn about the Inuit of Greenland by building their own kayaks.

■ A gallery at the University of Alaska at Anchorage was the site of an unusual exhibit in 1992 designed to give local artists the opportunity to express their most X-rated visions. For the adults-only exhibit, entitled "Eros Censored," artists were asked what they would create if they did not have to fear censorship.

■ The name of the northernmost campus in the country, formerly the North Slope Higher Education Center, was changed in September 1990 by local officials, who preferred an Eskimo name. It is now Arctic Sivunmum Ilisagvik College.

■ The oldest higher-education institution in Alaska is Sheldon Jackson College, founded in 1878.

ARIZONA

IN 1991, Republican Gov. Fife Symington, newly elected, began his term by pressing for the elimination of the Arizona Board of Regents, which governs the state's three public universities, in favor of a separate board for each institution.

By the time the Legislature met in 1992, he had retreated. But the Board of Regents is still under pressure—from the Governor and legislators—to evaluate the functions of its central office. Politicians say the board spends too little time on long-term planning and too much on routine matters. They want the regents to delegate more responsibilities to each university, an idea that is welcomed by university officials because it would give them the fiscal autonomy they say is essential in a tight economy.

The board is also considering re-

ARIZONA
Continued

form measures. One would allow high-school students who are capable of doing college-level work to enroll in college free. Additionally, the board is studying the creation of branch campuses and is offering bachelor's-degree programs at some community colleges to provide space for Arizona's growing student population. The board also reached an agreement for a student-exchange program between Arizona's universities and those in Sonora, Mexico.

The universities have still had to cope with less money for higher education than educators say is needed. Like most states, Arizona is struggling to meet increased demands with less money. All three state universities were forced to shrink their administrative and support staffs through layoffs and attrition. Although a committee of educators and legislators is studying the financing of education, no action has been taken.

In response to the enrollment growth, a legislative study released in June 1992 concluded that Arizona should consider creating a four-year-college system. Enrollment at the universities, now about 95,000, is expected nearly to double over the next 30 years. Supporters of a new system say it could focus on undergraduate education and therefore be more economical than universities.

The tougher economic climate has, of necessity, helped to smooth the rivalries that have long existed among the three universities. In 1992 the university presidents traveled together around the state to tell the public about the budget crisis in higher education. Alumni of the three institutions also waged a joint campaign to lobby legislators.

Tuition rates for students from outside the state continue to be an issue, as Arizona moves toward a policy that would have those who are not state residents pay for 100 per cent of the cost of their education. About 25 per cent of the students enrolled in state universities are not Arizonans. Currently, they bear 90 per cent of their educational costs.

While the state studies cost-saving measures, improving efficiency has also become an issue. The Joint Legislative Budget Committee is developing criteria to do the state's first-ever study of faculty teaching loads, an effort that evolved out of the public's perception that professors were spending too little time in the classroom.

Arizona is also pushing to become more of a national center for science. After several years of research, scientists at the University of Arizona are preparing to construct what will be the largest telescope mirror ever built in America. The 6.5-meter mirror won't be ready until 1994, but scientists say it is the kind that will be used in a new generation of compact, yet powerful, ground-based telescopes.

DEMOGRAPHICS

Population: 3,750,000   (Rank: 23)

Age distribution:
Up to 17 .... 26.9%
18 to 24 .... 10.4%
25 to 44 .... 31.9%
45 and older 30.8%

Racial and ethnic distribution:
American Indian 5.6%
Asian 1.5%
Black 3.0%

White 80.8%
Other and unknown 9.1%
Hispanic (may be any race) . 18.8%

Educational attainment of adults (highest level):
9th grade or less 9.0%
Some high school, no diploma 12.3%
High-school diploma 26.1%
Some college, no degree 25.4%
Associate degree 6.8%
Bachelor's degree 13.3%
Graduate or professional
  degree 7.0%

Proportion who speak a language other than English at home: 20.8%

Per-capita personal income: $16,579

Poverty rate:
All 15.7%
Under age 18 .... 22.0%
Age 18 and older 13.4%

New public high-school graduates in:
1992-93 (estimate) 29,690
2001-02 (estimate) 47,120

New GED diploma recipients: 9,978

High-school dropout rate: 14.4%

POLITICAL LEADERSHIP

Governor: Fife Symington (R), term ends 1994

Governor's higher-education aide: John Kelly, 1700 West Washington Street, Phoenix 85007; (602) 542-4331

U.S. Senators: Dennis DeConcini (D), term ends 1995; John S. McCain (R), term ends 1999

U.S. Representatives:
3 Democrats, 3 Republicans

Sam Coppersmith (D), Karan English (D), Jim Kolbe (R), Jon Kyl (R), Ed Pastor (D), Bob Stump (R)

Legislature: Senate, 12 Democrats, 18 Republicans; House, 25 Democrats, 35 Republicans

COLLEGES AND UNIVERSITIES

Higher education:
Public 4-year institutions 3
Public 2-year institutions 17
Private 4-year institutions 14
Private 2-year institutions 4
Total 38

Vocational institutions: 155

Statewide coordinating board:
Arizona Board of Regents
2020 North Central Avenue
Suite 230
Phoenix 85004
(602) 229-2500
Frank Besnette, executive director

Private-college association:
None

Institutions censured by the AAUP:
None

Institutions under NCAA sanctions:
None

FACULTY MEMBERS

Full-time faculty members by rank:
Professor 1,061
Associate professor 931
Assistant professor 828
Instructor 133
Lecturer 158
No rank 1,712
Total 4,823

ARIZONA
Continued

Full-time faculty members with tenure:
Men 1,736
Women 461
Total 2,197

Average pay of full-time professors

Public 4-year institutions:
Professor $59,957
Associate professor $44,293
Assistant professor $38,030
Instructor $24,399
No rank $23,426
All $45,918

Public 2-year institutions:
Professor .... n/a
Associate professor .... n/a
Assistant professor .... n/a
Instructor .... n/a
No rank $40,478
All $40,478

Private 4-year institutions:
Professor $40,733
Associate professor $35,791
Assistant professor $27,783
Instructor $20,635
No rank $20,160
All $32,438

STUDENTS

Enrollment:
At public 4-year institutions . 95,657
At public 2-year institutions   153,143
At private 4-year institutions   13,980
At private 2-year institutions . 1,955
Undergraduate 236,505
Graduate 26,792
Professional 1,438
American Indian 8,845
Asian 6,116
Black 7,585
Hispanic 29,618
White 205,676
Foreign 6,895
Total 264,735

Enrollment highlights:
Women 53.6%
Full-time 43.8%
Minority 20.2%
Foreign 2.6%
10-year change in total
  enrollment .... Up 30.6%

Proportion of enrollment made up of minority students:
At public 4-year institutions . 15.1%
At public 2-year institutions . 23.1%
At private 4-year institutions 21.5%
At private 2-year institutions 28.7%

Degrees awarded:
Associate 6,361
Bachelor's 14,265
Master's 5,178
Doctorate 545
Professional 408

Residence of new students: State residents made up 87% of all freshmen enrolled in Arizona; 96% of all Arizona residents who were freshmen attended college in their home state.

Test scores: Students averaged 20.9 on the A.C.T., which was taken by an estimated 31% of Arizona's high-school seniors.

Graduation rates at NCAA Division I institutions:
Arizona State University 44%
Northern Arizona University .. 33%
University of Arizona 45%

MONEY

Average tuition and fees:
At public 4-year institutions . $1,478

At public 2-year institutions .. $579
At private 4-year institutions $4,660
At private 2-year institutions $8,977

Expenditures:
Public institutions .. $1,446,388,000
Private institutions $90,409,000

State funds for higher-education operating expenses: $605,267,000
Two-year change: Up 1%

State spending on student aid:
Need-based: $3,328,000
Non–need-based: None
Other: None

Salary of chief executive of largest public 4-year campus:
Lattie F. Coor, Arizona State University: $150,003

Total spending on research and development by doctorate-granting universities: $260,187,000
Sources:
Federal government 47.0%
State and local governments .. 2.8%
Industry 6.9%
The institution itself 37.3%
Other 6.0%

Total federal spending on college- and university-based research and development: $115,683,000
Selected programs:
Department of Health
  and Human Services $47,968,000
National Science
  Foundation $24,963,000
Department of Defense $11,293,000
Department
  of Agriculture $3,100,000
Department of Energy .. $3,772,000

Largest endowment:
University of Arizona . $59,702,000

Top fund raisers:
University of Arizona . $44,631,000
Arizona State University $22,504,000
Maricopa County Community
  College $3,670,000

MISCELLANY

■ Arizona State University is home of the largest university meteorite collection in the world, housing 1,300 of the objects, most of which are about 4.5 billion years old. Only the British Museum and the Smithsonian Institution have larger collections.

■ A cartoonist at Walt Disney Studios drew the original "Sun Devil," Arizona State University's athletic mascot, as a favor to a former classmate. The logo made its first appearance at the university in November 1947, when it replaced a bulldog that had long adorned the masthead of the student newspaper.

■ For the past 20 years, the University of Arizona Garbage Project has been sifting and classifying garbage— all told, more than a quarter of a million pounds of the stuff.

■ The oldest institution of higher education in the state is the University of Arizona, founded in 1885.

ARKANSAS

During the 1992 Presidential campaign, Bill Clinton was able to point to a long list of his accomplishments in Arkansas education.

Mr. Clinton, a Democrat who had been Governor of Arkansas since 1978 (excluding a break from 1981 to 1983) made education the keystone of his

ARKANSAS
Continued

efforts to promote economic development and raise the state from poverty.

Under Mr. Clinton's leadership, the state strengthened elementary and secondary education with new standards that insure teachers are well prepared and that schools offer the kinds of mathematics, science, and foreign-language courses that students need for postsecondary education.

Higher-education officials say those school reforms, in turn, helped the state to increase its college-going rate and attract better-prepared students to the 21 public colleges and universities.

More than one-third of all Arkansas students still require remedial courses when they enter college, but state officials say the high proportion reflects the state's comprehensive program to assess students' readiness for college. Arkansas has been praised by independent education groups for its forthright approach to remedial education. A 1987 law requires colleges to assess entering students and report back to high schools on how their graduates fared in college.

Arkansas recently acted to improve the quality and availability of postsecondary technical education, which had been described by many of the state's leading business groups as antiquated and ill suited to train workers.

In 1991 the General Assembly and Mr. Clinton enacted a law to upgrade 14 of the state's 24 vocational-technical schools to colleges. By 1997 the 14 schools will be required to offer college-level courses and associate degrees. The goal of the law was to put high-quality technical education within driving distance of all prospective students.

As part of the change, oversight of the schools was given to the state's Board of Higher Education, the coordinating board for all postsecondary education. The board is made up of two bodies: the College Panel, which oversees programs and budgets of the technical and community colleges; and the University Panel, which handles the same duties for the state's 10 four-year public institutions. The director of higher education works for the board but is appointed by the Governor.

Money to finance the technical-college reforms is coming from an unlikely source—a half-per-cent increase in the corporate income tax that also was approved in 1991.

Business groups, which have strong influence in the legislature, had previously defeated attempts by Mr. Clinton to increase the corporate income tax. But the groups backed the 1991 tax after extracting an agreement from Mr. Clinton that the proceeds would be earmarked for the technical colleges.

Otherwise, most of Mr. Clinton's reforms have been financed with sales-tax increases—one cent in 1983 and an additional half-cent in 1991. Mr. Clinton's reliance on sales tax has angered some tax-fairness groups, which say he is too fearful of alienating influential corporate and natural-gas interests by pushing other levies, such as a tax on natural gas sold outside the state.

Public-school teachers benefited most from the sales-tax increases, but higher education has always received a share of the revenue. Most institutions used the money from the 1991 tax to buy new equipment and raise faculty salaries. The state has increased its spending on financial aid.

Arkansas has three private, historically black institutions and one public one, the University of Arkansas at Pine Bluff, which has been plagued in the past year by athletics and management scandals.

DEMOGRAPHICS

Population: 2,372,000   (Rank: 33)

Age distribution:
Up to 17 .... 26.4%
18 to 24 .... 10.2%
25 to 44 .... 29.3%
45 and older 34.2%

Racial and ethnic distribution:
American Indian 0.5%
Asian 0.5%
Black 15.9%
White 82.7%
Other and unknown 0.3%
Hispanic (may be any race) .. 0.8%

Educational attainment of adults (highest level):
9th grade or less 15.2%
Some high school, no diploma 18.4%
High-school diploma 32.7%
Some college, no degree 16.6%
Associate degree 3.7%
Bachelor's degree 8.9%
Graduate or professional
 degree 4.5%

Proportion who speak a language other than English at home: 2.8%

Per-capita personal income: $14,629

Poverty rate:
All 19.1%
Under age 18 .... 25.3%
Age 18 and older 16.8%

New public high-school graduates in:
1992-93 (estimate) 25,500
2001-02 (estimate) 26,450

New GED diploma recipients: 7,891

High-school dropout rate: 11.4%

POLITICAL LEADERSHIP

Governor: Lieut. Gov. Jim Guy Tucker (D) is expected to complete the term of Bill Clinton

Governor's higher-education aide:
Rob DeGostin, State Capitol, Little Rock 72201; (501) 682-2345

U.S. Senators: Dale Bumpers (D), term ends 1999; David Pryor (D), term ends 1997

U.S. Representatives:
2 Democrats, 2 Republicans
Jay Dickey (R), Tim Hutchinson (R), Blanche Lambert (D), Ray Thornton (D)

General Assembly: Senate, 30 Democrats, 5 Republicans; House, 89 Democrats, 10 Republicans, 1 Independent

COLLEGES AND UNIVERSITIES

Higher education:
Public 4-year institutions 10
Public 2-year institutions 10
Private 4-year institutions 10
Private 2-year institutions 5
Total 35

Vocational institutions: 100

Statewide coordinating board:
State Board of Higher Education
114 East Capitol
Little Rock 72201
(501) 324-9300
Diane S. Gilleland, director

ARKANSAS
Continued

Private-college association:
Independent Colleges of Arkansas
One Riverfront Place, Suite 610
North Little Rock 72114
(501) 378-0843
E. Kearney Dietz, president

Institutions censured by the AAUP:
Phillips County Community College, Southern Arkansas University, University of the Ozarks (governing board)

Institutions under NCAA sanctions:
None

FACULTY MEMBERS

Full-time faculty members by rank:
Professor 729
Associate professor 694
Assistant professor 786
Instructor 392
Lecturer 23
No rank 333
Total 2,957

Full-time faculty members with tenure:
Men 1,065
Women 340
Total 1,405

Average pay of full-time professors

Public 4-year institutions:
Professor $45,727
Associate professor $36,333
Assistant professor $31,151
Instructor $23,812
No rank $25,442
All $34,960

Public 2-year institutions:
Professor $32,756
Associate professor $26,331
Assistant professor $25,813
Instructor $21,258
No rank $27,042
All $26,811

Private 4-year institutions:
Professor $36,468
Associate professor $31,455
Assistant professor $27,333
Instructor $22,545
No rank .... n/a
All $31,410

STUDENTS

Enrollment:
At public 4-year institutions . 61,408
At public 2-year institutions . 17,237
At private 4-year institutions . 9,799
At private 2-year institutions . 1,981
Undergraduate 82,506
Graduate 6,364
Professional 1,555
American Indian 438
Asian 740
Black 12,188
Hispanic 431
White 75,157
Foreign 1,471
Total 90,425

Enrollment highlights:
Women 57.2%
Full-time 71.9%
Minority 15.5%
Foreign 1.6%
10-year change in total
  enrollment .... Up 16.5%

Proportion of enrollment made up of minority students:
At public 4-year institutions . 15.6%
At public 2-year institutions . 14.4%
At private 4-year institutions 12.5%
At private 2-year institutions 37.3%

Degrees awarded:
Associate 2,606

Bachelor's 7,475
Master's 1,691
Doctorate 135
Professional 324

Residence of new students: State residents made up 85% of all freshmen enrolled in Arkansas; 86% of all Arkansas residents who were freshmen attended college in their home state.

Test scores: Students averaged 19.9 on the A.C.T., which was taken by an estimated 60% of Arkansas's high-school seniors.

Graduation rates at NCAA Division I institutions:
Arkansas State University 31%
University of Arkansas
  at Fayetteville 36%
University of Arkansas
  at Little Rock .... n/a

MONEY

Average tuition and fees:
At public 4-year institutions . $1,418
At public 2-year institutions .. $648
At private 4-year institutions $4,464
At private 2-year institutions $2,482

Expenditures:
Public institutions $751,336,000
Private institutions ... $108,888,000

State funds for higher-education operating expenses: $411,827,000

Two-year change: Up 25%

State spending on student aid:
Need-based: $7,083,000
Non–need-based: $768,000
Other: $180,000

Salary of chief executive of largest public 4-year campus:
Daniel E. Ferritor, University of
  Arkansas at Fayetteville: $126,000

Total spending on research and development by doctorate-granting universities: $48,861,000
Sources:
Federal government 35.8%
State and local governments . 24.2%
Industry 8.3%
The institution itself 25.5%
Other 6.2%

Total federal spending on college- and university-based research and development: $23,586,000
Selected programs:
Department of Health
  and Human Services . $7,673,000
National Science
  Foundation $1,727,000
Department of Defense ... $729,000
Department
  of Agriculture $7,014,000
Department of Energy .. $1,125,000

Largest endowment:
Hendrix College $57,331,000

Top fund raisers:
University of Arkansas
  at Fayetteville $14,546,000
Arkansas College $8,892,000
Ouachita Baptist
  University $7,646,000

MISCELLANY

■ The chancellor of the University of Arkansas at Pine Bluff, Lawrence A. Davis, Jr., is the son of the campus's first chancellor, Lawrence A. Davis, Sr.

■ Former Sen. J. William Fulbright, the creator of the international scholarly and student exchanges that bear his name, served as president of the University of Arkansas from 1939 to 1941.

ARKANSAS
Continued

■ The University of Arkansas at Little Rock is the site of the Native American Press Archives, a collection of 250,000 items published since 1826 by American Indians.

■ The oldest institution of higher education in Arkansas is the University of the Ozarks, founded in 1834. It is affiliated with the United Presbyterian Church, USA.

CALIFORNIA

I T'S a nice place to visit. But you wouldn't want to be sick, indigent, homeless, go to school or college, or live here."

That sentiment, from a *Los Angeles Times* political cartoon, summed up the state of affairs in California in the summer of 1992, as Republican Gov. Pete Wilson and the Democrat-controlled Legislature haggled over which services to cut to avert a projected $10.7-billion deficit for fiscal year 1993. Meanwhile, as the gridlock dragged on for two months, state employees were paid with IOU's. Public colleges prepared for the fall term without knowing how much money they would get.

A budget was finally signed in early September. But its deep cuts to higher education, including student aid, and sharp tuition increases hammered the very principles that made California's public colleges and universities the envy of other states.

Many educators worried that the California Master Plan for Higher Education, adopted three decades ago to assure all qualified students a place in a two-year or four-year college or university, was being sacrificed to the state's fiscal crisis.

In the midst of the severe money shortage, enrollment continues to climb. The California Postsecondary Education Commission, the state's coordinating board, has estimated that enrollment will increase by 700,000 students over the next 13 years. Enrollment in public colleges stands at about 1.5 million, or more than one of every nine American college students.

The state budget cut all three levels of public higher education. The University of California system received $224-million less than in 1991-92, a 10.6-per-cent cut; the California State University system was cut by $125-million, 7.6 per cent; and the California Community Colleges took a 29-per-cent cut in state money. UC and the community colleges expected to restore some of their losses through other sources—including loans that will have to be repaid.

Each university system and community-college district is governed by its own board, and each determined how best to cope. California State University, 95 per cent of whose budget comes from the state, was hit the hardest.

Some 360,000 students are enrolled at 20 Cal State campuses. In the 1992-93 academic year, those students have fewer choices of courses, higher fees, longer lines, and much uncertainty.

By June 1992, some 2,200 layoff notices had been sent to system employees, including 340 tenured or tenure-track faculty members. At San Diego State University, 9 of 72 departments were slated for elimination and 193 faculty members notified of layoffs. At Fresno State University, 639 class sections were dropped. All layoffs of tenured and tenure-track faculty were rescinded in late summer after the CSU system found some extra money. But Chancellor Barry Munitz warned that faculty layoffs are likely in the coming year.

The president of San Francisco State, Robert A. Corrigan, compared the plight of the University of California and California State University systems to that of two friends jumping off a cliff—the only difference being that one of the friends, in this case UC, has a parachute.

Most educators agree that UC will weather California's budget problems better than CSU will. The system gets less than 30 per cent of its budget from the state, and has a $1-billion endowment. Still, UC officials complain that the state's contribution has been steadily decreasing, jeopardizing undergraduate education.

All three systems increased tuition sharply, spawning protests. Students at the University of California took over the auditorium at the Davis campus in January 1992, where regents met to pass the fee increase. By the time the fracas ended, five students had been arrested. Cal State students organized a two-day "teach-in" in late September. Several campuses participated, with San Diego State and San Francisco State staging the biggest events.

Even as the University of California was complaining about budget cuts, however, it faced public outrage over a retirement package totaling more than $2-million for its retiring president, David P. Gardner. Although there were angry demands for the withdrawal of the package—and for the resignation of the Board of Regents that approved it—the board held its ground. It did agree to changes in the policy for compensating top officials, including allowing a 20-day period for public comment on severance proposals.

Jack W. Peltason, chancellor of UC-Irvine, replaced Mr. Gardner.

The 107 California community colleges, which enroll more than a million students, are guaranteed a portion of the state's budget but get most of their funds from local taxes. They also were forced to cut back programs, raise fees, and rely increasingly on part-time faculty members to take the place of full-time professors.

Enrollment projections at four-year institutions were the impetus for talks about using community colleges to take some of the pressure off four-year campuses.

Governor Wilson vetoed a bill that would have allowed the University of California and California State University to accept qualified students but "redirect" some to two-year colleges for their first years of higher education. Those who volunteered for redirection would be assured of space at four-year colleges later. The state had estimated that such a policy could save $25-million a year beginning in 1993-94, since instruction costs are lower at community colleges.

Some educators applauded the proposal as a realistic way to deal with burgeoning enrollment. Others worried whether minority and poor students, who are already overrepresented at the two-year level, would be disproportionately diverted. Community-college officials, watching the state pare their budgets and seeing their classrooms crowded to overflowing, wondered how they could accommodate more students.

While public colleges in California are where most of the students are, private colleges are major players in

CALIFORNIA
Continued

higher education. They include the University of Southern California and Stanford University, the two largest, and smaller institutions such as Pomona and Mills Colleges.

The University of Southern California found itself in the eye of a storm in April 1992. Thousands of people, outraged by a jury's finding that police officers were not guilty of brutality in the beating of Los Angeles motorist Rodney G. King, rioted, looted, and set buildings ablaze. Much of the rioting took place near USC, but the campus was not harmed, and many students were involved in cleanup activities in the community.

Gerhard Casper, former provost and professor of law at the University of Chicago, took over as the president of Stanford University on September 1, 1992. Mr. Casper replaced Donald Kennedy, who announced in 1991, after a protracted controversy over management of federal research money, that he would step down in August 1992.

DEMOGRAPHICS

Population: 30,380,000   (Rank: 1)

Age distribution:
Up to 17 .... 26.9%
18 to 24 .... 10.9%
25 to 44 .... 34.7%
45 and older 27.5%

Racial and ethnic distribution:
American Indian 0.8%
Asian 9.6%
Black 7.4%
White 69.0%
Other and unknown 13.2%
Hispanic (may be any race) . 25.8%

Educational attainment of adults (highest level):
9th grade or less 11.2%
Some high school, no diploma 12.6%
High-school diploma 22.3%
Some college, no degree 22.6%
Associate degree 7.9%
Bachelor's degree 15.3%
Graduate or professional
  degree 8.1%

Proportion who speak a language other than English at home: 31.5%

Per-capita personal income: $20,847

Poverty rate:
All 12.5%
Under age 18 .... 18.2%
Age 18 and older 10.5%

New public high-school graduates in:
1992-93 (estimate) 243,550
2001-02 (estimate) 340,070

New GED diploma recipients: 39,226

High-school dropout rate: 14.2%

POLITICAL LEADERSHIP

Governor: Pete Wilson (R), term ends 1995

Governor's higher-education aide: Maureen G. DiMarco, 1121 L Street, Suite 600, Sacramento 95814; (916) 323-0611

U.S. Senators: Barbara Boxer (D), term ends 1999; Dianne Feinstein (D), term ends 1995

U.S. Representatives:
30 Democrats, 22 Republicans

Bill Baker (R), Xavier Becerra (D), Anthony C. Beilenson (D), Howard L. Berman (D), George E. Brown, Jr. (D), Ken Calvert (R), Gary Condit (D), C. Christopher Cox (R), Randy "Duke" Cunningham (R), Ronald V. Dellums (D), Julian C. Dixon (D), Calvin Dooley (D), John T. Doolittle (R), Robert K. Dornan (R), David Dreier (R), Don Edwards (D), Anna G. Eshoo (D), Vic Fazio (D), Bob Filner (D), Elton Gallegly (R), Dan Hamburg (D), Jane Harman (D), Wally Herger (R), Steve Horn (R), Michael Huffington (R), Duncan Hunter (R), Jay C. Kim (R), Tom Lantos (D), Richard H. Lehman (D), Jerry Lewis (R), Matthew G. Martinez (D), Robert T. Matsui (D), Al McCandless (R), Howard P. "Buck" McKeon (R), George Miller (D), Norman Y. Mineta (D), Carlos J. Moorhead (R), Ron Packard (R), Leon E. Panetta (D), Nancy Pelosi (D), Richard W. Pombo (R), Dana Rohrabacher (R), Lucille Roybal-Allard (D), Ed Royce (R), Lynn Schenk (D), Pete Stark (D), Bill Thomas (R), Esteban E. Torres (D), Walter R. Tucker (D), Maxine Waters (D), Henry A. Waxman (D), Lynn Woolsey (D)

Legislature: Senate, 23 Democrats, 13 Republicans, 2 Independents, 1 vacancy, 1 race undecided; House, 49 Democrats, 31 Republicans

COLLEGES AND UNIVERSITIES

Higher education:
Public 4-year institutions 31
Public 2-year institutions 107
Private 4-year institutions 142
Private 2-year institutions 30
Total 310

Vocational institutions: 852

Statewide coordinating board:
California Postsecondary Education Commission
1303 J Street, 5th Floor
Sacramento 95814
(916) 445-1000
Warren H. Fox, executive director

Private-college association:
Association of Independent California Colleges and Universities
1100 11th Street, Suite 315
Sacramento 95814
(916) 446-7626
Jonathan A. Brown, president

Institutions censured by the AAUP:
Loma Linda University, University of Judaism

Institution under NCAA sanctions:
University of the Pacific

FACULTY MEMBERS

Full-time faculty members by rank:
Professor 13,626
Associate professor 5,269
Assistant professor 5,101
Instructor 604
Lecturer 742
No rank 12,421
Total 37,763

Full-time faculty members with tenure:
Men 19,504
Women 6,491
Total 25,995

Average pay of full-time professors
Public 4-year institutions:
Professor $64,155
Associate professor $47,917
Assistant professor $39,787
Instructor $32,066
No rank $42,326
All $55,380

CALIFORNIA
Continued

Public 2-year institutions:
Professor $53,497
Associate professor $47,402
Assistant professor $47,181
Instructor $43,292
No rank $47,041
All $47,122

Private 4-year institutions:
Professor $62,277
Associate professor $44,469
Assistant professor $36,736
Instructor $28,481
No rank $35,015
All $48,804

STUDENTS

Enrollment:
At public 4-year institutions 496,757
At public 2-year
  institutions 1,057,921
At private 4-year institutions 203,820
At private 2-year institutions   11,499

Undergraduate 1,569,383
Graduate 169,074
Professional 31,540

American Indian 20,999
Asian 215,407
Black 114,787
Hispanic 222,724
White 1,130,301
Foreign 65,779

Total 1,769,997

Enrollment highlights:
Women 54.0%
Full-time 44.3%
Minority 33.7%
Foreign 3.7%
10-year change in total
  enrollment .... Down 1.2%

Proportion of enrollment made up of minority students:
At public 4-year institutions . 34.5%
At public 2-year institutions . 34.7%
At private 4-year institutions   25.0%
At private 2-year institutions   46.9%

Degrees awarded:
Associate 48,353
Bachelor's 98,157
Master's 34,529
Doctorate 4,747
Professional 7,814

Residence of new students: State residents made up 90% of all freshmen enrolled in California; 95% of all California residents who were freshmen attended college in their home state.

Test scores: Students averaged 900 on the S.A.T., which was taken by an estimated 46% of California's high-school seniors.

Graduation rates at NCAA Division I institutions:
California State University
  at Fresno 46%
California State University
  at Fullerton 39%
California State University
  at Long Beach 33%
California State University
  at Northridge 29%
California State University
  at Sacramento 37%
Loyola Marymount University . 67%
Pepperdine University 56%
Saint Mary's College
  of California 63%
San Diego State University 38%
San Jose State University 38%
Santa Clara University 79%
Stanford University 92%
University of California
  at Berkeley 73%

University of California
    at Irvine 57%
University of California
    at Los Angeles 71%
University of California
    at Santa Barbara 64%
University of the Pacific 60%
University of San Diego 53%
University of San Francisco ... 56%
University of Southern
    California 58%

MONEY

Average tuition and fees:
At public 4-year institutions . $1,220
At public 2-year institutions .. $114
At private 4-year institutions $10,863
At private 2-year institutions $7,942

Expenditures:
Public institutions . $11,230,941,000
Private institutions . $5,077,597,000

State funds for higher-education operating expenses: $4,841,606,000

Two-year change: Down 12%

State spending on student aid:
Need-based: $169,205,000
Non–need-based: None
Other: $52,163,000

Salary of chief executive of largest public 4-year campus:
Charles E. Young, University
   of California at Los Angeles:
   $175,000

Total spending on research and development by doctorate-granting universities: $2,007,361,000
Sources:
Federal government 68.2%
State and local governments .. 2.6%
Industry 4.5%
The institution itself 17.7%
Other 7.0%

Total federal spending on college- and university-based research and development: $1,317,370,000
Selected programs:
Department of Health
   and Human Services $709,269,000
National Science
   Foundation $199,756,000
Department of Defense $161,581,000
Department
   of Agriculture $15,363,000
Department of Energy . $78,587,000

Largest endowment:
Stanford University $2,043,000,000

Top fund raisers:
Stanford University .. $180,922,000
University of California
   at Berkeley $117,657,000
University of Southern
   California $94,304,000

MISCELLANY

■ With more than a million items, Loyola Marymount University boasts one of the largest picture-postcard collections in existence. The holdings include cards made of leather, woven grass, and tin; most were donated in 1967 by a Los Angeles photographer.

■ Monterey is the site of two institutions that focus on foreign languages. The Monterey Institute of International Studies, which offers master's degrees in international management, international-policy studies, language studies, and translation and interpretation, requires students to take many courses in languages other than their own. The Defense Language Institute provides training for 3,000 U.S. military personnel.

■ The University of California at Riverside is the home of the Eigh-

CALIFORNIA
Continued

teenth-Century Short Title Catalogue, an electronic bibliography with 315,000 records of books and monographs published in English from 1701 to 1800. Scholars can search the catalogue over the Research Libraries Information Network.

■ The oldest institutions of higher education in California are the University of the Pacific (an independent institution) and Santa Clara University (a Roman Catholic institution), both founded in 1851.

COLORADO

For the University of Colorado, the 1991-92 academic year was tough—and not simply because of the recession.

Among other things, the university system was criticized for the way it searched for a new system president; a coach at the Boulder campus was reprimanded for using his position to promote an anti-gay organization; and the university's Health Sciences Center was charged with paying its public-relations officers too much.

The controversies arose in a state where accountability and standards continue to be the watchwords of politicians and higher-education officials.

Gov. Roy Romer, a Democrat who became chairman of the National Governors' Association in 1992, helped create a committee on standards and assessment in elementary and secondary education and wants to see a similar national focus on higher education.

Mr. Romer proposed only a slight spending increase for colleges in 1991-92, but the institutions fared better in the General Assembly, which passed a higher postsecondary budget than the Governor had requested. For 1992-93, Mr. Romer was more generous, requesting a $25-million increase for higher education. This time, the General Assembly approved a $13-million increase, instead.

Community colleges continue to grow by leaps and bounds, and their leaders are demanding a larger share of the higher-education budget to keep up with growth. Those demands have occasionally caused friction with public four-year colleges.

While assessment of postsecondary education is a topic that observers predict will command attention in 1992-93, some legislative moves have already occurred on that front—at least one of which was prompted by a study by the Commission on Higher Education, the state's postsecondary coordinating board.

When the commission tracked the progress of freshmen who had entered public universities in 1986, it found that by 1990 only 19 per cent of the class had graduated. Although the study found that 44 per cent had graduated by 1991, some lawmakers were concerned about the figures.

That concern prompted the General Assembly to pass a law requiring that the higher-education commission examine whether impediments to graduation exist, and to report its findings to the legislature in 1993.

Another law passed in 1992 will provide "performance-based funding" to colleges. Under the law the commission will come up with a measure for examining colleges' performance—such as graduation rates—and financial bonuses will be provided based on how well colleges meet the standard. Legislators say the measure creates an additional opportunity for accountability, but some educators are concerned about how success will be measured.

DEMOGRAPHICS

Population: 3,377,000 (Rank: 26)

Age distribution:
Up to 17 .... 26.1%
18 to 24 .... 10.0%
25 to 44 .... 35.8%
45 and older 28.0%

Racial and ethnic distribution:
American Indian 0.8%
Asian 1.8%
Black 4.0%
White 88.2%
Other and unknown 5.1%
Hispanic (may be any race) . 12.9%

Educational attainment of adults (highest level):
9th grade or less 5.6%
Some high school, no diploma 10.0%
High-school diploma 26.5%
Some college, no degree 24.0%
Associate degree 6.9%
Bachelor's degree 18.0%
Graduate or professional
  degree 9.0%

Proportion who speak a language other than English at home: 10.5%

Per-capita personal income: $19,358

Poverty rate:
All 11.7%
Under age 18 .... 15.3%
Age 18 and older 10.4%

New public high-school graduates in:
1992-93 (estimate) 31,400
2001-02 (estimate) 36,170

New GED diploma recipients: 6,818

High-school dropout rate: 9.8%

POLITICAL LEADERSHIP

Governor: Roy Romer (D), term ends 1995

Governor's higher-education aide: Donna Chitwood, 136 State Capitol, Denver 80203; (303) 866-2155

U.S. Senators: Hank Brown (R), term ends 1997; Ben Nighthorse Campbell (D), term ends 1999

U.S. Representatives:
2 Democrats, 4 Republicans
Wayne Allard (R), Joel Hefley (R), Scott McInnis (R); Dan Schaefer (R), Patricia Schroeder (D), David E. Skaggs (D)

General Assembly: Senate, 16 Democrats, 19 Republicans; House, 31 Democrats, 34 Republicans

COLLEGES AND UNIVERSITIES

Higher education:
Public 4-year institutions 13
Public 2-year institutions 15
Private 4-year institutions 20
Private 2-year institutions 9
Total 57

Vocational institutions: 99

Statewide coordinating board:
Colorado Commission on
  Higher Education
1300 Broadway, 2nd Floor
Denver 80203
(303) 866-2723
David A. Longanecker, executive director

COLORADO
Continued

Private-college association:
Independent Higher Education
of Colorado
518 17th Street, Suite 387
Denver 80202
(303) 571-5559
Toni E. Worcester, executive director

Institutions censured by the AAUP:
None

Institutions under NCAA sanctions:
None

FACULTY MEMBERS

Full-time faculty members by rank:
Professor 1,844
Associate professor 1,299
Assistant professor 1,147
Instructor 199
Lecturer 50
No rank 852
Total 5,391

Full-time faculty members with tenure:
Men 2,708
Women 588
Total 3,296

Average pay of full-time professors

Public 4-year institutions:
Professor $52,275
Associate professor $40,850
Assistant professor $35,020
Instructor $25,959
No rank $29,188
All $43,262

Public 2-year institutions:
Professor $36,145
Associate professor $30,629
Assistant professor $27,495
Instructor $23,576
No rank $29,480
All $29,606

Private 4-year institutions:
Professor $53,005
Associate professor $40,057
Assistant professor $35,449
Instructor $27,424
No rank $34,041
All $42,974

STUDENTS

Enrollment:
At public 4-year institutions 128,616
At public 2-year institutions . 72,037
At private 4-year institutions 21,719
At private 2-year institutions . 4,759
Undergraduate 191,300
Graduate 32,806
Professional 3,025
American Indian 2,279
Asian 5,275
Black 6,646
Hispanic 17,078
White 191,283
Foreign 4,570
Total 227,131

Enrollment highlights:
Women 53.2%
Full-time 53.1%
Minority 14.1%
Foreign 2.0%
10-year change in total
  enrollment .... Up 39.4%

Proportion of enrollment made up of minority students:
At public 4-year institutions . 12.4%
At public 2-year institutions . 16.9%
At private 4-year institutions 12.4%
At private 2-year institutions 22.3%

Degrees awarded:
Associate 6,144
Bachelor's 16,435

Master's 5,099
Doctorate 718
Professional 794

Residence of new students: State residents made up 78% of all freshmen enrolled in Colorado; 80% of all Colorado residents who were freshmen attended college in their home state.

Test scores: Students averaged 21.3 on the A.C.T., which was taken by an estimated 61% of Colorado's high-school seniors.

Graduation rates at NCAA Division I institutions:
Colorado State University 56%
U.S. Air Force Academy 71%
University of Colorado
 at Boulder 61%

MONEY

Average tuition and fees:
At public 4-year institutions . $1,919
At public 2-year institutions .. $943
At private 4-year institutions $9,516
At private 2-year institutions $6,731

Expenditures:
Public institutions .. $1,374,188,000
Private institutions ... $250,811,000

State funds for higher-education operating expenses: $529,158,000
Two-year change: Up 4%

State spending on student aid:
Need-based: $13,442,000
Non–need-based: $10,838,000
Other: $2,014,000

Salary of chief executive of largest public 4-year campus:
James N. Corbridge, Jr., University of Colorado at Boulder: $123,900

Total spending on research and development by doctorate-granting universities: $249,958,000
Sources:
Federal government 72.0%
State and local governments .. 4.7%
Industry 6.4%
The institution itself 9.0%
Other 8.0%

Total federal spending on college- and university-based research and development: $168,905,000
Selected programs:
Department of Health
 and Human Services $80,860,000
National Science
 Foundation $30,233,000
Department of Defense $13,884,000
Department
 of Agriculture $6,030,000
Department of Energy .. $7,171,000

Largest endowment:
Colorado College $143,622,000

Top fund raisers:
University of Colorado $43,867,000
Colorado School
 of Mines $12,173,000
Colorado State
 University $11,827,000

MISCELLANY

■ Colorado State University in 1992 designated a new bridge on the campus as the Vietnam Era Memorial Bridge. It was topped with bricks from a university building that burned down in 1970 at the height of anti–Vietnam War protests on campus.

■ Regis University is offering an educational warranty that guarantees students a bachelor's degree in four years or free tuition until they gradu-

COLORADO
Continued

ate. To qualify for free tuition after four years, students must maintain a 2.0 grade-point average every semester.

■ A 10-foot-high steel sculpture of a paper airplane that appears to have been torn from a gigantic loose-leaf notebook, folded by gargantuan hands, and tossed out of the university library is a landmark on the University of Southern Colorado campus. The sculpture, which was designed by a student, is called "3-Fold Education."

■ The oldest institution of higher education in Colorado is the University of Denver, an independent institution founded in 1864.

CONNECTICUT

In Connecticut, public colleges continued to sing the budget blues in 1992, but the financial travails of private institutions often seemed more dramatic.

Wealthy Yale University began to lay off staff members and eliminate faculty positions. Wesleyan University nearly eliminated its policy of admitting students without regard to their financial need.

The financially troubled University of Bridgeport finally succumbed to the lures of an organization affiliated with the Rev. Sun Myung Moon's Unification Church and ceded control in exchange for money to keep the institution from closing.

Even with a new income tax, Connecticut didn't have enough money for its public institutions. The recession and layoffs in its defense industries had severely weakened the economy.

Nowhere was that more evident than in the state's appropriation for public higher education for 1992-93. The amount, $486-million, was 7 per cent below the 1990-91 level of support.

The continuing financial problems led to renewed calls from the General Assembly for greater cost savings in public higher education—and some action.

Connecticut lawmakers weighed several reorganization plans, including one that would have combined all public two-year and four-year institutions, except for the University of Connecticut, into a single administration.

Ultimately, lawmakers adopted a less-sweeping plan to merge the state's five two-year technical colleges with five of the 12 community colleges that are located near the technical colleges. Since 1990 the two-year institutions have been governed by a single Board of Trustees of Technical and Community Colleges, with the colleges maintaining their own administrations.

The technical colleges have been criticized for teaching skills that are out of date for the state's changing industrial base. Lawmakers said they hoped the merger would further push those colleges to upgrade their technical-training programs.

The legislature and Gov. Lowell P. Weicker, Jr., enacted new laws that will restrict public-college spending on administrative costs.

Despite its financial problems, higher education remains an important force in the state. Most faculty members belong to unions, which play an important role in state politics and were particularly active players in 1992, when they and Governor Weicker battled over pay and benefits for public employees.

The University of Connecticut is also adept at winning funds from the General Assembly. The university is governed by its own board, as are the four universities that make up the Connecticut State University System. The Board of Governors for Higher Education is the statewide coordinating board.

The influence of private colleges is also evident in state policy. Connecticut provides grants to private-college students and subsidizes cities and towns where the tax base is reduced by the presence of colleges.

DEMOGRAPHICS

Population: 3,291,000   (Rank: 27)

Age distribution:
Up to 17 .... 23.2%
18 to 24 .... 9.9%
25 to 44 .... 33.3%
45 and older 33.5%

Racial and ethnic distribution:
American Indian 0.2%
Asian 1.5%
Black 8.3%
White 87.0%
Other and unknown 2.9%
Hispanic (may be any race) .. 6.5%

Educational attainment of adults (highest level):
9th grade or less 8.4%
Some high school, no diploma 12.4%
High-school diploma 29.5%
Some college, no degree 15.9%
Associate degree 6.6%
Bachelor's degree 16.2%
Graduate or professional
  degree 11.0%

Proportion who speak a language other than English at home: 15.2%

Per-capita personal income: $26,022

Poverty rate:
All 6.8%
Under age 18 .... 10.7%
Age 18 and older 5.6%

New public high-school graduates in:
1992-93 (estimate) 25,670
2001-02 (estimate) 31,020

New GED diploma recipients: 5,306

High-school dropout rate: 9.0%

POLITICAL LEADERSHIP

Governor: Lowell P. Weicker, Jr. (Ind), term ends 1995

Governor's higher-education aide: Mark D. Waxenburg, State Capitol, Hartford 06106; (203) 566-4840

U.S. Senators: Christopher J. Dodd (D), term ends 1999; Joseph I. Lieberman (D), term ends 1995

U.S. Representatives:
3 Democrats, 3 Republicans
Rosa L. DeLauro (D), Gary A. Franks (R), Sam Gejdenson (D), Nancy L. Johnson (R), Barbara B. Kennelly (D), Christopher Shays (R)

General Assembly: Senate, 20 Democrats, 16 Republicans; House, 87 Democrats, 64 Republicans

CONNECTICUT
Continued

COLLEGES AND UNIVERSITIES

Higher education:
Public 4-year institutions 7
Public 2-year institutions 17
Private 4-year institutions 20
Private 2-year institutions 3
Total 47

Vocational institutions: 108

Statewide coordinating board:
Board of Governors for
  Higher Education
61 Woodland Street
Hartford 06105
(203) 566-5766
Andrew G. De Rocco,
commissioner of higher education

Private-college association:
Connecticut Conference
  of Independent Colleges
36 Gillett Street
Hartford 06105
(203) 522-0271
Michael A. Gerber, president

Institutions censured by the AAUP:
None

Institutions under NCAA sanctions:
None

FACULTY MEMBERS

Full-time faculty members by rank:
Professor 2,290
Associate professor 1,442
Assistant professor 1,502
Instructor 258
Lecturer 85
No rank 17
Total 5,594

Full-time faculty members with tenure:
Men 2,844
Women 786
Total 3,630

Average pay of full-time professors
Public 4-year institutions:
Professor $62,305
Associate professor $47,562
Assistant professor $38,958
Instructor $30,040
No rank .... n/a
All $51,222

Public 2-year institutions:
Professor $50,458
Associate professor $43,185
Assistant professor $36,863
Instructor $31,830
No rank .... n/a
All $43,335

Private 4-year institutions:
Professor $66,244
Associate professor $43,383
Assistant professor $36,560
Instructor $29,360
No rank $27,900
All $49,717

STUDENTS

Enrollment:
At public 4-year institutions . 64,920
At public 2-year institutions . 44,562
At private 4-year institutions 57,470
At private 2-year institutions . 1,578
Undergraduate 133,442
Graduate 31,878
Professional 3,210
American Indian 423
Asian 4,311
Black 9,937
Hispanic 5,620
White 143,434

Foreign 4,805
Total 168,530

Enrollment highlights:
Women 56.6%
Full-time 50.5%
Minority 12.4%
Foreign 2.9%
10-year change in total
 enrollment .... Up 5.6%

Proportion of enrollment made up of minority students:
At public 4-year institutions .. 9.4%
At public 2-year institutions . 16.7%
At private 4-year institutions 12.3%
At private 2-year institutions 12.5%

Degrees awarded:
Associate 4,721
Bachelor's 14,179
Master's 6,285
Doctorate 572
Professional 956

Residence of new students: State residents made up 78% of all freshmen enrolled in Connecticut; 62% of all Connecticut residents who were freshmen attended college in their home state.

Test scores: Students averaged 900 on the S.A.T., which was taken by an estimated 79% of Connecticut's high-school seniors.

Graduation rates at NCAA Division I institutions:
Central Connecticut State
 University 41%
Fairfield University 81%
University of Connecticut 66%
University of Hartford 51%
Yale University 94%

MONEY

Average tuition and fees:
At public 4-year institutions . $2,313
At public 2-year institutions .. $972
At private 4-year institutions $12,315
At private 2-year institutions $8,586

Expenditures:
Public institutions $811,282,000
Private institutions . $1,193,877,000

State funds for higher-education operating expenses: $486,239,000

Two-year change: Down 7%

State spending on student aid:
Need-based: $20,467,000
Non–need-based: $200,000
Other: $15,175,000

Salary of chief executive of largest public 4-year campus:
Harry J. Hartley, Jr., University
 of Connecticut: $150,542

Total spending on research and development by doctorate-granting universities: $298,076,000
Sources:
Federal government 63.9%
State and local governments .. 1.8%
Industry 4.5%
The institution itself 21.6%
Other 8.3%

Total federal spending on college- and university-based research and development: $189,462,000
Selected programs:
Department of Health
 and Human Services $146,427,000
National Science
 Foundation $16,282,000
Department of Defense . $8,511,000
Department
 of Agriculture $1,807,000
Department of Energy .. $9,800,000

Largest endowment:
Yale University $2,566,680,000

THE ALMANAC OF HIGHER EDUCATION • THE STATES

CONNECTICUT
Continued

Top fund raisers:
Yale University $132,417,000
Trinity College $8,766,000
Connecticut College $7,549,000

MISCELLANY

- Yale University houses the Fortunoff Video Archive for Holocaust Testimonies, a collection of some 2,200 videotaped accounts from survivors of the Nazi effort to exterminate Europe's Jews. About 500 have been cataloged and indexed, allowing scholars access from research libraries around the country.

- When Connecticut College placed Camille Paglia's controversial book, *Sexual Personae: Art and Decadence from Nefertiti to Emily Dickinson,* on its 1992 summer reading list, some faculty members objected. (The book has been sharply criticized by many feminists.) So the college added another book, Susan Faludi's *Backlash: The Undeclared War Against American Women,* to the list to be read and discussed in tandem with Ms. Paglia's book.

- Sacred Heart University in 1992 established a Center for Christian-Jewish Understanding aimed in part at examining the philosophical and theological differences between the two religions. The center will offer conferences, international activities, community lectures, and advanced academic courses for lay people and members of the clergy.

- Yale University, founded in 1701, is the oldest institution of higher education in Connecticut. In 1831 it had the distinction of running the nation's first endowment drive, which raised $107,000.

DELAWARE

DELAWARE, which likes to call itself the "small wonder" state, is home to big banking interests and major chemical-manufacturing operations. In recent years, it managed to attract new companies even while other parts of the country were feeling the first pinch of the recession. For a while, colleges here escaped the draconian cuts that plagued higher education in other states.

That changed in academic 1991-92, when the University of Delaware, Delaware State College, and Delaware Technical and Community College had their appropriations reduced by the General Assembly.

That action resulted in larger classes, staff reductions, and other cutbacks, including the elimination of the university's varsity wrestling program and alumni magazine.

While money was less plentiful, enrollment edged up as students sought higher education as a way to prepare themselves for whatever jobs were available.

Budget reductions and tuition increases continued into the 1992-93 academic year, as well.

Higher education did receive a boost in the form of the Work Force Development Grant Program. The program, started in December 1991, provides grants to adult part-time students who work for one or more employers, and to students who work full time for businesses that employ fewer than 100 workers. Qualified students receive a state grant that pays 65 per cent of their tuition, while the employer is asked to contribute 25 per cent. The institutions pay the remaining 10 per cent.

In September 1991, Republican Gov. Michael N. Castle, who was elected in 1989, reorganized the Postsecondary Education Commission, the statewide coordinating board that oversees the two public four-year institutions and the four-campus technical- and community-college system. Now called the Higher Education Commission, the 25-member board is charged with aligning the higher-education curriculum with elementary and secondary education and with the needs of employers.

Because of Delaware's two-term limit for governors, Mr. Castle could not run for re-election in 1992. In November, voters elected Tom Carper, a former Democratic Congressman, to a four-year term. Governor-elect Carper wants to promote cooperation among state government, businesses, and schools. He also wants to create a new scholarship program and an internship for students in state government offices.

The University of Delaware wound up in the middle of the "political correctness" debate when it barred two faculty members, Linda S. Gottfredson and Jan H. Blits, from seeking grants from the Pioneer Fund, a private foundation that a faculty committee contended was racist. The two were studying differences in intelligence based on race. In May 1992 the dispute was settled when the university reversed its decision and the professors received a year's paid leave of absence. Both said they had been subjected to pervasive harassment by others on the campus.

DEMOGRAPHICS

Population: 680,000   (Rank: 46)

Age distribution:
Up to 17 .... 24.7%
18 to 24 .... 11.0%
25 to 44 .... 32.9%
45 and older 31.3%

Racial and ethnic distribution:
American Indian 0.3%
Asian 1.4%
Black 16.9%
White 80.3%
Other and unknown 1.1%
Hispanic (may be any race) .. 2.4%

Educational attainment of adults (highest level):
9th grade or less 7.2%
Some high school, no diploma 15.3%
High-school diploma 32.7%
Some college, no degree 16.9%
Associate degree 6.5%
Bachelor's degree 13.7%
Graduate or professional
  degree 7.7%

Proportion who speak a language other than English at home: 6.9%

Per-capita personal income: $20,816

Poverty rate:
All 8.7%
Under age 18 .... 12.0%
Age 18 and older 7.6%

New public high-school graduates in:
1992-93 (estimate) 5,440
2001-02 (estimate) 6,970

New GED diploma recipients: 821

High-school dropout rate: 10.4%

DELAWARE
Continued

POLITICAL LEADERSHIP

Governor: Tom Carper (D), term ends 1997

Governor's higher-education aide: n/a

U.S. Senators: Joseph R. Biden, Jr. (D), term ends 1997; William V. Roth, Jr. (R), term ends 1995

U.S. Representative:
1 Republican
Michael N. Castle (R)

General Assembly: Senate, 15 Democrats, 6 Republicans; House, 18 Democrats, 23 Republicans

COLLEGES AND UNIVERSITIES

Higher education:
Public 4-year institutions 2
Public 2-year institutions 3
Private 4-year institutions 5
Private 2-year institutions 0
Total 10

Vocational institutions: 18

Statewide coordinating board:
Delaware Higher Education
  Commission
820 North French Street
Wilmington 19801
(302) 577-3240
John F. Corrozi, executive director

Private-college association:
None

Institution censured by the AAUP:
Wesley College

Institutions under NCAA sanctions:
None

FACULTY MEMBERS

Full-time faculty members by rank:
Professor 314
Associate professor 363
Assistant professor 345
Instructor 88
Lecturer 31
No rank 147
Total 1,288

Full-time faculty members with tenure:
Men 64
Women 48
Total 112

Average pay of full-time professors

Public 4-year institutions:
Professor $60,586
Associate professor $43,969
Assistant professor $35,558
Instructor $25,899
No rank .... n/a
All $44,231

Public 2-year institutions:
Professor .... n/a
Associate professor .... n/a
Assistant professor .... n/a
Instructor .... n/a
No rank $37,175
All $37,175

Private 4-year institutions:
Professor $46,294
Associate professor $45,347
Assistant professor $33,626
Instructor $26,741
No rank .... n/a
All $40,069

STUDENTS

Enrollment:
At public 4-year institutions . 23,424
At public 2-year institutions . 10,828

At private 4-year institutions . 7,752
At private 2-year institutions 0
Undergraduate 36,822
Graduate 3,309
Professional 1,873
American Indian 99
Asian 710
Black 4,710
Hispanic 546
White 35,155
Foreign 784
Total 42,004

Enrollment highlights:
Women 56.7%
Full-time 60.4%
Minority 14.7%
Foreign 1.9%
10-year change in total
 enrollment .... Up 27.5%

Proportion of enrollment made up of minority students:
At public 4-year institutions . 13.9%
At public 2-year institutions . 18.6%
At private 4-year institutions 11.8%
At private 2-year institutions ... n/a

Degrees awarded:
Associate 1,288
Bachelor's 3,539
Master's 791
Doctorate 114
Professional 329

Residence of new students: State residents made up 57% of all freshmen enrolled in Delaware; 74% of all Delaware residents who were freshmen attended college in their home state.

Test scores: Students averaged 895 on the S.A.T., which was taken by an estimated 66% of Delaware's high-school seniors.

Graduation rates at NCAA Division I institutions:
Delaware State College 29%
University of Delaware 68%

MONEY

Average tuition and fees:
At public 4-year institutions . $2,910
At public 2-year institutions .. $936
At private 4-year institutions $5,831
At private 2-year institutions ... n/a

Expenditures:
Public institutions $342,119,000
Private institutions $43,184,000

State funds for higher-education operating expenses: $122,469,000
Two-year change: Up 4%

State spending on student aid:
Need-based: $1,298,000
Non–need-based: $209,000
Other: $162,000

Salary of chief executive of largest public 4-year campus:
David P. Roselle, University
 of Delaware: salary n/a

Total spending on research and development by doctorate-granting universities: $40,119,000
Sources:
Federal government 43.8%
State and local governments .. 7.8%
Industry 11.0%
The institution itself 29.3%
Other 8.1%

Total federal spending on college- and university-based research and development: $17,922,000
Selected programs:
Department of Health
 and Human Services . $4,152,000

DELAWARE
Continued

National Science
   Foundation $4,896,000
Department of Defense . $2,010,000
Department
   of Agriculture $2,063,000
Department of Energy .. $1,000,000

Largest endowment:
University of Delaware $389,523,000

Top fund raisers:
University of Delaware $16,935,000
Delaware State College . $1,884,000
Goldey-Beacom College .. $904,000

MISCELLANY

■ The Wesley College public-relations office produces a weekly television quiz show, the "Texaco Star Academic Challenge," in which students from 37 high schools in Delaware make up teams to compete for top academic honors. Scholarships from five institutions of higher learning in Delaware are awarded to the winning and runner-up teams, with the winners receiving an all-expense-paid trip to Houston to compete in the national championships each June.

■ The University of Delaware claims to be the first to offer a junior year abroad. The program started in 1923 when eight University of Delaware juniors, accompanied by a French professor, set off to study the French language and customs in Nancy.

■ The oldest higher-education institution in the state is the University of Delaware, founded in 1833.

DISTRICT OF COLUMBIA

MAYOR Sharon Pratt Kelly found a way to unite colleges in the District of Columbia in 1992: the threat of taxes.

Facing a budget deficit, Mayor Kelly proposed—unsuccessfully—that colleges make special payments to the city in lieu of the property taxes from which they are exempt. Colleges said the plan would cost them $20-million a year and represented an intrusion on their tax-exempt status.

While the tax plan hasn't been enacted, it is typical of the sometimes rocky relationship between colleges and the city in a time when both town and gown are struggling for money.

District officials, for example, were furious when they discovered that the U.S. Senate, in its fiscal 1992 appropriations bill for the city, wanted to include $50-million over four years for the hospital at George Washington University. The House of Representatives blocked the provision, citing more pressing needs in Washington, but George Washington officials say they still want Congress to provide the money.

Howard University, meanwhile, had its own fight with Congress. Lawmakers had imposed tuition surcharges on the university's international students, and Howard officials are attempting to have the tuition payments eliminated or reduced.

The financial situation in 1992 was also troublesome for Washington's only public college, the University of the District of Columbia. Like all city agencies, it had a tight budget year. And public institutions in the Washington suburbs, like George Mason

University and the University of Maryland at College Park, also were short on cash.

As in years past, Washington's colleges were involved in debates over "political correctness" and academic freedom. Georgetown University—under pressure from some Catholic groups on and off the campus—revoked its recognition of a student group that supports abortion rights.

The president of Trinity College, Patricia A. McGuire, was a leading player in the debate over the policy of some accrediting groups requiring that campus reviews include evaluations of efforts to recruit and retain minority students and faculty members. Ms. McGuire said such policies were proper and necessary, in light of America's changing demographics.

DEMOGRAPHICS

Population: 598,000 (Rank: 48)

Age distribution:
Up to 17 .... 20.2%
18 to 24 .... 12.7%
25 to 44 .... 35.8%
45 and older 31.3%

Racial and ethnic distribution:
American Indian 0.2%
Asian 1.8%
Black 65.8%
White 29.6%
Other and unknown 2.5%
Hispanic (may be any race) .. 5.4%

Educational attainment of adults (highest level):
9th grade or less 9.6%
Some high school, no diploma 17.3%
High-school diploma 21.2%
Some college, no degree 15.6%
Associate degree 3.1%
Bachelor's degree 16.1%
Graduate or professional
 degree 17.2%

Proportion who speak a language other than English at home: 12.5%

Per-capita personal income: $24,063

Poverty rate:
All 16.9%
Under age 18 .... 25.5%
Age 18 and older 14.8%

New public high-school graduates in:
1992-93 (estimate) 2,790
2001-02 (estimate) 2,670

New GED diploma recipients: 734

High-school dropout rate: 13.9%

POLITICAL LEADERSHIP

Mayor: Sharon Pratt Kelly (D), term ends 1994

Mayor's higher-education aide:
Janette Harris, District Building, 1350 Pennsylvania Avenue, N.W., Suite 212, Washington 20004; (202) 727-0248

U.S. Senators: None

U.S. Representative:
Delegate Eleanor Holmes Norton (D); non-voting

Legislature: n/a

COLLEGES AND UNIVERSITIES

Higher education:
Public 4-year institutions 2
Public 2-year institutions 0
Private 4-year institutions 15
Private 2-year institutions 0
Total 17

DISTRICT OF COLUMBIA
Continued

Vocational institutions: 30

Statewide coordinating board:
Office of Postsecondary Education Research and Assistance
2100 Martin Luther King, Jr., Avenue, S.E.
Suite 401
Washington 20020
(202) 727-3685
Sheila Drews, acting chief

Private-college association:
Consortium of Universities of the Washington Metropolitan Area
One Dupont Circle, Suite 200
Washington 20036
(202) 331-8080
Monte P. Shepler, president

Institution censured by the AAUP:
Catholic University of America

Institutions under NCAA sanctions:
Howard University, University of the District of Columbia

FACULTY MEMBERS

Full-time faculty members by rank:
Professor 1,177
Associate professor 969
Assistant professor 940
Instructor 205
Lecturer 35
No rank 26
Total 3,352

Full-time faculty members with tenure:
Men 1,315
Women 386
Total 1,701

Average pay of full-time professors
Public 4-year institutions:
Professor $55,281
Associate professor $44,549
Assistant professor $35,927
Instructor $30,797
No rank .... n/a
All $45,057

Public 2-year institutions: n/a

Private 4-year institutions:
Professor $64,720
Associate professor $45,121
Assistant professor $37,087
Instructor $28,804
No rank $24,301
All $48,393

STUDENTS

Enrollment:
At public 4-year institutions . 12,595
At public 2-year institutions 0
At private 4-year institutions 68,074
At private 2-year institutions 0
Undergraduate 49,860
Graduate 22,525
Professional 8,284
American Indian 270
Asian 3,222
Black 24,770
Hispanic 2,406
White 40,977
Foreign 9,024
Total 80,669

Enrollment highlights:
Women 53.3%
Full-time 62.2%
Minority 42.8%
Foreign 11.2%
10-year change in total enrollment .... Down 6.9%

Proportion of enrollment made up of minority students:
At public 4-year institutions . 91.6%

At public 2-year institutions .... n/a
At private 4-year institutions   33.4%
At private 2-year institutions ... n/a

Degrees awarded:
Associate 403
Bachelor's 7,449
Master's 5,122
Doctorate 535
Professional 2,467

Residence of new students: Residents made up 18% of all freshmen enrolled in the District of Columbia; 50% of all District of Columbia residents who were freshmen attended college in the District.

Test scores: Students averaged 842 on the S.A.T., which was taken by an estimated 73% of the District of Columbia's high-school seniors.

Graduation rates at NCAA Division I institutions:
American University 68%
George Washington University   66%
Georgetown University........ 89%
Howard University 41%

MONEY

Average tuition and fees:
At public 4-year institutions .. $664
At public 2-year institutions .... n/a
At private 4-year institutions $11,939
At private 2-year institutions ... n/a

Expenditures:
Public institutions $111,468,000
Private institutions . $1,873,297,000

State funds for higher-education operating expenses: n/a
Two-year change: n/a

State spending on student aid:
Need-based: $1,010,000
Non–need-based: None
Other: None

Salary of chief executive of largest public 4-year campus:
Tilden J. LeMelle, University of the District of Columbia: $90,705

Total spending on research and development by doctorate-granting universities: $112,146,000
Sources:
Federal government 76.9%
Local government 0.4%
Industry 7.1%
The institution itself 9.4%
Other 6.1%

Total federal spending on college- and university-based research and development: $78,658,000
Selected programs:
Department of Health
  and Human Services $44,848,000
National Science
  Foundation $9,363,000
Department of Defense . $7,685,000
Department
  of Agriculture $1,027,000
Department of Energy .. $1,354,000

Largest endowment:
George Washington
  University $305,047,000

Top fund raisers:
Georgetown University $27,393,000
George Washington
  University $24,818,000
American University ... $6,156,000

MISCELLANY

■ Catholic University is raising money for its Italian American Heritage Center, which will sponsor academic programs and fellowships and have a museum and archives.

DISTRICT OF COLUMBIA
Continued

- The Library of Congress held a one-month exhibit in 1992 called "Revelations From the Russian Archives," displaying for the first time in the United States 300 once-secret documents that offered a behind-the-scenes look at the Soviet Union from its birth in 1917 to its death in 1991. The library made 25 of the documents available to scholars by computer.

- Mount Vernon College, a private institution for women, operates the Institute on Women and Work, an organization that studies ways to improve the work environment and status of professional women.

- The oldest institution of higher education in the District of Columbia is Georgetown University, a Roman Catholic institution founded in 1789. First called Georgetown College, it became a university in 1815 when it received the first university charter granted by the federal government. Georgetown's colors are blue and gray, representing the reunification of the North and South after the Civil War.

FLORIDA

For the first time ever, Florida came close to suspending much of its state government when debates over tax reform and spending cuts pushed the Legislature into fiscal 1993 without a budget.

State employees, including public-college faculty and staff members, came to work July 1, 1992, with no assurances of how they would be paid. The Legislature passed a budget later that day, ending talk that non-emergency services might be shut down temporarily.

The crisis was brought about by the recession and a tax structure that hasn't kept up with the state's explosive growth. Gov. Lawton Chiles, a Democrat, proposed a tax package, but it quickly ran into opposition from lawmakers, particularly Senate Republicans, who said the state needed to make government leaner rather than raise taxes.

The final budget increased spending by about $400-million, far less than the $2.5-billion that Mr. Chiles had proposed. Lawmakers also didn't approve the Governor's proposal to charge sales taxes on selected luxury services, while reducing some other taxes.

Higher education fared relatively well, with universities getting about $45-million more than in 1991-92.

Most of the new money was to pay for adding the equivalent of 5,500 full-time students to the system and continuing to develop the National High Magnetic Field Laboratory at Florida State University.

There was no money for salary increases; by the end of academic 1992-93, faculty members will have gone two and a half years without a raise and staff members will have gone three. The budget also increased undergraduate tuition by 15 per cent. As a result, the proportion of education costs that students must pay rose above a ceiling that legislators set in 1991.

Observers say the tax-reform issue is far from dead, and that more proposals are expected in 1993. No proposal is likely to introduce a personal income tax, the merest suggestion of which is generally considered political suicide.

Charles B. Reed, chancellor of the State University System, and Betty Castor, the education commissioner, stepped forward early as spokespersons for the Chiles tax package, which in some ways turned it into a crusade for education.

They were joined by several public-university presidents whose letters and speeches told how the financial pinch threatened programs on their campuses.

Florida, like many states, had cut the budgets of its government agencies in mid-year, when it became evident that tax revenues would not meet expectations. The cuts began in October 1990. By the time the budget debates were in full swing in the spring of 1992, the university system had lost $164-million to the cuts, but had added 18,000 students.

That forced the campuses to reduce their course offerings, enlarge classes, put a freeze on hiring, severely limit library purchases, and watch a few valued faculty members leave.

Mr. Reed and the Board of Regents called the losses intolerable, and less than two weeks after the 1992-93 budget passed, the regents voted to request a $300-million increase for 1993-94 to restore state support to the level at which it stood before the cuts began in late 1990.

The state's financial problems interfered with a widely heralded new law designed to give universities more control over their budgets in exchange for documentation of efficiency and quality.

As campus officials started gathering the reams of required statistics, some grumbled that the only change seemed to be an increase in paperwork, since the budget was too tight to allow much flexibility.

The state's overstretched budget took another hit when Hurricane Andrew tore across South Florida, causing billions of dollars in damage. Miami-Dade Community College, the University of Miami, and Florida International University all suffered from the blow. Money and supplies poured in from all over the country, including several campuses where students raised money.

The university system made little progress in 1992 on planning a 10th university for the fast-growing Fort Myers area in southwest Florida. The 1992-93 budget includes some planning money for the campus, which is supposed to open late in the decade to relieve enrollment pressures at the other colleges.

A major task for the regents and universities in 1992-93 is to produce a master plan for 1993-98.

Florida's 28 community colleges also felt the squeeze of tight budgets and rapid growth. One piece of proposed legislation would have turned some into four-year institutions. It failed, but only after a debate about the mission of two-year colleges.

That debate was fueled by the decision of Miami-Dade Community College to limit enrollment slightly for the fall 1991 term. The two-year colleges traditionally have accepted any Florida high-school graduate, and they provided a route by which students could later transfer to public universities for completion of their bachelor's degrees.

Several presidents of community colleges staunchly defended the "open door" policy, but the debate led to suggestions that the two-year colleges consider entrance standards to control enrollment and reduce their

FLORIDA
Continued

remedial burdens. And Miami-Dade resumed open admissions after voters approved a two-year property tax to benefit the college.

Florida's 28 community colleges are governed by their own boards, with oversight by the state Board of Community Colleges. The Board of Regents sets policy for the nine universities and works closely with the chancellor. The Postsecondary Education Planning Commission serves as an adviser and watchdog for both levels.

DEMOGRAPHICS

Population: 13,277,000   (Rank: 4)

Age distribution:
Up to 17 .... 22.6%
18 to 24 .... 9.1%
25 to 44 .... 30.4%
45 and older 38.0%

Racial and ethnic distribution:
American Indian 0.3%
Asian 1.2%
Black 13.6%
White 83.1%
Other and unknown 1.8%
Hispanic (may be any race) . 12.2%

Educational attainment of adults (highest level):
9th grade or less 9.5%
Some high school, no diploma 16.1%
High-school diploma 30.1%
Some college, no degree 19.4%
Associate degree 6.6%
Bachelor's degree 12.0%
Graduate or professional
  degree 6.3%

Proportion who speak a language other than English at home: 17.3%

Per-capita personal income: $18,992

Poverty rate:
All 12.7%
Under age 18 .... 18.7%
Age 18 and older 11.0%

New public high-school graduates in:
1992-93 (estimate) 78,640
2001-02 (estimate) 124,940

New GED diploma recipients: 35,673

High-school dropout rate: 14.3%

POLITICAL LEADERSHIP

Governor: Lawton Chiles (D), term ends 1995

Governor's higher-education aide: Debi Gallay, 301 Carlton Building, Tallahassee 32399; (904) 488-4512

U.S. Senators: Bob Graham (D), term ends 1999; Connie Mack (R), term ends 1995

U.S. Representatives:
10 Democrats, 13 Republicans
Jim Bacchus (D), Michael Bilirakis (R), Corinne Brown (D), Charles T. Canady (R), Peter Deutsch (D), Lincoln Diaz-Balart (R), Tillie Fowler (R), Sam M. Gibbons (D), Porter J. Goss (R), Alcee L. Hastings (D), Earl Hutto (D), Harry A. Johnston (D), Tom Lewis (R), Bill McCollum (R), John L. Mica (R), Carrie Meek (D), Dan Miller (R), Douglas "Pete" Peterson (D), Ileana Ros-Lehtinen (R), E. Clay Shaw, Jr. (R), Cliff Stearns (R), Karen L. Thurman (D), C.W. Bill Young (R)

Legislature: Senate, 20 Democrats, 20

Republicans; House, 71 Democrats, 49 Republicans

COLLEGES AND UNIVERSITIES

Higher education:
Public 4-year institutions 9
Public 2-year institutions 28
Private 4-year institutions 47
Private 2-year institutions 17
Total 101

Vocational institutions: 293

Statewide coordinating board:
Postsecondary Education
  Planning Commission
Florida Education Center
Tallahassee 32399
(904) 488-7894
William Proctor, executive director

Private-college association:
Independent Colleges and
  Universities of Florida
123 South Calhoun Street, Third Floor
Tallahassee 32301
(904) 681-3188
T. K. Wetherell, president

Institution censured by the AAUP:
Saint Leo College

Institutions under NCAA sanctions:
None

FACULTY MEMBERS

Full-time faculty members by rank:
Professor 3,697
Associate professor 2,934
Assistant professor 2,749
Instructor 1,428
Lecturer 113
No rank 2,117
Total 13,038

Full-time faculty members with tenure:
Men 5,224
Women 2,014
Total 7,238

Average pay of full-time professors
Public 4-year institutions:
Professor $55,305
Associate professor $40,240
Assistant professor $36,120
Instructor $27,000
No rank $24,880
All $43,855

Public 2-year institutions:
Professor $35,249
Associate professor $33,061
Assistant professor $29,351
Instructor $32,922
No rank $31,165
All $32,294

Private 4-year institutions:
Professor $46,478
Associate professor $36,304
Assistant professor $29,509
Instructor $22,444
No rank $33,336
All $35,881

STUDENTS

Enrollment:
At public 4-year institutions   176,989
At public 2-year institutions   262,829
At private 4-year institutions   91,939
At private 2-year institutions . 6,632
Undergraduate 478,315
Graduate 52,508
Professional 7,566
American Indian 1,616
Asian 10,871
Black 53,400
Hispanic 58,490
White 397,880
Foreign 16,132
Total 538,389

FLORIDA
Continued

Enrollment highlights:
Women 55.0%
Full-time 49.5%
Minority 23.8%
Foreign 3.0%
10-year change in total
 enrollment .... Up 30.7%

Proportion of enrollment made up of minority students:
At public 4-year institutions . 23.0%
At public 2-year institutions . 23.3%
At private 4-year institutions 26.1%
At private 2-year institutions 35.0%

Degrees awarded:
Associate 33,718
Bachelor's 35,494
Master's 10,802
Doctorate 1,251
Professional 2,138

Residence of new students: State residents made up 78% of all freshmen enrolled in Florida; 83% of all Florida residents who were freshmen attended college in their home state.

Test scores: Students averaged 884 on the S.A.T., which was taken by an estimated 50% of Florida's high-school seniors.

Graduation rates at NCAA Division I institutions:
Bethune-Cookman College 36%
Florida A&M University 34%
Florida International University 44%
Florida State University 51%
Jacksonville University 34%
Stetson University 61%
University of Central Florida .. 44%
University of Florida 56%
University of Miami 57%
University of South Florida ... 36%

MONEY

Average tuition and fees:
At public 4-year institutions . $1,337
At public 2-year institutions .. $788
At private 4-year institutions $7,992
At private 2-year institutions $4,751

Expenditures:
Public institutions .. $2,766,267,000
Private institutions . $1,162,843,000

State funds for higher-education operating expenses: $1,415,262,000
Two-year change: Down 9%

State spending on student aid:
Need-based: $27,162,000
Non–need-based: $45,512,000
Other: None

Salary of chief executive of largest public 4-year campus:
John V. Lombardi, University
 of Florida: $190,550

Total spending on research and development by doctorate-granting universities: $433,413,000
Sources:
Federal government 51.5%
State and local governments .. 7.7%
Industry 6.6%
The institution itself 28.2%
Other 6.1%

Total federal spending on college- and university-based research and development: $181,474,000
Selected programs:
Department of Health
 and Human Services $88,487,000
National Science
 Foundation $27,483,000
Department of Defense $19,349,000

Department
   of Agriculture $9,036,000
Department of Energy . $17,553,000

Largest endowment:
University of Florida
   Foundation $224,854,000

Top fund raisers:
University of Florida .. $59,614,000
University of Miami ... $50,242,000
Florida State University $18,168,000

MISCELLANY

■ Students at Eckerd College operate a volunteer Search and Rescue Team to assist boaters in distress. Created in 1971, the team handles about 250 calls for assistance every year.

■ The campus of Florida Southern College was designed by Frank Lloyd Wright in what the architect called a Florida interpretation of his "organic" style. The design features boldly horizontal buildings connected by covered walkways.

■ Florida Atlantic University President Anthony James Catanese ruled in 1992 that 34 cats that a group of biology professors wanted to remove from the campus be allowed to stay. The biologists were concerned that the cats were destroying the burrowing-owl population at the institution. The owl is an endangered species. The president said the cats could stay as long as they were immunized and neutered.

■ The oldest institution of higher education in the state is, depending on whom you ask, either Florida State University, founded in 1851 as Seminary West of the Suwannee, or the University of Florida, founded in 1853. The seminary underwent dramatic changes in 1857, when it became Florida State and held its first college-level classes.

GEORGIA

IN the fall of 1991, Gov. Zell Miller found out that his state was one of 13 in which college spending had dropped over a two-year period. He promised then that higher education, like Scarlett O'Hara in *Gone With the Wind*, would never go hungry again.

The Board of Regents, which oversees the 34 public colleges and universities in the University System of Georgia, appreciated the Democratic Governor's proclamation—especially since $79-million had been sliced from higher education in the fiscal 1992 budget.

For much of 1992, Mr. Miller set about making good on his promise, beginning by backing an $809-million higher-education budget for fiscal year 1993, about $7-million more than the budget approved for fiscal year 1992.

Faculty and staff members in the university system received some of the largesse: They won a 3-per-cent pay raise in 1992. That contrasts markedly with 1991, when the Governor vetoed a non-faculty pay raise and declined to give the commencement address at the University of Georgia after learning that protests were planned. (The Governor, a graduate of the university, delivered the 1992 address.)

In November, voters approved a state lottery for Georgia, largely be-

GEORGIA
Continued

cause Governor Miller promised that all proceeds would be spent on education programs. Some of the revenue will finance a grant program for college freshmen and sophomores with 3.0 grade-point averages and family incomes of less than $66,000 a year.

Under state guidelines, eligible freshmen would be awarded grants equivalent to tuition at any public college. As sophomores, students would qualify for "forgivable loans" equal to tuition if they had 3.0 averages as freshmen. Sophomores who maintained that average would not have to repay the loans.

Governor Miller and educators say the grant program will dramatically improve the state's college-going rate, which is among the country's lowest.

In 1992 the state created a program and a governing board for distance learning and "telemedicine," which will allow colleges, schools, and hospitals to provide classes and medical advice over two-way television. One project, already in existence, links the Medical College of Georgia with a rural hospital.

Another effort links public and private colleges, including Emory and Clark Atlanta Universities, in a partnership called the Research Alliance. The research will focus on genetics, environmental issues, and telecommunications.

While many educators believe its university system is enviable among Southern states, some say Georgia has more colleges than it can support. Nineteen of the public colleges offer four-year and graduate degrees, while 15 confer associate degrees. So far, though, legislators do not seem inclined to take up the argument that some colleges should be merged.

Meanwhile, the regents are reviewing their policy on granting regional university status, as state colleges in Columbus, Albany, Kennesaw, and Augusta push to become universities. Regents approved Valdosta State College's request for university status, and the transition is to occur by July 1, 1993. The General Assembly, which must approve the change, is expected to go along.

Regional universities focus on "regionally related" research and graduate programs for working professionals. They do not do the theoretical research or offer the advanced doctoral programs of institutions such as the University of Georgia, Georgia Institute of Technology, and Georgia State University.

Several historically black colleges, including three public institutions—Albany, Fort Valley, and Savannah State Colleges—are located in Georgia. It is not clear how a U.S. Supreme Court decision handed down in June 1992, which found that Mississippi had not done enough to desegregate its higher-education system, will affect Georgia.

The U.S. Education Department found in 1989 that the state was in compliance with federal anti-bias laws, but some advocates for black colleges maintain that those institutions still are not treated fairly.

The state is also home to well-known private black colleges, including Spelman and Morehouse Colleges.

DEMOGRAPHICS

Population: 6,623,000   (Rank: 11)

Age distribution:
Up to 17 .... 26.8%

18 to 24 .... 11.1%
25 to 44 .... 33.9%
45 and older 28.2%

Racial and ethnic distribution:
American Indian 0.2%
Asian 1.2%
Black 27.0%
White 71.0%
Other and unknown 0.7%
Hispanic (may be any race) .. 1.7%

Educational attainment of adults (highest level):
9th grade or less 12.0%
Some high school, no diploma 17.1%
High-school diploma 29.6%
Some college, no degree 17.0%
Associate degree 5.0%
Bachelor's degree 12.9%
Graduate or professional
  degree 6.4%

Proportion who speak a language other than English at home: 4.8%

Per-capita personal income: $17,436

Poverty rate:
All 14.7%
Under age 18 .... 20.1%
Age 18 and older 12.6%

New public high-school graduates in:
1992-93 (estimate) 58,580
2001-02 (estimate) 71,540

New GED diploma recipients: 15,527

High-school dropout rate: 14.1%

POLITICAL LEADERSHIP

Governor: Zell Miller (D), term ends 1995

Governor's higher-education aide:
W. Daniel Ebersole, State Capitol, Room 201, Atlanta 30334; (404) 651-7716

U.S. Senators: Paul Coverdell (R), term ends 1999; Sam Nunn (D), term ends 1997

U.S. Representatives:
7 Democrats, 4 Republicans
Sanford Bishop (D), Mac Collins (R), George (Buddy) Darden (D), Nathan Deal (D), Newt Gingrich (R), Don Johnson (D), Jack Kingston (R), John Lewis (D), John Linder (R), Cynthia McKinney (D), J. Roy Rowland (D)

General Assembly: Senate, 41 Democrats, 15 Republicans; House, 128 Democrats, 52 Republicans

COLLEGES AND UNIVERSITIES

Higher education:
Public 4-year institutions 20
Public 2-year institutions 29
Private 4-year institutions 30
Private 2-year institutions 16
Total 95

Vocational institutions: 128

Statewide coordinating board:
Board of Regents
University System of Georgia
244 Washington Street, S.W.
Atlanta 30334
(404) 656-2203
H. Dean Propst, chancellor

Private-college association:
Association of Private Colleges
  and Universities in Georgia
945 East Paces Ferry Road
Resurgens Plaza, Suite 1730
Atlanta 30326
(404) 233-5433
William W. Kelly, president

GEORGIA
Continued

Institutions censured by the AAUP:
None

Institutions under NCAA sanctions:
None

FACULTY MEMBERS

Full-time faculty members by rank:
Professor	1,945
Associate professor	2,184
Assistant professor	2,485
Instructor	807
Lecturer	31
No rank	196
Total	7,648

Full-time faculty members with tenure:
Men	2,581
Women	941
Total	3,522

Average pay of full-time professors

Public 4-year institutions:
Professor	$51,997
Associate professor	$39,733
Assistant professor	$34,006
Instructor	$24,952
No rank	n/a
All	$39,909

Public 2-year institutions:
Professor	$38,291
Associate professor	$34,628
Assistant professor	$29,473
Instructor	$25,284
No rank	$39,766
All	$31,709

Private 4-year institutions:
Professor	$48,928
Associate professor	$35,239
Assistant professor	$29,908
Instructor	$22,594
No rank	$33,705
All	$36,501

STUDENTS

Enrollment:
At public 4-year institutions	141,106
At public 2-year institutions	55,307
At private 4-year institutions	46,368
At private 2-year institutions	9,029
Undergraduate	214,413
Graduate	29,605
Professional	7,792
American Indian	548
Asian	4,241
Black	49,199
Hispanic	2,740
White	189,189
Foreign	5,893
Total	251,810

Enrollment highlights:
Women	54.4%
Full-time	66.3%
Minority	23.1%
Foreign	2.3%
10-year change in total enrollment	Up 36.7%

Proportion of enrollment made up of minority students:
At public 4-year institutions	18.4%
At public 2-year institutions	22.1%
At private 4-year institutions	36.7%
At private 2-year institutions	32.1%

Degrees awarded:
Associate	7,389
Bachelor's	21,402
Master's	6,427
Doctorate	800
Professional	1,835

Residence of new students: State residents made up 80% of all freshmen enrolled in Georgia; 83% of all Georgia residents who were freshmen attended college in their home state.

Test scores: Students averaged 842 on the S.A.T., which was taken by an estimated 65% of Georgia's high-school seniors.

Graduation rates at NCAA Division I institutions:
Georgia Institute of Technology 65%
Georgia Southern University .. 27%
Georgia State University 28%
Mercer University 38%
University of Georgia 60%

MONEY

Average tuition and fees:
At public 4-year institutions . $1,680
At public 2-year institutions .. $946
At private 4-year institutions $7,542
At private 2-year institutions $4,457

Expenditures:
Public institutions .. $1,769,744,000
Private institutions . $1,099,658,000

State funds for higher-education operating expenses: $951,726,000
Two-year change: Down 1%

State spending on student aid:
Need-based: $4,804,000
Non–need-based: $15,581,000
Other: $1,528,000

Salary of chief executive of largest public 4-year campus:
Charles B. Knapp, University of Georgia: $133,400 from state plus $16,000 from private sources

Total spending on research and development by doctorate-granting universities: $445,011,000
Sources:
Federal government 47.7%
State and local governments .. 9.6%
Industry 8.3%
The institution itself 32.0%
Other 2.4%

Total federal spending on college- and university-based research and development: $175,024,000
Selected programs:
Department of Health
 and Human Services $75,397,000
National Science
 Foundation $18,382,000
Department of Defense $42,674,000
Department
 of Agriculture $10,281,000
Department of Energy . $16,290,000

Largest endowment:
Emory University .. $1,289,630,000

Top fund raisers:
Emory University $45,136,000
Georgia Institute
 of Technology $32,183,000
University of Georgia . $23,271,000

MISCELLANY

■ Spelman College, founded in 1882, is the nation's oldest historically and predominantly black college for women.

■ The Southern Regional Education Board, an organization of government leaders and educators from 15 Southern states, has its headquarters in Atlanta.

■ Would-be cupids didn't just deliver chocolates on Emory University's campus on Valentine's Day in 1992. Students gave "condomgrams" to their sweethearts, as well. The 50-cent condom packages featured a "condom man" holding a bow and arrow.

■ The oldest institution of higher education in the state is the University of Georgia, founded in 1785.

HAWAII

ENCOMPASSING all of public higher education in the state, the University of Hawaii System has been the recipient of strong support from lawmakers and the public throughout its 83-year existence, particularly as programs in astronomy, environmental research, and Pacific Rim studies have expanded and gained widespread attention.

Democratic Gov. John Waihee, III, who was elected to a second term in 1990, also has championed the university. But for the 1992-93 academic year, his support came without an infusion of money. Instead, the university system had to take a $17-million budget cut.

Most of the impact will be felt at the university's Manoa campus, the oldest and largest in the system. University officials are already saying that a similar cut in the 1993-94 appropriation may force them to eliminate programs and limit enrollment.

Meanwhile, a group of lawmakers and business leaders want the Hilo campus to separate from the university system and form the Hawaii State University. The plan, under study by the Legislature, would mean a separate president, governing board, and budget for Hilo, which offers two- and four-year programs.

Backers say the move would bring Hilo more attention. They complain that under the University of Hawaii Board of Regents—which oversees three four-year campuses and seven community colleges—the Hilo campus is ignored. But skeptics doubt that another system could attract world-class faculty members or receive the financial support to thrive.

The Legislature in 1992 considered several bills to raise the number of tuition waivers awarded to native Hawaiians and other members of underrepresented minority groups, but the measures did not pass. Legislation that would have made it illegal for a non-accredited postsecondary institution to call itself a university or college also failed. Supporters said such a measure would crack down on "diploma mills."

DEMOGRAPHICS

Population: 1,135,000 (Rank: 40)

Age distribution:
Up to 17 .... 25.4%
18 to 24 .... 10.6%
25 to 44 .... 34.2%
45 and older 29.8%

Racial and ethnic distribution:
American Indian 0.5%
Asian 61.8%
Black 2.5%
White 33.4%
Other and unknown 1.9%
Hispanic (may be any race) .. 7.3%

Educational attainment of adults (highest level):
9th grade or less 10.1%
Some high school, no diploma 9.8%
High-school diploma 28.7%
Some college, no degree 20.1%
Associate degree 8.3%
Bachelor's degree 15.8%
Graduate or professional
  degree 7.1%

Proportion who speak a language other than English at home: 24.8%

Per-capita personal income: $21,190

Poverty rate:
All 8.3%
Under age 18 .... 11.6%
Age 18 and older 7.1%

New public high-school graduates in:
1992-93 (estimate) 9,490
2001-02 (estimate) 11,580

New GED diploma recipients: 1,361

High-school dropout rate: 7.5%

POLITICAL LEADERSHIP

Governor: John Waihee, III (D), term ends 1994

Governor's higher-education aide:
Patricia Brandt, State Capitol, Honolulu 96813; (808) 586-0102

U.S. Senators: Daniel K. Akaka (D), term ends 1995; Daniel K. Inouye (D), term ends 1999

U.S. Representatives:
2 Democrats, 0 Republicans
Neil Abercrombie (D), Patsy T. Mink (D)

Legislature: Senate, 22 Democrats, 3 Republicans; House, 47 Democrats, 4 Republicans

COLLEGES AND UNIVERSITIES

Higher education:
Public 4-year institutions 3
Public 2-year institutions 6
Private 4-year institutions 6
Private 2-year institutions 0
Total 15

Vocational institutions: 32

Statewide coordinating board:
University of Hawaii Board
  of Regents
Bachman Hall, Room 209
2444 Dole Street
Honolulu 96822
(808) 956-8213
Tatsuki Shiramizu, secretary of the board

Private-college association:
Hawaii Association of Independent
  Colleges and Universities
Hawaii Pacific University
1166 Fort Street
Honolulu 96813
(808) 544-0200
Helen Chapin, representative

Institutions censured by the AAUP:
None

Institutions under NCAA sanctions:
None

FACULTY MEMBERS

Full-time faculty members by rank:
Professor 433
Associate professor 367
Assistant professor 338
Instructor 101
Lecturer 0
No rank 590
Total 1,829

Full-time faculty members with tenure:
Men 750
Women 281
Total 1,031

Average pay of full-time professors
Public 4-year institutions:
Professor $59,939
Associate professor $45,457
Assistant professor $39,116
Instructor $29,831
No rank $38,647
All $47,053

HAWAII
Continued

Public 2-year institutions:
Professor .... n/a
Associate professor .... n/a
Assistant professor .... n/a
Instructor .... n/a
No rank $38,436
All $38,436

Private 4-year institutions:
Professor $29,782
Associate professor $25,974
Assistant professor $24,016
Instructor $19,463
No rank $29,792
All $26,068

STUDENTS

Enrollment:
At public 4-year institutions . 23,085
At public 2-year institutions . 19,979
At private 4-year institutions   10,708
At private 2-year institutions 0
Undergraduate 46,920
Graduate 6,408
Professional 444
American Indian 162
Asian 31,356
Black 1,457
Hispanic 1,002
White 16,132
Foreign 3,663
Total 53,772

Enrollment highlights:
Women 53.3%
Full-time 58.3%
Minority 67.8%
Foreign 6.8%
10-year change in total
    enrollment .... Up 14.0%

Proportion of enrollment made up of minority students:
At public 4-year institutions . 71.0%
At public 2-year institutions . 74.3%
At private 4-year institutions   46.0%
At private 2-year institutions ... n/a

Degrees awarded:
Associate 2,103
Bachelor's 3,720
Master's 1,007
Doctorate 114
Professional 113

Residence of new students: State residents made up 88% of all freshmen enrolled in Hawaii; 77% of all Hawaii residents who were freshmen attended college in their home state.

Test scores: Students averaged 878 on the S.A.T., which was taken by an estimated 56% of Hawaii's high-school seniors.

Graduation rates at NCAA Division I institution:
University of Hawaii 81%

MONEY

Average tuition and fees:
At public 4-year institutions . $1,290
At public 2-year institutions .. $413
At private 4-year institutions $4,448
At private 2-year institutions ... n/a

Expenditures:
Public institutions $424,473,000
Private institutions $35,223,000

State funds for higher-education operating expenses: $341,693,000
Two-year change: Up 9%

State spending on student aid:
Need-based: $661,000
Non–need-based: None
Other: None

**Salary of chief executive
of largest public 4-year campus:**
Paul C. Yuen (interim), University of Hawaii at Manoa: $120,000

Total spending on research and development by doctorate-granting universities: $76,525,000
Sources:
Federal government 55.8%
State and local governments . 35.9%
Industry 2.1%
The institution itself 4.7%
Other 1.6%

Total federal spending on college- and university-based research and development: $48,276,000
Selected programs:
Department of Health
  and Human Services $10,130,000
National Science
  Foundation $12,828,000
Department of Defense . $3,536,000
Department
  of Agriculture $4,340,000
Department of Energy .. $1,784,000

Largest endowment:
University of Hawaii .. $58,992,000

Top fund raisers:
University of Hawaii ... $9,980,000
Hawaii Pacific University . $956,000

MISCELLANY

■ The world's largest and most powerful optical telescope, the 10-meter W. M. Keck Telescope, was completed in April 1992 on Mauna Kea. The California Institute of Technology and the University of California, which constructed the telescope, have announced plans to build a second, identical instrument next to the Keck telescope.

■ Ukulele lessons are required for University of Hawaii students who want to become elementary teachers. It is important for students to learn to play the instrument because the ukulele is integral to the music of Hawaii.

■ The oldest institution of higher education in Hawaii is the University of Hawaii at Manoa, founded in 1907.

IDAHO

AT a time when many states have had to slash higher-education budgets by double-digit percentages, Idaho's colleges and universities are relatively fortunate: Their appropriation declined by less than 1 per cent in the 1992-93 academic year. But because state revenues grew at a slow rate in fiscal 1992, higher education may face more serious cuts in the future.

Educators had been fearful that a tax-limitation referendum, which would have limited property taxes to 1 per cent of assessed valuation, would put the brakes on spending for education. But voters defeated the so-called One Per Cent Initiative in November 1992.

Another measure to limit property taxes, passed in 1978, forces the Legislature to take money from other state operations to maintain financing for the public schools.

Residency requirements for students were tightened because of burgeoning enrollments at public colleges. That will bring the colleges more revenue, since non-resident tuition was increased in the 1991-92 academic year by an average of 19 per cent.

The state's two community colleges

IDAHO
Continued

are also seeing rapid growth. Although the colleges are supported by local property taxes, some officials say they may have to consider enrollment caps unless additional state support is forthcoming.

Some legislators continue to talk about changing the governance system for public colleges, advocating the adoption of a chancellor form of governance and the creation of a separate Board of Regents for postsecondary education. The same Board of Education currently oversees higher education and elementary and secondary education. It is called the Board of Regents in its postsecondary governance capacity.

Legislators backed a measure to allow a non-voting student member to serve on the Board of Education, but Democratic Gov. Cecil D. Andrus vetoed it. He said board members should represent the state in its entirety, not one constituency.

Idaho has four private non-profit colleges, all of which are affiliated with religious groups.

DEMOGRAPHICS

Population: 1,039,000   (Rank: 42)

Age distribution:
Up to 17 .... 30.7%
18 to 24 .... 9.9%
25 to 44 .... 29.9%
45 and older 29.5%

Racial and ethnic distribution:
American Indian 1.4%
Asian 0.9%
Black 0.3%
White 94.4%
Other and unknown 3.0%
Hispanic (may be any race) .. 5.3%

Educational attainment of adults (highest level):
9th grade or less 7.4%
Some high school, no diploma 12.9%
High-school diploma 30.4%
Some college, no degree 24.2%
Associate degree 7.5%
Bachelor's degree 12.4%
Graduate or professional
  degree 5.3%

Proportion who speak a language other than English at home: 6.4%

Per-capita personal income: $15,333

Poverty rate:
All 13.3%
Under age 18 .... 16.2%
Age 18 and older 11.9%

New public high-school graduates in:
1992-93 (estimate) 12,280
2001-02 (estimate) 12,460

New GED diploma recipients: 983

High-school dropout rate: 10.4%

POLITICAL LEADERSHIP

Governor: Cecil D. Andrus (D), term ends 1995

Governor's higher-education aide: Julie M. Cheever, Statehouse, Boise 83720; (208) 334-2100

U.S. Senators: Larry E. Craig (R), term ends 1997; Dirk Kempthorne (R), term ends 1999

U.S. Representatives:
1 Democrat, 1 Republican
Michael D. Crapo (R), Larry LaRocco (D)

Legislature: Senate, 12 Democrats, 23 Republicans; House, 20 Democrats, 50 Republicans

COLLEGES AND UNIVERSITIES

Higher education:
Public 4-year institutions	4
Public 2-year institutions	2
Private 4-year institutions	3
Private 2-year institutions	2
Total	11

Vocational institutions: 35

Statewide coordinating board:
Board of Regents
650 West State Street, Room 307
Boise 83720
(208) 334-2270
Rayburn Barton, executive director for higher education

Private-college association:
None

Institutions censured by the AAUP:
None

Institutions under NCAA sanctions:
None

FACULTY MEMBERS

Full-time faculty members by rank:
Professor	409
Associate professor	340
Assistant professor	343
Instructor	66
Lecturer	0
No rank	359
Total	1,517

Full-time faculty members with tenure:
Men	625
Women	157
Total	782

Average pay of full-time professors

Public 4-year institutions:
Professor	$43,033
Associate professor	$35,846
Assistant professor	$32,505
Instructor	$26,994
No rank	$28,948
All	$36,649

Public 2-year institutions:
Professor	$34,478
Associate professor	$31,473
Assistant professor	$27,557
Instructor	$23,575
No rank	$30,577
All	$30,532

Private 4-year institutions:
Professor	$31,398
Associate professor	$28,723
Assistant professor	n/a
Instructor	n/a
No rank	$27,616
All	$27,890

STUDENTS

Enrollment:
At public 4-year institutions	35,709
At public 2-year institutions	5,606
At private 4-year institutions	2,338
At private 2-year institutions	8,228
Undergraduate	44,683
Graduate	6,692
Professional	506
American Indian	485
Asian	706
Black	310
Hispanic	1,004
White	48,024
Foreign	1,352
Total	51,881

Enrollment highlights:
Women	54.2%
Full-time	66.9%
Minority	5.0%

IDAHO
Continued

Foreign 2.6%
10-year change in total
  enrollment .... Up 20.6%

Proportion of enrollment made up of minority students:
At public 4-year institutions .. 5.4%
At public 2-year institutions .. 4.1%
At private 4-year institutions . 5.0%
At private 2-year institutions . 3.2%

Degrees awarded:
Associate 2,979
Bachelor's 3,169
Master's 790
Doctorate 90
Professional 124

Residence of new students: State residents made up 59% of all freshmen enrolled in Idaho; 78% of all Idaho residents who were freshmen attended college in their home state.

Test scores: Students averaged 21.1 on the A.C.T., which was taken by an estimated 63% of Idaho's high-school seniors.

Graduation rates at NCAA Division I institutions:
Boise State University 19%
Idaho State University 48%
University of Idaho 42%

MONEY

Average tuition and fees:
At public 4-year institutions . $1,189
At public 2-year institutions .. $802
At private 4-year institutions $7,203
At private 2-year institutions $1,609

Expenditures:
Public institutions $314,398,000
Private institutions $69,032,000

State funds for higher-education operating expenses: $192,609,000
Two-year change: Up 5%

State spending on student aid:
Need-based: $507,000
Non–need-based: $252,000
Other: None

Salary of chief executive of largest public 4-year campus:
Charles P. Ruch, Boise State University: $102,000

Total spending on research and development by doctorate-granting universities: $36,570,000
Sources:
Federal government 39.3%
State and local governments . 22.3%
Industry 11.5%
The institution itself 26.2%
Other 0.7%

Total federal spending on college- and university-based research and development: $10,381,000
Selected programs:
Department of Health
  and Human Services ... $780,000
National Science
  Foundation $1,412,000
Department of Defense ... $375,000
Department
  of Agriculture $3,529,000
Department of Energy $101,000

Largest endowment:
University of Idaho ... $43,906,000

Top fund raisers:
College of Idaho $13,224,000

University of Idaho ... $11,325,000
Northwest Nazarene
  College $1,259,000

MISCELLANY

■ Boise State University claims to have the only university football field with blue artificial turf.

■ The North Idaho College *Sentinel* in 1992 won the Robert F. Kennedy Journalism Award, in the student category, for "outstanding coverage of the problems of the disadvantaged." The newspaper won the $1,000 top prize for a seven-part series on prejudice and discrimination on the campus. The series dealt with the problems experienced by handicapped students, homosexuals, and veterans, as well as by members of ethnic, racial, and religious minority groups.

■ Boise State University, located near a canyon that contains one of the country's largest populations of birds of prey, offers a highly specialized master's-degree program in raptor biology.

■ The oldest institution of higher education in Idaho is Ricks College, a Mormon institution founded in 1888.

ILLINOIS

COLLEGES and universities in Illinois seem to thrive on competition with each other—for students, for money, and for prestige.

While politicians and higher-education officials often decry such rivalry, the state's political traditions, its support for private colleges, and its decentralized system of higher-education governance all seem to encourage it.

Public colleges are supervised by five separate boards—the University of Illinois, Southern Illinois University, the Board of Governors, the Board of Regents, and the Illinois Board of Community Colleges.

That setup could change, however, if lawmakers decide to adopt one of two restructuring proposals recently forwarded to them by a committee appointed by Gov. Jim Edgar, a Republican who has been a strong supporter of higher education.

Advocates of restructuring say the changes would streamline governance, save money, and give campuses more authority. But political observers say the push for governance changes was inspired by politicians' displeasure with some recent actions of the boards. The Board of Regents has been criticized for increasing benefits for college presidents and the chancellor while pay for faculty and staff members has stayed flat. The Board of Governors has been under fire for engineering the controversial resignation of the president of Eastern Illinois University in Governor Edgar's home town.

Lawmakers will take up the governance issue in January 1993, and the traditional political rivalries between Chicago-area politicians and their downstate rivals are expected to affect the outcome. The debate could also create an opportunity for rival institutions to chip away at the political clout now wielded by the University of Illinois at Urbana-Champaign, one of the leading research universities in the nation.

The university is one of several public and private institutions that have tried to expand their presence to other areas of the state. A prime target is the

ILLINOIS
Continued

wealthy and growing suburbs that ring Chicago, which are home to many high-technology companies and the Argonne and Fermi National Laboratories. The university's action has caused some resentment at other institutions, notably Northern Illinois University and the Illinois Institute of Technology, a private institution, which want that educational market for themselves.

Turf battles among other public and private institutions have also flared up around Peoria and Rockford. The Board of Higher Education, the statewide coordinating board, has initiated a policy designed to mediate the disputes.

The board and lawmakers also remain very concerned about the quality of undergraduate education, improving productivity on campuses, and smoothing out procedures to make it easier for students to transfer from community colleges to four-year institutions.

The transfer issue is considered particularly important, since a high proportion of the minority students in Illinois enter higher education through the community colleges but do not complete baccalaureate degrees. In 1990, black and Hispanic students accounted for 19 per cent of the undergraduate population at community colleges but only 12 per cent of the transfers to state universities.

Illinois leaders are also concerned about the City Colleges of Chicago, a system that has specialized in educating minority students. The system's future has been in doubt since the Board of Trustees announced that it would not renew the contract of Nelvia Brady, who had been chancellor since 1988. Ms. Brady stepped down in April 1992 after disagreements with the board about how much control it should have over the system's management.

Until a successor to Ms. Brady is selected, a management team composed of three City College presidents, headed by Homer D. Franklin, president of Olive-Harvey College, is running the system. Observers expect a replacement to be named early in 1993.

Chicago, home to such institutions as DePaul and Loyola Universities, is also a center for Catholic higher education.

The Catholic colleges are just one segment of a politically influential private-college sector that includes such major research institutions as the University of Chicago and Northwestern University and small liberal-arts colleges like Knox and Lake Forest Colleges.

DEMOGRAPHICS

Population: 11,543,000   (Rank: 6)

Age distribution:
Up to 17 .... 26.0%
18 to 24 .... 10.3%
25 to 44 .... 32.5%
45 and older 31.2%

Racial and ethnic distribution:
American Indian 0.2%
Asian 2.5%
Black 14.8%
White 78.3%
Other and unknown 4.2%
Hispanic (may be any race) .. 7.9%

Educational attainment of adults (highest level):
9th grade or less 10.3%

Some high school, no diploma   13.5%
High-school diploma 30.0%
Some college, no degree 19.4%
Associate degree 5.8%
Bachelor's degree 13.6%
Graduate or professional
    degree 7.5%

Proportion who speak a language other than English at home: 14.2%

Per-capita personal income: $20,731

Poverty rate:
All 11.9%
Under age 18 .... 17.0%
Age 18 and older 10.1%

New public high-school graduates in:
1992-93 (estimate) 102,330
2001-02 (estimate) 108,110

New GED diploma recipients: 12,607

High-school dropout rate: 10.6%

POLITICAL LEADERSHIP

Governor: Jim Edgar (R), term ends 1995

Governor's higher-education aide: Mary Ann Louderback, State House, Floor 2½, Springfield 62706; (217) 782-2654

U.S. Senators: Carol Moseley Braun (D), term ends 1999; Paul Simon (D), term ends 1997

U.S. Representatives:
12 Democrats, 8 Republicans
Cardiss Collins (D), Jerry F. Costello (D), Philip M. Crane (R), Richard J. Durbin (D), Lane Evans (D), Thomas W. Ewing (R), Harris W. Fawell (R), Luis V. Gutierrez (D), J. Dennis Hastert (R), Henry J. Hyde (R), William O. Lipinski (D), Donald Manzullo (R), Robert H. Michel (R), John Porter (R), Glenn Poshard (D), Mel Reynolds (D), Dan Rostenkowski (D), Bobby L. Rush (D), George E. Sangmeister (D), Sidney R. Yates (D)

General Assembly: Senate, 27 Democrats, 32 Republicans; House, 67 Democrats, 51 Republicans

COLLEGES AND UNIVERSITIES

Higher education:
Public 4-year institutions 12
Public 2-year institutions 47
Private 4-year institutions 93
Private 2-year institutions 18
Total 170

Vocational institutions: 313

Statewide coordinating board:
Board of Higher Education
500 Reisch Building
Four West Old Capitol Square
Springfield 62701
(217) 782-2551
Richard D. Wagner,
executive director

Private-college association:
Federation of Independent Illinois
    Colleges and Universities
944 South Second Street
Springfield 62704
(217) 789-1400
Donald E. Fouts, president

Institution censured by the AAUP:
Illinois College of Optometry

Institution under NCAA sanctions:
University of Illinois
at Urbana-Champaign

FACULTY MEMBERS

Full-time faculty members by rank:
Professor 4,710

ILLINOIS
Continued

Associate professor 3,601
Assistant professor 3,692
Instructor 781
Lecturer 283
No rank 4,744
Total 17,811

Full-time faculty members with tenure:
Men 8,277
Women 2,816
Total 11,093

Average pay of full-time professors
Public 4-year institutions:
Professor $53,867
Associate professor $40,904
Assistant professor $34,794
Instructor $22,623
No rank $24,024
All $42,447

Public 2-year institutions:
Professor .... n/a
Associate professor .... n/a
Assistant professor .... n/a
Instructor .... n/a
No rank $40,239
All $40,239

Private 4-year institutions:
Professor $59,518
Associate professor $41,223
Assistant professor $35,106
Instructor $28,008
No rank $33,422
All $44,388

STUDENTS

Enrollment:
At public 4-year institutions   198,464
At public 2-year institutions   352,869
At private 4-year institutions 168,953
At private 2-year institutions . 8,960

Undergraduate 623,525
Graduate 88,688
Professional 17,033
American Indian 2,245
Asian 32,353
Black 89,218
Hispanic 48,932
White 541,347
Foreign 15,151
Total 729,246

Enrollment highlights:
Women 54.6%
Full-time 50.1%
Minority 24.2%
Foreign 2.1%
10-year change in total
  enrollment .... Up 13.2%

Proportion of enrollment made up of minority students:
At public 4-year institutions . 20.3%
At public 2-year institutions . 28.1%
At private 4-year institutions   19.3%
At private 2-year institutions   44.4%

Degrees awarded:
Associate 23,327
Bachelor's 49,757
Master's 19,288
Doctorate 2,409
Professional 4,412

Residence of new students: State residents made up 92% of all freshmen enrolled in Illinois; 85% of all Illinois residents who were freshmen attended college in their home state.

Test scores: Students averaged 20.8 on the A.C.T., which was taken by an estimated 54% of Illinois's high-school seniors.

Graduation rates at NCAA Division I institutions:
Bradley University 64%

Chicago State University 13%
DePaul University 59%
Eastern Illinois University 53%
Illinois State University 46%
Loyola University of Chicago . 60%
Northeastern Illinois University 19%
Northern Illinois University ... 52%
Northwestern University 88%
Southern Illinois University
 at Carbondale 41%
University of Illinois at Chicago 32%
University of Illinois
 at Urbana-Champaign 78%
Western Illinois University 42%

MONEY

Average tuition and fees:
At public 4-year institutions . $2,465
At public 2-year institutions .. $906
At private 4-year institutions $8,853
At private 2-year institutions $5,279

Expenditures:
Public institutions .. $3,310,763,000
Private institutions . $3,544,542,000

State funds for higher-education operating expenses: $1,718,849,000

Two-year change: Down 1%

State spending on student aid:
Need-based: $184,707,000
Non–need-based: $20,624,000
Other: $4,158,000

Salary of chief executive of largest public 4-year campus:
Morton W. Weir, University of
 Illinois at Urbana-Champaign:
 $133,600

Total spending on research and development by doctorate-granting universities: $647,863,000

Sources:
Federal government 54.4%
State and local governments .. 5.9%
Industry 6.8%
The institution itself 25.3%
Other 7.6%

Total federal spending on college- and university-based research and development: $351,598,000

Selected programs:
Department of Health
 and Human Services $163,567,000
National Science
 Foundation $84,733,000
Department of Defense $34,909,000
Department
 of Agriculture $8,287,000
Department of Energy . $36,800,000

Largest endowment:
University of Chicago $1,080,462,000

Top fund raisers:
University of Chicago . $82,185,000
Northwestern
 University $70,850,000
University of Illinois
 at Urbana-Champaign $62,900,000

MISCELLANY

■ Those familiar book characters Dick, Jane, and Spot were created in 1930 by William S. Gray, a professor at the University of Chicago who studied the reading habits of children.

■ For the past nine years, the University of Illinois at Urbana-Champaign has sponsored the Insect Fear Film Festival, a look at bugs as portrayed through creepy Grade B movies. Along with showings of such films as *The Fly, Return of the Fly,* and *The Nest,* a film about mutant cockroaches, the festival features presentations on real insects by faculty members.

■ Northern Illinois University's steel band—in which all of the instru-

ILLINOIS
Continued

ments are made from 55-gallon oil drums—claims to be the first on an American college campus. It was founded in 1973.

■ MacCormac Junior College, a private institution in Chicago, has the country's oldest program in Court Reporting Studies; it began in 1912.

■ The oldest higher-education institution in Illinois is McKendree College, which was founded in 1828 and is affiliated with the United Methodist Church.

INDIANA

ONLY a few years ago, Indiana educators were lamenting that high-school graduates in their state had one of the lowest rates of college participation in the country.

But Gov. Evan Bayh, a Democrat who at 37 is one of the country's youngest governors, gave a high priority to attracting more graduates to the state's colleges when he was elected in 1988. Supporters say Governor Bayh's attention—and efforts by private and public colleges and several higher-education advocacy groups—seems to be having an effect.

But some educators say students are enrolling in the state's two- and four-year institutions for another reason: the recession, which has led to a loss of jobs in industry, which accounts for most of Indiana's jobs.

In fact, the full-time-equivalent enrollment increase at state colleges—from 158,493 in 1980-81 to 176,080 in 1990-91—is almost certain to drive a debate in the General Assembly on how to change the distribution of student aid in the 1993-95 biennium to accommodate more students, even as the state's resources shrink.

College officials are also concerned because a 1987 grant from the Lilly Endowment, which enabled Indiana to provide aid to lower- and middle-income residents who attend state institutions, will expire in the middle of the 1992-93 academic year. Officials would like the state to pick up the slack, but that, they say, is doubtful, given all the other pulls on state money.

Indiana's economy got a boost when United Airlines said it would build an $800-million maintenance facility at Indianapolis International Airport. To prepare its residents for some of the more than 6,000 jobs the facility will provide, the state will spend about $6-million over the next three years to expand training programs in aviation mechanics.

The Governor scored a big victory in 1992 with the enactment by lawmakers of the Educational and Work Force Development Initiatives. Among the law's provisions are one requiring high-school sophomores to take a basic-skills test and one requiring young people to stay in school until they reach 17, or until they pass the basic-skills examination. Although geared mostly to elementary and secondary education, the law also contains provisions for a basic core curriculum among public colleges to make it easier for students to transfer credits from one to another, beginning in the 1992-93 academic year.

The Commission for Higher Education is the statewide coordinating board for postsecondary education.

The seven public systems are governed by individual boards.

The University of Notre Dame, DePauw University, Valparaiso University, and Wabash College are among Indiana's many private colleges. Such institutions have been lobbying for significant fee increases by their public counterparts to close the gap between the costs of public and private education.

DEMOGRAPHICS

Population: 5,610,000 (Rank: 14)

Age distribution:
Up to 17	26.1%
18 to 24	10.9%
25 to 44	31.5%
45 and older	31.6%

Racial and ethnic distribution:
American Indian	0.2%
Asian	0.7%
Black	7.8%
White	90.6%
Other and unknown	0.7%
Hispanic (may be any race)	1.8%

Educational attainment of adults (highest level):
9th grade or less	8.5%
Some high school, no diploma	15.8%
High-school diploma	38.2%
Some college, no degree	16.6%
Associate degree	5.3%
Bachelor's degree	9.2%
Graduate or professional degree	6.4%

Proportion who speak a language other than English at home: 4.8%

Per-capita personal income: $17,179

Poverty rate:
All	10.7%
Under age 18	14.2%
Age 18 and older	9.4%

New public high-school graduates in:
1992-93 (estimate)	56,790
2001-02 (estimate)	59,460

New GED diploma recipients: 12,520

High-school dropout rate: 11.4%

POLITICAL LEADERSHIP

Governor: Evan Bayh (D), term ends 1997

Governor's higher-education aide: Judy Wolpe, Indiana Government Center South, Room E204, 10 North Senate Avenue, Indianapolis 46204; (317) 233-3919

U.S. Senators: Daniel R. Coats (R), term ends 1999; Richard G. Lugar (R), term ends 1995

U.S. Representatives:
7 Democrats, 3 Republicans
Steve Buyer (R), Dan Burton (R), Lee H. Hamilton (D), Andrew Jacobs, Jr. (D), Jill L. Long (D), Frank McCloskey (D), John T. Myers (R), Tim Roemer (D), Philip R. Sharp (D), Peter J. Visclosky (D)

General Assembly: Senate, 22 Democrats, 28 Republicans; House, 55 Democrats, 45 Republicans

COLLEGES AND UNIVERSITIES

Higher education:
Public 4-year institutions	14
Public 2-year institutions	14
Private 4-year institutions	41
Private 2-year institutions	11
Total	80

INDIANA
Continued

Vocational institutions: 130

Statewide coordinating board:
Commission for Higher Education
101 West Ohio Street, Suite 550
Indianapolis 46204
(317) 232-1900
Clyde Ingle, commissioner for higher education

Private-college association:
Independent Colleges of Indiana
101 West Ohio Street, Suite 440
Indianapolis 46204
(317) 684-4292
T. K. Olson, president

Institution censured by the AAUP:
Concordia Theological Seminary

Institutions under NCAA sanctions:
None

FACULTY MEMBERS

Full-time faculty members by rank:
Professor 2,708
Associate professor 2,378
Assistant professor 2,552
Instructor 479
Lecturer 273
No rank 595
Total 8,985

Full-time faculty members with tenure:
Men 3,491
Women 933
Total 4,424

Average pay of full-time professors
Public 4-year institutions:
Professor $55,966
Associate professor $41,374
Assistant professor $34,014
Instructor $22,087
No rank .... n/a
All $41,975

Public 2-year institutions:
Professor $37,476
Associate professor $32,182
Assistant professor $28,013
Instructor $24,675
No rank $24,487
All $27,169

Private 4-year institutions:
Professor $50,962
Associate professor $38,372
Assistant professor $32,795
Instructor $25,186
No rank $39,463
All $40,268

STUDENTS

Enrollment:
At public 4-year institutions   186,318
At public 2-year institutions . 36,611
At private 4-year institutions   56,441
At private 2-year institutions .   3,645

Undergraduate 246,902
Graduate 30,770
Professional 5,343

American Indian 720
Asian 3,913
Black 15,323
Hispanic 4,380
White 251,389
Foreign 7,290
Total 283,015

Enrollment highlights:
Women 52.7%
Full-time 64.6%
Minority 8.8%
Foreign 2.6%
10-year change in total
  enrollment .... Up 14.4%

Proportion of enrollment made up of minority students:
At public 4-year institutions .. 8.6%
At public 2-year institutions .. 9.7%
At private 4-year institutions . 8.8%
At private 2-year institutions   12.2%

Degrees awarded:
Associate 8,947
Bachelor's 27,625
Master's 7,407
Doctorate 1,040
Professional 1,443

Residence of new students: State residents made up 75% of all freshmen enrolled in Indiana; 88% of all Indiana residents who were freshmen attended college in their home state.

Test scores: Students averaged 868 on the S.A.T., which was taken by an estimated 58% of Indiana's high-school seniors.

Graduation rates at NCAA Division I institutions:
Ball State University 48%
Butler University 56%
Indiana State University 37%
Indiana University
    at Bloomington 54%
Purdue University 68%
University of Evansville 52%
University of Notre Dame 93%
Valparaiso University 69%

MONEY

Average tuition and fees:
At public 4-year institutions . $2,067
At public 2-year institutions . $1,423
At private 4-year institutions $8,451
At private 2-year institutions $6,756

Expenditures:
Public institutions .. $2,186,604,000
Private institutions ... $773,866,000

State funds for higher-education operating expenses: $894,242,000
Two-year change: Up 2%

State spending on student aid:
Need-based: $50,054,000
Non–need-based: $909,000
Other: None

Salary of chief executive of largest public 4-year campus:
Steven C. Beering, Purdue University main campus: $172,000

Total spending on research and development by doctorate-granting universities: $240,696,000
Sources:
Federal government 56.1%
State and local governments .. 8.1%
Industry 7.5%
The institution itself 21.6%
Other 6.7%

Total federal spending on college- and university-based research and development: $138,349,000
Selected programs:
Department of Health
    and Human Services $59,013,000
National Science
    Foundation $37,860,000
Department of Defense . $5,564,000
Department
    of Agriculture $9,298,000
Department of Energy . $14,258,000

Largest endowment:
University of Notre
    Dame $637,234,000

Top fund raisers:
Indiana University $90,901,000
University of Notre
    Dame $46,432,000
Purdue University $32,568,000

INDIANA
Continued

MISCELLANY

■ In February 1992 Indiana University sponsored a research conference on Wendell L. Willkie, a 1913 graduate who would have been 100 years old in 1992.

■ The trustees of Wabash College voted in March 1992 to keep the institution's policy of admitting only male students.

■ The all-male Rose-Hulman Institute of Technology will begin admitting women in 1995. The engineering institute wants to broaden the pool of students in light of a decline in the number of high-school graduates.

■ The oldest institution of higher education in Indiana is Vincennes University, a two-year college founded in 1801 as the Jefferson Academy and renamed in 1806.

IOWA

IN higher education, Iowa is a state of contrasts:

The population is small, yet the state supports two major research universities, the University of Iowa and Iowa State University.

The proportion of Iowa high-school graduates pursuing postsecondary education far exceeds the national average—67 per cent *vs.* 59 per cent—yet only 17 per cent of Iowa's adults hold four-year degrees.

Although agriculture is still a key part of the state's economy and the focus of much university research, colleges and universities also are engaged in several well-respected literary and scientific endeavors. The Iowa Writers' Workshop at the University of Iowa is renowned as a spawning ground for young authors. Researchers at Iowa State have been responsible for many significant developments in the biological sciences and technology, including one that has helped to revolutionize communications: A graduate student invented a device integral to facsimile machines.

The University of Iowa still bears the scars of a tragedy that took place in November 1991: A distraught graduate student killed three professors, an administrator, a student, and then himself. Another student was wounded and is now a quadriplegic. The university has named a walkway in memory of the administrator.

Iowa lawmakers have long been known for their generous support of higher education, although booms and busts in the farm economy often define the intensity of that support. In the mid-1980's and again in the early 1990's, tight budgets put pressure on institutions to consolidate and prune their academic programs. Gov. Terry E. Branstad, a Republican who has been in office through both cycles, is considered an advocate for public colleges. The Governor and legislators have also been vocal in pressing colleges to improve undergraduate education and to make it easier for community-college graduates to transfer to four-year institutions.

Demographic projections suggest the state will be wrestling with financial issues for the next decade. The population, which decreased in the 1980's to 2.77 million from 2.91 million, is expected to creep up to about

2.8 million by 2000, while its median age increases. That means there could be a pool of non-traditional-aged students eager for higher education at the same time the institutions face greater competition for state funds—from state health-care agencies and other departments that serve an aging population.

Iowans consider private colleges an integral part of their higher-education system, and the private institutions are influential in education policy making, particularly in insuring adequate financial support for state student-aid programs. The private colleges enroll more than a quarter of all students in postsecondary education and confer nearly half of all the baccalaureate degrees. Most of the private colleges are small, liberal-arts institutions, such as Grinnell and Coe.

Drake University, a private research institution, has demonstrated considerable political muscle at the federal level. Like the two public research universities, Drake has been notably successful in winning noncompetitive research grants from Congress.

Northern Iowa University, the third institution under the governance of the state Board of Regents, began as a teacher-training college and is still known for its expertise in that field. But interest in education has not necessarily meant interest in the teacher-training establishment.

In March 1992, Drake and the three public universities withdrew their teacher-education programs from the National Council for Accreditation of Teacher Education, saying the council's standards were too prescriptive and costly.

Community colleges, known in Iowa as "area colleges," are governed by locally elected boards of trustees, but the state's Board of Education, acting as the State Board of Community Colleges, also has a role in overseeing them.

DEMOGRAPHICS

Population: 2,795,000   (Rank: 30)

Age distribution:
Up to 17 .... 26.0%
18 to 24 .... 10.1%
25 to 44 .... 29.8%
45 and older 34.1%

Racial and ethnic distribution:
American Indian 0.3%
Asian 0.9%
Black 1.7%
White 96.6%
Other and unknown 0.5%
Hispanic (may be any race) .. 1.2%

Educational attainment of adults (highest level):
9th grade or less 9.2%
Some high school, no diploma 10.7%
High-school diploma 38.5%
Some college, no degree 17.0%
Associate degree 7.7%
Bachelor's degree 11.7%
Graduate or professional
  degree 5.2%

Proportion who speak a language other than English at home: 3.9%

Per-capita personal income: $17,296

Poverty rate:
All 11.5%
Under age 18 .... 14.3%
Age 18 and older 10.5%

New public high-school graduates in:
1992-93 (estimate) 30,890
2001-02 (estimate) 32,040

IOWA
Continued

New GED diploma recipients: 5,305

High-school dropout rate: 6.6%

POLITICAL LEADERSHIP

Governor: Terry E. Branstad (R), term ends 1995

Governor's higher-education aide: Phil Dunshee, State House, Des Moines 50319; (515) 281-5211

U.S. Senators: Charles E. Grassley (R), term ends 1999; Tom Harkin (D), term ends 1997

U.S. Representatives:
1 Democrat, 4 Republicans
Fred Grandy (R), Jim Leach (R), Jim Ross Lightfoot (R), Jim Nussle (R), Neal Smith (D)

General Assembly: Senate, 26 Democrats, 24 Republicans; House, 49 Democrats, 51 Republicans

COLLEGES AND UNIVERSITIES

Higher education:
Public 4-year institutions 3
Public 2-year institutions 15
Private 4-year institutions 35
Private 2-year institutions 5
Total 58

Vocational institutions: 72

Statewide coordinating boards:
State Board of Regents
East 12th Street and Grand Avenue
Old State Historical Building
Des Moines 50319
(515) 281-3934
R. Wayne Richey, executive director

Board of Education
Division of Community Colleges
East 14th Street and Grand Avenue
Grimes State Office Building
Des Moines 50319
(515) 281-8260
Joann Horton, administrator

Private-college association:
Iowa Association of Independent Colleges and Universities
505 Fifth Avenue
Suite 1030
Des Moines 50309
(515) 282-3175
John V. Hartung, president

Institution censured by the AAUP:
University of Osteopathic Medicine and Health Sciences

Institutions under NCAA sanctions:
None

FACULTY MEMBERS

Full-time faculty members by rank:
Professor 1,558
Associate professor 1,118
Assistant professor 1,391
Instructor 433
Lecturer 5
No rank 750
Total 5,255

Full-time faculty members with tenure:
Men 2,232
Women 561
Total 2,793

Average pay of full-time professors
Public 4-year institutions:
Professor $62,120

Associate professor $46,603
Assistant professor $37,789
Instructor $25,773
No rank .... n/a
All $47,944

Public 2-year institutions:
Professor $35,730
Associate professor $30,287
Assistant professor $29,422
Instructor $28,030
No rank $30,682
All $30,745

Private 4-year institutions:
Professor $42,426
Associate professor $34,091
Assistant professor $29,217
Instructor $24,082
No rank $27,461
All $34,196

STUDENTS

Enrollment:
At public 4-year institutions . 67,957
At public 2-year institutions . 49,877
At private 4-year institutions   50,352
At private 2-year institutions . 2,329
Undergraduate 144,984
Graduate 19,452
Professional 6,079
American Indian 441
Asian 2,430
Black 4,044
Hispanic 1,587
White 155,204
Foreign 6,809
Total 170,515

Enrollment highlights:
Women 53.4%
Full-time 70.4%
Minority 5.2%
Foreign 4.0%
10-year change in total
    enrollment .... Up 21.4%

Proportion of enrollment made up of minority students:
At public 4-year institutions .. 5.9%
At public 2-year institutions .. 4.2%
At private 4-year institutions . 5.3%
At private 2-year institutions . 4.8%

Degrees awarded:
Associate 7,888
Bachelor's 16,129
Master's 3,006
Doctorate 604
Professional 1,427

Residence of new students: State residents made up 83% of all freshmen enrolled in Iowa; 88% of all Iowa residents who were freshmen attended college in their home state.

Test scores: Students averaged 21.7 on the A.C.T., which was taken by an estimated 64% of Iowa's high-school seniors.

Graduation rates at NCAA Division I institutions:
Drake University 57%
Iowa State University 59%
University of Iowa 63%
University of Northern Iowa .. 59%

MONEY

Average tuition and fees:
At public 4-year institutions . $1,880
At public 2-year institutions . $1,298
At private 4-year institutions $8,703
At private 2-year institutions $5,119

Expenditures:
Public institutions .. $1,617,626,000
Private institutions ... $490,214,000

State funds for higher-education operating expenses: $601,983,000
Two-year change: Up 3%

IOWA
Continued

State spending on student aid:
Need-based: $34,873,000
Non–need-based: $629,000
Other: $26,375,000

Salary of chief executive of largest public 4-year campus:
Hunter R. Rawlings III, University of Iowa: $175,000

Total spending on research and development by doctorate-granting universities: $232,147,000
Sources:
Federal government 48.8%
State and local governments . 12.7%
Industry 5.3%
The institution itself 29.0%
Other 4.2%

Total federal spending on college- and university-based research and development: $106,735,000
Selected programs:
Department of Health
 and Human Services $68,189,000
National Science
 Foundation $11,332,000
Department of Defense . $3,106,000
Department
 of Agriculture $11,490,000
Department of Energy .. $1,383,000

Largest endowment:
Grinnell College $292,928,000

Top fund raisers:
University of Iowa $36,614,000
Iowa State University . $31,016,000
Drake University $16,522,000

MISCELLANY

■ In 1855, eight years after it was founded, the University of Iowa became the nation's first public institution to admit women and men on an equal basis.

■ An Iowa farm owner and music teacher who "simply couldn't spend all her income" left an estate worth about $10-million to Simpson College in 1992. The bequest from Amy Robertson, a 1921 graduate and a Simpson trustee, was the largest the college had ever received. It included about 1,500 acres of farmland, cash and tax-free bonds, and leases on Texas oil wells.

■ A group of undergraduates from Luther College in 1992 won first place among 14 teams in the first annual national barbershop-quartet competition for college-age men. The quartet, the Water Street Junction, sang "Goodbye, My Coney Island Baby" to take the title.

■ The oldest higher-education institution in Iowa is Loras College, a Roman Catholic institution founded in 1839.

KANSAS

A tax-reform package pushed through the Kansas Legislature in 1990 has not resulted in the additional revenue that higher-education officials had hoped for. Nonetheless, the Board of Regents is engaged in long-term planning to move the populist state, where farming is the dominant industry and universities must fight charges of elitism, into the 21st century.

The regents coordinate all higher

education and act as the governing board for the six state universities.

In academic 1992-93 the state universities will receive a $55-million infusion as their portion of a $185-million windfall that Kansas received after the federal government recalculated its payments for indigent-patient care. The money will be used for building repairs and renovations at several of the universities.

As far as the regents are concerned, the money could not have come at a better time. In a March 1992 report on space and construction needs, they pointed out that while building costs had increased by 400 per cent since 1961, money in the Kansas Educational Building Fund had increased by less than 150 per cent.

The report identified 10 "high priority" projects to improve facilities, including the reconstruction of Hoch Auditorium at the University of Kansas, which was ravaged by fire in the summer of 1991.

While construction and renovation have been identified as priorities, officials have also managed to put new programs in place that they hope will make higher education more responsive to the needs of the state's labor force. The board lifted a moratorium on new programs by approving offerings in electronics technology and education.

Rapidly increasing tuition has forced the regents to consider changes in the distribution of student aid, a subject they expect to take up in detail before the end of 1992. An amendment under consideration would tie the award of state scholarships to high-school students' completion of a core curriculum recommended by the board.

Some regents also continue to talk about bringing community colleges, which are locally governed, under the board's authority to improve coordination between two- and four-year colleges. No action has been taken, however.

Meanwhile, the regents expect to complete a study of the system's mission—and the role of each institution—by December 1992. The document will be used to guide the universities in the next decade.

DEMOGRAPHICS

Population: 2,495,000 (Rank: 32)

Age distribution:
Up to 17 .... 26.9%
18 to 24 .... 10.1%
25 to 44 .... 31.3%
45 and older 31.6%

Racial and ethnic distribution:
American Indian 0.9%
Asian 1.3%
Black 5.8%
White 90.1%
Other and unknown 2.0%
Hispanic (may be any race) .. 3.8%

Educational attainment of adults (highest level):
Less than 9th grade 7.7%
Some high school, no degree 11.0%
High-school diploma 32.8%
Some college, no degree 21.9%
Associate degree 5.4%
Bachelor's degree 14.1%
Graduate or professional
  degree 7.0%

Proportion who speak a language other than English at home: 5.7%

Per-capita personal income: $18,322

Poverty rate:
All 11.5%

KANSAS
Continued

Under age 18 .... 14.3%
Age 18 and older 10.4%

New public high-school graduates in:
1992-93 (estimate) 25,160
2001-02 (estimate) 29,640

New GED diploma recipients: 5,328

High-school dropout rate: 8.7%

POLITICAL LEADERSHIP

Governor: Joan Finney (D), term ends 1995

Governor's higher-education aide:
Gary Reser, State Capitol, Second Floor, Topeka 66612; (913) 296-6691

U.S. Senators: Bob Dole (R), term ends 1999; Nancy Landon Kassebaum (R), term ends 1997

U.S. Representatives:
2 Democrats, 2 Republicans
Dan Glickman (D), Jan Meyers (R), Pat Roberts (R), Jim Slattery (D)

Legislature: Senate, 14 Democrats, 26 Republicans; House, 59 Democrats, 66 Republicans

COLLEGES AND UNIVERSITIES

Higher education:
Public 4-year institutions 8
Public 2-year institutions 21
Private 4-year institutions 21
Private 2-year institutions 3
Total 53

Vocational institutions: 67

Statewide coordinating board:
Kansas Board of Regents
Capitol Tower
400 Southwest Eighth Avenue
Suite 609
Topeka 66603
(913) 296-3421
Stanley Z. Koplik, executive director

Private-college association:
Kansas Independent College Association
Capitol Federal Building, Room 515
700 Kansas Avenue
Topeka 66603
(913) 235-9877
Robert N. Kelly, executive director

Institutions censured by the AAUP:
None

Institutions under NCAA sanctions:
None

FACULTY MEMBERS

Full-time faculty members by rank:
Professor 1,205
Associate professor 915
Assistant professor 1,108
Instructor 252
Lecturer 33
No rank 1,146
Total 4,659

Full-time faculty members with tenure:
Men 1,961
Women 516
Total 2,477

Average pay of full-time professors
Public 4-year institutions:
Professor $50,058
Associate professor $38,234
Assistant professor $32,596
Instructor $24,380

No rank .... n/a
All $39,869

Public 2-year institutions:
Professor $34,105
Associate professor $30,793
Assistant professor $27,601
Instructor $24,289
No rank $31,433
All $31,337

Private 4-year institutions:
Professor $30,163
Associate professor $26,308
Assistant professor $23,504
Instructor $20,137
No rank $18,129
All $25,263

STUDENTS

Enrollment:
At public 4-year institutions . 90,164
At public 2-year institutions . 58,953
At private 4-year institutions   13,280
At private 2-year institutions ..   978
Undergraduate 142,003
Graduate 19,209
Professional 2,163
American Indian 1,969
Asian 2,717
Black 6,796
Hispanic 3,534
White 143,023
Foreign 5,336
Total 163,375

Enrollment highlights:
Women 55.1%
Full-time 57.3%
Minority 9.5%
Foreign 3.3%
10-year change in total
  enrollment .... Up 19.6%

Proportion of enrollment made up of minority students:
At public 4-year institutions .. 8.4%
At public 2-year institutions . 10.4%

At private 4-year institutions   10.7%
At private 2-year institutions   37.5%

Degrees awarded:
Associate 5,547
Bachelor's 12,428
Master's 3,309
Doctorate 346
Professional 566

Residence of new students: State residents made up 82% of all freshmen enrolled in Kansas; 90% of all Kansas residents who were freshmen attended college in their home state.

Test scores: Students averaged 21.1 on the A.C.T., which was taken by an estimated 69% of Kansas' high-school seniors.

Graduation rates at NCAA Division I institutions:
Kansas State University 47%
University of Kansas 54%
Wichita State University 45%

MONEY

Average tuition and fees:
At public 4-year institutions . $1,569
At public 2-year institutions .. $748
At private 4-year institutions $5,997
At private 2-year institutions $4,135

Expenditures:
Public institutions .. $1,131,558,000
Private institutions ... $135,958,000

State funds for higher-education operating expenses: $465,860,000
Two-year change: Up 3%

State spending on student aid:
Need-based: $6,552,000
Non–need-based: $32,000
Other: $29,000

KANSAS
Continued

Salary of chief executive of largest public 4-year campus:
Gene A. Budig, University of Kansas: $142,000

Total spending on research and development by doctorate-granting universities: $114,651,000
Sources:
Federal government 37.9%
State and local governments . 22.3%
Industry 6.6%
The institution itself 29.2%
Other 4.0%

Total federal spending on college- and university-based research and development: $44,005,000
Selected programs:
Department of Health
  and Human Services $21,472,000
National Science
  Foundation $5,950,000
Department of Defense . $1,465,000
Department
  of Agriculture $5,139,000
Department of Energy .. $2,504,000

Largest endowment:
Kansas University Endowment
  Association $235,107,000

Top fund raisers:
University of Kansas .. $29,968,000
Kansas State University $17,444,000
Wichita State University $7,524,000

MISCELLANY

■ Wichita State University's National Institute for Aviation Research produces periodic reports on the quality of airlines in the United States.

■ Emporia State University opened the National Teachers Hall of Fame in 1992. Retired or practicing teachers will be selected to nominate outstanding schoolteachers from across the country, whose pictures will be placed in the hall.

■ The first television station in Kansas began operating at Kansas State University in January 1948. Today the university beams science and language classes to high schools in several states via satellite.

■ The oldest higher-education institution in Kansas is Highland Community College, which was chartered in 1857. The oldest four-year institution in the state is Baker University, a United Methodist institution, which received its charter just three days after Highland.

KENTUCKY

THE new Governor of Kentucky, Brereton C. Jones, moved quickly in 1992 to keep his pledge to remove gubernatorial cronyism from the selection of college governing-board members.

With the strong backing of Governor Jones, a Democrat, the General Assembly established a seven-member commission to make nominations to the boards—making a reality of an idea that had been a goal of reform-minded politicians and educators for several years.

Politicians and college leaders say the one act that may have provoked legislators finally to enact the measure was a decision by former Gov. Wallace G. Wilkinson to name himself to a six-year term on the University of Kentucky Board of Trustees just before he left office in December 1991. Mr. Wilkinson had earned praise for his far-reaching school reforms but was strongly criticized by legislators and others for appointing his political allies to some key higher-education posts.

Under the law, all board appointments, including Mr. Wilkinson's, were vacated as of June 30, and Governor Jones selected new trustees for the eight public colleges and the Council on Higher Education, the statewide coordinating board. About half of the old members were reappointed, with the remaining seats going to newcomers.

The appointment law was the highlight of an otherwise disappointing legislative session for public higher education because of the state's difficult budget situation. The only significant increase in financing went for a proposal by Governor Jones that will require public colleges to develop ways to measure the effectiveness of their teaching, research, and public service.

While public-college budgets have been cut and tuition increased to make up the lost state support, Kentucky's leaders have not abandoned their efforts to extend higher education to as many of its citizens as possible.

In addition to 14 community colleges run under the auspices of the University of Kentucky, many of the state's other public colleges are operating or opening new off-campus centers designed to bring higher education closer to students. Governor Jones is also moving ahead with the development of a statewide telecommunications network that will help promote distance learning.

The colleges also remain deeply involved with school-reform efforts, such as helping school districts develop family-and-youth resource centers. But some higher-education leaders fear the cuts in financing will hamper the colleges' participation.

Private colleges, which include small, church-related institutions, also are assisting the public schools. Rivalries between the public- and private-college sectors have been minimal, largely because the private institutions are liberal-arts–oriented, while the public colleges emphasize programs in professional education and research.

The two major research institutions, the University of Kentucky and the University of Louisville, historically have vied for primacy in the state, but are gradually developing distinct orientations, with Louisville assuming a stronger urban mission.

The role of Kentucky State University, a historically black institution, has caused some contention. In 1991, amid rumors that some trustees wanted to convert the institution to a community college, about 75 students took over the administration building to protest any changes in the university's mission. State officials say they are committed to preserving Kentucky State as a black-oriented institution.

In recent years, legislators and higher-education officials have pressed the other institutions to increase their enrollment of minority students and their hiring of minority faculty members.

Perhaps because of the strong interest that legislators and governors take in public higher education, Kentucky has long been a low-tuition state, where public funds make up more than 40 per cent of the institutions' budgets and tuition just 14 per cent.

KENTUCKY
Continued

But that might soon change. Over the next year, the Council on Higher Education will study whether a more equitable approach might be to raise tuition and increase financial aid, rather than the state's continuing to provide a heavy subsidy to students who could afford to pay more.

DEMOGRAPHICS

Population: 3,713,000   (Rank: 24)

Age distribution:
Up to 17 .... 25.8%
18 to 24 .... 10.8%
25 to 44 .... 31.6%
45 and older 31.8%

Racial and ethnic distribution:
American Indian 0.2%
Asian 0.5%
Black 7.1%
White 92.0%
Other and unknown 0.2%
Hispanic (may be any race) .. 0.6%

Educational attainment of adults (highest level):
9th grade or less 19.0%
Some high school, no diploma 16.4%
High-school diploma 31.8%
Some college, no degree 15.2%
Associate degree 4.1%
Bachelor's degree 8.1%
Graduate or professional
    degree 5.5%

Proportion who speak a language other than English at home: 2.5%

Per-capita personal income: $15,626

Poverty rate:
All 19.0%
Under age 18 .... 24.8%
Age 18 and older 17.0%

New public high-school graduates in:
1992-93 (estimate) 34,080
2001-02 (estimate) 33,170

New GED diploma recipients: 12,613

High-school dropout rate: 13.3%

POLITICAL LEADERSHIP

Governor: Brereton C. Jones (D), term ends 1995

Governor's higher-education aide: Sherry K. Jelsma, State Capitol, Room 132, Frankfort 40601; (502) 564-2611

U.S. Senators: Wendell H. Ford (D), term ends 1999; Mitch McConnell (R), term ends 1997

U.S. Representatives:
4 Democrats, 2 Republicans
Scotty Baesler (D), Tom Barlow (D), Jim Bunning (R), Romano L. Mazzoli (D), William H. Natcher (D), Harold Rogers (R)

General Assembly: Senate, 25 Democrats, 13 Republicans; House, 72 Democrats, 28 Republicans

COLLEGES AND UNIVERSITIES

Higher education:
Public 4-year institutions 8
Public 2-year institutions 14
Private 4-year institutions 25
Private 2-year institutions 15
Total 62

Vocational institutions: 119

Statewide coordinating board:
Council on Higher Education
1050 U.S. 127 South, Suite 101
Frankfort 40601
(502) 564-3553
Gary S. Cox, executive director

Private-college association:
Council of Independent Kentucky
  Colleges and Universities
P.O. Box 668
Danville 40423
(606) 236-3533
John W. Frazer, executive director

Institution censured by the AAUP:
Murray State University

Institutions under NCAA sanctions:
None

FACULTY MEMBERS

Full-time faculty members by rank:
Professor 1,512
Associate professor 1,481
Assistant professor 1,516
Instructor 590
Lecturer 74
No rank 76
Total 5,249

Full-time faculty members with tenure:
Men 2,171
Women 854
Total 3,025

Average pay of full-time professors
Public 4-year institutions:
Professor $48,242
Associate professor $38,515
Assistant professor $32,931
Instructor $25,174
No rank $27,712
All $38,818

Public 2-year institutions:
Professor $38,078
Associate professor $30,210
Assistant professor $25,447
Instructor $23,662
No rank .... n/a
All $28,463

Private 4-year institutions:
Professor $38,018
Associate professor $30,657
Assistant professor $26,348
Instructor $21,948
No rank $24,973
All $30,086

STUDENTS

Enrollment:
At public 4-year institutions   106,421
At public 2-year institutions . 40,674
At private 4-year institutions   24,982
At private 2-year institutions . 5,775

Undergraduate 155,271
Graduate 18,093
Professional 4,488

American Indian 506
Asian 1,343
Black 10,491
Hispanic 738
White 162,549
Foreign 2,225
Total 177,852

Enrollment highlights:
Women 58.1%
Full-time 64.0%
Minority 7.4%
Foreign 1.3%
10-year change in total
  enrollment .... Up 24.3%

Proportion of enrollment made up of minority students:
At public 4-year institutions .. 7.7%
At public 2-year institutions .. 7.4%
At private 4-year institutions . 4.7%
At private 2-year institutions   15.0%

KENTUCKY
Continued

Degrees awarded:
Associate 5,387
Bachelor's 12,225
Master's 3,681
Doctorate 320
Professional 1,127

Residence of new students: State residents made up 88% of all freshmen enrolled in Kentucky; 90% of all Kentucky residents who were freshmen attended college in their home state.

Test scores: Students averaged 20.0 on the A.C.T., which was taken by an estimated 61% of Kentucky's high-school seniors.

Graduation rates at NCAA Division I institutions:
Eastern Kentucky University .. 34%
Morehead State University 38%
Murray State University 39%
University of Kentucky 47%
University of Louisville 27%
Western Kentucky University . 40%

MONEY

Average tuition and fees:
At public 4-year institutions . $1,444
At public 2-year institutions .. $771
At private 4-year institutions $5,200
At private 2-year institutions $4,662

Expenditures:
Public institutions .. $1,236,680,000
Private institutions ... $251,329,000

State funds for higher-education operating expenses: $621,794,000

Two-year change: Up 2%

State spending on student aid:
Need-based: $21,075,000
Non–need-based: None
Other: $6,444,000

Salary of chief executive of largest public 4-year campus:
Donald C. Swain, University of Louisville: $155,000

Total spending on research and development by doctorate-granting universities: $90,880,000
Sources:
Federal government 42.1%
State and local governments .. 7.4%
Industry 8.9%
The institution itself 36.6%
Other 5.0%

Total federal spending on college- and university-based research and development: $38,185,000
Selected programs:
Department of Health
  and Human Services $19,116,000
National Science
  Foundation $4,898,000
Department of Defense ... $554,000
Department
  of Agriculture $8,634,000
Department of Energy .. $3,270,000

Largest endowment:
Berea College $286,279,000

Top fund raisers:
Berea College $13,333,000
University of Louisville $11,164,000
Southern Baptist
  Theological Seminary $9,144,000

MISCELLANY

■ Berea College, established in 1855 to serve needy students from Appalachia, charges no tuition but has a compulsory work program for each student to help offset the lack of tuition revenue.

■ Morehead State University began work in 1935 on the 11,000 feet of underground steam tunnels that warm its main campus, but construction wasn't completed until 1979.

■ The oldest higher-education institution in the state is Transylvania University, founded in 1780. Kentucky's 1857-58 legislature repealed the bill establishing Transylvania as a university, and it operated until 1865 as a high school. Since then it has been a liberal-arts college.

LOUISIANA

Louisiana's colleges and universities started the 1991-92 academic year terrified that a former Ku Klux Klan leader, David Duke, would be elected Governor, bringing humiliation on the state and prompting many students and faculty members—particularly those who are not white—to leave the state.

Mr. Duke, a Republican, lost the race to former Gov. Edwin W. Edwards, a flamboyant, populist Democrat.

While the election results were heartening to higher-education officials, their institutions continued to face many problems.

Since the price of oil fell in the mid-1980's, Louisiana's economy has been in terrible shape. Public colleges have experienced a series of budget cuts, forcing campuses to eliminate class sections and leave many vacant positions unfilled.

Governor Edwards ordered another cut in the fall of 1992, touching off protests at many campuses. The Governor said he sympathized with the colleges but had no choice, given that many parts of the state budget are protected by law from cuts.

Complicating the situation has been the state's decentralized—and, many say, duplicative—higher-education structure. Louisiana has a coordinating board, the Louisiana Board of Regents, and three governing boards. While the governing boards in many states handle specific types of institutions, such as research universities or community colleges, all three of Louisiana's systems contain different types of colleges.

Some lawmakers would like to see a more centralized structure. But the supporters of Southern University, the nation's only historically black college system, have fought off the idea repeatedly.

The state's flagship campus—Louisiana State University—has been torn between a push from faculty members to improve its academic quality and Louisiana's strong populist traditions. In 1988, after years of debate, the university adopted its first admissions requirements besides a high-school diploma, and professors say they are starting to see better-prepared students in their classes.

Remedial education and low graduation rates remain key issues in the state, however, as many public schools do not provide good training for college-bound students.

A major issue for Louisiana in the 1992-93 academic year is college desegregation. A federal judge threw out a desegregation case against the state in 1990, but that action was based on an appeals-court decision that the U.S. Supreme Court overruled in 1992, in a case involving Mississippi's colleges and universities.

LOUISIANA
Continued

Past attempts to deal with desegregation issues in Louisiana have been bitterly divisive, and the process is not likely to be easy—especially as long as money remains tight. Many black politicians say Louisiana's predominantly white power structure will use desegregation as an excuse to cut state support to the black colleges.

While most Louisiana students attend public colleges, the state also has several important private institutions, including Loyola and Tulane Universities and the historically black Dillard and Xavier Universities.

DEMOGRAPHICS

Population: 4,252,000 (Rank: 21)

Age distribution:
Up to 17 .... 29.0%
18 to 24 .... 10.9%
25 to 44 .... 31.3%
45 and older 28.8%

Racial and ethnic distribution:
American Indian 0.4%
Asian 1.0%
Black 30.8%
White 67.3%
Other and unknown 0.5%
Hispanic (may be any race) .. 2.2%

Educational attainment of adults (highest level):
9th grade or less 14.7%
Some high school, no diploma 17.0%
High-school diploma 31.7%
Some college, no degree 17.2%
Associate degree 3.3%
Bachelor's degree 10.5%
Graduate or professional
   degree 5.6%

Proportion who speak a language other than English at home: 10.1%

Per-capita personal income: $15,046

Poverty rate:
All 23.6%
Under age 18 .... 31.4%
Age 18 and older 20.3%

New public high-school graduates in:
1992-93 (estimate) 33,600
2001-02 (estimate) 30,190

New GED diploma recipients: 7,305

High-school dropout rate: 12.5%

POLITICAL LEADERSHIP

Governor: Edwin W. Edwards (D), term ends 1996

Governor's higher-education aide: Sally Clausen, Office of the Governor, P.O. Box 94004, Baton Rouge 70804; (504) 342-0998

U.S. Senators: John B. Breaux (D), term ends 1999; J. Bennett Johnston (D), term ends 1997

U.S. Representatives:
4 Democrats, 3 Republicans
Richard H. Baker (R), Cleo Fields (D), Jimmy Hayes (D), William J. Jefferson (D), Robert L. Livingston (R), Jim McCrery (R), W.J. (Billy) Tauzin (D)

Legislature: Senate, 34 Democrats, 5 Republicans; House, 88 Democrats, 16 Republicans, 1 Independent

COLLEGES AND UNIVERSITIES

Higher education:
Public 4-year institutions 14

Public 2-year institutions 6
Private 4-year institutions 12
Private 2-year institutions 4
Total 36

Vocational institutions: 167

Statewide coordinating board:
Louisiana Board of Regents
153rd Riverside Mall
Suite 129
Baton Rouge 70801
(504) 342-4253
Sammie W. Cosper, commissioner of higher education

Private-college association:
Louisiana Association of Independent Colleges and Universities
650 North 10th Street
Baton Rouge 70802
(504) 389-9885
William Arceneaux, president

Institutions censured by the AAUP:
None

Institutions under NCAA sanctions:
Northwestern State University,
Southeastern Louisiana University,
Tulane University

FACULTY MEMBERS

Full-time faculty members by rank:
Professor 1,522
Associate professor 1,546
Assistant professor 1,973
Instructor 877
Lecturer 17
No rank 71
Total 6,006

Full-time faculty members with tenure:
Men 2,466
Women 901
Total 3,367

Average pay of full-time professors
Public 4-year institutions:
Professor $48,401
Associate professor $38,321
Assistant professor $32,547
Instructor $24,229
No rank $22,541
All $36,705

Public 2-year institutions:
Professor $38,025
Associate professor $32,941
Assistant professor $28,815
Instructor $25,203
No rank $28,218
All $29,878

Private 4-year institutions:
Professor $55,509
Associate professor $41,922
Assistant professor $32,282
Instructor $24,982
No rank $25,000
All $41,362

STUDENTS

Enrollment:
At public 4-year institutions   136,635
At public 2-year institutions . 21,655
At private 4-year institutions   26,067
At private 2-year institutions . 2,242
Undergraduate 160,555
Graduate 20,271
Professional 5,773
American Indian 856
Asian 2,683
Black 44,738
Hispanic 3,448
White 130,361
Foreign 4,513
Total 186,599

Enrollment highlights:
Women 56.7%
Full-time 71.7%
Minority 28.4%

LOUISIANA
Continued

Foreign 2.4%
10-year change in total
  enrollment .... Up 16.6%

Proportion of enrollment made up of minority students:
At public 4-year institutions . 27.3%
At public 2-year institutions . 30.9%
At private 4-year institutions 31.6%
At private 2-year institutions 34.9%

Degrees awarded:
Associate 2,642
Bachelor's 15,905
Master's 3,993
Doctorate 405
Professional 1,459

Residence of new students: State residents made up 83% of all freshmen enrolled in Louisiana; 87% of all Louisiana residents who were freshmen attended college in their home state.

Test scores: Students averaged 19.4 on the A.C.T., which was taken by an estimated 68% of Louisiana's high-school seniors.

Graduation rates at NCAA Division I institutions:
Centenary College of Louisiana 47%
Grambling State University ... 49%
Louisiana State University 33%
Louisiana Tech University 39%
McNeese State University 29%
Nicholls State University 19%
Northeast Louisiana University 26%
Northwestern State University   12%
Southeastern Louisiana
  University 20%
Southern University 25%
Tulane University 67%
University of New Orleans 19%
University of Southwestern
  Louisiana 31%

MONEY

Average tuition and fees:
At public 4-year institutions . $1,791
At public 2-year institutions .. $852
At private 4-year institutions $9,783
At private 2-year institutions $5,671

Expenditures:
Public institutions .. $1,286,648,000
Private institutions ... $531,135,000

State funds for higher-education operating expenses: $620,791,000
Two-year change: Up 6%

State spending on student aid:
Need-based: $4,717,000
Non–need-based: $697,000
Other: $9,800,000

Salary of chief executive of largest public 4-year campus:
William E. Davis, Louisiana State
  University: $126,360

Total spending on research and development by doctorate-granting universities: $207,038,000
Sources:
Federal government 40.0%
State and local governments . 21.1%
Industry 4.9%
The institution itself 26.6%
Other 7.4%

Total federal spending on college- and university-based research and development: $69,265,000
Selected programs:
Department of Health
  and Human Services $42,666,000
National Science
  Foundation $6,289,000

Department of Defense . $2,653,000
Department
   of Agriculture $5,658,000
Department of Energy .. $2,183,000

Largest endowment:
Tulane University $234,066,000

Top fund raisers:
Tulane University $27,568,000
Xavier University
   of Louisiana $5,474,000
Loyola University $4,600,000

MISCELLANY

■ Capitalizing on the state's environmental problems, Tulane and Xavier Universities have decided to use Louisiana as a laboratory. They formed a partnership to create the Tulane/Xavier Center For Bioenvironmental Research. Researchers will examine the effects of exposure to hazardous substances.

■ Xavier University is the nation's only historically black college with a Roman Catholic affiliation. The university was second in the nation in placing black students in medical school, according to the Association of American Medical Colleges. Only Howard University, with an undergraduate enrollment four times as large, recorded more.

■ The University of Southwestern Louisiana in 1992 denied Jeff Gremillion the opportunity to be editor of the yearbook for a second year because of anger over pictures he placed in the 1992 edition, including one of a partly nude woman and another of a bulldog sitting on an American flag.

■ The oldest higher-education institution in the state is Centenary College of Louisiana. It was founded in 1825 and is affiliated with the United Methodist Church.

MAINE

MAINE'S push to make higher education more widely available to its citizens was severely tested by the recession.

But the tough economic times that forced deep budget cuts, pay freezes, and steep tuition increases also inspired some creative efforts designed to aid current and prospective students.

After the seven-campus University of Maine System raised tuition in the middle of the 1991-92 academic year, the state's student-loan agency jumped in and offered $2-million in emergency loans to help students pay the higher costs.

The tuition increase was prompted by cuts in state support—cuts that followed years of generous state financing for public colleges. In 1991-92, however, the university system's appropriation fell 20 per cent below the level it had reached two years earlier. Nonetheless, the system's chancellor, Robert L. Woodbury, promised to avoid tuition increases for the 1992-93 academic year, saying the system must remain affordable.

Tuition may still be beyond the reach of some Mainers. Voters rejected a ballot initiative, proposed by the Legislature, that would have floated $9.9-million in bonds to pay tuition at any of the state's six technical colleges for as many as 3,000 unemployed people.

Research focused on the university's geographic and historic interests—such as pulp and paper studies,

MAINE
Continued

marine sciences, and Canadian studies—remains a priority in the state. In addition, the system continues to make extensive use of interactive television to extend higher education to far corners of the state.

Another hopeful sign for higher education is the state's continued commitment to financial aid. That commitment also reflects the strong influence of private colleges, since many Maine residents who wish to attend those institutions need aid to pay for them. Several of the private institutions, including Bates, Bowdoin, and Colby Colleges, predate the public institutions and draw most of their students from out of state.

In addition to the university system and the Maine Technical College System, the state operates the Maine Maritime Academy. Each is governed by its own Board of Trustees.

DEMOGRAPHICS

Population: 1,235,000 (Rank: 39)

Age distribution:
Up to 17 .... 25.1%
18 to 24 .... 10.0%
25 to 44 .... 32.5%
45 and older 32.4%

Racial and ethnic distribution:
American Indian 0.5%
Asian 0.5%
Black 0.4%
White 98.4%
Other and unknown 0.1%
Hispanic (may be any race) .. 0.6%

Educational attainment of adults (highest level):
9th grade or less 8.8%
Some high school, no diploma 12.4%
High-school diploma 37.1%
Some college, no degree 16.1%
Associate degree 6.9%
Bachelor's degree 12.7%
Graduate or professional
  degree 6.1%

Proportion who speak a language other than English at home: 9.2%

Per-capita personal income: $17,454

Poverty rate:
All 10.8%
Under age 18 .... 13.8%
Age 18 and older 9.8%

New public high-school graduates in:
1992-93 (estimate) 12,280
2001-02 (estimate) 13,740

New GED diploma recipients: 3,423

High-school dropout rate: 8.3%

POLITICAL LEADERSHIP

Governor: John R. McKernan, Jr. (R), term ends 1995

Governor's higher-education aide:
Fred Douglas, State House, Station 23, Augusta 04333; (207) 287-5803

U.S. Senators: William S. Cohen (R), term ends 1997; George J. Mitchell (D), term ends 1995

U.S. Representatives:
1 Democrat, 1 Republican
Thomas H. Andrews (D), Olympia J. Snowe (R)

Legislature: Senate, 20 Democrats, 15 Republicans; House, 90 Democrats, 61 Republicans

COLLEGES AND UNIVERSITIES

Higher education:
Public 4-year institutions 8
Public 2-year institutions 6
Private 4-year institutions 12
Private 2-year institutions 5
Total 31

Vocational institutions: 18

Statewide coordinating board:
University of Maine System
Board of Trustees
107 Maine Avenue
Bangor 04401
(207) 947-0336
Robert L. Woodbury, chancellor

Private-college association:
Maine Independent Colleges
  Association
Thomas College
West River Road
Waterville 04901
(207) 873-0771
George R. Spann, president

Institution censured by the AAUP:
Husson College

Institutions under NCAA sanctions:
None

FACULTY MEMBERS

Full-time faculty members by rank:
Professor 494
Associate professor 530
Assistant professor 540
Instructor 77
Lecturer 28
No rank 254
Total 1,923

Full-time faculty members with tenure:
Men 779
Women 224
Total 1,003

Average pay of full-time professors

Public 4-year institutions:
Professor $50,110
Associate professor $39,811
Assistant professor $33,735
Instructor $24,493
No rank $18,419
All $40,122

Public 2-year institutions:
Professor .... n/a
Associate professor .... n/a
Assistant professor .... n/a
Instructor .... n/a
No rank $31,775
All $31,775

Private 4-year institutions:
Professor $53,759
Associate professor $38,296
Assistant professor $31,657
Instructor $26,686
No rank $29,222
All $39,463

STUDENTS

Enrollment:
At public 4-year institutions . 34,616
At public 2-year institutions .. 6,884
At private 4-year institutions 14,262
At private 2-year institutions . 1,424
Undergraduate 51,787
Graduate 4,771
Professional 628
American Indian 398
Asian 418
Black 296
Hispanic 195
White 55,487
Foreign 392
Total 57,186

Enrollment highlights:
Women 57.9%

MAINE
Continued

Full-time 56.8%
Minority 2.3%
Foreign 0.7%
10-year change in total
  enrollment .... Up 32.2%

Proportion of enrollment made up of minority students:
At public 4-year institutions .. 1.7%
At public 2-year institutions .. 2.7%
At private 4-year institutions . 3.7%
At private 2-year institutions . 0.8%

Degrees awarded:
Associate 1,859
Bachelor's 4,944
Master's 731
Doctorate 34
Professional 162

Residence of new students: State residents made up 71% of all freshmen enrolled in Maine; 70% of all Maine residents who were freshmen attended college in their home state.

Test scores: Students averaged 882 on the S.A.T., which was taken by an estimated 66% of Maine's high-school seniors.

Graduation rates at NCAA Division I institution:
University of Maine 50%

MONEY

Average tuition and fees:
At public 4-year institutions . $2,263
At public 2-year institutions . $1,497
At private 4-year institutions $10,928
At private 2-year institutions $3,899

Expenditures:
Public institutions $344,435,000
Private institutions ... $186,175,000

State funds for higher-education operating expenses: $172,985,000
Two-year change: Down 7%

State spending on student aid:
Need-based: $5,044,000
Non–need-based: None
Other: None

Salary of chief executive of largest public 4-year campus:
Frederick E. Hutchinson, University of Maine: $123,165

Total spending on research and development by doctorate-granting universities: $23,605,000
Sources:
Federal government 38.3%
State and local governments .. 3.8%
Industry 19.8%
The institution itself 35.0%
Other 3.1%

Total federal spending on college- and university-based research and development: $10,197,000
Selected programs:
Department of Health
  and Human Services ... $608,000
National Science
  Foundation $1,931,000
Department of Defense ... $213,000
Department
  of Agriculture $3,053,000
Department of Energy $77,000

Largest endowment:
Bowdoin College $161,556,000

Top fund raisers:
Bowdoin College $19,443,000

University of Maine ... $7,499,000
Colby College $6,552,000

MISCELLANY

- In 1992 Peter Marbach, development officer at Unity College, obtained 32 solar panels that were once used by the Carter White House and installed them on the roof of the college's cafeteria.

- Scraps from the University of Maine salad bar are helping generate electricity. Manure from the university's dairy farm, combined with food waste, creates a gas that generates about $10,000 worth of electricity annually.

- Bowdoin College is the oldest higher-education institution in Maine. It was founded in 1794.

MARYLAND

MARYLAND created a new structure for public higher education in 1988 and then spent the next few years putting in place major changes in the way the state finances student aid and community colleges.

But it seems as if the system—like most four-year-olds—just can't stay still.

In 1992, college officials were again pushing proposals for mergers, governance changes, curricular reform, and even a plan from one institution for a new relationship with the state. At the same time, public-college students and faculty members continued to protest state budget cuts and the resulting mid-year tuition increases.

In a year when lawmakers raised taxes and even then found that state revenues would be insufficient, the proposals that promised to save the state money were among the most popular.

St. Mary's College of Maryland, for example, won approval to become a "state related" institution after college leaders assured legislators and Gov. William Donald Schaefer, a Democrat, that they would not ask for ever-increasing appropriations from the state if the college could be protected from future budget cuts.

Under the new law, St. Mary's was granted greater autonomy over spending, and the right to double its tuition charges over the next five years.

St. Mary's and Morgan State University are the only four-year public institutions in Maryland that were not placed under the expanded University of Maryland System in 1988.

Fears of higher costs helped to kill another proposal, which would have merged the University of Maryland's Baltimore County and downtown Baltimore campuses into a single institution geared toward research in science, health, and technology.

The president of the State Senate said Maryland could not afford another research institution to compete with the University of Maryland at College Park. The leaders of the two Baltimore-area campuses say they will pursue the merger proposal again in 1993.

The College Park campus has had its problems. With state appropriations dwindling, the university went through an extensive review of academic programs and decided to eliminate its College of Human Ecology and seven departments. Eventually the moves will save the campus more than $6.3-million, which will be used

MARYLAND
Continued

to strengthen other academic programs.

The opposition to the Baltimore merger illustrates how regional politics often influence higher-education policy in Maryland. Controversy over another proposed merger shows how racial issues, too, have been a factor.

The Maryland Higher Education Commission, the statewide coordinating board, had suggested merging two of the state's four historically black institutions, Morgan State University and Coppin State College. But the proposal was dropped when a committee appointed to study the merger advised against it. Black legislators and others objected to the merger, saying it would deprive black students of educational opportunities at a time when Maryland is still under a federal court order to desegregate its higher-education system.

The commission has not been shy about using its authority to help set higher-education policy, most notably in 1992 when it severely restricted the creation of new academic programs on four-year campuses. Since July 1992, with the state's abolition of community-college boards of trustees, the commission also has been responsible for overseeing the state's 19 community colleges.

Along with the commission and the University of Maryland System, private institutions like Washington and Hood Colleges enjoy considerable clout in state political circles because of the work of a well-organized private-college lobby. Other institutions enjoy favor because of their prestige, notably St. John's College, which is known for its "great books" curriculum, and the Johns Hopkins University, a nationally respected research university.

DEMOGRAPHICS

Population: 4,860,000   (Rank: 19)

Age distribution:
Up to 17 .... 24.7%
18 to 24 .... 10.0%
25 to 44 .... 35.1%
45 and older 30.1%

Racial and ethnic distribution:
American Indian 0.3%
Asian 2.9%
Black 24.9%
White 71.0%
Other and unknown 0.9%
Hispanic (may be any race) .. 2.6%

Educational attainment of adults (highest level):
9th grade or less 7.9%
Some high school, no diploma 13.7%
High-school diploma 28.1%
Some college, no degree 18.6%
Associate degree 5.2%
Bachelor's degree 15.6%
Graduate or professional
  degree 10.9%

Proportion who speak a language other than English at home: 8.9%

Per-capita personal income: $22,189

Poverty rate:
All 8.3%
Under age 18 .... 11.3%
Age 18 and older 7.3%

New public high-school graduates in:
1992-93 (estimate) 38,690
2001-02 (estimate) 52,730

New GED diploma recipients: 6,211

High-school dropout rate: 10.9%

POLITICAL LEADERSHIP

Governor: William Donald Schaefer (D), term ends 1995

Governor's higher-education aide: Nancy Grasmick, 201 West Baltimore Street, Baltimore 21201; 410-333-2100

U.S. Senators: Barbara A. Mikulski (D), term ends 1999; Paul S. Sarbanes (D), term ends 1995

U.S. Representatives:
4 Democrats, 4 Republicans
Roscoe G. Bartlett (R), Helen Delich Bentley (R), Benjamin L. Cardin (D), Wayne T. Gilchrest (R), Steny H. Hoyer (D), Kweisi Mfume (D), Constance A. Morella (R), Albert R. Wynn (D)

General Assembly: Senate, 38 Democrats, 9 Republicans; House, 116 Democrats, 25 Republicans

COLLEGES AND UNIVERSITIES

Higher education:
Public 4-year institutions 14
Public 2-year institutions 19
Private 4-year institutions 21
Private 2-year institutions 3
Total 57

Vocational institutions: 153

Statewide coordinating board:
Maryland Higher Education
   Commission
Jeffrey Building
16 Francis Street
Annapolis 21401
(410) 974-2971

Shaila R. Aery, secretary of higher education

Private-college association:
Maryland Independent College
   and University Association
208 Duke of Gloucester Street
Annapolis 21401
(410) 269-0306
J. Elizabeth Garraway, president

Institutions censured by the AAUP:
Maryland Institute College of Art, New Community College of Baltimore

Institution under NCAA sanctions:
University of Maryland
at College Park

FACULTY MEMBERS

Full-time faculty members by rank:
Professor 2,092
Associate professor 1,807
Assistant professor 1,849
Instructor 449
Lecturer 200
No rank 216
Total 6,613

Full-time faculty members with tenure:
Men 2,780
Women 997
Total 3,777

Average pay of full-time professors

Public 4-year institutions:
Professor $60,952
Associate professor $46,006
Assistant professor $38,240
Instructor $28,248
No rank $22,112
All $46,028

Public 2-year institutions:
Professor $48,561

MARYLAND
Continued

Associate professor $40,205
Assistant professor $32,606
Instructor $27,555
No rank $30,884
All $40,313

Private 4-year institutions:
Professor $61,122
Associate professor $39,972
Assistant professor $33,623
Instructor $26,934
No rank $31,683
All $42,484

STUDENTS

Enrollment:
At public 4-year institutions   110,830
At public 2-year institutions   109,953
At private 4-year institutions   38,174
At private 2-year institutions ..   743
Undergraduate 219,707
Graduate 36,207
Professional 3,786
American Indian 817
Asian 11,429
Black 44,292
Hispanic 4,726
White 190,880
Foreign 7,556
Total 259,700

Enrollment highlights:
Women 56.6%
Full-time 46.3%
Minority 24.3%
Foreign 2.9%
10-year change in total
  enrollment .... Up 15.5%

Proportion of enrollment made up of minority students:
At public 4-year institutions . 27.9%
At public 2-year institutions . 24.2%
At private 4-year institutions   14.4%
At private 2-year institutions   16.3%

Degrees awarded:
Associate 7,429
Bachelor's 18,493
Master's 6,469
Doctorate 824
Professional 1,122

Residence of new students: State residents made up 83% of all freshmen enrolled in Maryland; 75% of all Maryland residents who were freshmen attended college in their home state.

Test scores: Students averaged 907 on the S.A.T., which was taken by an estimated 66% of Maryland's high-school seniors.

Graduation rates at NCAA Division I institutions:
Coppin State College 16%
Loyola College 70%
Morgan State University 28%
Mount Saint Mary's College ... 70%
Towson State University 51%
U.S. Naval Academy 77%
University of Maryland
  Baltimore County 35%
University of Maryland
  at College Park 57%
University of Maryland
  Eastern Shore 16%

MONEY

Average tuition and fees:
At public 4-year institutions . $2,287
At public 2-year institutions . $1,244
At private 4-year institutions $10,698
At private 2-year institutions $6,101

Expenditures:
Public institutions .. $1,576,934,000
Private institutions . $1,356,011,000

State funds for higher-education operating expenses: $788,159,000

Two-year change: Down 3%

State spending on student aid:
Need-based: $16,652,000
Non–need-based: $5,449,000
Other: $135,000

Salary of chief executive of largest public 4-year campus:
William E. Kirwan, University of Maryland at College Park: $143,377

Total spending on research and development by doctorate-granting universities: $977,593,000
Sources:
Federal government 74.1%
State and local governments .. 7.3%
Industry 4.3%
The institution itself 11.1%
Other 3.1%

Total federal spending on college- and university-based research and development: $589,856,000
Selected programs:
Department of Health
 and Human Services $235,025,000
National Science
 Foundation $31,082,000
Department of Defense $272,701,000
Department
 of Agriculture $5,999,000
Department of Energy . $10,636,000

Largest endowment:
Johns Hopkins
 University $561,433,000

Top fund raisers:
Johns Hopkins
 University $100,437,000
University of Maryland $24,421,000
Washington College $4,798,000

MISCELLANY

■ Hood College, a private liberal-arts institution for women that is celebrating its centennial in 1992-93, has frozen its prices. To help families strapped by the economic downturn, Hood kept its 1992-93 charges at the 1991-92 level of $12,078 for tuition and $5,675 for room and board.

■ To see how computer music will stand the test of time, students at the Peabody Institute of the Johns Hopkins University in 1991 sealed samples of their compositions and an assortment of musical software, including compact and optical disks, in a time capsule. Students undertook the project to mark the creation of Peabody's new master's-degree program in electronic and computer music.

■ Students from the University of Maryland at College Park are helping to restore 350-year-old Kiplin Hall in North Yorkshire, England. It was the home of George Calvert, whose son founded the Maryland colony.

■ The oldest institution of higher education in Maryland is Washington College, founded in 1782 and said to be the only institution of higher education to which George Washington gave his express consent for the use of his name.

MASSACHUSETTS

EVEN in 1992, a year in which the recession hurt public colleges nationwide, the financial woes of Massachusetts' colleges stand out. From academic 1990-91 through

MASSACHUSETTS
Continued

1992-93, state support for higher education in the Bay State dropped by 10 per cent, the third-biggest loss in the country.

The effects of the cuts are visible at public colleges throughout the state. Tuition is up. Class sizes are up. The number of classes offered is down. Morale—of students, faculty members, and administrators—is way down.

Educators say their state colleges were poorly prepared for the recession. Public higher education has traditionally taken a back seat to the state's prestigious private colleges, and it was only in the mid-1980's that Massachusetts lawmakers began a concerted effort to improve the quality of the public institutions.

The immediate outlook is not encouraging. The recession is still taking a toll, and Gov. William F. Weld, a Republican, has vowed to balance the state's budget with program cuts rather than tax increases.

For public higher education, Governor Weld and his Secretary of Education, Piedad F. Robertson, say that specialization is the key to preserving quality. They are encouraging colleges, particularly the regional four-year institutions, to develop more distinct missions and to eliminate academic programs that do not meet pressing demands.

Theoretically, the plan has broad support. But few colleges have volunteered to eliminate programs, and legislators take a proprietary interest in those offered by colleges in the districts they represent.

Money woes were not restricted to public colleges in 1992. State support for financial aid to private-college students was cut dramatically, forcing private institutions to find other sources of money for their students.

Harvard University discovered in 1992 that it was not immune to the financial problems plaguing many research universities. It closed the 1991 fiscal year with a $42-million deficit in its $1.2-billion budget. It delayed the start of a long-awaited fund-raising campaign that is believed to have a goal of $2-billion.

In contrast, women's colleges in Massachusetts are on a fund-raising streak. Wellesley College in 1992 set a new record for fund-raising by a private liberal-arts college when it closed its capital campaign with $167-million in gifts and pledges. In 1991 Mount Holyoke ended a campaign with $138-million, and in 1989 Smith College finished a campaign that raised $163-million.

Several private institutions are undergoing transitions in their leadership. Harvard has a new president, Neil L. Rudenstine. At Tufts University, John A. DiBiaggio, formerly president of Michigan State University, succeeded Jean Mayer. Brandeis University, which has been divided over how much its Jewish identity should define the institution, installed a new president in 1992, Samuel O. Thier. And Francis C. Oakley announced in October 1992 that he would retire as president of Williams College in December 1993.

The University of Massachusetts also has a new president—Michael K. Hooker, formerly president of the University of Maryland–Baltimore County.

Private colleges in Massachusetts, like their counterparts elsewhere, are involved in the debates over "political correctness" and the treatment of women and members of minority groups on campus.

Harvard had major protests in 1992 over allegations of discrimination against female, black, and gay students. The literature faculty at the Massachusetts Institute of Technology has been torn by allegations that faculty members who disagree with certain literary and political theories are isolated. At Clark University, an associate professor of philosophy, Christina Hoff Sommers, has emerged as a national critic of political correctness and what she views as the excesses of academic feminism.

DEMOGRAPHICS

Population: 5,996,000   (Rank: 13)

Age distribution:
Up to 17 .... 22.9%
18 to 24 .... 11.2%
25 to 44 .... 33.7%
45 and older 32.2%

Racial and ethnic distribution:
American Indian 0.2%
Asian 2.4%
Black 5.0%
White 89.8%
Other and unknown 2.6%
Hispanic (may be any race) .. 4.8%

Educational attainment of adults (highest level):
9th grade or less 8.0%
Some high school, no diploma 12.0%
High-school diploma 29.7%
Some college, no degree 15.8%
Associate degree 7.2%
Bachelor's degree 16.6%
Graduate or professional
   degree 10.6%

Proportion who speak a language other than English at home: 15.2%

Per-capita personal income: $23,003

Poverty rate:
All 8.9%
Under age 18 .... 13.2%
Age 18 and older 7.7%

New public high-school graduates in:
1992-93 (estimate) 46,260
2001-02 (estimate) 54,970

New GED diploma recipients: 10,849

High-school dropout rate: 8.5%

POLITICAL LEADERSHIP

Governor: William F. Weld (R), term ends 1995

Governor's higher-education aide:
Piedad F. Robertson, One Ashburton Place, Room 1401, Boston 02108; (617) 727-1313

U.S. Senators: Edward M. Kennedy (D), term ends 1995; John F. Kerry (D), term ends 1997

U.S. Representatives:
8 Democrats, 2 Republicans
Peter I. Blute (R), Barney Frank (D), Joseph P. Kennedy, II (D), Edward J. Markey (D), Martin T. Meehan (D), Joe Moakley (D), Richard E. Neal (D), John W. Olver (D), Gerry E. Studds (D), Peter G. Torkildsen (R)

General Court: Senate, 31 Democrats, 9 Republicans; House, 124 Democrats, 35 Republicans, 1 Independent

COLLEGES AND UNIVERSITIES

Higher education:
Public 4-year institutions 14
Public 2-year institutions 17

MASSACHUSETTS
Continued

Private 4-year institutions 71
Private 2-year institutions 14
Total 116

Vocational institutions: 157

Statewide coordinating board:
Higher Education Coordinating Council
One Ashburton Place
Room 1401
Boston 02108
(617) 727-7785
Peter M. Mitchell, interim chancellor

Private-college association:
Association of Independent Colleges and Universities in Massachusetts
11 Beacon Street, Suite 1224
Boston 02108
(617) 742-5147
Clare M. Cotton, president

Institutions censured by the AAUP:
American International College, Bridgewater State College, Dean Junior College, Nichols College

Institution under NCAA sanctions:
University of Lowell

FACULTY MEMBERS

Full-time faculty members by rank:
Professor 6,139
Associate professor 4,248
Assistant professor 3,832
Instructor 554
Lecturer 541
No rank 257
Total 15,571

Full-time faculty members with tenure:
Men 6,918
Women 2,224
Total 9,142

Average pay of full-time professors
Public 4-year institutions:
Professor $54,551
Associate professor $44,719
Assistant professor $36,137
Instructor $28,209
No rank .... n/a
All $46,965

Public 2-year institutions:
Professor $40,742
Associate professor $32,647
Assistant professor $29,462
Instructor $26,824
No rank $30,698
All $35,873

Private 4-year institutions:
Professor $69,231
Associate professor $45,978
Assistant professor $38,668
Instructor $30,621
No rank $30,053
All $51,004

STUDENTS

Enrollment:
At public 4-year institutions   110,031
At public 2-year institutions . 74,641
At private 4-year institutions 220,711
At private 2-year institutions   13,491
Undergraduate 333,956
Graduate 72,005
Professional 12,913
American Indian 1,220
Asian 16,144
Black 18,376
Hispanic 12,501
White 349,516
Foreign 21,117
Total 418,874

Enrollment highlights:
Women 55.1%

Full-time 62.6%
Minority 12.1%
Foreign 5.0%
10-year change in total
  enrollment .... Up 0.1%

Proportion of enrollment made up of minority students:
At public 4-year institutions .. 8.0%
At public 2-year institutions . 13.4%
At private 4-year institutions 13.4%
At private 2-year institutions 17.4%

Degrees awarded:
Associate 13,316
Bachelor's 43,559
Master's 17,827
Doctorate 2,122
Professional 3,657

Residence of new students: State residents made up 68% of all freshmen enrolled in Massachusetts; 79% of all Massachusetts residents who were freshmen attended college in their home state.

Test scores: Students averaged 902 on the S.A.T., which was taken by an estimated 80% of Massachusetts' high-school seniors.

Graduation rates at NCAA Division I institutions:
Boston College 85%
Boston University 62%
College of the Holy Cross 87%
Harvard University 94%
Northeastern University 47%
University of Massachusetts
  at Amherst 63%

MONEY

Average tuition and fees:
At public 4-year institutions . $2,580
At public 2-year institutions . $1,528
At private 4-year institutions $12,446
At private 2-year institutions $7,750

Expenditures:
Public institutions .. $1,357,588,000
Private institutions . $4,922,923,000

State funds for higher-education operating expenses: $625,380,000
Two-year change: Down 10%

State spending on student aid:
Need-based: $23,748,000
Non–need-based: None
Other: $16,241,000

Salary of chief executive of largest public 4-year campus:
Richard D. O'Brien, University
  of Massachusetts at Amherst:
  $123,500

Total spending on research and development by doctorate-granting universities: $898,808,000
Sources:
Federal government 72.2%
State and local governments .. 1.6%
Industry 9.6%
The institution itself 6.0%
Other 10.7%

Total federal spending on college- and university-based research and development: $635,891,000
Selected programs:
Department of Health
  and Human Services $283,414,000
National Science
  Foundation $124,325,000
Department of Defense $102,031,000
Department
  of Agriculture $15,021,000
Department of Energy . $60,385,000

Largest endowment:
Harvard University $4,669,683,000

Top fund raisers:
Harvard University .. $195,583,000

MASSACHUSETTS
Continued

Massachusetts Institute
  of Technology $110,308,000
Boston University $40,771,000

MISCELLANY

- The Bunting Institute at Radcliffe College is the country's first and largest multidisciplinary think tank for women. Founded some 30 years ago, it has provided fellowships to more than 1,000 female academics and artists.

- Middlesex Community College in Massachusetts used to be housed—at least in part—inside a Veteran's Hospital. The state finally moved the programs out of the hospital to other buildings adjacent to the hospital grounds.

- Harvard University has refused to let a company sell condoms emblazoned with its insignia. The company said its product would help the university encourage students to practice safe sex. But Harvard officials said the university might face legal problems if the condoms proved defective.

- Harvard University, founded in 1636, is the country's oldest institution of higher education.

MICHIGAN

Michigan has had a tradition of strong public and private colleges, with generally stable leadership. But several of its postsecondary institutions began the 1992-93 academic year in search of presidents.

Perhaps the best-known departing president is John A. DiBiaggio, who left Michigan State University after a protracted clash with the Board of Trustees over control of the athletics programs. Mr. DiBiaggio is now president of Tufts University.

The president of Central Michigan University since 1988, Edward B. Jakubauskas, opted to leave at the end of the 1991-92 academic year after "no confidence" votes by the Academic Senate, the faculty union, and department heads. The groups had criticized Mr. Jakubauskas' handling of a budget shortfall.

At Olivet College, racial discord between black and white students, which sparked a mass exodus of black students in the spring of 1992, brought on the resignation of President Donald A. Morris, who also had been stung by a "no confidence" vote by faculty members.

Meanwhile, at Ferris State University, President Helen Popovich received an overwhelming vote of "no confidence" by faculty members in 1992, but she remained at the institution. Faculty members have faulted her efforts to reduce Ferris State's deficit.

Despite the campus unrest and a tight budget, higher education in Michigan has been spared the cutbacks imposed on other state agencies by Republican Gov. John M. Engler and state lawmakers, who passed a "stay even" budget of $1.3-billion for the 1992-93 fiscal year. The appropriation bill also contains language that calls for the public colleges and universities to improve undergraduate education and attract more non-traditional and part-time students.

Additionally, the state is promoting

collaborative efforts among community and four-year colleges. An example is a project that links state universities with Northwestern Michigan College, a two-year institution, to determine how the universities can offer more programs to students who live in that part of the state.

Financial-aid policies were little changed in 1991-92, but the state did suspend its prepaid-tuition program, which was created by Gov. James J. Blanchard in 1986. The program has stopped taking new participants, waiting for the outcome of a state appeal of an Internal Revenue Service decision requiring income-tax payments on its earnings. In July 1992, a federal district court upheld the IRS ruling, casting more doubt on the future of the program. The state was expected to appeal.

The 1991-92 academic year saw the formation of the Citizens Council for Michigan Public Universities, a coalition of business and civic leaders that promotes increased support for higher education.

Each public college and university in Michigan, which has no strong statewide coordination, is run by an independent governing board. The boards for the University of Michigan, Michigan State, and Wayne State Universities are selected in statewide elections. Community colleges are governed by local boards.

DEMOGRAPHICS

Population: 9,368,000 (Rank: 8)

Age distribution:
Up to 17 .... 26.5%
18 to 24 .... 10.6%
25 to 44 .... 32.2%
45 and older 30.7%

Racial and ethnic distribution:
American Indian 0.6%
Asian 1.1%
Black 13.9%
White 83.4%
Other and unknown 0.9%
Hispanic (may be any race) .. 2.2%

Educational attainment of adults (highest level):
9th grade or less 7.8%
Some high school, no diploma 15.5%
High-school diploma 32.3%
Some college, no degree 20.4%
Associate degree 6.7%
Bachelor's degree 10.9%
Graduate or professional
  degree 6.4%

Proportion who speak a language other than English at home: 6.6%

Per-capita personal income: $18,655

Poverty rate:
All 13.1%
Under age 18 .... 18.6%
Age 18 and older 11.1%

New public high-school graduates in:
1992-93 (estimate) 85,960
2001-02 (estimate) 92,010

New GED diploma recipients: 14,111

High-school dropout rate: 10.0%

POLITICAL LEADERSHIP

Governor: John M. Engler (R), term ends 1995

Governor's higher-education aide: Georgia Van Adestine, Governor's

MICHIGAN
Continued

Office, P.O. Box 30013, Lansing 48909; (517) 335-7824

U.S. Senators: Carl Levin (D), term ends 1997; Donald W. Riegle, Jr. (D), term ends 1995

U.S. Representatives:
10 Democrats, 6 Republicans
James A. Barcia (D), David E. Bonior (D), Dave Camp (R), Bob Carr (D), Barbara-Rose Collins (D), John Conyers, Jr. (D), John D. Dingell (D), William D. Ford (D), Paul B. Henry (R), Peter Hoekstra (R), Dale E. Kildee (D), Joe Knollenberg (R), Sander M. Levin (D), Nick Smith (R), Bart Stupak (D), Fred Upton (R)

Legislature: Senate, 18 Democrats, 20 Republicans; House, 54 Democrats, 56 Republicans

COLLEGES AND UNIVERSITIES

Higher education:
Public 4-year institutions	15
Public 2-year institutions	29
Private 4-year institutions	50
Private 2-year institutions	3
Total	97

Vocational institutions: 278

Statewide coordinating board:
State Department of Education
P.O. Box 30008
Lansing 48909
(517) 335-4933
Gary D. Hawks, deputy superintendent for postsecondary education

Private-college association:
Association of Independent Colleges and Universities of Michigan
650 Michigan National Tower
Lansing 48933
(517) 372-9160
Edward O. Blews, Jr., president

Institutions censured by the AAUP:
Hillsdale College, Olivet College, University of Detroit Mercy

Institution under NCAA sanctions:
University of Michigan

FACULTY MEMBERS

Full-time faculty members by rank:
Professor	3,887
Associate professor	3,127
Assistant professor	3,088
Instructor	607
Lecturer	379
No rank	3,105
Total	14,193

Full-time faculty members with tenure:
Men	4,868
Women	1,157
Total	6,025

Average pay of full-time professors

Public 4-year institutions:
Professor	$57,693
Associate professor	$44,335
Assistant professor	$37,841
Instructor	$27,375
No rank	$27,104
All	$46,407

Public 2-year institutions:
Professor	$41,747
Associate professor	$37,348
Assistant professor	$31,204
Instructor	$25,118
No rank	$32,816
All	$32,793

Private 4-year institutions:
Professor $41,914
Associate professor $33,525
Assistant professor $28,357
Instructor $23,071
No rank $33,545
All $34,078

STUDENTS

Enrollment:
At public 4-year institutions   259,879
At public 2-year institutions   227,480
At private 4-year institutions   79,599
At private 2-year institutions   . 2,845
Undergraduate 500,739
Graduate 58,624
Professional 10,440
American Indian 3,547
Asian 10,693
Black 56,786
Hispanic 9,094
White 475,505
Foreign 14,178
Total 569,803

Enrollment highlights:
Women 55.1%
Full-time 50.8%
Minority 14.4%
Foreign 2.5%
10-year change in total
   enrollment .... Up 9.5%

Proportion of enrollment made up of minority students:
At public 4-year institutions . 13.0%
At public 2-year institutions . 14.6%
At private 4-year institutions   18.2%
At private 2-year institutions   18.9%

Degrees awarded:
Associate 21,156
Bachelor's 42,428
Master's 13,297
Doctorate 1,313
Professional 2,418

Residence of new students: State residents made up 85% of all freshmen enrolled in Michigan; 91% of all Michigan residents who were freshmen attended college in their home state.

Test scores: A.C.T. score n/a

Graduation rates at NCAA Division I institutions:
Central Michigan University ... 53%
Eastern Michigan University .. 36%
Michigan State University 66%
University of Detroit Mercy ... 48%
University of Michigan 82%
Western Michigan University .. 44%

MONEY

Average tuition and fees:
At public 4-year institutions . $2,635
At public 2-year institutions . $1,124
At private 4-year institutions $6,885
At private 2-year institutions $4,749

Expenditures:
Public institutions .. $4,076,519,000
Private institutions ... $637,849,000

State funds for higher-education operating expenses: $1,539,460,000
Two-year change: Up 4%

State spending on student aid:
Need-based: $81,577,000
Non–need-based: None
Other: $1,900,000

Salary of chief executive of largest public 4-year campus:
Gordon Guyer (interim), Michigan
   State University: $157,000

Total spending on research and development by doctorate-granting universities: $527,070,000
Sources:
Federal government 52.4%

MICHIGAN
Continued

State and local governments .. 7.0%
Industry 8.5%
The institution itself 24.3%
Other 7.8%

Total federal spending on college- and university-based research and development: $274,276,000

Selected programs:
Department of Health
  and Human Services $155,239,000
National Science
  Foundation $48,718,000
Department of Defense $16,585,000
Department
  of Agriculture $14,228,000
Department of Energy . $11,846,000

Largest endowment:
University of Michigan $500,430,000

Top fund raisers:
University of Michigan $94,789,000
Michigan State
  University $53,554,000
Wayne State University $15,255,000

MISCELLANY

■ The Walter P. Reuther Library of Labor and Urban Affairs at Wayne State University houses the world's largest collection on labor history, including the archives of the United Auto Workers of America.

■ Northern Michigan University is home to one of three U.S. Olympic Education Centers—the only one on a college campus.

■ Michigan State University is the only university in the United States with three medical schools. Aspiring medical doctors, veterinarians, and osteopathic physicians can all get their degrees from Michigan State.

■ The oldest institution of higher education in the state is the University of Michigan, founded in 1817.

MINNESOTA

IN the summer of 1992, Minnesota did what many states dare not even talk about: It shut down a public college.

But the closing of one campus of 1,000 students, the University of Minnesota's agriculture-oriented branch at Waseca, in a system that enrolls more than 220,000 is unlikely to have a profound impact on higher education. The state still has 63 other public-college campuses.

Several years of serious budget problems, however, are forcing Minnesotans to rethink their philosophy toward postsecondary education, particularly the unofficial policy that all students should be able to attend college within 35 miles of their homes.

Although other campus closings are not yet in the offing, the institutions and the state have taken steps that could lead to dramatic changes. Chief among them was a decision to merge the four-year, community, and technical colleges into a single system by 1995. The merger is an attempt to reduce expensive duplication. The University of Minnesota, a constitutionally chartered institution, was not included in the merger, but it, too, is examining programs with an eye toward eliminating duplication.

Some lawmakers and Gov. Arne H. Carlson, a Republican, still have reservations about the merger. They worry that the unique mission of technical colleges could be lost in a giant system, and are skeptical that the merger will actually save money. But a legislative attempt in 1992 to undo the merger failed, and state officials are working to put the new system into place.

Meanwhile, a panel of legislators, students, community leaders, and college officials appointed by Governor Carlson has highlighted other topics that could soon move up on the state's higher-education agenda.

The panel, the Commission on Post-Secondary Education, has called on the state to give financial rewards to colleges that are innovative and teach their students well. The commission also recommended that the state increase requirements for graduation from high school and that it prohibit postsecondary-education funds from being used to pay for the costs of remedial courses for recent high-school graduates. If students need such courses, the commission said, their school districts should pay for them.

The push for academic quality followed a decision by the State University System to impose tougher admissions standards beginning in 1994.

The renewed emphasis on standards at the four-year institutions, coupled with their plans to curtail enrollment growth, is also putting new pressures on the state's 20-campus Minnesota Community College System. About half of the community colleges' students enroll with the goal of transferring to a four-year college.

The financial pressures on the public colleges have given new ammunition to an argument advanced by private colleges: that Minnesota should change its philosophy toward financing higher education. The private colleges say the state should devote more money to financial aid rather than subsidize low public-college tuition.

The Minnesota Private College Council, the private-college lobby, says the state's seemingly egalitarian low-tuition policy is actually regressive. Some legislators are beginning to agree. A bill that would have dramatically shifted spending priorities in that direction was introduced in 1992, but failed to pass the Legislature.

That setback aside, private colleges, including Macalester College and several institutions affiliated with the Lutheran Church, generally enjoy great influence in the state's political and cultural life. One sign of that influence is the state's generous financial programs, which are open to private-college students. Another is the state's willingness to allow private colleges to participate in an offshoot of the state's "school choice" program. The program allows 11th- and 12th-graders to receive high-school credit for the courses they take at colleges, and participating colleges are reimbursed by school districts.

DEMOGRAPHICS

Population: 4,432,000   (Rank: 20)

Age distribution:
Up to 17 .... 26.8%
18 to 24 .... 9.8%
25 to 44 .... 33.2%
45 and older 30.2%

Racial and ethnic distribution:
American Indian 1.1%
Asian 1.8%
Black 2.2%
White 94.4%
Other and unknown 0.5%
Hispanic (may be any race) .. 1.2%

MINNESOTA
Continued

Educational attainment of adults (highest level):
9th grade or less 8.6%
Some high school, no diploma 9.0%
High-school diploma 33.0%
Some college, no degree 19.0%
Associate degree 8.6%
Bachelor's degree 15.6%
Graduate or professional
  degree 6.3%

Proportion who speak a language other than English at home: 5.6%

Per-capita personal income: $19,125

Poverty rate:
All 10.2%
Under age 18 .... 12.7%
Age 18 and older 9.3%

New public high-school graduates in:
1992-93 (estimate) 48,530
2001-02 (estimate) 60,610

New GED diploma recipients: 6,151

High-school dropout rate: 6.4%

POLITICAL LEADERSHIP

Governor: Arne H. Carlson (R), term ends 1995

Governor's higher-education aide:
Curt Johnson, 130 Capitol Building, St. Paul 55155; (612) 296-3391

U.S. Senators: Dave Durenberger (R), term ends 1995; Paul D. Wellstone (D), term ends 1997

U.S. Representatives:
6 Democrats, 2 Republicans
Rod Grams (R), David Minge (D), James L. Oberstar (D), Timothy J. Penny (D), Collin C. Peterson (D), Jim Ramstad (R), Martin Olav Sabo (D), Bruce F. Vento (D)

Legislature: Senate, 45 Democrats, 22 Republicans; House, 87 Democrats, 47 Republicans

COLLEGES AND UNIVERSITIES

Higher education:
Public 4-year institutions 10
Public 2-year institutions 26
Private 4-year institutions 34
Private 2-year institutions 8
Total 78

Vocational institutions: 113

Statewide coordinating board:
Minnesota Higher Education
  Coordinating Board
400 Capitol Square Building
550 Cedar Street
St. Paul 55101
(612) 296-9665
David R. Powers, executive director

Private-college association:
Minnesota Private College Council
401 Galtier Plaza
Box 40
175 Fifth Street East
St. Paul 55101
(612) 228-9061
David B. Laird, Jr., president

Institutions censured by the AAUP: None

Institution under NCAA sanctions: University of Minnesota–Twin Cities

FACULTY MEMBERS

Full-time faculty members by rank:
Professor 2,190

Associate professor 1,658
Assistant professor 1,716
Instructor 432
Lecturer 9
No rank 1,281
Total 7,286

Full-time faculty members with tenure:
Men 2,925
Women 824
Total 3,749

Average pay of full-time professors
Public 4-year institutions:
Professor $55,625
Associate professor $42,723
Assistant professor $35,252
Instructor $26,181
No rank .... n/a
All $44,975

Public 2-year institutions:
Professor $40,000
Associate professor $39,755
Assistant professor $33,256
Instructor $27,498
No rank $39,762
All $39,536

Private 4-year institutions:
Professor $47,897
Associate professor $36,759
Assistant professor $31,118
Instructor $26,718
No rank .... n/a
All $37,351

STUDENTS

Enrollment:
At public 4-year institutions   133,622
At public 2-year institutions . 65,589
At private 4-year institutions   50,224
At private 2-year institutions . 4,354
Undergraduate 222,683
Graduate 25,361
Professional 5,745
American Indian 2,002
Asian 4,948
Black 4,143
Hispanic 1,936
White 235,231
Foreign 5,529
Total 253,789

Enrollment highlights:
Women 54.9%
Full-time 60.1%
Minority 5.2%
Foreign 2.2%
10-year change in total
  enrollment .... Up 22.8%

Proportion of enrollment made up of minority students:
At public 4-year institutions .. 5.0%
At public 2-year institutions .. 5.6%
At private 4-year institutions . 5.3%
At private 2-year institutions . 6.9%

Degrees awarded:
Associate 7,674
Bachelor's 22,881
Master's 4,366
Doctorate 750
Professional 1,561

Residence of new students: State residents made up 80% of all freshmen enrolled in Minnesota; 82% of all Minnesota residents who were freshmen attended college in their home state.

Test scores: Students averaged 21.4 on the A.C.T., which was taken by an estimated 59% of Minnesota's high-school seniors.

Graduation rates at NCAA Division I institution:
University of Minnesota–Twin
  Cities 34%

MONEY

Average tuition and fees:
At public 4-year institutions . $2,216

MINNESOTA
Continued

At public 2-year institutions . $1,578
At private 4-year institutions $9,507
At private 2-year institutions $7,664

Expenditures:
Public institutions .. $1,802,133,000
Private institutions ... $753,255,000

State funds for higher-education operating expenses: $965,288,000

Two-year change: Down 4%

State spending on student aid:
Need-based: $77,678,000
Non–need-based: None
Other: $1,595,000

Salary of chief executive of largest public 4-year campus:
Nils Hasselmo, University
   of Minnesota–Twin Cities: $152,300

Total spending on research and development by doctorate-granting universities: $292,046,000
Sources:
Federal government 49.2%
State and local governments . 16.2%
Industry 6.2%
The institution itself 18.3%
Other 10.0%

Total federal spending on college- and university-based research and development: $141,748,000

Selected programs:
Department of Health
   and Human Services $92,215,000
National Science
   Foundation $20,975,000
Department of Defense $10,057,000
Department
   of Agriculture $7,242,000
Department of Energy .. $4,560,000

Largest endowment:
Macalester College ... $390,024,000

Top fund raisers:
University
   of Minnesota $109,132,000
Mayo Foundation $41,436,000
St. Olaf College $11,908,000

MISCELLANY

■ Concordia College holds a "Corn Feed" every year before its students return. The college sponsors the party for the local community, and residents eat thousands of ears of corn.

■ In 1991, Bemidji State University became the first public university in the country to open an on-campus apartment building exclusively for single parents and their children.

■ At a time when many institutions are cutting back, the University of Saint Thomas opened a new campus in Minneapolis in 1992. An atrium at the new facility features what is said to be the largest fresco in the United States.

■ Minnesotans disagree over which institution of higher education is the oldest in the state. The University of Minnesota–Twin Cities was chartered in 1851 but did not admit a freshman class until 1869. Hamline University was chartered in 1854 and commenced classes that same year.

MISSISSIPPI

IN a landmark decision, the U.S. Supreme Court ruled in June 1992 that Mississippi's public colleges and universities remained illegally segregated. It ordered lower federal courts to supervise state efforts to desegregate.

The decision capped years of legal battles involving the state, the U.S. Justice Department, and civil-rights leaders.

Mississippi officials maintained that the state had met its legal obligations by ending racial limitations on where students could enroll, and by making "good faith" efforts to attract more black students to the predominantly white institutions.

The Supreme Court disagreed, saying that key elements of Mississippi's higher-education system needed more judicial scrutiny, which it predicted would lead to changes in some policies. Specifically, the Court criticized the state's use of standardized test scores in admissions decisions and the widespread duplication of academic programs at nearby predominantly white and historically black institutions.

The Court also suggested that Mississippi might not need eight public four-year colleges and universities, and that maintaining all those institutions—three of which are historically black—may perpetuate segregation.

Despite the Supreme Court decision, it may be years before Mississippi fully desegregates its colleges. The first major plan put forth to meet the Court's orders set off a huge controversy in the state, with many people threatening to take the case back to court.

The plan was proposed by the Board of Trustees of State Institutions of Higher Learning, the governing board for the eight four-year institutions. The board recommended merging some colleges—historically black Mississippi Valley State University and predominantly white Delta State University, among them—and closing several professional schools.

As of late 1992, the board's proposal was under consideration by federal courts.

Community colleges, which were not covered by the desegregation ruling, are governed by the State Board for Community and Junior Colleges.

Mississippi's college leaders, particularly Higher Education Commissioner W. Ray Cleere, have been pushing to improve the academic quality of their institutions through tougher admissions standards and closer links between colleges and the public schools. The campaign has been controversial because many say that, until the public schools improve, it is unreasonable for the colleges to expect much more of high-school graduates.

Another major roadblock to improving Mississippi higher education has been lack of money. The state has been in a recession, and Governor Kirk Fordice, a Republican, is a staunch fiscal conservative. Budget cuts, program eliminations, and tuition increases have become the norm for the state's colleges.

In 1992 the colleges had one bit of good financial news when the Legislature overrode Governor Fordice's veto of a bill to raise the sales tax to 7 per cent, from 6 per cent, and to designate the new funds for education at all levels. Even with the additional revenue, however, colleges will still have less money than was appropriated for the 1990-91 academic year.

Private higher education in Mississippi consists largely of liberal-arts, religiously affiliated institutions, such as Blue Mountain, Millsaps, Mississippi, Tougaloo, and William Carey Colleges.

MISSISSIPPI
Continued

DEMOGRAPHICS

Population: 2,592,000 (Rank: 31)

Age distribution:
Up to 17 .... 29.0%
18 to 24 .... 11.5%
25 to 44 .... 29.2%
45 and older 30.3%

Racial and ethnic distribution:
American Indian 0.3%
Asian 0.5%
Black 35.6%
White 63.5%
Other and unknown 0.1%
Hispanic (may be any race) .. 0.6%

Educational attainment of adults (highest level):
9th grade or less 15.6%
Some high school, no diploma 20.1%
High-school diploma 27.5%
Some college, no degree 16.9%
Associate degree 5.2%
Bachelor's degree 9.7%
Graduate or professional
  degree 5.1%

Proportion who speak a language other than English at home: 2.8%

Per-capita personal income: $13,328

Poverty rate:
All 25.2%
Under age 18 .... 33.6%
Age 18 and older 21.7%

New public high-school graduates in:
1992-93 (estimate) 23,180
2001-02 (estimate) 23,520

New GED diploma recipients: 6,053

High-school dropout rate: 11.8%

POLITICAL LEADERSHIP

Governor: Kirk Fordice (R), term ends 1996

Governor's higher-education aide: Jeanne Forrester, State Capitol, P.O. Box 139, Jackson 39205; (601) 359-3150

U.S. Senators: Thad Cochran (R), term ends 1997; Trent Lott (R), term ends 1995

U.S. Representatives:
5 Democrats, 0 Republicans
Mike Espy (D), G. V. (Sonny) Montgomery (D), Mike Parker (D), Gene Taylor (D), Jamie L. Whitten (D)

Legislature: Senate, 39 Democrats, 13 Republicans; House, 93 Democrats, 27 Republicans, 2 Independents

COLLEGES AND UNIVERSITIES

Higher education:
Public 4-year institutions 9
Public 2-year institutions 20
Private 4-year institutions 12
Private 2-year institutions 5
Total 46

Vocational institutions: 48

Statewide coordinating boards:
Board of Trustees of State Institutions
  of Higher Learning
3825 Ridgewood Road
Jackson 39211
(601) 982-6611
W. Ray Cleere, commissioner

State Board for Community
  and Junior Colleges
3825 Ridgewood Road

Jackson 39211
(601) 982-6518
Olon E. Ray, executive director

Private-college association:
Mississippi Association
of Independent Colleges
P.O. Drawer 1198
Clinton 39060
(601) 925-3400
Johnnie Ruth Hudson,
executive director

Institutions censured by the AAUP:
None

Institution under NCAA sanctions:
Jackson State University

FACULTY MEMBERS

Full-time faculty members by rank:
Professor	670
Associate professor	637
Assistant professor	821
Instructor	353
Lecturer	11
No rank	1,428
Total	3,920

Full-time faculty members with tenure:
Men	818
Women	275
Total	1,093

Average pay of full-time professors

Public 4-year institutions:
Professor	$43,350
Associate professor	$34,948
Assistant professor	$30,691
Instructor	$21,720
No rank	n/a
All	$33,717

Public 2-year institutions:
Professor	n/a
Associate professor	n/a
Assistant professor	n/a
Instructor	n/a
No rank	$28,195
All	$28,195

Private 4-year institutions:
Professor	$46,320
Associate professor	$34,978
Assistant professor	$29,166
Instructor	$19,894
No rank	n/a
All	$34,888

STUDENTS

Enrollment:
At public 4-year institutions	58,781
At public 2-year institutions	50,257
At private 4-year institutions	10,640
At private 2-year institutions	3,205
Undergraduate	110,333
Graduate	10,415
Professional	2,135
American Indian	377
Asian	783
Black	33,699
Hispanic	395
White	85,699
Foreign	1,930
Total	122,883

Enrollment highlights:
Women	56.4%
Full-time	75.9%
Minority	29.1%
Foreign	1.6%
10-year change in total enrollment	Up 20.0%

Proportion of enrollment made up of minority students:
At public 4-year institutions	30.8%
At public 2-year institutions	25.8%
At private 4-year institutions	31.4%
At private 2-year institutions	44.7%

Degrees awarded:
Associate	4,995
Bachelor's	8,808

MISSISSIPPI
Continued

Master's 2,370
Doctorate 293
Professional 477

Residence of new students: State residents made up 87% of all freshmen enrolled in Mississippi; 92% of all Mississippi residents who were freshmen attended college in their home state.

Test scores: Students averaged 18.6 on the A.C.T., which was taken by an estimated 72% of Mississippi's high-school seniors.

Graduation rates at NCAA Division I institutions:
Alcorn State University 47%
Jackson State University 18%
Mississippi State University ... 52%
Mississippi Valley State
  University 39%
University of Mississippi 48%
University of Southern
  Mississippi 40%

MONEY

Average tuition and fees:
At public 4-year institutions . $1,927
At public 2-year institutions .. $722
At private 4-year institutions $5,238
At private 2-year institutions $3,721

Expenditures:
Public institutions $922,574,000
Private institutions $93,959,000

State funds for higher-education operating expenses: $437,215,000
Two-year change: Up 3%

State spending on student aid:
Need-based: $1,175,000
Non–need-based: $71,000
Other: None

Salary of chief executive of largest public 4-year campus:
Donald W. Zacharias, Mississippi State University: $102,000

Total spending on research and development by doctorate-granting universities: $85,229,000
Sources:
Federal government 47.3%
State and local governments . 24.3%
Industry 9.6%
The institution itself 11.1%
Other 7.6%

Total federal spending on college- and university-based research and development: $36,277,000
Selected programs:
Department of Health
  and Human Services . $8,545,000
National Science
  Foundation $4,684,000
Department of Defense . $1,925,000
Department
  of Agriculture $10,476,000
Department of Energy .. $5,115,000

Largest endowment:
University of Mississippi $46,052,000

Top fund raisers:
Mississippi State
  University $11,122,000
University of Mississippi $10,716,000
Mississippi College $4,495,000

MISCELLANY

■ The Mississippi University for Women is one of two state-supported institutions in the country whose primary mission is the education of women. The other is Texas Woman's University.

- The University of Mississippi has the federal government's only legal marijuana farm. Officials of the university's Marijuana Project grow the plants on a 5.6-acre plot for research on medical and other uses.

- Mississippi State University played the leading research and development role in establishing the $2.7-billion commercial catfish industry in the United States. The industry was created entirely from scratch on the basis of scientific research, which led to the development of special feeds, demonstrated the nutritional value of catfish, and showed that the fish could be produced and preserved safely.

- The oldest institution of higher education in the state is Mississippi College, a Southern Baptist institution founded in 1826.

MISSOURI

In the "Show Me" state, skepticism typically runs high. That may explain voters' resounding defeat of a tax increase in November 1991 that would have provided nearly $200-million for higher education.

But college officials contend that the defeat of "Proposition B" does not indicate that voters are against higher education; they are against taxes.

With that in mind, the Coordinating Board for Higher Education created the Task Force on Critical Choices for Higher Education, a group that comprises the heads of the governing boards of all public four-year institutions and some public two-year and private-college board chairpersons, as well.

Its purpose is to advise the board on how best to prepare students for college; how to control the cost of higher education; how to revamp governing boards; how to reshape the missions of Missouri's colleges and universities; how to improve institutional accountability, including examinations of retention and graduation rates, faculty productivity and workloads; and how to assess student achievement.

One of the group's key proposals is that admission standards at the University of Missouri be toughened. The standards were adopted by the Board of Curators, the university's governing board, and will go into effect by fall 1997.

Controlling the cost of higher education is an issue in Missouri. Public colleges got a boost in August 1992 when voters approved an amendment to the state Constitution requiring that all revenue generated by the state's lottery be put into elementary, secondary, and postsecondary education. That could total $80-million to $140-million a year.

Higher education had had a high priority in the administration of former Gov. John Ashcroft, a Republican who once taught at the college level.

Although Mr. Ashcroft was barred from seeking a third term in 1992, higher education seems likely to maintain its high profile in the administration of Mel Carnahan, a Democrat who was elected in November.

Within his first 90 days in office, Mr. Carnahan promised a study of public colleges, the results of which will be used to improve higher education. He also proposed a Universal College Revolving Fund to make loans to students at public or private colleges who make satisfactory progress toward degrees.

The University of Missouri system

MISSOURI
Continued

is governed by the Board of Curators, and each of the nine other public four-year institutions and 10 community colleges has its own board. Many of the private colleges in the state are small and religiously affiliated, although two, Saint Louis University and Washington University, are known nationwide for their strong research missions.

Relations between public and private institutions are generally good, with the state giving some direct aid to private colleges to provide special programs. The coordinating board encourages the sectors to work together, recently approving joint programs in nursing, elementary education, and business administration offered by Mineral Area Community College and Central Methodist College.

DEMOGRAPHICS

Population: 5,158,000   (Rank: 15)

Age distribution:
Up to 17 .... 26.0%
18 to 24 .... 9.9%
25 to 44 .... 31.0%
45 and older 33.1%

Racial and ethnic distribution:
American Indian 0.4%
Asian 0.8%
Black 10.7%
White 87.7%
Other and unknown 0.4%
Hispanic (may be any race) .. 1.2%

Educational attainment of adults (highest level):
9th grade or less 11.6%
Some high school, no diploma 14.5%
High-school diploma 33.1%
Some college, no degree 18.4%
Associate degree 4.5%
Bachelor's degree 11.7%
Graduate or professional
  degree 6.1%

Proportion who speak a language other than English at home: 3.8%

Per-capita personal income: $17,928

Poverty rate:
All 13.3%
Under age 18 .... 17.7%
Age 18 and older 11.8%

New public high-school graduates in:
1992-93 (estimate) 46,930
2001-02 (estimate) 52,730

New GED diploma recipients: 8,543

High-school dropout rate: 11.4%

POLITICAL LEADERSHIP

Governor: Mel Carnahan (D), term ends 1997

Governor's higher-education aide: n/a

U.S. Senators: Christopher S. Bond (R), term ends 1999; John C. Danforth (R), term ends 1995

U.S. Representatives:
6 Democrats, 3 Republicans
William L. Clay (D), Pat Danner (D), Bill Emerson (R), Richard A. Gephardt (D), Mel Hancock (R), Ike Skelton (D), James M. Talent (R), Harold L. Volkmer (D), Alan Wheat (D)

General Assembly: Senate, 20 Democrats, 13 Republicans, 1 vacancy; House, 100 Democrats, 63 Republicans

COLLEGES AND UNIVERSITIES

Higher education:
Public 4-year institutions 13
Public 2-year institutions 14
Private 4-year institutions 55
Private 2-year institutions 11
Total 93

Vocational institutions: 193

Statewide coordinating board:
Coordinating Board for
  Higher Education
101 Adams Street
Jefferson City 65101
(314) 751-2361
Charles J. McClain, commissioner of higher education

Private-college association:
Independent Colleges and
  Universities of Missouri
514 Earth City Expressway, Suite 244
Earth City 63045
(314) 739-4770
Charles V. Gallagher, president

Institutions censured by the AAUP:
Concordia Seminary,
Metropolitan Community Colleges

Institutions under NCAA sanctions:
None

FACULTY MEMBERS

Full-time faculty members by rank:
Professor 2,079
Associate professor 1,718
Assistant professor 2,016
Instructor 574
Lecturer 98
No rank 730
Total 7,215

Full-time faculty members with tenure:
Men 2,935
Women 772
Total 3,707

Average pay of full-time professors
Public 4-year institutions:
Professor $49,135
Associate professor $39,254
Assistant professor $33,893
Instructor $26,252
No rank $31,693
All $39,031

Public 2-year institutions:
Professor $47,653
Associate professor $40,971
Assistant professor $33,706
Instructor $29,171
No rank $30,108
All $34,915

Private 4-year institutions:
Professor $49,201
Associate professor $35,492
Assistant professor $30,792
Instructor $23,018
No rank $26,562
All $36,860

STUDENTS

Enrollment:
At public 4-year institutions   125,270
At public 2-year institutions . 74,823
At private 4-year institutions   85,310
At private 2-year institutions . 4,004
Undergraduate 245,658
Graduate 34,368
Professional 9,381
American Indian 1,132
Asian 4,487
Black 23,050
Hispanic 3,434
White 250,758
Foreign 6,546
Total 289,407

Enrollment highlights:
Women 54.8%

MISSOURI
Continued

Full-time 56.3%
Minority 11.3%
Foreign 2.3%
10-year change in total
  enrollment .... Up 23.4%

Proportion of enrollment made up of minority students:
At public 4-year institutions .. 9.6%
At public 2-year institutions . 13.2%
At private 4-year institutions 11.7%
At private 2-year institutions 24.2%

Degrees awarded:
Associate 6,909
Bachelor's 24,628
Master's 8,607
Doctorate 619
Professional 2,283

Residence of new students: State residents made up 79% of all freshmen enrolled in Missouri; 85% of all Missouri residents who were freshmen attended college in their home state.

Test scores: Students averaged 21.0 on the A.C.T., which was taken by an estimated 67% of Missouri's high-school seniors.

Graduation rates at NCAA Division I institutions:
Saint Louis University 61%
Southeast Missouri State
  University 33%
Southwest Missouri State
  University 35%
University of Missouri
  at Columbia 54%
University of Missouri
  at Kansas City 46%

MONEY

Average tuition and fees:
At public 4-year institutions . $1,733
At public 2-year institutions .. $891
At private 4-year institutions $7,487
At private 2-year institutions $5,208

Expenditures:
Public institutions .. $1,349,451,000
Private institutions . $1,340,923,000

State funds for higher-education operating expenses: $590,483,000

Two-year change: 0%

State spending on student aid:
Need-based: $10,125,000
Non–need-based: $9,515,000
Other: $260,000

Salary of chief executive of largest public 4-year campus:
Charles A. Kiesler, University
  of Missouri at Columbia: $150,000
  plus a $50,000 one-time bonus

Total spending on research and development by doctorate-granting universities: $281,133,000

Sources:
Federal government 54.2%
State and local governments .. 6.6%
Industry 10.0%
The institution itself 21.2%
Other 8.1%

Total federal spending on college- and university-based research and development: $169,883,000

Selected programs:
Department of Health
  and Human Services $134,675,000
National Science
  Foundation $13,352,000
Department of Defense . $3,237,000
Department
  of Agriculture $8,795,000

Largest endowment:
Washington
  University $1,442,616,000

Top fund raisers:
Washington University $50,307,000
University of Missouri
  at Columbia $20,733,000
University of Missouri
  at Kansas City $8,608,000

MISCELLANY

■ Selmo Park, the president's residence at Central Missouri State University, is named after "Old Selmo," a slave who helped the builder, Edmund Augustus Nickerson, escape from prison during the Civil War. Built in 1866, the house was bought 60 years later by the university's Board of Regents.

■ Lincoln University, a historically black institution that opened its doors in 1866, is believed to be the only college founded by black Civil War veterans. Men of the 62nd and 65th Colored Infantries donated more than $6,000 to start the institution, which was known as Lincoln Institute until 1921.

■ Winston Churchill popularized the phrase Iron Curtain in a speech at Westminster College on March 5, 1946. (A museum containing the most extensive collection of Churchilliana in the United States is adjacent to the campus.)

■ Harris-Stowe State College is the only college in the nation not attached to a larger university where all of the students are enrolled in teacher-education programs.

■ The oldest higher-education institution in Missouri is Saint Louis University, a Roman Catholic institution founded in 1818.

MONTANA

THE Montana University System is continuing its perennial struggle for improved financial support.

The system of universities, community colleges, and vocational-technical centers began the 1991-93 biennium with a 14-per-cent budget increase, which officials considered insufficient to make up for past years of low support. Even that largesse didn't last long, however.

In a January 1992 special session, the Legislature cut the system's budget by almost 6 per cent. An additional 4 per cent was removed during a special legislative session called in July to deal with the state's large budget deficit.

Much of the January cut was made up with a tuition increase, but legislators advised the Board of Regents of Higher Education against imposing another increase to offset the summer cut. Higher-education officials warned that they would have to eliminate classes and make some layoffs if the budget was cut too deeply.

Montana is one of only a few states without a sales tax. A proposal to put a sales-tax measure on the November ballot to raise state revenues was considered in the special session. But lawmakers rejected the measure, asserting that voters were in no mood for new taxes of any kind.

The cuts in higher education came despite recommendations by a citizens' committee appointed by the outgoing Governor, Republican Stan Stephens. The group had urged increasing support for the university system by $9-million a year for five years. The system has long complained that its

MONTANA
Continued

support lags behind that of comparable institutions in other states.

The citizens' panel also recommended reducing enrollments by about 22 per cent over five years as a way to raise per-student spending to the averages at similar institutions in other states.

Presidents of Montana's colleges and universities responded with specific proposals to cut enrollments, stirring the ire of some legislators.

The Higher Education Commissioner, John M. Hutchinson, and system officials are working on other recommendations by the citizens' panel, including the development of a statewide telecommunications system for higher education, the expansion of campus research and public-service programs, and the institution of several measures to gauge academic quality.

Montana's new Governor, Marc Racicot, a Republican, has promised to work with university officials to raise academic standards. He also opposes suggestions that some branches of the university system be closed.

The regents govern all public institutions in the state. The state also has several small, private colleges.

The University of Montana continued its folksy practice of sending a busload of university representatives, including the president, to communities across this sparsely populated state to recruit students and build public support.

DEMOGRAPHICS

Population: 808,000 (Rank: 44)

Age distribution:
Up to 17 .... 27.6%
18 to 24 .... 8.9%
25 to 44 .... 31.2%
45 and older 32.3%

Racial and ethnic distribution:
American Indian 6.0%
Asian 0.5%
Black 0.3%
White 92.7%
Other and unknown 0.5%
Hispanic (may be any race) .. 1.5%

Educational attainment of adults (highest level):
9th grade or less 8.1%
Some high school, no diploma 10.9%
High-school diploma 33.5%
Some college, no degree 22.1%
Associate degree 5.6%
Bachelor's degree 14.1%
Graduate or professional
  degree 5.7%

Proportion who speak a language other than English at home: 5.0%

Per-capita personal income: $15,675

Poverty rate:
All 16.1%
Under age 18 .... 20.5%
Age 18 and older 14.4%

New public high-school graduates in:
1992-93 (estimate) 9,220
2001-02 (estimate) 9,260

New GED diploma recipients: 1,740

High-school dropout rate: 8.1%

POLITICAL LEADERSHIP

Governor: Marc Racicot (R), term ends 1997

Governor's higher-education aide:
n/a

U.S. Senators: Max Baucus (D), term ends 1997; Conrad R. Burns (R), term ends 1995

U.S. Representative:
1 Democrat
Pat Williams (D)

Legislature: Senate, 30 Democrats, 20 Republicans; House, 47 Democrats, 53 Republicans

COLLEGES AND UNIVERSITIES

Higher education:
Public 4-year institutions 6
Public 2-year institutions 8
Private 4-year institutions 3
Private 2-year institutions 2
Total 19

Vocational institutions: 43

Statewide coordinating board:
Montana University System
2500 Broadway
Helena 59620
(406) 444-6570
John M. Hutchinson,
commissioner of higher education

Private-college association:
None

Institutions censured by the AAUP:
None

Institutions under NCAA sanctions:
None

FACULTY MEMBERS

Full-time faculty members by rank:
Professor 427
Associate professor 339
Assistant professor 374
Instructor 74
Lecturer 8
No rank 120
Total 1,342

Full-time faculty members with tenure:
Men 630
Women 131
Total 761

Average pay of full-time professors
Public 4-year institutions:
Professor $40,520
Associate professor $33,644
Assistant professor $29,918
Instructor $23,766
No rank .... n/a
All $34,404

Public 2-year institutions:
Professor .... n/a
Associate professor .... n/a
Assistant professor .... n/a
Instructor .... n/a
No rank $26,628
All $24,641

Private 4-year institutions:
Professor $33,082
Associate professor $27,317
Assistant professor $23,387
Instructor $20,009
No rank .... n/a
All $26,680

STUDENTS

Enrollment:
At public 4-year institutions . 28,015
At public 2-year institutions .. 3,850
At private 4-year institutions . 3,046
At private 2-year institutions .. 965
Undergraduate 32,187
Graduate 3,479
Professional 210
American Indian 2,427
Asian 120

MONTANA
Continued

Black 114
Hispanic 280
White 32,200
Foreign 735
Total 35,876

Enrollment highlights:
Women 52.9%
Full-time 73.2%
Minority 8.4%
Foreign 2.0%
10-year change in total
  enrollment .... Up 2.0%

Proportion of enrollment made up of minority students:
At public 4-year institutions .. 4.4%
At public 2-year institutions . 22.2%
At private 4-year institutions . 5.7%
At private 2-year institutions 74.9%

Degrees awarded:
Associate 782
Bachelor's 3,862
Master's 709
Doctorate 71
Professional 71

Residence of new students: State residents made up 86% of all freshmen enrolled in Montana; 72% of all Montana residents who were freshmen attended college in their home state.

Test scores: Students averaged 21.6 on the A.C.T., which was taken by an estimated 54% of Montana's high-school seniors.

Graduation rates at NCAA Division I institutions:
Montana State University ...... n/a
University of Montana 27%

MONEY

Average tuition and fees:
At public 4-year institutions . $1,553
At public 2-year institutions .. $964
At private 4-year institutions $5,565
At private 2-year institutions $1,140

Expenditures:
Public institutions $218,231,000
Private institutions $27,990,000

State funds for higher-education operating expenses: $125,863,000
Two-year change: Up 8%

State spending on student aid:
Need-based: $395,000
Non–need-based: None
Other: None

Salary of chief executive of largest public 4-year campus:
Michael P. Malone, Montana State
  University: $94,340

Total spending on research and development by doctorate-granting universities: $34,980,000
Sources:
Federal government 35.8%
State and local governments . 22.5%
Industry 12.2%
The institution itself 29.0%
Other 0.5%

Total federal spending on college- and university-based research and development: $13,041,000
Selected programs:
Department of Health
  and Human Services . $2,386,000
National Science
  Foundation $5,190,000
Department of Defense ... $239,000

Department
    of Agriculture $2,963,000
Department of Energy $51,000

Largest endowment:
University of Montana
    Foundation $22,079,000

Top fund raisers:
Montana College of Mineral Science
    and Technology $1,429,000
Eastern Montana College . $698,000
College of Great Falls $551,000

MISCELLANY

■ The University of Montana made news in 1992 when one of its football players reached what is believed to be the first-ever financial settlement with the National Collegiate Athletic Association in the association's drug-testing program. The NCAA agreed to settle after a state judge ruled that it had violated its own procedures in determining that Steve Premock had used anabolic steroids.

■ Western Montana College received a $280,000 foundation grant to help develop telecommunications links among scattered rural elementary and secondary schools. The program now connects more than 100 one-room and two-room schools.

■ American Indians are the largest minority group in Montana. Seven colleges in the state are controlled by tribal councils.

■ The oldest institution of higher education in Montana is Rocky Mountain College, an interdenominational institution founded in 1878.

NEBRASKA

O N Saturdays in the fall, Nebraskans will drive for hours to get to Lincoln if they have tickets to University of Nebraska football games.

But because few students are willing to endure such commutes on a daily basis, educators and politicians are constantly balancing demands for academic programs throughout the state with Nebraska's continuing budget problems.

Traditionally, the University of Nebraska at Lincoln has dominated higher education in the state and it continues to do so, offering a wide array of academic programs, with particular strength in agriculture. But increasingly, citizens who live far from Lincoln are demanding that more attention be paid to campuses in their areas.

That trend was evident in 1991, when lawmakers decided to merge Kearney State College into the University of Nebraska system. Some supporters of the Lincoln campus of the University of Nebraska worry that the addition of another institution to the system will decrease the amount of money their campus receives.

Money has not been plentiful for any Nebraska college in recent years. Because of shortfalls, public colleges had to reduce their budgets by 2 per cent in academic 1991-92 and by 1 per cent for 1992-93. More and potentially larger cuts are expected, so institutions are raising tuition. Even with that additional revenue, students expect larger and fewer classes.

State leaders hope to save money—without reducing the quality of higher education—by giving new authority to

NEBRASKA
Continued

the state's coordinating board, the Coordinating Commission for Postsecondary Education.

In 1992 the commission adopted rules to limit the creation of new academic programs in the state. Under the rules, the commission will approve new programs only if they are central to the mission of the institution that wants to offer them and if the institution has adequate resources.

The coordinating board is also working with the new Midwestern Higher Education Commission to develop reciprocity agreements with other states, so that specialized programs may be offered only in a few places in the region.

Although most students in Nebraska attend public colleges and universities, the state also has a number of private institutions, many of which are affiliated with religious groups. These institutions include the College of Saint Mary; Dana, Doane, and Hastings Colleges; and Nebraska Wesleyan University.

DEMOGRAPHICS

Population: 1,593,000   (Rank: 36)

Age distribution:
Up to 17 .... 27.3%
18 to 24 .... 9.8%
25 to 44 .... 30.8%
45 and older 32.0%

Racial and ethnic distribution:
American Indian 0.8%
Asian 0.8%
Black 3.6%
White 93.8%
Other and unknown 1.0%
Hispanic (may be any race) .. 2.3%

Educational attainment of adults (highest level):
9th grade or less 8.0%
Some high school, no diploma 10.2%
High-school diploma 34.7%
Some college, no degree 21.1%
Associate degree 7.1%
Bachelor's degree 13.1%
Graduate or professional
   degree 5.9%

Proportion who speak a language other than English at home: 4.8%

Per-capita personal income: $17,718

Poverty rate:
All 11.1%
Under age 18 .... 13.8%
Age 18 and older 10.1%

New public high-school graduates in:
1992-93 (estimate) 17,390
2001-02 (estimate) 18,730

New GED diploma recipients: 2,517

High-school dropout rate: 7.0%

POLITICAL LEADERSHIP

Governor: E. Benjamin Nelson (D), term ends 1995

Governor's higher-education aide: Andrew F. Cunningham, P.O. Box 94601, Lincoln 68509; (402) 471-2742

U.S. Senators: J. James Exon (D), term ends 1997; J. Robert Kerrey (D), term ends 1995

U.S. Representatives:
1 Democrat, 2 Republicans

Bill Barrett (R), Doug Bereuter (R), Peter Hoagland (D)

Unicameral: Non-partisan legislature

COLLEGES AND UNIVERSITIES

Higher education:
Public 4-year institutions 7
Public 2-year institutions 11
Private 4-year institutions 15
Private 2-year institutions 1
Total 34

Vocational institutions: 45

Statewide coordinating board:
Coordinating Commission for
  Postsecondary Education
140 North Eighth Street, Suite 300
P.O. Box 95005
Lincoln 68509
(402) 471-2847
Bruce G. Stahl, executive director

Private-college association:
Association of Independent Colleges
  and Universities of Nebraska
521 South 14th Street, Suite 302
Lincoln 68508
(402) 434-2818
Thomas J. O'Neill, Jr., president

Institutions censured by the AAUP:
None

Institutions under NCAA sanctions:
None

FACULTY MEMBERS

Full-time faculty members by rank:
Professor 710
Associate professor 642
Assistant professor 800
Instructor 219
Lecturer 10
No rank 386
Total 2,767

Full-time faculty members with tenure:
Men 1,142
Women 258
Total 1,400

Average pay of full-time professors
Public 4-year institutions:
Professor $52,850
Associate professor $40,393
Assistant professor $35,340
Instructor $25,510
No rank $18,601
All $41,233

Public 2-year institutions:
Professor .... n/a
Associate professor .... n/a
Assistant professor .... n/a
Instructor .... n/a
No rank $27,393
All $27,393

Private 4-year institutions:
Professor $42,301
Associate professor $34,208
Assistant professor $28,507
Instructor $21,926
No rank .... n/a
All $32,879

STUDENTS

Enrollment:
At public 4-year institutions . 60,692
At public 2-year institutions . 33,922
At private 4-year institutions 17,885
At private 2-year institutions .. 332
Undergraduate 97,878
Graduate 12,210
Professional 2,743
American Indian 729
Asian 1,178
Black 2,723
Hispanic 1,559
White 104,620

NEBRASKA
Continued

Foreign 2,022
Total 112,831

Enrollment highlights:
Women 54.9%
Full-time 55.7%
Minority 5.6%
Foreign 1.8%
10-year change in total
 enrollment .... Up 26.1%

Proportion of enrollment made up of minority students:
At public 4-year institutions .. 4.9%
At public 2-year institutions .. 6.0%
At private 4-year institutions . 7.1%
At private 2-year institutions 11.8%

Degrees awarded:
Associate 2,678
Bachelor's 8,677
Master's 1,713
Doctorate 230
Professional 658

Residence of new students: State residents made up 86% of all freshmen enrolled in Nebraska; 85% of all Nebraska residents who were freshmen attended college in their home state.

Test scores: Students averaged 21.2 on the A.C.T., which was taken by an estimated 74% of Nebraska's high-school seniors.

Graduation rates at NCAA Division I institutions:
Creighton University 64%
University of Nebraska
 at Lincoln 48%

MONEY

Average tuition and fees:
At public 4-year institutions . $1,592
At public 2-year institutions .. $990
At private 4-year institutions $6,893
At private 2-year institutions ... n/a

Expenditures:
Public institutions $762,480,000
Private institutions ... $226,173,000

State funds for higher-education operating expenses: $358,591,000
Two-year change: Up 9%

State spending on student aid:
Need-based: $2,352,000
Non–need-based: None
Other: None

Salary of chief executive of largest public 4-year campus:
Graham B. Spanier, University of
 Nebraska at Lincoln: $146,000

Total spending on research and development by doctorate-granting universities: $105,373,000
Sources:
Federal government 32.6%
State and local governments . 26.5%
Industry 10.5%
The institution itself 26.7%
Other 3.6%

Total federal spending on college- and university-based research and development: $29,379,000
Selected programs:
Department of Health
 and Human Services $14,546,000
National Science
 Foundation $2,998,000
Department of Defense ... $829,000
Department
 of Agriculture $6,559,000
Department of Energy $322,000

Largest endowment:
University of Nebraska $201,153,000

Top fund raisers:
University of Nebraska $39,912,000
Creighton University ... $9,084,000
Union College $2,240,000

MISCELLANY

- The University of Nebraska Center for Great Plains Studies, founded in 1976, is a clearinghouse for scholarship, teaching, and public-outreach programs on the region. It offers what is thought to be the nation's only major in Great Plains studies.

- Creighton University's Hereditary Cancer Institute is the home of what may be the world's largest cancer registry. The institute has a data base of more than 4,000 families whose members have suffered from some form of hereditary cancer. Using the information it collects, officials at the institute counsel family members on the disease.

- Nebraska was the first state to adopt a law that requires the National Collegiate Athletic Association to meet certain due-process standards when it investigates public colleges in the state.

- Students at Nebraska Wesleyan University taking a course in sociological research are required to write letters home to their parents. The professor who teaches the class says he thinks students are better able to see the link between sociology and their everyday lives by writing letters that explain what they are learning.

- The oldest institution of higher education in Nebraska is Peru State College, founded in 1867.

NEVADA

NEVADA'S public universities continue to try to convince the Legislature that they need more money to attract and keep high-caliber faculty members and build strong academic programs. But, considering the state's budget picture, that will be a hard sell to lawmakers and Democratic Gov. Bob Miller.

The University of Nevada's two campuses, at Las Vegas and Reno, as well as the four community colleges, must absorb an 8-per-cent budget cut in fiscal 1992-93. That will result in tuition increases, cuts in operating budgets, and delays in making building repairs. And the Governor has asked that the university system cut an additional $6-million from its budget, on top of the 8-per-cent cut.

Despite the cuts, Nevada has increased higher-education spending faster than other states for the third year in a row. The state spent 27 per cent more on education in 1992-93 than it did two years ago, according to a study by the Center for Higher Education at Illinois State University.

Although educators expect money to command a great deal of legislative attention, that will not be the lawmakers' only focus. In May 1992, they approved an inquiry into the forced resignation of Jerry Tarkanian, the basketball-coaching legend at the University of Nevada at Las Vegas. The investigation will also take up charges of ticket scalping and the relationship between the Las Vegas campus and its foundation, a private fund-raising arm. Earlier in 1992, Rollie Massimino was recruited from Villanova University to coach Las Vegas's Runnin' Rebels, a basketball program with a

NEVADA
Continued

history of scrapes with the National Collegiate Athletic Association.

Mr. Tarkanian's resignation was seen as a victory for faculty members and administrators at UNLV who want the institution to place more emphasis on academics and less on athletics. But Mr. Tarkanian's continuing popularity in the state indicates that many Nevadans may not approve of the change in priorities.

The state's community colleges and four-year universities often compete for resources. The same rivalry has pitted Reno against Las Vegas. But a 1991 report on the state's community colleges, which enroll more than half of the college students in Nevada, may ultimately improve the two-year institutions' position.

The report, "Changing with the Times, Challenging the Future," found that the community colleges would increasingly be asked to provide programs to improve workers' skills. Yet the report warned that the community colleges would face serious shortages of faculty members in science and technology.

To recognize that community colleges are an integral part of education in the state, the University of Nevada System changed its name in 1992 to the University and Community College System of Nevada. The system's elected Board of Regents oversees four-year and two-year campuses alike.

Sierra Nevada College is the state's only non-profit private college.

DEMOGRAPHICS

Population: 1,284,000   (Rank: 38)

Age distribution:
Up to 17 .... 25.1%
18 to 24 .... 9.4%
25 to 44 .... 34.8%
45 and older 30.7%

Racial and ethnic distribution:
American Indian 1.6%
Asian 3.2%
Black 6.6%
White 84.3%
Other and unknown 4.4%
Hispanic (may be any race) . 10.4%

Educational attainment of adults (highest level):
9th grade or less 6.0%
Some high school, no diploma 15.2%
High-school diploma 31.5%
Some college, no degree 25.8%
Associate degree 6.2%
Bachelor's degree 10.1%
Graduate or professional
   degree 5.2%

Proportion who speak a language other than English at home: 13.2%

Per-capita personal income: $19,783

Poverty rate:
All 10.2%
Under age 18 .... 13.3%
Age 18 and older 9.1%

New public high-school graduates in:
1992-93 (estimate) 9,890
2001-02 (estimate) 16,740

New GED diploma recipients: 2,734

High-school dropout rate: 15.2%

POLITICAL LEADERSHIP

Governor: Bob Miller (D), term ends 1995

Governor's higher-education aide:
Scott M. Craigie, Executive Chamber, Capitol Complex, Carson City 89710; (702) 687-5670

U.S. Senators: Richard H. Bryan (D), term ends 1995; Harry Reid (D), term ends 1999

U.S. Representatives:
1 Democrat, 1 Republican
James H. Bilbray (D), Barbara F. Vucanovich (R)

Legislature: Senate, 10 Democrats, 10 Republicans, 1 race undecided; House, 29 Democrats, 13 Republicans

COLLEGES AND UNIVERSITIES

Higher education:
Public 4-year institutions 2
Public 2-year institutions 4
Private 4-year institutions 1
Private 2-year institutions 2
Total 9

Vocational institutions: 55

Statewide coordinating board:
University and Community College
  System of Nevada
2601 Enterprise Road
Reno 89512
(702) 784-4901
Mark H. Dawson, chancellor

Private-college association:
None

Institutions censured by the AAUP:
None

Institutions under NCAA sanctions:
None

FACULTY MEMBERS

Full-time faculty members by rank:
Professor 288
Associate professor 249
Assistant professor 248
Instructor 56
Lecturer 140
No rank 147
Total 1,128

Full-time faculty members with tenure:
Men 448
Women 122
Total 570

Average pay of full-time professors
Public 4-year institutions:
Professor $57,490
Associate professor $45,160
Assistant professor $37,551
Instructor $39,520
No rank .... n/a
All $43,777

Public 2-year institutions:
Professor $41,986
Associate professor .... n/a
Assistant professor .... n/a
Instructor $32,022
No rank $36,018
All $36,434

Private 4-year institutions:
Professor $40,388
Associate professor $25,311
Assistant professor $27,138
Instructor .... n/a
No rank $24,000
All $31,445

STUDENTS

Enrollment:
At public 4-year institutions . 29,424
At public 2-year institutions . 31,818
At private 4-year institutions .. 313
At private 2-year institutions .. 173
Undergraduate 56,215
Graduate 5,333
Professional 180
American Indian 1,043

NEVADA
Continued

Asian	2,559
Black	2,931
Hispanic	3,408
White	50,910
Foreign	877
Total	61,728

Enrollment highlights:

Women	56.3%
Full-time	29.9%
Minority	16.3%
Foreign	1.4%
10-year change in total enrollment	Up 52.6%

Proportion of enrollment made up of minority students:

At public 4-year institutions	13.4%
At public 2-year institutions	19.2%
At private 4-year institutions	1.0%
At private 2-year institutions	15.8%

Degrees awarded:

Associate	949
Bachelor's	2,235
Master's	543
Doctorate	38
Professional	49

Residence of new students: State residents made up 89% of all freshmen enrolled in Nevada; 86% of all Nevada residents who were freshmen attended college in their home state.

Test scores: Students averaged 20.9 on the A.C.T., which was taken by an estimated 42% of Nevada's high-school seniors.

Graduation rates at NCAA Division I institutions:

University of Nevada at Las Vegas	29%
University of Nevada at Reno	32%

MONEY

Average tuition and fees:

At public 4-year institutions	$1,275
At public 2-year institutions	$651
At private 4-year institutions	$6,200
At private 2-year institutions	n/a

Expenditures:

Public institutions	$281,018,000
Private institutions	$3,893,000

State funds for higher-education operating expenses: $207,572,000

Two-year change: Up 27%

State spending on student aid:
Need-based: $377,000
Non–need-based: None
Other: None

Salary of chief executive of largest public 4-year campus:
Robert C. Maxson, University of Nevada at Las Vegas: $154,000

Total spending on research and development by doctorate-granting universities: $38,301,000

Sources:

Federal government	54.0%
State and local governments	6.3%
Industry	11.9%
The institution itself	24.0%
Other	3.8%

Total federal spending on college- and university-based research and development: $23,111,000

Selected programs:

Department of Health and Human Services	$3,429,000
National Science Foundation	$4,353,000
Department of Defense	$154,000

Department
   of Agriculture $1,380,000
Department of Energy .. $3,411,000

Largest endowment:
University of Nevada .. $67,079,000

Top fund raisers:
data not reported

MISCELLANY

- Sierra Nevada College, on the North Shore of Lake Tahoe within minutes of 14 downhill ski areas, offers the nation's only four-year program in ski-business and resort management. The six-year-old program now caters to 50 students who complete internships at ski resorts as far away as Japan.

- In 1968, Howard R. Hughes, who owned property in Nevada, donated money to the state to study the feasibility of a statewide community-college system. Nevada's Legislature had approved the study, but allocated no money for it. Mr. Hughes donated $250,000 to pay for the study and to bail out Nevada's only two-year institution, a private college in serious financial trouble. Nevada now has four state-run community colleges, including the college that Mr. Hughes saved 24 years ago.

- The only Basque-studies program in the Western Hemisphere is at the University of Nevada at Reno. Primarily a research institute, the program sponsors four to six visiting researchers in each academic year.

- The oldest institution of higher education in the state is the University of Nevada at Reno, founded in 1874.

NEW HAMPSHIRE

ALTHOUGH the recession hammered New Hampshire's economy in 1991 and 1992, its public colleges and universities found something to celebrate: two consecutive years of record enrollments.

The growth proved beneficial. The additional tuition income helped offset a 3.5-per-cent cut in funds that was imposed by the state in November 1991.

Higher-education officials had their fingers crossed that they could finish 1992 without another budget reduction, but they were fairly confident they would have to take a cut of some size before the fiscal year ends in June 1993.

New Hampshire's four-year colleges raised tuition by 5.5 per cent in 1991-92 and again in 1992-93—a low rate for public systems in New England.

State support for public colleges and universities is relatively low. The five-college University System of New Hampshire received only $56-million from the state in 1991-92 and 1992-93. New Hampshire ranks 50th of all states in financing for higher education, measured either as spending per capita or as a percentage of personal income.

New Hampshire has no sales tax or personal income tax. And although several 1992 gubernatorial candidates favored a sales tax, the candidate who won, Steve Merrill, a Republican, opposed increasing any taxes to raise money for higher education.

The New Hampshire Industrial Research Center, a collaborative effort between the University of New Hampshire and Dartmouth College, in

NEW HAMPSHIRE
Continued

1992 began helping small businesses in product development and testing. Lawmakers created the center in 1991 to include colleges in the economic-development effort.

Dartmouth bucked recessionary trends by starting a five-year, $425-million capital campaign that raised $184-million in its first eight months. The money will pay for scholarships, endowed professorships, fellowships, construction, and operating expenses.

Some of the money will help finance expensive curricular changes, including requirements that students study world cultures, take interdisciplinary courses, and complete a major senior-year project directed by a faculty member.

The University System of New Hampshire is run by a Board of Trustees and includes five universities and four-year colleges. The state grants the board much authority to make budgetary and policy decisions.

The state also has a system of seven vocational-technical colleges, run by its own board. That system has much less budgetary and operating autonomy than the four-year institutions.

DEMOGRAPHICS

Population: 1,105,000   (Rank: 41)

Age distribution:
Up to 17 .... 25.3%
18 to 24 .... 10.1%
25 to 44 .... 34.8%
45 and older 29.7%

Racial and ethnic distribution:
American Indian 0.2%
Asian 0.8%
Black 0.6%
White 98.0%
Other and unknown 0.3%
Hispanic (may be any race) .. 1.0%

Educational attainment of adults (highest level):
9th grade or less 6.7%
Some high school, no diploma 11.2%
High-school diploma 31.7%
Some college, no degree 18.0%
Associate degree 8.1%
Bachelor's degree 16.4%
Graduate or professional
    degree 7.9%

Proportion who speak a language other than English at home: 8.7%

Per-capita personal income: $21,760

Poverty rate:
All 6.4%
Under age 18 .... 7.4%
Age 18 and older 6.1%

New public high-school graduates in:
1992-93 (estimate) 9,440
2001-02 (estimate) 13,150

New GED diploma recipients: 2,276

High-school dropout rate: 9.4%

POLITICAL LEADERSHIP

Governor: Steve Merrill (R), term ends 1995

Governor's higher-education aide: n/a

U.S. Senators: Judd Gregg (R), term ends 1999; Bob Smith (R), term ends 1997

U.S. Representatives:
1 Democrat, 1 Republican
Dick Swett (D), Bill Zeliff (R)

General Court: Senate, 11 Democrats, 13 Republicans; House, 139 Democrats, 257 Republicans, 1 Independent, 3 Libertarians

COLLEGES AND UNIVERSITIES

Higher education:
Public 4-year institutions 5
Public 2-year institutions 7
Private 4-year institutions 12
Private 2-year institutions 4
Total 28

Vocational institutions: 26

Statewide coordinating board:
New Hampshire Postsecondary
  Education Commission
Two Industrial Park Drive
Concord 03301
(603) 271-2555
James A. Busselle, executive director

Private-college association:
None

Institutions censured by the AAUP:
None

Institutions under NCAA sanctions:
None

FACULTY MEMBERS

Full-time faculty members by rank:
Professor 668
Associate professor 609
Assistant professor 528
Instructor 69
Lecturer 15
No rank 29
Total 1,918

Full-time faculty members with tenure:
Men 784
Women 241
Total 1,025

Average pay of full-time professors
Public 4-year institutions:
Professor $52,290
Associate professor $41,196
Assistant professor $33,490
Instructor $29,320
No rank $28,000
All $41,977

Public 2-year institutions:
Professor $33,100
Associate professor $27,781
Assistant professor $26,426
Instructor $20,210
No rank .... n/a
All $30,582

Private 4-year institutions:
Professor $59,303
Associate professor $38,146
Assistant professor $32,724
Instructor $25,343
No rank $23,432
All $42,839

STUDENTS

Enrollment:
At public 4-year institutions . 23,799
At public 2-year institutions .. 8,364
At private 4-year institutions 24,546
At private 2-year institutions . 2,801
Undergraduate 50,942
Graduate 7,885
Professional 683
American Indian 229
Asian 760
Black 669
Hispanic 490
White 56,522
Foreign 840
Total 59,510

Enrollment highlights:
Women 54.5%
Full-time 62.9%

NEW HAMPSHIRE
Continued

Minority 3.7%
Foreign 1.4%
10-year change in total
  enrollment .... Up 27.2%

Proportion of enrollment made up of minority students:
At public 4-year institutions .. 1.9%
At public 2-year institutions .. 2.1%
At private 4-year institutions . 5.7%
At private 2-year institutions . 5.2%

Degrees awarded:
Associate 2,512
Bachelor's 6,745
Master's 1,944
Doctorate 83
Professional 165

Residence of new students: State residents made up 49% of all freshmen enrolled in New Hampshire; 58% of all New Hampshire residents who were freshmen attended college in their home state.

Test scores: Students averaged 923 on the S.A.T., which was taken by an estimated 76% of New Hampshire's high-school seniors.

Graduation rates at NCAA Division I institutions:
Dartmouth College 95%
University of New Hampshire . 66%

MONEY
Average tuition and fees:
At public 4-year institutions . $3,110
At public 2-year institutions . $1,899
At private 4-year institutions $11,154
At private 2-year institutions $5,547

Expenditures:
Public institutions $259,157,000
Private institutions ... $363,330,000

State funds for higher-education operating expenses: $74,026,000
Two-year change: Up 1%

State spending on student aid:
Need-based: $840,000
Non–need-based: $10,000
Other: $694,000

Salary of chief executive of largest public 4-year campus:
Dale F. Nitzschke, University of New Hampshire: $130,000

Total spending on research and development by doctorate-granting universities: $69,731,000
Sources:
Federal government 63.9%
State and local governments .. 5.7%
Industry 5.3%
The institution itself 16.5%
Other 8.5%

Total federal spending on college- and university-based research and development: $52,386,000
Selected programs:
Department of Health
  and Human Services $27,689,000
National Science
  Foundation $5,826,000
Department of Defense . $2,712,000
Department
  of Agriculture $1,966,000
Department of Energy .. $1,281,000

Largest endowment:
Dartmouth College ... $594,582,000

Top fund raisers:
Dartmouth College $56,594,000
University
  of New Hampshire ... $4,111,000
Colby-Sawyer College .. $3,616,000

MISCELLANY

■ A marine biologist at the University of New Hampshire is a two-time award winner for music videos about crustaceans. In 1991 Randy Olson won an award at the New England Film and Video Festival for *Lobstahs,* a short film on how to eat lobsters. In 1992 he won the same award for *Barnacles Tell No Lies,* a five-minute video that provides entertaining tidbits about the tiny invertebrates.

■ The covered bridge that spans the Contoocook River on the New England College campus was the first to be constructed by a college.

■ The Dartmouth College medical school in 1992 established the C. Everett Koop Institute to provide a base for Dr. Koop, the outspoken Surgeon General in the Reagan Administration, to help reform medical education and American health care.

■ Dartmouth College, founded in 1769, is the oldest higher-education institution in New Hampshire.

NEW JERSEY

Gov. Jim Florio came into the Governor's office in 1990 facing a $3-billion revenue shortfall. He promised sweeping educational and tax reforms. Those included plans to equalize state spending in school districts and increase sales and property taxes—moves that ultimately made him one of the least popular governors in the country only a year after his election.

The dust has settled, but optimism is still in short supply. Many educators and lawmakers complain that increases in the cost of higher education, coupled with reduced state spending, have placed it out of the reach of the average citizen. Added to that was a vote by the Legislature in May 1992 to cut the sales tax by 1 cent on the dollar. That necessitated massive cuts in all state-government agencies.

The Legislature passed a budget for fiscal year 1993 that calls for spending more than $1-billion on higher education, but directs reductions in some accounts to support negotiated salary increases and other mandatory payments elsewhere in the budget. The budget is about $67-million less than what Mr. Florio recommended, and will result in layoffs at colleges and universities, the elimination of many class sections, and reduced student-support services.

In the case of Rutgers University, less money will mean 300 assistant-professor positions will go unfilled, and the purchase of some 30,000 library books will be postponed.

Some good news for students followed angry protests at the state house that occurred near the end of the 1991-92 academic year, when hundreds of college students decried tuition increases. The students were pressuring lawmakers to approve Mr. Florio's Tuition Stabilization Incentive Grant Program. In the end, it won legislative approval. Through the program, colleges that keep tuition increases to 4.5 per cent can share in a $30-million pool.

Meanwhile, Edward D. Goldberg, the chancellor of higher education, is asking for an amendment to the state constitution guaranteeing every citizen a right to a "quality, affordable college education." Legislators may

NEW JERSEY
Continued

not jump to support that, fearing that it would increase state costs. But the idea has sparked discussions about the future of higher education in the Garden State.

The Board of Higher Education, the statewide coordinating body for public and private postsecondary education, in 1992 lowered the requirements for designating colleges as universities, eliminating the prerequisite that a university offer at least three doctoral programs. Eight public and private institutions in New Jersey are called universities.

Critics have accused the board of caving in to political pressure from state lawmakers, who have threatened to grant university status to several colleges by special legislation. Opponents say the change will cheapen the term "university."

Supporters say the name change only validates the status of comprehensive public and private colleges in the state, and will help attract students.

Glassboro State College has a new name, but not because of a state policy. The college has been renamed Rowan College of New Jersey, in recognition of a businessman who pledged in July 1992 to give $100-million to the institution. The gift is among the largest ever made to any college in the country.

Amid the debate about the future of higher education in the state, the Department of Higher Education received rave reviews for leadership and efficiency from a management consulting firm. That may silence, at least for a while, the perennial talk of merging the agency with the state's Education Department, which oversees elementary and secondary schools.

DEMOGRAPHICS

Population: 7,760,000 (Rank: 9)

Age distribution:
Up to 17 .... 23.7%
18 to 24 .... 9.6%
25 to 44 .... 33.1%
45 and older 33.5%

Racial and ethnic distribution:
American Indian 0.2%
Asian 3.5%
Black 13.4%
White 79.3%
Other and unknown 3.6%
Hispanic (may be any race) .. 9.6%

Educational attainment of adults (highest level):
9th grade or less 9.4%
Some high school, no diploma 13.9%
High-school diploma 31.1%
Some college, no degree 15.5%
Associate degree 5.2%
Bachelor's degree 16.0%
Graduate or professional
  degree 8.8%

Proportion who speak a language other than English at home: 19.5%

Per-capita personal income: $25,666

Poverty rate:
All 7.6%
Under age 18 .... 11.3%
Age 18 and older 6.4%

New public high-school graduates in:
1992-93 (estimate) 62,070
2001-02 (estimate) 69,270

New GED diploma recipients: 8,430

High-school dropout rate: 9.6%

POLITICAL LEADERSHIP

Governor: Jim Florio (D), term ends 1994

Governor's higher-education aide:
Marisa Quinn, State House, CN-001, Trenton 08625; (609) 777-1243

U.S. Senators: Bill Bradley (D), term ends 1997; Frank R. Lautenberg (D), term ends 1995

U.S. Representatives:
7 Democrats, 6 Republicans
Robert E. Andrews (D), Bob Franks (R), Dean A. Gallo (R), William J. Hughes (D), Herbert C. Klein (D), Robert Menendez (D), Frank Pallone, Jr. (D), Donald M. Payne (D), Marge Roukema (R), H. James Saxton (R), Christopher H. Smith (R), Robert G. Torricelli (D), Dick Zimmer (R)

Legislature: Senate, 13 Democrats, 27 Republicans; House, 22 Democrats, 58 Republicans

COLLEGES AND UNIVERSITIES

Higher education:
Public 4-year institutions 14
Public 2-year institutions 19
Private 4-year institutions 22
Private 2-year institutions 4
Total 59

Vocational institutions: 168

Statewide coordinating board:
Board of Higher Education
20 West State Street, CN542
Trenton 08625
(609) 292-4310
Edward D. Goldberg, chancellor

Private-college association:
Association of Independent Colleges and Universities in New Jersey
797 Springfield Avenue
P.O. Box 206
Summit 07901
(908) 277-3738
John B. Wilson, president

Institutions censured by the AAUP:
Camden County College,
Rider College

Institution under NCAA sanctions:
Upsala College

FACULTY MEMBERS

Full-time faculty members by rank:
Professor 2,768
Associate professor 2,590
Assistant professor 2,347
Instructor 558
Lecturer 195
No rank 27
Total 8,485

Full-time faculty members with tenure:
Men 3,362
Women 1,321
Total 4,683

Average pay of full-time professors
Public 4-year institutions:
Professor $64,494
Associate professor $48,948
Assistant professor $38,459
Instructor $27,408
No rank $53,082
All $50,329

Public 2-year institutions:
Professor $52,743
Associate professor $45,125
Assistant professor $36,532
Instructor $32,091
No rank $24,050
All $42,030

Private 4-year institutions:
Professor $63,477

NEW JERSEY
Continued

Associate professor $42,446
Assistant professor $34,844
Instructor $26,188
No rank $57,219
All $47,557

STUDENTS

Enrollment:
At public 4-year institutions   137,691
At public 2-year institutions   123,910
At private 4-year institutions   58,672
At private 2-year institutions . 3,674
Undergraduate 276,320
Graduate 41,464
Professional 6,163
American Indian 776
Asian 14,340
Black 33,113
Hispanic 21,642
White 241,666
Foreign 12,410
Total 323,947

Enrollment highlights:
Women 55.1%
Full-time 50.2%
Minority 22.4%
Foreign 3.8%
10-year change in total
  enrollment .... Up 0.7%

Proportion of enrollment made up of minority students:
At public 4-year institutions . 22.7%
At public 2-year institutions . 23.7%
At private 4-year institutions   18.1%
At private 2-year institutions   35.3%

Degrees awarded:
Associate 9,935
Bachelor's 22,859
Master's 7,246
Doctorate 855
Professional 1,763

Residence of new students: State residents made up 86% of all freshmen enrolled in New Jersey; 58% of all New Jersey residents who were freshmen attended college in their home state.

Test scores: Students averaged 891 on the S.A.T., which was taken by an estimated 75% of New Jersey's high-school seniors.

Graduation rates at NCAA Division I institutions:
Fairleigh Dickinson University   39%
Monmouth College 50%
Princeton University 95%
Rider College 58%
Rutgers University
  at New Brunswick 72%
Saint Peter's College 45%
Seton Hall University 60%

MONEY

Average tuition and fees:
At public 4-year institutions . $2,860
At public 2-year institutions . $1,235
At private 4-year institutions $10,281
At private 2-year institutions $5,874

Expenditures:
Public institutions .. $2,165,562,000
Private institutions ... $944,968,000

State funds for higher-education operating expenses: $1,177,880,000
Two-year change: Up 10%

State spending on student aid:
Need-based: $111,762,000
Non–need-based: $7,624,000
Other: $119,000

**Salary of chief executive
of largest public 4-year campus:**
Francis L. Lawrence, Rutgers
  University at New Brunswick:
  $180,000

**Total spending on research and
development by doctorate-granting
universities:** $319,797,000
Sources:
Federal government 42.2%
State and local governments . 14.5%
Industry 5.5%
The institution itself 30.1%
Other 7.7%

**Total federal spending on college-
and university-based research
and development:** $139,264,000
Selected programs:
Department of Health
  and Human Services $67,435,000
National Science
  Foundation $28,775,000
Department of Defense $17,922,000
Department
  of Agriculture $4,552,000
Department of Energy .. $7,939,000

Largest endowment:
Princeton University $2,624,082,000

Top fund raisers:
Princeton University .. $88,288,000
Rutgers University ... $27,600,000
New Jersey Institute
  of Technology $7,225,000

MISCELLANY

■ In 1992 Princeton University established a wildlife-research center in Kenya on a 48,500-acre cattle ranch owned by an alumnus. The unfenced ranch is home to elephants, lions, leopards, baboons, vervet monkeys, zebras, buffalo, gazelles, giraffes, and other animals. Research at the center, which Princeton will operate with four other research institutions, focuses on wildlife management.

■ Students at Monmouth College had an unusual complaint in 1992: They wanted more essays and problem-solving questions on their tests. And faculty members decided that the students had a point. Two-thirds of the Faculty Council voted in favor of a non-binding resolution recommending that professors stop using multiple-choice questions exclusively.

■ Since 1991 the National Football League has used a continuing-education program developed by Fairleigh Dickinson University to prepare its 1,600 players for second careers. Under one option, players take classes at colleges near their teams' stadiums but receive credit toward degrees at the institutions they originally attended. Fairleigh Dickinson created the program in 1985 for the New York Giants.

■ Princeton University is the oldest institution of higher education in New Jersey. It was founded in 1746.

NEW MEXICO

HIGHER education in New Mexico did not benefit from any ground-breaking initiatives in the 1992 legislative session, or more-than-usual attention from Democratic Gov. Bruce D. King. But public universities and colleges in the "Land of Enchantment" did get something that might make educators in other states envious: more money.

While the New Mexico Commission on Higher Education initially rec-

NEW MEXICO
Continued

ommended a 12.6-per-cent increase in spending at the six four-year campuses and 16 community colleges, the state gave the colleges a 4.5-per-cent increase for the 1993 fiscal year, a reflection of the state's relatively flat rate of growth. Meanwhile, educators point out, enrollment at the institutions continues to outpace spending, straining budgets and campus facilities.

Commissioners, who are appointed by the Governor, had hoped that part of the increase could be spent on improving conditions at New Mexico State University's chemistry laboratory, a facility that scientists say is inadequate and possibly dangerous. Officials at the university have been pushing since 1988 for money to renovate and expand various facilities, without success.

In November 1992, voters approved a statewide general-obligation bond issue of $91.7-million, nearly $60-million of which will be used to construct and renovate buildings on college campuses, including the state university's chemistry lab. Educators had crossed their fingers and lobbied extensively to secure passage of the referendum, because voters defeated a request for $27.5-million for campus renovations in 1990.

The University of New Mexico continues to be pushed by legislators to do a better job of recruiting Hispanic faculty members and administrators. The university's enrollment is 22 per cent Hispanic and 3.5 per cent American Indian. But of the full-time and part-time faculty members, 8 per cent are Hispanic. Although that is above the 2-per-cent national average, lawmakers believe that because the state has one of the highest Hispanic populations in America, the university should be doing more.

UNM President Richard E. Peck has said attracting more Hispanic faculty members is a priority, as is expanding the university's programs in Latin American and Southwestern regional studies.

The Commission on Higher Education is the statewide coordinating board for postsecondary education. New Mexico has 11 governing boards for public colleges.

The state has two federally supported colleges for American Indians—the Institute of American Indian and Alaska Native Culture and Arts Development and the Southwestern Indian Polytechnic Institute. The state also has three private, non-profit colleges.

DEMOGRAPHICS

Population: 1,548,000   (Rank: 37)

Age distribution:
Up to 17 .... 29.6%
18 to 24 .... 9.9%
25 to 44 .... 31.9%
45 and older 28.6%

Racial and ethnic distribution:
American Indian 8.9%
Asian 0.9%
Black 2.0%
White 75.6%
Other and unknown 12.6%
Hispanic (may be any race) . 38.2%

Educational attainment of adults (highest level):
9th grade or less 11.4%
Some high school, no diploma 13.5%
High-school diploma 28.7%
Some college, no degree 20.9%
Associate degree 5.0%

Bachelor's degree 12.1%
Graduate or professional
  degree 8.3%

Proportion who speak a language other than English at home: 35.5%

Per-capita personal income: $14,644

Poverty rate:
All 20.6%
Under age 18 .... 27.8%
Age 18 and older 17.6%

New public high-school graduates in:
1992-93 (estimate) 15,400
2001-02 (estimate) 17,710

New GED diploma recipients: 4,161

High-school dropout rate: 11.7%

POLITICAL LEADERSHIP

Governor: Bruce D. King (D), term ends 1995

Governor's higher-education aide:
Chuck Spath, Governor's Office, Capitol Building, Suite 400, Santa Fe 87503; (505) 827-3000

U.S. Senators: Jeff Bingaman (D), term ends 1995; Pete V. Domenici (R), term ends 1997

U.S. Representatives:
1 Democrat, 2 Republicans
Bill Richardson (D), Steven H. Schiff (R), Joe Skeen (R)

Legislature: Senate, 27 Democrats, 15 Republicans; House, 52 Democrats, 18 Republicans

COLLEGES AND UNIVERSITIES

Higher education:
Public 4-year institutions 6
Public 2-year institutions 16
Private 4-year institutions 5
Private 2-year institutions 1
Total 28

Vocational institutions: 43

Statewide coordinating board:
Commission on Higher Education
1068 Cerrillos Road
Santa Fe 87501
(505) 827-7383
Danny K. Earp, deputy executive director

Private-college association:
New Mexico Independent College Association
650 Granada Street
Santa Fe 87501
(505) 986-1199
Robert E. Rhodes, executive director

Institutions censured by the AAUP: None

Institutions under NCAA sanctions: None

FACULTY MEMBERS

Full-time faculty members by rank:
Professor 578
Associate professor 528
Assistant professor 606
Instructor 163
Lecturer 106
No rank 241
Total 2,222

Full-time faculty members with tenure:
Men 852
Women 224
Total 1,076

Average pay of full-time professors
Public 4-year institutions:
Professor $49,035

NEW MEXICO
Continued

Associate professor $38,122
Assistant professor $33,316
Instructor $24,575
No rank $24,898
All $39,437

Public 2-year institutions:
Professor $32,985
Associate professor $31,906
Assistant professor $28,956
Instructor $25,853
No rank $26,923
All $27,768

Private 4-year institutions:
Professor $34,053
Associate professor $29,247
Assistant professor $25,048
Instructor .... n/a
No rank $32,668
All $30,949

STUDENTS

Enrollment:
At public 4-year institutions . 48,013
At public 2-year institutions . 35,486
At private 4-year institutions . 1,917
At private 2-year institutions ... 180
Undergraduate 74,853
Graduate 10,133
Professional 610
American Indian 4,596
Asian 1,125
Black 2,176
Hispanic 23,635
White 52,573
Foreign 1,491
Total 85,596

Enrollment highlights:
Women 55.6%
Full-time 52.8%
Minority 37.5%
Foreign 1.7%
10-year change in total
  enrollment .... Up 46.9%

Proportion of enrollment made up of minority students:
At public 4-year institutions . 33.2%
At public 2-year institutions . 43.6%
At private 4-year institutions 29.4%
At private 2-year institutions 44.7%

Degrees awarded:
Associate 2,455
Bachelor's 5,022
Master's 1,838
Doctorate 223
Professional 179

Residence of new students: State residents made up 84% of all freshmen enrolled in New Mexico; 82% of all New Mexico residents who were freshmen attended college in their home state.

Test scores: Students averaged 20.1 on the A.C.T., which was taken by an estimated 56% of New Mexico's high-school seniors.

Graduation rates at NCAA Division I institutions:
New Mexico State University . 37%
University of New Mexico 27%

MONEY

Average tuition and fees:
At public 4-year institutions . $1,409
At public 2-year institutions .. $536
At private 4-year institutions $8,187
At private 2-year institutions $3,594

Expenditures:
Public institutions $828,157,000
Private institutions $28,022,000

State funds for higher-education operating expenses: $364,895,000

Two-year change: Up 9%

State spending on student aid:
Need-based: $7,888,000
Non–need-based: $3,967,000
Other: $1,986,000

Salary of chief executive of largest public 4-year campus:
Richard E. Peck, University
   of New Mexico: $146,000

Total spending on research and development by doctorate-granting universities: $151,927,000

Sources:
Federal government 56.4%
State and local governments .. 9.7%
Industry 14.2%
The institution itself 12.8%
Other 6.9%

Total federal spending on college- and university-based research and development: $69,397,000

Selected programs:
Department of Health
   and Human Services $11,859,000
National Science
   Foundation $8,914,000
Department of Defense $18,112,000
Department
   of Agriculture $2,383,000
Department of Energy .. $9,985,000

Largest endowment:
University of New Mexico
   and Foundation $68,251,000

Top fund raisers:
University of New
   Mexico $14,347,000
New Mexico State
   University $2,171,000

MISCELLANY

■ St. John's College, whose curriculum focuses on the "great books" of Western culture, announced it would establish the Institute for the Study of Eastern Classics at its Santa Fe campus in 1992. The institute offers an intensive one-year program for graduate students interested in studying the classic texts of India and China.

■ The Los Alamos National Laboratory, one of three national laboratories that the University of California operates for the U.S. Department of Energy, grew out of federal nuclear research in the 1940's that led to the development of the atomic bomb.

■ The University of New Mexico's Archaeology Field School, founded in 1927, is the oldest program of its type in the nation.

■ The oldest institution of higher education in the state is the New Mexico State University main campus, founded in 1888.

NEW YORK

HIGHER education in New York, distinctive for its diversity and sophistication, is a victim of a steady, if not deliberate, retreat by the state.

State officials say that most of the problems are tied to New York's budget difficulties, and that financial support will bounce back when the economy improves.

But leaders in higher education worry that New York is moving away from its strong commitment to its vast

NEW YORK
Continued

public-college sector and to its private colleges, which range from major research institutions like Columbia, Cornell, and New York Universities, to respected religious institutions like the Union and Jewish Theological Seminaries, to colleges of the arts such as Cooper Union and the Juilliard School.

Circumstances in recent years give higher-education leaders and students little comfort.

Known for having developed and sustained two giant public-university systems that together comprise 85 institutions and enroll nearly 600,000 students, New York has spent the last several years slashing the state's share of the budgets for those systems. The cutbacks have led to layoffs, enrollment limits, sharp reductions in academic programs, and, of course, tuition increases.

Long regarded as a national leader in financial aid—both because of the amount it spends and the way its programs are open to graduate students— New York has cut the size of student grants and tightened eligibility, so that fewer middle-class students will get aid.

Spending on another program, which provides direct state aid to private colleges, has also shrunk dramatically. In the late 1980's, New York spent more than $100-million on such aid. For 1992-93, the budget is $39-million.

The loss of the aid has been especially unsettling for small liberal-arts colleges, including Colgate University, Vassar College, and the College of St. Rose.

The state's cutbacks have been devastating to the State University of New York and the City University of New York. Both systems were forced to raise their tuition rates dramatically, but each took steps to try to make those increases as palatable as possible.

At SUNY, Chancellor D. Bruce Johnstone continued to press for authority to charge different rates of tuition at different campuses. He has long contended that the system's four research campuses—in Albany, Binghamton, Buffalo, and Stony Brook— should charge higher tuition than do the 12 comprehensive colleges and 14 specialized and technical colleges.

At CUNY, which had no tuition until 1976 and which still prides itself as the college for the immigrants and working class of New York City, Chancellor W. Ann Reynolds tried to soften the impact of the latest increase with an unusual plan: Full-time students who enrolled before June 1992 will see their tuition go up $300 from $1,850; new students will pay $600 more but are promised that if they earn their baccalaureate degree, they'll get their final semester free, as an incentive to finish college.

The CUNY student body has a substantial number of black, Hispanic, and Caribbean students, many of whom fear the state's commitment to public higher education is weakening at the very time minority students are enrolling in greater numbers.

That issue will soon become a matter for the courts to decide. In March 1992 about 50 students, faculty members, and staff members filed a class-action lawsuit against Gov. Mario M. Cuomo and the state. It accuses New York of giving financial preferences to SUNY because it is "predominantly white." About 64 per cent of CUNY students are members of racial-minority groups; at SUNY the figure is about 13 per cent.

Some CUNY faculty members also said the university's low-income and minority students would suffer under a new set of standards that will require them to take certain college preparatory courses in high school or complete them at CUNY. The requirements will be phased in over 10 years, starting in the fall of 1993.

CUNY's work with New York City on such pressing urban issues as care for AIDS patients and school reform has earned the system some fame. But most of its publicity has centered on controversies and tragedy at one of the university's oldest campuses, City College.

In 1992, City College removed Leonard Jeffries from his chairmanship of the black-studies department, after enduring months of criticism for not responding sooner to complaints that he had made anti-Semitic speeches.

City College has also been criticized for failing to prepare properly for a celebrity basketball game at which nine people were trampled to death in December 1991.

Although their lobbying was not successful in 1992, faculty unions and student groups are well organized and politically active.

Higher education in New York also benefits from the state's role as a center for philanthropy and artistic life. The New York Public Library is based there, as are the Ford, Mellon, and Rockefeller Foundations and the Carnegie Corporation.

Separate boards of trustees govern SUNY and CUNY. Both systems also operate community colleges, which depend on local communities for a share of their budgets, and professional schools.

DEMOGRAPHICS

Population: 18,058,000 (Rank: 2)

Age distribution:
Up to 17 .... 24.2%
18 to 24 .... 10.4%
25 to 44 .... 32.7%
45 and older 32.7%

Racial and ethnic distribution:
American Indian 0.3%
Asian 3.9%
Black 15.9%
White 74.4%
Other and unknown 5.5%
Hispanic (may be any race) . 12.3%

Educational attainment of adults (highest level):
9th grade or less 10.2%
Some high school, no diploma 15.0%
High-school diploma 29.5%
Some college, no degree 15.7%
Associate degree 6.5%
Bachelor's degree 13.2%
Graduate or professional
  degree 9.9%

Proportion who speak a language other than English at home: 23.3%

Per-capita personal income: $22,471

Poverty rate:
All 13.0%
Under age 18 .... 19.1%
Age 18 and older 11.1%

New public high-school graduates in:
1992-93 (estimate) 131,610
2001-02 (estimate) 143,970

New GED diploma recipients: 32,668

High-school dropout rate: 9.9%

NEW YORK
Continued

POLITICAL LEADERSHIP

Governor: Mario M. Cuomo (D), term ends 1995

Governor's higher-education aide: Robert Lowry, State Capitol, Executive Chamber, Room 239, Albany 12224; (518) 486-6475

U.S. Senators: Alfonse M. D'Amato (R), term ends 1999; Daniel Patrick Moynihan (D), term ends 1995

U.S. Representatives:
18 Democrats, 13 Republicans
Gary L. Ackerman (D), Sherwood L. Boehlert (R), Eliot L. Engel (D), Hamilton Fish, Jr. (R), Floyd H. Flake (D), Benjamin A. Gilman (R), Maurice D. Hinchey (D), George J. Hochbrueckner (D), Amo Houghton (R), Peter T. King (R), John J. La-Falce (D), Rick A. Lazio (R), David A. Levy (R), Nita M. Lowey (D), Carolyn B. Maloney (D), Thomas J. Manton (D), John M. McHugh (R), Michael R. McNulty (D), Susan Molinari (R), Jerrold Nadler (D), Major R. Owens (D), Bill Paxon (R), Jack Quinn (R), Charles B. Rangel (D), Charles E. Schumer (D), José E. Serrano (D), Louise M. Slaughter (D), Gerald B. H. Solomon (R), Edolphus Towns (D), Nydia M. Velazquez (D), James T. Walsh (R)

Legislature: Senate, 27 Democrats, 34 Republicans; House, 100 Democrats, 49 Republicans, 1 race undecided

COLLEGES AND UNIVERSITIES

Higher education:
Public 4-year institutions	42
Public 2-year institutions	48
Private 4-year institutions	186
Private 2-year institutions	48
Total	324

Vocational institutions: 312

Statewide coordinating board:
New York State Education Department
Cultural Education Center
Room 5B28
Albany 12230
(518) 474-5851
Donald J. Nolan, deputy commissioner for higher and professional education

Private-college association:
Commission on Independent Colleges and Universities in New York
17 Elk Street
P.O. Box 7289
Albany 12224
(518) 436-4781
C. Mark Lawton, president

Institutions censured by the AAUP:
New York University,
State University of New York,
Yeshiva University

Institution under NCAA sanctions:
Syracuse University

FACULTY MEMBERS

Full-time faculty members by rank:
Professor	12,182
Associate professor	9,859
Assistant professor	8,912
Instructor	1,831
Lecturer	1,193
No rank	482
Total	34,459

Full-time faculty members with tenure:
Men	16,051

Women 5,517
Total 21,568

Average pay of full-time professors
Public 4-year institutions:
Professor $64,593
Associate professor $49,042
Assistant professor $38,861
Instructor $30,965
No rank .... n/a
All $50,914

Public 2-year institutions:
Professor $53,459
Associate professor $43,390
Assistant professor $35,975
Instructor $28,581
No rank .... n/a
All $43,373

Private 4-year institutions:
Professor $61,185
Associate professor $43,464
Assistant professor $35,700
Instructor $26,860
No rank $33,066
All $46,120

STUDENTS

Enrollment:
At public 4-year institutions   359,381
At public 2-year institutions   248,392
At private 4-year institutions   399,282
At private 2-year institutions   28,268
Undergraduate 842,045
Graduate 167,024
Professional 26,254
American Indian 3,882
Asian 48,965
Black 111,845
Hispanic 74,635
White 748,696
Foreign 47,300
Total 1,035,323

Enrollment highlights:
Women 55.8%
Full-time 62.3%

Minority 24.2%
Foreign 4.6%
10-year change in total
 enrollment .... Up 4.3%

Proportion of enrollment made up of minority students:
At public 4-year institutions . 30.0%
At public 2-year institutions . 21.8%
At private 4-year institutions 19.2%
At private 2-year institutions 41.5%

Degrees awarded:
Associate 48,814
Bachelor's 89,067
Master's 37,150
Doctorate 3,805
Professional 7,145

Residence of new students: State residents made up 64% of all freshmen enrolled in New York; 80% of all New York residents who were freshmen attended college in their home state.

Test scores: Students averaged 882 on the S.A.T., which was taken by an estimated 75% of New York's high-school seniors.

Graduation rates at NCAA Division I institutions:
Canisius College 56%
City University of New York
 Brooklyn College 25%
Colgate University 87%
Columbia University 97%
Cornell University 87%
Fordham University 73%
Hofstra University 56%
Iona College 61%
Long Island University
 Brooklyn Center 28%
Manhattan College 70%
Marist College 61%
Niagara University 57%
Saint Bonaventure University . 70%
Saint Francis College 29%

NEW YORK
Continued

Saint John's University 63%
Siena College 79%
State University of New York
  at Buffalo 50%
Syracuse University 62%
U.S. Military Academy 78%
Wagner College 32%

MONEY

Average tuition and fees:
At public 4-year institutions . $1,587
At public 2-year institutions . $1,419
At private 4-year institutions $10,340
At private 2-year institutions $5,926

Expenditures:
Public institutions .. $5,058,750,000
Private institutions . $7,640,442,000

State funds for higher-education operating expenses: $2,689,086,000
Two-year change: Down 5%

State spending on student aid:
Need-based: $449,800,000
Non–need-based: $13,358,000
Other: $385,000

Salary of chief executive of largest public 4-year campus:
William R. Greiner, State University of New York at Buffalo: $133,775

Total spending on research and development by doctorate-granting universities: $1,410,700,000
Sources:
Federal government 65.0%
State and local governments .. 5.4%
Industry 5.5%
The institution itself 12.6%
Other 11.5%

Total federal spending on college- and university-based research and development: $851,970,000
Selected programs:
Department of Health
  and Human Services $560,894,000
National Science
  Foundation $139,658,000
Department of Defense $56,306,000
Department
  of Agriculture $10,908,000
Department of Energy . $44,829,000

Largest endowment:
Columbia University $1,525,904,000

Top fund raisers:
Cornell University ... $177,075,000
Columbia University . $128,242,000
New York University .. $87,555,000

MISCELLANY

■ A windmill installed at Hamilton College in 1992 is generating heat and light for one residence hall. The 120-foot-tall structure, a gift from the class of 1991, is expected to cut Hamilton's electricity bill by about $4,000 a year.

■ The trustees of Hartwick College changed the official seal in 1992 after some charged that the old seal, which showed the founder of Hartwick Seminary resting one hand on the shoulder of an Indian while handing him a book, was historically inaccurate and demeaning to American Indians. The college now uses the original seal of the seminary, which closed in 1948. It depicts the Sower from biblical parables.

■ Mary Clark Stuart, the new president of the College of Mount Saint Vincent, is the first lay president of the institution, which was founded in

1910 by the Sisters of Charity of New York.

■ The oldest higher-education institution in New York is Columbia University, founded in 1754.

NORTH CAROLINA

North Carolina's quickly diversifying economy has helped mitigate the impact of the recession on the state's public colleges. The economic growth has been fueled in part by the "Research Triangle," comprising major universities whose research and expertise have helped attract high-technology companies to the state. In turn, the research park has brought the University of North Carolina system attention from around the country for the partnership between industry and education.

In 1992-93, the UNC system also received a boost from the General Assembly, which passed a budget of over $1-billion for the colleges, about $43-million higher than the 1991-92 appropriation.

Still, UNC found itself in need of additional revenue and raised tuition for the 1992-93 academic year. Students attending four-year colleges paid 6 per cent more than they did in 1991-92. At community colleges, students paid 15 per cent more in 1992-93.

With the election in November 1992 of Democrat Jim Hunt as Governor, observers expected more attention to education. Mr. Hunt, who was Governor from 1977 through 1985, has said he wants to make a long-term financial commitment to community colleges, which have complained about not receiving enough state support. He also proposed providing job-training vouchers that would allow students to attend, tuition-free, the first and last quarters of any vocational program offered by a two-year college.

What colleges really need, educators say, are new buildings. The system has not started a state-financed building since 1988. Legislators had proposed a statewide referendum in the fall of 1992 on a $300-million bond issue for construction projects. But they decided that, given the recession, it would be best to delay the vote until 1993, although North Carolina has one of the lowest debt loads in the country.

The lion's share of the bond issue would have gone to the University of North Carolina at Chapel Hill, which requested some $44-million for buildings to house the schools of business administration and social work, an addition to the School of Dentistry, and other projects.

Some legislators said the bond issue also would have helped North Carolina's five public black colleges, where capital improvements have often lagged behind those at predominantly white institutions. Included in the request for bond money were projects at North Carolina A&T State University, which sought $7.7-million for a technology building and $4.6-million to renovate the library.

A feud erupted at Appalachian State University, between students and faculty members on the one hand and the administration on the other, over its request for $9.5-million in bond money for a student center and arena. Opponents of the center complained that the university was placing athletic needs over academic concerns. Instead, they wanted the money to finance a new science building. The fracas culminated when six stu-

NORTH CAROLINA
Continued

dents chained themselves to a water fountain in the chancellor's office in May 1992. The administration later dropped its plan to request bond money for the center.

Community-college officials hope that Governor-elect Hunt's focus on long-term financial support of the colleges will help them raise faculty salaries.

A state commission, warning that faculty pay ranked among the nation's lowest, urged three years ago that $135-million in new money be invested in the 58-college system. Legislators agreed that conditions should be improved, but have since given the two-year colleges only $20-million toward the goal.

The effect on North Carolina of a landmark U.S. Supreme Court ruling in June 1992—that Mississippi had not done enough to desegregate its public colleges and universities—is unclear. Some college officials maintain the Court ruling will have little impact because the state already is taking steps to improve its public black institutions.

Black students ended a year-long protest at Chapel Hill in October 1992, when university officials agreed to seek money to build a black cultural center. The controversy gained attention in 1992 when members of the football team spoke out on the issue and staged rallies.

North Carolina has a strong tradition of private higher education, including research universities such as Duke and Wake Forest Universities and liberal-arts institutions such as Davidson and Salem Colleges and Johnson C. Smith University.

DEMOGRAPHICS

Population: 6,737,000   (Rank: 10)

Age distribution:
Up to 17 .... 24.4%
18 to 24 .... 11.5%
25 to 44 .... 32.5%
45 and older 31.6%

Racial and ethnic distribution:
American Indian 1.2%
Asian 0.8%
Black 22.0%
White 75.6%
Other and unknown 0.5%
Hispanic (may be any race) .. 1.2%

Educational attainment of adults (highest level):
9th grade or less 12.7%
Some high school, no diploma 17.3%
High-school diploma 29.0%
Some college, no degree 16.8%
Associate degree 6.8%
Bachelor's degree 12.0%
Graduate or professional
   degree 5.4%

Proportion who speak a language other than English at home: 3.9%

Per-capita personal income: $16,853

Poverty rate:
All 13.0%
Under age 18 .... 17.2%
Age 18 and older 11.6%

New public high-school graduates in:
1992-93 (estimate) 60,720
2001-02 (estimate) 63,790

New GED diploma recipients: 13,331

High-school dropout rate: 12.5%

POLITICAL LEADERSHIP

Governor: Jim Hunt (D), term ends 1997

Governor's higher-education aide: n/a

U.S. Senators: Lauch Faircloth (R), term ends 1999; Jesse Helms (R), term ends 1997

U.S. Representatives:
8 Democrats, 4 Republicans
Eva Clayton (D), Cass Ballenger (R), Howard Coble (R), W.G. (Bill) Hefner (D), H. Martin Lancaster (D), J. Alex McMillan (R), Stephen L. Neal (D), David Price (D), Charlie Rose (D), Charles H. Taylor (R), Tim Valentine (D), Melvin Watt (D)

General Assembly: Senate, 39 Democrats, 11 Republicans; House, 78 Democrats, 42 Republicans

COLLEGES AND UNIVERSITIES

Higher education:
Public 4-year institutions 16
Public 2-year institutions 58
Private 4-year institutions 37
Private 2-year institutions 14
Total 125

Vocational institutions: 76

Statewide coordinating boards:
University of North Carolina
General Administration
P.O. Box 2688
Chapel Hill 27515
(919) 962-6981
C. D. Spangler, Jr., president

State Department of Community Colleges
200 West Jones Street
Raleigh 27603
(919) 733-7051
Robert W. Scott, president

Private-college association:
North Carolina Association of Independent Colleges and Universities
879A Washington Street
Raleigh 27605
(919) 832-5817
A. Hope Williams, president

Institutions censured by the AAUP:
Chowan College, Southeastern Baptist Theological Seminary, Wingate College

Institutions under NCAA sanctions:
None

FACULTY MEMBERS

Full-time faculty members by rank:
Professor 2,748
Associate professor 2,300
Assistant professor 2,376
Instructor 442
Lecturer 528
No rank 1,281
Total 9,675

Full-time faculty members with tenure:
Men 3,368
Women 985
Total 4,353

Average pay of full-time professors
Public 4-year institutions:
Professor $56,374
Associate professor $42,659
Assistant professor $36,175
Instructor $34,642
No rank .... n/a
All $43,035
Public 2-year institutions:
Professor .... n/a

NORTH CAROLINA
Continued

Associate professor .... n/a
Assistant professor .... n/a
Instructor .... n/a
No rank $26,141
All $26,141

Private 4-year institutions:
Professor $46,812
Associate professor $35,261
Assistant professor $28,874
Instructor $23,232
No rank $24,448
All $35,798

STUDENTS

Enrollment:
At public 4-year institutions 148,698
At public 2-year institutions 136,559
At private 4-year institutions 61,522
At private 2-year institutions . 5,211
Undergraduate 316,240
Hispanic 2,528
White 273,874
Foreign 4,852
Total 351,990

Enrollment highlights:
Women 56.0%
Full-time 63.4%
Minority 21.1%
Foreign 1.4%
10-year change in total
  enrollment .... Up 22.4%

Proportion of enrollment made up of minority students:
At public 4-year institutions . 21.4%
At public 2-year institutions . 20.1%
At private 4-year institutions 21.2%
At private 2-year institutions 35.1%

Degrees awarded:
Associate 10,647
Bachelor's 27,288
Master's 6,015
Doctorate 861
Professional 1,597

Residence of new students: State residents made up 81% of all freshmen enrolled in North Carolina; 94% of all North Carolina residents who were freshmen attended college in their home state.

Test scores: Students averaged 855 on the S.A.T., which was taken by an estimated 57% of North Carolina's high-school seniors.

Graduation rates at NCAA Division I institutions:
Appalachian State University .. 53%
Campbell University 42%
Davidson College 89%
Duke University 92%
East Carolina University 45%
North Carolina A&T State
  University 40%
North Carolina State University 59%
University of North Carolina
  at Asheville 33%
University of North Carolina
  at Chapel Hill 76%
University of North Carolina
  at Charlotte 50%
University of North Carolina
  at Greensboro 50%
University of North Carolina
  at Wilmington 42%
Wake Forest University 81%
Western Carolina University .. 41%

MONEY

Average tuition and fees:
At public 4-year institutions . $1,112
At public 2-year institutions .. $334
At private 4-year institutions $7,826
At private 2-year institutions $4,964

Expenditures:
Public institutions .. $2,420,825,000
Private institutions . $1,599,803,000

State funds for higher-education operating expenses: $1,541,926,000

Two-year change: Up 4%

State spending on student aid:
Need-based: $3,919,000
Non–need-based: $24,218,000
Other: $37,188,000

Salary of chief executive of largest public 4-year campus:
Larry K. Monteith, North Carolina State University: $124,160

Total spending on research and development by doctorate-granting universities: $441,860,000
Sources:
Federal government 62.6%
State and local governments . 14.7%
Industry 9.8%
The institution itself 9.2%
Other 3.6%

Total federal spending on college- and university-based research and development: $305,255,000

Selected programs:
Department of Health
  and Human Services $213,230,000
National Science
  Foundation $32,861,000
Department of Defense $18,325,000
Department
  of Agriculture $12,150,000
Department of Energy .. $6,958,000

Largest endowment:
Duke University $527,635,000

Top fund raisers:
Duke University $113,693,000

University of North Carolina
  at Chapel Hill $53,050,000
North Carolina State
  University $29,532,000

MISCELLANY

■ Duke University officials in April 1992 announced the first birth in the Western hemisphere of a rare primate known as the aye-aye. Duke scientists say the birth represents an important step in saving the endangered aye-aye and in learning how to build a captive population that could be used to repopulate its native Madagascar.

■ Librarians at the University of North Carolina at Chapel Hill and Duke and North Carolina State Universities are collaborating on the creation of a major collection of volumes on life in the South. The effort, called Documenting the Contemporary South, will include materials on Southern folklore, literature, and industries.

■ The Burlington Textiles Library at North Carolina State University has among its holdings a collection of 472 unusual socks donated by the owner of a textile-machinery company.

■ The oldest institution of higher education in North Carolina is Salem College, a Moravian institution founded in 1772.

NORTH DAKOTA

To cut costs, the North Dakota University System in 1992 gave each of its 11 public colleges and universities responsibility for ad-

NORTH DAKOTA
Continued

ministering selected statewide programs.

Each campus will direct programs in which it is already strong. The University of North Dakota, for example, will coordinate interactive television and library networks for all campuses. North Dakota State University will lead economic-development programs for all colleges.

The system's chancellor, Douglas Treadway, said the move would streamline management and keep the system office from becoming too centralized.

It came none too soon. Outgoing Gov. George A. Sinner announced in July 1992 that state agencies must cut their budgets by 10 per cent for the 1993-95 biennium. Each campus will decide where to make cuts, a process that officials say will be hard because the system is already stretched thin from years of no budget growth.

The cuts will end a brief period of prosperity for higher education. The state's appropriation for its colleges and universities jumped by 13 per cent for the 1991-93 biennium, enabling the system to freeze tuition at all institutions for the fall of 1992. But tuition increases may be necessary in 1993-94 to offset the newest cuts.

The new Governor, Edward Schafer, a Republican, says he opposes raising taxes to help higher education.

Because North Dakota is large and sparsely populated, higher-education officials are always looking for ways to increase people's access to a college education. They have been building an interactive-video network to broadcast courses around the state. Now that all 11 public campuses are linked, the officials are discussing whether to include public schools and the community colleges that serve Indian tribes.

The North Dakota Board of Higher Education already showed its innovative bent in 1990 when it became the first in the country to adopt the "Total Quality Management" business philosophy for the entire university system.

The chancellor and higher-education board govern the North Dakota University System, which includes six four-year universities and five two-year campuses. The state also has five community colleges controlled by Indian tribes.

DEMOGRAPHICS

Population: 635,000   (Rank: 47)

Age distribution:
Up to 17 .... 27.2%
18 to 24 .... 10.6%
25 to 44 .... 30.4%
45 and older 31.5%

Racial and ethnic distribution:
American Indian 4.1%
Asian 0.5%
Black 0.6%
White 94.6%
Other and unknown 0.3%
Hispanic (may be any race) .. 0.7%

Educational attainment of adults (highest level):
9th grade or less 15.0%
Some high school, no diploma 8.3%
High-school diploma 28.0%
Some college, no degree 20.5%
Associate degree 10.0%
Bachelor's degree 13.5%
Graduate or professional
  degree 4.5%

Proportion who speak a language other than English at home: 7.9%

Per-capita personal income: $15,605

Poverty rate:
All 14.4%
Under age 18 .... 17.1%
Age 18 and older 13.3%

New public high-school graduates in:
1992-93 (estimate) 7,470
2001-02 (estimate) 7,520

New GED diploma recipients: 858

High-school dropout rate: 4.6%

POLITICAL LEADERSHIP

Governor: Edward Schafer (R), term ends 1996

Governor's higher-education aide: n/a

U.S. Senators: Jocelyn Burdick (D), term ends 1993; Byron L. Dorgan, term ends 1999

U.S. Representative:
1 Democrat
Earl Pomeroy (D)

Legislative Assembly: Senate, 25 Democrats, 24 Republicans; House, 33 Democrats, 65 Republicans

COLLEGES AND UNIVERSITIES

Higher education:
Public 4-year institutions 6
Public 2-year institutions 9
Private 4-year institutions 4
Private 2-year institutions 1
Total 20

Vocational institutions: 20

Statewide coordinating board:
North Dakota University System
600 East Boulevard Avenue
State Capitol Building, 10th Floor
Bismarck 58505
(701) 224-2960
Douglas Treadway, chancellor

Private-college association:
North Dakota Independent College Fund
Box 6082
Jamestown College
Jamestown 58401
(701) 252-3467
Robert L. Richardson, executive director

Institutions censured by the AAUP:
None

Institutions under NCAA sanctions:
None

FACULTY MEMBERS

Full-time faculty members by rank:
Professor 263
Associate professor 311
Assistant professor 416
Instructor 155
Lecturer 40
No rank 196
Total 1,381

Full-time faculty members with tenure:
Men 533
Women 146
Total 679

Average pay of full-time professors
Public 4-year institutions:
Professor $42,931
Associate professor $35,782
Assistant professor $30,964
Instructor $26,512

NORTH DAKOTA
Continued

No rank .... n/a
All $34,391

Public 2-year institutions:
Professor .... n/a
Associate professor $32,835
Assistant professor $28,296
Instructor $27,456
No rank $29,323
All $29,438

Private 4-year institutions:
Professor $34,504
Associate professor $29,515
Assistant professor $26,460
Instructor $20,942
No rank $17,273
All $26,250

STUDENTS

Enrollment:
At public 4-year institutions . 27,277
At public 2-year institutions .. 7,413
At private 4-year institutions . 2,980
At private 2-year institutions .. 208
Undergraduate 35,214
Graduate 2,169
Professional 495
American Indian 1,616
Asian 285
Black 246
Hispanic 195
White 34,380
Foreign 1,156
Total 37,878

Enrollment highlights:
Women 49.4%
Full-time 79.8%
Minority 6.4%
Foreign 3.1%
10-year change in total
 enrollment .... Up 11.2%

Proportion of enrollment made up of minority students:
At public 4-year institutions .. 3.5%
At public 2-year institutions . 14.2%
At private 4-year institutions . 5.5%
At private 2-year institutions 100.0%

Degrees awarded:
Associate 1,875
Bachelor's 4,202
Master's 620
Doctorate 71
Professional 109

Residence of new students: State residents made up 71% of all freshmen enrolled in North Dakota; 84% of all North Dakota residents who were freshmen attended college in their home state.

Test scores: Students averaged 20.7 on the A.C.T., which was taken by an estimated 75% of North Dakota's high-school seniors.

Graduation rates at NCAA Division I institutions: n/a

MONEY

Average tuition and fees:
At public 4-year institutions . $1,930
At public 2-year institutions . $1,584
At private 4-year institutions $5,389
At private 2-year institutions ... n/a

Expenditures:
Public institutions $357,832,000
Private institutions $25,646,000

State funds for higher-education operating expenses: $145,535,000
Two-year change: Up 12%

State spending on student aid:
Need-based: $1,600,000

Non–need-based: $324,000
Other: None

Salary of chief executive of largest public 4-year campus:
Kendall Baker, University
  of North Dakota: $115,000

Total spending on research and development by doctorate-granting universities: $29,966,000
Sources:
Federal government 69.5%
State and local governments .. 3.5%
Industry 9.5%
The institution itself 13.4%
Other 4.1%

Total federal spending on college- and university-based research and development: $22,429,000
Selected programs:
Department of Health
  and Human Services ... $847,000
National Science
  Foundation $1,124,000
Department of Defense ... $550,000
Department
  of Agriculture $5,830,000
Department of Energy .. $8,819,000

Largest endowment:
University of North Dakota
  Foundation $19,144,000

Top fund raiser:
Jamestown College $1,357,000

MISCELLANY

■ More than 15,000 musical arrangements used on the Lawrence Welk television shows have been donated to North Dakota State University, along with the late band leader's office furniture, photographs, scrapbooks, and other memorabilia. University officials plan to exhibit the materials in the library and perhaps feature the music in concerts.

■ Since 1970, Bismarck State College has offered an electrical-lineworkers program. The three-semester certificate program focuses on electrical theory, safe work procedures, and climbing skills. The college leases a 20-acre tract where students set up underground electrical systems, put up power lines and poles, and learn to operate a substation.

■ Five of North Dakota's two-year colleges are controlled by Indian Tribes—Fort Berthold, Little Hoop, Standing Rock, and Turtle Mountain Community Colleges, and United Tribes Technical College.

■ The oldest institution of higher education in North Dakota is the University of North Dakota in Grand Forks, founded in 1883.

OHIO

THOSE who believe student activism is dead should have visited Ohio in academic 1991-92.

Thousands of students, from Bowling Green State University to Miami University, converged twice on the State House in Columbus, to blast Republican Gov. George V. Voinovich's threats to cut millions from higher-education budgets. Those demonstrations were supplemented by rallies on campuses across the state.

Although the Governor may have heard the students' slogans, the state's $520-million deficit spoke to him louder. Mr. Voinovich ordered a $316-million reduction in total spending in the second year of Ohio's bien-

OHIO
Continued

nial budget, forcing colleges to absorb $170-million in cuts from the $1.5-billion higher-education budget for fiscal year 1993. That was on top of reductions totaling $102-million that public colleges sustained in two previous rounds of cuts.

In July 1992 the Ohio Board of Regents, the statewide coordinating agency, allowed public colleges to raise tuition by 9 per cent or $225, whichever would be greater. The Ohio State University, the largest public system, with some 50,000 students, took the biggest hit, losing $45-million. It raised tuition by $231 a year.

Despite its problems, Ohio has managed to keep student-aid programs above the budget-cutting fray. However, educators will not be able to open the state's need-based assistance program to part-time students, as they had hoped to do. Those funds were used to make up for losses in state support to universities.

Mr. Voinovich has degrees from both Ohio University and Ohio State, but he does not appear to be fond of how the state's colleges are operating. The Governor and legislators have been pushing public colleges to conduct their business more efficiently. To that end, the regents established a "Managing for the Future Task Force" in 1991 to identify areas of possible cost savings.

In a report in July 1992, the group recommended wide-ranging changes in higher education, including adopting systemwide goals, fostering partnerships between colleges, and removing tuition caps. The report also suggested that the Board of Regents be given more power to eliminate duplicate programs and establish faculty-workload policies and performance evaluations to reward good teaching. Some recommendations, including a suggestion that technical colleges and university branch campuses in the same locations be consolidated and converted to community colleges, will require legislative action.

While money commands much attention in Ohio, the predicament of 18 community-college presidents, investigated for making illegal campaign contributions through a two-year-college association, is still making news. Most of the presidents have been offered the chance to plead guilty to the least severe charges and have their guilty pleas expunged from their records under a "diversion program" for first-time offenders. But four former and current presidents, and the former executive director of the Ohio Technical and Community College Association, are going to trial on charges of theft and tampering with records.

They deny wrongdoing, as do the other presidents, who say they accepted the diversion program to avoid lengthy legal battles.

In Ohio's decentralized system, the public colleges, many of which maintain branch campuses, have their own governing boards.

The state's higher-education mix also includes many well-known private institutions. Among them are Oberlin and Kenyon Colleges, the College of Wooster, and Case Western Reserve University.

DEMOGRAPHICS

Population: 10,939,000   (Rank: 7)

Age distribution:
Up to 17 .... 25.8%

18 to 24 .... 10.3%
25 to 44 .... 31.6%
45 and older 32.3%

Racial and ethnic distribution:
American Indian 0.2%
Asian 0.8%
Black 10.6%
White 87.8%
Other and unknown 0.5%
Hispanic (may be any race) .. 1.3%

Educational attainment of adults (highest level):
9th grade or less 7.9%
Some high school, no diploma 16.4%
High-school diploma 36.3%
Some college, no degree 17.0%
Associate degree 5.3%
Bachelor's degree 11.1%
Graduate or professional
  degree 5.9%

Proportion who speak a language other than English at home: 5.4%

Per-capita personal income: $17,770

Poverty rate:
All 12.5%
Under age 18 .... 17.8%
Age 18 and older 10.7%

New public high-school graduates in:
1992-93 (estimate) 107,060
2001-02 (estimate) 111,700

New GED diploma recipients: 19,969

High-school dropout rate: 8.9%

POLITICAL LEADERSHIP

Governor: George V. Voinovich (R), term ends 1995

Governor's higher-education aide:
Tally Krum, 77 South High Street, 30th Floor, Columbus 43266; (614) 644-0868

U.S. Senators: John Glenn (D), term ends 1999; Howard M. Metzenbaum (D), term ends 1995

U.S. Representatives:
10 Democrats, 9 Republicans
Douglas Applegate (D), John A. Boehner (R), Sherrod Brown (D), Eric D. Fingerhut (D), Paul E. Gillmor (R), Bill Gradison (R), Tony P. Hall (D), David L. Hobson (R), Martin R. Hoke (R), David Mann (D), Marcy Kaptur (D), John R. Kasich (R), Michael G. Oxley (R), Deborah Pryce (R), Ralph Regula (R), Tom Sawyer (D), Louis Stokes (D), Ted Strickland (D), James A. Traficant, Jr. (D)

General Assembly: Senate, 13 Democrats, 20 Republicans; House, 53 Democrats, 46 Republicans

COLLEGES AND UNIVERSITIES

Higher education:
Public 4-year institutions 25
Public 2-year institutions 36
Private 4-year institutions 65
Private 2-year institutions 28
Total 154

Vocational institutions: 312

Statewide coordinating board:
Ohio Board of Regents
30 East Broad Street
3600 State Office Tower
Columbus 43266
(614) 466-6000
Elaine H. Hairston, chancellor

Private-college association:
Association of Independent Colleges and Universities of Ohio
17 South High Street, Suite 1020

OHIO
Continued

Columbus 43215
(614) 228-2196
Larry H. Christman, president

Institutions censured by the AAUP:
None

Institution under NCAA sanctions:
Miami University

FACULTY MEMBERS

Full-time faculty members by rank:
Professor	4,724
Associate professor	4,620
Assistant professor	4,448
Instructor	1,096
Lecturer	89
No rank	592
Total	15,569

Full-time faculty members with tenure:
Men	7,525
Women	2,098
Total	9,623

Average pay of full-time professors

Public 4-year institutions:
Professor	$60,661
Associate professor	$45,099
Assistant professor	$36,934
Instructor	$27,936
No rank	n/a
All	$47,142

Public 2-year institutions:
Professor	$43,576
Associate professor	$38,797
Assistant professor	$32,823
Instructor	$27,431
No rank	$33,048
All	$34,951

Private 4-year institutions:
Professor	$47,816
Associate professor	$35,908
Assistant professor	$30,450
Instructor	$23,416
No rank	$22,955
All	$36,832

STUDENTS

Enrollment:
At public 4-year institutions	288,809
At public 2-year institutions	136,787
At private 4-year institutions	111,493
At private 2-year institutions	17,698
Undergraduate	480,616
Graduate	62,155
Professional	12,016
American Indian	1,422
Asian	7,354
Black	45,237
Hispanic	5,466
White	481,358
Foreign	13,950
Total	554,787

Enrollment highlights:
Women	53.2%
Full-time	61.0%
Minority	11.0%
Foreign	2.5%
10-year change in total enrollment	Up 13.4%

Proportion of enrollment made up of minority students:
At public 4-year institutions	10.0%
At public 2-year institutions	11.8%
At private 4-year institutions	11.1%
At private 2-year institutions	19.7%

Degrees awarded:
Associate	17,547
Bachelor's	47,017
Master's	13,051
Doctorate	1,696
Professional	3,071

Residence of new students: State residents made up 86% of all freshmen enrolled in Ohio; 87% of all Ohio residents who were freshmen attended college in their home state.

Test scores: Students averaged 20.9 on the A.C.T., which was taken by an estimated 54% of Ohio's high-school seniors.

Graduation rates at NCAA Division I institutions:
Bowling Green State University 54%
Cleveland State University 35%
Kent State University 41%
Miami University 75%
Ohio State University 53%
Ohio University 53%
University of Akron 42%
University of Cincinnati 45%
University of Dayton 70%
University of Toledo 37%
Wright State University 29%
Xavier University 62%
Youngstown State University .. 37%

MONEY

Average tuition and fees:
At public 4-year institutions . $2,622
At public 2-year institutions . $1,768
At private 4-year institutions $8,729
At private 2-year institutions $6,093

Expenditures:
Public institutions .. $3,726,135,000
Private institutions . $1,402,876,000

State funds for higher-education operating expenses: $1,376,490,000

Two-year change: Down 7%

State spending on student aid:
Need-based: $61,000,000
Non–need-based: $24,668,000
Other: None

Salary of chief executive of largest public 4-year campus:
E. Gordon Gee, Ohio State University main campus: $160,476

Total spending on research and development by doctorate-granting universities: $457,189,000
Sources:
Federal government 57.0%
State and local governments . 10.1%
Industry 8.2%
The institution itself 13.5%
Other 11.2%

Total federal spending on college- and university-based research and development: $252,157,000

Selected programs:
Department of Health
  and Human Services $134,894,000
National Science
  Foundation $30,580,000
Department of Defense $36,439,000
Department
  of Agriculture $8,112,000
Department of Energy .. $5,772,000

Largest endowment:
Case Western Reserve
  University $442,722,000

Top fund raisers:
Ohio State University . $74,296,000
Case Western Reserve
  University $49,771,000
University of Cincinnati $30,457,000

MISCELLANY

■ The University of Toledo received $450,000 in 1992 to endow a visiting professorship in Catholic thought. It is believed to be the first public university to endow a faculty position in Roman Catholic studies.

■ Wilberforce University, founded in 1856, was the first co-educational institution for blacks.

■ Case Western Reserve University operates the Cleveland Free-Net, the

OHIO
Continued

nation's first public computer system. Established in 1986, the system has data bases in more than 350 areas, including arts, education, and health. It provides, free of charge, electronic mail, discussion groups, and schedules of community events, among other things. Its 88 telephone lines handle 6,500 calls a day.

■ The oldest higher-education institution in the state is Ohio University, founded in 1804.

OKLAHOMA

In Oklahoma, even the people who run the colleges go to class. Since 1991 all appointees to public-college governing boards and the state Board of Regents have been required by law to complete a mini-course on financial and management issues that affect higher education.

The Regents Education Program reflects an emphasis on higher standards that Oklahoma higher-education officials have been pushing in recent years. That push is also evident in such programs as the Board of Regents' Academic Scholars Program for top high-school graduates who attend college in the state and in the tougher admissions standards now going into effect at four-year institutions.

The campaign sometimes runs afoul of the state's populist traditions. The idea of tougher admissions requirements alarmed some legislators, who feared families of high-school graduates would be angry if they could not get into a university because they were not academically prepared.

But those concerns are expected to shrink as elementary and secondary schools start putting into place many of the new programs authorized under a massive public-school reform law that makes more college-preparatory classes available in secondary schools.

Debates over tuition policy, however, continue to flare. The Board of Regents has been trying to raise tuition so that it covers a greater share of students' education costs, but the notion is still unpopular with students and legislators.

Political figures credit the Board of Regents, the statewide governing board for higher education, and Chancellor Hans Brisch with providing some badly needed polish to higher education's image. In the late 1980's, athletics scandals and stories about questionable spending by university-related foundations dominated most of the higher-education news.

Higher-education leaders say they are grateful for the support they have received from the Legislature and from Gov. David Walters, a Democrat. But they're not satisfied.

The colleges say they need more than $1-billion for capital expenditures. For the past two years higher-education leaders have been lobbying for $200- to $300-million in state financing to begin making renovations and improvements. It had been nearly 25 years since the public colleges got a big infusion of money for such work.

The colleges got some satisfaction in November 1992, when voters approved a $350-million facilities bond issue that included $258-million for higher education.

While the prestige of the Board of Regents has grown in the last five years, the state's 17 individually governed public colleges and universities still remain politically influential, particularly with lawmakers from their regions.

Politics even come into play in regions without their own public university, as evidenced by a continuing debate over who should run the University Center at Tulsa, at which four institutions offer courses. The regents now control it, but various legislative proposals have called for making the center independent or placing it under Oklahoma State University or the University of Oklahoma.

Oklahoma's best-known private institution, Oral Roberts University, is also in Tulsa.

DEMOGRAPHICS

Population: 3,175,000 (Rank: 28)

Age distribution:
Up to 17 .... 26.6%
18 to 24 .... 10.3%
25 to 44 .... 30.6%
45 and older 32.5%

Racial and ethnic distribution:
American Indian 8.0%
Asian 1.1%
Black 7.4%
White 82.1%
Other and unknown 1.3%
Hispanic (may be any race) .. 2.7%

Educational attainment of adults (highest level):
9th grade or less 9.8%
Some high school, no diploma 15.6%
High-school diploma 30.5%
Some college, no degree 21.3%
Associate degree 5.0%
Bachelor's degree 11.8%
Graduate or professional
    degree 6.0%

Proportion who speak a language other than English at home: 5.0%

Per-capita personal income: $15,541

Poverty rate:
All 16.7%
Under age 18 .... 21.7%
Age 18 and older 14.9%

New public high-school graduates in:
1992-93 (estimate) 30,300
2001-02 (estimate) 33,360

New GED diploma recipients: 6,293

High-school dropout rate: 10.4%

POLITICAL LEADERSHIP

Governor: David Walters (D), term ends 1995

Governor's higher-education aide:
Sandy Garrett, 2500 North Lincoln Boulevard, Suite 121, Oklahoma City 73105; (405) 521-4886

U.S. Senators: David L. Boren (D), term ends 1997; Don Nickles (R), term ends 1999

U.S. Representatives:
4 Democrats, 2 Republicans
Bill Brewster (D), Glenn English (D), James M. Inhofe (R), Ernest Jim Istook (R), Dave McCurdy (D), Mike Synar (D)

Legislature: Senate, 37 Democrats, 11 Republicans; House, 69 Democrats, 32 Republicans

COLLEGES AND UNIVERSITIES

Higher education:
Public 4-year institutions 14
Public 2-year institutions 15

OKLAHOMA
Continued

Private 4-year institutions 13
Private 2-year institutions 6
Total 48

Vocational institutions: 86

Statewide coordinating board:
Oklahoma State Regents
 for Higher Education
500 Education Building
State Capitol Complex
Oklahoma City 73105
(405) 524-9100
Hans Brisch, chancellor

Private-college association:
Oklahoma Association of
 Independent Colleges and
 Universities
114 East Sheridan, Suite 101
Oklahoma City 73104
(405) 235-0587
position of president vacant

Institutions censured by the AAUP:
Southern Nazarene University,
University of Central Oklahoma

Institutions under NCAA sanctions:
Oklahoma State University,
University of Tulsa

FACULTY MEMBERS

Full-time faculty members by rank:
Professor 1,012
Associate professor 933
Assistant professor 1,155
Instructor 404
Lecturer 44
No rank 912
Total 4,460

Full-time faculty members with tenure:
Men 1,563
Women 469
Total 2,032

Average pay of full-time professors
Public 4-year institutions:
Professor $47,320
Associate professor $39,213
Assistant professor $33,943
Instructor $27,630
No rank $25,971
All $37,921

Public 2-year institutions:
Professor $33,370
Associate professor $30,380
Assistant professor $29,196
Instructor $26,967
No rank $30,822
All $30,342

Private 4-year institutions:
Professor $46,997
Associate professor $37,632
Assistant professor $31,441
Instructor $22,596
No rank $21,911
All $37,535

STUDENTS

Enrollment:
At public 4-year institutions . 92,945
At public 2-year institutions . 58,128
At private 4-year institutions 17,758
At private 2-year institutions . 4,390
Undergraduate 149,148
Graduate 20,741
Professional 3,332
American Indian 9,609
Asian 2,904
Black 11,816
Hispanic 2,635
White 140,865
Foreign 5,392
Total 173,221

Enrollment highlights:
Women 53.8%
Full-time 59.4%
Minority 16.1%
Foreign 3.1%
10-year change in total
  enrollment .... Up 8.1%

Proportion of enrollment made up of minority students:
At public 4-year institutions . 15.9%
At public 2-year institutions . 15.9%
At private 4-year institutions   14.4%
At private 2-year institutions   28.1%

Degrees awarded:
Associate 6,204
Bachelor's 13,601
Master's 3,943
Doctorate 408
Professional 923

Residence of new students: State residents made up 91% of all freshmen enrolled in Oklahoma; 90% of all Oklahoma residents who were freshmen attended college in their home state.

Test scores: Students averaged 20.1 on the A.C.T., which was taken by an estimated 60% of Oklahoma's high-school seniors.

Graduation rates at NCAA Division I institutions:
Oklahoma State University 43%
University of Oklahoma 41%
University of Tulsa 49%

MONEY

Average tuition and fees:
At public 4-year institutions . $1,340
At public 2-year institutions .. $864
At private 4-year institutions $5,852
At private 2-year institutions $5,732

Expenditures:
Public institutions $973,213,000
Private institutions ... $262,526,000

State funds for higher-education operating expenses: $557,532,000
Two-year change: Up 12%

State spending on student aid:
Need-based: $14,193,000
Non–need-based: $4,077,000
Other: $20,558,000

Salary of chief executive of largest public 4-year campus:
Richard L. Van Horn, University
  of Oklahoma at Norman: $152,880

Total spending on research and development by doctorate-granting universities: $130,650,000
Sources:
Federal government 28.3%
State and local governments .. 5.9%
Industry 5.3%
The institution itself 53.9%
Other 6.7%

Total federal spending on college- and university-based research and development: $35,866,000
Selected programs:
Department of Health
  and Human Services $11,372,000
National Science
  Foundation $4,979,000
Department of Defense . $4,463,000
Department
  of Agriculture $5,986,000
Department of Energy .. $6,445,000

Largest endowment:
University of Tulsa ... $319,492,000

Top fund raisers:
University of Oklahoma $27,460,000

THE ALMANAC OF HIGHER EDUCATION • THE STATES

OKLAHOMA
Continued

Oklahoma State
  University $14,259,000
Oklahoma City
  University $4,538,000

MISCELLANY

■ A replica of a landmark building at Oklahoma State University—Old Central—has been built on the university's sister campus in Kameoka, Japan.

■ The University of Oklahoma Press is publishing a series of books devoted to new American Indian literature and criticism.

■ In an effort to curb a rash of bookbag thefts, the University of Oklahoma has been placing "dummy" book bags equipped with loud alarms in dormitories, cafeterias, and the student union. Anyone who picks up one of the bags is greeted by a shriek of 110 decibels.

■ The oldest institution of higher education in Oklahoma is Bacone College, founded in 1880.

OREGON

Oregon's Gov. Barbara Roberts had some blunt advice in 1992 for worried faculty members at public colleges: Stop "whining," she said, about the devastating cuts being made to higher education because of a new property-tax limit and get out there to build support for other kinds of revenue.

The Governor said she wasn't being callous, just realistic about the political climate for a tax-reform package that would fill the gap left by the tax limitation, which the voters approved in 1990. Since the limitation, known as Measure 5, was passed, the state has assumed many of the costs for public schools, community colleges, and other government services previously financed with local property taxes.

For the Oregon State System of Higher Education, which includes eight public, four-year institutions, the impact has been crushing. Tuition increased by an average of 40 per cent, academic programs and in some cases entire departments and schools were eliminated, and student-aid budgets were pushed to their limits.

Governor Roberts, a Democrat, wanted the Legislative Assembly to put a tax-reform measure on the September 15 ballot. But lawmakers rejected her proposal, prompting higher-education officials to fear that the damage done to their institutions by budget cuts would be be irreparable. For the 1993-95 budget cycle, the institutions have been told to expect 20 per cent less from the state than in 1991-93, and college presidents have already come forward with plans that involve hundreds of layoffs and the elimination of even more programs.

State higher-education officials are also reconsidering whether the state should continue to subsidize tuition for all students or redirect more state funds into student-aid programs aimed directly at those with the greatest financial need.

Students, not surprisingly, have been organizing to demand increased state support. In addition to the established Oregon Student Lobby, a group called Students of Oregon United to

Rescue College Education has been organized.

The budget squeeze has given new impetus to the state's push for greater cooperation between public and private institutions in the Portland metropolitan area and throughout the state. The Joint Graduate School of Engineering, for example, involves the three public research institutions—the University of Oregon and Oregon and Portland State Universities—and the private Oregon Graduate Institute. Improving opportunities for advanced courses in engineering was a particular priority for the state's high-technology industry, a group with significant political clout.

Beyond their concern with budget problems, higher-education officials had worried that voters would approve a constitutional amendment that declared homosexuality abnormal and perverse and required public schools and colleges to present that position in the classroom. In November 1992, voters defeated the measure, which opponents said would have restricted free speech on campuses and affected everything from classroom discussion to the purchase of library books.

The state is also developing a regional library network that will include public institutions and private liberal-arts institutions, such as Reed College and Lewis and Clark College.

Oregon also is focusing on ways to link public schools with higher education. In 1991 the state created a new tracking system for high-school students designed to assess their mastery of basic skills in the 10th grade and then allow them to pursue either a college-preparatory or career-oriented curriculum. Students in the career track will be encouraged to continue their education at community colleges. Governor Roberts is also considering changes in educational governance that could lead to the creation of a single coordinating board to oversee all public and postsecondary education.

DEMOGRAPHICS

Population: 2,922,000 (Rank: 29)

Age distribution:
Up to 17 .... 25.6%
18 to 24 .... 9.3%
25 to 44 .... 32.6%
45 and older 32.4%

Racial and ethnic distribution:
American Indian 1.4%
Asian 2.4%
Black 1.6%
White 92.8%
Other and unknown 1.8%
Hispanic (may be any race) .. 4.0%

Educational attainment of adults (highest level):
9th grade or less 6.2%
Some high school, no diploma 12.3%
High-school diploma 28.9%
Some college, no degree 25.0%
Associate degree 6.9%
Bachelor's degree 13.6%
Graduate or professional
 degree 7.0%

Proportion who speak a language other than English at home: 7.3%

Per-capita personal income: $17,575

Poverty rate:
All 12.4%
Under age 18 .... 15.8%
Age 18 and older 11.3%

New public high-school graduates in:
1992-93 (estimate) 25,530
2001-02 (estimate) 29,650

OREGON
Continued

New GED diploma recipients: 8,723

High-school dropout rate: 11.8%

POLITICAL LEADERSHIP

Governor: Barbara Roberts (D), term ends 1995

Governor's higher-education aide: Marilynne Keyser, 160 State Capitol, Salem 97310; (503) 378-2068

U.S. Senators: Mark O. Hatfield (R), term ends 1997; Bob Packwood (R), term ends 1999

U.S. Representatives:
4 Democrats, 1 Republican
Peter A. DeFazio (D), Elizabeth Furse (D), Michael J. Kopetski (D), Bob Smith (R), Ron Wyden (D)

Legislative Assembly: Senate, 16 Democrats, 14 Republicans; House, 28 Democrats, 32 Republicans

COLLEGES AND UNIVERSITIES

Higher education:
Public 4-year institutions	8
Public 2-year institutions	13
Private 4-year institutions	24
Private 2-year institutions	1
Total	46

Vocational institutions: 103

Statewide coordinating board:
Oregon Office of Educational Policy and Planning
225 Winter Street, N.E.
Salem 97310
(503) 378-3921

David Young, administrator for academic degrees and program review

Private-college association:
Oregon Independent Colleges Association
7100 Southwest Hampton Street
Suite 222
Portland 97223
(503) 639-4541
Gary K. Andeen, executive director

Institutions censured by the AAUP: None

Institutions under NCAA sanctions: None

FACULTY MEMBERS

Full-time faculty members by rank:
Professor	1,081
Associate professor	935
Assistant professor	895
Instructor	195
Lecturer	36
No rank	1,510
Total	4,652

Full-time faculty members with tenure:
Men	2,031
Women	733
Total	2,764

Average pay of full-time professors

Public 4-year institutions:
Professor	$45,488
Associate professor	$36,727
Assistant professor	$31,206
Instructor	$24,247
No rank	$21,247
All	$37,147

Public 2-year institutions:
Professor	$37,860
Associate professor	$32,692

Assistant professor $30,564
Instructor $27,235
No rank $33,852
All $33,724

Private 4-year institutions:
Professor $45,619
Associate professor $34,793
Assistant professor $29,083
Instructor $23,912
No rank $22,448
All $35,983

STUDENTS

Enrollment:
At public 4-year institutions . 68,500
At public 2-year institutions . 76,827
At private 4-year institutions 21,080
At private 2-year institutions .. 234
Undergraduate 146,982
Graduate 15,970
Professional 3,689
American Indian 1,694
Asian 6,321
Black 2,153
Hispanic 2,990
White 145,797
Foreign 7,686
Total 166,641

Enrollment highlights:
Women 52.9%
Full-time 56.8%
Minority 8.3%
Foreign 4.6%
10-year change in total
  enrollment .... Up 5.8%

Proportion of enrollment made up of minority students:
At public 4-year institutions .. 9.0%
At public 2-year institutions .. 7.6%
At private 4-year institutions . 8.5%
At private 2-year institutions . 6.8%

Degrees awarded:
Associate 4,769
Bachelor's 12,586
Master's 3,276
Doctorate 452
Professional 928

Residence of new students: State residents made up 82% of all freshmen enrolled in Oregon; 92% of all Oregon residents who were freshmen attended college in their home state.

Test scores: Students averaged 925 on the S.A.T., which was taken by an estimated 55% of Oregon's high-school seniors.

Graduation rates at NCAA Division I institutions:
Oregon State University 50%
University of Oregon 46%
University of Portland 57%

MONEY

Average tuition and fees:
At public 4-year institutions . $1,906
At public 2-year institutions .. $794
At private 4-year institutions $9,606
At private 2-year institutions $7,570

Expenditures:
Public institutions .. $1,219,341,000
Private institutions ... $256,067,000

State funds for higher-education operating expenses: $485,482,000
Two-year change: Up 16%

State spending on student aid:
Need-based: $11,852,000
Non–need-based: None
Other: None

Salary of chief executive of largest public 4-year campus:
Myles Brand, University of Oregon: $113,556

OREGON
Continued

Total spending on research and development by doctorate-granting universities: $171,550,000

Sources:
Federal government 62.6%
State and local governments . 13.2%
Industry 3.7%
The institution itself 11.1%
Other 9.4%

Total federal spending on college- and university-based research and development: $95,772,000

Selected programs:
Department of Health
  and Human Services $42,061,000
National Science
  Foundation $18,858,000
Department of Defense . $8,532,000
Department
  of Agriculture $9,375,000
Department of Energy .. $4,107,000

Largest endowment:
Reed College $97,802,000

Top fund raisers:
Oregon State University $24,277,000
University of Oregon .. $14,577,000
Reed College $7,399,000

MISCELLANY

■ Western Oregon State College claims to have the tallest tree on any college campus: It is a 122-foot, 6-inch sequoia.

■ In exchange for working as volunteer fire fighters in Corvallis, Ore., a group of Oregon State University students gets rent-free housing.

■ Students help operate a small nuclear reactor that is used for research projects at Reed College. The reactor is the only one in the country at a college without a graduate school. The students must go through a year of training to earn an operator's license.

■ The oldest higher-education institution in Oregon is Willamette University, founded by Christian missionaries in 1842.

PENNSYLVANIA

PENNSYLVANIA, complain many in higher education, continues to rank near the bottom nationally in its spending per student. That will not change in the 1992-93 academic year.

The state has been hit hard by the recession. Its largest city, Philadelphia, teetered at the edge of bankruptcy in 1990. Finances being what they are, Democratic Gov. Robert P. Casey has asked all government agencies, including colleges, to bite the bullet. Even so, public higher education in the Keystone State has escaped the wholesale cutbacks that have plagued colleges elsewhere.

The 14 state-owned universities, which include former teachers' colleges, such as Millersville, Clarion, and Mansfield Universities, and four "state related" institutions—Pennsylvania State, Lincoln, and Temple Universities, and the University of Pittsburgh—are coping with 1992-93 appropriations that are down by 3.5 per cent from the 1991-92 fiscal year.

Even with the budget cuts, educators at state-owned and state-related institutions know their plight could have been far worse. Mr. Casey recommended that the state end its practice of providing direct aid to 11 private colleges in the Philadelphia area, including the University of Pennsylvania, Drexel and Hahnemann Universities, and the Philadelphia College of Textiles & Science. Although the state Senate's budget included some private-college aid, the final budget adopted by the General Assembly did not include the appropriation.

Mr. Casey had argued that given the state's severe budget problems and his unwillingness to raise taxes, such an appropriation, which totaled $76-million in 1991-92, was a luxury the state could no longer afford.

One of the most visible victims may be the University of Pennsylvania's School of Veterinary Medicine, which receives 40 per cent of its budget from the government and is the only such school in the state. Penn officials say that without state money, they will have to close the school by 1996.

A few private-college presidents were hopeful that legislators would restore some aid when they convened in the fall of 1992. But by late November, nothing had changed, forcing several presidents to scale back programs, lay off workers, and raise tuition to make up for the loss of state aid.

The private-college aid may have fallen victim to a report by the Legislative Black Caucus, which took all of the state's colleges and universities to task for failing to provide more opportunities to black students. More blacks were enrolled in colleges 10 years ago than today, the report said. One legislator has suggested providing money to colleges for recruitment and retention activities, based on how well the colleges have performed. Annually, the institutions get more than $1-million from the state for those purposes.

Many state lawmakers are still fuming after the disclosure of a benefit package that Wesley Posvar, president of Pitt, received from the institution when he retired in 1991. That prompted Governor Casey and many legislators to press state-related colleges for more details about their finances and the salaries of top officials. The legislature passed a law in 1992 requiring such disclosure.

Legislators also approved a measure that set up two state-backed college-savings plans. Under one, parents can purchase tax-exempt bonds for the college expenses of their children. Through a "Tuition Account Program," parents can gear their contributions to the existing tuition rates at any public university.

The 14 state-owned institutions are overseen by the Board of Governors, while each of the state-related universities is governed by its own board.

DEMOGRAPHICS

Population: 11,961,000   (Rank: 5)

Age distribution:
Up to 17 .... 23.7%
18 to 24 .... 10.1%
25 to 44 .... 30.9%
45 and older 35.3%

Racial and ethnic distribution:
American Indian 0.1%
Asian 1.2%
Black 9.2%
White 88.5%
Other and unknown 1.0%
Hispanic (may be any race) .. 2.0%

Educational attainment of adults (highest level):
9th grade or less 9.4%
Some high school, no diploma 15.9%
High-school diploma 38.6%

PENNSYLVANIA
Continued

Some college, no degree 12.9%
Associate degree 5.2%
Bachelor's degree 11.3%
Graduate or professional
  degree 6.6%

Proportion who speak a language other than English at home: 7.3%

Per-capita personal income: $19,306

Poverty rate:
All 11.1%
Under age 18 .... 15.7%
Age 18 and older 9.7%

New public high-school graduates in:
1992-93 (estimate) 101,700
2001-02 (estimate) 114,050

New GED diploma recipients: 20,378

High-school dropout rate: 9.1%

POLITICAL LEADERSHIP

Governor: Robert P. Casey (D), term ends 1995

Governor's higher-education aide:
Helen D. Wise, State Capitol, Room 238, Harrisburg 17120; (717) 787-2500

U.S. Senators: Arlen Specter (R), term ends 1999; Harris Wofford (D), term ends 1995

U.S. Representatives:
11 Democrats, 10 Republicans
Lucien E. Blackwell (D), Robert A. Borski (D), William F. Clinger, Jr. (R), William J. Coyne (D), Thomas M. Foglietta (D), George W. Gekas (R), Bill Goodling (R), Jim Greenwood (R), Tim Holden (D), Paul E. Kanjorksi (D), Ron Klink (D), Joseph M. McDade (R), Paul McHale (D), Marjorie Margolies Mezvinsky (D), Austin J. Murphy (D), John P. Murtha (D), Thomas J. Ridge (R), Rick Santorum (R), Bud Shuster (R), Robert S. Walker (R), Curt Weldon (R)

General Assembly: Senate, 25 Democrats, 25 Republicans; House, 105 Democrats, 98 Republicans

COLLEGES AND UNIVERSITIES

Higher education:
Public 4-year institutions 43
Public 2-year institutions 20
Private 4-year institutions 101
Private 2-year institutions 56
Total 220

Vocational institutions: 314

Statewide coordinating board:
State Department of Education
333 Market Street, 12th Floor
Harrisburg 17126
(717) 787-5041
Charles R. Fuget, commissioner for postsecondary and higher education

Private-college association:
Commission for Independent Colleges
  and Universities of Pennsylvania
800 North Third Street, Suite 404
Harrisburg 17102
(717) 232-8649
Brian C. Mitchell, president

Institution censured by the AAUP:
Grove City College

Institution under NCAA sanctions:
Lock Haven University of Pennsylvania

FACULTY MEMBERS

Full-time faculty members by rank:
Professor	6,505
Associate professor	6,013
Assistant professor	6,309
Instructor	1,432
Lecturer	184
No rank	222
Total	20,665

Full-time faculty members with tenure:
Men	9,880
Women	2,675
Total	12,555

Average pay of full-time professors

Public 4-year institutions:
Professor	$58,031
Associate professor	$44,245
Assistant professor	$35,619
Instructor	$27,665
No rank	$30,415
All	$44,618

Public 2-year institutions:
Professor	$45,373
Associate professor	$39,007
Assistant professor	$33,831
Instructor	$27,909
No rank	$35,387
All	$38,392

Private 4-year institutions:
Professor	$58,541
Associate professor	$41,653
Assistant professor	$34,597
Instructor	$26,829
No rank	$33,721
All	$43,805

STUDENTS

Enrollment:
At public 4-year institutions	235,271
At public 2-year institutions	108,207
At private 4-year institutions	214,417
At private 2-year institutions	46,165
Undergraduate	514,387
Graduate	75,979
Professional	13,694
American Indian	1,011
Asian	13,588
Black	44,009
Hispanic	7,709
White	523,157
Foreign	14,586
Total	604,060

Enrollment highlights:
Women	54.0%
Full-time	63.0%
Minority	11.3%
Foreign	2.4%
10-year change in total enrollment	Up 19.0%

Proportion of enrollment made up of minority students:
At public 4-year institutions	10.1%
At public 2-year institutions	13.2%
At private 4-year institutions	8.5%
At private 2-year institutions	24.7%

Degrees awarded:
Associate	17,760
Bachelor's	60,495
Master's	14,821
Doctorate	2,036
Professional	3,462

Residence of new students: State residents made up 77% of all freshmen enrolled in Pennsylvania; 82% of all Pennsylvania residents who were freshmen attended college in their home state.

Test scores: Students averaged 877 on the S.A.T., which was taken by an estimated 68% of Pennsylvania's high-school seniors.

Graduation rates at NCAA Division I institutions:
Bucknell University 87%

PENNSYLVANIA
Continued

Drexel University 70%
Duquesne University 69%
La Salle University 67%
Lafayette College 87%
Lehigh University 86%
Pennsylvania State University . 74%
Robert Morris College......... 56%
Saint Francis College 51%
Saint Joseph's University 73%
Temple University 45%
University of Pennsylvania 90%
University of Pittsburgh 60%
Villanova University 83%

MONEY

Average tuition and fees:
At public 4-year institutions . $3,401
At public 2-year institutions . $1,505
At private 4-year institutions $9,848
At private 2-year institutions $6,314

Expenditures:
Public institutions .. $3,390,869,000
Private institutions . $4,437,071,000

State funds for higher-education operating expenses: $1,388,920,000

Two-year change: 0%

State spending on student aid:
Need-based: $158,613,000
Non–need-based: $568,000
Other: None

Salary of chief executive of largest public 4-year campus:
Joab Thomas, Pennsylvania State University main campus: salary n/a

Total spending on research and development by doctorate-granting universities: $829,518,000

Sources:
Federal government 62.1%
State and local governments .. 3.8%
Industry 11.9%
The institution itself 15.2%
Other 7.0%

Total federal spending on college- and university-based research and development: $536,674,000

Selected programs:
Department of Health
  and Human Services $294,998,000
National Science
  Foundation $66,056,000
Department of Defense $116,533,000
Department
  of Agriculture $8,384,000
Department of Energy . $18,707,000

Largest endowment:
University
  of Pennsylvania $825,601,000

Top fund raisers:
University
  of Pennsylvania $143,384,000
Pennsylvania State
  University $61,368,000
Carnegie Mellon
  University $46,864,000

MISCELLANY

■ Every spring, alumni, students, and professors at Juniata College join the maple-syrup harvest at the college's Environmental Studies Field Station. Tapping 600 to 800 trees, the volunteers make about 100 gallons of syrup.

■ A graveyard filled with textbooks from years past circles Alumni Hall at Widener University. For 62 years, graduating classes from what was then the Pennsylvania Military College buried their textbooks, placing a tombstone over the resting place. The tradition ended when the institution became a civilian, liberal-arts college in 1962. But officials at Widener, which became a university in 1979, let the graveyard remain.

■ To attract bright students, Lebanon Valley College is offering scholarships linked to an applicant's high-school class rank. Those in the top 10 per cent received a 50-per-cent discount on Lebanon Valley's $12,500 tuition in 1992-93. Students in the top 20 per cent paid one-third less, and those in the top 30 per cent paid one-quarter less.

■ The University of Pennsylvania, founded in 1740, is the nation's oldest full-fledged university. (Harvard, which dates to 1636, was founded as a college.)

RHODE ISLAND

IN a state steeped in patrician tradition, Rhode Island's public colleges have always had to battle for respect—and money.

The state has only three public institutions—the University of Rhode Island, Rhode Island College, and the Community College of Rhode Island—and they are often overshadowed by such nationally renowned private institutions as Brown University and the Rhode Island School of Design.

Even though the state's economy has been dragged down by the recession—or perhaps because of that circumstance—the public-college sector has emerged as a scrappy and savvy advocate for preserving its share of shrinking state resources.

Their scrappiness has not prevented all budget reductions. State spending for public higher education has declined by 7 per cent since 1990-91. But lawmakers and Gov. Bruce Sundlun, a Democrat who was re-elected in November, have tried to insulate higher education from the deepest cuts.

Much of the credit belongs to the students of public colleges, who have borne the brunt of state reductions by paying higher tuition. In 1991 they formed Rhode Island Students for Education to fight further budget cuts.

Legislators continue to be sensitive to students' concern about high tuition and reduced course offerings. But one of Governor Sundlun's proposals to raise revenue—extending the state's 7-per-cent sales tax to textbooks—died in the General Assembly in 1992.

The lawmakers are far less sympathetic to the entreaties of college faculty members, who also have paid a financial price by having pay raises deferred. Several legislators have questioned whether the faculty members' workload is too light.

To improve relations, the institutions and the Board of Governors for Higher Education want professors to join the Higher Education–Legislative Network, which is designed to help lawmakers make use of faculty expertise.

One program that remains popular with legislators is an effort called the Rhode Island Children's Crusade. Financed with private and public funds, it pays the costs of a college education for needy students who stay off drugs and attain good grades.

Unlike other states where private colleges have a strong presence and students from both sectors are able to participate in state aid programs, Rhode Island has seen few tensions between the public and private sectors. That is so, in part, because cam-

RHODE ISLAND
Continued

pus leaders have been willing to let each institution carve its own niche.

In fact, the Board of Governors, the statewide coordinating and governing board, recently approved the creation of a new law school at a private institution, Roger Williams College, without any objections from the University of Rhode Island, even though the state has no public law school. The state university has been more interested in programs related to its mission as a land-grant and sea-grant institution. Its School of Oceanography is among the most prestigious in the nation.

DEMOGRAPHICS

Population: 1,004,000   (Rank: 43)

Age distribution:
Up to 17 .... 22.9%
18 to 24 .... 11.6%
25 to 44 .... 32.2%
45 and older 33.4%

Racial and ethnic distribution:
American Indian 0.4%
Asian 1.8%
Black 3.9%
White 91.4%
Other and unknown 2.5%
Hispanic (may be any race) .. 4.6%

Educational attainment of adults (highest level):
9th grade or less 11.1%
Some high school, no diploma 16.9%
High-school diploma 29.5%
Some college, no degree 15.0%
Associate degree 6.3%
Bachelor's degree 13.5%
Graduate or professional degree 7.8%

Proportion who speak a language other than English at home: 17.0%

Per-capita personal income: $19,207

Poverty rate:
All 9.6%
Under age 18 .... 13.8%
Age 18 and older 8.3%

New public high-school graduates in:
1992-93 (estimate) 7,280
2001-02 (estimate) 8,980

New GED diploma recipients: 2,654

High-school dropout rate: 11.1%

POLITICAL LEADERSHIP

Governor: Bruce Sundlun (D), term ends 1995

Governor's higher-education aide: Scott Wolf, State House, Room 111, Providence 02903; (401) 277-2080 extension 321

U.S. Senators: John H. Chafee (R), term ends 1995; Claiborne Pell (D), term ends 1997

U.S. Representatives:
1 Democrat, 1 Republican
Ronald K. Machtley (R), John F. Reed (D)

General Assembly: Senate, 36 Democrats, 11 Republicans, 3 races undecided; House, 80 Democrats, 11 Republicans, 9 races undecided

COLLEGES AND UNIVERSITIES

Higher education:
Public 4-year institutions 2

Public 2-year institutions 1
Private 4-year institutions 9
Private 2-year institutions 0
Total 12

Vocational institutions: 25

Statewide coordinating board:
Office of Higher Education
301 Promenade Street
Providence 02908
(401) 277-6560
Americo W. Petrocelli, commissioner of higher education

Private-college association:
Rhode Island Independent
　Higher Education Association
Charles-Orms Building, Suite 120
10 Orms Street
Providence 02904
(401) 272-8270
Robert J. McKenna, president

Institutions censured by the AAUP:
None

Institutions under NCAA sanctions:
None

FACULTY MEMBERS

Full-time faculty members by rank:
Professor 1,148
Associate professor 675
Assistant professor 665
Instructor 65
Lecturer 45
No rank 99
Total 2,697

Full-time faculty members with tenure:
Men 1,169
Women 407
Total 1,576

Average pay of full-time professors
Public 4-year institutions:
Professor $54,779
Associate professor $43,286
Assistant professor $36,698
Instructor $33,952
No rank .... n/a
All $46,351

Public 2-year institutions:
Professor $42,978
Associate professor $34,453
Assistant professor $29,050
Instructor $24,376
No rank .... n/a
All $37,706

Private 4-year institutions:
Professor $63,462
Associate professor $44,597
Assistant professor $36,668
Instructor $29,053
No rank $40,870
All $49,161

STUDENTS

Enrollment:
At public 4-year institutions . 25,730
At public 2-year institutions . 16,620
At private 4-year institutions   35,923
At private 2-year institutions 0
Undergraduate 68,499
Graduate 9,467
Professional 307
American Indian 222
Asian 1,891
Black 2,558
Hispanic 1,606
White 69,974
Foreign 2,022
Total 78,273

Enrollment highlights:
Women 54.6%
Full-time 63.4%
Minority 8.2%
Foreign 2.6%

RHODE ISLAND
Continued

10-year change in total
  enrollment . . . . Up 17.1%

Proportion of enrollment made up of minority students:
At public 4-year institutions . . 5.7%
At public 2-year institutions . . 9.9%
At private 4-year institutions . 9.3%
At private 2-year institutions . . . n/a

Degrees awarded:
Associate 3,495
Bachelor's 8,789
Master's 1,795
Doctorate 190
Professional 82

Residence of new students: State residents made up 44% of all freshmen enrolled in Rhode Island; 70% of all Rhode Island residents who were freshmen attended college in their home state.

Test scores: Students averaged 881 on the S.A.T., which was taken by an estimated 70% of Rhode Island's high-school seniors.

Graduation rates at NCAA Division I institutions:
Brown University 92%
Providence College 81%
University of Rhode Island 58%

MONEY

Average tuition and fees:
At public 4-year institutions . $2,311
At public 2-year institutions . $1,100
At private 4-year institutions $10,885
At private 2-year institutions . . . n/a

Expenditures:
Public institutions $287,194,000
Private institutions . . . $486,764,000

State funds for higher-education operating expenses: $118,911,000
Two-year change: Down 7%

State spending on student aid:
Need-based: $9,084,000
Non–need-based: $53,000
Other: $424,000

Salary of chief executive of largest public 4-year campus:
Robert L. Carothers, University of Rhode Island: $112,000

Total spending on research and development by doctorate-granting universities: $82,634,000
Sources:
Federal government 69.5%
State and local governments . . 6.2%
Industry 5.3%
The institution itself 16.0%
Other 3.0%

Total federal spending on college- and university-based research and development: $51,828,000
Selected programs:
Department of Health
  and Human Services $16,213,000
National Science
  Foundation $13,786,000
Department of Defense $10,222,000
Department
  of Agriculture $1,233,000
Department of Energy . . $3,305,000

Largest endowment:
Brown University $431,444,000

Top fund raisers:
Brown University $51,482,000

University of Rhode
  Island $6,040,000
Rhode Island School
  of Design $3,226,000

MISCELLANY

■ Roger Williams College will open the state's first school of law in August 1993.

■ At the request of administrators and female faculty members at Brown University, a federal court in 1992 vacated a consent decree that had governed faculty hiring and promotion for 14 years. The decree, which settled a sex-discrimination suit against the university, set goals and timetables for the hiring of female faculty members.

■ The oldest institution of higher education in Rhode Island is Brown University, founded in 1764.

SOUTH CAROLINA

WHEN John M. Palms became president of the University of South Carolina in 1991, his first mandate was to restore the institution's reputation. The 13-year presidency of James B. Holderman had been marked by personal scandals and charges of free spending that shook the public's faith in the university.

Now that much of that faith has been restored, Mr. Palms is pressing forward to make the university a premier research institution. But, given the state's persistent lack of money, the president will have to accomplish that goal without additional resources.

Mr. Palms contends that reorganization is one necessary step. He wants to break ties with the three four-year colleges in the system and concentrate more resources on the Columbia campus and the system's five two-year colleges.

In June 1992, the Board of Trustees backed his proposal to let the Coastal Carolina campus go free, but the board wanted time to study similar plans for campuses at Aiken and Spartanburg.

The General Assembly must approve the changes, and several lawmakers want to use the opportunity to revamp higher education in the state. Some complain that, with 12 public four-year colleges and 21 two-year colleges, South Carolina has more higher education than it can afford.

In addition to 33 public campuses, which include Clemson University and the Citadel, the state has about 30 private colleges.

Higher education in South Carolina is undergoing a transformation in other ways. The Commission on Higher Education, the coordinating body, is pushing for a policy that for the first time would provide need-based aid to students attending public colleges. The proposal will be presented to the General Assembly in its 1993 session.

Legislators have also been interested in the performance of South Carolina students and colleges. In the 1992-93 academic year, colleges must report their graduation and dropout rates to the commission and the General Assembly.

Yet another change in policy elevated six former colleges to university status in early 1992. Supporters of the switch say the move will help the institutions attract faculty members and students.

South Carolina State University, the only public historically black insti-

SOUTH CAROLINA
Continued

tution of higher education, is one of the colleges that achieved university status. Some legislators have been pressing for a management audit because of gaps in the university's financial records, but its supporters say suspicions of wrongdoing are unfounded.

It is unclear how South Carolina State, along with the predominantly white colleges, will be affected by a U.S. Supreme Court decision in June 1992 that Mississippi had not done enough to desegregate its colleges.

Public- and private-college officials, recognizing that both sectors need more support from the state, have formed the Business Advisory Council to lobby for all of higher education.

DEMOGRAPHICS

Population: 3,560,000   (Rank: 25)

Age distribution:
Up to 17 .... 26.3%
18 to 24 .... 11.5%
25 to 44 .... 32.1%
45 and older 30.0%

Racial and ethnic distribution:
American Indian 0.2%
Asian 0.6%
Black 29.8%
White 69.0%
Other and unknown 0.3%
Hispanic (may be any race) .. 0.9%

Educational attainment of adults (highest level):
9th grade or less 13.6%
Some high school, no diploma 18.1%
High-school diploma 29.5%
Some college, no degree 15.8%
Associate degree 6.3%
Bachelor's degree 11.2%
Graduate or professional degree 5.4%

Proportion who speak a language other than English at home: 3.5%

Per-capita personal income: $15,467

Poverty rate:
All 15.4%
Under age 18 .... 21.0%
Age 18 and older 13.3%

New public high-school graduates in:
1992-93 (estimate) 33,130
2001-02 (estimate) 36,020

New GED diploma recipients: 6,060

High-school dropout rate: 11.7%

POLITICAL LEADERSHIP

Governor: Carroll A. Campbell, Jr. (R), term ends 1995

Governor's higher-education aide: Janice Trawick, P.O. Box 11369, Columbia 29211; (803) 734-9818

U.S. Senators: Ernest F. Hollings (D), term ends 1999; Strom Thurmond (R), term ends 1997

U.S. Representatives:
3 Democrats, 3 Republicans
James E. Clyburn (D), Butler Derrick (D), Bob Inglis (R), Arthur Ravenel, Jr. (R), Floyd D. Spence (R), John M. Spratt, Jr. (D)

General Assembly: Senate, 29 Democrats, 16 Republicans, 1 race undecided; House, 73 Democrats, 50 Republicans, 1 Independent

COLLEGES AND UNIVERSITIES

Higher education:
Public 4-year institutions 12
Public 2-year institutions 21
Private 4-year institutions 20
Private 2-year institutions 11
Total 64

Vocational institutions: 56

Statewide coordinating board:
Commission on Higher Education
1333 Main Street, Suite 200
Columbia 29201
(803) 253-6260
Fred R. Sheheen, commissioner

Private-college association:
South Carolina College Council
P.O. Box 12007
Columbia 29211
(803) 799-7122
Arthur M. Bjontegard, Jr., president

Institutions censured by the AAUP:
None

Institutions under NCAA sanctions:
None

FACULTY MEMBERS

Full-time faculty members by rank:
Professor 1,359
Associate professor 1,293
Assistant professor 1,252
Instructor 399
Lecturer 56
No rank 1,161
Total 5,520

Full-time faculty members with tenure:
Men 1,977
Women 625
Total 2,602

Average pay of full-time professors

Public 4-year institutions:
Professor $52,146
Associate professor $40,026
Assistant professor $33,509
Instructor $24,046
No rank .... n/a
All $40,541

Public 2-year institutions:
Professor $40,403
Associate professor $33,431
Assistant professor $28,594
Instructor $24,143
No rank $27,168
All $27,649

Private 4-year institutions:
Professor $39,327
Associate professor $32,251
Assistant professor $26,571
Instructor $21,902
No rank $28,363
All $31,510

STUDENTS

Enrollment:
At public 4-year institutions . 81,303
At public 2-year institutions . 49,831
At private 4-year institutions 23,787
At private 2-year institutions . 4,381
Undergraduate 139,982
Graduate 16,829
Professional 2,491
American Indian 334
Asian 1,494
Black 31,177
Hispanic 911
White 122,964
Foreign 2,422
Total 159,302

Enrollment highlights:
Women 56.5%
Full-time 68.5%
Minority 21.6%
Foreign 1.5%

SOUTH CAROLINA
Continued

10-year change in total
enrollment .... Up 20.2%

Proportion of enrollment made up of minority students:
At public 4-year institutions . 17.6%
At public 2-year institutions . 24.4%
At private 4-year institutions 25.3%
At private 2-year institutions 43.9%

Degrees awarded:
Associate 5,202
Bachelor's 13,215
Master's 3,828
Doctorate 342
Professional 587

Residence of new students: State residents made up 80% of all freshmen enrolled in South Carolina; 89% of all South Carolina residents who were freshmen attended college in their home state.

Test scores: Students averaged 831 on the S.A.T., which was taken by an estimated 59% of South Carolina's high-school seniors.

Graduation rates at NCAA Division I institutions:
Charleston Southern University 17%
Citadel 72%
Clemson University 71%
College of Charleston 31%
Furman University 76%
South Carolina State University 51%
University of South Carolina
  Coastal Carolina College 27%
University of South Carolina
  at Columbia 60%
Winthrop University 46%

MONEY

Average tuition and fees:
At public 4-year institutions . $2,317
At public 2-year institutions .. $813
At private 4-year institutions $6,434
At private 2-year institutions $5,110

Expenditures:
Public institutions .. $1,324,647,000
Private institutions ... $297,112,000

State funds for higher-education operating expenses: $633,379,000

Two-year change: Down 1%

State spending on student aid:
Need-based: $16,966,000
Non-need-based: None
Other: $1,258,000

Salary of chief executive of largest public 4-year campus:
John M. Palms, University of South Carolina at Columbia: $135,503

Total spending on research and development by doctorate-granting universities: $137,269,000

Sources:
Federal government 33.3%
State and local governments . 12.7%
Industry 9.4%
The institution itself 37.1%
Other 7.6%

Total federal spending on college- and university-based research and development: $42,705,000

Selected programs:
Department of Health
  and Human Services $22,093,000
National Science
  Foundation $6,986,000
Department of Defense . $3,435,000
Department
  of Agriculture $5,705,000
Department of Energy .. $1,459,000

Largest endowment:
Furman University $87,867,000

Top fund raisers:
University of South Carolina
  at Columbia $22,701,000
Clemson University ... $21,666,000
Furman University $7,497,000

MISCELLANY

■ The University of South Carolina decided to save money in 1992 by ending the practice of hiring a performer for $18,300 to dress up as the university's mascot, a gamecock called "Cocky." Instead, two or three students will receive $500 scholarships to do the job.

■ The original charter of the College of Charleston was signed by three signers of the Declaration of Independence and three signers of the U.S. Constitution.

■ The oldest higher-education institution in South Carolina is the College of Charleston, founded in 1770. It became a university with the addition of a graduate program, called the University of Charleston, in July 1992.

SOUTH DAKOTA

THE biggest higher-education challenge for South Dakota these days is making more college-degree programs available in Sioux Falls.

Sioux Falls is not only the largest city in the state but also the largest in the Upper Great Plains region without a public college.

In 1991 the state Board of Regents established the Sioux Falls Center, where several different public institutions offer baccalaureate programs in nursing and technology, and limited graduate work in business.

Now several state institutions, including the University of South Dakota and South Dakota State University, want to add more programs, but state officials are trying to insure the expansion does not unnecessarily duplicate courses already offered by the several small private colleges in the region.

South Dakota has no state-operated community colleges. It relies instead on seven public four-year institutions to provide such education. That has been a cost saver for the state and has worked well for most students, since most of the colleges are located along South Dakota's populous eastern and western borders.

The arrangement has been less convenient to students in rural communities, who cannot easily commute to a campus, but higher-education leaders say the situation will soon improve when they begin using a new telecommunications network for distance learning.

The strong American Indian presence in the state is also reflected in higher education. Four tribally controlled institutions operate in South Dakota, including one that changed from a college to a university in 1992—Sinte Gleska University.

In 1992 lobbyists for the South Dakota Tribal Association sought $500,000 from the state to support the colleges, since the institutions enroll about 200 non-Indian students. Gov. George S. Mickelson and some legislators said they were sympathetic but rejected the appeal, saying it was an inappropriate use of state funds.

On the whole the Legislature and Governor have been strong supporters of higher education. Mr. Mickel-

SOUTH DAKOTA
Continued

son, a Republican, has been especially interested in research as a way to promote economic development.

With help from the federal government and South Dakota's own commitment of funds, the state is making strides in expanding the research capacity of its universities. As would be expected in a state where farming and mining are still mainstays of the economy, much of the research relates to agriculture. But institutions also have been expanding into non-agricultural fields.

DEMOGRAPHICS

Population: 703,000 (Rank: 45)

Age distribution:
Up to 17 .... 28.6%
18 to 24 .... 9.8%
25 to 44 .... 29.6%
45 and older 32.1%

Racial and ethnic distribution:
American Indian 7.3%
Asian 0.4%
Black 0.5%
White 91.6%
Other and unknown 0.2%
Hispanic (may be any race) .. 0.8%

Educational attainment of adults (highest level):
Less than 9th grade 13.4%
Some high school, no degree . 9.5%
High-school diploma 33.7%
Some college, no degree 18.8%
Associate degree 7.4%
Bachelor's degree 12.3%
Graduate or professional
  degree 4.9%

Proportion who speak a language other than English at home: 6.5%

Per-capita personal income: $16,071

Poverty rate:
All 15.9%
Under age 18 .... 20.4%
Age 18 and older 14.0%

New public high-school graduates in:
1992-93 (estimate) 7,700
2001-02 (estimate) 8,570

New GED diploma recipients: 1,113

High-school dropout rate: 7.7%

POLITICAL LEADERSHIP

Governor: George S. Mickelson (R), term ends 1995

Governor's higher-education aide: James Soyer, 500 East Capitol, Pierre 57501; (605) 773-3661

U.S. Senators: Thomas A. Daschle (D), term ends 1999; Larry Pressler (R), term ends 1997

U.S. Representative:
1 Democrat
Tim Johnson (D)

Legislature: Senate, 20 Democrats, 15 Republicans; House, 29 Democrats, 41 Republicans

COLLEGES AND UNIVERSITIES

Higher education:
Public 4-year institutions 7
Public 2-year institutions 1
Private 4-year institutions 10
Private 2-year institutions 1
Total 19

Vocational institutions: 20

Statewide coordinating board:
Board of Regents
207 East Capitol Avenue
Pierre 57501
(605) 773-3455
Howell Todd, executive director

Private-college association:
South Dakota Association
 of Independent Colleges
P.O. Box 645
1501 South Prairie
Sioux Falls 57101
(605) 331-6684
Tom Johnson, board member

Institutions censured by the AAUP:
None

Institutions under NCAA sanctions:
None

FACULTY MEMBERS

Full-time faculty members by rank:
Professor 355
Associate professor 242
Assistant professor 372
Instructor 134
Lecturer 8
No rank 24
Total 1,135

Full-time faculty members with tenure:
Men 435
Women 103
Total 538

Average pay of full-time professors
Public 4-year institutions:
Professor $41,359
Associate professor $33,491
Assistant professor $29,685
Instructor $22,221
No rank .... n/a
All $33,607

Public 2-year institutions:
Professor .... n/a
Associate professor .... n/a
Assistant professor .... n/a
Instructor .... n/a
No rank $18,628
All $18,628

Private 4-year institutions:
Professor $35,159
Associate professor $27,944
Assistant professor $24,735
Instructor $22,240
No rank $26,741
All $27,442

STUDENTS

Enrollment:
At public 4-year institutions . 26,451
At public 2-year institutions ... 145
At private 4-year institutions . 7,363
At private 2-year institutions .. 249
Undergraduate 30,197
Graduate 3,564
Professional 447
American Indian 1,912
Asian 198
Black 250
Hispanic 94
White 31,106
Foreign 648
Total 34,208

Enrollment highlights:
Women 56.0%
Full-time 71.4%
Minority 7.3%
Foreign 1.9%
10-year change in total
 enrollment .... Up 4.4%

Proportion of enrollment made up of minority students:
At public 4-year institutions .. 5.6%
At public 2-year institutions . 85.5%
At private 4-year institutions 12.0%
At private 2-year institutions . 0.4%

Degrees awarded:
Associate 791

SOUTH DAKOTA
Continued

Bachelor's 3,617
Master's 769
Doctorate 44
Professional 102

Residence of new students: State residents made up 72% of all freshmen enrolled in South Dakota; 72% of all South Dakota residents who were freshmen attended college in their home state.

Test scores: Students averaged 21.0 on the A.C.T., which was taken by an estimated 69% of South Dakota's high-school seniors.

Graduation rates at NCAA Division I institutions: n/a

MONEY

Average tuition and fees:
At public 4-year institutions . $1,854
At public 2-year institutions . $1,920
At private 4-year institutions $6,346
At private 2-year institutions $4,515

Expenditures:
Public institutions $184,153,000
Private institutions $79,252,000

State funds for higher-education operating expenses: $104,472,000

Two-year change: Up 16%

State spending on student aid:
Need-based: $480,000
Non–need-based: $90,000
Other: None

Salary of chief executive of largest public 4-year campus: Robert T. Wagner, South Dakota State University: $93,118

Total spending on research and development by doctorate-granting universities: $14,342,000
Sources:
Federal government 47.9%
State and local governments . 40.3%
Industry 2.6%
The institution itself 6.8%
Other 2.3%

Total federal spending on college- and university-based research and development: $5,791,000
Selected programs:
Department of Health
   and Human Services ... $627,000
National Science
   Foundation $1,798,000
Department of Defense $30,000
Department
   of Agriculture $2,430,000
Department of Energy 0

Largest endowment:
University of South
   Dakota $15,817,000

Top fund raisers:
University of South
   Dakota $4,276,000
South Dakota State
   University $3,443,000
Augustana College $3,319,000

MISCELLANY

■ In its Shrine to Music Museum, the University of South Dakota houses more than 4,000 instruments, including one of the two Stradivari guitars still in existence.

■ Augustana College is home to the Center for Western Studies. Founded in 1970, it helps preserve the historical and cultural record of the upper Great Plains.

■ The oldest institution of higher education in South Dakota is the North American Baptist Seminary, founded in 1858.

TENNESSEE

As educators in Tennessee saw another legislative session come to a close in May 1992, they witnessed Democratic Gov. Ned Ray McWherter's failure once more to get a state income tax.

Mr. McWherter has pushed for the tax since he was elected to a second term in 1990. He says he wants to improve the state's public schools and colleges but needs more money to do it. While higher-education officials generally are behind him, lawmakers and voters are less enthusiastic.

Despite the income-tax defeat, the session proved to be a relatively good one for public colleges and universities, which began the 1992-93 academic year with a budget that was 9 per cent higher than the previous year's. Students, however, are paying fees that are as much as 7 per cent above those in the 1991-92 academic year, and the Tennessee Higher Education Commission is considering changes in its tuition and financial-aid policies that may alter the proportion of education costs that students are expected to pay.

As elsewhere, accountability in higher education is an issue in Tennessee. A law passed in 1992 requires universities and colleges to report annually to lawmakers on how well students are faring. The "report card" will include data on the number of students in remedial courses and students' test scores on professional examinations.

Legislators considered a bill giving the Board of Regents more authority in the hiring of university presidents and other campus officials, but it lacked support. The bill was proposed after controversy at East Tennessee State University, where board members were unhappy that a presidential candidate whom they preferred was not recommended by a search committee of faculty members, students, and community representatives.

Other legislators advocate a "superboard" that would oversee the state's 10 four-year colleges. The University of Tennessee system has its own governing board, while other colleges are under the state Board of Regents. Some officials complain that the set-up gives the University of Tennessee an unfair advantage.

Relations between private and public colleges are more strained than in the past, as private institutions seek additional financial aid for their students. The private colleges—which include several historically black institutions, including Fisk University and Meharry Medical College—produce nearly one-third of all college graduates in Tennessee.

A committee continues to monitor how well the state is doing in following a court order to desegregate public colleges. Educators are considering how Tennessee will be affected by a June 1992 U.S. Supreme Court ruling that Mississippi had not done enough to desegregate its colleges.

DEMOGRAPHICS

Population: 4,953,000 (Rank: 18)

Age distribution:
Up to 17 .... 24.8%
18 to 24 .... 10.7%

TENNESSEE
Continued

25 to 44 .... 32.1%
45 and older 32.4%

Racial and ethnic distribution:
American Indian 0.2%
Asian 0.7%
Black 16.0%
White 83.0%
Other and unknown 0.2%
Hispanic (may be any race) .. 0.7%

Educational attainment of adults (highest level):
9th grade or less 16.0%
Some high school, no diploma 17.0%
High-school diploma 30.0%
Some college, no degree 16.9%
Associate degree 4.2%
Bachelor's degree 10.5%
Graduate or professional
   degree 5.4%

Proportion who speak a language other than English at home: 2.9%

Per-capita personal income: $16,486

Poverty rate:
All 15.7%
Under age 18 .... 21.0%
Age 18 and older 13.9%

New public high-school graduates in:
1992-93 (estimate) 43,710
2001-02 (estimate) 44,870

New GED diploma recipients: 11,759

High-school dropout rate: 13.4%

POLITICAL LEADERSHIP

Governor: Ned Ray McWherter (D), term ends 1995

Governor's higher-education aide: Billy Stair, G12 State Capitol, Nashville 37243; (615) 741-5098

U.S. Senators: Jim Sasser (D), term ends 1995; (Governor McWherter is expected to appoint a Democrat to replace Al Gore.)

U.S. Representatives:
6 Democrats, 3 Republicans
Bob Clement (D), Jim Cooper (D), John J. Duncan, Jr. (R), Harold E. Ford (D), Bart Gordon (D), Marilyn Lloyd (D), James H. Quillen (R), Don Sundquist (R), John Tanner (D)

General Assembly: Senate, 20 Democrats, 13 Republicans; House, 63 Democrats, 36 Republicans

COLLEGES AND UNIVERSITIES

Higher education:
Public 4-year institutions 10
Public 2-year institutions 14
Private 4-year institutions 42
Private 2-year institutions 21
Total 87

Vocational institutions: 125

Statewide coordinating board:
Tennessee Higher
   Education Commission
Parkway Towers, Suite 1900
404 James Robertson Parkway
Nashville 37243
(615) 741-7562
Arliss L. Roaden, executive director

Private-college association:
Tennessee Independent Colleges
   and Universities
611 Commerce Street, Suite 2912
Nashville 37203
(615) 242-6400
Hans C. Giesecke, president

Institutions censured by the AAUP:
None

Institution under NCAA sanctions:
University of Tennessee
at Knoxville

FACULTY MEMBERS

Full-time faculty members by rank:
Professor 2,354
Associate professor 1,998
Assistant professor 1,892
Instructor 892
Lecturer 54
No rank 80
Total 7,270

Full-time faculty members with tenure:
Men 3,245
Women 1,016
Total 4,261

Average pay of full-time professors

Public 4-year institutions:
Professor $50,613
Associate professor $40,250
Assistant professor $33,813
Instructor $23,772
No rank .... n/a
All $41,089

Public 2-year institutions:
Professor $39,384
Associate professor $33,499
Assistant professor $29,567
Instructor $24,647
No rank $25,734
All $30,509

Private 4-year institutions:
Professor $48,836
Associate professor $34,714
Assistant professor $29,323
Instructor $21,255
No rank $23,233
All $35,883

STUDENTS

Enrollment:
At public 4-year institutions   109,944
At public 2-year institutions . 65,105
At private 4-year institutions   46,032
At private 2-year institutions . 5,157
Undergraduate 198,709
Graduate 22,285
Professional 5,244
American Indian 476
Asian 2,283
Black 31,240
Hispanic 1,302
White 186,541
Foreign 4,396
Total 226,238

Enrollment highlights:
Women 54.4%
Full-time 65.1%
Minority 15.9%
Foreign 1.9%
10-year change in total
  enrollment .... Up 10.6%

Proportion of enrollment made up of minority students:
At public 4-year institutions . 15.1%
At public 2-year institutions . 15.4%
At private 4-year institutions   17.4%
At private 2-year institutions   26.4%

Degrees awarded:
Associate 5,642
Bachelor's 17,577
Master's 4,839
Doctorate 626
Professional 1,289

Residence of new students: State residents made up 79% of all freshmen enrolled in Tennessee; 85% of all Tennessee residents who were freshmen attended college in their home state.

Test scores: Students averaged 20.1 on the A.C.T., which was taken by an

TENNESSEE
Continued

estimated 64% of Tennessee's high-school seniors.

Graduation rates at NCAA Division I institutions:
Austin Peay State University .. 29%
East Tennessee State
  University 34%
Memphis State University 32%
Middle Tennessee State
  University 34%
Tennessee State University 21%
Tennessee Technological
  University 49%
University of Tennessee
  at Chattanooga 30%
University of Tennessee
  at Knoxville 51%
Vanderbilt University 77%

MONEY

Average tuition and fees:
At public 4-year institutions . $1,518
At public 2-year institutions .. $848
At private 4-year institutions $6,889
At private 2-year institutions $4,203

Expenditures:
Public institutions .. $1,519,680,000
Private institutions . $1,005,210,000

State funds for higher-education operating expenses: $747,525,000
Two-year change: Up 5%

State spending on student aid:
Need-based: $13,086,000
Non–need-based: $330,000
Other: $5,875,000

Salary of chief executive of largest public 4-year campus:
William T. Snyder, University of Tennessee at Knoxville: $126,000

Total spending on research and development by doctorate-granting universities: $232,121,000
Sources:
Federal government 59.0%
State and local governments . 13.2%
Industry 4.7%
The institution itself 16.8%
Other 6.2%

Total federal spending on college- and university-based research and development: $133,724,000
Selected programs:
Department of Health
  and Human Services $88,097,000
National Science
  Foundation $9,419,000
Department of Defense . $6,803,000
Department
  of Agriculture $7,431,000
Department of Energy . $13,998,000

Largest endowment:
Vanderbilt University $613,207,000

Top fund raisers:
Vanderbilt University . $50,478,000
University of Tennessee $32,002,000
University of the South . $7,433,000

MISCELLANY

■ Memphis State University's Center for Applied Psychological Research is one of the nation's leading sources of information about tobacco use and its effect on metabolism and body weight. Studies done by psychology professors affiliated with the center have been included in several recent reports by the Surgeon General.

■ While jeans may be the clothing of

choice on most college campuses, faculty members and some students at the University of the South don academic gowns when they go to class. Students earn the right to wear gowns when they join the Order of the Gownsmen by earning a 3.4 in their freshman year and maintaining the required GPA throughout their remaining years.

■ The oldest institutions of higher education in the state are the University of Tennessee at Knoxville and Tusculum College, both founded in 1794.

TEXAS

SINCE the oil bust of the mid-1980's, Texas has worked to diversify its economy, focusing on high-technology businesses with links to the research and expertise of the University of Texas and Texas A&M University Systems.

Texas expected another boon with the construction of the Superconducting Supercollider, and it promised to contribute $1-billion for the project—a key reason the U.S. Department of Energy selected the state as the site for it. The project had a close call in June 1992, when the House of Representatives voted to end construction. But the Senate voted in August 1992 to continue financing it.

The $8.25-billion effort may be headed for more trouble with Bill Clinton's assumption of the Presidency. Although Mr. Clinton supports the SSC, its advocates fear he won't fight for it as President Bush did.

Few would dispute Texas' overall success in attracting high-tech industries and projects. But for all the benefit that such growth has brought to the state, it has not insulated colleges from tight budgets and the need to streamline. Higher-education officials are in the second year of a $5.7-billion biennial budget. Colleges started out with about $3-million more than they had in the previous budget, but the Legislature cut their allocations by 3.2 per cent in early 1992. Many college officials fear another setback in 1993, as lawmakers try to make up a projected $5-billion deficit.

Spending on higher education represents 16.6 per cent of the state's revenue and accounts for the lion's share of non-mandatory state spending. Therefore, educators feel the state's colleges, universities, and medical schools are especially vulnerable, even with the support of Democratic Gov. Ann W. Richards, elected in 1990 and viewed positively by many in higher education.

Hans Mark, who retired as chancellor of the University of Texas System in September 1992, noted that over the past eight years, state appropriations for higher education had increased by only 1 per cent when adjusted for inflation. Mr. Mark was replaced by William H. Cunningham, the former president of the university's Austin campus.

The state's public colleges—most notably the UT and A&M Systems, which have the largest endowments of public-university systems anywhere—have by necessity become adept at fund raising. For instance, in fall 1991, the University of Texas Southwestern Medical Center at Dallas received four donations totaling $85-million. And in the spring of 1992, Texas A&M University received land on Guam, valued at $52-million, from an alumnus.

While university officials are

TEXAS
Continued

pleased with their fund-raising success, they complain that legislators use that financial prowess to argue against large increases in state funds for postsecondary education.

Realizing that money is becoming tighter, some institutions are taking steps now that they hope will lead to savings later. In June 1992, for example, the University of Houston at Clear Lake eliminated eight academic programs and 45 staff positions.

Part of the restructuring is related to lawmakers' interest in accountability. Many legislators are pressing for "strategic planning," in which educators would prepare goals that would be used to set budgeting priorities.

Legislators also want to provide appropriations based on performance in all state agencies, but particularly in higher education. In performance-based financing, colleges would receive a portion of their appropriation based on a number of criteria, including graduation rates.

Ethnic and racial issues are always present in Texas, particularly among Hispanics, who complain that the state doesn't do enough to recruit minority students to its colleges. In January 1992, a state district judge ruled that the Texas higher-education system discriminated against residents of South Texas, a mostly Hispanic region, and gave the state until May 1993 to correct the inequities. The state is appealing that decision; but in the interim, the plaintiffs have issued a plan to create dozens of new master's and doctoral programs at the border colleges.

The plan would cost the state $200-million a year for the next decade.

Among the state's public colleges are two historically black institutions: Prairie View A&M and Texas Southern Universities. The U.S. Supreme Court ruled in June 1992 that Mississippi had not done enough to desegregate its higher-education system, but it is unclear what impact, if any, that ruling will have on Texas.

Several private institutions are major players in Texas higher education, including Southern Methodist, Texas Christian, and Rice Universities.

Another well-known private institution, Baylor University, won a big victory in November 1991 when the Baptist General Convention of Texas voted to alter the group's relationship with the university in a way that Baylor officials say will assure academic freedom for the institution. Fundamentalist Baptists had aggressively campaigned against the move.

DEMOGRAPHICS

Population: 17,349,000   (Rank: 3)

Age distribution:
Up to 17 .... 28.6%
18 to 24 .... 10.9%
25 to 44 .... 33.3%
45 and older 27.2%

Racial and ethnic distribution:
American Indian 0.4%
Asian 1.9%
Black 11.9%
White 75.2%
Other and unknown 10.6%
Hispanic (may be any race) . 25.5%

Educational attainment of adults (highest level):
9th grade or less 13.5%
Some high school, no diploma 14.4%
High-school diploma 25.6%
Some college, no degree 21.1%

Associate degree 5.2%
Bachelor's degree 13.9%
Graduate or professional
   degree 6.5%

Proportion who speak a language other than English at home: 25.4%

Per-capita personal income: $17,230

Poverty rate:
All 18.1%
Under age 18 .... 24.3%
Age 18 and older 15.6%

New public high-school graduates in:
1992-93 (estimate) 174,660
2001-02 (estimate) 193,850

New GED diploma recipients: 39,944

High-school dropout rate: 12.9%

POLITICAL LEADERSHIP

Governor: Ann W. Richards (D), term ends 1995

Governor's higher-education aide:
Beverly Salas, Box 12428, Austin 78711; (512) 463-1877

U.S. Senators: Lloyd Bentsen (D), term ends 1995; Phil Gramm (R), term ends 1997

U.S. Representatives:
21 Democrats, 9 Republicans
Michael A. Andrews (D), Bill Archer (R), Dick Armey (R), Joe L. Barton (R), Henry Bonilla (R), Jack Brooks (D), John Bryant (D), Jim Chapman (D), Ronald D. Coleman (D), Larry Combest (R), E de la Garza (D), Tom DeLay (R), Chet Edwards (D), Jack Fields (R), Martin Frost (D), Pete Geren (D), Henry B. Gonzalez (D), Gene Green (D), Ralph M. Hall (D), Eddie Bernice Johnson (D), Sam Johnson (R), Greg Laughlin (D), Solomon P. Ortiz (D), J.J. Pickle (D), Bill Sarpalius (D), Lamar Smith (R), Charles W. Stenholm (D), Frank Tejeda (D), Craig A. Washington (D), Charles Wilson (D)

Legislature: Senate, 18 Democrats, 13 Republicans; House, 92 Democrats, 57 Republicans, 1 vacancy

COLLEGES AND UNIVERSITIES

Higher education:
Public 4-year institutions 40
Public 2-year institutions 65
Private 4-year institutions 57
Private 2-year institutions 10
Total 172

Vocational institutions: 372

Statewide coordinating board:
Texas Higher Education
   Coordinating Board
P.O. Box 12788
Austin 78711
(512) 483-6100
Kenneth H. Ashworth, commissioner

Private-college association:
Independent Colleges and
   Universities of Texas
P.O. Box 13105
Austin 78711
(512) 472-9522
Carol L. McDonald, president

Institutions censured by the AAUP:
Amarillo College, Blinn College, Frank Phillips College, Houston Baptist University, Southwestern Adventist College, University of Texas of the Permian Basin

Institutions under NCAA sanctions:
Lamar University, Texas A&M

TEXAS
Continued

University, University of Texas at El Paso, University of Texas–Pan American

FACULTY MEMBERS

Full-time faculty members by rank:
Professor 5,636
Associate professor 4,710
Assistant professor 4,702
Instructor 1,374
Lecturer 1,113
No rank 4,560
Total 22,095

Full-time faculty members with tenure:
Men 7,616
Women 2,380
Total 9,996

Average pay of full-time professors

Public 4-year institutions:
Professor $54,694
Associate professor $40,353
Assistant professor $34,130
Instructor $25,312
No rank $30,382
All $41,351

Public 2-year institutions:
Professor $40,290
Associate professor $35,851
Assistant professor $32,680
Instructor $27,588
No rank $33,280
All $33,439

Private 4-year institutions:
Professor $52,271
Associate professor $38,560
Assistant professor $32,438
Instructor $23,204
No rank $22,042
All $40,273

STUDENTS

Enrollment:
At public 4-year institutions   417,777
At public 2-year institutions   384,537
At private 4-year institutions   94,305
At private 2-year institutions . 4,818
Undergraduate 788,613
Graduate 96,926
Professional 15,898
American Indian 3,006
Asian 27,907
Black 80,458
Hispanic 148,296
White 617,626
Foreign 24,144
Total 901,437

Enrollment highlights:
Women 53.3%
Full-time 54.5%
Minority 29.6%
Foreign 2.7%
10-year change in total
  enrollment .... Up 28.5%

Proportion of enrollment made up of minority students:
At public 4-year institutions . 27.7%
At public 2-year institutions . 33.1%
At private 4-year institutions 22.6%
At private 2-year institutions 42.5%

Degrees awarded:
Associate 22,828
Bachelor's 60,472
Master's 18,047
Doctorate 2,268
Professional 4,109

Residence of new students: State residents made up 92% of all freshmen enrolled in Texas; 95% of all Texas residents who were freshmen attended college in their home state.

Test scores: Students averaged 876

on the S.A.T., which was taken by an estimated 44% of Texas' high-school seniors.

Graduation rates at NCAA Division I institutions:
Baylor University 66%
Lamar University 18%
Prairie View A&M University .. n/a
Rice University 84%
Sam Houston State University . 33%
Southern Methodist University 69%
Southwest Texas State
   University 28%
Stephen F. Austin State
   University 39%
Texas A&M University 65%
Texas Christian University 57%
Texas Southern University 9%
Texas Tech University 38%
University of Houston .... n/a
University of North Texas 35%
University of Texas at Arlington 26%
University of Texas at Austin .. 58%
University of Texas at El Paso . 26%
University of Texas–
   Pan American 12%
University of Texas
   at San Antonio 19%

MONEY

Average tuition and fees:
At public 4-year institutions .. $986
At public 2-year institutions .. $495
At private 4-year institutions $6,497
At private 2-year institutions $4,394

Expenditures:
Public institutions .. $5,604,164,000
Private institutions . $1,397,222,000

State funds for higher-education operating expenses: $2,802,348,000
Two-year change: Up 9%

State spending on student aid:
Need-based: $29,755,000
Non–need-based: None
Other: $106,211,000

Salary of chief executive of largest public 4-year campus:
Robert M. Berdahl, University of Texas at Austin: salary n/a

Total spending on research and development by doctorate-granting universities: $1,123,816,000
Sources:
Federal government 46.5%
State and local governments . 11.6%
Industry 6.9%
The institution itself 22.5%
Other 12.5%

Total federal spending on college- and university-based research and development: $469,460,000
Selected programs:
Department of Health
   and Human Services $264,463,000
National Science
   Foundation $48,276,000
Department of Defense $59,139,000
Department
   of Agriculture $21,839,000
Department of Energy . $26,584,000

Largest endowment:
University of Texas
   System $3,374,301,000

Top fund raisers:
University of Texas
   at Austin $68,056,000
Texas A&M University $44,713,000
University of Houston . $43,916,000

MISCELLANY

■ Arte Público Press, a publishing unit at the University of Houston, has begun a 10-year, $20-million project to recover, catalog, and publish lost, forgotten, and deteriorating Hispanic-

TEXAS
Continued

American literary works from the colonial period through 1960.

■ Shelley Fisher Fishkin, a professor of American studies at the University of Texas at Austin, has prompted a re-examination of the Mark Twain classic *Huckleberry Finn* by writing that the character of Huck was based on a black child. Oxford University Press will publish Ms. Fishkin's book on the topic, *Was Huck Black? Mark Twain and African-American Voices,* in 1993.

■ In recognition of "Community College Month," South Plains College officials awarded scholarship certificates to 27 newborns in 1992. The infants were dubbed "the Class of 2010." If they graduate from high school, they can use their $1,000 scholarship certificates at the two-year college.

■ A dispute between Texas Methodists and Baptists obscures any higher-education institution's clear claim to being the oldest in the state. Southwestern University, a private liberal-arts college affiliated with the United Methodist Church, was founded in 1840 as Rutersville College. Baylor University, a private institution affiliated with the Baptist General Convention of Texas, was chartered in 1845. Baylor officials note that although Rutersville received its charter earlier, the college was closed during the Civil War. They say Baylor is the state's oldest higher-education institution in continuous operation.

UTAH

In Utah, where higher education has long been esteemed by the public and lawmakers, the nine-institution System of Higher Education is projecting a 40-per-cent increase in enrollment by 2000.

Such growth—and a lack of money to keep up with it—is placing enormous burdens on Utah's public colleges and universities and causing the Board of Regents to rethink the state's tradition of providing access to all students who want to go to college.

In the 1991-92 academic year the regents adopted several measures to cap enrollment, including stricter admission standards, and eliminated state-supported remedial courses at the universities. The Board of Regents is the governing and coordinating unit for all of higher education.

Under tough new residency standards adopted by the board in April 1992 for out-of-state students, a student must prove that Utah will be his or her permanent home after graduation. Also, students who move to Utah and enroll in a public college in their first year in the state will have to pay non-resident tuition for the entire length of their enrollment.

Some critics argue that cutting the number of students from outside Utah will result in a less diverse student population. But supporters say the institutions' first allegiance should be to the state's residents.

Utah's newly elected Governor, Mike Leavitt, a Republican, believes residents should be given priority for admission to the state's universities. He also advocates raising admissions requirements so fewer students will need remediation in college.

One response to the enrollment crunch has been a plan by Utah Valley Community College to become a four-year institution. President Kerry Romesburg has pushed that alternative as a way to provide more educational opportunities to residents of Utah County, where the only four-year institution is Brigham Young University, founded by the Mormon Church. Although Brigham Young has produced many of the state's business and political leaders—including the outgoing Republican Governor, Norman H. Bangerter, and Sen. Orrin G. Hatch, also a Republican—more and more of its students are coming from across the nation.

While supporters of the proposal to convert Utah Valley to a four-year institution say it would provide more opportunities for local residents to earn baccalaureate degrees, opponents worry that the college's job-training role would be lost.

Utah faculty members generate millions of dollars in research money for their institutions. Utah State University is strong in space and agricultural research, while the University of Utah is a leader in research on artificial organs and genetics.

However, the University of Utah's research efforts have not been without problems. In 1991 the university publicized researchers' claims that nuclear-fusion energy could be created from a simple experiment. Scientists elsewhere criticized the university for going public before nuclear physicists could review the claims. In the end, the state shut down its National Cold Fusion Institute because it could no longer attract outside support.

DEMOGRAPHICS

Population: 1,770,000   (Rank: 35)

Age distribution:
Up to 17 .... 36.3%
18 to 24 .... 11.8%
25 to 44 .... 29.1%
45 and older 22.8%

Racial and ethnic distribution:
American Indian 1.4%
Asian 1.9%
Black 0.7%
White 93.8%
Other and unknown 2.2%
Hispanic (may be any race) .. 4.9%

Educational attainment of adults (highest level):
9th grade or less 3.4%
Some high school, no diploma 11.5%
High-school diploma 27.2%
Some college, no degree 27.9%
Associate degree 7.8%
Bachelor's degree 15.4%
Graduate or professional
 degree 6.8%

Proportion who speak a language other than English at home: 7.8%

Per-capita personal income: $14,625

Poverty rate:
All 11.4%
Under age 18 .... 12.5%
Age 18 and older 10.7%

New public high-school graduates in:
1992-93 (estimate) 24,860
2001-02 (estimate) 26,181

New GED diploma recipients: 801

High-school dropout rate: 8.7%

POLITICAL LEADERSHIP

Governor: Mike Leavitt (R), term ends 1997

UTAH
Continued

Governor's higher-education aide:
n/a

U.S. Senators: Robert F. Bennett (R), term ends 1999; Orrin G. Hatch (R), term ends 1995

U.S. Representatives:
2 Democrats, 1 Republican
James V. Hansen (R), Bill Orton (D), Karen Shepherd (D)

Legislature: Senate, 11 Democrats, 18 Republicans; House, 26 Democrats, 49 Republicans

COLLEGES AND UNIVERSITIES

Higher education:
Public 4-year institutions	4
Public 2-year institutions	5
Private 4-year institutions	2
Private 2-year institutions	4
Total	15

Vocational institutions: 38

Statewide coordinating board:
Utah System of Higher Education
355 West North Temple
Three Triad Center, Suite 550
Salt Lake City 84180
(801) 538-5247
Wm. Rolfe Kerr, commissioner of higher education

Private-college association:
None

Institution censured by the AAUP:
Westminster College of Salt Lake City

Institutions under NCAA sanctions:
None

FACULTY MEMBERS

Full-time faculty members by rank:
Professor	1,094
Associate professor	940
Assistant professor	817
Instructor	291
Lecturer	36
No rank	159
Total	3,337

Full-time faculty members with tenure:
Men	1,717
Women	287
Total	2,004

Average pay of full-time professors

Public 4-year institutions:
Professor	$48,566
Associate professor	$36,050
Assistant professor	$31,451
Instructor	$24,704
No rank	n/a
All	$38,483

Public 2-year institutions:
Professor	$33,391
Associate professor	$30,931
Assistant professor	$28,288
Instructor	$24,677
No rank	$27,916
All	$28,606

Private 4-year institutions:
Professor	$50,111
Associate professor	$39,780
Assistant professor	$32,913
Instructor	$26,650
No rank	$28,855
All	$41,157

STUDENTS

Enrollment:
At public 4-year institutions	57,529
At public 2-year institutions	28,579
At private 4-year institutions	33,687
At private 2-year institutions	1,508

Undergraduate 110,637
Graduate 9,464
Professional 1,202
American Indian 1,322
Asian 2,243
Black 661
Hispanic 2,233
White 110,150
Foreign 4,694
Total 121,303

Enrollment highlights:
Women 48.8%
Full-time 64.0%
Minority 5.5%
Foreign 3.9%
10-year change in total
  enrollment .... Up 29.1%

Proportion of enrollment made up of minority students:
At public 4-year institutions .. 5.9%
At public 2-year institutions .. 8.8%
At private 4-year institutions . 2.0%
At private 2-year institutions . 9.7%

Degrees awarded:
Associate 3,750
Bachelor's 10,907
Master's 2,479
Doctorate 361
Professional 380

Residence of new students: State residents made up 64% of all freshmen enrolled in Utah; 90% of all Utah residents who were freshmen attended college in their home state.

Test scores: Students averaged 21.0 on the A.C.T., which was taken by an estimated 65% of Utah's high-school seniors.

Graduation rates at NCAA Division I institutions:
Brigham Young University 39%
Southern Utah University 66%
University of Utah 33%
Utah State University 52%
Weber State University 11%

MONEY

Average tuition and fees:
At public 4-year institutions . $1,524
At public 2-year institutions . $1,173
At private 4-year institutions $2,182
At private 2-year institutions $4,319

Expenditures:
Public institutions $914,771,000
Private institutions ... $252,753,000

State funds for higher-education operating expenses: $345,888,000
Two-year change: Up 13%

State spending on student aid:
Need-based: $1,042,000
Non–need-based: $1,396,000
Other: $9,400,000

Salary of chief executive of largest public 4-year campus:
Arthur K. Smith, University of Utah: $135,200

Total spending on research and development by doctorate-granting universities: $187,076,000
Sources:
Federal government 67.7%
State and local governments .. 9.1%
Industry 3.9%
The institution itself 15.6%
Other 3.6%

Total federal spending on college- and university-based research and development: $122,880,000
Selected programs:
Department of Health
  and Human Services $47,417,000
National Science
  Foundation $13,396,000

UTAH
Continued

Department of Defense	$48,369,000
Department of Agriculture	$2,957,000
Department of Energy	$5,465,000

Largest endowment:
University of Utah ... $78,223,000

Top fund raisers:
University of Utah	$46,461,000
Utah State University	$5,640,000
Dixie College	$3,442,000

MISCELLANY

■ Phi Beta Kappa rejected in 1992 Brigham Young University's application to become a member of the national honor society. The organization said the university's religious philosophy was not compatible with academic freedom. BYU's mission statement says that education that does not emphasize Jesus Christ is "inadequate."

■ Doctors at the University Hospital at the University of Utah performed the first successful artificial-heart operation in 1982. Barney Clark, the recipient of the Jarvik-7 artificial heart, lived for 112 days.

■ Utah State University is the home of "Dr. Lent's Leech Lab," named for Charles M. Lent, a professor of biology who is an authority on the feeding behavior of leeches. Because parts of the brains of leeches are similar to those of humans, Mr. Lent says his work may have applications for such ailments as Parkinson's disease.

■ The oldest institution of higher education in the state is the University of Utah, founded in 1850.

VERMONT

As economic problems continued to slam New England in 1992, Vermont found itself with a $60-million deficit and a need to slash 1992-93 budgets throughout the state government.

Higher education's share of the slash was 3 per cent, with each college or university asked to set its own priorities for the cutbacks.

Tuition for Vermont residents rose 17 per cent at the University of Vermont and 6 to 8 per cent in the Vermont State Colleges System. The university had raised tuition by more than 15 per cent for the 1991-92 year and already was considered elitist by some people because of its high tuition and large proportion of out-of-state students.

Vermont's Democratic Governor, Howard Dean, wants the state to pay for educating medical students who agree to practice in rural Vermont after graduating. Mr. Dean was re-elected in November 1992.

The University of Vermont and Johnson State College got new presidents after enduring campus controversies in 1991. The university's interim president, Thomas P. Salmon, is a former Governor and member of the state House of Representatives. He is regarded as a political asset for the university.

His predecessor, George H. Davis, resigned after slightly less than one year as president. That year was marked by disruptive controversies, involving, among other things, the construction of a shantytown on the campus green and a student takeover of the president's office. Both protests stemmed from complaints that the university was too slow in seeking racial diversity.

Middlebury College, a private, liberal-arts institution, also got a new president in 1992. The former president, Timothy Light, resigned abruptly after being criticized for his handling of layoffs. He was replaced by John M. McCardell, Jr., who has held several faculty and administrative posts at Middlebury since 1976 and is popular on the campus.

Another of Vermont's private, liberal-arts institutions, Bennington College, also made the news in 1992. A group of students took over the president's office for a week in May to protest faculty cuts planned for 1993-94 to reduce a $1.5-million deficit. Students said the financial problems had been caused by mismanagement. Despite the protests, the faculty cuts, along with some in administrative posts, will be carried out.

Vermont, like other New England states, has long put a high value on private higher education. The state still provides financial help for eligible residents to attend any college in any state, public or private.

The University of Vermont itself was a private institution until 1955. It received only limited money from the state until that year, when financial problems forced it to forge stronger ties with the state. The university still receives less than 15 per cent of its budget from the state.

The university is run by a Board of Trustees. A separate board fulfills the same role for the three four-year colleges and two two-year colleges in the state-college system.

DEMOGRAPHICS

Population: 567,000 (Rank: 50)

Age distribution:
Up to 17 .... 25.6%
18 to 24 .... 11.1%
25 to 44 .... 33.2%
45 and older 30.2%

Racial and ethnic distribution:
American Indian 0.3%
Asian 0.6%
Black 0.3%
White 98.6%
Other and unknown 0.1%
Hispanic (may be any race) .. 0.7%

Educational attainment of adults (highest level):
9th grade or less 8.7%
Some high school, no diploma 10.6%
High-school diploma 34.6%
Some college, no degree 14.7%
Associate degree 7.2%
Bachelor's degree 15.4%
Graduate or professional
   degree 8.9%

Proportion who speak a language other than English at home: 5.8%

Per-capita personal income: $17,997

Poverty rate:
All 9.9%
Under age 18 .... 12.0%
Age 18 and older 9.1%

New public high-school graduates in:
1992-93 (estimate) 5,180
2001-02 (estimate) 6,270

New GED diploma recipients: 1,264

High-school dropout rate: 8.0%

POLITICAL LEADERSHIP

Governor: Howard Dean (D), term ends 1995

VERMONT
Continued

Governor's higher-education aide:
James Bressor, Pavilion Office Building, 109 State Street, Montpelier 05609; (802) 828-3333

U.S. Senators: James M. Jeffords (R), term ends 1995; Patrick J. Leahy (D), term ends 1999

U.S. Representative:
1 Socialist
Bernard Sanders (Socialist)

General Assembly: Senate, 14 Democrats, 16 Republicans; House, 87 Democrats, 57 Republicans, 4 Independents, 2 Progressives

COLLEGES AND UNIVERSITIES

Higher education:
Public 4-year institutions 4
Public 2-year institutions 2
Private 4-year institutions 13
Private 2-year institutions 3
Total 22

Vocational institutions: 11

Statewide coordinating boards:
Vermont State Colleges
P.O. Box 359
Waterbury 05676
(802) 241-2520
Charles Bunting, chancellor

University of Vermont
85 South Prospect Street
Burlington 05405
(802) 656-3186
Thomas P. Salmon, interim president

Private-college association:
Association of Vermont
 Independent Colleges
Two Prospect Street
Montpelier 05602
(802) 223-1662
Alan H. Weiss, executive director

Institutions censured by the AAUP:
None

Institutions under NCAA sanctions:
None

FACULTY MEMBERS

Full-time faculty members by rank:
Professor 385
Associate professor 391
Assistant professor 429
Instructor 51
Lecturer 56
No rank 192
Total 1,504

Full-time faculty members with tenure:
Men 625
Women 139
Total 764

Average pay of full-time professors
Public 4-year institutions:
Professor $54,647
Associate professor $41,294
Assistant professor $33,172
Instructor $27,151
No rank $34,752
All $42,272

Public 2-year institutions:
Professor $36,767
Associate professor $31,277
Assistant professor $23,607
Instructor $21,303
No rank .... n/a
All $27,546

Private 4-year institutions:
Professor $49,266
Associate professor $36,819
Assistant professor $31,712

Instructor $26,742
No rank $30,063
All $36,154

STUDENTS

Enrollment:
At public 4-year institutions . 16,075
At public 2-year institutions .. 4,835
At private 4-year institutions   13,462
At private 2-year institutions . 2,026
Undergraduate 31,646
Graduate 4,137
Professional 615
American Indian 131
Asian 569
Black 375
Hispanic 428
White 34,178
Foreign 717
Total 36,398

Enrollment highlights:
Women 56.8%
Full-time 68.0%
Minority 4.2%
Foreign 2.0%
10-year change in total
  enrollment .... Up 18.8%

Proportion of enrollment made up of minority students:
At public 4-year institutions .. 3.8%
At public 2-year institutions .. 1.1%
At private 4-year institutions . 6.2%
At private 2-year institutions . 1.6%

Degrees awarded:
Associate 1,262
Bachelor's 4,517
Master's 1,002
Doctorate 59
Professional 87

Residence of new students: State residents made up 43% of all freshmen enrolled in Vermont; 63% of all Vermont residents who were freshmen attended college in their home state.

Test scores: Students averaged 897 on the S.A.T., which was taken by an estimated 69% of Vermont's high-school seniors.

Graduation rates at NCAA Division I institution:
University of Vermont 76%

MONEY

Average tuition and fees:
At public 4-year institutions . $4,092
At public 2-year institutions . $2,424
At private 4-year institutions $10,649
At private 2-year institutions $6,768

Expenditures:
Public institutions $260,371,000
Private institutions ... $245,813,000

State funds for higher-education operating expenses: $54,912,000
Two-year change: Down 3%

State spending on student aid:
Need-based: $11,292,000
Non–need-based: None
Other: $10,000

Salary of chief executive of largest public 4-year campus:
Thomas P. Salmon (interim),
  University of Vermont: $125,000

Total spending on research and development by doctorate-granting universities: $45,162,000
Sources:
Federal government 67.7%
State and local governments .. 5.3%
Industry 7.7%
The institution itself 14.5%
Other 4.9%

VERMONT
Continued

Total federal spending on college- and university-based research and development: $31,687,000

Selected programs:
Department of Health
 and Human Services $26,000,000
National Science
 Foundation $1,504,000
Department of Defense ... $355,000
Department
 of Agriculture $2,980,000
Department of Energy $588,000

Largest endowment:
Middlebury College .. $209,182,000

Top fund raisers:
Middlebury College ... $10,981,000
Norwich University $5,818,000
St. Michael's College ... $2,925,000

MISCELLANY

■ Middlebury College was the first to award a degree to a black man, Alexander Lucius Twilight, in 1823.

■ At Sterling College, a small, private two-year institution that focuses on resource management and environmental studies, most students stay on the campus over the Thanksgiving holiday and enjoy a feast featuring food from the college farm.

■ The New England Culinary Institute has an annual Quadrathlon in which teams compete in a combination of sports and cooking. Team members from culinary schools around the country race bicycles carrying ingredients to a kitchen and then race their finished meals to a panel of judges.

■ The oldest institution of higher education in the state is the University of Vermont, founded in 1791.

VIRGINIA

B Y some measures, Virginia's public colleges continue to be the envy of many other states. The University of Virginia and the College of William and Mary have top-notch student bodies and faculties, historic campuses, and exceptionally loyal alumni.

Other Virginia institutions, such as George Mason University, have made names for themselves in different ways. George Mason is nationally known as a model for institutions in growing suburban areas in the way it meets local needs and forges bonds with the business community.

Despite those successes, the past few years have not been easy for Virginia higher education. The recession, which hit Virginia later than the rest of the nation, is now in full force.

Gov. L. Douglas Wilder, a Democrat, and most lawmakers find the idea of tax increases anathema, so budget cuts have been the order of the day. In total, the higher-education budget has been cut 22 per cent since 1990. As a result, tuition has been rising rapidly, although the state has tried to minimize the impact by providing more money for student aid.

Colleges got a bit of good news in November 1992, when voters approved a measure to authorize the state to issue millions of dollars in bonds for state facilities, including many at public colleges.

Although the General Assembly has not had much money in recent years, that fact has not stopped it from expressing its interest in higher education—usually by asking the State Council of Higher Education to study various issues and prepare policy options for the colleges and lawmakers to consider.

In 1992 the General Assembly asked for reports on faculty workloads, graduation rates, prepaid-tuition programs, and student aid. The council is the statewide coordinating agency for higher education; institutions have their own governing boards.

Governor Wilder is also not shy about pressing his agenda on colleges. He has pushed colleges to divest themselves of stock in companies with South African ties, to lower their tuition, and to do more to fight illegal drug use on their campuses.

In 1992 he urged colleges to keep a closer watch on athletics programs after the University of Virginia acknowledged that improper loans had been made to student athletes in the 1980's.

The scandal was particularly upsetting to Virginia officials because the university had prided itself on maintaining high academic standards in its athletics program.

An issue of continuing importance in Virginia is desegregation. While college officials have maintained that the state institutions have desegregated, it is not clear how a recent Supreme Court case on Mississippi desegregation will affect Virginia. Two of the state's public institutions—Norfolk and Virginia State Universities—are historically black.

Private colleges in Virginia include Emory and Henry, Hampden-Sydney, and Hollins Colleges; and Hampton, Liberty, and Washington and Lee Universities. Liberty, along with much of the Rev. Jerry Falwell's religious organization, has been experiencing financial problems.

DEMOGRAPHICS

Population: 6,286,000 (Rank: 12)

Age distribution:
Up to 17 .... 24.5%
18 to 24 .... 11.2%
25 to 44 .... 34.6%
45 and older 29.8%

Racial and ethnic distribution:
American Indian 0.2%
Asian 2.6%
Black 18.8%
White 77.4%
Other and unknown 0.9%
Hispanic (may be any race) .. 2.6%

Educational attainment of adults (highest level):
9th grade or less 11.2%
Some high school, no diploma 13.7%
High-school diploma 26.6%
Some college, no degree 18.5%
Associate degree 5.5%
Bachelor's degree 15.4%
Graduate or professional
  degree 9.1%

Proportion who speak a language other than English at home: 7.3%

Per-capita personal income: $20,082

Poverty rate:
All 10.2%
Under age 18 .... 13.3%
Age 18 and older 9.2%

New public high-school graduates in:
1992-93 (estimate) 56,520
2001-02 (estimate) 67,250

New GED diploma recipients: 10,264

High-school dropout rate: 10.0%

VIRGINIA
Continued

POLITICAL LEADERSHIP

Governor: L. Douglas Wilder (D), term ends 1994

Governor's higher-education aide: James W. Dyke, Jr., P.O. Box 1475, Richmond 23212; (804) 786-1151

U.S. Senators: Charles S. Robb (D), term ends 1995; John Warner (R), term ends 1997

U.S. Representatives:
7 Democrats, 4 Republicans
Herbert H. Bateman (R), Thomas J. Bliley, Jr. (R), Rick Boucher (D), Leslie L. Byrne (D), Robert W. Goodlatte (R), James P. Moran, Jr. (D), Lewis F. Payne, Jr. (D), Owen B. Pickett (D), Robert C. Scott (D), Norman Sisisky (D), Frank R. Wolf (R)

General Assembly: Senate, 22 Democrats, 18 Republicans; House, 58 Democrats, 41 Republicans, 1 Independent

COLLEGES AND UNIVERSITIES

Higher education:
Public 4-year institutions 15
Public 2-year institutions 24
Private 4-year institutions 33
Private 2-year institutions 11
Total 83

Vocational institutions: 149

Statewide coordinating board:
State Council of Higher Education for Virginia
James Monroe Building
101 North 14th Street
Richmond 23219
(804) 225-2600
Gordon K. Davies, director

Private-college association:
Council of Independent Colleges in Virginia
P.O. Box 1005
118 East Main Street
Bedford 24523
(703) 586-0606
Robert B. Lambeth, Jr., president

Institutions censured by the AAUP:
Virginia Community College System

Institution under NCAA sanctions:
Hampton University

FACULTY MEMBERS

Full-time faculty members by rank:
Professor 2,959
Associate professor 3,243
Assistant professor 2,866
Instructor 799
Lecturer 67
No rank 40
Total 9,974

Full-time faculty members with tenure:
Men 3,932
Women 994
Total 4,926

Average pay of full-time professors
Public 4-year institutions:
Professor $61,146
Associate professor $46,120
Assistant professor $37,706
Instructor $28,648
No rank $26,156
All $47,650

Public 2-year institutions:
Professor $42,256

Associate professor $37,289
Assistant professor $32,708
Instructor $28,120
No rank $22,420
All $35,361

Private 4-year institutions:
Professor $47,115
Associate professor $35,860
Assistant professor $29,796
Instructor $22,890
No rank $12,215
All $36,269

STUDENTS

Enrollment:
At public 4-year institutions   160,200
At public 2-year institutions   131,086
At private 4-year institutions   57,899
At private 2-year institutions . 4,257
Undergraduate 302,072
Graduate 45,177
Professional 6,193
American Indian   860
Asian 11,400
Black 49,566
Hispanic 4,803
White 280,786
Foreign 6,027
Total 353,442

Enrollment highlights:
Women 55.3%
Full-time 55.4%
Minority 19.2%
Foreign 1.7%
10-year change in total
  enrollment .... Up 26.0%

Proportion of enrollment made up of minority students:
At public 4-year institutions . 19.4%
At public 2-year institutions . 18.0%
At private 4-year institutions   19.3%
At private 2-year institutions   42.7%

Degrees awarded:
Associate 8,378
Bachelor's 27,119
Master's 7,159
Doctorate   839
Professional 1,732

Residence of new students: State residents made up 68% of all freshmen enrolled in Virginia; 78% of all Virginia residents who were freshmen attended college in their home state.

Test scores: Students averaged 893 on the S.A.T., which was taken by an estimated 63% of Virginia's high-school seniors.

Graduation rates at NCAA Division I institutions:
College of William and Mary .. 85%
George Mason University 43%
James Madison University 79%
Liberty University 36%
Old Dominion University 48%
Radford University 50%
University of Richmond 83%
University of Virginia 90%
Virginia Commonwealth
  University 42%
Virginia Military Institute 67%
Virginia Polytechnic Institute
  and State University 71%

MONEY

Average tuition and fees:
At public 4-year institutions . $2,691
At public 2-year institutions   .. $867
At private 4-year institutions $7,621
At private 2-year institutions $4,852

Expenditures:
Public institutions .. $2,682,902,000
Private institutions ... $609,665,000

State funds for higher-education operating expenses: $934,776,000
Two-year change: Down 13%

VIRGINIA
Continued

State spending on student aid:
Need-based: $7,390,000
Non–need-based: $19,230,000
Other: None

Salary of chief executive of largest public 4-year campus:
James D. McComas, Virginia Polytechnic Institute and State University: $106,714 from state plus $43,919 from private donations

Total spending on research and development by doctorate-granting universities: $321,547,000

Sources:
Federal government 52.9%
State and local governments . 17.0%
Industry 8.1%
The institution itself 14.5%
Other 7.5%

Total federal spending on college- and university-based research and development: $166,017,000

Selected programs:
Department of Health
  and Human Services $80,710,000
National Science
  Foundation $19,933,000
Department of Defense $14,639,000
Department
  of Agriculture $6,974,000
Department of Energy . $11,550,000

Largest endowment:
University of Virginia $507,002,000

Top fund raisers:
University of Virginia . $54,043,000
Virginia Polytechnic Institute
  and State University $25,833,000
Washington and Lee
  University $19,823,000

MISCELLANY

■ Under a new partnership intended to promote racial harmony and an understanding of cultural diversity, students from historically black Virginia Union University and predominantly white Lynchburg College are sharing dormitories, attending conferences together, and staging joint artistic performances.

■ Southern Seminary College, a private, two-year institution for women, has a national reputation for its equitation program. Its riding team has won numerous awards in Intercollegiate Horse Association competitions.

■ Virginia's highest mountain, Mount Rogers, is named for the founder of the Massachusetts Institute of Technology, William Barston Rogers. Before moving to Massachusetts, Rogers was a professor of natural philosophy at the University of Virginia and the first state geologist.

■ The oldest institution of higher education in Virginia—and the second oldest in the nation—is the College of William and Mary, which will celebrate its 300th anniversary in 1993.

WASHINGTON

CONTINUING an activist streak, the State of Washington nearly became a laboratory for a new approach to higher-education finance in 1992. But a legislative proposal that would have raised public-college tuition and significantly expanded financial aid for students at public and private colleges fell victim to political and budgetary considerations that have come to influence higher-education policy making.

Indeed, higher education has figured prominently in the state's deliberations on ways to avert a deficit—and not always to the colleges' advantage. In fact, early in 1992, college leaders feared that legislators and then-Gov. Booth Gardner, a Democrat, would try to balance the state budget by cutting higher-education appropriations and raising tuition without any increase in financial aid.

Ultimately, public colleges were spared major cuts. The financial-aid reform died when student groups successfully lobbied to eliminate the tuition increases and when public colleges, led by the University of Washington, the state's premier research institution, quietly fought the measure.

The public institutions opposed the proposal to redirect state money from public-college programs to student aid, which also would have benefited students at private colleges.

The issue of how to apportion state financial aid remains a sticking point in Washington. Some private-college officials complain that the state's formula does not take into account the higher costs of their institutions.

The financial-aid debates reflect the state's interest in making higher education more accessible to its citizens, and Washington has taken several steps in recent years to accomplish that.

In 1990 the University of Washington and Washington State and Central Washington Universities opened five branch campuses in the populous Vancouver, Spokane, and Puget Sound regions. The branch campuses are supposed to reach more minority and part-time students. Of the state's six public, four-year institutions, only the main branches of the University of Washington and Evergreen State College are in densely populated areas—Seattle and Olympia, respectively.

The state has also improved its two-year institutions, coinciding with then-Governor Gardner's interest in improving the training of Washington's work force. Since 1991 five vocational-technical institutions formerly run by local school boards have been placed under the same board that had previously overseen community colleges. The board is now called the State Board for Community and Technical Colleges.

Like the community colleges, each technical college is governed by its own board of trustees.

Washington's newly elected Governor, Mike Lowry, a Democrat, advocated lifting enrollment caps at the universities and said the state should spend more on public schools so students would be better prepared for college.

The Higher Education Coordinating Board, which oversees four-year institutions, continues to look into ways in which colleges can work better with public schools and to encourage colleges to improve undergraduate education.

Washington also continues to attract a large number of Asian immigrants, placing greater demand for classes in English as a second language on the community colleges, which have historically provided basic-skills and literacy training in addition to more traditional associate-degree-level courses.

DEMOGRAPHICS

Population: 5,018,000 (Rank: 16)

WASHINGTON
Continued

Age distribution:
Up to 17 .... 26.2%
18 to 24 .... 9.7%
25 to 44 .... 34.2%
45 and older 29.9%

Racial and ethnic distribution:
American Indian 1.7%
Asian 4.3%
Black 3.1%
White 88.5%
Other and unknown 2.4%
Hispanic (may be any race) .. 4.4%

Educational attainment of adults (highest level):
9th grade or less 5.5%
Some high school, no diploma 10.7%
High-school diploma 27.9%
Some college, no degree 25.0%
Associate degree 7.9%
Bachelor's degree 15.9%
Graduate or professional
 degree 7.0%

Proportion who speak a language other than English at home: 9.0%

Per-capita personal income: $19,484

Poverty rate:
All 10.9%
Under age 18 .... 14.5%
Age 18 and older 9.7%

New public high-school graduates in:
1992-93 (estimate) 46,340
2001-02 (estimate) 62,170

New GED diploma recipients: 9,523

High-school dropout rate: 10.6%

POLITICAL LEADERSHIP

Governor: Mike Lowry (D), term ends 1997

Governor's higher-education aide: n/a

U.S. Senators: Slade Gorton (R), term ends 1995; Patty Murray (D), term ends 1999

U.S. Representatives:
8 Democrats, 1 Republican
Maria Cantwell (D), Norm Dicks (D), Jennifer Dunn (R), Thomas S. Foley (D), Jay Inslee (D), Mike Kreidler (D), Jim McDermott (D), Al Swift (D), Jolene Unsoeld (D)

Legislature: Senate, 28 Democrats, 21 Republicans; House, 66 Democrats, 32 Republicans

COLLEGES AND UNIVERSITIES

Higher education:
Public 4-year institutions 6
Public 2-year institutions 27
Private 4-year institutions 20
Private 2-year institutions 4
Total 57

Vocational institutions: 117

Statewide coordinating board:
Higher Education Coordinating Board
917 Lakeridge Way
P.O. Box 43430
Olympia 98504
(206) 753-3241
Ann Daley, executive director

Private-college association:
Washington Friends of
 Higher Education
600 Tower Building
1809 Seventh Avenue

Seattle 98101
(206) 624-9093
David M. Irwin, president

Institutions censured by the AAUP:
None

Institutions under NCAA sanctions:
None

FACULTY MEMBERS

Full-time faculty members by rank:
Professor	1,795
Associate professor	1,304
Assistant professor	995
Instructor	101
Lecturer	144
No rank	2,508
Total	6,847

Full-time faculty members with tenure:
Men	3,649
Women	1,106
Total	4,755

Average pay of full-time professors

Public 4-year institutions:
Professor	$53,019
Associate professor	$39,592
Assistant professor	$34,973
Instructor	$26,926
No rank	$36,767
All	$43,780

Public 2-year institutions:
Professor	n/a
Associate professor	n/a
Assistant professor	n/a
Instructor	n/a
No rank	$33,156
All	$33,156

Private 4-year institutions:
Professor	$44,693
Associate professor	$36,241
Assistant professor	$30,627
Instructor	$25,405
No rank	$16,217
All	$36,647

STUDENTS

Enrollment:
At public 4-year institutions	81,433
At public 2-year institutions	146,199
At private 4-year institutions	33,503
At private 2-year institutions	2,143
Undergraduate	240,208
Graduate	19,922
Professional	3,148
American Indian	3,854
Asian	15,424
Black	7,361
Hispanic	6,122
White	225,213
Foreign	5,304
Total	263,278

Enrollment highlights:
Women	55.9%
Full-time	57.0%
Minority	12.7%
Foreign	2.0%
10-year change in total enrollment	Down 13.3%

Proportion of enrollment made up of minority students:
At public 4-year institutions	13.9%
At public 2-year institutions	12.3%
At private 4-year institutions	11.4%
At private 2-year institutions	15.4%

Degrees awarded:
Associate	14,319
Bachelor's	18,359
Master's	5,284
Doctorate	632
Professional	852

Residence of new students: State residents made up 89% of all freshmen enrolled in Washington; 92% of all Washington residents who were fresh-

WASHINGTON
Continued

men attended college in their home state.

Test scores: Students averaged 916 on the S.A.T., which was taken by an estimated 50% of Washington's high-school seniors.

Graduation rates at NCAA Division I institutions:
Gonzaga University 52%
Eastern Washington University 34%
University of Washington 60%
Washington State University .. 51%

MONEY

Average tuition and fees:
At public 4-year institutions . $1,823
At public 2-year institutions .. $844
At private 4-year institutions $9,463
At private 2-year institutions $6,743

Expenditures:
Public institutions .. $1,922,673,000
Private institutions ... $330,200,000

State funds for higher-education operating expenses: $909,892,000

Two-year change: Up 6%

State spending on student aid:
Need-based: $23,483,000
Non–need-based: None
Other: $876,000

Salary of chief executive of largest public 4-year campus:
William P. Gerberding, University of Washington: $115,382 from state plus $52,930 from private donations

Total spending on research and development by doctorate-granting universities: $312,169,000

Sources:
Federal government 73.8%
State and local governments .. 3.0%
Industry 7.9%
The institution itself 12.0%
Other 3.3%

Total federal spending on college- and university-based research and development: $240,010,000

Selected programs:
Department of Health
 and Human Services $148,170,000
National Science
 Foundation $32,251,000
Department of Defense $23,360,000
Department
 of Agriculture $8,468,000
Department of Energy .. $9,840,000

Largest endowment:
University
 of Washington $198,343,000

Top fund raisers:
University
 of Washington $102,832,000
Washington State
 University $25,970,000
Pacific Lutheran
 University $6,284,000

MISCELLANY

■ Spokane Falls Community College didn't want students to be embarrassed or intimidated when they worked out at the institution's new fitness center. So in 1991 it adopted a dress code that bars such apparel as halter tops, leotards, short shorts, and sleeveless "muscle shirts."

■ Crosby House, Gonzaga University's alumni center, was once the home of the singer Bing Crosby. He attended the college and dropped out a few months short of earning a degree.

The college boasts a Crosby collection that includes several gold records and an Academy Award.

- Evergreen State College's mascot is a geoduck, the largest known burrowing mollusk in the world. The school's motto is "Omnia Extares," which, loosely translated from the Latin, means "Let it all hang out."

- The oldest institution of higher education in Washington is Whitman College, founded in 1859.

WEST VIRGINIA

POLITICIANS in West Virginia spend a lot of time evaluating the way the state's public colleges function.

In 1989, acting on a recommendation from the Carnegie Foundation for the Advancement of Teaching, West Virginia divided its colleges into two systems: the University of West Virginia System for research universities and professional schools, and the State College System for the other institutions.

The theory was that the reorganization would eliminate the duplication of academic programs and help colleges find ways to improve the state's economy, which has been plagued by a decline in the coal industry and a long-standing belief of many citizens that they didn't need a college education.

Some progress has been made. In 1992 the state created a grant program for public colleges, seeking to develop applied-technology and job-training programs. The state's public colleges are also creating links to the public schools by improving teacher-education programs and helping schools offer more Advanced Placement classes. The new boards for the two systems have been working to develop better-defined missions for the colleges.

Many politicians and educators, however, say the reorganization has not lived up to expectations. The state continues to operate three medical schools—despite repeated requests from lawmakers that they be merged to save money.

Competition among institutions for academic programs remains intense—particularly with the state facing tight budgets.

So, once again, the state is seeking a study of higher education. Gov. Gaston Caperton, a Democrat, and legislators have created a 17-member Higher Education Advocacy Team, which is supposed to develop a strategic plan for the state's colleges.

Governor Caperton was re-elected in 1992. During his campaign, he was criticized for supporting tax increases. While the increases are highly unpopular in the state, colleges would probably have faced much more severe budget cuts without them.

While West Virginia colleges must make do with a limited supply of state funds, they have fared well in gaining "earmarked" money from the federal government.

In appropriations bills for fiscal 1992, Congress provided more than $65-million to two West Virginia institutions—West Virginia University and Wheeling Jesuit College. That was more earmarked money than any other state received.

The largesse was due largely to Sen. Robert C. Byrd, a West Virginia Democrat who had pledged that he would use his position as chairman of the Senate Appropriations Committee to

WEST VIRGINIA
Continued

steer as much money as possible to his home state.

DEMOGRAPHICS

Population: 1,801,000   (Rank: 34)

Age distribution:
Up to 17	24.3%
18 to 24	10.4%
25 to 44	29.9%
45 and older	35.5%

Racial and ethnic distribution:
American Indian	0.1%
Asian	0.4%
Black	3.1%
White	96.2%
Other and unknown	0.1%
Hispanic (may be any race)	0.5%

Educational attainment of adults (highest level):
9th grade or less	16.8%
Some high school, no diploma	17.3%
High-school diploma	36.6%
Some college, no degree	13.2%
Associate degree	3.8%
Bachelor's degree	7.5%
Graduate or professional degree	4.8%

Proportion who speak a language other than English at home: 2.6%

Per-capita personal income: $14,301

Poverty rate:
All	19.7%
Under age 18	26.2%
Age 18 and older	17.5%

New public high-school graduates in:
1992-93 (estimate)	20,340
2001-02 (estimate)	16,140

New GED diploma recipients: 4,155

High-school dropout rate: 10.9%

POLITICAL LEADERSHIP

Governor: Gaston Caperton (D), term ends 1997

Governor's higher-education aides: Charles W. Manning and Paul Marion, 1018 Kanawha Boulevard East, Suite 700, Charleston 25301; (304) 558-2177

U.S. Senators: Robert C. Byrd (D), term ends 1995; John D. Rockefeller, IV (D), term ends 1997

U.S. Representatives:
3 Democrats, 0 Republicans
Alan B. Mollohan (D), Nick J. Rahall, II (D), Bob Wise (D)

Legislature: Senate, 32 Democrats, 2 Republicans; House, 79 Democrats, 21 Republicans

COLLEGES AND UNIVERSITIES

Higher education:
Public 4-year institutions	12
Public 2-year institutions	4
Private 4-year institutions	9
Private 2-year institutions	3
Total	28

Vocational institutions: 51

Statewide coordinating boards:
University System of West Virginia
1018 Kanawha Boulevard East
Suite 700
Charleston 25301
(304) 558-2177
Charles W. Manning, chancellor

State College System of West Virginia
1018 Kanawha Boulevard East

Suite 700
Charleston 25301
(304) 558-2177
Paul Marion, chancellor

Private-college association:
West Virginia Association
  of Independent Colleges
Security Building, Suite 1106
100 Capitol Street
Charleston 25301
(304) 345-5525
Robert F. Prather, president

Institutions censured by the AAUP:
None

Institutions under NCAA sanctions:
None

FACULTY MEMBERS

Full-time faculty members by rank:
Professor 792
Associate professor 687
Assistant professor 764
Instructor 246
Lecturer 63
No rank 0
Total 2,552

Full-time faculty members with tenure:
Men 1,114
Women 413
Total 1,527

Average pay of full-time professors
Public 4-year institutions:
Professor $44,756
Associate professor $36,313
Assistant professor $29,534
Instructor $22,645
No rank .... n/a
All $35,610
Public 2-year institutions:
Professor $36,090
Associate professor $29,533
Assistant professor $24,356
Instructor $19,001
No rank .... n/a
All $27,610
Private 4-year institutions:
Professor $34,662
Associate professor $30,069
Assistant professor $25,974
Instructor $23,131
No rank .... n/a
All $28,904

STUDENTS

Enrollment:
At public 4-year institutions . 63,362
At public 2-year institutions . 10,746
At private 4-year institutions . 7,880
At private 2-year institutions . 2,802
Undergraduate 74,660
Graduate 8,839
Professional 1,291
American Indian 139
Asian 688
Black 3,160
Hispanic 360
White 78,795
Foreign 1,648
Total 84,790

Enrollment highlights:
Women 55.4%
Full-time 68.5%
Minority 5.2%
Foreign 1.9%
10-year change in total
  enrollment .... Up 3.4%

Proportion of enrollment made up of minority students:
At public 4-year institutions .. 5.4%
At public 2-year institutions .. 3.6%
At private 4-year institutions . 5.7%
At private 2-year institutions . 7.3%

Degrees awarded:
Associate 2,841

WEST VIRGINIA
Continued

Bachelor's 7,414
Master's 1,740
Doctorate 128
Professional 302

Residence of new students: State residents made up 71% of all freshmen enrolled in West Virginia; 85% of all West Virginia residents who were freshmen attended college in their home state.

Test scores: Students averaged 19.8 on the A.C.T., which was taken by an estimated 52% of West Virginia's high-school seniors.

Graduation rates at NCAA Division I institutions:
Marshall University 39%
West Virginia University 55%

MONEY

Average tuition and fees:
At public 4-year institutions . $1,543
At public 2-year institutions .. $930
At private 4-year institutions $8,751
At private 2-year institutions $2,767

Expenditures:
Public institutions $493,825,000
Private institutions $96,910,000

State funds for higher-education operating expenses: $284,606,000

Two-year change: Up 3%

State spending on student aid:
Need-based: $5,806,000
Non–need-based: None
Other: $8,917,000

Salary of chief executive of largest public 4-year campus:
Neil S. Bucklew, West Virginia University: $104,608

Total spending on research and development by doctorate-granting universities: $46,946,000
Sources:
Federal government 42.0%
State and local governments .. 2.6%
Industry 21.4%
The institution itself 30.3%
Other 3.7%

Total federal spending on college- and university-based research and development: $22,240,000
Selected programs:
Department of Health
　and Human Services . $5,503,000
National Science
　Foundation $1,333,000
Department of Defense ... $211,000
Department
　of Agriculture $4,225,000
Department of Energy .. $5,278,000

Largest endowment:
West Virginia University
　Foundation $70,940,000

Top fund raisers:
West Virginia University $14,620,000
Marshall University $4,710,000
Davis and Elkins College $2,746,000

MISCELLANY

■ Every fall, West Virginia University's mechanical-engineering department sponsors a "Fall Fruit Fling," in which students drop pumpkins from a 120-foot-high building. Students design protective devices aimed at keeping the pumpkins intact. Those that survive the crash are judged on the originality of the protective designs and on how close they come to their targets.

■ In 1989, in extreme financial straits, Salem College became the first institution to merge with a Japanese university and changed its name to Salem-Teikyo University. With half the students American and the other half Japanese, Salem-Teikyo's mission is "to educate a world citizen who acquires a wide knowledge without prejudice and makes decisions with an international point of view."

■ Students and faculty members at West Virginia Wesleyan College have reported encounters with ghosts in at least four buildings on the 88-acre campus of the quiet, Methodist, liberal-arts college. Many of the stories center on the 86-year-old Lynch-Raine administration building, where a student reportedly hanged himself in the 1960's. Other stories come from students in Agnes Howard Hall, a dormitory named for a Wesleyan student who died in 1920.

■ Some dispute exists over the oldest college in West Virginia. Marshall University and West Liberty State College were founded in 1837. But Bethany College says those two institutions did not become bachelor's-degree-granting institutions until years later. Bethany believes its 1840 charter makes it the oldest institution of higher education in the state.

WISCONSIN

IN Wisconsin, higher education is everybody's business.

Faculty members in the University of Wisconsin System routinely pressure the Legislature for higher salaries. Student groups routinely lobby for limits on tuition increases and for policies against sexual harassment on campuses. And legislators themselves often speak out against university policies that they say keep undergraduates from completing their education on time and that allow faculty members to pursue too many research and consulting interests that take them away from the classroom.

The activity reflects Wisconsin's populist traditions and the statewide importance of the university system, which serves more than 132,000 students on 26 two-year and four-year campuses, and nearly a million others through extension programs.

The geographic breadth of the system has long been one of its greatest strengths, bringing it broad political support. But recent budget pressures have caused some state officials to question whether the state can afford so many higher-education opportunities.

The issue was highlighted in the spring of 1992, when the newly appointed president of the Board of Regents was quoted as saying that the state should consider closing campuses, particularly in the north and northwest, where the university's Eau Claire, River Falls, Stout, and Superior campuses are located. He later said he had been misquoted, but university officials say they do expect to eliminate some duplicative programs at those campuses, or find ways to offer some programs within regions.

Under its new president, Katharine C. Lyall, the university is also undertaking what it terms a "reinvestment plan" that calls for re-allocating more than $26-million of the system's budget between 1992 and 1995 to seven goals, including greater computeriza-

WISCONSIN
Continued

tion, upgrading of laboratories and equipment, and increasing faculty pay.

One area that remains contentious is tuition.

Although university officials maintain that their proposed increases are often well below those proposed at other major Midwestern universities, the state's active and well-organized student lobby, the United Council of Wisconsin Student Governments, has worked unsuccessfully for a legislative cap on increases. Such a measure was proposed in 1992, but was strongly opposed by the university systems as too inflexible. It was not enacted.

The council has been a strong voice behind many of the system's efforts in recent years to make the campuses more accommodating to female, minority, and gay students.

The university was one of the first in the nation to adopt a "hate speech" code to penalize students who use racist, sexist, or homophobic slurs. That code was challenged by civil-liberties groups and ruled an unconstitutional infringement on free speech by a federal court in October 1991.

The university was developing a new code in 1992 when the U.S. Supreme Court issued a ruling that appeared to limit the right of public colleges to adopt such codes. In light of the ruling, the Board of Regents repealed the code in September 1992.

Student and faculty groups have been particularly active in the nationwide effort to end discrimination against gays in the Reserve Officers Training Corps.

The Wisconsin Board of Regents is the governing board for the entire system. The Board of Vocational, Technical, and Adult Education supervises technical colleges.

Wisconsin provides no direct support to its private colleges but does maintain a separate financial-aid program for students who attend those institutions, such as Alverno College and Lawrence and Marquette Universities.

DEMOGRAPHICS

Population: 4,955,000   (Rank: 17)

Age distribution:
Up to 17 .... 26.5%
18 to 24 .... 10.2%
25 to 44 .... 31.8%
45 and older 31.5%

Racial and ethnic distribution:
American Indian 0.8%
Asian 1.1%
Black 5.0%
White 92.2%
Other and unknown 0.9%
Hispanic (may be any race) .. 1.9%

Educational attainment of adults (highest level):
9th grade or less 9.5%
Some high school, no diploma 11.9%
High-school diploma 37.1%
Some college, no degree 16.7%
Associate degree 7.1%
Bachelor's degree 12.1%
Graduate or professional
  degree 5.6%

Proportion who speak a language other than English at home: 5.8%

Per-capita personal income: $17,939

Poverty rate:
All 10.7%

Under age 18 .... 14.9%
Age 18 and older 9.2%

New public high-school graduates in:
1992-93 (estimate) 49,970
2001-02 (estimate) 60,090

New GED diploma recipients: 3,948

High-school dropout rate: 7.1%

POLITICAL LEADERSHIP

Governor: Tommy G. Thompson (R), term ends 1995

Governor's higher-education aide:
Thomas Fonfara, State Capitol, P.O. Box 7863, Madison 53707; (608) 266-1212

U.S. Senators: Russell D. Feingold (D), term ends 1999; Herb Kohl (D), term ends 1995

U.S. Representatives:
4 Democrats, 5 Republicans
Les Aspin (D), Thomas M. Barrett (D), Steve Gunderson (R), Gerald D. Kleczka (D), Scott L. Klug (R), David R. Obey (D), Tom Petri (R), Toby Roth (R), F. James Sensenbrenner, Jr. (R)

Legislature: Senate, 18 Democrats, 15 Republicans; House, 52 Democrats, 47 Republicans

COLLEGES AND UNIVERSITIES

Higher education:
Public 4-year institutions 13
Public 2-year institutions 17
Private 4-year institutions 28
Private 2-year institutions 3
Total 61

Vocational institutions: 90

Statewide coordinating board:
University of Wisconsin System
1720 Van Hise Hall
1220 Linden Drive
Madison 53706
(608) 262-2321
Katharine C. Lyall, president

Private-college association:
Wisconsin Association of Independent Colleges and Universities
25 West Main Street, Suite 583
Madison 53703
(608) 256-7761
Rolf Wegenke, president

Institution censured by the AAUP:
Marquette University

Institutions under NCAA sanctions:
None

FACULTY MEMBERS

Full-time faculty members by rank:
Professor 2,664
Associate professor 2,011
Assistant professor 2,010
Instructor 240
Lecturer 259
No rank 2,928
Total 10,112

Full-time faculty members with tenure:
Men 4,024
Women 927
Total 4,951

Average pay of full-time professors
Public 4-year institutions:
Professor $53,527
Associate professor $40,368
Assistant professor $35,844
Instructor $29,155
No rank .... n/a
All $43,894

THE ALMANAC OF HIGHER EDUCATION • THE STATES

WISCONSIN
Continued

Public 2-year institutions:
Professor $43,490
Associate professor $36,246
Assistant professor $30,058
Instructor $25,553
No rank $37,964
All $37,699

Private 4-year institutions:
Professor $45,692
Associate professor $38,019
Assistant professor $31,136
Instructor $22,396
No rank $30,309
All $36,320

STUDENTS

Enrollment:
At public 4-year institutions   152,691
At public 2-year institutions   100,838
At private 4-year institutions   45,095
At private 2-year institutions . 1,150
Undergraduate 266,775
Graduate 29,452
Professional 3,547
American Indian 2,050
Asian 4,991
Black 10,667
Hispanic 4,692
White 271,096
Foreign 6,278
Total 299,774

Enrollment highlights:
Women 54.7%
Full-time 63.6%
Minority 7.6%
Foreign 2.1%
10-year change in total
   enrollment .... Up 11.4%

Proportion of enrollment made up of minority students:
At public 4-year institutions .. 6.1%
At public 2-year institutions .. 9.6%
At private 4-year institutions . 8.4%
At private 2-year institutions . 2.3%

Degrees awarded:
Associate 8,549
Bachelor's 25,888
Master's 5,599
Doctorate 784
Professional 1,023

Residence of new students: State residents made up 84% of all freshmen enrolled in Wisconsin; 88% of all Wisconsin residents who were freshmen attended college in their home state.

Test scores: Students averaged 21.7 on the A.C.T., which was taken by an estimated 59% of Wisconsin's high-school seniors.

Graduation rates at NCAA Division I institutions:
Marquette University 73%
University of Wisconsin
   at Green Bay 31%
University of Wisconsin
   at Madison 66%
University of Wisconsin
   at Milwaukee 36%

MONEY

Average tuition and fees:
At public 4-year institutions . $1,951
At public 2-year institutions . $1,234
At private 4-year institutions $8,237
At private 2-year institutions $4,768

Expenditures:
Public institutions .. $2,307,325,000
Private institutions ... $588,850,000

State funds for higher-education operating expenses: $902,988,000
Two-year change: Up 7%

State spending on student aid:
Need-based: $42,595,000
Non–need-based: $1,183,000
Other: $1,944,000

Salary of chief executive of largest public 4-year campus:
Donna E. Shalala, University of Wisconsin at Madison: $120,300

Total spending on research and development by doctorate-granting universities: $363,364,000
Sources:
Federal government 57.5%
State and local governments . 16.3%
Industry 4.7%
The institution itself 13.1%
Other 8.5%

Total federal spending on college- and university-based research and development: $198,712,000
Selected programs:
Department of Health
  and Human Services $107,744,000
National Science
  Foundation $36,789,000
Department of Defense . $7,786,000
Department
  of Agriculture $7,778,000
Department of Energy . $16,647,000

Largest endowment:
University of Wisconsin
  Foundation $144,780,000

Top fund raisers:
University of Wisconsin
  at Madison $128,395,000
Marquette University .. $17,478,000
Beloit College $7,276,000

MISCELLANY

■ A Kuwaiti prince who graduated from the University of Wisconsin–Parkside is offering two $1,000 scholarships for Kenosha, Wis., residents who served in the Persian Gulf war. The prince, Sabah al-Sabah, said: "I'll never forget the love I got from the Kenosha community during my UW–Parkside years."

■ Administrators at Viterbo College fired the entire staff of the student newspaper in 1992 because the editors had published parodies about condoms and ads for a clinic's abortion-counseling services. The college is affiliated with the Roman Catholic Church. College officials said that the newspaper, *The Lumen,* had "shocked the sensibilities of many students, faculty, staff, and administrators."

■ Ninety-one diaries believed to contain the oldest continuous account of rural life in America have been donated to the University of Wisconsin's Eau Claire campus. The diaries were kept in the late 19th and 20th centuries by a farmer and businessman and his sons.

■ The oldest institution of higher education in Wisconsin is Nashotah House, an Episcopal seminary founded in 1842.

WYOMING

KEEPING track of higher education in Wyoming is easy. But the politics behind the system sometimes are hard to follow—particularly when financing proposals affect the state's influential energy interests.

The only institution in the state that grants four-year degrees is the University of Wyoming. The state has

WYOMING
Continued

seven public, two-year colleges, governed by the Wyoming Community College Commission. Wyoming is the only state with no private, non-profit institutions of higher learning.

The University of Wyoming enjoys strong support from lawmakers as well as from Gov. Michael Sullivan, a Democrat. But a downturn in the state's oil and coal industries kept the Legislature from providing any increase in financing for the 1992-93 academic year, and the university is weighing proposals to raise fees and eliminate programs.

The energy industries were influential in killing a legislative proposal that would have instituted a statewide tax to finance increases for the the two-year colleges. Community-college financing is a recurring issue, and often confounding to those who say the existing system is inequitable.

Currently, only the seven counties where the colleges are located assess taxes to support them, even though the institutions also serve students in the state's 16 other counties through off-campus centers.

Backers of the community colleges have been trying for years to expand the tax base to the other counties. But the energy companies, fearful that taxes would require them to increase their prices to non-competitive levels to cover higher costs, have succeeded in defeating such measures in the Legislature and in local referenda.

The state's budget problems also slowed the growth of the Wyoming Educational Trust Fund, which lawmakers created in 1991 with an initial contribution of $10-million. The state contributed no new money to the fund in 1992. Planned as a $50-million endowment, the fund provides income to the university, community colleges, and public schools for innovative programs.

Budget problems, however, didn't deprive Wyoming of all its momentum. Under the direction of the state's new Postsecondary Planning and Coordinating Council, the community colleges and university have taken several steps to make it easier for students to transfer to the four-year institution.

The council is chaired by Governor Sullivan and includes legislators, university and community-college leaders, and other top education officials.

DEMOGRAPHICS

Population: 460,000 (Rank: 51)

Age distribution:
Up to 17 .... 29.6%
18 to 24 .... 9.6%
25 to 44 .... 32.8%
45 and older 28.0%

Racial and ethnic distribution:
American Indian 2.1%
Asian 0.6%
Black 0.8%
White 94.2%
Other and unknown 2.3%
Hispanic (may be any race) .. 5.7%

Educational attainment of adults (highest level):
9th grade or less 5.7%
Some high school, no diploma 11.2%
High-school diploma 33.2%
Some college, no degree 24.2%
Associate degree 6.9%
Bachelor's degree 13.1%
Graduate or professional
  degree 5.7%

Proportion who speak a language other than English at home: 5.7%

Per-capita personal income: $16,937

Poverty rate:
All 11.9%
Under age 18 .... 14.4%
Age 18 and older 10.8%

New public high-school graduates in:
1992-93 (estimate) 5,670
2001-02 (estimate) 4,840

New GED diploma recipients: 1,304

High-school dropout rate: 6.9%

POLITICAL LEADERSHIP

Governor: Michael Sullivan (D), term ends 1995

Governor's higher-education aide: Scott Farris, Governor's Office, State Capitol, Cheyenne 82002; (307) 777-7434

U.S. Senators: Alan K. Simpson (R), term ends 1997; Malcolm Wallop (R), term ends 1995

U.S. Representative:
1 Republican
Craig Thomas (R)

Legislature: Senate, 10 Democrats, 20 Republicans; House, 19 Democrats, 41 Republicans

COLLEGES AND UNIVERSITIES

Higher education:
Public 4-year institutions 1
Public 2-year institutions 7
Private 4-year institutions 0
Private 2-year institutions 1
Total 9

Vocational institutions: 12

Statewide coordinating board:
Wyoming Postsecondary Education Planning and Coordinating Council
State Capitol
Cheyenne 82002
(307) 777-7434
Gov. Michael Sullivan, chairman

Private-college association:
None

Institutions censured by the AAUP:
None

Institutions under NCAA sanctions:
None

FACULTY MEMBERS

Full-time faculty members by rank:
Professor 244
Associate professor 158
Assistant professor 192
Instructor 58
Lecturer 40
No rank 330
Total 1,022

Full-time faculty members with tenure:
Men 417
Women 121
Total 538

Average pay of full-time professors
Public 4-year institutions:
Professor $51,005
Associate professor $40,055
Assistant professor $36,298
Instructor $35,868
No rank .... n/a
All $42,133

Public 2-year institutions:
Professor $34,048

WYOMING
Continued

Associate professor $34,576
Assistant professor $27,447
Instructor $23,296
No rank $28,947
All $28,930

Private 4-year institutions: n/a

STUDENTS

Enrollment:
At public 4-year institutions . 12,517
At public 2-year institutions . 18,106
At private 4-year institutions 0
At private 2-year institutions .. 703
Undergraduate 28,212
Graduate 2,894
Professional 220
American Indian 444
Asian 184
Black 284
Hispanic 905
White 28,952
Foreign 557
Total 31,326

Enrollment highlights:
Women 56.3%
Full-time 54.0%
Minority 5.9%
Foreign 1.8%
10-year change in total
  enrollment .... Up 48.1%

Proportion of enrollment made up of minority students:
At public 4-year institutions .. 5.5%
At public 2-year institutions .. 6.1%
At private 4-year institutions ... n/a
At private 2-year institutions . 6.6%

Degrees awarded:
Associate 1,629
Bachelor's 1,646
Master's 361
Doctorate 58
Professional 67

Residence of new students: State residents made up 77% of all freshmen enrolled in Wyoming; 81% of all Wyoming residents who were freshmen attended college in their home state.

Test scores: Students averaged 21.2 on the A.C.T., which was taken by an estimated 61% of Wyoming's high-school seniors.

Graduation rates at NCAA Division I institution:
University of Wyoming 42%

MONEY

Average tuition and fees:
At public 4-year institutions . $1,148
At public 2-year institutions .. $662
At private 4-year institutions ... n/a
At private 2-year institutions $7,500

Expenditures:
Public institutions $227,131,000
Private institutions $4,104,000

State funds for higher-education operating expenses: $122,152,000
Two-year change: Down 2%

State spending on student aid:
Need-based: $220,000
Non–need-based: None
Other: None

Salary of chief executive of largest public 4-year campus:
Terry P. Roark, University of Wyoming: $119,940

Total spending on research and development by doctorate-granting universities: $22,831,000

Sources:
Federal government 53.5%
State and local governments .. 9.0%
Industry 8.8%
The institution itself 27.7%
Other 1.0%

Total federal spending on college- and university-based research and development: $9,731,000

Selected programs:
Department of Health
 and Human Services . $1,004,000
National Science
 Foundation $4,545,000
Department of Defense . $1,042,000
Department
 of Agriculture $1,632,000
Department of Energy $324,000

Largest endowment:
University of Wyoming $45,291,000

Top fund raiser:
University of Wyoming . $7,272,000

MISCELLANY

■ A new library on Easter Island was named in 1991 for the late William Mulloy, an anthropologist at the University of Wyoming who spent much of his career doing research on the island's shrines and monuments and restoring them. Mulloy died in 1978.

■ Casper College has won four national team championships in rodeo.

■ Northwest College, a two-year public college, takes new students through an intensive one-week orientation each fall. Programs include swimming and hiking trips in Yellowstone National Park and sessions on stress management.

■ The oldest institution of higher education in the state is the University of Wyoming, founded in 1886.

Sources and Notes

THE statistics in this Almanac are meant to provide a broad view of higher education in the 50 states and the District of Columbia.

The figures are comparable from state to state, and, in all cases, they were the latest available at press time.

The time covered by the statistics varies from item to item. For example, the racial and ethnic distribution of the adult population of the states was gathered from the decennial census in 1990.

The U.S. Department of Education typically releases statistics from its surveys of colleges and universities one to three years after collecting the data. As a consequence, the latest figures on academic degrees conferred cover 1989-90.

Many statistics that would be useful to educators and policy makers are not available for every state.

For example, the Education Department does not collect information to show, on a comparable basis across the states, the proportion of high-school students who go on to college, or the proportion of college students who complete their degrees. Some states do collect such information, but those figures are not included in this Almanac because they would not always be comparable.

Because of rounding, figures may not add to 100 per cent. The designation "n/a" indicates that data are not available or not applicable. In some instances, U.S. totals may include data on service schools and outlying areas that are not shown separately.

DEMOGRAPHICS

Population:
SOURCE: Census Bureau
DATE: 1991

Age distribution:
SOURCE: Census Bureau
DATE: 1991

Racial and ethnic distribution:
SOURCE: Census Bureau
DATE: 1990

Educational attainment of adults (highest level):
SOURCE: Census Bureau
DATE: 1990
NOTE: Figures cover persons 25 years and older.

Proportion who speak a language other than English at home:
SOURCE: Census Bureau
DATE: 1990
NOTE: Figures cover persons 5 years and older who "sometimes or always" speak a language other than English at home.

Per-capita personal income:
SOURCE: U.S. Department of Commerce
DATE: 1991

Poverty rate:
SOURCE: Census Bureau
DATE: 1990

New public high-school graduates:
SOURCE: U.S. Department
of Education
NOTE: The figures cover only graduates of public high schools, which account for about 89 per cent of all high-school graduates.

New GED diploma recipients:
SOURCE: American Council
on Education
DATE: 1991
NOTE: General Education Development diplomas are high-school equivalency certificates awarded to high-school dropouts who pass the GED test.

High-school dropout rate:
SOURCE: Census Bureau
DATE: 1990
NOTE: The figures represent the proportion of 16- to 19-year-olds who are not high-school graduates and who are not enrolled in school.

POLITICAL LEADERSHIP

Governor:
SOURCE: National Governors'
Association

Governor's higher-education aide:
SOURCES: National Governors'
Association; *Chronicle of Higher Education* reporting

U.S. Senators:
SOURCE: Secretary of the Senate;
Associated Press

U.S. Representatives:
SOURCE: Clerk of the House
of Representatives; Associated Press

Legislature:
SOURCE: National Conference
of State Legislatures
NOTE: Figures represent the strength of state legislatures as of November 1992.

COLLEGES AND UNIVERSITIES

Higher education:
SOURCE: U.S. Department
of Education
DATE: 1990-91
NOTE: The figures include public, private non-profit, and private for-profit institutions accredited at the college level by an agency recognized by the U.S. Department of Education. Public institutions include colleges and universities controlled by local and state governments, as well as military academies and other institutions operated by the federal government. The figures include approximately 300 private for-profit institutions.

Vocational institutions:
SOURCE: U.S. Department
of Education
DATE: 1990-91
NOTE: Figure includes public, private non-profit, and private for-profit non-collegiate institutions that offer post-secondary education.

Statewide coordinating board:
SOURCES: State Higher Education
Executive Officers; *Chronicle of Higher Education* reporting
NOTE: These organizations are responsible for planning for public colleges and universities. Some boards also have governing authority. Those that do are indicated in the state narratives.

Private-college association:
SOURCES: National Association

SOURCES & NOTES
Continued

of Independent Colleges and Universities; *Chronicle of Higher Education* reporting

Institutions censured by the AAUP:
SOURCE: American Association of University Professors
DATE: Action as of June 1992
NOTE: The AAUP censures institutions when it finds that they have violated its standards of academic freedom and tenure. The standards seek to protect the rights of faculty members to free speech without fear of penalty, and to due process in appointment, promotion, and tenure decisions. The standards are included in the 1940 Statement of Principles of Academic Freedom and Tenure, which was developed by the AAUP and the Association of American Colleges and endorsed by more than 100 other academic organizations. Censure was imposed on administrative officers at all institutions listed except at those noted.

Institutions under NCAA sanctions:
SOURCE: National Collegiate Athletic Association
DATE: Action as of November 1992

FACULTY MEMBERS

Full-time faculty members by rank and tenure status:
SOURCE: U.S. Department of Education
DATE: 1990-91
NOTE: Figures cover full-time members of the instructional staff on 9- and 10-month contracts only. Those faculty members account for 86 per cent of all full-time college professors. Figures do not include medical-school faculty members.

Average pay of full-time professors:
SOURCE: U.S. Department of Education
DATE: 1990-91
NOTE: Figures cover full-time members of the instructional staff on 9- and 10-month contracts only. Those faculty members account for 86 per cent of all full-time college professors. Figures do not include medical-school faculty members. The average for all faculty members includes the category of lecturer, which is not shown separately.

STUDENTS

Enrollment:
SOURCE: U.S. Department of Education
DATE: Fall 1990
NOTE: The full definitions of the racial and ethnic categories are as follows: American Indian and Alaskan native; Asian and Pacific Islander; black, non-Hispanic; Hispanic; and white, non-Hispanic. Foreign students are non-resident aliens studying in the United States on a temporary basis.

Enrollment highlights:
SOURCE: U.S. Department of Education
NOTE: The change in enrollment is from fall 1980 to fall 1990. The other figures are from fall 1990. All proportions are based on total enrollment with one exception: The proportion of students who are minority-group members covers only U.S. citizens.

Proportion of enrollment made up of minority students:
SOURCE: U.S. Department of Education
DATE: Fall 1990

Degrees awarded:
SOURCE: U.S. Department of Education
DATE: 1989-90

Residence of new students:
SOURCE: U.S. Department of Education
DATE: Fall 1988
NOTE: The figures cover freshmen only.

Test scores:
SOURCES: *Chronicle of Higher Education* reporting; College Board
DATES: 1991 for A.C.T.; 1992 for S.A.T.
NOTE: The A.C.T. (American College Testing Program's A.C.T. Assessment) is scored on a scale from 1 to 36. The S.A.T.—the College Board's Scholastic Aptitude Test—is scored on a scale from 400 to 1,600. For each state, one score is given, depending on which test was taken by the larger number of students.

Graduation rates at NCAA Division I institutions:
SOURCE: National Collegiate Athletic Association
NOTE: These figures were compiled by the NCAA as part of a federal requirement to collect information on graduation rates of all students and student-athletes at the 297 institutions that play in Division I, the top competitive level. The figures represent the proportion of full-time freshmen in 1984-85 who earned a bachelor's degree within six years. The figures include both athletes and non-athletes.

MONEY

Average tuition and fees:
SOURCE: U.S. Department of Education
DATE: 1990-91
NOTE: Figures cover undergraduate charges and are weighted by fall 1990 full-time-equivalent undergraduate enrollment. The figures for public institutions represent charges to state residents.

Expenditures:
SOURCE: U.S. Department of Education
DATE: 1989-90

State funds for higher-education operating expenses:
SOURCE: Edward R. Hines, Illinois State University
DATE: 1992-93
NOTE: Figures include state tax funds appropriated for colleges and universities, for student aid, and for governing and coordinating boards. They do not include funds for capital outlays and money from sources other than state taxes, such as student fees or appropriations from local governments.

State spending on student aid:
SOURCE: National Association of State Scholarship and Grant Programs
DATE: 1991-92
NOTE: "Need-based" aid covers scholarships awarded on the basis of a student's financial situation. "Non-need-based" aid includes scholarships given to reward meritorious students, to encourage students to major in particular disciplines, and to reduce the difference in tuition costs between public and private institutions. The category of "other" aid includes spending for work-study, loan-forgiveness, and loan programs. The statistics cover aid to both undergraduate and graduate students. The figures include most of the money that states

SOURCES & NOTES
Continued

spend on student financial aid. However, some states may spend more on programs that are not specifically identified as student-aid programs.

Salary of chief executive of largest public 4-year campus:
SOURCE: *Chronicle of Higher Education* reporting
DATE: 1992-93
NOTE: Institutions were selected on the basis of fall 1990 enrollment as reported by the U.S. Department of Education.

Total spending on research and development by doctorate-granting universities:
SOURCE: National Science Foundation
DATE: Fiscal year 1990
NOTE: Figures cover spending in science and engineering, and exclude spending in such disciplines as the arts, education, and the humanities.

Total federal spending on college- and university-based research and development:
SOURCE: National Science Foundation
DATE: Fiscal year 1990
NOTE: Figures cover federal obligations, which are funds set aside for payments. Institutions do not always receive them in the year in which they were obligated. Figures include only spending for science and engineering projects, and exclude spending in such disciplines as the arts, education, and the humanities.

Largest endowment:
SOURCES: National Association of College and University Business Officers; *Chronicle of Higher Education* reporting
DATE: As of June 30, 1991

Top fund raisers:
SOURCE: Council for Aid to Education
DATE: 1990-91
NOTE: Figures are based on a survey of 1,059 institutions, which together received about 85 per cent of all private contributions to colleges and universities. Rankings of institutions may be heavily influenced by the timing of fund drives, unusually large gifts, and other factors.

MISCELLANY

SOURCE: *Chronicle of Higher Education* reporting

Enrollment by Race

THE TABLE that follows shows the distribution of enrollment by racial and ethnic group in fall 1990 at more than 3,000 colleges and universities.

The distribution is based on each institution's total enrollment, including full-time and part-time students and undergraduate and graduate students. The total enrollment appears in the last column.

The institutions are listed in alphabetical order by state. Institutions that are part of state systems of higher education appear under the system name.

The figures were compiled by the U.S. Department of Education, which conducts an annual survey of enrollment by race. The table omits about 500 institutions that did not provide complete information to the Education Department.

Because of rounding, the figures may not add to 100 per cent.

The full definitions of the racial and ethnic groups are as follows: American Indian or Alaskan native; Asian or Pacific Islander; black, non-Hispanic; Hispanic; and white, non-Hispanic. Figures in those groups cover both U.S. citizens and resident aliens. Foreign students include all non-resident aliens who are enrolled in U.S. colleges and universities, regardless of their racial or ethnic backgrounds.

ALABAMA	American Indian	Asian	Black	Hispanic	White	Foreign	Total
Alabama A&M U	0.0%	0.6%	77.4%	0.2%	14.2%	7.6%	4,886
Alabama Aviation and Tech C	2.0	1.3	11.5	1.5	83.1	0.6	539
Alabama Christian Sch of Religion	0.0	0.0	20.2	0.0	79.8	0.0	104
Alabama State U	0.0	0.2	97.4	0.3	1.5	0.5	4,587
Athens State C	0.4	0.4	6.4	0.2	92.2	0.4	2,770
Auburn U							
Main campus	0.2	0.7	3.9	0.6	91.3	3.3	21,537
Montgomery	0.1	1.9	16.7	0.1	80.9	0.4	6,261
Bessemer State Tech C	0.0	0.2	25.4	0.1	74.2	0.0	1,730
Birmingham Southern C	0.1	1.7	11.3	0.2	86.2	0.6	1,902
Bishop State CC	0.1	0.3	59.4	0.0	39.0	1.1	2,057
Brewer State JC	0.0	0.1	9.2	0.0	90.8	0.0	1,114
C A Fredd State Tech C	0.0	0.0	93.9	0.0	6.1	0.0	279
Carver State Tech C	0.2	0.6	83.9	0.0	15.3	0.0	535
Central Alabama CC	0.5	0.1	15.5	0.1	83.5	0.2	2,097
Chattahoochee Valley State CC	0.1	0.8	26.7	1.4	71.0	0.0	1,685
Chauncey Sparks State Tech C	0.4	0.8	46.4	0.0	52.4	0.0	506

ALABAMA, cont.

	American Indian	Asian	Black	Hispanic	White	Foreign	Total
CC of the Air Force	0.0%	0.0%	17.8%	0.0%	82.2%	0.0%	29,567
Concordia C	0.0	0.0	100.0	0.0	0.0	0.0	380
Douglas MacArthur State Tech C	0.5	0.2	19.3	0.0	80.0	0.0	560
Draughons JC	0.0	0.0	55.0	0.0	45.0	0.0	189
Enterprise State JC	0.6	2.2	12.5	2.2	82.4	0.0	2,108
Gadsden State CC	0.2	0.3	11.6	0.5	81.2	6.3	5,478
George C Wallace State CC Dothan	0.3	0.6	11.7	0.3	87.0	0.1	3,755
George C Wallace State CC Selma	0.2	0.2	31.6	0.1	67.6	0.2	1,678
Harry M Ayers State Tech C	0.0	0.2	10.4	0.0	89.0	0.4	529
Hobson State Tech C	0.2	0.0	43.3	0.0	56.5	0.0	593
Huntingdon C	0.1	2.0	6.8	0.3	89.6	1.1	791
International Bible C	0.0	0.0	15.9	0.0	81.7	2.4	82
J F Drake State Tech C	0.1	0.5	36.4	0.1	62.9	0.0	852
Jacksonville State U	0.3	0.5	16.4	0.6	80.7	1.5	8,448
James H Faulkner State JC	0.5	0.4	8.5	0.2	90.2	0.2	3,109
Jefferson Davis CC	1.3	0.1	20.9	0.2	77.2	0.3	1,054
Jefferson State CC	0.2	0.4	10.3	0.3	88.0	0.8	6,636
John C Calhoun State CC	0.8	0.5	10.6	0.5	87.2	0.3	7,833
John M Patterson State Tech C	0.0	1.2	32.7	0.3	65.8	0.0	681
Judson C	0.0	0.0	4.5	0.3	94.9	0.3	312
Lawson State CC	0.0	0.0	96.4	0.0	3.6	0.0	1,711
Livingston U	0.4	0.0	27.4	0.3	70.4	1.5	1,921
Lurleen B Wallace State JC	0.2	0.0	13.5	0.1	85.1	1.0	1,256
Marion Military Inst	0.0	1.6	18.7	2.4	76.4	0.8	246
Miles C	0.0	0.2	99.7	0.0	0.2	0.0	584
Mobile C	0.5	0.0	13.3	0.2	83.8	2.2	1,325
National Education Center National Inst of Tech	0.0	0.0	52.8	1.0	46.1	0.0	193
Northeast Alabama State JC	0.6	0.3	0.8	0.1	98.0	0.2	1,546
Northwest Alabama CC	0.6	0.1	3.4	0.1	95.8	0.1	1,940
Oakwood C	0.0	0.0	89.7	0.0	0.0	10.3	1,266
Patrick Henry State JC	0.3	0.4	16.3	0.0	82.9	0.0	1,160
Reid State Tech C	0.5	0.0	27.2	0.0	72.3	0.0	364
RETS Electronic Inst	0.0	0.0	90.3	0.0	9.7	0.0	72
Samford U	0.1	1.0	6.0	0.5	92.5	0.0	4,164
Shelton State CC	0.0	1.8	21.0	0.4	76.8	0.0	5,112
Shoals CC	0.7	0.3	10.2	0.1	88.7	0.0	2,185
Snead State JC	0.1	0.1	0.7	0.2	99.0	0.0	1,691
Southeastern Bible C	0.0	0.0	5.3	0.0	92.1	2.6	152
Southern JC Birmingham	0.0	0.0	97.7	0.0	2.3	0.0	512
Southern JC Huntsville	0.7	0.5	33.4	2.1	63.0	0.3	916
Southern Union State JC	0.1	0.6	16.0	0.2	82.8	0.3	2,896
Southwest State Tech C	0.2	1.3	28.7	0.2	69.6	0.0	1,027
Spring Hill C	0.3	1.1	7.2	3.3	86.7	1.3	1,305
Stillman C	0.0	0.6	99.1	0.0	0.3	0.0	770
Talladega C	0.1	0.1	97.2	0.4	2.1	0.0	667
Trenholm State Tech C	0.0	0.0	78.8	0.0	21.2	0.0	783
Troy State U							
Main campus	0.4	0.4	15.9	0.8	81.7	0.8	5,024
Dothan	0.4	0.8	7.0	1.2	90.4	0.3	1,933
Montgomery	0.5	1.1	23.5	1.5	73.4	0.1	2,736
Tuskegee U	0.0	0.8	92.2	2.6	2.5	1.9	3,510
U of Alabama Tuscaloosa	0.3	0.7	8.9	0.7	85.0	4.5	19,794

	American Indian	Asian	Black	Hispanic	White	Foreign	Total
Birmingham	0.1%	1.2%	15.3%	0.3%	79.2%	3.9%	15,356
Huntsville	0.4	2.8	5.0	1.0	87.0	3.8	8,139
U of Montevallo	0.3	0.3	7.3	0.6	90.8	0.6	3,250
U of North Alabama	0.3	0.2	7.5	0.3	91.7	0.5	5,622
U of South Alabama	0.6	1.6	10.0	0.8	81.8	5.2	11,584
Walker C	0.0	0.0	3.0	0.0	96.9	0.1	909
Walker State Tech C	0.8	0.0	7.2	0.5	91.4	0.0	969
Wallace State CC Hanceville	0.0	0.0	2.0	0.0	97.9	0.0	4,043

ALASKA

Alaska Bible C	4.7	2.8	3.8	0.9	84.0	3.8	106
Alaska JC	15.0	1.5	18.0	4.6	60.9	0.0	394
Alaska Pacific U	6.3	2.9	5.8	3.2	79.9	1.9	1,266
Sheldon Jackson C	27.6	1.1	1.8	2.5	65.5	1.5	275
U of Alaska							
Anchorage	5.2	2.8	4.2	2.3	84.3	1.1	17,490
Fairbanks	15.5	1.7	2.2	1.5	76.2	2.9	7,592
Southeast	12.5	2.9	0.6	1.5	81.6	0.8	2,710

ARIZONA

Al Collins Graphic Design Sch	4.6	0.0	5.3	8.0	81.1	1.1	475
American Graduate Sch of International Management	2.4	3.5	4.0	4.8	53.5	31.8	1,557
American Indian Bible C	72.2	2.4	0.0	5.6	9.5	10.3	126
Arizona C of the Bible	0.9	0.9	2.8	3.8	88.7	2.8	106
Arizona State U	1.2	3.0	2.4	6.3	81.9	5.1	42,936
Arizona Western C	1.7	0.8	2.7	41.5	53.1	0.1	4,911
Cochise C	1.1	3.5	5.8	25.2	64.3	0.0	4,542
DeVry Inst of Tech	3.0	6.2	4.3	11.1	73.2	2.2	2,647
Eastern Arizona C	6.3	0.6	2.3	18.3	72.4	0.0	4,568
Frank Lloyd Wright Sch of Architecture	0.0	0.0	3.3	0.0	63.3	33.3	30
ITT Tech Inst Phoenix	5.1	1.0	10.9	17.9	65.1	0.0	312
ITT Tech Inst Tucson	5.5	1.6	5.1	19.1	68.8	0.0	256
Maricopa County CC Dist							
Gateway CC	3.6	1.9	4.7	11.3	77.7	0.7	6,821
Glendale CC	1.0	2.5	2.4	9.8	83.2	0.9	18,512
Mesa CC	1.9	2.6	2.4	8.2	83.6	1.2	19,818
Paradise Valley CC	0.8	1.7	0.5	4.0	92.4	0.5	5,557
Phoenix CC	3.0	2.2	5.2	14.7	74.3	0.6	12,837
Rio Salado CC	2.0	1.2	3.5	9.1	83.9	0.2	10,480
Scottsdale CC	2.4	1.3	1.2	3.4	91.0	0.7	9,612
South Mountain CC	2.6	1.3	15.5	33.6	46.7	0.4	3,288
Mohave CC	2.2	1.0	0.1	3.6	93.0	0.1	4,945
National Education Center Arizona Automotive Inst	5.9	1.5	5.4	18.5	68.6	0.0	912
Northern Arizona U	5.2	1.0	1.4	7.1	83.2	2.1	16,992
Northland Pioneer C	25.0	0.4	1.2	6.5	66.8	0.0	5,656
Pima CC	2.5	2.0	3.4	22.4	67.6	2.3	28,766
Prescott C	6.9	0.2	0.5	3.4	88.7	0.3	593
Southwestern C	1.5	0.7	2.9	1.5	91.2	2.2	137
U of Arizona	1.3	3.4	2.0	9.3	78.5	5.6	35,729
Western International U	0.3	9.8	11.3	6.1	47.5	25.0	1,245
Yavapai C	6.2	1.1	0.9	5.8	84.8	1.1	6,003

THE ALMANAC OF HIGHER EDUCATION • ENROLLMENT BY RACE

ARKANSAS

	American Indian	Asian	Black	Hispanic	White	Foreign	Total
Arkansas Baptist C	0.0%	0.0%	97.9%	0.0%	2.1%	0.0%	291
Arkansas C	0.1	0.4	3.1	0.6	95.6	0.2	833
Arkansas State U							
Main campus	0.2	0.9	11.1	0.2	86.2	1.3	9,264
Beebe	2.6	0.7	5.0	0.6	91.1	0.0	1,520
Arkansas Tech U	0.7	0.4	1.9	0.4	95.9	0.6	4,062
Capital City JC of Business	0.0	0.8	44.1	0.8	54.2	0.0	236
Central Baptist C	0.5	0.5	2.5	0.0	96.5	0.0	201
Crowley's Ridge C	0.0	0.0	2.1	0.0	97.2	0.7	144
East Arkansas CC	0.1	0.3	31.6	0.5	67.5	0.0	1,467
Garland County CC	0.8	0.3	6.2	0.4	92.1	0.1	1,886
Harding U	0.4	0.2	2.0	0.6	93.5	3.3	3,228
Henderson State U	0.4	0.2	13.6	0.4	85.1	0.3	4,042
Hendrix C	0.1	1.1	5.6	0.6	90.8	1.9	1,006
John Brown U	1.0	0.5	0.5	1.1	86.5	10.3	912
Mississippi County CC	0.0	1.7	17.9	1.2	79.3	0.0	1,878
North Arkansas CC	0.3	0.3	0.1	0.2	99.1	0.0	1,725
Ouachita Baptist U	0.0	0.8	5.1	0.2	92.7	1.3	1,313
Phillips County CC	0.4	0.2	45.1	0.3	53.9	0.0	1,467
Shorter C	0.0	0.0	81.5	0.0	4.4	14.1	135
Southern Arkansas U							
Main campus	0.3	0.8	18.7	0.6	79.1	0.5	2,492
El Dorado	0.4	0.3	16.2	0.1	83.1	0.0	791
Tech	0.0	0.4	18.8	0.1	80.7	0.0	920
Southern Tech C Little Rock	0.0	0.0	32.8	0.3	66.9	0.0	628
U of Arkansas							
Fayetteville	1.1	1.4	4.7	0.6	88.5	3.7	14,732
Little Rock	0.2	1.0	11.3	0.8	84.7	2.0	11,232
Medical Sciences	0.2	2.5	6.7	0.6	88.1	1.8	1,408
Monticello	0.7	0.3	12.9	0.9	85.3	0.0	2,108
Pine Bluff	0.1	0.2	83.7	0.2	15.6	0.1	3,672
U of Central Arkansas	0.0	0.0	9.8	0.0	89.6	0.5	8,396
U of the Ozarks	0.4	0.4	3.4	0.4	81.8	13.5	731
Westark CC	1.1	2.1	2.4	0.6	93.7	0.0	5,166
Williams Baptist C	0.7	0.1	1.3	0.3	95.4	2.2	690

CALIFORNIA

	American Indian	Asian	Black	Hispanic	White	Foreign	Total
American Academy of Dramatic Arts West	1.4	2.2	3.6	5.8	87.0	0.0	138
American Baptist Seminary of the West	0.0	8.3	39.6	4.2	33.3	14.6	48
American Conservatory Theatre	0.6	1.7	12.6	2.9	82.3	0.0	175
American Film Inst-Center for Advanced Film and Television Studies	0.0	1.6	4.9	1.1	75.8	16.5	182
Art Center C of Design	0.6	16.2	1.0	6.2	62.8	13.1	1,266
Art Inst of Southern California	5.5	12.6	0.0	5.5	70.1	6.3	127
Azusa Pacific U	0.8	5.2	3.4	6.2	74.6	9.8	3,159
Bethany C	0.2	4.9	1.1	11.1	81.9	0.9	470
Biola U	0.3	12.8	2.8	4.7	71.6	7.7	2,574
Brooks C	1.1	8.6	10.1	10.9	63.7	5.6	534
Brooks Inst	0.0	12.9	0.0	2.4	83.5	1.2	85
California C of Arts and Crafts	0.5	9.0	2.5	3.3	74.0	10.6	1,109
Cal C of Podiatric Medicine	0.0	15.1	4.0	5.4	69.5	6.0	351
California Family Study Center	0.0	2.8	3.2	5.3	88.3	0.4	283

	American Indian	Asian	Black	Hispanic	White	Foreign	Total
California Inst of the Arts	0.4%	5.5%	5.8%	4.9%	75.5%	7.9%	1,018
Cal Inst of Integral Studies ...	0.6	5.7	1.9	1.9	87.4	2.5	522
California Inst of Tech	0.2	14.0	0.9	1.8	57.8	25.4	1,861
California Lutheran U	0.4	3.4	2.4	6.6	82.1	5.0	2,969
California Sch of Professional Psychology							
Berkeley	0.2	4.8	4.1	3.9	85.3	1.7	517
Fresno	0.3	3.9	3.0	5.6	85.8	1.5	337
Los Angeles	1.2	5.8	7.8	10.2	72.7	2.4	502
San Diego	0.8	2.5	1.9	5.3	88.8	0.8	528
Cal Western Sch of Law	0.2	4.5	0.8	2.2	91.2	1.1	830
Chapman U	0.2	5.5	2.7	3.7	80.1	7.6	2,256
Chapman U Academic Centers	0.4	5.3	7.0	11.4	74.3	1.5	5,803
Christ C Irvine	0.3	3.7	2.9	5.4	77.9	9.8	592
Christian Heritage C	0.6	5.5	4.6	3.1	82.9	3.4	327
Church Divinity Sch of the Pacific	0.0	3.3	1.1	0.0	92.3	3.3	91
Claremont Graduate Sch	0.5	5.1	3.9	4.2	76.8	9.5	1,676
Claremont McKenna C	0.6	12.8	4.5	8.1	69.8	4.1	849
Cleveland Chiropractic C	0.0	10.9	3.5	8.0	75.0	2.7	376
Cogswell Polytechnical C	1.4	25.1	5.7	6.8	60.6	0.4	279
Coleman C	0.7	7.3	6.1	9.7	74.3	2.0	891
C of Notre Dame	0.2	10.0	4.8	6.8	71.5	6.7	1,156
C of Oceaneering	0.0	11.1	9.4	39.3	37.6	2.6	117
C of Osteopathic Medicine of the Pacific	0.4	15.8	3.3	6.4	73.9	0.2	486
Columbia C Hollywood	0.0	6.6	5.1	7.7	50.5	30.1	196
D-Q U	71.5	1.2	0.6	13.4	12.8	0.6	172
Deep Springs C	0.0	3.8	7.7	7.7	80.8	0.0	26
DeVry Inst of Tech Los Angeles	0.4	19.1	12.0	32.8	33.5	2.3	1,886
Dominican C of San Rafael ..	0.3	3.5	3.2	5.9	81.5	5.6	712
Dominican Sch of Philosophy and Theology ..	0.0	7.2	4.3	10.1	66.7	11.6	69
Don Bosco Tech Inst	0.4	18.8	0.0	69.2	10.9	0.7	276
Fashion Inst of Design and Merchandising							
Los Angeles	0.1	24.1	5.0	18.8	40.0	12.0	1,584
Sherman Oaks	0.2	16.4	5.5	15.6	58.3	4.1	1,110
Fielding Inst	0.1	1.2	4.4	1.9	87.9	4.5	751
Fuller Theological Seminary .	0.1	11.4	4.4	5.0	67.6	11.4	2,159
Golden Gate Baptist Seminary	0.2	11.9	5.1	2.4	73.4	7.0	545
Golden Gate U	0.3	11.3	6.5	3.9	69.6	8.4	7,564
Graduate Theological Union .	0.5	2.5	1.8	2.0	76.0	17.2	396
Harvey Mudd C	0.0	19.0	1.0	4.6	73.6	1.7	583
Hebrew Union C Jewish Inst of Religion	0.0	0.0	0.0	0.0	100.0	0.0	65
Holy Names C	0.3	4.8	17.0	6.7	56.6	14.5	890
Humphreys C	0.8	4.4	4.8	14.2	74.7	1.2	521
Inst of Transpersonal Psychology	0.0	5.7	1.3	3.2	89.8	0.0	157
International Sch of Theology	0.0	6.0	0.0	2.0	88.0	4.0	100
ITT Tech Inst Buena Park	0.4	13.6	5.0	13.2	61.4	6.5	841
ITT Tech Inst Sacramento	0.0	8.0	5.9	13.9	72.1	0.0	323
ITT Tech Inst Van Nuys	0.0	12.1	10.4	37.2	37.7	2.5	355
ITT Tech Inst West Covina	0.9	15.9	11.4	48.9	23.0	0.0	687
Jesuit Sch of Theology Berkeley	0.6	3.1	0.6	5.0	70.0	20.6	160

CALIFORNIA, cont.

	American Indian	Asian	Black	Hispanic	White	Foreign	Total
Kelsey-Jenney C	0.0%	12.8%	10.9%	45.5%	29.6%	1.2%	594
LIFE Bible C	0.3	9.4	2.9	9.4	77.1	0.9	341
Life Chiropractic C West	2.3	8.6	1.0	4.4	81.7	1.8	383
Lincoln U	0.5	6.2	1.9	1.9	18.6	70.8	370
Loma Linda U	0.2	20.6	3.9	5.2	55.8	14.4	2,481
Los Angeles C of Chiropractic	0.7	9.9	1.8	6.3	75.0	6.2	947
Loyola Marymount U	0.5	10.8	4.3	11.4	70.4	2.6	6,430
Manor Fashion Inst	0.0	0.0	15.4	0.0	84.6	0.0	26
Marymount C	0.7	5.8	5.0	11.6	54.2	22.7	1,076
Master's C	0.6	2.8	2.4	2.0	89.9	2.3	1,004
Menlo C	0.4	7.9	1.6	0.8	79.6	9.7	494
Mennonite Brethren Bible Seminary	0.0	1.7	0.9	1.7	51.3	44.3	115
Mills C	0.6	8.7	6.8	4.0	72.6	7.2	1,042
Monterey Inst of International Studies	0.3	4.2	1.7	4.3	61.3	28.2	698
Mount Saint Mary's C	0.3	11.7	10.1	31.9	43.9	2.0	1,177
National Hispanic U	0.0	0.4	3.7	94.2	0.4	1.2	242
National U	0.8	6.5	9.4	5.9	72.2	5.3	8,836
New C of California	2.4	6.1	9.1	9.1	70.1	3.2	739
Northrop U	0.2	40.0	4.0	10.3	33.9	11.6	1,276
Occidental C	0.6	13.2	4.6	9.2	69.7	2.8	1,672
Otis / Parsons Sch of Art and Design	2.2	19.0	3.8	7.7	57.1	10.2	783
Pacific Christian C	0.2	5.4	2.1	5.0	84.3	3.1	483
Pacific Coast C	0.1	5.2	17.6	33.8	41.9	1.4	977
Pacific Graduate Sch of Psychology	0.9	4.1	1.6	3.5	89.2	0.6	316
Pacific Lutheran Theological Seminary	0.0	3.3	2.5	0.8	86.8	6.6	121
Pacific Oaks C	1.5	3.2	8.3	7.9	77.6	1.5	469
Pacific Sch of Religion	0.5	6.5	4.3	1.6	74.7	12.4	186
Pacific Union C	0.6	17.2	3.2	8.1	65.1	5.7	1,770
Palmer C of Chiropractic West	0.2	7.2	0.7	2.4	77.8	11.8	585
Patten C	0.4	9.1	18.5	10.8	61.2	0.0	492
Pepperdine U	0.9	6.5	4.6	5.1	77.4	5.5	7,193
Pitzer C	0.5	5.4	5.4	8.8	70.7	9.2	828
Point Loma Nazarene C	0.5	3.4	2.2	5.2	85.1	3.6	2,252
Pomona C	0.6	12.8	4.8	8.5	67.6	5.8	1,384
Queen of Holy Rosary C	0.7	6.7	1.5	3.7	87.4	0.0	270
RAND Graduate Sch of Policy Studies	0.0	16.7	1.9	0.0	81.5	0.0	54
Saint Joseph's C	0.0	33.3	7.1	21.4	21.4	16.7	42
Saint Mary's C of California	0.5	3.4	4.0	5.7	83.2	3.2	3,940
Samuel Merritt C	1.6	8.4	3.1	4.7	79.1	3.1	191
San Francisco Art Inst	0.7	3.4	1.5	2.8	82.5	9.1	715
San Francisco Conservatory of Music	0.8	12.2	3.5	5.5	49.4	28.6	255
San Francisco Theological Seminary	0.0	4.2	3.6	1.1	60.0	31.1	615
San Jose Christian C	0.4	32.3	3.4	5.1	54.0	4.7	235
Santa Clara U	0.4	16.2	2.0	6.4	68.7	6.3	7,701
Sch of Theology at Claremont	1.2	18.9	10.4	2.4	52.2	14.9	249
Scripps C	0.5	10.6	2.7	8.7	75.2	2.4	634
Shasta Bible C	0.0	0.0	0.0	0.0	100.0	0.0	43
Sierra U	2.2	1.1	0.0	1.1	95.6	0.0	90

	American Indian	Asian	Black	Hispanic	White	Foreign	Total
Simpson C	0.9%	6.3%	0.7%	1.6%	89.3%	1.2%	429
Southern California C	0.7	4.4	2.4	9.7	80.1	2.8	919
Southern Cal C of Optometry	0.0	46.5	0.3	4.4	48.0	0.8	383
Southwestern U Sch of Law	0.5	8.6	2.4	5.1	83.4	0.0	1,103
Stanford U	0.8	13.1	5.6	7.2	58.9	14.4	14,724
Starr King Sch for the Ministry	0.0	0.0	0.0	0.0	100.0	0.0	45
U S International U	0.5	4.4	4.8	5.6	61.0	23.7	2,254
U of California							
Berkeley	1.1	23.9	6.3	12.1	49.4	7.2	30,634
Davis	0.9	21.1	3.7	7.6	62.8	3.9	23,890
Irvine	0.5	33.2	2.9	9.4	49.6	4.4	16,808
Los Angeles	0.8	23.6	6.3	13.1	50.9	5.4	36,420
Riverside	0.6	25.2	3.2	9.6	57.8	3.7	8,708
San Diego	0.8	19.6	2.9	9.8	62.7	4.1	17,790
San Francisco	0.7	23.1	4.2	7.1	61.8	3.0	3,812
Santa Barbara	1.2	11.2	3.2	10.2	71.0	3.1	18,385
Santa Cruz	1.2	10.3	3.0	10.1	73.5	2.0	10,054
U of Judaism	0.0	1.4	0.7	8.6	82.7	6.5	139
U of LaVerne	0.6	6.4	9.1	12.8	69.0	2.2	6,130
U of Redlands	0.5	6.0	6.3	8.0	77.2	2.0	3,043
U of San Diego	0.4	5.2	1.7	7.6	81.8	3.2	6,024
U of San Francisco	0.6	11.9	5.9	6.3	65.0	10.2	6,708
U of the Pacific	0.6	16.4	2.6	5.3	70.5	4.6	5,486
U of West Los Angeles	1.0	6.3	24.6	8.0	60.0	0.1	703
West Coast Christian C	2.6	8.6	1.3	25.2	53.0	9.3	151
West Coast U	0.0	9.8	7.0	8.2	55.4	19.7	1,205
Western State U C of Law							
Orange County	0.5	7.2	3.9	9.9	78.4	0.1	1,538
San Diego	1.4	5.3	3.6	7.3	82.4	0.2	590
Westmont C	0.6	3.0	1.3	3.9	90.5	0.8	1,268
Whittier C	1.1	6.4	3.3	10.6	75.3	3.3	1,840
Woodbury U	0.6	11.5	6.6	19.0	48.7	13.5	1,024
Yeshiva Ohr Elchonon Chabad West Coast Talmudical Seminary	0.0	0.0	0.0	0.0	80.8	19.2	26

COLORADO

Aims CC	1.3	0.9	0.4	11.6	85.7	0.0	8,833
Arapahoe CC	1.1	1.5	1.2	5.1	89.2	2.0	7,470
Bel-Rea Inst of Animal Tech	2.2	0.0	1.3	3.6	92.0	0.9	224
Beth-El C of Nursing	0.4	4.1	1.6	4.1	89.8	0.0	245
Blair JC	0.3	0.0	14.1	7.9	77.3	0.3	693
Colorado Christian U	0.1	0.9	3.6	3.4	90.0	1.9	852
Colorado C	1.1	2.4	1.4	4.7	87.0	3.4	1,952
Colorado Inst of Art	1.7	2.0	11.0	9.6	75.7	0.1	1,327
Colorado Mountain C	0.9	0.6	0.7	4.7	90.6	2.5	9,699
Colorado Northwestern CC	0.6	0.6	0.9	4.3	93.5	0.1	1,440
Colorado Sch of Mines	1.0	2.1	1.1	7.1	77.7	11.0	2,865
Colorado State U Sys							
Colorado State U	0.9	2.2	1.5	3.8	88.6	2.9	26,828
Fort Lewis C	9.8	0.7	0.4	3.8	83.3	2.0	3,935
U of Southern Colorado	0.7	1.1	2.9	22.3	70.0	3.0	4,365
Colorado Tech	0.9	1.8	6.2	4.7	81.6	4.9	1,248
CC of Aurora	1.4	3.1	13.8	6.3	74.9	0.5	4,098
CC of Denver	1.3	4.7	11.4	22.1	58.7	1.8	5,712

COLORADO, cont.

	American Indian	Asian	Black	Hispanic	White	Foreign	Total
Denver Conservative Baptist Seminary	0.0%	1.9%	1.9%	2.1%	90.5%	3.7%	536
Denver Inst of Tech	2.5	1.1	10.4	12.7	73.1	0.3	761
Denver Tech C	1.9	2.3	20.7	7.5	67.6	0.0	639
Front Range CC	1.7	3.2	1.1	9.4	83.5	1.1	9,706
Iliff Sch of Theology	1.9	3.4	5.6	1.6	83.1	4.4	320
ITT Tech Inst	0.0	3.1	7.3	8.7	80.8	0.0	287
Lamar CC	1.1	0.2	2.0	10.1	86.2	0.4	969
Morgan CC	1.0	0.0	0.0	5.9	92.6	0.4	908
National Tech U	0.6	8.9	2.0	3.3	85.1	0.0	1,443
National Theatre Conservatory	0.0	0.0	7.0	2.3	90.7	0.0	43
Nazarene Bible C	0.5	0.7	3.8	1.7	92.5	0.9	424
Northeastern JC	0.3	0.3	0.4	3.7	95.4	0.0	3,686
Otero JC	1.0	1.1	7.2	28.2	61.3	1.3	838
Parks JC	1.4	1.2	5.5	19.7	72.1	0.0	968
Pikes Peak CC	1.7	2.3	9.8	8.6	77.3	0.2	7,788
Pueblo CC	1.5	0.2	1.8	28.8	67.2	0.4	2,863
Red Rocks CC	1.3	1.0	1.3	6.6	87.8	2.0	6,477
Regis U	0.4	1.6	4.2	8.1	84.9	0.8	5,495
Rocky Mountain C of Art and Design	0.5	0.0	3.7	4.6	89.4	1.8	217
Saint Thomas Seminary	0.0	0.7	0.7	15.6	83.0	0.0	135
State C's in Colorado							
Adams State C	0.9	0.8	1.9	14.0	82.2	0.2	5,235
Mesa State C	0.8	0.3	0.8	5.7	90.5	1.8	4,610
Metropolitan State C Denver	0.5	2.8	4.8	9.1	82.5	0.3	17,400
Western State C	0.6	0.7	1.5	3.4	92.9	0.9	2,402
Tech Trades Inst Colorado Springs	0.0	2.2	15.2	9.8	72.8	0.0	184
Tech Trades Inst Grand Junction	0.6	0.0	0.0	8.4	91.0	0.0	178
Trinidad State JC	0.5	0.2	1.8	36.0	57.9	3.6	1,550
U S Air Force Academy	0.8	3.2	6.7	5.5	82.9	0.9	4,416
U of Colorado							
Boulder	0.6	4.4	1.8	4.9	84.9	3.5	28,600
Colorado Springs	0.6	2.6	2.4	4.7	89.1	0.5	6,646
Denver	0.6	4.8	2.9	5.4	84.3	2.0	11,512
Health Sciences Center	0.6	3.0	2.0	5.0	87.8	1.6	1,805
U of Denver	0.7	2.0	2.9	3.5	83.8	7.1	7,534
U of Northern Colorado	0.3	1.2	1.5	5.3	90.5	1.2	12,413
Yeshiva Toras Chaim Talmudical Seminary	0.0	0.0	0.0	0.0	88.2	11.8	34

CONNECTICUT

	American Indian	Asian	Black	Hispanic	White	Foreign	Total
Albertus Magnus C	0.1	1.1	11.2	4.4	79.7	3.5	734
Asnuntuck CC	0.4	1.6	5.4	2.2	89.3	1.0	1,838
Briarwood C	0.0	0.3	12.5	1.5	85.8	0.0	393
Bridgeport Engineering Inst	0.0	4.6	5.3	4.8	85.4	0.0	417
Connecticut C	0.1	2.5	3.1	2.3	87.0	5.0	1,978
Connecticut State U Sys							
Central Connecticut State U	0.1	1.8	4.2	2.3	91.0	0.6	13,798
Eastern Connecticut State U	0.7	1.0	4.6	2.9	89.7	1.1	4,475
Southern Conn State U	0.1	0.8	5.9	1.7	90.0	1.5	13,612
Western Conn State U	0.8	1.8	3.7	2.3	91.0	0.3	6,245
Fairfield U	0.0	1.9	1.2	1.8	94.5	0.5	4,821

	American Indian	Asian	Black	Hispanic	White	Foreign	Total
Greater Hartford CC	0.2%	3.0%	30.1%	13.6%	50.1%	3.0%	3,068
Greater New Haven Tech C	0.1	2.0	8.1	5.6	83.6	0.6	715
Hartford C for Women	0.0	1.6	14.0	4.9	71.2	8.2	243
Hartford Graduate Center	0.2	2.9	2.1	1.5	92.2	1.2	2,383
Hartford Seminary	0.0	3.4	19.0	0.6	77.1	0.0	179
Hartford State Tech C	0.1	6.4	8.9	5.3	78.7	0.6	872
Holy Apostles C and Seminary	0.0	3.2	3.2	4.5	89.1	0.0	221
Housatonic CC	0.4	2.3	21.5	15.0	59.5	1.3	2,396
Manchester CC	0.4	2.0	5.4	2.8	89.0	0.4	6,488
Mattatuck CC	0.2	0.9	5.0	4.1	89.3	0.5	4,269
Middlesex CC	0.5	1.1	3.5	2.8	91.8	0.3	3,228
Mitchell C	0.2	0.4	4.7	3.5	86.3	4.9	942
Mohegan CC	0.6	1.2	4.1	2.5	91.4	0.3	3,194
Northwestern Connecticut CC	0.1	0.7	1.2	0.5	97.0	0.5	2,204
Norwalk CC	0.2	2.0	14.5	9.8	69.0	4.5	3,698
Norwalk State Tech C	0.0	5.9	15.0	8.9	69.8	0.3	978
Paier C of Art	0.0	0.0	1.3	0.0	96.4	2.3	309
Quinebaug Valley CC	0.0	0.9	0.6	6.1	92.4	0.1	1,270
Quinnipiac C	0.1	0.5	1.9	1.1	96.3	0.2	3,405
Sacred Heart U	0.0	2.0	6.0	4.5	86.1	1.5	4,266
Saint Joseph C	0.1	0.7	5.9	2.9	90.4	0.0	1,870
South Central CC	0.3	1.6	16.7	6.5	73.2	1.7	4,014
Teikyo Post U	0.0	0.9	5.0	1.2	92.0	1.0	2,082
Thames Valley State Tech C	0.6	1.9	2.7	3.5	90.9	0.3	947
Trinity C	0.0	5.2	5.5	3.1	84.1	2.1	2,135
Tunxis CC	0.2	1.3	2.1	2.6	92.5	1.4	3,882
U S Coast Guard Academy	1.1	5.4	1.6	2.9	87.5	1.6	950
U of Bridgeport	0.1	2.2	8.5	3.1	76.3	9.9	4,278
U of Connecticut							
Main campus	0.4	3.5	3.5	2.9	86.6	3.1	25,497
Health Center	0.6	6.0	3.7	3.9	84.9	0.8	483
U of Hartford	0.1	1.3	5.1	2.2	84.4	6.9	7,882
U of New Haven	0.1	1.6	6.5	1.9	83.4	6.4	6,063
Waterbury State Tech C	0.1	2.8	2.6	2.6	91.7	0.2	1,501
Wesleyan U	0.1	6.3	7.2	3.0	80.4	3.0	3,419
Yale U	0.3	9.4	5.9	4.0	68.7	11.7	10,994

DELAWARE

Delaware State C	0.4	0.5	59.6	1.2	36.3	2.0	2,606
Delaware Tech and CC							
Southern	0.6	0.6	14.0	2.8	81.3	0.7	2,989
Stanton-Wilmington	0.2	2.2	13.7	2.1	81.1	0.8	5,983
Terry	0.8	1.8	16.1	1.4	79.9	0.1	1,856
Goldey-Beacom C	0.2	3.5	9.7	1.4	85.2	0.0	1,886
U of Delaware	0.2	1.9	4.6	0.8	89.4	3.2	20,818
Wesley C	0.3	2.1	11.4	1.2	84.9	0.0	1,165
Widener U Delaware	0.0	1.0	6.3	1.6	91.2	0.0	1,032
Widener U Sch of Law	0.0	1.0	2.8	1.6	94.7	0.0	1,873
Wilmington C	0.1	0.6	13.0	1.2	85.0	0.1	1,796

DISTRICT OF COLUMBIA

American U	0.5	3.5	6.8	4.1	72.8	12.4	11,258
Catholic U	0.1	3.2	4.8	3.5	80.3	8.2	6,638
Corcoran Sch of Art	0.3	6.1	8.6	5.7	69.1	10.2	314
De Sales Sch of Theology	0.0	0.0	18.4	7.9	73.7	0.0	38
Defense Intelligence C	0.0	2.8	4.5	2.5	81.0	9.3	605

D.C., cont.

	American Indian	Asian	Black	Hispanic	White	Foreign	Total
Dominican House of Studies	0.0%	0.0%	2.0%	2.0%	92.2%	3.9%	51
Gallaudet U	0.3	1.3	6.4	3.1	77.6	11.3	2,014
George Washington U	0.8	6.3	6.7	2.7	70.9	12.7	19,103
Georgetown U	0.2	4.8	7.1	4.3	75.3	8.2	11,525
Mount Vernon C	0.2	2.5	14.5	4.1	70.5	8.1	482
Oblate C	0.0	5.0	5.0	7.5	75.0	7.5	40
Southeastern U	0.3	8.7	49.5	2.8	8.9	29.7	606
Strayer C	0.5	8.8	42.4	3.7	29.6	15.0	2,916
Trinity C	0.3	12.9	20.6	4.1	62.2	0.0	1,089
U of the District of Columbia	0.0	2.0	83.0	3.0	4.0	8.0	11,990
Wesley Theological Seminary	0.0	3.9	20.4	0.8	73.9	1.0	383

FLORIDA

Barry U	0.1	1.3	10.9	21.3	58.9	7.4	5,902
Bethune Cookman C	0.0	0.3	95.8	0.3	0.6	3.0	2,342
Briarcliffe C	0.0	0.0	12.6	71.3	12.6	3.6	167
Caribbean Center for Advanced Studies Miami Inst of Psychology	0.0	0.8	7.4	56.0	33.7	2.1	243
Clearwater Christian C	1.0	1.2	1.0	3.8	89.3	3.8	419
C of Boca Raton	0.4	2.1	2.4	6.9	74.6	13.5	954
Eckerd C	0.3	1.3	1.8	2.3	83.6	10.6	1,344
Embry-Riddle Aeronautical U	0.7	2.7	5.2	4.7	83.7	2.9	10,813
Flagler Career Inst	0.0	0.8	23.3	3.5	72.0	0.4	257
Flagler C	0.0	0.0	1.3	0.7	98.0	0.0	1,228
Florida Baptist Theological C	0.5	0.5	4.5	0.7	92.6	1.4	443
Florida Bible C	0.0	0.7	0.7	2.8	88.1	7.7	143
Florida Christian C	0.0	0.0	4.2	0.0	95.8	0.0	118
Florida C	0.3	0.8	2.9	2.1	91.7	2.1	373
Florida Inst of Tech	0.3	1.6	3.5	4.9	77.1	12.6	5,929
Florida Southern C	0.0	0.4	2.3	1.1	93.9	2.2	2,684
Fort Lauderdale C Tallahassee	0.0	1.1	24.7	21.3	51.7	1.1	352
Hobe Sound Bible C	0.0	0.0	0.0	0.0	84.1	15.9	176
International Academy of Merchandising and Design	0.5	0.5	6.5	8.7	82.1	1.6	184
ITT Tech Inst	0.5	0.9	8.6	12.3	77.6	0.0	559
Jacksonville U	0.2	2.5	5.0	4.0	85.3	3.0	2,517
Liberty Bible C	0.0	0.0	4.7	2.7	89.3	3.4	149
Miami Christian C	0.0	0.9	30.7	22.7	42.2	3.6	225
National Education Center Bauder	0.1	2.3	27.3	11.2	50.7	8.3	724
National Education Center Tampa Tech Inst	0.1	2.1	20.7	9.2	66.8	1.2	1,114
New England Inst of Tech Palm Beach	0.0	0.6	18.6	9.1	70.6	1.1	649
Nova U	0.2	1.1	11.1	9.0	72.3	6.4	9,562
Orlando C	0.8	0.6	24.0	11.1	62.3	1.1	2,127
Palm Beach Atlantic C	0.2	1.2	5.7	4.1	86.9	1.8	1,535
Phillips JC	0.1	0.5	15.6	2.9	80.9	0.0	855
Prospect Hall C	0.0	0.8	48.8	7.3	41.2	1.9	260
Regional Seminary of Saint Vincent De Paul	0.0	0.0	0.0	27.2	58.7	14.1	92
Ringling Sch of Art and Design	0.7	1.4	1.2	5.2	88.9	2.6	576
Rollins C	0.2	2.1	3.9	4.3	87.9	1.5	3,590

	American Indian	Asian	Black	Hispanic	White	Foreign	Total
Saint John Vianney C Seminary	0.0%	2.5%	2.5%	35.0%	45.0%	15.0%	40
Saint Leo C	1.7	2.2	20.2	4.7	70.5	0.6	5,308
Saint Thomas U	0.1	1.2	15.0	45.2	33.7	4.8	2,659
Southeastern Academy	0.6	2.2	18.8	4.6	73.9	0.0	720
Southeastern C of the Assemblies of God	0.4	0.8	1.3	4.4	91.7	1.3	1,192
Spurgeon Baptist Bible C	0.0	0.0	0.0	2.4	95.1	2.4	41
State U Sys of Florida							
Florida A&M U	0.0	0.7	86.6	1.7	9.4	1.6	8,344
Florida Atlantic U	0.0	2.9	6.1	6.3	80.3	4.3	12,767
Florida International U	0.1	2.7	9.0	42.8	40.1	5.3	22,466
Florida State U	0.2	1.5	7.0	3.9	84.6	2.8	28,170
U of Central Florida	0.2	3.5	4.1	5.8	84.0	2.4	21,541
U of Florida	0.1	3.4	6.0	5.3	80.2	4.8	35,477
U of North Florida	0.2	3.3	7.2	2.3	86.0	0.9	8,021
U of South Florida	0.1	2.7	4.6	5.5	84.7	2.3	32,326
U of West Florida	0.3	2.2	5.0	1.5	88.9	2.2	7,877
Stetson U	0.5	1.2	2.4	3.3	89.8	2.9	3,003
Talmudic C of Florida	0.0	0.0	0.0	0.0	100.0	0.0	56
Tampa C	0.4	1.1	18.4	12.0	61.6	6.5	909
Trinity C	0.0	0.0	5.3	1.3	87.4	6.0	151
United Electronics Inst	0.6	0.8	21.9	5.8	70.3	0.5	620
U of Miami	0.2	3.4	6.9	18.7	60.6	10.2	13,841
U of Sarasota	0.0	1.1	20.0	1.1	75.8	2.1	95
U of Tampa	0.4	1.4	3.4	6.4	85.2	3.3	2,503
Warner Southern C	0.0	0.9	9.1	1.5	84.9	3.6	470
Webber C	0.4	0.9	13.4	3.6	72.3	9.4	224

GEORGIA

	American Indian	Asian	Black	Hispanic	White	Foreign	Total
Abraham Baldwin Agricultural C	0.0	0.2	10.4	0.1	87.6	1.6	2,497
Agnes Scott C	0.2	2.4	9.6	1.9	82.8	3.2	593
Albany State C	0.3	0.4	82.2	0.2	17.0	0.0	2,405
American C for the Applied Arts	0.0	1.0	26.7	3.3	58.3	10.8	705
Andrew C	0.0	0.0	17.6	1.0	62.4	19.0	306
Armstrong State C	0.3	1.2	13.3	1.2	83.4	0.7	4,170
Art Inst of Atlanta	0.2	1.2	26.0	1.3	70.5	0.9	1,288
Atlanta Christian C	0.0	3.3	11.5	0.0	83.6	1.6	183
Atlanta C of Art	0.3	2.4	14.1	1.3	77.6	4.3	375
Atlanta Metropolitan C	0.1	0.7	92.7	0.1	0.9	5.4	1,620
Augusta C	0.3	2.1	15.4	1.1	80.3	0.8	5,185
Bainbridge C	0.0	0.1	17.5	0.1	82.3	0.0	898
Ben Hill-Irwin Tech Inst	0.0	0.0	19.5	0.0	80.5	0.0	528
Berry C	0.2	0.4	1.9	0.8	95.2	1.4	1,805
Brenau C	0.0	0.8	8.9	0.9	87.6	1.8	1,838
Brewton-Parker C	0.2	0.2	22.6	0.4	75.8	0.7	1,870
Brunswick C	0.3	0.5	16.3	0.8	81.5	0.7	1,441
Chattahoochee Tech Inst	0.1	4.3	12.5	1.4	81.7	0.0	1,401
Clark Atlanta U	0.0	0.6	94.9	0.2	1.2	3.1	3,508
Clayton State C	0.2	1.5	15.4	1.0	81.3	0.6	4,140
Columbia Theological Seminary	0.0	4.4	6.5	0.3	84.0	4.8	619
Columbus C	0.2	2.2	18.2	2.0	75.9	1.4	4,154
Columbus Tech Inst	0.4	1.5	45.0	3.2	50.0	0.0	856
Coosa Valley Tech Inst	0.1	0.4	8.7	0.3	90.4	0.0	927

GEORGIA, cont.

	American Indian	Asian	Black	Hispanic	White	Foreign	Total
Covenant C	0.2%	0.2%	3.8%	1.3%	90.4%	4.1%	606
Crandall JC	0.0	0.0	59.6	0.0	40.3	0.2	544
Dalton C	0.1	0.4	2.1	0.2	97.2	0.0	2,500
Darton C	0.4	0.7	17.7	0.3	80.8	0.1	2,123
Dekalb C	0.6	2.9	20.5	1.4	73.0	1.7	13,944
DeKalb Tech Inst	0.4	1.4	20.2	0.8	76.5	0.7	3,672
DeVry Inst of Tech	0.8	2.4	63.4	1.7	30.7	1.0	3,121
Draughon's C	0.0	1.8	78.3	3.6	16.2	0.0	277
East Georgia C	0.2	0.2	17.8	0.2	81.7	0.0	617
Emmanuel C	0.0	1.5	14.7	0.5	83.3	0.0	395
Emmanuel C Sch of Christian Ministries	0.0	0.0	0.0	0.0	100.0	0.0	51
Emory U	0.1	3.8	7.7	1.6	80.8	6.1	9,390
Floyd JC	0.2	0.5	6.3	0.2	92.7	0.0	2,017
Fort Valley State C	0.0	0.1	92.7	0.2	5.2	1.7	2,158
Gainesville C	0.2	0.6	3.5	0.4	94.2	1.1	2,482
Georgia C	0.2	0.8	15.6	0.6	81.3	1.4	4,948
Georgia Inst of Tech	0.1	6.5	6.9	2.7	75.6	8.2	12,241
Georgia Military C	0.7	1.0	33.0	2.3	63.0	0.0	1,892
Georgia Southern U	0.1	0.5	12.6	0.5	85.2	1.2	12,249
Georgia Southwestern C	0.1	0.4	16.0	0.3	81.2	2.0	2,225
Georgia State U	0.3	2.8	16.4	1.8	75.8	2.8	23,336
Gordon C	0.2	0.3	16.6	0.7	81.7	0.6	1,480
Gwinnett Tech Inst	0.5	4.5	3.3	2.3	89.4	0.0	2,575
Heart of Georgia Tech Inst	0.0	0.0	23.9	0.0	75.8	0.3	293
Inst of Paper Science and Tech	0.0	1.7	3.3	0.0	90.0	5.0	60
Interdenominational Theological Center	0.0	0.0	96.9	0.0	0.0	3.1	294
Kennesaw State C	0.3	1.0	3.8	1.2	92.5	1.2	10,018
LaGrange C	0.1	0.7	8.6	0.4	85.7	4.5	993
Lanier Tech Inst	0.0	0.9	9.7	1.3	88.1	0.0	455
Life C	0.5	0.8	2.1	4.6	88.8	3.2	1,867
Macon C	0.5	1.0	20.1	0.9	77.4	0.1	4,210
Medical C of Georgia	0.1	3.1	8.4	1.3	82.4	4.7	2,426
Mercer U	0.4	1.9	13.9	2.0	79.2	2.6	5,868
Middle Georgia C	0.2	0.6	15.5	0.1	83.3	0.3	1,505
Morehouse C	0.0	0.0	99.9	0.0	0.0	0.1	2,720
Morehouse Sch of Medicine	0.0	4.8	82.8	2.8	9.0	0.7	145
Moultrie Area Tech Inst	0.7	0.2	20.8	0.7	77.5	0.0	812
North Georgia C	0.2	0.3	1.6	0.3	97.2	0.5	2,518
Oglethorpe U	0.1	3.1	5.8	1.5	85.3	4.2	1,095
Pickens Tech Inst	0.0	0.0	0.5	0.0	98.9	0.6	629
Piedmont C	0.4	0.4	4.8	0.2	90.7	3.4	495
Reinhardt C	0.0	0.0	1.4	0.0	96.0	2.6	768
Savannah C of Art and Design	0.0	1.0	7.7	1.1	85.8	4.4	1,977
Savannah State C	0.0	0.2	84.8	0.0	11.7	3.2	2,319
Shorter C	0.0	1.4	4.8	0.3	91.4	2.1	858
South C	0.0	0.4	49.7	1.1	48.8	0.0	465
South Georgia C	0.0	0.8	16.9	0.4	80.8	1.1	1,107
Southern C of Tech	0.1	3.0	15.3	1.0	78.0	2.6	4,007
Spelman C	0.0	0.0	98.1	0.0	0.1	1.8	1,710
Thomas C	0.3	0.0	17.5	0.6	81.1	0.6	360
Toccoa Falls C	0.0	1.1	0.4	2.3	88.7	7.5	790
Truett McConnell C	0.0	0.5	7.9	0.0	91.0	0.6	1,631
U of Georgia	0.1	1.2	5.3	0.8	88.7	3.7	28,395
Upson Tech Inst	0.3	0.0	34.5	0.0	65.2	0.0	287

	American Indian	Asian	Black	Hispanic	White	Foreign	Total
Valdosta State C	0.2%	0.3%	15.9%	0.5%	82.4%	0.7%	7,144
Valdosta Tech Inst	0.4	0.6	26.0	0.2	72.8	0.0	857
Waycross C	0.0	0.1	9.9	0.3	89.4	0.3	669
Wesleyan C	0.2	1.8	9.6	2.2	80.8	5.5	511
West Georgia C	0.2	0.4	13.7	0.6	84.4	0.7	7,068
Young Harris C	0.0	0.0	0.2	0.0	99.8	0.0	435

HAWAII

	American Indian	Asian	Black	Hispanic	White	Foreign	Total
Brigham Young U Hawaii	0.4	25.9	9.6	3.6	44.4	16.1	2,117
Chaminade U of Honolulu	0.2	30.9	8.6	3.1	53.7	3.5	2,408
Hawaii Loa C	0.0	26.4	9.6	3.3	44.5	16.2	550
Hawaii Pacific U	0.3	21.7	10.3	4.3	42.4	21.0	5,557
International C and Graduate Sch of Theology	0.0	32.9	6.6	0.0	46.1	14.5	76
U of Hawaii							
Manoa	0.2	64.0	0.8	0.9	25.3	8.8	18,799
West Oahu	0.5	63.5	2.1	1.4	32.2	0.3	652

IDAHO

	American Indian	Asian	Black	Hispanic	White	Foreign	Total
Boise Bible C	3.9	1.3	1.3	0.0	93.4	0.0	76
Boise State U	0.6	1.9	0.7	2.9	93.1	0.9	13,367
C of Idaho	0.7	2.7	0.3	2.3	92.5	1.5	1,176
C of Southern Idaho	0.6	0.6	0.6	3.0	87.4	7.9	2,786
Idaho State U	1.5	1.3	0.6	1.9	93.0	1.6	9,139
ITT Tech Inst	0.5	1.2	0.2	3.0	95.2	0.0	433
Lewis-Clark State C	2.5	0.3	0.3	0.3	94.6	2.0	2,667
North Idaho C	1.4	0.5	0.6	0.6	96.2	0.6	2,820
Northwest Nazarene C	0.7	1.2	0.6	1.3	95.2	1.0	1,086
Ricks C	0.5	1.1	0.2	1.2	92.9	4.1	7,795
U of Idaho	0.8	1.5	0.9	1.8	90.7	4.2	10,536

ILLINOIS

	American Indian	Asian	Black	Hispanic	White	Foreign	Total
Alfred Adler Inst of Chicago	0.0	0.5	4.1	1.0	90.7	3.6	194
American Academy of Art	0.5	4.1	3.5	8.8	82.4	0.7	739
American Conservatory of Music	0.0	6.4	8.0	4.0	60.0	21.6	125
Augustana C	0.0	1.5	3.0	1.4	91.1	3.0	2,253
Aurora U	0.2	3.4	12.2	4.8	79.2	0.2	2,116
Barat C	0.0	2.9	4.6	1.9	90.4	0.1	678
Belleville Area C	0.6	2.0	6.1	1.3	89.6	0.3	14,180
Bethany Theological Seminary	0.0	0.0	0.0	8.4	80.0	11.6	95
Black Hawk C							
East	0.0	0.1	0.9	0.4	98.3	0.3	768
Quad Cities	0.2	0.7	5.7	4.5	88.9	0.0	5,811
Blackburn C	0.2	0.2	9.6	0.9	84.2	4.8	438
Blessing-Rieman C of Nursing	0.0	0.0	2.9	0.0	97.1	0.0	103
Board of Governors U's							
Chicago State U	0.2	0.8	82.4	3.4	12.7	0.6	7,152
Eastern Illinois U	0.2	0.6	4.7	0.8	92.9	0.9	11,116
Governors State U	0.2	0.8	20.3	2.0	76.2	0.5	5,592
Northeastern Illinois U	0.3	8.7	10.5	12.7	66.8	1.1	10,453
Western Illinois U	0.2	0.9	7.6	1.3	86.4	3.7	13,747
Bradley U	0.0	2.0	6.4	1.3	84.8	5.5	6,065
Carl Sandburg C	0.3	0.7	4.9	1.4	92.0	0.6	2,639
Catholic Theological Union	0.0	3.4	3.1	3.7	69.8	20.0	325

ILLINOIS, cont.

	American Indian	Asian	Black	Hispanic	White	Foreign	Total
Chicago C of Osteopathic Medicine	0.4%	10.8%	2.1%	1.7%	84.9%	0.0%	471
Chicago Sch of Professional Psychology	0.0	3.3	2.5	5.7	85.2	3.3	122
Chicago Theological Seminary	0.0	8.5	31.2	0.5	59.8	0.0	199
City C's of Chicago							
City-Wide C	0.7	6.7	46.8	22.4	23.4	0.0	9,604
Harold Washington C	0.7	10.1	60.6	10.4	18.1	0.0	8,310
Harry S Truman C	0.8	17.8	12.2	36.8	32.5	0.0	16,460
Kennedy-King C	0.7	2.3	68.9	21.8	6.4	0.0	9,508
Malcolm X C	0.7	4.6	49.4	37.3	8.1	0.0	9,602
Olive-Harvey C	0.6	0.8	79.6	16.0	3.1	0.0	8,763
Richard J Daley C	0.4	2.8	22.7	31.5	42.6	0.0	8,335
Wilbur Wright C	0.6	9.7	12.3	24.8	52.6	0.0	8,294
C of Du Page	0.1	7.3	2.3	5.3	84.9	0.0	29,185
C of Lake County	0.4	3.0	6.9	10.1	79.6	0.0	13,526
C of Saint Francis	0.2	0.7	2.4	1.2	95.5	0.0	3,998
Columbia C	0.3	3.1	24.3	8.4	62.7	1.2	6,795
Concordia U	0.2	1.8	5.0	2.0	90.6	0.3	1,310
Danville Area CC	0.1	0.8	9.0	1.6	88.5	0.1	3,533
De Paul U	0.2	6.0	8.7	5.2	78.4	1.5	15,711
DeVry Inst of Tech Chicago	0.3	12.2	31.8	20.3	33.5	1.9	3,303
DeVry Inst of Tech Lombard	0.3	6.3	10.7	4.1	78.2	0.4	2,512
Dr William Scholl C of Podiatric Medicine	0.5	5.3	7.4	4.8	78.8	3.2	378
Elgin CC	0.3	3.1	3.4	4.3	88.7	0.2	7,066
Elmhurst C	0.2	1.6	3.2	1.7	92.6	0.7	3,006
Eureka C	0.2	0.0	3.6	1.8	94.1	0.2	441
Forest Inst of Professional Psychology	0.8	2.0	3.6	2.4	91.3	0.0	253
Garrett-Evangelical Theological Seminary	0.4	4.6	9.6	1.3	69.2	14.9	478
Gem City C	0.0	0.0	1.2	0.0	98.8	0.0	84
Greenville C	0.2	0.6	5.5	2.5	89.1	2.0	837
Harrington Inst of Interior Design	0.0	3.0	3.5	3.7	89.1	0.7	404
Highland CC	0.0	0.6	3.1	0.4	95.8	0.1	3,258
Illinois Benedictine C	0.2	5.9	8.7	3.1	82.0	0.0	2,631
Illinois Board of Regents U's							
Illinois State U	0.2	1.4	5.7	1.1	90.3	1.2	22,662
Northern Illinois U	0.3	3.7	6.0	2.8	84.5	2.7	24,509
Sangamon State U	0.2	1.0	5.8	0.8	90.5	1.9	4,347
Illinois Central C	0.2	1.3	5.1	0.9	92.4	0.1	12,718
Illinois C	0.0	0.9	1.4	0.5	97.0	0.3	888
Illinois C of Optometry	0.0	11.3	2.0	4.0	78.6	4.0	547
Illinois Eastern CC's	0.0	0.3	0.5	0.9	98.2	0.1	8,556
Illinois Inst of Tech	0.0	12.4	10.3	4.5	61.8	10.9	6,501
Illinois Medical Training Center	0.0	1.9	79.8	7.5	10.2	0.5	371
Illinois Sch of Professional Psychology	0.2	0.6	3.8	3.2	91.5	0.6	468
Illinois Valley CC	0.1	1.1	3.0	1.8	93.9	0.1	4,207
Inst for Clinical Social Work	0.0	3.2	1.6	0.0	95.2	0.0	62
International Academy of Merchandising and Design	0.5	3.8	17.0	4.9	72.9	0.7	547
ITT Tech Inst Schaumburg	0.3	3.2	9.8	7.4	79.3	0.0	377
John A Logan C	0.3	0.7	4.5	0.4	93.8	0.2	5,216
John Marshall Law Sch	0.1	1.6	4.1	2.4	91.3	0.4	1,280

	American Indian	Asian	Black	Hispanic	White	Foreign	Total
John Wood CC	0.0%	0.7%	4.1%	0.7%	93.9%	0.5%	2,743
Joliet JC	0.3	1.1	8.5	4.1	85.8	0.1	9,645
Judson C	0.0	1.4	5.0	2.1	89.8	1.7	576
Kaes C	0.0	0.0	10.2	32.7	57.1	0.0	49
Kankakee CC	0.1	0.7	8.1	0.6	90.5	0.1	3,789
Kaskaskia C	0.5	0.3	5.1	1.0	93.0	0.1	3,269
Keller Graduate Sch of Management	1.0	2.5	4.2	1.0	91.3	0.0	1,786
Kendall C	0.0	1.3	14.0	3.2	77.9	3.5	371
Kishwaukee C	0.4	1.9	4.9	4.2	88.2	0.3	3,035
Knowledge Systems Inst	0.0	57.7	7.7	0.0	34.6	0.0	26
Knox C	0.5	4.9	5.1	1.6	81.6	6.3	945
Lake Forest C	0.2	3.1	5.9	0.8	88.5	1.5	1,103
Lake Forest Graduate Sch of Management	0.0	2.4	1.6	1.0	95.1	0.0	627
Lake Land C	0.3	0.4	3.3	0.8	94.8	0.4	4,437
Lewis and Clark CC	0.3	0.5	4.7	0.3	94.1	0.1	5,886
Lewis U	0.3	1.3	17.8	4.7	75.4	0.5	3,708
Lexington Inst of Hospitality Careers	0.0	0.0	14.7	26.5	50.0	8.8	34
Lincoln Christian C	0.0	0.5	0.5	0.5	95.8	2.8	616
Lincoln C	0.2	1.7	12.2	1.6	84.2	0.0	1,489
Lincoln Land CC	0.1	0.5	4.8	0.5	94.0	0.1	7,717
Loyola U of Chicago	0.2	8.9	8.1	5.6	77.1	0.2	14,780
Loyola U Mallinckrodt	0.0	6.7	7.2	4.4	71.1	10.6	180
Lutheran Sch of Theology Chicago	0.0	0.8	6.2	3.4	77.4	12.2	385
MacCormac C	0.0	1.5	5.6	40.1	50.0	2.8	464
MacMurray C	0.3	0.5	29.0	5.0	65.1	0.1	1,116
McCormick Theological Seminary	0.0	14.0	7.1	9.6	64.2	5.1	592
McHenry County C	0.1	0.4	0.2	4.7	94.4	0.2	3,768
McKendree C	0.7	0.4	13.8	1.1	82.8	1.2	1,229
Meadville / Lombard Theological Sch	0.0	2.7	0.0	2.7	89.2	5.4	37
Mennonite C of Nursing	0.0	1.7	3.4	1.7	93.2	0.0	118
Metropolitan Business C	0.0	0.0	86.0	3.2	10.8	0.0	93
Midstate C	0.0	1.4	6.2	0.5	91.8	0.0	417
Millikin U	0.2	0.8	2.7	0.5	95.9	0.1	1,859
Monmouth C	0.0	7.3	9.1	1.7	81.6	0.3	656
Montay C	0.9	3.6	26.1	14.1	54.7	0.6	468
Moody Bible Inst	0.2	2.0	1.8	1.6	85.3	9.1	1,480
Moraine Valley CC	0.2	1.3	3.8	3.6	90.9	0.2	13,601
Morrison Inst of Tech	0.0	0.0	3.8	4.7	91.5	0.0	211
Morton C	0.2	2.6	0.9	28.5	67.5	0.3	4,195
Mundelein C	0.3	2.5	20.6	10.3	65.9	0.4	1,030
NAES C	82.1	0.0	0.0	0.0	17.9	0.0	95
National C of Chiropractic	0.4	2.9	1.8	1.9	86.1	7.0	797
National-Louis U	0.3	3.7	14.2	5.6	76.1	0.1	6,714
North Central C	0.1	2.3	5.7	1.4	90.4	0.1	2,577
North Park C and Theological Seminary	0.0	4.3	5.0	4.1	86.1	0.6	1,035
Northern Baptist Theological Seminary	0.0	2.8	15.1	13.3	40.8	28.0	218
Northwestern U	0.2	8.8	5.9	2.0	75.2	7.8	17,041
Oakton CC	0.2	9.7	3.2	3.0	83.8	0.0	12,395
Olivet Nazarene U	0.2	1.3	3.7	1.1	91.7	2.0	1,670

ILLINOIS, cont.

	American Indian	Asian	Black	Hispanic	White	Foreign	Total
Parkland C	1.3%	2.3%	7.6%	1.3%	85.9%	1.6%	8,570
Parks C of Saint Louis U	0.0	2.0	3.1	1.5	84.4	9.0	1,120
Phillips C Chicago	1.1	0.0	68.1	20.9	9.9	0.0	91
Prairie State C	0.4	1.0	23.2	4.7	70.5	0.1	5,123
Principia C	0.0	0.5	0.6	0.3	88.3	10.3	634
Quincy C	0.0	0.6	2.1	1.2	95.7	0.5	1,270
Ray C of Design	0.0	6.1	22.6	10.3	56.8	4.2	659
Rend Lake C	0.2	0.3	2.6	0.5	96.4	0.0	3,766
Richland CC	0.2	0.8	8.0	0.4	90.6	0.0	3,801
Rock Valley C	0.3	1.7	4.5	2.2	91.0	0.3	8,730
Rockford C	0.3	0.9	1.2	1.1	94.6	1.9	1,512
Rosary C	0.2	1.8	7.4	5.8	81.8	3.0	1,846
Rush U	0.2	10.9	5.4	1.5	79.4	2.6	1,144
Saint Augustine C	0.0	0.1	0.3	99.3	0.3	0.0	1,455
Saint Francis Medical Center C of Nursing	0.0	0.9	1.7	0.9	96.5	0.0	115
Saint Joseph C of Nursing	0.0	4.2	5.0	1.7	89.1	0.0	119
Sauk Valley CC	0.4	1.1	4.7	4.6	89.2	0.0	3,109
Sch of the Art Inst of Chicago	0.5	6.3	4.6	4.3	79.2	5.1	2,129
Shawnee CC	0.1	0.4	18.0	0.2	81.3	0.0	1,575
Shimer C	0.0	0.0	10.1	1.4	88.4	0.0	69
South Suburban C	0.6	1.1	26.9	5.4	66.1	0.0	8,581
Southeastern Illinois C	0.4	0.3	14.4	2.2	82.5	0.2	3,032
Southern Illinois U							
Edwardsville	0.3	1.0	12.3	1.0	83.7	1.7	11,686
Carbondale	0.4	1.6	9.5	1.8	78.9	7.9	24,078
Spertus C of Judaica	0.0	1.0	19.6	1.4	77.5	0.5	209
Spoon River C	0.2	0.6	3.9	0.5	94.1	0.8	1,970
Springfield C	0.0	0.3	6.6	0.3	92.5	0.3	332
State CC	0.1	0.5	97.3	0.2	1.9	0.0	1,236
Taylor Business Inst	0.0	1.9	28.0	8.2	60.4	1.4	207
Trinity Christian C	0.5	0.5	6.8	0.5	90.1	1.5	546
Trinity C	0.0	3.5	8.2	1.7	85.5	1.1	898
Trinity Evangelical Divinity Sch	0.1	6.9	4.1	1.1	78.2	9.6	1,457
Triton C	0.3	3.8	16.4	11.9	66.8	0.8	16,759
U of Chicago	0.2	9.1	3.8	2.1	74.2	10.6	10,867
U of Health Sciences Chicago Medical Sch	0.2	15.6	5.2	1.3	72.7	5.0	906
U of Illinois							
Chicago	0.3	14.2	10.2	9.6	59.8	6.0	24,959
Urbana-Champaign	0.2	8.4	5.8	3.5	75.0	7.2	38,163
U of Saint Mary of the Lake Mundelein Seminary	0.0	2.8	0.3	4.5	85.9	6.6	290
Waubonsee CC	0.8	0.8	5.2	15.4	77.8	0.1	6,089
West Suburban C of Nursing	0.0	8.3	8.3	0.0	80.6	2.8	36
Wheaton C	0.1	4.6	1.1	1.3	91.0	2.0	2,533
William Rainey Harper C	0.2	4.8	1.6	5.4	86.3	1.7	16,509

INDIANA

Ancilla C	0.0	0.3	0.8	0.6	98.1	0.2	618
Anderson U	1.3	0.4	4.3	0.2	93.4	0.3	2,124
Ball State U	0.2	0.6	4.0	0.7	93.2	1.3	20,343
Bethel C	0.1	0.1	4.4	0.1	94.4	0.7	699
Butler U	0.2	1.8	6.6	1.3	90.1	0.1	3,905
Calumet C of Saint Joseph	0.5	0.8	21.0	16.2	61.2	0.2	974

	American Indian	Asian	Black	Hispanic	White	Foreign	Total
Christian Theological Seminary	0.0%	0.7%	9.0%	1.4%	86.0%	2.9%	279
Commonwealth Business C							
Main campus	0.0	0.3	9.7	1.4	88.6	0.0	289
La Porte	0.0	0.0	4.9	1.0	94.2	0.0	103
Concordia Theological Seminary	0.3	1.0	2.8	0.5	92.5	2.8	389
Davenport C Merrillville	0.0	0.8	23.5	8.6	66.6	0.4	476
Davenport C South Bend	0.0	1.8	14.7	3.3	80.2	0.0	334
DePauw U	0.2	1.5	5.7	1.0	90.0	1.6	2,347
Earlham C	0.1	2.6	4.7	1.0	89.8	1.8	1,221
Franklin C	0.1	0.7	1.8	0.7	95.6	1.1	880
George Rogers Clark C	1.2	0.0	53.5	0.0	45.3	0.0	86
Goshen Biblical Seminary	0.0	0.0	3.2	2.1	77.9	16.8	95
Goshen C	0.3	1.1	2.3	2.5	86.1	7.7	1,107
Grace C	0.2	0.5	0.5	0.5	97.7	0.8	643
Grace Theological Seminary	0.6	2.4	1.8	0.6	90.2	4.3	164
Holy Cross C	0.0	0.0	6.4	1.6	90.6	1.4	437
Huntington C	0.0	0.3	1.2	0.0	92.2	6.3	601
Indiana Inst of Tech	0.1	1.2	14.5	1.6	73.2	9.5	1,107
Indiana State U	0.2	0.5	6.5	0.6	86.6	5.6	11,781
Indiana U Sys							
Bloomington	0.2	2.3	3.7	1.6	86.9	5.4	35,451
East	0.2	0.4	2.7	0.5	95.9	0.3	2,053
Kokomo	0.4	0.6	2.8	1.1	95.0	0.2	3,332
Northwest	0.1	0.7	19.9	7.1	71.9	0.3	5,075
Purdue U Indianapolis	0.2	2.1	7.2	1.0	88.5	1.0	27,517
Purdue U Fort Wayne	0.2	0.9	3.4	1.0	93.7	0.8	11,889
South Bend	0.1	1.0	4.6	0.8	92.1	1.5	7,215
Southeast	0.2	0.2	1.6	0.2	97.6	0.2	5,642
Indiana Wesleyan U	0.2	0.3	7.6	0.8	90.1	0.9	2,719
International Business C Fort Wayne	0.0	0.0	4.8	2.0	93.3	0.0	504
International Business C Indianapolis	0.0	0.4	9.2	1.3	89.0	0.0	228
ITT Tech Inst Evansville	0.0	0.2	5.1	0.0	94.7	0.0	488
ITT Tech Inst Fort Wayne	0.2	0.7	9.5	2.6	87.1	0.0	1,067
ITT Tech Inst Indianapolis	0.3	0.5	12.5	1.0	85.8	0.0	1,050
Lockyear C	0.0	0.0	40.0	0.7	59.3	0.0	135
Lutheran C of Health Professions	0.2	0.2	2.5	0.2	96.8	0.0	408
Manchester C	0.0	0.5	2.0	1.0	94.5	1.9	1,097
Marian C	0.4	0.8	12.0	0.6	84.6	1.5	1,242
Mennonite Biblical Seminary	0.0	0.0	0.0	2.4	52.4	45.1	82
Mid-America C of Funeral Services	0.0	0.0	4.9	0.0	95.1	0.0	82
Oakland City C	0.1	0.3	0.8	0.4	98.4	0.0	732
Purdue U							
Main campus	0.4	2.8	3.2	1.5	86.0	6.2	37,588
Calumet	0.5	1.2	9.0	8.1	81.2	0.1	8,506
North Central	0.6	0.5	2.7	1.2	95.0	0.0	3,446
Rose-Hulman Inst of Tech	0.0	1.8	0.6	0.6	93.4	3.6	1,419
Saint Francis C	0.8	1.1	4.6	1.1	91.9	0.5	879
Saint Joseph's C	0.1	0.4	3.9	1.2	93.9	0.6	1,033
Saint Mary-of-the-Woods C	0.3	0.4	2.1	0.9	95.1	1.2	1,040
Saint Mary's C	0.1	0.9	0.6	2.0	95.2	1.2	1,718
Saint Meinrad C	0.0	1.7	0.0	2.6	86.2	9.5	116

INDIANA, cont.

	American Indian	Asian	Black	Hispanic	White	Foreign	Total
Saint Meinrad Sch of Theology	0.0%	1.0%	2.0%	5.9%	90.2%	1.0%	102
Summit Christian C	0.0	0.0	6.9	1.3	91.2	0.5	376
Taylor U	0.1	0.5	0.8	0.5	96.0	2.0	1,718
Tri-State U	0.2	1.6	1.6	0.7	85.8	10.1	1,193
U of Evansville	0.1	0.9	2.8	0.3	91.6	4.2	2,933
U of Indianapolis	0.3	4.4	11.1	0.5	80.9	2.7	3,391
U of Southern Indiana	0.3	0.3	2.6	0.3	95.7	0.8	6,480
Valparaiso U	0.1	1.1	1.8	1.0	94.4	1.7	3,864
Vincennes U	0.1	0.2	4.5	1.7	91.6	1.9	9,162
Wabash C	0.2	1.5	4.2	0.9	89.3	3.7	854

IOWA

	American Indian	Asian	Black	Hispanic	White	Foreign	Total
American Inst of Business	0.0	1.3	1.4	0.9	96.4	0.0	1,054
Briar Cliff C	0.1	0.3	1.3	1.4	96.1	0.8	1,122
Buena Vista C	0.0	0.6	0.4	0.5	98.5	0.0	2,332
Central U of Iowa	0.0	1.1	1.1	0.8	94.5	2.5	1,503
Clarke C	0.1	0.2	3.8	0.5	94.4	1.0	876
Coe C	0.0	0.9	2.0	0.5	89.0	7.7	1,250
Cornell C	0.4	1.5	1.4	2.0	92.5	2.2	1,140
Des Moines CC	0.2	1.6	2.8	0.8	94.0	0.5	10,553
Divine Word C	0.0	60.3	1.7	1.7	15.5	20.7	58
Dordt C	0.0	2.0	0.5	0.1	85.8	11.7	1,054
Drake U	0.2	1.3	2.7	1.0	92.8	1.9	8,029
Eastern Iowa CC Dist	0.5	1.0	3.0	1.8	93.1	0.6	5,744
Emmaus Bible C	0.0	0.0	1.3	4.0	70.9	23.8	151
Faith Baptist Bible C and Seminary	1.0	2.4	1.4	1.4	93.9	0.0	295
Graceland C	0.6	1.6	6.2	1.6	87.0	3.0	2,371
Grand View C	0.6	2.7	3.9	0.8	90.3	1.7	1,420
Grinnell C	0.1	3.9	4.7	1.4	81.7	8.2	1,278
Hamilton Tech C	0.2	0.5	5.1	3.1	90.8	0.2	414
Hawkeye Inst of Tech	0.5	0.8	3.2	0.3	95.0	0.1	1,820
Indian Hills CC	0.3	0.5	0.6	0.0	98.6	0.1	3,015
Iowa Central CC	0.0	1.3	2.9	0.6	95.2	0.0	2,224
Iowa Lakes CC	0.1	0.5	1.2	0.2	97.9	0.0	1,634
Iowa Methodist Sch of Nursing	0.0	1.0	1.5	0.0	97.6	0.0	205
Iowa State U	0.1	1.4	2.3	1.0	86.6	8.6	25,737
Iowa Valley CC	1.1	0.0	3.3	0.2	95.3	0.0	2,344
Iowa Wesleyan C	0.1	0.5	5.7	0.8	86.3	6.6	914
Iowa Western CC	0.2	0.6	1.4	0.7	97.1	0.1	3,288
Kirkwood CC	0.2	1.3	2.1	0.0	94.1	2.3	8,623
Lincoln Tech Inst	0.0	0.0	2.8	0.0	97.2	0.0	107
Loras C	0.0	1.8	1.8	0.5	95.9	0.0	1,905
Luther C	0.0	1.4	0.8	0.3	92.8	4.7	2,216
Maharishi International U	0.4	0.9	1.0	1.2	75.8	20.7	2,533
Marycrest C	0.0	1.0	3.5	1.5	91.9	2.2	1,793
Morningside C	1.7	1.7	2.5	0.7	93.4	0.0	1,356
Mount Mercy C	0.1	0.3	0.5	0.1	98.4	0.5	1,528
Mount Saint Clare C	1.0	1.6	2.6	0.3	91.0	3.5	311
National Education Center National Inst of Tech	1.0	3.6	5.8	1.0	88.3	0.3	309
North Iowa Area CC	0.1	0.3	2.1	0.9	96.5	0.1	2,771
Northeast Iowa CC	0.5	0.5	0.1	0.0	98.9	0.0	1,829
Northwest Iowa Tech C	1.2	0.4	0.4	0.0	98.1	0.0	521

	American Indian	Asian	Black	Hispanic	White	Foreign	Total
Northwestern C	0.0%	0.7%	0.4%	0.0%	93.1%	5.8%	1,064
Palmer C of Chiropractic	0.4	0.7	0.7	1.2	88.4	8.5	1,662
Saint Ambrose U	0.5	0.6	3.3	1.7	93.0	0.9	2,323
Simpson C	0.1	0.3	1.0	0.3	97.9	0.2	1,735
Southeastern CC	0.1	0.6	2.2	0.9	96.2	0.0	2,683
Southwestern CC	0.0	0.3	3.2	0.3	95.2	0.9	1,150
Teikyo Westmar U	0.2	0.6	6.1	0.3	67.4	25.4	653
U of Dubuque	0.6	1.2	4.7	0.9	80.0	12.6	1,121
U of Iowa	0.3	2.7	2.7	1.6	86.0	6.6	28,785
U of Northern Iowa	0.1	0.6	1.9	0.5	95.3	1.7	13,435
U of Osteopathic Medicine and Health Sciences	0.3	6.6	3.9	2.0	86.5	0.8	1,179
Upper Iowa U	0.1	0.9	3.7	0.8	94.1	0.4	2,215
Vennard C	0.0	0.7	0.0	0.7	96.6	2.1	145
Waldorf C	0.2	0.8	3.1	0.5	91.4	4.1	654
Wartburg C	0.1	0.4	1.8	0.1	90.3	7.2	1,440
Wartburg Theological Seminary	0.9	0.9	1.3	2.6	86.9	7.4	229
Western Iowa Tech CC	2.7	1.4	0.8	1.1	93.7	0.2	1,678
William Penn C	0.1	1.4	2.2	2.0	93.6	0.7	737

KANSAS

	American Indian	Asian	Black	Hispanic	White	Foreign	Total
Allen County CC	0.4	0.8	1.6	0.5	96.4	0.2	1,458
American Career C	3.1	0.0	16.3	3.1	75.5	2.0	98
Baker U	0.3	0.7	3.7	1.6	91.7	1.9	1,365
Barclay C	0.0	1.0	1.0	2.0	90.9	5.1	99
Barton County CC	0.4	0.7	7.2	2.2	89.3	0.3	3,224
Benedictine C	0.9	0.5	2.5	3.1	88.7	4.3	795
Bethany C	0.3	0.0	2.9	1.1	93.1	2.6	653
Bethel C	0.7	1.6	4.8	1.1	86.4	5.4	559
Butler County CC	1.4	1.6	6.0	1.3	88.1	1.5	4,688
Central Baptist Theological Seminary	0.8	0.0	15.8	0.0	80.8	2.5	120
Central C	2.5	2.9	2.9	5.0	86.1	0.4	238
Cloud County CC	0.6	0.4	1.7	1.0	96.1	0.2	2,337
Coffeyville CC	1.3	0.8	12.1	0.3	84.6	0.8	2,015
Colby CC	0.0	0.2	0.6	1.1	97.6	0.5	2,163
Cowley County CC	2.0	0.6	3.1	2.8	91.3	0.3	2,503
Dodge City CC	0.4	1.0	2.3	5.9	90.3	0.2	2,428
Donnelly C	1.0	1.8	53.3	7.9	19.3	16.8	394
Emporia State U	0.3	0.5	2.5	1.5	92.7	2.5	6,072
Fort Hays State U	0.5	1.5	1.0	1.1	95.9	0.0	5,500
Fort Scott CC	0.6	0.1	4.4	0.7	93.2	1.1	1,766
Garden City CC	0.1	1.0	3.1	7.0	88.7	0.0	2,195
Haskell Indian JC	100.0	0.0	0.0	0.0	0.0	0.0	831
Hesston C	0.4	1.6	2.5	2.9	75.3	17.3	486
Highland CC	1.5	0.2	3.5	1.1	93.7	0.0	1,743
Hutchinson CC	0.7	0.2	3.6	3.0	92.1	0.4	3,887
Independence CC	1.0	1.3	4.8	1.6	88.6	2.7	1,928
Johnson County CC	0.4	2.2	2.1	1.8	93.2	0.3	13,740
Kansas City C Bible Sch	0.0	6.1	0.0	2.0	83.7	8.2	49
Kansas City Kansas CC	0.5	1.2	20.0	3.6	74.7	0.0	4,985
Kansas Newman C	1.5	0.7	5.3	5.1	85.3	2.0	955
Kansas State U	0.3	1.4	3.3	1.8	87.9	5.2	21,137
Kansas State U Salina	0.1	0.6	1.0	1.8	95.8	0.6	674
Kansas Wesleyan U	0.6	1.2	8.2	3.0	84.9	2.0	801

KANSAS, cont.

	American Indian	Asian	Black	Hispanic	White	Foreign	Total
Labette CC	2.1%	0.5%	3.6%	0.9%	92.2%	0.7%	2,465
Manhattan Christian C	0.0	0.5	1.0	1.0	95.6	2.0	205
McPherson C	0.6	0.6	3.0	1.3	89.0	5.4	464
MidAmerica Nazarene C	0.2	1.0	1.9	0.7	93.7	2.4	1,240
Neosho County CC	0.8	0.6	4.4	2.4	91.4	0.5	1,215
Ottawa U							
Kansas City	0.5	5.8	4.9	6.8	82.0	0.0	1,913
Ottawa	1.7	0.4	6.2	1.3	78.0	12.5	536
Pittsburg State U	1.5	2.4	2.2	1.3	89.0	3.6	5,912
Pratt CC	0.1	0.2	2.0	1.8	95.7	0.2	1,218
Saint Mary C	2.3	1.4	22.0	4.9	67.0	2.3	983
Saint Mary of the Plains C	0.7	0.6	4.5	7.3	83.0	3.9	1,071
Seward County CC	0.3	1.5	2.8	4.4	90.9	0.0	1,490
Southwestern C	1.1	0.4	8.1	3.4	86.9	0.0	702
Tabor C	0.2	0.2	4.4	2.5	88.4	4.2	432
U of Kansas							
Main campus	0.6	2.0	2.6	1.7	85.7	7.3	26,434
Medical Center	0.4	5.8	2.1	2.3	87.5	2.0	2,473
Washburn U of Topeka	0.8	1.8	5.3	3.8	86.8	1.5	6,485
Wichita State U	1.0	3.7	4.6	2.8	82.1	5.8	16,151

KENTUCKY

	American Indian	Asian	Black	Hispanic	White	Foreign	Total
Alice Lloyd C	0.0	0.2	0.4	0.0	99.5	0.0	548
Asbury C	0.3	0.8	1.3	0.8	94.3	2.5	1,042
Asbury Theological Seminary	0.3	0.7	0.7	0.3	91.7	6.3	671
Bellarmine C	0.0	0.4	1.5	0.6	97.2	0.4	3,907
Berea C	0.1	0.9	10.5	0.7	82.4	5.4	1,535
Brescia C	0.0	0.4	1.6	0.1	97.3	0.5	731
Campbellsville C	0.5	0.5	6.1	0.1	91.8	1.1	853
Career Com JC of Business	0.0	0.0	48.5	0.0	51.5	0.0	66
Centre C	0.0	1.4	1.6	0.7	96.0	0.2	858
Clear Creek Baptist Bible C	0.0	0.0	0.0	0.0	100.0	0.0	139
Cumberland C	0.3	0.2	5.8	0.3	90.7	2.6	1,812
Eastern Kentucky U	0.2	0.3	5.5	0.3	93.0	0.8	15,290
Georgetown C	0.1	0.4	1.8	0.3	96.1	1.4	1,595
Kentucky Christian C	0.0	0.0	0.4	0.0	98.4	1.2	566
Kentucky C of Business	0.0	0.0	11.0	0.6	88.5	0.0	712
Kentucky Mountain Bible C	1.4	4.3	4.3	0.0	89.9	0.0	69
Kentucky State U	0.2	0.2	44.9	0.3	53.1	1.3	2,506
Kentucky Wesleyan C	0.0	0.8	4.1	0.1	94.1	0.8	707
Lees C	0.0	2.6	4.0	0.6	92.9	0.0	352
Lexington Theological							
Seminary	0.0	0.0	10.3	0.0	87.1	2.6	116
Lindsey Wilson C	0.2	1.1	5.9	0.2	92.2	0.5	1,327
Louisville Presbyterian							
Theological Seminary	0.0	2.3	0.0	0.0	94.3	3.4	175
Louisville Tech Inst	0.0	0.0	5.6	1.2	93.0	0.2	500
Mid-Continent Baptist Bible C	0.0	0.0	3.4	2.2	92.1	2.2	89
Midway C	0.0	0.0	2.3	0.0	96.2	1.4	556
Morehead State U	0.1	0.2	3.4	0.2	95.4	0.8	8,605
Murray State U	0.2	0.4	4.2	0.2	93.5	1.4	8,079
National Education Center							
Kentucky C of Tech	0.0	0.3	27.1	0.6	72.0	0.0	339
Northern Kentucky U	0.1	0.3	1.4	0.2	97.4	0.6	11,254
Pikeville C	0.0	0.0	0.9	0.0	98.7	0.4	972
RETS Electronic Inst	0.0	0.0	25.1	0.0	74.9	0.0	338

	American Indian	Asian	Black	Hispanic	White	Foreign	Total
Saint Catharine C	0.4%	0.0%	11.6%	0.0%	82.4%	5.6%	233
Spalding U	0.1	0.8	9.9	0.3	88.8	0.2	1,059
Sue Bennett C	1.0	0.0	2.9	0.2	95.4	0.6	517
Sullivan C	0.5	0.0	16.9	0.4	80.9	1.3	1,713
Thomas More C	0.2	0.2	3.5	0.2	94.8	1.1	1,297
Transylvania U	0.0	1.8	2.1	0.5	94.8	0.7	1,091
Union C	0.5	0.1	4.9	0.0	94.3	0.2	1,022
U of Kentucky	0.2	1.2	3.5	0.5	90.6	4.0	22,538
U of Kentucky CC Sys							
Ashland CC	0.7	0.2	0.7	0.1	98.4	0.0	3,057
Elizabethtown CC	0.8	1.6	6.8	1.5	89.2	0.1	3,356
Hazard CC	1.9	0.5	1.8	0.1	95.7	0.0	1,314
Henderson CC	0.6	0.2	4.4	0.2	94.4	0.1	1,363
Hopkinsville CC	0.6	0.8	12.0	1.6	85.0	0.0	1,823
Jefferson CC	0.3	0.8	12.0	0.3	86.4	0.1	10,234
Lexington CC	1.0	0.5	4.8	0.4	93.2	0.1	4,580
Madisonville CC	0.3	0.2	4.7	0.1	94.6	0.0	2,134
Maysville CC	0.8	0.6	1.6	0.0	97.1	0.0	1,024
Owensboro CC	0.9	0.4	2.5	0.1	96.1	0.0	2,415
Paducah CC	0.4	0.4	3.7	0.2	95.3	0.0	2,788
Prestonsburg CC	0.4	0.2	0.6	0.1	98.6	0.1	2,438
Somerset CC	1.5	0.5	0.4	0.2	97.3	0.0	2,085
Southeast CC	0.5	0.5	2.1	0.1	96.6	0.0	2,063
U of Louisville	0.3	1.9	9.3	0.8	85.9	1.8	22,979
Watterson C	0.0	0.0	20.6	0.0	79.4	0.0	160
Western Kentucky U	0.1	0.7	5.1	0.4	93.5	0.2	15,170

LOUISIANA

Bossier Parish CC	0.0	0.2	12.0	1.3	86.5	0.0	3,335
Centenary C of Louisiana	0.5	0.7	7.3	1.0	88.8	1.7	998
Delgado CC	1.8	2.1	31.5	4.8	58.4	1.4	11,614
Dillard U	0.0	0.0	100.0	0.0	0.0	0.0	1,998
Grambling State U	0.2	0.0	94.9	0.0	3.5	1.3	6,485
Louisiana C	0.2	0.7	5.7	0.6	91.7	1.2	1,075
Louisiana State U Sys							
A&M C	0.3	2.4	7.2	1.6	83.4	5.1	26,112
Alexandria	0.6	0.5	8.2	0.5	90.2	0.0	2,404
Eunice	0.4	0.1	11.3	0.6	87.7	0.0	2,261
Medical Center	0.1	5.2	8.0	2.3	82.0	2.4	2,538
Shreveport	0.6	1.7	9.6	0.7	87.2	0.2	4,107
U of New Orleans	0.5	2.6	12.3	4.7	77.8	2.1	15,322
Louisiana Tech U	0.3	0.9	14.3	0.8	81.5	2.3	10,004
Loyola U	0.6	1.9	10.9	6.3	78.1	2.2	5,400
McNeese State U	0.6	0.5	12.9	1.0	84.0	1.1	7,671
New Orleans Baptist							
Theological Seminary	0.0	1.0	8.4	4.6	85.7	0.3	1,461
Nicholls State U	0.8	0.1	10.3	1.3	87.1	0.3	7,356
Northeast Louisiana U	0.6	1.6	15.4	0.2	79.4	2.7	10,686
Northwestern State U	1.0	1.0	19.7	1.6	76.5	0.3	7,323
Notre Dame Seminary							
Graduate Sch of Theology	0.0	21.3	3.7	1.9	65.7	7.4	108
Our Lady of Holy Cross C	0.8	1.1	17.2	3.5	77.4	0.1	1,047
Phillips JC	0.0	0.2	29.9	3.1	66.5	0.2	965
Saint Bernard Parish CC	1.2	0.4	3.1	2.4	92.9	0.0	1,021
Saint Joseph Seminary C	0.0	6.7	1.5	3.7	87.3	0.7	134
Southeastern Louisiana U	0.3	0.3	5.9	0.9	92.0	0.6	10,262

LOUISIANA, cont.

	American Indian	Asian	Black	Hispanic	White	Foreign	Total
Southern Tech C Lafayette ...	0.0%	0.9%	35.8%	0.6%	62.5%	0.2%	640
Southern Tech C Shreveport .	0.0	0.0	41.7	0.4	57.8	0.1	984
Southern U and A&M C Sys							
Baton Rouge	0.0	0.2	93.2	0.3	4.1	2.2	8,941
New Orleans	0.0	0.8	91.3	0.3	5.6	1.9	4,064
Shreveport Bossier City	0.0	0.0	91.5	0.0	8.3	0.2	1,020
U of Southwestern Louisiana	0.2	1.2	16.6	0.9	76.6	4.6	15,764
Xavier U	0.0	0.5	90.7	0.6	5.5	2.7	2,943

MAINE

	American Indian	Asian	Black	Hispanic	White	Foreign	Total
Andover C	0.0	1.1	0.2	0.0	98.6	0.0	435
Bangor Theological Seminary	0.0	0.0	0.0	0.7	98.6	0.7	141
Bates C	0.3	3.8	2.4	1.1	90.5	1.9	1,572
Beal C	0.0	0.0	0.0	0.0	100.0	0.0	353
Bowdoin C	0.1	3.1	3.9	2.5	87.7	2.7	1,399
Casco Bay C	0.0	0.7	0.0	0.4	98.9	0.0	272
Central Maine Medical Center							
Sch of Nursing	1.2	0.0	0.0	2.3	96.5	0.0	86
Central Maine Tech C	0.1	0.1	0.0	0.1	99.6	0.0	782
Colby C	0.1	2.7	1.8	1.4	92.1	1.9	1,767
C of the Atlantic	0.0	0.9	0.0	1.3	95.6	2.2	227
Eastern Maine Tech C	1.4	0.1	0.2	0.0	98.3	0.0	1,328
Husson C	0.9	0.5	1.5	0.5	95.6	1.1	1,850
Kennebec Valley Tech C	0.4	0.6	0.0	0.0	98.9	0.0	1,136
Maine Maritime Academy	0.5	0.3	0.5	0.2	92.2	6.3	603
Mid-State C	0.0	0.0	0.0	0.0	100.0	0.0	278
Northern Maine Tech C	3.5	0.4	0.1	0.2	95.8	0.0	1,217
Portland Sch of Art	0.3	1.0	0.0	0.3	98.4	0.0	305
Saint Joseph's C	0.2	0.5	0.4	0.2	98.7	0.0	3,753
Southern Maine Tech C	0.5	2.9	0.2	0.1	96.2	0.1	2,101
Thomas C	0.0	0.3	0.3	0.0	98.7	0.7	1,026
Unity C	0.0	0.0	0.0	0.0	98.2	1.8	398
U of Maine							
Main campus	1.1	0.5	0.4	0.3	97.4	0.2	13,278
Augusta	0.4	0.1	0.1	0.0	99.4	0.0	4,773
Farmington	0.2	0.3	0.2	0.1	99.3	0.0	2,438
Fort Kent	0.5	0.2	0.4	0.2	96.1	2.6	571
Machias	2.5	0.1	0.2	0.1	93.4	3.8	1,008
Presque Isle	0.8	0.3	1.6	0.1	92.1	5.1	1,458
U of Southern Maine	0.5	0.4	0.2	0.2	98.6	0.1	10,487
U of New England	0.2	1.1	0.2	1.0	95.9	1.4	1,259
Washington County Tech C ..	5.6	0.0	0.0	0.0	94.4	0.0	320
Westbrook C	0.0	0.4	0.0	0.2	95.2	4.2	565

MARYLAND

	American Indian	Asian	Black	Hispanic	White	Foreign	Total
Allegany CC	0.1	0.3	1.6	0.5	97.5	0.0	2,650
Anne Arundel CC	0.4	1.8	8.0	1.4	88.0	0.4	12,148
Baltimore Hebrew U	0.0	0.0	0.8	0.0	99.2	0.0	263
Baltimore International							
Culinary C	0.0	1.0	19.8	3.1	75.1	1.0	293
Capitol C	0.0	10.0	18.3	1.8	66.2	3.7	737
Catonsville CC	0.3	2.1	15.4	0.8	81.0	0.4	12,766
Cecil CC	0.3	0.7	2.9	0.6	95.3	0.2	1,525
Charles County CC	0.4	1.6	8.8	1.1	87.9	0.1	5,282
Chesapeake C	0.1	0.2	9.5	0.3	89.6	0.1	2,064
C of Notre Dame	0.0	1.2	14.3	1.5	81.5	1.6	2,617

	American Indian	Asian	Black	Hispanic	White	Foreign	Total
Columbia Union C	0.0%	5.7%	36.8%	4.1%	49.8%	3.6%	1,338
Dundalk CC	0.7	1.2	10.3	0.6	87.2	0.0	3,410
Eastern Christian C	0.0	0.0	9.1	0.0	90.9	0.0	22
Essex CC	0.3	1.8	7.8	0.7	89.4	0.0	11,016
Frederick CC	0.2	1.0	4.1	1.0	92.9	0.9	3,976
Garrett CC	0.0	0.0	2.3	0.2	97.5	0.0	652
Goucher C	0.2	4.9	4.0	3.3	85.5	2.0	891
Hagerstown Business C	0.0	0.6	3.9	0.0	95.6	0.0	360
Hagerstown JC	0.2	0.7	6.7	0.5	91.9	0.0	3,353
Harford CC	0.4	1.6	7.2	1.0	89.8	0.0	5,102
Hood C	0.2	2.1	6.1	1.8	88.0	1.8	1,988
Howard CC	0.4	4.3	12.2	1.4	80.7	0.9	4,445
Johns Hopkins U	0.3	7.6	5.5	1.4	77.6	7.6	13,363
Loyola C	0.0	1.9	3.2	1.1	92.7	1.1	6,355
Maryland C of Art and Design	0.0	6.7	30.0	1.1	60.0	2.2	90
Maryland Inst C of Art	0.0	3.7	6.7	2.1	84.9	2.6	1,381
Montgomery C							
Germantown	0.3	4.7	6.4	2.7	84.7	1.2	3,183
Rockville	0.4	11.5	9.5	5.7	65.9	6.9	14,361
Takoma Park	1.9	7.0	33.4	5.8	44.5	7.3	4,805
Morgan State U	0.2	0.5	91.8	0.3	3.8	3.4	4,693
Mount Saint Mary's C	0.2	1.1	4.0	1.3	93.2	0.1	1,807
Ner Israel Rabbinical C	0.0	0.0	0.0	0.0	100.0	0.0	370
New CC of Baltimore	0.5	1.7	74.6	0.7	18.6	3.8	4,743
Peabody Inst							
of Johns Hopkins U	0.0	4.1	3.5	0.2	69.7	22.6	492
Prince George's CC	0.4	4.7	48.1	2.3	43.5	0.9	13,087
St John's C	0.0	4.1	2.3	1.8	89.6	2.3	442
Saint Mary's C	0.1	2.3	7.1	1.0	88.2	1.3	1,568
Saint Mary's Seminary and U	0.0	0.7	19.4	0.3	78.9	0.7	304
Sojourner-Douglass C	0.0	0.0	96.0	0.0	2.4	1.6	253
Uniformed Services U							
of the Health Sciences	0.4	7.6	3.4	3.4	81.1	4.2	794
U S Naval Academy	0.7	4.7	6.0	6.3	81.4	0.9	4,368
U of Maryland Sys							
C Park	0.2	8.7	9.7	2.9	71.3	7.2	34,829
Baltimore County	0.3	8.1	12.1	1.5	74.7	3.4	10,146
Baltimore	0.2	6.9	11.5	1.7	75.8	3.9	4,727
Eastern Shore	0.1	1.0	69.6	0.6	22.5	6.0	2,067
U C	0.5	6.0	19.0	2.8	69.3	2.5	14,476
Bowie State U	0.2	3.4	64.9	0.8	29.3	1.4	4,188
Coppin State C	0.2	1.2	90.7	0.4	4.7	2.8	2,578
Frostburg State U	0.2	0.7	7.3	0.7	90.7	0.5	5,019
Salisbury State U	0.1	1.1	5.9	0.5	92.1	0.2	5,734
Towson State U	0.2	2.0	7.7	1.1	87.5	1.4	15,035
U of Baltimore	0.3	2.1	15.8	1.0	78.8	2.0	5,770
Villa Julie C	0.1	1.4	14.6	0.5	83.4	0.0	1,596
Washington Bible C	0.2	6.1	38.2	0.4	46.3	8.7	458
Washington C	0.0	0.8	1.2	0.7	95.4	1.9	1,046
Washington Theological							
Union	0.0	2.2	2.6	5.7	89.5	0.0	229
Western Maryland C	0.1	0.4	4.4	0.8	93.5	0.9	2,222
Wor-Wic Tech CC	0.1	0.4	20.1	0.4	79.1	0.0	1,385

MASSACHUSETTS

American International C	0.0	1.1	6.1	2.0	88.1	2.7	1,829
Amherst C	0.1	9.8	6.1	7.1	74.6	2.4	1,598

MASS., cont.

	American Indian	Asian	Black	Hispanic	White	Foreign	Total
Andover Newton Theological Sch	0.0%	0.7%	5.0%	3.7%	85.2%	5.5%	458
Anna Maria C	0.0	1.3	2.5	1.6	92.7	1.9	1,412
Aquinas C Milton	0.0	0.6	2.1	1.2	96.2	0.0	341
Aquinas C Newton	0.0	2.7	7.9	5.8	82.5	1.0	291
Arthur D Little Management Education Inst	0.0	1.5	0.0	1.5	3.0	93.9	66
Assumption C	0.1	2.4	2.0	2.2	92.9	0.4	2,974
Babson C	0.0	1.7	1.1	1.5	92.4	3.4	3,090
Bay Path C	0.3	5.9	3.5	3.1	86.5	0.7	577
Bay State C	0.0	0.9	5.7	6.0	86.0	1.4	566
Becker C Leicester	0.0	6.1	2.1	1.9	88.6	1.3	474
Becker C Worcester	0.0	1.9	2.8	0.5	94.7	0.0	1,196
Bentley C	0.1	2.5	1.7	2.3	89.4	4.0	7,436
Berklee C of Music	1.1	1.5	3.5	2.1	65.7	26.0	2,731
Boston Architectural Center	0.8	1.7	1.8	14.3	81.4	0.0	945
Boston C	0.2	5.5	3.8	4.1	82.6	3.8	14,506
Boston Conservatory	0.8	1.1	4.4	2.2	78.2	13.2	363
Boston U	0.2	8.5	3.5	3.3	72.6	11.9	27,996
Bradford C	0.0	2.1	2.5	2.3	86.8	6.4	439
Brandeis U	0.1	4.9	3.2	2.3	79.7	9.9	3,791
Cambridge C	0.5	1.7	22.5	3.3	71.2	0.8	824
Clark U	0.2	3.7	2.1	2.0	81.8	10.2	3,286
C of Our Lady of Elms	0.1	1.1	2.3	3.0	91.4	2.2	1,116
C of the Holy Cross	0.1	1.6	3.9	2.3	91.8	0.3	2,693
Conway Sch of Landscape Design	0.0	0.0	0.0	0.0	94.4	5.6	18
Curry C	0.1	0.5	3.7	1.4	92.5	1.8	1,216
Dean JC	0.1	1.5	2.6	1.5	93.4	0.9	2,532
Eastern Nazarene C	0.0	2.8	6.8	5.2	83.0	2.2	917
Emerson C	0.1	0.8	2.3	1.9	90.0	5.0	2,692
Emmanuel C	0.0	4.2	11.0	4.6	73.4	6.8	1,079
Endicott C	0.3	2.5	1.5	2.3	88.4	5.0	868
Episcopal Divinity Sch	0.0	4.1	2.0	2.0	80.6	11.2	98
Fisher C	0.5	1.7	8.4	2.3	84.8	2.2	2,084
Forsyth Sch of Dental Hygienists	0.0	1.7	0.0	0.8	97.5	0.0	119
Franklin Inst of Boston	0.5	10.7	9.2	3.4	72.9	3.4	413
Gordon C	0.1	2.1	1.3	1.7	91.7	3.1	1,146
Gordon-Conwell Theological Seminary	0.1	6.3	20.0	12.9	57.4	3.3	855
Hampshire C	0.4	2.1	2.7	3.3	88.7	2.9	1,313
Harvard U	0.3	6.0	4.9	3.5	74.6	10.7	22,851
Hebrew C	0.0	0.0	0.0	2.3	82.6	15.1	86
Hellenic C Holy Cross Greek Orthodox Sch of Theology	0.0	0.7	0.0	0.0	81.1	18.2	148
Laboure C	0.0	1.6	14.4	1.8	82.2	0.0	444
Lasell C	0.0	1.3	1.3	4.3	79.9	13.2	447
Lesley C	0.4	1.4	4.1	2.1	86.3	5.6	5,495
Marian Court JC	0.0	0.5	1.6	2.6	95.2	0.0	189
Massachusetts Higher Education Coordinating Council							
U of Lowell	0.2	4.5	2.0	1.5	86.7	5.2	14,259
U of Mass Amherst	0.2	2.8	2.8	2.8	85.1	6.3	26,025
U of Mass Boston	0.4	5.0	9.7	3.5	79.1	2.3	13,723
U of Mass Dartmouth	0.4	1.3	2.6	1.0	92.7	2.0	7,343

	American Indian	Asian	Black	Hispanic	White	Foreign	Total
U of Mass Worcester	0.4%	3.6%	1.8%	1.1%	93.2%	0.0%	556
Bridgewater State C	0.4	0.6	1.4	1.0	96.2	0.5	8,821
Massachusetts C of Art	0.3	5.4	2.8	2.9	85.0	3.7	1,846
Mass Maritime Academy	0.2	1.3	0.8	1.5	90.6	5.5	598
North Adams State C	0.2	0.4	1.9	0.7	96.9	0.0	2,421
Salem State C	0.4	0.9	2.5	1.6	94.1	0.6	9,810
Westfield State C	0.3	0.5	2.7	1.3	95.3	0.0	5,292
Berkshire CC	0.1	0.8	2.0	0.5	94.6	2.1	2,621
Bristol CC	0.5	1.0	2.6	1.5	93.8	0.5	4,999
Bunker Hill CC	0.3	11.9	14.9	6.1	63.2	3.7	5,606
Cape Cod CC	0.8	0.4	1.2	1.8	95.6	0.2	4,326
Greenfield CC	0.1	1.6	0.8	1.1	95.6	0.7	2,351
Holyoke CC	0.7	0.8	2.6	4.7	90.7	0.6	5,318
Massachusetts Bay CC	0.2	1.9	6.2	2.5	86.3	2.9	4,662
Massasoit CC	0.4	1.2	6.0	0.9	91.3	0.1	6,670
Mount Wachusett CC	0.4	1.0	2.8	3.4	91.1	1.4	3,680
North Shore CC	0.2	1.6	4.2	6.2	87.8	0.0	5,780
Northern Essex CC	0.9	1.5	0.3	8.4	88.6	0.2	6,647
Quinsigamond CC	0.5	2.3	2.9	5.2	88.9	0.2	4,703
Roxbury CC	0.2	8.9	66.3	12.7	11.7	0.2	1,886
Springfield Tech CC	0.7	1.5	9.5	7.3	80.6	0.4	5,866
Massachusetts C of Pharmacy and Allied Health Sciences	0.4	10.8	5.4	6.2	61.4	15.8	1,139
Massachusetts Inst of Tech	0.3	12.1	3.8	4.4	57.7	21.8	9,628
Mass Sch of Professional Psychology	0.0	0.6	0.6	0.0	97.0	1.8	166
Merrimack C	0.0	2.2	1.5	2.0	91.0	3.2	3,507
MGH Inst of Health Professions	0.0	0.3	0.0	0.3	95.9	3.4	295
Montserrat C of Art	0.0	1.8	1.3	1.8	95.2	0.0	227
Mount Holyoke C	0.1	5.6	3.4	2.7	77.9	10.2	1,931
New England C of Optometry	0.0	7.9	4.7	4.7	74.1	8.6	382
New England Conservatory of Music	0.7	4.9	2.7	2.6	65.0	24.2	739
New England Sch of Law	0.2	0.7	1.5	1.4	96.0	0.2	1,187
Newbury C	0.0	4.9	14.0	15.3	62.1	3.7	4,282
Nichols C	0.1	0.5	0.6	0.8	96.7	1.4	1,945
Northeastern U	0.4	2.8	5.7	1.6	82.6	6.9	30,510
Pine Manor C	0.0	1.3	3.6	2.9	75.8	16.4	549
Pope John XXIII National Seminary	0.0	0.0	0.0	0.0	95.5	4.5	44
Regis C	0.0	1.0	2.0	4.5	86.9	5.7	1,145
Saint Hyacinth C and Seminary	0.0	0.0	0.0	4.3	95.7	0.0	23
Simmons C	0.2	2.2	2.9	2.0	89.2	3.5	2,817
Simon's Rock C of Bard	0.4	4.3	5.3	3.9	82.6	3.6	281
Smith C	0.3	8.6	4.1	3.2	77.7	6.1	3,058
Springfield C	0.1	0.4	4.9	2.3	89.0	3.3	3,577
Stonehill C	0.0	0.3	0.6	0.4	98.0	0.7	3,025
Tufts U	0.2	16.8	7.2	5.9	60.3	9.6	7,895
Wellesley C	0.4	19.5	7.1	4.0	63.8	5.4	2,277
Wentworth Inst of Tech	0.2	4.7	8.0	2.4	79.1	5.7	3,902
Western New England C	0.1	1.2	2.8	1.5	93.6	0.8	5,404
Weston Sch of Theology	0.0	2.0	2.6	0.0	89.5	5.9	153
Wheaton C	0.5	3.7	2.3	1.2	88.3	4.0	1,262

MASS., cont.

	American Indian	Asian	Black	Hispanic	White	Foreign	Total
Williams C	0.1%	8.4%	7.6%	4.3%	75.5%	4.0%	2,056
Worcester Polytechnic Inst	0.1	4.8	0.6	0.8	85.8	7.9	3,911

MICHIGAN

	American Indian	Asian	Black	Hispanic	White	Foreign	Total
Adrian C	0.2	0.9	2.7	1.9	92.4	1.9	1,180
Albion C	0.1	3.2	2.2	0.4	93.4	0.8	1,569
Alma C	0.2	0.9	1.5	1.1	95.0	1.3	1,229
Alpena CC	0.3	0.4	1.9	0.7	96.8	0.0	2,309
Andrews U	0.5	6.9	15.7	5.8	53.6	17.5	2,877
Aquinas C	0.5	0.8	5.1	1.7	91.1	0.9	2,629
Baker C Sys							
Flint	0.9	0.8	13.1	1.5	83.7	0.0	3,506
Muskegon	1.0	0.3	8.4	2.0	88.3	0.0	1,877
Owosso	0.2	0.4	0.2	1.4	97.8	0.0	954
Bay De Noc CC	2.1	0.1	0.0	0.3	97.6	0.0	2,166
Calvin C	0.2	1.9	1.1	0.6	87.4	8.8	4,260
Calvin Theological Seminary	2.6	6.1	2.6	2.2	51.8	34.6	228
Center for Creative Studies C of Art and Design	0.4	2.9	8.1	1.7	85.1	1.8	1,002
Center for Humanistic Studies	0.0	0.0	8.2	0.0	91.8	0.0	73
Central Michigan U	0.5	0.5	2.4	0.9	94.9	0.8	18,286
Charles S Mott CC	1.2	0.6	14.2	1.7	82.1	0.1	9,963
Cleary C	0.6	0.2	13.8	4.0	80.3	1.0	976
Concordia C	0.2	1.6	8.0	1.0	88.4	0.8	611
Cranbrook Academy of Art	0.0	2.8	0.7	4.9	78.2	13.4	142
Davenport C	1.0	1.3	5.0	2.1	90.5	0.1	3,821
Davenport C Lansing	0.7	0.8	11.3	5.3	81.6	0.2	2,886
Delta C	0.5	0.5	6.9	3.4	88.6	0.1	11,114
Detroit C of Business							
Dearborn	0.4	0.7	50.6	2.3	45.7	0.3	2,709
Warren	0.8	1.0	44.9	0.6	52.6	0.1	1,938
Detroit C of Law	0.0	1.7	9.4	0.8	86.3	1.8	659
Eastern Michigan U	0.3	1.3	7.5	1.3	85.5	4.1	25,011
Ferris State U	0.5	0.7	6.3	1.0	89.8	1.7	12,037
Glen Oaks CC	0.8	0.7	1.1	0.5	96.8	0.1	1,428
GMI Engineering and Management Inst	0.4	6.3	5.6	1.6	80.2	6.0	3,203
Gogebic CC	1.0	0.5	3.0	0.3	95.1	0.1	1,339
Grace Bible C	0.8	0.8	0.8	2.4	88.2	7.1	127
Grand Rapids Baptist C and Seminary	0.0	0.3	1.0	0.2	96.3	2.1	894
Grand Rapids JC	0.9	1.4	5.9	2.0	89.5	0.3	12,054
Grand Valley State U	0.4	0.9	4.7	1.5	92.0	0.5	11,725
Great Lakes Bible C	1.4	0.7	4.9	0.0	93.0	0.0	142
Great Lakes JC of Business	0.3	0.0	6.5	3.4	89.7	0.0	2,082
Henry Ford CC	0.5	1.7	14.9	2.3	80.4	0.2	16,147
Hillsdale C	0.0	0.0	1.5	0.0	96.8	1.7	1,110
Hope C	0.3	1.3	1.2	1.0	93.2	3.0	2,813
Jackson CC	0.7	0.6	10.9	2.3	85.4	0.1	6,487
Jordan C	0.3	0.6	57.8	1.3	40.1	0.0	2,322
Kalamazoo C	0.4	6.0	2.5	0.6	87.0	3.4	1,263
Kalamazoo Valley CC	0.6	0.9	6.8	1.3	88.8	1.7	10,492
Kellogg CC	0.6	0.7	6.5	1.0	90.6	0.6	5,815
Kendall C of Art and Design	0.7	2.1	2.3	2.0	92.3	0.6	701
Kirtland CC	1.3	0.2	3.1	1.0	94.3	0.0	1,271
Lake Michigan C	1.0	1.1	11.9	1.4	84.2	0.3	3,422

	American Indian	Asian	Black	Hispanic	White	Foreign	Total
Lake Superior State U	3.7%	0.3%	0.6%	0.4%	69.0%	26.0%	3,407
Lansing CC	0.8	1.8	6.3	2.4	87.6	1.1	22,343
Lawrence Inst of Tech	0.7	2.0	7.0	1.2	86.9	2.3	5,469
Lewis C of Business	0.0	0.0	100.0	0.0	0.0	0.0	233
Macomb CC	0.4	1.2	1.7	0.7	95.8	0.2	31,538
Madonna C	0.3	0.9	11.0	1.8	83.7	2.4	4,392
Marygrove C	0.3	0.8	76.2	0.6	21.6	0.4	1,241
Mercy C	0.2	0.6	44.7	0.7	52.5	1.2	2,056
Michigan Christian C	0.0	0.4	15.3	0.7	82.5	1.1	268
Michigan State U	0.5	2.3	6.9	1.6	83.4	5.3	44,307
Michigan Tech U	0.5	1.2	1.1	0.6	90.0	6.5	6,497
Mid Michigan CC	1.2	0.3	0.5	0.9	96.9	0.3	1,925
Monroe County CC	0.4	0.4	0.9	1.1	97.2	0.1	3,313
Montcalm CC	0.3	0.3	3.6	1.4	94.4	0.0	2,040
Muskegon CC	1.9	0.4	7.1	2.1	88.4	0.2	5,119
Nazareth C	0.2	0.6	6.7	0.9	91.5	0.0	638
North Central Michigan C	3.0	0.2	0.0	0.4	96.4	0.0	1,932
Northern Michigan U	2.1	0.4	1.6	0.6	94.7	0.7	8,505
Northwestern Michigan C	1.7	0.5	0.1	0.5	97.0	0.2	4,391
Northwood Inst	0.0	0.2	11.4	0.6	87.6	0.2	1,601
Oakland CC	0.6	1.7	10.1	1.6	85.7	0.4	28,069
Oakland U	0.2	2.7	5.6	0.9	89.6	0.9	12,400
Olivet C	0.0	0.1	8.6	0.7	90.6	0.0	754
Reformed Bible C	1.1	1.7	0.6	1.1	61.1	34.3	175
Sacred Heart Major Seminary C and Theologate	0.0	0.0	9.3	0.4	88.0	2.3	258
Saginaw Valley State U	0.6	0.6	5.3	3.1	89.7	0.6	6,179
Saint Mary's C	0.0	1.4	6.2	0.5	90.1	1.8	433
Schoolcraft C	0.4	0.8	2.4	0.9	95.0	0.6	9,177
Siena Heights C	0.4	0.5	4.9	3.6	89.0	1.5	1,837
Southwestern Michigan C	0.8	0.6	6.0	1.3	87.5	3.8	2,551
Spring Arbor C	0.4	0.4	16.4	1.1	80.4	1.5	1,644
St Clair County CC	0.6	0.1	1.9	1.1	95.2	1.0	4,467
Suomi C	3.8	0.8	10.4	0.9	79.6	4.5	530
Thomas M Cooley Law Sch	0.0	1.0	3.1	2.1	93.3	0.5	1,542
U of Detroit	0.3	2.4	20.3	1.5	66.6	8.9	5,699
U of Michigan							
Ann Arbor	0.4	7.2	6.7	3.0	76.3	6.4	36,391
Dearborn	0.6	3.4	6.5	1.8	86.8	1.0	7,684
Flint	1.0	1.1	7.5	1.4	88.9	0.0	6,593
Walsh C of Accountancy and Business Administration	0.2	1.9	4.7	0.7	92.2	0.3	3,326
Washtenaw CC	0.9	3.1	11.4	1.7	82.6	0.2	10,975
Wayne County CC	1.0	1.3	67.2	2.1	27.7	0.8	11,986
Wayne State U	0.5	3.7	22.5	1.8	66.3	5.2	33,872
West Shore CC	1.0	0.5	0.9	1.4	96.2	0.0	1,305
Western Michigan U	0.3	1.0	5.0	0.8	88.3	4.6	26,989
Western Theological Seminary	0.0	0.0	0.7	0.7	92.4	6.2	145
William Tyndale C	0.0	0.5	38.0	0.3	60.2	1.0	382
Yeshiva Beth Yehuda Yeshiva Gedolah of Greater Detroit	0.0	0.0	0.0	0.0	100.0	0.0	38

MINNESOTA

Alexandria Tech C	0.8	0.4	0.0	0.3	98.5	0.0	1,585
Bethany Lutheran C	0.3	1.0	3.2	0.0	95.2	0.3	311
Bethel C	0.3	1.8	0.7	0.4	96.6	0.1	1,791

MINNESOTA, cont.

	American Indian	Asian	Black	Hispanic	White	Foreign	Total
Bethel Theological Seminary	0.0%	3.2%	2.6%	0.4%	89.1%	4.6%	495
Carleton C	0.3	7.1	3.1	2.4	86.5	0.6	1,857
C of Associated Arts	0.7	2.1	0.7	0.7	95.1	0.7	144
C of Saint Benedict	0.4	1.3	0.6	1.1	94.7	1.9	1,916
C of Saint Catherine							
Saint Catherine campus	0.8	1.6	1.0	1.1	93.6	2.0	2,519
Saint Mary's campus	1.4	1.0	3.6	1.1	93.0	0.0	840
C of Saint Scholastica	2.6	0.7	0.2	0.3	95.7	0.6	1,966
Concordia C Saint Paul	0.2	4.7	2.8	1.0	90.9	0.5	1,235
Concordia C Moorhead	0.7	1.0	0.3	0.3	94.4	3.3	2,948
Dakota County Tech C	0.6	2.0	0.7	0.5	96.2	0.0	1,782
Dr Martin Luther C	1.1	0.2	0.5	0.5	97.3	0.5	442
Gustavus Adolphus C	0.1	1.0	1.2	0.3	95.7	1.8	2,371
Hamline U	0.4	2.4	2.2	0.8	92.5	1.7	2,514
Luther Northwestern							
Theological Seminary	0.3	0.1	0.5	0.4	95.0	3.6	746
Macalester C	0.8	2.5	4.3	2.4	80.7	9.2	1,853
Mayo Foundation							
Mayo Graduate Sch	0.0	2.1	1.0	0.0	79.2	17.7	96
Mayo Graduate Sch							
of Medicine	0.6	6.3	1.4	4.4	71.7	15.5	1,082
Mayo Medical Sch	1.3	7.0	1.3	3.8	86.7	0.0	158
Mayo Sch of Health-							
Related Sciences	0.0	1.9	0.5	0.0	97.7	0.0	214
Medical Inst of Minnesota	0.6	1.1	4.7	0.0	93.6	0.0	534
Minneapolis C of Art Design	0.3	5.9	2.2	1.3	90.0	0.3	712
Minnesota Bible C	0.0	5.2	0.0	1.0	87.5	6.3	96
Minnesota CC's Sys							
Anoka-Ramsey CC	0.6	0.8	0.6	0.3	97.5	0.1	6,688
Arrowhead CC Region							
Hibbing CC	2.6	0.1	0.3	0.2	96.6	0.1	2,047
Itasca CC	6.2	0.2	0.4	0.2	92.9	0.1	1,423
Mesabi CC	6.9	0.2	0.8	0.3	91.7	0.2	1,536
Rainy River CC	16.1	0.0	1.6	0.3	81.8	0.2	626
Vermilion CC	3.9	0.0	2.4	0.5	92.9	0.3	634
Austin CC	0.2	0.9	0.3	0.6	97.3	0.6	1,244
Brainerd CC	2.3	0.4	0.9	0.2	95.9	0.3	1,837
Fergus Falls CC	0.4	0.3	0.5	0.2	98.2	0.4	1,228
Inver Hills CC	0.2	1.0	0.9	0.9	96.9	0.1	5,136
Lakewood CC	0.2	2.4	2.8	0.5	93.8	0.2	6,217
Minneapolis CC	2.7	2.7	15.0	1.3	75.0	3.3	4,064
Normandale CC	0.1	1.8	0.8	0.3	96.2	0.6	8,851
North Hennepin CC	0.3	0.5	0.8	0.4	95.8	2.2	6,163
Northland CC	4.6	0.6	1.5	0.7	92.3	0.3	905
Rochester CC	0.3	2.2	0.8	0.4	94.9	1.4	4,156
Willmar CC	0.4	0.4	0.1	0.6	98.5	0.0	1,380
Worthington CC	0.0	0.9	0.7	0.2	97.2	0.9	851
National Education Center							
Brown Inst	1.1	2.1	6.0	1.1	89.6	0.0	1,409
North Central Bible C	0.2	1.1	2.8	1.9	91.3	2.7	1,182
Northwest Tech Inst	0.0	2.3	0.0	0.0	97.7	0.0	177
Northwestern C	0.3	1.5	1.2	0.4	94.7	1.9	950
Northwestern C							
of Chiropractic	0.2	0.4	0.2	1.3	89.5	8.4	522
Northwestern Electronics Inst	0.9	2.6	1.7	0.9	93.9	0.0	543
Oak Hills Bible C	1.4	0.7	0.0	0.0	95.8	2.1	144
Pillsbury Baptist Bible C	0.0	0.3	1.1	1.1	96.5	1.1	367

	American Indian	Asian	Black	Hispanic	White	Foreign	Total
Rasmussen Business C	0.6%	0.0%	0.6%	0.0%	98.5%	0.3%	326
Saint John's U	0.1	1.6	1.5	0.8	93.5	2.5	2,035
Saint Mary's C	0.8	1.3	1.1	0.8	93.6	2.4	2,167
Saint Olaf C	0.2	2.9	0.9	0.6	93.4	2.0	3,097
Saint Paul Bible C	0.0	7.2	0.6	0.4	91.3	0.6	516
Saint Paul Tech C	1.6	12.3	9.7	4.1	72.1	0.3	2,369
State U Sys of Minnesota							
Bemidji State U	3.9	0.0	0.3	0.3	92.7	2.8	5,424
Mankato State U	0.2	1.3	0.8	0.5	94.9	2.3	16,575
Metropolitan State U	0.6	1.5	4.1	1.1	92.6	0.0	5,221
Moorhead State U	0.9	0.8	0.2	0.5	95.5	2.2	8,900
Saint Cloud State U	0.3	0.8	0.7	0.4	96.9	0.9	17,075
Southwest State U	0.4	0.5	1.7	0.3	95.9	1.2	3,055
Winona State U	0.4	1.3	0.8	0.5	94.0	3.0	7,707
U of Minnesota							
Twin Cities	0.6	3.4	1.9	1.0	88.5	4.5	57,168
Duluth	1.0	1.0	0.7	0.4	95.4	1.4	10,329
Morris	1.7	2.5	1.7	1.1	92.8	0.3	2,168
Waseca	0.1	0.1	1.0	0.2	98.2	0.5	1,042
U of Saint Thomas	0.3	1.7	1.4	0.8	94.7	1.0	9,805
United Theological Seminary	0.5	0.0	1.4	1.0	96.2	1.0	210
Walden U	0.5	2.4	1.7	0.9	94.5	0.0	422
William Mitchell C of Law	0.6	1.5	3.7	1.9	91.9	0.3	1,152
Willmar Tech C	0.1	0.9	0.1	2.6	96.2	0.0	1,413
Winona Tech C	0.8	0.6	0.5	0.3	96.4	1.4	631

MISSISSIPPI

Alcorn State U	0.0	0.1	94.4	0.5	5.1	0.0	2,863
Belhaven C	0.3	0.7	8.9	0.8	85.5	3.8	868
Blue Mountain C	0.0	0.0	8.6	0.3	90.5	0.6	347
Clarke C	0.0	0.0	21.8	0.8	77.4	0.0	133
Coahoma CC	0.0	0.0	97.3	0.0	2.7	0.0	1,351
Copiah-Lincoln JC							
Natchez	0.4	0.2	26.3	0.0	73.1	0.0	472
Wesson	0.2	0.3	26.0	0.1	73.5	0.0	1,494
Delta State U	0.1	0.5	21.5	0.1	77.9	0.0	3,995
East Central CC	6.4	0.0	19.9	0.0	73.8	0.0	1,303
East Mississippi CC	0.0	0.2	32.5	0.5	66.8	0.0	1,085
Hinds CC Raymond	0.1	0.6	34.8	0.2	64.1	0.2	8,747
Holmes CC	0.1	0.3	19.3	0.2	80.0	0.0	2,073
Itawamba CC	0.0	0.1	14.5	0.0	85.3	0.0	3,281
Jackson State U	0.1	2.0	92.1	0.1	4.0	1.7	6,837
Jones County JC	0.3	0.0	17.4	0.1	82.1	0.0	4,122
Magnolia Bible C	0.0	0.0	40.5	2.7	56.8	0.0	37
Mary Holmes C	0.0	0.0	98.9	0.0	0.0	1.1	742
Meridian CC	0.3	0.6	24.1	0.2	74.8	0.0	2,952
Millsaps C	0.0	1.7	4.2	0.5	93.2	0.4	1,410
Mississippi C	0.3	0.6	13.3	0.4	85.3	0.2	3,620
Mississippi Delta JC	0.0	0.3	42.3	0.1	57.3	0.0	2,123
Mississippi Gulf Coast JC	1.1	0.8	14.2	1.2	82.8	0.0	9,524
Mississippi State U	0.4	1.1	11.8	0.3	81.7	4.8	14,391
Mississippi U for Women	0.5	0.2	18.4	0.1	80.6	0.1	2,407
Mississippi Valley State U	0.0	0.0	99.5	0.0	0.5	0.1	1,873
Northeast Mississippi CC	0.0	0.1	11.4	0.0	88.4	0.0	2,955
Northwest Mississippi CC	0.0	0.0	20.9	0.0	79.1	0.0	3,893
Pearl River JC	0.5	0.4	24.9	0.3	73.9	0.0	3,362

MISSISSIPPI, cont.

	American Indian	Asian	Black	Hispanic	White	Foreign	Total
Phillips JC Gulfport	0.0%	1.6%	25.4%	0.5%	72.4%	0.0%	1,172
Phillips JC Jackson	0.2	0.5	43.3	0.2	55.9	0.0	639
Reformed Theological Seminary	0.0	5.0	4.4	0.2	76.3	14.1	617
Rust C	0.0	0.0	96.7	0.0	1.6	1.8	1,021
Southeastern Baptist C	0.0	0.0	8.6	0.0	91.4	0.0	70
Southwest Mississippi CC	0.0	0.0	21.5	0.0	78.5	0.0	1,520
Tougaloo C	0.0	0.1	99.7	0.0	0.2	0.0	956
U of Mississippi							
Main campus	0.1	0.5	9.0	0.2	85.2	5.0	11,288
Medical Center	0.1	1.9	9.8	0.5	83.6	4.1	1,637
U of Southern Mississippi	0.2	0.6	13.3	0.4	83.6	1.9	13,490
Wesley Biblical Seminary	0.0	0.0	11.3	0.0	79.0	9.7	62
Wesley C	0.0	0.0	5.2	3.4	91.4	0.0	58
William Carey C	0.3	0.6	30.5	1.3	65.6	1.7	1,574
Wood JC	0.0	0.6	9.4	0.0	86.5	3.5	519

MISSOURI

	American Indian	Asian	Black	Hispanic	White	Foreign	Total
Aquinas Inst of Theology	0.0	0.0	1.2	1.2	93.0	4.7	86
Assemblies of God Theological Seminary	0.0	0.9	0.5	3.2	88.4	6.9	216
Avila C	0.7	0.3	8.9	2.1	85.9	2.1	1,367
Baptist Bible C	0.0	0.7	0.5	1.6	96.8	0.4	825
Barnes Hospital Sch of Nursing	0.0	0.7	2.0	0.0	97.3	0.0	297
Calvary Bible C	2.2	0.4	2.2	1.1	93.0	1.1	273
Central Bible C	0.2	1.3	1.6	1.8	94.5	0.6	1,091
Central Christian C of the Bible	0.0	2.7	0.0	0.0	97.3	0.0	74
Central Methodist C	0.0	0.2	7.2	0.2	91.1	1.2	887
Central Missouri State U	0.1	0.5	6.7	0.6	89.1	3.1	11,429
Cleveland Chiropractic C	0.3	1.7	1.3	2.0	90.6	4.0	297
C of the Ozarks	0.0	0.0	0.8	0.0	97.3	1.9	1,512
Columbia C	1.4	1.7	14.4	3.1	76.6	2.8	4,214
Conception Seminary C	0.0	2.9	1.0	3.9	92.2	0.0	103
Concordia Seminary	0.0	1.2	0.8	0.8	93.7	3.5	489
Cottey C	0.9	0.9	0.0	1.1	87.1	10.1	348
Covenant Theological Seminary	0.3	3.2	3.8	0.0	85.4	7.3	316
Crowder C	2.3	0.5	1.1	1.2	94.8	0.1	1,608
Culver-Stockton C	0.0	0.2	4.2	0.2	94.0	1.5	1,129
DeVry Inst of Tech	0.7	3.7	11.4	1.3	82.3	0.7	1,747
Drury C	0.3	0.6	1.8	0.6	95.9	0.8	3,501
East Central C	0.1	0.2	0.7	0.1	98.8	0.0	2,915
Eden Theological Seminary	0.0	1.5	8.5	1.5	84.9	3.5	199
Evangel C	0.3	0.5	3.0	0.6	94.7	0.8	1,540
Fontbonne C	0.0	1.4	13.5	0.9	79.8	4.4	1,139
Forest Inst of Professional Psychology	4.7	0.0	0.9	1.9	91.5	0.9	106
Hannibal-La Grange C	0.4	0.3	1.8	0.3	96.7	0.5	1,010
Harris-Stowe State C	0.2	0.7	76.6	0.3	21.2	1.0	1,973
ITT Tech Inst	0.0	1.1	22.8	1.3	74.3	0.6	544
Jefferson C	0.1	0.3	0.4	0.2	98.9	0.0	3,936
Kansas City Art Inst	0.3	1.6	3.5	4.2	88.3	2.1	575
Kemper Military Sch and C	1.1	4.8	45.0	3.2	45.0	1.1	189
Kenrick Seminary	0.0	1.5	0.0	0.0	97.1	1.5	68

	American Indian	Asian	Black	Hispanic	White	Foreign	Total
Kirksville C of Osteopathic Medicine	0.6%	7.0%	0.4%	5.4%	85.4%	1.3%	542
Lincoln U	0.6	0.4	23.0	0.5	73.3	2.2	3,619
Lindenwood C	0.7	1.6	10.4	0.8	86.3	0.3	2,431
Logan C of Chiropractic	0.4	1.9	1.9	1.3	85.7	8.7	679
Maryville C	0.2	0.6	2.9	0.4	92.7	3.1	3,274
Metropolitan CC's Sys							
Longview CC	0.4	0.7	5.4	1.2	92.2	0.1	9,625
Maple Woods CC	0.3	0.9	0.9	1.4	96.3	0.1	4,753
Penn Valley CC	0.5	2.0	36.2	3.7	54.6	3.0	5,778
Midwestern Baptist Theological Seminary	0.2	0.7	2.3	0.2	94.9	1.6	428
Mineral Area C	0.2	0.5	1.9	0.2	97.1	0.2	2,649
Missouri Baptist C	0.5	1.0	11.8	0.2	82.9	3.6	1,059
Missouri Southern State C	1.9	0.5	1.1	0.6	95.7	0.1	6,016
Missouri Valley C	0.3	0.9	19.4	3.8	74.6	1.0	1,054
Missouri Western State C	1.3	0.5	4.3	1.1	92.8	0.1	4,555
Moberly Area CC	0.3	0.3	6.7	0.6	91.0	1.2	1,518
Nazarene Theological Seminary	0.3	1.5	2.1	1.2	89.4	5.6	339
North Central Missouri C	0.1	0.2	1.0	0.1	98.6	0.0	903
Northeast Missouri State U	0.0	0.4	3.8	0.5	92.5	2.8	6,150
Northwest Missouri State U	1.4	0.2	2.1	0.4	93.8	2.2	6,093
Ozark Christian C	0.5	0.2	1.1	0.3	97.0	0.9	634
Phillips JC	0.7	0.3	19.9	1.7	77.4	0.0	296
Platt JC	0.5	0.0	4.0	1.5	94.1	0.0	202
Ranken Tech Inst	0.6	4.0	23.3	1.8	69.2	1.1	1,414
Research C of Nursing	0.0	0.6	6.7	5.5	87.1	0.0	163
Rockhurst C	0.3	1.9	7.7	3.2	86.4	0.5	2,801
Saint Charles County CC	0.1	0.7	1.1	0.5	97.4	0.1	3,505
Saint Louis Christian C	0.0	0.0	4.6	0.0	89.3	6.1	131
Saint Louis C of Pharmacy	0.0	2.8	1.9	0.1	94.7	0.5	752
Saint Louis CC	0.2	1.0	16.4	0.5	81.5	0.4	32,347
Saint Louis U	0.2	3.3	5.6	2.0	83.4	5.6	12,891
Saint Paul Sch of Theology	0.0	1.1	7.4	1.1	88.1	2.2	269
Southeast Missouri State U	0.2	0.4	6.7	0.2	89.2	3.2	8,801
Southwest Baptist U	0.3	0.8	1.1	0.3	96.2	1.2	2,948
Southwest Missouri State U	0.3	0.9	1.8	0.5	95.8	0.6	19,480
Southwest Mo State U W Plains	0.4	0.5	0.1	0.0	98.9	0.1	855
State Fair CC	0.3	0.6	3.6	1.1	94.4	0.0	2,369
Stephens C	0.0	1.7	2.9	1.4	94.0	0.0	1,191
Tarkio C	0.0	0.7	17.5	5.2	76.5	0.2	1,075
Three Rivers CC	0.2	0.0	2.1	0.2	97.5	0.0	2,062
U of Missouri							
Columbia	0.3	1.6	4.0	0.9	86.8	6.4	25,058
Kansas City	0.7	4.1	7.0	1.8	81.8	4.7	11,263
Rolla	0.2	5.8	3.2	1.3	82.9	6.7	5,440
Saint Louis	0.1	2.6	9.8	0.9	86.3	0.3	15,393
Webster U	0.4	1.1	11.5	2.8	82.9	1.3	8,745
Wentworth Military Academy	0.3	1.8	7.6	0.6	89.7	0.0	331
Westminster C	0.5	0.6	1.5	0.5	96.7	0.1	784
William Jewell C	0.1	0.5	1.9	0.4	96.2	0.7	2,056
William Woods C	0.0	0.0	0.3	0.0	98.8	0.9	767

MONTANA

Blackfeet CC	96.2	0.0	0.0	0.0	3.8	0.0	264
Carroll C	1.2	0.8	0.5	1.2	93.9	2.5	1,207

MONTANA, cont.

	American Indian	Asian	Black	Hispanic	White	Foreign	Total
C of Great Falls	5.0%	0.5%	0.6%	0.9%	89.2%	3.8%	1,081
Dawson CC	1.7	0.0	0.2	0.8	97.1	0.3	648
Dull Knife Memorial C	80.4	0.0	0.0	0.0	19.6	0.0	281
Flathead Valley CC	3.2	0.6	0.0	1.3	94.5	0.4	1,823
Fort Belknap C	91.1	0.0	0.0	0.0	8.9	0.0	135
Fort Peck CC	83.3	0.0	0.0	0.0	16.7	0.0	246
Miles CC	3.1	0.2	0.0	0.2	95.2	1.4	585
Montana U Sys							
Eastern Montana C	4.8	0.3	0.2	1.5	92.6	0.5	3,953
Montana C of Mineral Science and Tech	0.9	0.3	0.1	0.6	93.6	4.5	1,930
Montana State U	2.1	0.3	0.3	0.7	94.4	2.2	10,392
Northern Montana C	9.3	0.1	0.6	0.5	89.1	0.4	1,761
Western Montana C	1.5	0.3	0.1	0.4	97.8	0.0	1,100
Rocky Mountain C	3.0	1.1	0.8	1.5	88.9	4.7	758
Salish Kootenai CC	72.5	0.0	0.0	0.0	27.3	0.1	684
Stone Child C	100.0	0.0	0.0	0.0	0.0	0.0	138

NEBRASKA

	American Indian	Asian	Black	Hispanic	White	Foreign	Total
Bellevue C	0.8	0.9	6.2	2.7	87.1	2.3	2,048
Bishop Clarkson C	0.0	1.4	2.3	1.0	95.3	0.0	511
Central CC	0.5	0.3	0.2	0.9	98.2	0.0	10,915
Chadron State C	1.5	0.1	0.4	0.6	96.8	0.7	3,059
C of Saint Mary	0.2	0.5	3.4	1.0	94.9	0.1	1,280
Concordia Teachers C	0.2	0.2	0.6	0.4	97.3	1.2	818
Creighton U	0.2	4.2	2.9	2.8	86.4	3.4	6,168
Dana C	0.2	0.6	5.5	0.2	88.2	5.3	507
Doane C	0.1	0.6	1.0	1.0	93.8	3.6	1,229
Gateway Electronics Inst	0.0	1.5	9.0	1.2	88.3	0.0	332
Grace C of the Bible	0.8	1.6	1.2	0.4	93.0	3.1	257
Hastings C	0.0	0.6	2.6	0.7	95.4	0.6	965
McCook CC	0.1	0.1	0.8	0.7	97.5	0.8	864
Metropolitan Tech CC	1.1	1.8	8.4	2.4	86.4	0.0	8,516
Mid-Plains CC	0.4	0.4	0.4	2.0	96.6	0.1	2,027
Midland Lutheran C	0.1	0.6	2.6	0.4	94.6	1.7	960
Nebraska Christian C	0.0	0.8	0.0	2.3	95.5	1.5	133
Nebraska Indian CC	73.3	0.0	0.0	0.0	26.7	0.0	329
Nebraska Methodist C of Nursing and Allied Health	0.3	0.0	1.6	0.8	97.3	0.0	364
Nebraska Wesleyan U	0.5	0.7	1.4	1.1	96.4	0.0	1,691
Northeast CC	0.1	0.0	0.3	0.1	99.3	0.1	2,815
Peru State C	0.5	0.5	3.9	0.3	94.4	0.5	1,526
Southeast CC							
Beatrice	0.1	0.8	1.1	0.0	96.5	1.4	710
Lincoln	0.4	1.4	1.2	1.0	95.8	0.1	4,689
Milford	0.2	0.0	0.2	0.2	99.4	0.0	972
Union C	0.8	1.5	1.8	1.8	88.3	5.8	617
U of Nebraska							
Kearney	0.4	0.3	0.6	1.3	96.9	0.5	9,894
Lincoln	0.3	1.0	1.8	1.1	90.7	5.1	24,453
Medical Center	0.3	3.4	2.0	1.6	89.9	2.7	2,444
Omaha	0.3	1.2	4.3	1.7	91.5	1.0	15,804
C of Tech Agriculture	0.0	0.0	0.0	0.7	99.3	0.0	145
Wayne State C	0.3	0.3	1.1	0.2	97.7	0.4	3,512
Western Nebraska CC	1.6	0.1	0.8	4.8	92.6	0.2	1,940
York C	0.9	0.6	6.2	1.5	88.4	2.4	337

	American Indian	Asian	Black	Hispanic	White	Foreign	Total
NEVADA							
Morrison C Reno	1.4%	3.4%	4.1%	6.1%	83.7%	1.4%	147
Sierra Nevada C	0.3	0.0	0.3	0.3	94.6	4.5	313
U of Nevada Sys							
U of Nevada Las Vegas	0.6	4.5	5.8	5.1	82.6	1.4	17,937
U of Nevada Reno	1.0	3.0	1.6	2.9	87.5	4.1	11,487
CC of South Nevada	1.1	4.8	8.9	8.3	76.8	0.0	14,161
Northern Nevada CC	3.9	0.5	1.5	4.7	89.5	0.0	2,599
Truckee Meadows CC	4.0	5.6	2.7	5.1	81.2	1.3	9,737
Western Nevada CC	3.3	2.8	2.6	6.7	84.6	0.1	5,321
NEW HAMPSHIRE							
Castle C	0.0	0.3	1.4	1.7	96.6	0.0	290
Colby-Sawyer C	0.0	2.1	1.0	0.2	96.7	0.0	515
Daniel Webster C	0.0	0.8	1.0	0.8	96.3	1.1	996
Dartmouth C	2.1	5.9	4.9	2.9	76.6	7.7	4,859
Franklin Pierce C	0.1	0.8	1.4	1.1	95.7	0.9	3,587
Franklin Pierce Law Center	0.5	1.5	0.2	0.2	92.1	5.4	406
Hesser C	0.0	1.6	3.4	0.9	92.8	1.5	1,999
Magdalen C	1.7	1.7	3.4	3.4	89.7	0.0	58
McIntosh C	0.0	1.3	2.5	0.2	94.6	1.3	448
New England C	0.0	0.4	0.1	0.3	97.3	1.8	1,146
New Hampshire C	0.1	1.6	1.4	1.1	95.2	0.6	6,403
New Hampshire Tech C Berlin	0.0	0.4	0.2	0.0	99.4	0.0	489
NH Tech C Claremont	0.0	0.2	0.0	0.2	99.6	0.0	557
NH Tech C Laconia	0.4	0.2	0.1	0.3	99.1	0.0	1,068
NH Tech C Manchester	0.5	0.8	1.1	0.3	97.3	0.0	1,842
NH Tech C Nashua	0.0	1.8	0.9	0.6	96.6	0.0	950
NH Tech C Stratham	1.0	2.1	1.5	0.6	94.5	0.2	971
New Hampshire Tech Inst	0.0	0.5	0.7	0.0	98.7	0.1	2,487
Notre Dame C	0.5	0.5	0.3	0.3	98.3	0.1	1,153
Rivier C	0.0	1.4	0.9	1.4	95.2	1.0	2,687
Saint Anselm C	0.0	0.3	0.3	0.3	98.8	0.4	1,986
U of New Hampshire Sys							
U of NH Main campus	0.3	0.8	0.4	0.6	96.3	1.6	13,260
Keene State C	0.6	0.3	0.4	0.6	97.7	0.5	4,350
Plymouth State C	0.2	0.6	0.3	0.5	98.2	0.3	4,360
Sch for Lifelong Learning	0.4	0.5	0.3	0.4	98.3	0.2	1,405
U of NH Manchester	0.9	0.5	0.5	0.7	97.4	0.0	424
White Pines C	0.0	0.0	0.0	0.0	76.6	23.4	64
NEW JERSEY							
Assumption C for Sisters	0.0	37.1	0.0	8.6	54.3	0.0	35
Atlantic CC	0.3	1.7	10.3	3.4	83.1	1.3	5,001
Bergen CC	0.1	5.9	4.6	9.3	75.4	4.6	12,119
Berkeley C of Business	0.0	1.1	10.0	14.8	74.0	0.1	1,444
Beth Medrash Govoha	0.0	0.0	0.0	0.8	93.1	6.1	1,393
Bloomfield C	0.1	2.6	43.4	9.3	43.7	0.9	1,646
Brookdale CC	0.2	3.2	5.7	3.5	87.0	0.6	11,885
Burlington County C	0.3	1.8	14.7	2.7	79.7	0.8	6,710
Caldwell C	0.0	2.2	6.3	5.1	82.8	3.6	1,187
Camden County C	0.1	2.9	12.1	2.8	81.5	0.6	12,010
Centenary C	0.1	0.1	6.6	1.9	86.5	4.7	846
C of Saint Elizabeth	0.0	2.9	7.5	10.3	77.0	2.3	1,154
County C of Morris	0.2	3.8	3.1	3.6	87.1	2.1	9,422

NEW JERSEY, cont.

	American Indian	Asian	Black	Hispanic	White	Foreign	Total
Cumberland County C	1.3%	0.4%	11.6%	9.3%	76.1%	1.4%	2,475
DeVry Tech Inst	0.2	3.8	23.8	12.9	58.8	0.6	1,990
Drew U	0.4	4.0	6.2	2.2	82.6	4.7	2,276
Essex County C	0.3	1.8	61.5	16.5	15.5	4.4	6,706
Fairleigh Dickinson U	0.4	3.9	8.2	3.8	80.0	3.6	11,784
Felician C	0.4	7.5	7.8	7.7	74.0	2.6	730
Georgian Court C	0.3	0.8	3.0	2.7	93.0	0.1	2,315
Glassboro State C	0.5	1.3	8.8	3.1	85.4	1.0	9,668
Gloucester County C	0.2	1.5	7.1	1.2	87.9	2.2	4,372
Hudson County CC	0.1	10.4	13.8	48.6	25.0	2.0	2,830
Jersey City State C	0.1	6.6	16.1	15.3	57.8	4.1	7,681
Katharine Gibbs Sch	0.0	2.9	30.8	11.7	53.8	0.8	240
Kean C of New Jersey	0.1	3.0	13.1	10.3	71.8	1.7	13,303
Mercer County CC	0.3	2.6	13.7	5.3	77.1	1.1	8,774
Middlesex County C	0.6	9.5	8.0	8.8	71.5	1.7	11,019
Monmouth C	0.1	3.0	4.1	2.4	86.2	4.3	4,274
Montclair State C	0.5	2.5	7.7	8.7	78.6	2.0	13,067
New Brunswick Theological Seminary	0.0	2.8	41.0	3.5	50.7	2.1	144
New Jersey Inst of Tech	0.1	14.7	8.3	8.2	49.9	18.8	7,667
Ocean County C	0.2	1.2	2.4	2.9	93.3	0.1	7,424
Passaic County CC	0.2	6.1	22.1	44.0	21.5	6.1	3,268
Princeton Theological Seminary	0.1	9.1	6.9	1.1	72.5	10.2	792
Princeton U	0.3	8.5	5.5	4.0	68.1	13.6	6,483
Ramapo C of New Jersey	0.2	2.7	8.7	3.0	82.1	3.3	4,519
Raritan Valley CC	0.3	3.4	4.2	2.2	89.9	0.0	5,380
Rider C	0.5	1.1	5.1	2.6	90.0	0.8	5,727
Rutgers U							
Camden	0.3	3.5	8.6	3.0	83.9	0.7	5,328
New Brunswick	0.2	8.7	7.9	5.7	71.8	5.7	33,016
Newark	0.2	8.9	17.9	10.3	57.8	4.9	9,336
Saint Peter's C	0.1	7.9	8.1	16.2	66.7	1.0	3,356
Salem CC	1.3	0.7	10.8	2.3	82.4	2.6	1,356
Seton Hall U	0.1	2.6	8.4	5.3	82.6	1.0	9,926
Stockton State C	0.3	2.3	9.8	2.5	84.8	0.3	5,639
Sussex County CC Commission	0.0	1.0	0.6	0.8	97.6	0.0	1,946
Thomas Edison State C	0.4	0.9	7.9	3.1	84.2	3.5	7,813
Trenton State C	0.1	2.0	7.8	3.3	85.1	1.6	7,403
Union County C	0.0	1.4	15.1	6.7	58.7	18.0	9,980
U of Medicine and Dentistry of New Jersey	0.1	10.9	9.3	5.2	66.1	8.4	3,215
Upsala C	0.0	3.5	29.8	5.6	58.5	2.5	1,138
Warren CC Commission	0.2	0.2	1.9	1.1	95.2	1.4	1,233
Westminster Choir C	0.0	1.7	6.4	2.3	77.7	11.9	345
William Paterson C	0.2	1.5	6.0	5.5	86.2	0.6	10,036

NEW MEXICO

Albuquerque Tech-VI CC	1.0	2.9	6.3	34.9	52.8	2.0	9,739
C of Santa Fe	8.8	1.9	1.7	29.1	57.5	1.0	1,051
C of the Southwest	0.4	0.4	2.2	14.9	76.8	5.4	276
Eastern New Mexico U							
Main campus	1.5	0.7	5.5	18.5	72.2	1.5	3,619
Clovis	0.8	1.0	4.2	19.9	73.8	0.3	4,609

ENROLLMENT BY RACE • THE ALMANAC OF HIGHER EDUCATION

	American Indian	Asian	Black	Hispanic	White	Foreign	Total
Inst of American Indian and Alaska Native Culture and Arts Development	81.7%	0.0%	0.5%	2.4%	11.1%	4.3%	208
New Mexico Highlands U	3.6	0.4	2.7	69.2	23.5	0.7	2,445
NM Inst of Mining and Tech	1.8	2.2	0.5	13.7	69.1	12.6	1,306
New Mexico JC	0.4	0.4	3.7	17.6	77.4	0.5	2,438
New Mexico State U							
Main campus	2.4	0.6	1.5	27.3	65.1	3.1	14,812
Alamogordo	3.4	1.3	4.1	16.5	74.8	0.0	1,759
Carlsbad	1.9	0.4	0.8	24.9	71.9	0.1	1,077
Dona Ana	3.1	0.4	2.6	42.0	51.1	0.9	3,290
Grants	22.3	0.0	0.6	26.6	50.5	0.0	467
Northern New Mexico CC	7.7	0.4	0.6	71.7	19.5	0.1	1,628
Parks C	8.3	1.1	3.3	31.7	55.0	0.6	180
Saint John's C	0.2	1.5	0.9	4.7	91.7	1.1	469
San Juan C	24.3	0.2	0.3	10.7	64.0	0.6	3,025
Santa Fe CC	3.5	0.4	0.3	48.1	47.7	0.0	2,704
U of New Mexico							
Main campus	3.5	2.0	1.9	21.7	69.0	1.8	23,950
Gallup	71.7	0.1	0.5	9.5	18.0	0.1	2,060
Valencia	2.3	0.6	0.9	37.9	57.8	0.4	2,033
Western New Mexico U	2.1	0.5	1.9	39.0	55.1	1.4	1,881

NEW YORK

	American Indian	Asian	Black	Hispanic	White	Foreign	Total
Adelphi U	0.1	2.9	9.8	4.7	80.9	1.6	8,749
Albany C of Pharmacy	0.3	4.6	1.3	1.0	90.9	1.8	672
Albany Law Sch	0.4	3.1	3.5	1.5	90.8	0.7	826
Albany Medical C	0.0	17.0	2.6	2.3	75.6	2.5	610
American Acad McAllister Inst of Funeral Service	0.0	0.0	31.3	3.7	63.4	1.5	134
American Academy of Dramatic Arts	0.0	0.9	3.8	4.7	77.4	13.2	212
American Center for the Alexander Technique	0.0	0.0	3.1	6.2	90.6	0.0	32
Bank Street C of Education	0.3	2.1	17.0	10.1	69.7	0.9	755
Bard C	0.0	1.5	2.3	2.2	88.2	5.7	1,114
Barnard C	0.0	19.5	3.5	4.1	70.6	2.3	2,173
Berkeley C	0.0	1.9	17.0	8.5	72.6	0.0	577
Berkeley Sch of New York	0.0	2.8	23.9	32.5	40.4	0.5	834
Boricua C	0.0	0.1	5.9	93.4	0.6	0.0	1,100
Bramson ORT Tech Inst	0.0	0.0	1.5	2.6	95.9	0.0	1,096
Briarcliffe Sch	0.0	0.0	13.1	12.0	69.8	5.2	659
Brooklyn Law Sch	0.0	6.3	3.6	6.0	84.0	0.0	1,426
Bryant & Stratton Business Inst Albany	0.5	1.4	26.3	1.7	69.0	1.2	422
Bryant & Stratton Business Inst Rochester	0.8	1.2	15.5	3.8	78.3	0.3	1,177
Bryant & Stratton Business Inst Syracuse	0.5	0.8	12.7	0.2	85.9	0.0	1,176
Canisius C	0.4	0.9	4.8	1.2	91.2	1.6	4,693
Cazenovia C	0.9	1.3	7.0	1.6	89.0	0.2	1,072
Central Yeshiva Tomchei Tmimim Lubavitch America	0.0	0.0	0.0	0.0	56.2	43.8	427
Christ the King Seminary	0.0	0.0	1.1	0.0	98.9	0.0	94
City U of New York							
Baruch C	0.1	21.5	23.6	17.7	28.9	8.1	15,854

THE ALMANAC OF HIGHER EDUCATION • ENROLLMENT BY RACE

NEW YORK, cont.

	American Indian	Asian	Black	Hispanic	White	Foreign	Total
City U of New York, cont.							
Brooklyn C	0.1%	9.1%	20.6%	10.0%	57.5%	2.7%	16,602
Bronx CC	0.5	2.9	47.2	44.3	3.8	1.3	6,427
City C	0.3	13.8	35.3	26.2	14.6	9.6	14,090
C of Staten Island	0.5	4.4	9.3	5.4	76.8	3.4	12,185
Graduate Sch	0.0	3.4	5.2	5.1	64.4	21.9	4,027
Hunter C	0.4	9.0	20.1	18.9	49.0	2.6	19,645
Hostos CC	0.1	1.1	15.3	81.6	1.3	0.6	4,263
John Jay C of Criminal Justice	0.3	2.8	36.1	28.6	31.1	1.0	8,671
Kingsborough CC	0.2	3.6	21.4	11.7	61.1	2.0	13,808
LaGuardia C	0.3	9.9	27.8	38.2	16.0	7.9	9,171
Lehman C	0.9	3.4	30.2	36.4	28.3	0.9	10,238
Manhattan CC	0.3	7.8	56.1	25.6	7.8	2.4	14,823
Medgar Evers C	0.2	0.8	88.6	5.9	0.9	3.5	3,533
New York City Tech C	0.2	8.2	54.0	23.2	11.9	2.6	10,904
Queens C	0.1	10.7	8.5	11.6	63.5	5.5	18,071
Queens C Law Sch	0.2	4.6	15.0	9.1	70.3	0.9	461
Queensborough CC	0.4	9.4	21.4	16.1	48.1	4.6	12,186
York C	0.1	6.8	61.7	14.6	6.7	10.1	5,729
Clarkson U	0.2	2.2	0.8	0.6	87.5	8.8	3,386
Cochran Sch of Nursing	0.0	6.0	25.0	8.3	60.7	0.0	84
Colgate Rochester-Bexley Hall-Crozer Divinity Sch Seminary	0.9	0.9	11.8	0.5	84.4	1.4	211
Colgate U	0.3	4.9	4.5	2.4	83.7	4.2	2,710
C for Human Services	2.1	0.5	69.3	18.6	9.4	0.2	866
C of Aeronautics	0.0	18.5	23.3	26.6	26.6	5.0	1,315
C of Insurance	0.0	10.1	10.3	6.9	70.3	2.4	710
C of Mount Saint Vincent	0.1	4.3	9.5	13.7	70.7	1.7	1,022
C of Saint Rose	0.0	0.2	1.0	0.2	97.4	1.2	3,685
Columbia U	0.2	9.7	4.6	4.4	68.4	12.8	18,242
Teachers C	0.2	3.5	10.8	6.3	67.9	11.3	4,258
Concordia C	0.0	0.5	7.6	3.3	69.4	19.1	576
Cooper Union	0.1	26.4	5.4	6.1	58.4	3.7	1,036
Cornell U							
Endowed C's	0.3	12.0	4.0	4.1	68.2	11.4	11,533
Statutory C's	0.5	5.1	6.8	5.2	73.5	9.0	9,304
Culinary Inst of America	0.5	2.0	2.9	1.5	92.2	0.9	1,822
D'Youville C	0.8	0.9	8.0	3.2	80.5	6.5	1,482
Daemen C	0.6	0.9	14.8	3.4	79.4	0.9	1,946
Dominican C of Blauvelt	0.0	3.1	6.6	3.9	86.3	0.0	1,495
Edna McConnell Clark Sch of Nursing	0.0	1.6	73.4	4.7	20.3	0.0	64
Empire State Baptist Seminary	0.0	0.0	23.1	0.0	76.9	0.0	13
Five Towns C	0.0	0.9	24.0	4.6	70.1	0.4	541
Fordham U	0.1	2.9	6.8	6.6	79.8	3.8	13,158
Friends World C	0.0	1.2	4.8	1.2	85.9	6.9	248
Graduate Sch of Political Management	0.0	1.6	18.0	4.9	73.8	1.6	61
Hamilton C	0.2	3.5	3.1	3.1	85.6	4.5	1,658
Hartwick C	0.3	1.0	1.2	0.9	95.2	1.5	1,552
Helene Fuld Sch of Nursing	0.0	3.4	80.7	2.9	13.0	0.0	207
Hilbert C	0.4	0.6	7.0	0.7	91.3	0.0	715
Hobart and William Smith C's	0.3	1.4	4.1	2.4	89.7	2.1	1,848
Hofstra U	0.5	3.1	5.8	3.7	86.4	0.5	12,431

	American Indian	Asian	Black	Hispanic	White	Foreign	Total
Holy Trinity Orthodox Seminary	0.0%	0.0%	0.0%	0.0%	57.9%	42.1%	38
Houghton C	0.6	0.9	1.7	0.4	91.5	4.8	1,178
Inst of Design and Construction	0.0	4.6	24.6	18.9	50.9	1.1	175
Iona C	0.2	1.7	14.4	8.1	75.2	0.4	7,594
Ithaca C	0.1	0.8	1.8	1.5	94.7	1.1	6,432
Jamestown Business C	0.0	0.6	1.0	0.3	98.1	0.0	312
Jewish Theological Seminary of America	0.0	0.0	0.4	0.0	94.4	5.1	450
Juilliard Sch	0.3	11.9	4.5	3.4	51.7	28.3	1,026
King's C	0.2	3.2	6.1	4.6	82.0	3.8	495
Laboratory Inst of Merchandising	0.0	1.5	10.3	9.8	76.0	2.5	204
Le Moyne C	0.4	1.3	2.5	1.2	93.7	0.9	2,355
Long Island U C W Post	0.2	1.4	5.4	3.1	84.9	5.0	8,694
Southhampton	1.0	1.1	7.1	3.4	86.0	1.3	1,251
Manhattan C	0.0	5.4	3.6	8.7	79.2	3.1	3,794
Manhattan Sch of Music	0.1	9.8	3.5	3.8	50.9	31.9	818
Manhattanville C	0.5	1.9	4.2	4.6	83.4	5.4	1,581
Mannes C of Music	0.0	17.4	10.7	3.6	59.3	9.1	582
Maria C	0.0	0.7	3.7	1.1	94.3	0.2	916
Marist C	0.1	2.4	9.4	6.4	81.0	0.6	4,980
Maryknoll Sch of Theology	0.0	11.1	1.4	4.2	62.5	20.8	72
Marymount C	0.1	1.7	14.0	12.2	68.5	3.6	1,124
Marymount Manhattan C	0.2	3.8	15.8	13.8	62.9	3.6	1,332
Mater Dei C	9.7	0.4	3.5	1.5	84.5	0.5	547
Medaille C	0.2	0.1	27.2	4.0	68.3	0.2	1,105
Mercy C Main campus	0.4	1.5	20.3	27.4	48.0	2.4	4,806
Mesivta of Eastern Parkway Rabbinical Seminary	0.0	0.0	0.0	0.0	100.0	0.0	45
Molloy C	0.1	0.7	7.4	5.1	86.7	0.0	1,635
Monroe C	0.1	0.6	37.0	52.3	9.9	0.2	2,407
Mount Saint Mary C	0.3	0.8	8.2	3.5	85.4	1.8	1,428
Mount Sinai Sch of Medicine	0.0	14.9	4.6	6.7	73.8	0.0	504
Nazareth C of Rochester	0.2	0.5	2.2	0.9	95.9	0.4	2,822
New Sch for Social Research	0.2	7.1	7.0	5.0	70.5	10.3	6,321
New York Chiropractic C	0.1	2.0	2.3	5.4	89.1	1.0	690
NY C of Podiatric Medicine	0.7	8.0	15.7	5.5	67.5	2.7	415
New York Inst of Tech Main campus	0.2	3.8	5.8	4.2	70.5	15.5	6,944
Central Islip	0.3	1.0	8.7	4.1	75.7	10.3	1,888
Metropolitan	0.3	6.3	15.2	9.2	28.4	40.6	2,483
New York Law Sch	0.0	3.8	4.7	5.0	86.2	0.4	1,372
New York Medical C	0.5	13.5	10.6	5.0	68.9	1.5	1,310
NY Sch of Interior Design	0.0	3.4	4.2	2.6	84.9	4.8	643
NY Theological Seminary	0.0	21.6	37.7	14.7	23.0	3.0	361
Niagara U	0.3	0.4	3.9	0.7	79.3	15.5	3,063
Nyack C	0.0	13.5	7.7	6.8	68.0	4.1	784
Olean Business Inst	0.6	0.0	0.6	0.0	98.9	0.0	176
Pace U New York	0.5	10.3	14.0	11.8	53.2	10.3	8,487
Pleasantville-Briarcliff	0.8	2.2	3.1	5.0	86.6	2.4	4,145
White Plains	0.5	4.6	5.0	4.6	83.7	1.6	4,109
Paul Smith's C of Arts and Science	0.4	0.0	1.4	0.9	92.0	5.3	792

NEW YORK, cont.

	American Indian	Asian	Black	Hispanic	White	Foreign	Total
Phillip Beth Israel Sch of Nursing	0.0%	18.8%	37.2%	8.9%	34.0%	1.0%	191
Plaza Business Inst	0.0	6.8	31.2	21.2	40.1	0.7	706
Polytechnic U	0.1	27.9	7.1	5.5	44.4	14.9	3,696
Pratt Inst	0.1	10.3	10.7	6.9	58.5	13.5	3,384
Rabbinical Seminary of America	0.0	0.0	0.0	0.0	100.0	0.0	176
Rabbinical Seminary of M'kor Chaim	0.0	0.0	0.0	0.0	100.0	0.0	93
Rensselaer Polytechnic Inst	0.2	10.0	2.6	3.0	72.6	11.6	6,692
Rika Breuer Teachers Seminary	0.0	0.0	0.0	0.0	97.4	2.6	77
Roberts Wesleyan C	0.2	0.4	5.3	1.5	85.1	7.5	970
Rochester Business Inst	0.2	0.4	48.5	6.7	44.2	0.0	495
Rockefeller U	0.0	4.7	1.6	0.8	60.2	32.8	128
Russell Sage C	0.4	1.5	6.5	2.3	88.9	0.5	4,272
Saint Bernard's Inst	0.0	0.7	2.2	1.5	94.9	0.7	137
Saint Bonaventure U	0.4	0.3	0.9	0.7	96.5	1.3	2,772
Saint Elizabeth Hospital Sch of Nursing	0.0	0.0	1.8	0.0	98.2	0.0	171
Saint Francis C	0.2	1.8	21.1	11.3	60.4	5.2	1,743
Saint John Fisher C	0.3	1.4	3.2	1.5	93.3	0.4	2,504
Saint John's U	0.3	6.6	8.5	8.1	72.4	4.1	19,105
Saint Joseph's C							
Main campus	0.0	8.1	36.6	6.0	49.0	0.2	827
Suffolk	0.0	0.4	3.5	7.8	88.3	0.0	1,936
Saint Joseph's Seminary and C	0.0	0.0	0.0	2.9	93.8	3.3	272
Saint Lawrence U	1.0	0.7	2.5	0.9	91.8	3.2	2,091
Saint Thomas Aquinas C	0.0	1.2	2.6	3.3	92.9	0.1	2,077
Sarah Lawrence C	0.3	4.3	5.4	4.4	85.0	0.7	1,193
Sch of Visual Arts	0.1	4.8	5.7	4.9	77.7	6.8	4,804
Seminary of the Immaculate Conception	0.0	2.0	1.0	2.0	95.0	0.0	202
Sh'or Yoshuv Rabbinical C	0.0	5.7	6.6	4.7	75.5	7.5	106
Siena C	0.0	1.0	1.3	1.6	95.7	0.4	3,454
Skidmore C	0.2	2.6	5.6	3.6	86.6	1.5	2,605
State U of New York							
Albany	0.1	4.0	7.7	5.0	79.7	3.5	17,400
Binghamton	0.1	6.6	4.9	4.1	79.9	4.4	12,202
Buffalo	0.4	4.9	5.6	2.6	79.3	7.1	27,638
Stony Brook	0.2	11.6	7.1	5.4	67.8	7.9	17,624
C at Brockport	0.3	0.7	4.7	1.5	92.1	0.8	9,661
C at Buffalo	0.4	0.9	8.7	2.9	86.0	1.0	12,952
C at Cortland	0.2	0.6	2.1	1.6	95.0	0.5	7,238
C at Fredonia	0.6	0.7	2.3	1.7	94.4	0.3	5,041
C at Geneseo	0.3	1.5	1.8	1.6	94.8	0.1	5,599
C at New Paltz	0.3	2.2	6.5	4.8	83.8	2.4	8,610
C at Old Westbury	0.4	5.0	27.0	9.5	56.1	2.0	4,260
C at Oneonta	0.1	1.0	1.8	1.9	94.6	0.5	6,317
C at Oswego	0.2	1.1	3.5	2.0	92.9	0.3	8,942
C at Plattsburgh	0.3	1.1	2.9	1.5	93.0	1.3	6,543
C at Potsdam	1.0	0.9	1.3	0.9	95.2	0.6	4,830
C at Purchase	0.1	1.7	3.4	3.4	90.0	1.5	4,619
Health Science Center Brooklyn	0.2	9.6	24.8	2.9	57.2	5.3	1,642
Health Science Center Syracuse	0.3	5.5	7.3	2.4	81.0	3.5	1,027

	American Indian	Asian	Black	Hispanic	White	Foreign	Total
C of Environmental Science and Forestry	0.3%	0.6%	0.9%	1.1%	88.6%	8.6%	1,715
Maritime C	0.1	5.1	1.9	5.4	73.1	14.4	821
C of Optometry	0.0	16.1	3.1	3.8	70.6	6.3	286
C of Ceramics Alfred U	0.7	1.8	2.5	1.6	87.9	5.5	854
Inst of Tech Utica-Rome	0.2	1.4	2.4	1.0	93.4	1.6	2,542
C of Tech Alfred	0.5	0.9	3.2	0.7	94.4	0.4	3,700
C of Tech Canton	0.9	0.5	3.4	1.5	93.5	0.2	2,662
C of Tech and Ag Cobleskill	0.1	0.5	4.8	3.0	91.6	0.0	2,630
C of Tech Farmingdale	0.3	2.5	10.1	5.5	81.6	0.1	11,102
C of Tech and Ag Morrisville	0.3	0.5	5.4	1.9	91.5	0.3	3,289
C of Tech Delhi	0.2	1.3	4.4	2.7	91.4	0.0	2,374
Empire State C	0.3	0.9	8.1	4.5	85.2	0.9	6,894
Adirondack CC	0.2	0.2	0.4	0.7	98.3	0.1	3,378
Broome CC	0.1	1.4	2.1	0.5	94.0	1.9	6,433
Cayuga County CC	0.2	0.2	2.9	0.9	95.7	0.1	2,904
Clinton CC	0.4	0.9	6.8	2.8	88.9	0.3	2,140
Columbia-Greene CC	0.4	0.2	3.5	2.0	93.6	0.2	1,696
CC of the Finger Lakes	0.4	0.3	1.5	0.8	96.9	0.1	3,866
Corning CC	0.4	0.2	3.4	1.2	94.7	0.1	3,693
Dutchess CC	0.3	2.4	8.4	3.3	85.0	0.6	7,076
Erie CC							
City	1.2	1.4	24.8	6.3	66.2	0.1	3,682
North	0.4	0.8	4.6	0.5	92.5	1.1	6,603
South	0.6	0.3	0.5	0.6	97.8	0.2	3,518
Fashion Inst of Tech	0.3	15.1	14.1	11.2	56.6	2.8	12,098
Fulton-Montgomery CC	1.6	0.3	2.1	2.3	90.6	3.0	2,001
Genesee CC	0.1	0.1	0.9	0.2	98.8	0.0	3,572
Herkimer County CC	0.0	0.0	1.0	0.1	98.7	0.2	2,412
Hudson Valley CC	0.3	0.9	3.7	0.8	94.2	0.2	9,401
Jamestown CC	1.0	0.4	1.2	0.7	96.1	0.5	4,647
Jefferson CC	0.3	1.1	5.7	2.9	90.0	0.0	2,482
Mohawk Valley CC	0.3	0.9	5.9	1.8	89.7	1.3	6,467
Monroe CC	0.5	2.2	8.9	2.9	84.9	0.7	13,545
Nassau CC	0.3	2.0	10.3	5.1	81.2	1.1	21,537
Niagara County CC	1.0	0.4	4.5	0.6	92.8	0.7	5,265
North Country CC	0.7	0.3	4.0	1.3	93.1	0.7	1,483
Onondaga CC	1.0	1.4	5.9	0.9	90.0	0.9	8,309
Orange County CC	0.5	1.3	5.4	5.2	87.4	0.2	5,425
Rockland CC	0.4	4.0	15.2	5.8	71.5	3.2	8,021
Schenectady County CC	0.2	0.6	4.0	1.0	94.2	0.0	3,234
Suffolk County CC							
Ammerman	0.2	1.3	1.8	3.0	93.7	0.0	12,395
Eastern	0.2	0.8	2.6	1.5	95.0	0.0	2,440
Western	0.3	0.9	7.0	8.1	83.6	0.0	5,055
Sullivan County CC	0.1	1.1	17.2	6.5	68.0	7.2	2,090
Tompkins-Cortland CC	0.4	1.7	2.7	1.2	92.9	1.1	2,775
Ulster County CC	0.1	1.0	6.7	3.0	88.8	0.5	2,927
Westchester CC	0.3	3.3	14.9	7.4	73.2	0.9	10,043
Stenotype Academy	0.0	0.8	39.4	11.4	48.4	0.0	738
Syracuse U							
Main campus	0.2	2.9	5.1	2.1	83.0	6.8	21,900
Utica C	0.5	0.9	6.7	2.0	89.6	0.4	2,553
Tech Career Insts	0.0	41.0	31.7	12.9	9.8	4.6	1,897
Tobe-Coburn Sch of Fashion Careers	0.6	5.1	13.1	20.5	60.8	0.0	176

NEW YORK, cont.

	American Indian	Asian	Black	Hispanic	White	Foreign	Total
Torah Temimah Talmudical Seminary	0.0%	0.0%	0.0%	0.0%	99.4%	0.6%	176
Trocaire C	1.0	0.3	6.2	0.8	91.1	0.5	970
Union C	0.0	3.8	1.8	2.2	90.8	1.5	2,877
Union Theological Seminary	0.7	3.1	11.6	2.7	73.8	8.2	294
U of Rochester	0.1	5.8	4.5	2.4	77.9	9.4	9,291
Vassar C	0.1	8.0	7.3	4.2	77.3	3.2	2,453
Villa Maria C	0.2	0.4	7.9	0.6	90.4	0.6	519
Wadhams Hall Seminary and C	2.3	0.0	2.3	0.0	95.5	0.0	44
Wagner C	0.0	0.7	5.7	1.6	78.5	13.5	1,538
Webb Inst of Naval Architecture	0.0	1.3	0.0	0.0	98.7	0.0	78
Wells C	0.0	1.6	5.0	2.4	90.0	1.0	381
Westchester Business Inst	0.5	1.0	30.1	17.0	51.0	0.5	1,111
Wood Sch	0.0	2.2	25.4	49.0	23.4	0.0	492
Yeshiva Derech Chaim	0.0	0.0	0.0	0.0	99.3	0.7	153
Yeshiva Karlin Stolin Beth Aaron V'Israel Rabbinical Inst	0.0	0.0	0.0	0.0	96.8	3.2	63

NORTH CAROLINA

	American Indian	Asian	Black	Hispanic	White	Foreign	Total
Alamance CC	0.2	0.6	16.3	0.3	82.5	0.1	3,569
Anson CC	0.1	0.1	28.0	0.9	70.8	0.0	885
Asheville-Buncombe Tech CC	0.5	0.4	5.3	0.6	92.9	0.3	3,467
Barton C	0.1	0.2	9.2	0.5	88.8	1.2	1,718
Beaufort County CC	0.0	0.1	22.3	0.2	77.5	0.0	1,194
Belmont Abbey C	0.6	1.4	4.4	1.9	89.1	2.6	1,022
Bennett C	0.0	0.0	96.4	0.0	0.3	3.2	586
Bladen CC	1.0	0.2	29.4	0.5	68.9	0.0	591
Blue Ridge CC	0.1	0.5	4.1	0.8	94.5	0.1	1,449
Brevard C	0.4	0.5	5.3	0.8	86.6	6.4	779
Brunswick CC	0.3	0.1	13.8	1.0	84.3	0.6	712
Caldwell CC and Tech Inst	0.1	0.2	3.4	0.2	96.0	0.1	2,613
Campbell U	0.7	20.3	6.6	1.4	70.5	0.5	5,043
Cape Fear CC	0.4	0.6	12.4	0.6	85.7	0.4	2,783
Carteret CC	0.7	1.0	10.5	0.6	87.3	0.1	1,444
Catawba C	0.1	0.7	7.4	0.4	90.8	0.5	967
Catawba Valley CC	0.2	1.2	6.1	0.7	91.7	0.1	3,161
Cecils JC	1.5	0.0	21.9	0.9	75.8	0.0	343
Central Carolina CC	0.7	0.5	19.5	0.6	78.6	0.1	2,804
Central Piedmont CC	0.4	2.3	17.0	0.6	77.8	1.9	16,311
Chowan C	0.1	0.3	30.6	0.8	62.1	6.1	889
Cleveland CC	0.2	0.5	17.7	0.2	81.5	0.0	1,506
Coastal Carolina CC	0.6	2.1	15.0	4.2	78.1	0.1	3,388
C of the Albemarle	0.4	0.6	16.7	0.6	81.9	0.0	1,627
Craven CC	0.5	1.0	18.4	1.8	78.2	0.1	2,193
Davidson C	0.2	2.2	4.2	1.1	88.9	3.5	1,508
Davidson County CC	0.2	0.5	7.2	0.2	91.8	0.0	2,313
Duke U	0.2	4.4	5.9	2.4	80.1	7.0	11,293
Durham Tech CC	0.3	2.1	34.0	1.2	61.7	0.6	4,812
East Coast Bible C	0.0	4.0	7.5	1.0	87.4	0.0	199
Edgecombe CC	0.2	0.1	46.5	0.2	52.8	0.2	1,696
Elon C	0.1	0.7	5.0	0.6	92.8	0.8	3,263
Fayetteville Tech CC	2.3	2.1	28.7	3.3	63.6	0.1	5,488
Forsyth Tech CC	0.2	1.0	21.9	0.4	76.4	0.1	4,896
Gardner-Webb C	0.1	0.3	12.0	0.4	87.0	0.2	2,074

	American Indian	Asian	Black	Hispanic	White	Foreign	Total
Gaston C	0.1%	0.6%	10.2%	0.3%	88.6%	0.0%	3,503
Greensboro C	0.3	1.2	12.1	0.5	85.7	0.3	1,116
Guilford C	0.6	0.7	5.1	0.7	90.4	2.5	1,753
Guilford Tech CC	0.7	1.7	18.2	0.5	79.0	0.0	6,996
Halifax CC	2.0	0.1	37.8	0.2	58.9	1.0	815
Haywood CC	0.2	0.0	1.1	0.0	98.8	0.0	1,236
High Point C	0.0	0.8	5.3	0.8	92.6	0.6	2,308
Isothermal CC	0.1	0.5	9.4	0.3	89.5	0.3	1,576
James Sprunt CC	0.3	0.1	31.2	0.1	68.2	0.1	946
John Wesley C	0.0	0.0	10.1	1.3	88.6	0.0	79
Johnson C Smith U	0.0	0.0	100.0	0.0	0.0	0.0	1,182
Johnston CC	0.1	0.5	16.0	0.2	83.0	0.2	2,413
Lees-McRae C	0.0	0.3	8.7	0.9	88.8	1.3	863
Lenoir CC	0.2	0.2	27.5	0.5	71.5	0.1	2,138
Lenoir-Rhyne C	0.2	0.2	4.6	0.5	93.2	1.3	1,648
Livingstone C	0.0	0.0	96.9	0.0	0.4	2.6	682
Louisburg C	0.1	0.3	8.3	0.0	91.0	0.2	891
Mars Hill C	0.5	0.2	6.4	0.1	91.5	1.3	1,331
Martin CC	0.0	0.4	31.3	0.1	67.9	0.1	677
Mayland CC	0.6	0.2	2.2	0.1	96.8	0.0	813
Meredith C	0.1	0.3	2.8	0.4	94.0	2.3	2,245
Methodist C	0.6	3.0	10.8	2.1	82.7	0.7	1,254
Mitchell CC	0.1	0.4	10.7	0.8	88.0	0.0	1,431
Montgomery CC	1.1	0.9	18.0	0.4	79.6	0.0	543
Montreat-Anderson C	0.3	0.8	5.4	0.5	88.6	4.4	387
Mount Olive C	0.1	0.5	17.4	0.9	81.1	0.0	755
Nash CC	2.1	0.1	20.7	0.1	77.0	0.1	1,549
North Carolina Wesleyan C	0.3	0.2	14.8	0.4	83.4	0.9	1,436
Pamlico CC	0.0	0.0	19.5	0.8	79.7	0.0	133
Peace C	0.2	1.2	1.2	0.0	97.2	0.2	434
Pfeiffer C	0.2	0.8	7.4	0.8	89.6	1.1	958
Phillips JC Charlotte	0.0	1.6	81.3	0.0	17.2	0.0	128
Phillips JC Fayetteville	0.6	0.0	66.5	4.8	28.1	0.0	310
Phillips JC Hardbarger	1.1	1.6	86.0	0.9	10.4	0.0	643
Piedmont Bible C	0.0	0.3	2.7	0.7	95.3	1.0	298
Piedmont CC	0.8	0.5	39.6	0.5	58.6	0.0	1,081
Pitt CC	0.4	0.4	22.1	0.2	76.8	0.2	4,211
Queens C	0.3	0.9	7.9	0.8	87.3	2.7	1,579
Randolph CC	0.1	0.6	5.0	0.1	94.0	0.1	1,426
Richmond CC	5.7	0.6	23.2	0.2	70.4	0.0	1,002
Roanoke Bible C	0.0	0.0	4.4	0.0	95.6	0.0	113
Roanoke-Chowan CC	1.6	0.0	45.6	0.2	52.5	0.0	432
Robeson CC	37.0	0.3	20.3	0.4	42.0	0.0	1,470
Rockingham CC	0.2	0.3	15.6	0.3	83.3	0.3	1,817
Rowan-Cabarrus CC	0.4	0.8	10.7	0.4	87.8	0.0	2,991
Saint Andrews Presbyterian C	0.6	0.7	6.5	1.4	87.3	3.5	718
Saint Augustine's C	0.0	0.0	99.8	0.0	0.2	0.0	1,900
Saint Mary's C	0.0	0.3	2.0	0.3	94.5	2.9	344
Salem C	0.3	0.8	2.1	0.3	95.4	1.1	724
Sampson CC	1.5	0.4	25.5	0.7	71.8	0.0	948
Sandhills CC	2.9	0.4	17.2	0.4	79.1	0.0	2,145
Shaw U	0.2	0.1	91.9	0.1	7.7	0.0	1,846
Southeastern Baptist Theological Seminary	0.6	1.4	4.3	1.4	92.2	0.0	644
Southeastern CC	3.9	0.3	18.4	0.1	77.4	0.0	1,547
Southwestern CC	10.7	0.3	0.9	0.2	87.8	0.1	1,345
Stanly CC	1.0	0.3	10.1	0.1	88.2	0.3	1,303

N.C., cont.

	American Indian	Asian	Black	Hispanic	White	Foreign	Total
Surry CC	0.1%	0.2%	5.4%	0.3%	93.9%	0.1%	2,816
Tri-County CC	1.4	0.0	1.1	0.1	97.4	0.0	912
U of North Carolina							
Asheville	0.4	0.8	3.9	0.7	93.6	0.7	3,271
Chapel Hill	0.6	2.6	8.6	0.8	84.2	3.0	23,878
Charlotte	0.6	2.1	11.1	0.7	83.2	2.2	14,699
Greensboro	0.3	0.8	10.5	0.7	86.5	1.2	12,882
Wilmington	0.4	0.8	7.1	0.5	91.0	0.2	7,567
Appalachian State U	0.2	0.5	4.4	0.5	94.1	0.4	11,931
East Carolina U	0.5	1.1	9.1	0.6	88.2	0.6	17,564
Elizabeth City State U	0.1	0.3	75.3	0.2	23.6	0.5	1,746
Fayetteville State U	1.0	1.0	66.0	1.5	30.5	0.0	3,337
North Carolina A&T State U	0.2	0.6	84.7	0.2	12.7	1.7	6,595
North Carolina Central U	0.3	0.6	83.3	0.1	15.1	0.6	5,482
NC Sch of the Arts	0.8	1.9	8.6	2.5	81.3	4.9	486
North Carolina State U	0.3	2.8	8.7	0.8	83.3	4.1	27,199
Pembroke State U	23.8	0.8	11.1	0.5	63.4	0.4	3,133
Western Carolina U	1.5	0.7	4.3	0.2	92.0	1.3	6,411
Winston-Salem State U	0.2	0.4	82.1	0.1	17.1	0.0	2,517
Vance-Granville CC	0.8	0.4	37.2	0.5	61.1	0.0	2,309
Wake Forest U	0.3	1.6	6.3	0.3	89.4	1.9	5,477
Wake Tech CC	0.4	2.0	17.9	0.8	77.7	1.2	6,129
Warren Wilson C	0.5	2.1	3.1	0.3	87.3	6.6	573
Wayne CC	0.3	0.9	22.0	0.6	76.2	0.0	2,364
Western Piedmont CC	0.3	0.8	5.1	0.2	93.5	0.0	2,709
Wilkes CC	0.0	0.4	5.2	0.3	94.0	0.0	2,023
Wilson Tech CC	0.1	0.4	23.2	0.1	76.2	0.1	1,308
Wingate C	0.2	0.7	7.8	0.4	89.7	1.3	1,558

NORTH DAKOTA

	American Indian	Asian	Black	Hispanic	White	Foreign	Total
Fort Bethold CC	83.2	0.0	0.0	0.0	16.8	0.0	155
Jamestown C	1.1	0.7	1.0	0.0	92.1	5.1	899
Little Hoop CC	85.5	0.0	0.0	0.0	14.5	0.0	165
Medcenter One C of Nursing	0.0	0.0	0.0	1.2	98.8	0.0	84
North Dakota U Sys							
U of North Dakota							
Main campus	1.9	1.3	0.4	0.7	93.0	2.7	11,659
Lake	2.2	0.7	4.8	0.9	90.7	0.7	996
Williston	4.1	0.4	0.0	0.8	93.8	0.8	714
ND State U Main campus	0.6	0.8	0.3	0.2	94.9	3.2	8,707
ND State U Bottineau	7.1	0.2	0.4	0.4	82.7	9.1	452
Dickinson State U	1.3	0.1	0.3	0.2	96.7	1.3	1,429
Mayville State U	1.7	0.1	1.2	0.1	91.7	5.1	763
Minot State U	2.4	0.3	1.4	1.2	85.2	9.5	3,637
ND State C of Science	1.7	0.8	1.1	0.1	95.7	0.6	2,116
Valley City State U	0.6	0.2	0.8	0.6	95.5	2.3	1,082
Bismarck State C	2.2	0.1	0.1	0.2	97.0	0.4	2,304
Standing Rock CC	91.1	0.0	0.0	0.0	8.9	0.0	202
Trinity Bible C	2.5	0.0	0.5	2.5	94.2	0.3	394
U of Mary	5.0	0.7	0.7	0.6	92.5	0.4	1,603

OHIO

	American Indian	Asian	Black	Hispanic	White	Foreign	Total
Air Force Inst of Tech	0.0	0.2	3.6	0.1	92.1	3.9	915
Antioch U	0.4	1.5	6.9	2.5	85.2	3.4	671
Antonelli Inst of Art and Photography	0.0	0.0	18.1	0.6	81.3	0.0	171

	American Indian	Asian	Black	Hispanic	White	Foreign	Total
Art Academy of Cincinnati ...	0.0%	0.4%	4.5%	0.4%	93.9%	0.8%	247
Athenaeum of Ohio	0.0	0.0	2.4	0.0	97.6	0.0	290
Baldwin-Wallace C	0.1	0.7	5.1	0.5	92.9	0.8	4,870
Belmont Tech C	0.1	0.0	1.1	0.0	98.6	0.2	1,618
Bliss C West	0.0	0.7	16.3	0.7	82.3	0.0	147
Bluffton C	0.0	0.3	2.0	0.0	94.0	3.7	684
Borromeo C	0.0	0.0	1.9	7.4	90.7	0.0	54
Bowling Green State U							
Main campus	0.1	0.8	3.8	1.1	92.7	1.5	18,657
Firelands	0.1	0.1	1.7	1.0	97.0	0.1	1,446
Bradford Sch	0.0	0.0	5.8	0.0	94.2	0.0	156
Bryant and Stratton							
Business Inst	0.5	1.3	4.8	2.5	90.9	0.0	395
Capital U	0.0	0.8	8.0	0.4	89.9	0.8	3,235
Career Com C of Business ...	0.0	1.0	67.6	0.0	31.4	0.0	102
Case Western Reserve U	0.2	5.6	5.9	0.7	74.5	12.9	8,213
Cedarville C	0.3	0.7	0.7	0.6	96.9	0.9	1,918
Central Ohio Tech C	0.3	0.3	1.7	0.5	97.2	0.1	1,555
Central State U	0.3	0.0	89.5	0.0	4.9	5.2	2,886
Chatfield C	0.0	0.0	0.0	0.0	100.0	0.0	129
Cincinnati Bible C and							
Seminary	0.0	0.8	2.7	0.1	94.2	2.2	873
Cincinnati C of Mortuary							
Science	0.0	0.0	10.8	0.0	89.2	0.0	120
Cincinnati Metropolitan C	0.0	0.0	58.3	0.0	41.2	0.5	204
Cincinnati Tech C	0.4	1.1	17.2	0.4	80.9	0.0	4,883
Circleville Bible C	0.0	0.0	6.5	0.0	93.5	0.0	170
Clark State CC	0.1	0.7	7.6	0.3	91.2	0.1	2,718
Cleveland Inst of Art	0.0	4.1	4.5	2.0	88.5	0.8	488
Cleveland Inst of Electronics .	0.3	0.7	16.1	1.5	81.2	0.2	10,405
Cleveland Inst of Music	0.2	1.6	3.0	1.6	78.9	14.5	427
Cleveland State U	0.5	1.7	12.8	1.8	80.6	2.5	19,214
C of Mount Saint Joseph	0.4	1.0	4.5	0.3	91.6	2.2	2,648
C of Wooster	0.1	1.0	5.4	0.5	86.0	7.0	1,877
Columbus C of Art and Design	0.4	2.2	5.8	2.5	87.2	1.8	1,631
Columbus State CC	0.3	1.6	16.0	1.0	80.1	1.0	13,290
Davis JC	0.0	0.5	16.0	2.4	80.6	0.5	376
Defiance C	0.2	0.3	5.8	2.0	90.1	1.6	964
Denison U	0.0	1.3	4.5	1.0	91.4	1.8	2,035
DeVry Inst of Tech	0.1	1.5	16.0	0.9	80.9	0.6	2,716
Dyke C	0.1	0.6	46.3	1.7	50.2	1.1	1,316
Edison State CC	0.3	0.6	1.3	0.7	97.0	0.1	3,325
ETI Tech C Cleveland	0.0	1.8	40.7	3.2	54.3	0.0	622
ETI Tech C Niles	0.0	0.0	8.1	0.0	91.9	0.0	135
Franciscan U of Steubenville .	0.1	0.9	1.1	3.8	87.0	7.1	1,574
Franklin U	0.1	1.6	14.0	0.6	82.2	1.5	4,005
God's Bible Sch and C	0.0	1.7	0.0	0.0	94.3	4.0	176
Hebrew Union C Jewish							
Inst of Religion	0.0	0.0	0.0	0.0	91.9	8.1	123
Heidelberg C	0.2	2.4	1.7	1.2	89.7	4.7	1,286
Hiram C	0.1	0.7	5.2	0.3	93.4	0.3	1,341
Hocking Tech C	0.0	0.0	0.8	0.0	97.6	1.6	5,212
International C							
of Broadcasting	0.0	0.0	27.9	0.0	72.1	0.0	86
ITT Tech Inst	0.2	0.2	11.5	0.4	87.7	0.0	479
Jefferson Tech C	0.1	0.0	3.2	0.1	96.6	0.1	1,630
John Carroll U	0.2	1.6	3.2	1.0	93.5	0.5	4,547

OHIO, cont.

	American Indian	Asian	Black	Hispanic	White	Foreign	Total
Kent State U							
Main campus	0.1%	0.7%	5.4%	0.6%	91.1%	2.1%	24,434
Ashtabula	0.0	0.1	2.2	0.2	97.5	0.0	906
East Liverpool	0.0	0.0	1.3	0.0	98.7	0.0	684
Geauga	0.2	0.0	1.8	0.0	98.0	0.0	546
Salem	0.0	0.0	0.6	0.0	99.4	0.0	840
Stark	0.0	0.1	2.3	0.1	97.3	0.0	2,164
Trumbull	0.1	0.4	4.9	0.4	94.3	0.0	1,686
Tuscarawas	0.0	0.1	0.4	0.1	99.4	0.0	1,241
Kenyon C	0.0	3.0	2.4	1.0	92.3	1.2	1,523
Kettering C of Medical Arts	0.1	1.4	4.0	1.0	93.2	0.4	730
Lake Erie C	0.0	1.2	3.2	0.2	95.3	0.0	894
Lakeland CC	0.3	0.6	1.9	0.3	96.9	0.0	8,806
Lima Tech C	0.3	0.4	4.9	1.0	93.4	0.0	2,521
Lorain County CC	0.3	0.5	6.0	5.0	88.0	0.1	7,026
Lourdes C	0.0	0.4	4.4	1.6	93.6	0.0	1,049
Malone C	0.1	0.3	4.1	0.2	95.1	0.3	1,555
Marietta C	0.1	0.1	0.7	0.1	97.3	1.7	1,383
Marion Tech C	0.4	0.8	3.6	0.8	94.3	0.1	1,564
Medical C of Ohio	0.0	11.7	5.3	1.3	81.7	0.0	832
Methodist Theological Sch	0.0	2.5	12.4	0.0	83.8	1.2	241
Miami-Jacobs JC of Business	0.0	0.7	31.9	1.0	66.4	0.0	599
Miami U							
Hamilton	0.0	0.6	2.7	0.2	96.4	0.0	2,073
Middletown	0.1	0.4	2.3	0.2	96.8	0.2	2,038
Oxford	0.1	1.6	2.6	0.5	93.9	1.4	15,835
Mount Union C	0.1	0.6	5.5	0.4	88.3	5.1	1,389
Mount Vernon Nazarene C	0.0	0.7	0.8	0.4	97.4	0.8	1,056
Muskingum Area Tech C	0.4	0.0	2.6	0.3	96.7	0.0	2,435
Muskingum C	0.3	1.2	0.8	0.3	96.8	0.6	1,175
North Central Tech C	0.3	0.5	3.9	0.7	94.5	0.1	2,275
Northeastern Ohio U's							
C of Medicine	0.2	25.6	1.7	1.4	71.1	0.0	418
Northwest Tech C	0.5	0.2	0.4	3.1	95.8	0.0	1,993
Notre Dame C	0.1	0.8	28.1	1.7	68.6	0.7	848
Oberlin C	0.2	8.1	8.3	3.1	75.3	4.9	2,902
Ohio C of Podiatric Medicine	0.6	5.2	16.4	6.7	69.1	2.1	330
Ohio Dominican C	0.2	0.6	12.1	1.7	75.5	10.0	1,365
Ohio Northern U	0.0	1.2	2.8	0.6	93.8	1.5	2,648
Ohio State U							
Main campus	0.2	2.8	5.4	1.3	84.7	5.6	54,087
Ag Tech Inst	0.3	0.0	2.2	0.4	96.3	0.8	738
Lima	0.1	0.8	1.8	1.0	96.3	0.0	1,357
Mansfield	0.2	0.2	2.4	0.6	96.6	0.0	1,309
Marion	0.2	0.5	4.7	0.5	94.2	0.0	1,100
Newark	0.2	0.8	1.5	0.5	97.0	0.1	1,567
Ohio U							
Main campus	0.2	0.4	3.9	0.5	87.7	7.3	18,505
Belmont	0.3	0.1	0.7	0.0	99.0	0.0	1,061
Chillicothe	0.1	0.1	1.4	0.2	98.1	0.2	1,614
Ironton	0.3	0.1	1.0	0.1	98.2	0.2	1,785
Lancaster	0.3	0.0	2.0	0.1	97.4	0.0	2,027
Zanesville	0.3	0.0	2.4	0.1	97.1	0.1	1,534
Ohio Wesleyan U	0.1	1.2	4.3	0.9	85.2	8.2	2,045
Otterbein C	0.1	0.6	3.1	0.6	93.9	1.7	2,453
Owens Tech C	0.4	0.5	6.7	2.2	90.1	0.2	6,857
Pontifical C Josephinum	0.0	2.2	1.5	3.7	80.1	12.5	136

	American Indian	Asian	Black	Hispanic	White	Foreign	Total
Rabbinical C of Telshe	0.0%	1.0%	7.2%	0.0%	88.7%	3.1%	97
RETS Tech Center	0.3	0.8	8.5	0.3	90.2	0.0	388
Saint Mary Seminary	0.0	0.0	0.0	0.0	100.0	0.0	72
Shawnee State U	0.6	0.3	4.6	0.3	94.0	0.2	3,180
Southeastern Business C	0.0	0.0	4.6	0.0	95.4	0.0	87
Southern Ohio C							
Cincinnati	0.0	0.0	35.8	0.0	64.2	0.0	232
Fairfield	0.2	0.2	8.7	0.5	90.5	0.0	620
Southern State CC	0.3	0.1	0.8	0.2	98.6	0.1	1,567
Stark Tech C	0.5	0.3	6.8	0.2	92.2	0.1	3,996
Terra Tech C	0.3	0.0	1.0	3.4	95.1	0.1	2,303
Tiffin U	0.0	0.2	6.9	0.2	89.2	3.5	896
Trinity Lutheran Seminary	0.0	0.0	3.4	1.3	91.6	3.8	238
United Theological Seminary	0.4	0.8	22.6	0.0	74.5	1.6	491
U of Cincinnati							
Main campus	0.2	2.3	9.1	0.7	83.8	3.9	31,013
Clermont	0.5	0.4	1.4	0.5	97.1	0.1	1,409
Raymond Walters	0.7	1.3	7.7	0.7	89.1	0.4	4,078
U of Dayton	0.1	1.3	4.5	1.4	91.6	1.0	11,493
U of Findlay	0.5	0.1	13.3	3.1	82.8	0.2	2,024
U of Rio Grande	0.1	0.0	1.1	0.0	97.6	1.2	1,937
U of Toledo	0.7	1.0	6.9	1.5	83.9	5.9	24,691
Urbana U	0.9	0.8	31.5	0.6	65.0	1.2	852
Ursuline C	0.0	1.1	14.3	1.8	82.2	0.6	1,604
Virginia Marti C of Fashion and Art	0.0	0.0	24.2	3.1	72.7	0.0	161
Walsh C	0.0	0.0	3.2	2.3	91.8	2.7	1,458
Washington Tech C	0.4	0.1	1.3	0.0	98.2	0.0	2,660
West Side Inst of Tech	0.5	0.8	21.0	2.2	75.2	0.3	367
Wilberforce U	0.0	0.1	98.8	0.0	0.4	0.7	809
Wilmington C	0.0	0.0	19.4	0.1	79.1	1.4	2,027
Wittenberg U	0.0	0.9	4.0	0.5	90.7	3.9	2,377
Wooster Business C	0.1	0.2	38.5	1.3	59.9	0.0	827
Wright State U							
Main campus	0.2	1.8	5.8	0.7	89.5	2.0	16,393
Lake	0.0	0.1	0.1	0.3	99.3	0.1	880
Xavier U	0.1	1.9	7.7	1.8	87.2	1.2	6,678
Youngstown State U	0.1	0.4	6.8	1.0	90.3	1.4	15,454

OKLAHOMA

Bartlesville Wesleyan C	2.7	1.2	2.1	1.7	86.3	6.0	480
Cameron U	4.2	2.4	13.3	4.0	75.4	0.7	5,276
Carl Albert State C	14.8	0.1	2.7	0.4	81.9	0.1	1,253
Connors State C	11.1	0.4	10.2	0.8	77.5	0.0	1,910
East Central U	9.7	0.4	2.9	0.7	86.0	0.3	4,183
Eastern Oklahoma State C	16.3	0.2	4.6	1.0	77.5	0.4	1,784
El Reno JC	4.2	1.1	5.4	1.4	87.7	0.2	1,177
Flaming Rainbow U	55.6	1.6	4.8	0.0	38.1	0.0	63
Hillsdale Free Will Baptist C	1.8	2.4	5.9	1.2	88.2	0.6	170
Langston U	2.0	0.5	51.6	0.8	44.8	0.3	2,792
Murray State C	9.5	0.2	4.2	0.9	85.1	0.1	1,251
Northeastern Okla A&M C	13.8	0.4	10.0	0.5	74.5	0.7	2,558
Northeastern State U	17.1	0.3	4.1	0.8	76.8	0.9	8,849
Northern Oklahoma C	8.1	0.2	2.2	1.0	88.2	0.3	1,892
Northwestern State U	1.9	0.1	3.1	1.2	93.2	0.5	1,746
Oklahoma City CC	3.4	2.7	5.6	1.9	85.7	0.7	8,015

OKLAHOMA, cont.

	American Indian	Asian	Black	Hispanic	White	Foreign	Total
Okla JC of Business and Tech	2.0%	0.9%	29.0%	2.2%	62.2%	3.7%	542
Oklahoma Mission Baptist C	2.4	0.6	6.7	2.4	87.9	0.0	165
Oklahoma Panhandle State U	0.8	0.5	3.7	6.0	88.7	0.3	1,275
Oklahoma State U							
Main campus	3.5	1.6	2.4	0.9	84.3	7.2	19,827
Oklahoma City	3.3	3.1	5.6	1.3	86.1	0.5	4,139
C of Osteopathic Medicine	5.6	2.2	4.4	3.3	84.4	0.0	270
Oral Roberts U	0.7	2.3	21.3	3.7	65.9	6.1	3,172
Phillips U	1.1	0.8	4.0	0.7	84.1	9.1	964
Rogers State C	12.8	0.6	1.3	0.5	80.6	4.2	2,476
Rose State C	4.0	2.5	14.7	2.3	76.1	0.3	8,245
Saint Gregory's C	6.3	2.2	3.7	5.2	74.5	8.1	271
Southeastern Okla State U	28.6	2.4	4.0	0.9	63.8	0.4	3,971
Southwestern Okla State U	3.0	1.4	2.0	1.5	91.8	0.3	5,373
Tulsa JC	2.8	1.2	5.9	1.2	88.8	0.0	17,955
U of Central Oklahoma	2.2	1.6	7.2	1.1	83.3	4.6	14,232
U of Oklahoma							
Norman	3.0	2.8	5.2	1.9	81.0	6.2	20,774
Health Science Center	5.2	3.7	4.9	2.2	81.4	2.6	2,818
U of Science and Arts							
of Oklahoma	7.4	1.0	3.6	1.1	85.5	1.4	1,559
U of Tulsa	2.8	1.6	3.9	1.3	81.9	8.4	4,575
Western Oklahoma State C	2.0	1.0	7.4	5.9	83.5	0.1	1,869

OREGON

	American Indian	Asian	Black	Hispanic	White	Foreign	Total
Bassist C	0.0	6.9	1.2	2.3	88.4	1.2	173
Central Oregon CC	2.5	0.4	0.0	0.7	95.6	0.8	3,036
Chemeketa CC	1.3	2.1	0.9	2.6	91.5	1.6	9,172
Clackamas CC	0.3	1.6	0.4	0.9	96.6	0.3	6,437
Clatsop CC	2.1	3.5	0.2	2.8	91.4	0.0	1,156
Columbia Christian C	0.4	2.1	3.9	0.7	92.9	0.0	280
Concordia C	0.5	2.0	3.8	0.9	76.2	16.7	816
Eugene Bible C	1.4	1.4	1.4	2.1	93.8	0.0	146
George Fox C	0.5	1.4	1.5	2.4	89.6	4.6	1,062
ITT Tech Inst	0.5	4.2	2.5	2.9	89.9	0.0	554
Lane CC	2.0	2.1	1.0	1.7	91.0	2.2	8,407
Lewis and Clark C	0.9	4.0	1.4	1.0	86.6	6.2	3,525
Linfield C	0.8	2.6	0.8	0.4	92.0	3.4	2,225
Linn-Benton CC	0.8	1.0	0.4	0.8	95.9	1.2	6,132
Marylhurst C	0.8	1.2	0.6	1.1	95.8	0.6	1,031
Mount Angel Seminary	0.0	11.5	2.2	17.3	69.1	0.0	139
Mt Hood CC	0.9	3.2	1.3	1.2	92.6	0.8	7,480
Multnomah Sch of Bible	0.8	1.8	1.1	1.0	88.9	6.4	621
National C of Naturopathic							
Medicine	0.0	0.6	1.3	1.3	84.4	12.3	154
Northwest Christian C	0.4	2.7	0.8	1.9	91.1	3.1	257
Oregon Graduate Inst							
of Science and Tech	0.0	9.9	0.0	0.0	65.1	25.0	292
Oregon Health Science U	0.6	7.8	1.0	1.3	85.5	3.8	1,356
Oregon Polytechnic Inst	0.9	2.1	0.4	3.4	93.2	0.0	234
Pacific Northwest C of Art	0.5	0.5	0.0	2.1	92.7	4.1	193
Pacific U	0.8	11.0	0.9	2.2	81.7	3.4	1,522
Portland CC	0.7	6.4	3.1	2.2	86.5	1.1	21,888
Reed C	0.5	5.0	1.1	2.3	87.4	3.6	1,330
Rogue CC	1.1	0.4	0.2	1.5	96.6	0.1	2,312
Southwestern Oregon CC	1.6	1.2	0.2	0.9	95.9	0.2	2,846

	American Indian	Asian	Black	Hispanic	White	Foreign	Total
Treasure Valley CC	1.0%	1.3%	0.2%	7.9%	88.1%	1.5%	3,065
Umpqua CC	1.0	1.0	0.7	1.7	93.7	1.9	2,067
U of Portland	0.6	6.4	1.4	1.7	79.0	10.9	2,460
Warner Pacific C	1.1	2.6	4.3	0.9	84.8	6.3	462
Western Baptist C	0.7	1.2	0.2	1.4	96.4	0.0	417
Western Conservative Baptist Seminary	0.4	9.0	1.3	1.3	85.8	2.1	521
Western Evangelical Seminary	0.0	3.4	2.7	1.4	85.6	6.8	146
Western States Chiropractic C	0.5	1.9	0.7	1.9	85.1	9.8	417
Willamette U	0.4	5.0	1.0	2.2	84.6	6.8	2,337

PENNSYLVANIA

	American Indian	Asian	Black	Hispanic	White	Foreign	Total
Academy of the New Church	0.0	2.9	0.0	0.0	71.8	25.3	170
Albert Einstein Medical Center	0.0	0.0	11.1	0.0	88.9	0.0	27
Albright C	0.1	2.7	2.3	0.9	89.8	4.2	1,763
Allegheny C	0.1	1.7	3.4	1.3	89.6	4.0	1,817
Allentown C of Saint Francis De Sales	0.1	0.5	0.5	0.8	97.7	0.5	1,856
Alvernia C	0.3	0.5	2.2	1.2	95.8	0.1	1,099
American C	0.0	0.0	0.0	0.0	100.0	0.0	370
American Inst of Design	0.0	0.0	32.2	3.1	64.7	0.0	357
Annenberg Research Inst	0.0	8.3	0.0	0.0	91.7	0.0	12
Antonelli Inst of Art and Photography	0.0	1.0	12.6	2.0	84.3	0.0	198
Art Inst of Philadelphia	0.2	0.6	12.8	2.5	83.8	0.1	1,311
Art Inst of Pittsburgh	0.3	0.5	6.8	0.9	91.5	0.0	2,523
Baptist Bible C and Seminary	0.1	0.7	1.4	1.0	96.6	0.1	711
Beaver C	0.0	1.4	7.0	1.1	89.3	1.2	2,253
Berean Inst	0.0	2.1	94.1	2.9	0.8	0.0	239
Biblical Theological Seminary	0.0	21.7	2.5	1.5	69.0	5.4	203
Bradford Sch	0.2	0.8	13.6	2.6	82.8	0.0	500
Bradley Academy for Visual Arts	0.0	0.7	12.9	2.2	84.2	0.0	272
Bryn Mawr C	0.2	9.8	5.0	2.4	76.1	6.5	1,885
Bucknell U	0.1	1.6	2.1	1.3	93.3	1.6	3,463
Bucks County CC	0.1	1.4	1.6	0.8	96.1	0.0	11,164
Butler County CC	0.0	0.3	0.7	0.4	98.6	0.0	3,214
Cabrini C	0.1	0.9	2.2	0.6	95.5	0.7	1,477
Carlow C	0.9	0.4	13.5	0.7	83.7	0.8	1,208
Carnegie Mellon U	0.2	3.1	3.0	0.6	81.4	11.7	7,225
Cedar Crest C	0.3	0.4	0.8	1.1	95.3	2.0	982
Central Pa Business Sch	0.0	0.6	13.3	2.6	83.5	0.0	656
Chatham C	0.0	2.5	8.2	0.9	84.3	4.0	643
Chestnut Hill C	0.2	0.9	8.8	3.9	83.9	2.4	1,189
CHI Inst	0.0	1.2	7.8	2.4	88.7	0.0	424
Clarissa Sch of Fashion Design	0.0	3.3	18.0	0.0	75.4	3.3	61
C Misericordia	0.0	0.2	1.2	0.5	97.6	0.6	1,513
CC of Allegheny County	0.3	0.8	10.0	0.3	88.2	0.4	20,553
CC of Beaver County	0.2	0.2	3.5	0.3	95.8	0.0	2,836
CC of Philadelphia	0.5	6.0	40.2	4.7	48.6	0.0	15,151
Curtis Inst of Music	0.0	10.4	2.4	1.2	51.8	34.1	164
Dean Inst of Tech	0.0	0.0	20.5	0.0	79.5	0.0	112
Delaware County CC	0.1	1.0	5.1	0.3	93.2	0.3	9,193
Delaware Valley C	0.1	0.4	2.6	0.2	95.6	1.2	1,098
Dickinson C	0.1	2.5	0.9	1.3	94.6	0.6	2,061

PA., cont.

	American Indian	Asian	Black	Hispanic	White	Foreign	Total
Dickinson Sch of Law	0.4%	1.4%	2.0%	0.4%	94.8%	1.1%	555
Drexel U	0.2	7.7	6.2	1.3	77.7	6.9	11,926
Du Bois Business C	0.0	0.0	0.0	0.0	100.0	0.0	278
Duquesne U	0.3	1.0	2.0	0.7	95.4	0.6	7,443
Eastern Baptist Theological Seminary	0.0	1.7	31.4	3.1	58.5	5.2	287
Eastern C	0.2	1.2	7.6	1.0	82.4	7.6	1,367
Elizabethtown C	0.1	0.8	1.1	0.4	96.8	0.9	1,806
Erie Business Center	0.4	1.2	8.1	0.0	90.3	0.0	258
Evangelical Sch of Theology	0.0	0.0	0.0	0.0	97.7	2.3	88
Faith Theological Seminary	0.0	90.0	5.0	0.0	5.0	0.0	20
Franklin and Marshall C	0.1	5.0	2.6	1.6	85.9	4.9	1,796
Gannon U	0.1	1.4	2.3	0.3	94.7	1.2	4,595
Geneva C	0.2	0.9	8.1	0.2	89.9	0.7	1,488
Gettysburg C	0.0	0.9	2.2	0.7	94.8	1.4	2,074
Gratz C	0.0	0.0	0.4	0.0	95.1	4.5	512
Grove City C	0.0	0.0	0.0	0.0	100.0	0.0	2,138
Gwynedd-Mercy C	0.1	1.4	4.3	0.9	91.4	1.9	1,980
Hahnemann U	0.3	8.1	11.6	2.6	75.8	1.6	2,096
Harcum JC	0.0	0.4	9.3	1.3	80.6	8.3	687
Harrisburg Area CC	0.2	2.3	5.4	1.1	90.2	0.8	8,355
Haverford C	0.0	8.5	5.3	4.5	81.7	0.0	1,147
Holy Family C	0.0	0.8	1.7	1.2	95.0	1.2	2,050
Hussian Sch of Art	0.0	0.0	12.6	2.3	85.1	0.0	174
ICS Center for Degree Studies	0.1	0.7	13.1	2.6	83.5	0.1	4,313
ICS International Correspondence Schs	0.1	0.6	32.3	3.7	62.6	0.6	20,727
Immaculata C	0.1	1.1	2.3	1.5	93.8	1.2	2,368
Information Computer Systems Inst	1.5	0.0	1.5	4.5	92.4	0.0	66
Johnson Tech Inst	0.0	1.1	0.3	0.3	98.3	0.0	361
Juniata C	0.3	1.9	0.9	0.2	93.8	3.0	1,134
Keystone JC	0.5	0.6	2.8	0.6	92.7	2.8	1,232
King's C	0.2	0.5	0.3	0.4	98.4	0.2	2,258
La Roche C	0.0	0.6	1.5	0.3	97.4	0.2	1,858
La Salle U	0.0	1.4	8.7	2.0	87.8	0.0	6,333
Lackawanna JC	0.6	0.9	2.1	0.3	96.0	0.1	775
Lafayette C	0.1	2.5	3.1	1.1	89.2	4.0	2,288
Lancaster Bible C	0.0	0.5	3.1	0.8	95.7	0.0	392
Lancaster Theological Seminary	0.0	0.9	7.0	1.4	89.2	1.4	213
Lebanon Valley C	0.0	0.8	0.9	0.3	97.2	0.8	1,244
Lehigh County CC	0.1	1.6	1.3	1.6	94.6	0.7	4,145
Lehigh U	0.0	3.7	1.8	1.5	85.8	7.2	6,647
Lincoln Tech Inst Allentown	0.0	0.0	0.7	1.3	97.3	0.7	449
Lincoln Tech Inst Philadelphia	0.0	0.0	11.8	2.4	85.8	0.0	127
Lincoln U	0.0	0.1	90.5	1.2	6.2	2.0	1,374
Lutheran Theological Seminary Gettysburg	0.0	0.4	2.5	0.8	94.1	2.1	236
Lutheran Theological Seminary Philadelphia	0.0	1.4	30.1	0.5	66.0	1.9	209
Luzerne County CC	0.0	0.6	1.6	0.4	97.2	0.1	6,530
Lycoming C	0.0	1.5	0.7	0.2	97.1	0.5	1,255
Manor JC	0.0	0.2	7.6	1.5	83.2	7.6	476
Marywood C	0.2	0.5	0.6	0.9	97.1	0.7	3,087
Medical C of Pennsylvania	0.2	13.2	5.5	3.2	74.1	3.9	568

	American Indian	Asian	Black	Hispanic	White	Foreign	Total
Mercyhurst C	1.1%	0.5%	3.4%	0.1%	92.7%	2.1%	2,058
Messiah C	0.0	1.7	2.0	1.3	92.9	2.0	2,239
Montgomery County CC	0.5	3.2	4.9	0.9	90.4	0.0	8,172
Moore C of Art and Design	0.0	7.3	5.2	2.6	84.9	0.0	578
Moravian C	0.0	1.6	1.8	1.0	95.5	0.0	1,787
Mount Aloysius JC	0.0	0.7	0.7	2.2	96.4	0.1	1,487
Muhlenberg C	0.0	2.6	1.5	1.2	93.7	1.0	2,028
National Education Center Vale Tech Inst	0.0	0.7	12.0	2.4	84.9	0.0	417
Neumann C	0.0	0.6	4.9	1.1	93.1	0.3	1,262
New Castle Business Sch	0.0	0.0	14.3	0.0	85.7	0.0	35
Northampton County Area CC	0.3	1.5	2.1	3.2	92.3	0.6	5,535
Northeastern Christian JC	0.0	0.5	36.0	0.5	51.1	11.8	186
Palmer Sch	0.0	1.4	13.9	16.7	68.1	0.0	72
Peirce JC	0.1	1.1	45.2	2.8	49.0	1.9	1,133
Penn Tech Inst	0.0	0.4	4.3	0.0	95.3	0.0	253
Pennco Tech	0.0	0.4	12.2	2.5	84.8	0.0	475
Pennsylvania C of Optometry	0.5	7.8	7.9	2.1	80.3	1.4	631
Pa C of Podiatric Medicine	0.0	4.0	6.7	4.6	80.3	4.3	371
Pa C of Straight Chiropractic	0.0	0.0	4.0	0.0	94.9	1.0	99
Pennsylvania C of Tech	0.1	0.1	1.3	0.2	98.2	0.0	4,343
Pennsylvania Inst of Tech	0.0	2.4	30.0	1.4	66.1	0.0	416
Pennsylvania State U							
Main campus	0.1	2.9	3.2	1.5	87.5	4.7	38,864
Allentown	0.0	4.0	1.0	1.6	93.4	0.0	697
Altoona	0.1	1.1	3.1	0.8	94.8	0.1	2,509
Beaver	0.1	1.1	4.7	0.9	93.2	0.1	1,030
Berks	0.0	2.4	1.3	1.7	94.5	0.1	1,665
Delaware	0.2	2.4	9.3	0.9	87.2	0.1	1,811
Du Bois	0.1	0.4	0.1	0.4	99.0	0.0	1,045
Erie Behrend C	0.2	1.6	4.0	0.9	93.4	0.0	2,987
Fayette	0.5	0.5	1.6	0.1	97.2	0.0	945
Great Valley	0.8	4.8	4.6	1.2	88.1	0.5	1,093
Harrisburg Capital C	0.1	2.0	2.7	0.8	93.7	0.7	3,416
Hazleton	0.1	1.9	1.5	2.2	94.2	0.1	1,308
Hershey Medical Center	0.2	6.9	5.1	2.0	80.0	5.9	494
McKeesport	0.2	1.2	6.6	0.5	91.5	0.0	1,343
Mont Alto	0.2	3.8	2.9	0.8	92.3	0.0	900
New Kensington	0.1	0.5	1.7	0.1	97.6	0.0	1,144
Ogontz	0.1	3.2	4.3	0.9	91.5	0.0	3,207
Schuylkill	0.0	2.0	1.8	1.0	95.1	0.2	1,139
Shenango Valley	0.3	0.3	3.3	0.3	95.9	0.0	1,192
Wilkes-Barre	0.1	0.9	0.8	0.5	97.7	0.0	990
Worthington-Scranton	0.1	1.0	0.2	0.3	98.5	0.0	1,364
York	0.1	2.2	1.3	0.5	95.9	0.0	1,920
Philadelphia C of Bible	0.6	3.4	8.7	2.7	81.4	3.1	641
Philadelphia C of Osteopathic Medicine	0.0	3.9	3.9	1.6	90.2	0.5	828
Philadelphia C of Pharmacy and Science	0.0	11.0	3.3	0.5	81.9	3.4	1,659
Philadelphia C of Textiles and Science	0.0	2.6	9.5	0.9	82.2	4.9	3,320
Pinebrook JC	0.0	4.3	6.8	2.6	80.3	6.0	117
Pittsburgh Inst of Aeronautics	0.1	0.3	0.8	0.5	98.2	0.2	1,031
Pittsburgh Tech Inst	0.0	1.4	3.6	0.0	94.9	0.0	276
Pittsburgh Theological Seminary	0.0	3.1	6.9	0.6	89.3	0.0	319

PA., cont.

	American Indian	Asian	Black	Hispanic	White	Foreign	Total
Point Park C	0.0%	0.6%	8.9%	0.3%	84.8%	5.3%	2,977
Reading Area CC	0.8	1.2	6.8	5.6	85.0	0.5	2,337
Reformed Presbyterian Theological Seminary	0.0	1.5	33.8	0.0	64.7	0.0	68
RETS Education Center	0.0	0.0	13.2	1.8	85.1	0.0	228
Robert Morris C	0.1	0.3	3.9	0.2	94.9	0.7	5,326
Rosemont C	0.1	1.8	3.1	0.3	93.2	1.5	681
Saint Charles Borromeo Seminary	0.0	1.8	7.5	1.6	88.0	1.1	442
Saint Francis C	0.1	0.7	1.6	0.3	97.2	0.1	1,763
Saint Joseph's U	0.0	1.8	6.2	1.7	86.4	3.8	6,622
Saint Vincent C	0.0	0.3	1.2	0.9	96.7	0.9	1,147
Saint Vincent Seminary	0.0	1.5	0.0	0.0	94.0	4.5	67
Sawyer Sch	0.0	1.1	12.9	0.3	85.5	0.1	697
Seton Hill C	0.2	1.2	3.2	4.2	90.5	0.7	1,037
Spring Garden C	0.2	5.2	12.6	1.0	79.7	1.2	898
State Sys of Higher Education							
Bloomsburg U of Pa	0.1	0.7	2.3	0.6	95.8	0.6	7,484
California U of Pa	0.1	0.6	4.0	0.4	94.1	0.9	6,531
Cheyney U of Pa	0.2	0.6	93.3	0.9	3.3	1.7	1,738
Clarion U of Pa	0.1	0.2	2.4	0.3	94.7	2.3	6,618
East Stroudsburg U of Pa	0.2	1.3	2.5	1.3	93.1	1.5	5,456
Edinboro U of Pa	0.2	0.3	3.4	0.4	93.4	2.3	8,131
Indiana U of Pa	0.1	1.2	4.7	0.5	91.0	2.5	14,398
Kutztown U of Pa	0.2	0.8	3.5	1.3	93.1	1.1	7,742
Lock Haven U of Pa	0.3	0.2	2.8	0.5	94.6	1.6	3,520
Mansfield U of Pa	0.2	0.3	3.8	0.3	94.2	1.1	3,182
Millersville U of Pa	0.1	1.5	5.0	1.4	90.9	1.1	7,789
Shippensburg U of Pa	0.1	1.2	2.8	0.6	94.6	0.7	6,592
Slippery Rock U of Pa	0.2	0.3	3.3	0.4	94.9	0.9	7,825
West Chester U of Pa	0.1	1.8	5.6	0.8	90.0	1.7	12,076
Susquehanna U	0.1	0.3	1.2	1.1	96.2	1.1	1,751
Swarthmore C	0.2	7.4	6.7	3.2	77.2	5.4	1,330
Temple U	0.3	5.2	15.6	2.4	72.0	4.6	29,714
Thaddeus Stevens State Sch of Tech	0.0	2.6	17.9	3.3	76.2	0.0	491
Thiel C	0.0	0.4	4.9	0.1	92.7	1.9	943
Thomas Jefferson U	0.5	8.7	8.6	1.9	78.5	1.8	2,364
Tracey-Warner Sch	0.0	0.6	29.0	2.8	67.0	0.6	176
Triangle Tech Pittsburgh	0.0	0.0	7.3	0.0	92.7	0.0	452
Trinity Episcopal Sch for Ministry	0.0	0.0	0.9	0.0	95.4	3.7	108
U of the Arts	0.4	3.1	7.0	2.0	82.1	5.4	1,310
U of Pennsylvania	0.3	7.5	5.2	2.4	72.4	12.2	21,868
U of Pittsburgh							
Main campus	0.1	2.3	6.6	0.6	85.3	5.2	28,120
Bradford	0.1	0.7	3.6	0.6	94.9	0.1	1,204
Greensburg	0.1	0.5	1.4	0.0	97.8	0.1	1,504
Johnstown	0.0	0.4	2.5	0.6	96.5	0.0	3,210
Titusville	0.0	0.0	0.5	0.5	99.0	0.0	393
U of Scranton	0.1	0.8	0.2	0.5	95.6	2.7	5,116
Ursinus C	0.2	1.3	1.5	0.7	95.8	0.6	2,316
Valley Forge Christian C	0.4	4.3	3.3	4.1	87.4	0.6	491
Valley Forge Military JC	0.0	4.3	6.4	3.6	76.4	9.3	140
Villanova U	0.1	1.6	2.2	1.0	93.7	1.4	11,577
Washington and Jefferson C	0.2	1.4	3.8	0.8	93.3	0.5	1,198

	American Indian	Asian	Black	Hispanic	White	Foreign	Total
Watterson Sch of Business and Tech	0.0%	0.5%	53.9%	9.7%	35.5%	0.5%	217
Waynesburg C	0.1	0.8	4.6	0.3	94.1	0.1	1,244
Westminster C	0.0	0.3	1.0	0.1	98.5	0.1	1,594
Westminster Theological Seminary	0.6	19.6	4.5	0.6	57.7	17.0	530
Westmoreland County CC	0.1	0.3	1.1	0.0	98.5	0.0	5,795
Widener U	0.1	2.4	5.4	1.0	89.8	1.3	5,896
Wilkes U	0.0	0.6	0.9	0.3	97.7	0.5	3,627
Williamson Free Sch of Mechanical Trades	0.0	0.3	3.2	0.6	95.3	0.6	340
Wilson C	0.0	0.4	0.7	0.2	97.2	1.4	943
York C	0.0	0.9	1.2	0.7	97.0	0.3	4,588

RHODE ISLAND

	American Indian	Asian	Black	Hispanic	White	Foreign	Total
Brown U	0.2	9.6	5.9	3.7	70.6	10.0	7,577
Bryant C	0.1	0.8	0.7	1.1	96.6	0.8	5,219
CC of Rhode Island	0.6	1.8	4.2	3.2	89.8	0.3	16,620
Johnson & Wales U	0.3	2.1	7.7	2.4	82.3	5.1	7,592
New England Inst of Tech	0.0	1.5	2.7	0.0	95.6	0.1	2,041
Providence C	0.0	0.4	1.9	1.0	96.2	0.5	5,351
Rhode Island C	0.2	1.2	2.1	1.5	94.6	0.4	9,683
Rhode Island Sch of Design	0.3	7.0	2.3	2.6	78.6	9.2	1,909
Roger Williams C	0.0	1.1	0.7	0.9	95.8	1.4	3,823
Salve Regina U	0.0	0.2	0.6	0.2	97.8	1.1	2,411
U of Rhode Island	0.3	1.9	2.2	1.6	91.2	2.9	16,047

SOUTH CAROLINA

	American Indian	Asian	Black	Hispanic	White	Foreign	Total
Aiken Tech C	0.6	0.8	32.6	0.5	65.2	0.3	1,903
Anderson C	0.0	0.0	11.9	0.0	85.7	2.4	968
Benedict C	0.0	0.0	99.2	0.0	0.1	0.7	1,478
Central Wesleyan C	0.3	0.4	10.7	0.0	87.4	1.2	934
Charleston Southern U	0.9	0.7	22.0	0.6	75.9	0.0	2,158
Chesterfield-Marlboro Tech C	1.3	0.4	27.1	0.2	71.0	0.0	852
Citadel Military C of SC	0.4	1.1	8.8	0.4	88.7	0.6	3,801
Claflin C	0.0	0.1	98.9	0.1	0.1	0.8	913
Clemson U	0.1	0.9	6.5	0.7	87.8	4.0	15,714
Clinton JC	0.0	0.0	100.0	0.0	0.0	0.0	88
Coker C	0.3	0.3	27.7	1.4	68.9	1.4	775
C of Charleston	0.3	1.3	7.1	0.5	89.8	1.0	7,726
Columbia Bible C and Seminary	0.1	2.1	3.2	1.2	85.6	7.7	961
Columbia C	0.0	0.6	19.2	0.4	79.3	0.4	1,190
Converse C	0.4	0.4	4.3	1.7	92.1	1.2	1,134
Denmark Tech C	0.0	0.2	97.4	0.3	1.9	0.2	617
Erskine C and Seminary	0.1	0.6	9.4	0.4	86.8	2.6	681
Florence-Darlington Tech C	0.1	0.1	25.2	0.2	74.3	0.2	2,324
Francis Marion C	0.3	0.4	13.6	0.2	85.0	0.5	3,886
Furman U	0.0	0.9	4.3	0.5	94.3	0.0	3,312
Greenville Tech C	0.1	0.9	13.3	0.3	85.1	0.3	7,917
Horry-Georgetown Tech C	0.5	0.6	16.9	0.4	81.6	0.1	1,984
Johnson & Wales U Charleston	0.0	1.6	18.5	1.8	78.0	0.2	567
Lander C	0.1	0.4	14.8	0.4	82.6	1.6	2,309
Limestone C	0.3	0.8	17.5	0.4	81.0	0.0	1,195

THE ALMANAC OF HIGHER EDUCATION • ENROLLMENT BY RACE

S.C., cont.

	American Indian	Asian	Black	Hispanic	White	Foreign	Total
Lutheran Theological Southern Seminary	0.0%	0.0%	8.1%	0.0%	91.9%	0.0%	161
Medical U of South Carolina	0.4	2.6	7.2	0.9	88.0	0.8	1,781
Midlands Tech C	0.3	1.0	27.2	0.9	70.7	0.0	7,546
Morris C	0.0	0.0	99.9	0.0	0.1	0.0	760
Newberry C	0.0	0.4	16.9	0.8	81.7	0.1	709
Nielsen Electronics Inst	0.0	0.0	72.8	0.0	27.2	0.0	169
North Greenville C	1.5	0.0	41.8	0.8	55.1	0.8	392
Orangeburg-Calhoun Tech C	0.3	0.5	41.3	0.0	57.8	0.2	1,504
Phillips JC Charleston	0.0	0.0	84.0	0.0	16.0	0.0	400
Phillips JC Greenville	0.0	0.0	82.8	0.0	17.2	0.0	198
Phillips JC Spartanburg	0.0	0.0	84.6	0.0	15.4	0.0	240
Piedmont Tech C	0.2	0.4	27.8	0.2	71.4	0.0	2,144
Presbyterian C	0.0	0.3	4.3	0.2	94.8	0.4	1,133
Sherman C of Straight Chiropractic	0.7	2.0	2.0	2.0	87.8	5.4	147
South Carolina State C	0.0	0.4	94.1	0.0	5.3	0.1	4,822
Spartanburg Methodist C	0.0	1.0	21.4	0.0	76.2	1.5	932
Spartanburg Tech C	0.1	1.1	16.9	0.3	81.6	0.0	2,276
Sumter Area Tech C	0.2	1.0	34.7	1.6	62.5	0.0	1,929
Tech C of the Lowcountry	1.5	1.4	34.6	0.9	59.9	1.7	1,210
Tri-County Tech C	0.2	0.4	9.9	0.3	88.3	0.9	2,935
Trident Tech C	0.5	2.5	17.7	1.2	77.8	0.3	6,939
U of South Carolina							
Columbia	0.1	1.5	12.5	0.8	80.9	4.1	25,613
Aiken	0.1	1.0	14.4	0.8	83.2	0.4	2,966
Beaufort	0.3	1.2	11.8	2.3	84.2	0.1	896
Coastal Carolina	0.2	0.6	7.2	0.6	89.9	1.4	4,080
Lancaster	0.1	0.4	9.0	0.1	90.2	0.1	984
Salkehatchie	0.4	0.1	37.5	0.2	61.6	0.1	831
Sumter	0.1	1.1	18.0	1.1	77.7	2.0	1,260
Union	0.3	0.3	12.8	0.3	86.4	0.0	368
Spartanburg	0.1	0.9	8.8	0.3	88.7	1.2	3,501
Voorhees C	0.0	0.0	98.9	0.0	0.0	1.1	566
Williamsburg Tech C	0.2	0.0	43.1	0.0	56.7	0.0	503
Winthrop C	0.2	0.5	14.6	0.5	82.2	2.0	5,104
Wofford C	0.1	1.4	8.1	0.4	89.4	0.7	1,066
York Tech C	0.4	0.5	16.6	0.4	82.0	0.0	2,909

SOUTH DAKOTA

	American Indian	Asian	Black	Hispanic	White	Foreign	Total
Augustana C	0.4	0.3	0.7	0.3	95.5	2.8	2,113
Dakota Wesleyan U	5.4	0.4	0.8	0.1	92.5	0.7	706
Huron U	5.2	0.2	8.7	1.4	79.2	5.2	424
Kilian CC	0.0	0.4	0.0	0.0	99.6	0.0	249
Mount Marty C	1.3	0.6	0.7	1.0	96.4	0.0	947
National C Rapid City	13.7	2.6	3.5	1.2	78.6	0.4	723
National C Sioux Falls	2.9	0.8	8.2	5.2	82.8	0.0	1,239
North American Baptist Seminary	0.0	1.3	0.6	0.0	88.3	9.7	154
Oglala Lakota C	84.7	0.0	0.0	0.0	15.3	0.0	757
Presentation C	13.6	0.0	0.2	0.5	84.5	1.2	588
Sinte Gleska C	74.7	0.0	0.0	0.0	25.3	0.0	494
Sioux Falls C	0.5	0.2	0.4	0.6	97.4	0.7	937
SD State Board of Regents Sys							
U of South Dakota	2.1	0.8	0.9	0.3	94.9	1.0	7,627
Black Hills State U	2.8	0.4	0.3	0.5	95.7	0.3	2,545

	American Indian	Asian	Black	Hispanic	White	Foreign	Total
Dakota State U	0.4%	0.5%	1.0%	0.2%	97.9%	0.1%	1,303
Northern State U	4.1	0.4	0.1	0.0	95.4	0.0	3,346
SD Sch of Mines and Tech	1.6	0.8	0.5	0.4	85.0	11.7	2,322
South Dakota State U	0.9	0.5	0.4	0.1	96.2	2.0	8,551

TENNESSEE

	American Indian	Asian	Black	Hispanic	White	Foreign	Total
American Baptist C	0.0	0.0	14.1	0.0	83.5	2.4	206
Aquinas JC	0.0	0.7	6.9	1.5	90.1	0.7	405
Belmont U	0.1	0.5	3.6	0.3	91.6	3.9	2,812
Bethel C	0.0	0.0	9.8	0.0	89.6	0.7	613
Bristol U	0.0	0.0	12.9	0.0	85.1	2.0	255
Career Com C of Business	0.0	0.0	8.3	0.0	91.7	0.0	96
Carson-Newman C	0.2	0.2	3.1	0.4	95.6	0.5	2,109
Christian Brothers U	0.1	1.9	19.1	0.6	75.9	2.4	1,765
Church of God Sch of Theology	0.0	1.6	2.6	7.9	70.4	17.5	189
Crichton C	0.3	0.0	26.2	0.0	72.6	0.9	328
Cumberland U	0.0	1.0	14.7	0.4	80.3	3.5	687
David Lipscomb U	0.1	0.2	3.0	0.2	95.3	1.1	2,427
Draughons JC of Business	0.2	2.4	26.1	0.0	70.8	0.5	418
Draughons JC Chattanooga	0.0	0.0	23.1	0.0	76.9	0.0	234
Draughons JC Johnson City	0.0	0.0	7.2	0.0	92.8	0.0	125
Draughons JC Kingsport	0.0	0.0	1.7	0.0	98.3	0.0	180
Draughons JC Knoxville	0.6	0.6	16.1	0.0	82.7	0.0	353
Draughons JC Memphis	0.6	0.6	72.6	0.3	25.9	0.0	328
Edmondson JC of Business	0.3	0.6	30.4	0.0	68.7	0.0	674
Emmanuel Sch of Religion	0.0	0.0	0.0	0.6	94.9	4.4	158
Fisk U	0.0	0.0	97.8	0.0	0.1	2.1	911
Free Will Baptist Bible C	0.4	0.0	0.4	1.6	97.2	0.4	252
Freed-Hardeman U	0.2	0.7	4.4	0.3	91.8	2.6	1,183
Harding U Graduate Sch of Religion	0.0	0.0	8.8	0.6	89.3	1.3	159
Hiwassee C	0.0	8.0	8.0	0.8	83.1	0.0	522
ITT Tech Inst	0.0	1.3	14.2	0.5	83.9	0.0	598
Jackson State CC	0.0	1.0	13.6	0.0	85.4	0.0	3,256
John A Gupton C	0.0	4.3	10.6	0.0	85.1	0.0	47
Johnson Bible C	0.0	0.2	1.1	0.4	97.2	1.1	457
King C	0.0	0.8	0.2	3.4	88.2	7.4	527
Knoxville Business C	0.3	0.3	30.3	0.0	69.1	0.0	350
Knoxville C	0.0	0.3	99.1	0.1	0.6	0.0	1,266
Lambuth U	0.1	0.0	14.3	0.3	80.2	5.1	769
Lane C	0.0	0.2	98.9	0.0	0.8	0.2	530
Lee C	1.4	0.8	1.5	2.3	89.9	4.1	1,748
Lemoyne-Owen C	0.0	0.0	98.9	0.0	0.2	0.9	1,066
Lincoln Memorial U	0.1	0.2	1.2	0.1	89.7	8.8	1,819
Martin Methodist C	0.8	0.5	16.2	0.5	76.9	5.1	390
Maryville C	0.4	0.2	4.5	1.1	86.0	7.8	841
McKenzie C	0.0	0.5	34.0	0.0	65.5	0.0	203
Meharry Medical C	0.0	6.7	78.7	1.6	6.4	6.6	623
Memphis C of Art	0.4	1.5	10.7	0.4	80.5	6.6	272
Memphis Theological Seminary	0.0	0.0	28.6	0.0	69.2	2.3	133
Mid-America Baptist Theological Seminary	0.0	0.0	1.6	0.0	95.3	3.0	430

TENNESSEE, cont.

	American Indian	Asian	Black	Hispanic	White	Foreign	Total
Milligan C	0.1%	0.6%	1.5%	1.1%	95.8%	0.9%	814
O'More C of Design	0.0	0.0	2.5	0.8	95.1	1.6	122
Rhodes C	0.1	2.8	4.1	0.4	91.7	0.9	1,407
Southern C of Optometry	0.3	3.2	1.4	0.6	94.5	0.0	345
Southern C of Seventh-Day Adventists	0.3	3.8	6.0	4.6	82.1	3.3	1,534
State U & CC Sys of Tennessee							
Austin Peay State U	0.4	1.3	17.3	2.4	78.0	0.6	6,347
East Tennessee State U	0.3	0.5	3.2	0.3	94.6	1.0	11,590
Memphis State U	0.2	0.6	17.9	0.3	77.6	3.5	20,681
Middle Tennessee State U	0.2	0.5	8.1	0.5	88.5	2.1	14,865
Tennessee State U	0.1	2.8	62.1	0.5	34.5	0.0	7,393
Tennessee Tech U	0.1	0.9	3.4	0.4	92.5	2.6	8,140
Chattanooga State Tech CC	0.3	0.7	10.1	0.4	88.4	0.1	8,843
Cleveland State CC	0.2	0.6	4.5	0.5	94.4	0.0	3,315
Columbia State CC	0.1	0.5	6.5	0.4	92.1	0.3	3,402
Dyersburg State CC	0.6	0.2	12.0	0.3	87.0	0.0	1,993
Motlow State CC	0.3	0.4	5.5	0.5	92.5	0.8	2,782
Nashville State Tech Inst	0.2	1.5	14.8	0.6	82.7	0.3	5,974
Northeast State Tech CC	0.1	0.1	1.2	0.0	98.6	0.0	2,826
Pellissippi State Tech CC	0.2	1.0	4.4	0.5	93.3	0.6	5,983
Roane State CC	0.3	0.4	2.9	0.2	96.1	0.0	4,928
Shelby State CC	0.2	0.7	55.0	0.5	43.5	0.2	4,763
State Tech Inst Memphis	0.3	1.3	30.1	0.8	67.2	0.3	8,768
Volunteer State CC	0.4	0.5	5.7	0.4	93.0	0.0	4,160
Walters State CC	0.4	0.3	2.8	0.3	96.2	0.0	4,112
Tennessee Inst of Electronics	0.0	0.0	25.0	0.0	75.0	0.0	64
Tennessee Temple U	0.1	1.4	3.7	1.7	90.8	2.3	1,071
Tennessee Wesleyan C	0.2	0.7	7.6	1.0	85.0	5.6	605
Tomlinson C	0.0	0.0	6.8	6.4	77.1	9.6	249
Trevecca Nazarene C	0.1	0.4	21.1	0.5	77.4	0.5	1,795
Tusculum C	0.0	1.0	4.6	1.5	92.2	0.7	718
Union U	0.0	0.0	8.2	0.0	90.9	0.8	2,010
U of the South	0.0	0.7	1.0	0.3	95.5	2.5	1,164
U of Tennessee							
Chattanooga	0.3	1.7	9.4	0.8	86.0	1.7	7,725
Knoxville	0.2	1.2	5.0	0.5	89.9	3.3	26,055
Martin	0.2	0.6	14.4	0.3	81.0	3.6	5,363
Memphis	0.1	3.7	9.0	0.8	82.4	4.0	1,785
Vanderbilt U	0.2	2.6	4.7	0.9	85.4	6.2	9,161
William Jennings Bryan C	0.0	0.8	3.2	0.2	94.0	1.8	502

TEXAS

	American Indian	Asian	Black	Hispanic	White	Foreign	Total
Abilene Christian U	0.2	2.1	3.3	2.2	91.7	0.4	4,053
Alamo CC Dist							
Palo Alto C	0.3	0.8	5.0	54.9	38.3	0.7	4,087
St Philip's C	0.4	1.6	24.5	39.3	33.9	0.2	5,204
San Antonio C	0.4	1.8	5.2	43.9	47.7	0.9	20,083
Alvin CC	0.4	1.0	7.3	11.2	79.7	0.4	3,787
Amarillo C	0.6	1.7	3.6	10.2	83.7	0.2	5,949
Amber U	0.5	1.5	23.3	3.4	71.3	0.0	1,493
American Trades Inst	0.0	2.4	18.4	36.8	41.2	1.2	1,147
Angelina C	0.6	0.5	10.9	2.4	85.5	0.0	3,115
Angelo State U	0.3	0.8	4.3	10.9	82.2	1.5	6,298
Arlington Baptist C	0.0	2.0	6.6	10.2	79.1	2.0	196
Art Inst of Dallas	1.0	2.5	9.9	13.9	72.1	0.6	1,170

	American Indian	Asian	Black	Hispanic	White	Foreign	Total
Austin C	0.3%	2.8%	2.2%	4.8%	88.6%	1.3%	1,230
Austin CC	0.4	4.0	5.9	15.1	73.7	0.8	24,251
Austin Presbyterian Theological Seminary	0.0	0.8	7.0	4.5	85.6	2.1	243
Baptist Missionary Assn Theological Seminary	0.0	1.4	14.3	2.9	80.0	1.4	70
Bauder Fashion C	0.4	3.6	14.0	15.8	65.6	0.7	279
Baylor C of Dentistry	0.7	13.8	3.5	6.5	73.9	1.6	429
Baylor C of Medicine	0.0	14.8	1.7	5.1	67.5	10.9	999
Baylor U	0.3	3.3	3.0	3.7	88.0	1.6	12,014
Bee County C	0.4	0.8	2.6	50.0	45.9	0.3	2,250
Blinn C	0.2	0.9	7.0	7.5	82.1	2.3	6,849
Brazosport C	0.4	1.6	6.4	13.2	78.0	0.5	3,460
Central Texas C	0.5	3.7	19.0	10.3	64.4	2.0	4,815
Cisco JC	0.1	0.8	8.7	6.8	83.7	0.0	2,067
Clarendon C	0.4	0.0	3.3	5.1	91.0	0.2	974
C of the Mainland	0.5	1.2	13.5	11.2	72.2	1.4	3,540
Collin County CC	0.3	2.3	3.2	4.1	90.0	0.2	9,059
Commonwealth Inst of Funeral Service	0.0	0.0	10.3	2.6	73.1	14.1	78
Concordia Lutheran C	0.1	1.0	6.8	7.2	84.4	0.4	678
Cooke County C	0.5	0.7	3.2	3.8	90.3	1.5	3,084
Criswell C	0.0	2.4	6.5	4.3	77.7	9.0	368
Dallas Baptist U	0.7	1.6	19.1	4.3	68.9	5.5	2,333
Dallas Christian C	0.0	0.0	0.0	6.1	90.9	3.0	99
Dallas County CC Sys							
Brookhaven C	0.4	6.4	8.0	8.7	75.4	1.1	8,502
Cedar Valley C	0.2	0.7	38.7	4.7	55.6	0.1	3,147
Eastfield C	0.5	4.6	10.8	9.2	74.4	0.5	9,525
El Centro C	0.7	2.5	42.9	11.1	41.3	1.5	5,660
Mountain View C	0.5	3.1	19.5	17.6	58.9	0.4	6,239
North Lake C	0.6	4.3	7.8	8.0	78.8	0.5	6,283
Richland C	0.4	6.8	8.3	6.6	76.6	1.2	12,567
Dallas Theological Seminary .	0.2	6.0	8.0	1.3	75.3	9.2	1,216
Del Mar C	0.3	1.0	3.0	49.0	46.5	0.2	10,538
DeVry Inst of Tech	0.4	5.5	21.6	16.1	54.8	1.5	2,292
East Texas Baptist U	0.3	1.0	8.1	1.1	87.0	2.5	924
East Texas State U	0.5	0.5	9.6	2.7	82.6	4.0	7,840
East Texas State U Texarkana	0.3	0.2	8.0	0.4	90.5	0.6	1,257
El Paso CC	0.5	0.6	3.1	77.6	17.8	0.4	17,081
Episcopal Theological Seminary of the Southwest	1.4	0.0	1.4	2.9	85.7	8.6	70
Frank Phillips C	0.9	0.4	3.3	5.4	88.1	1.8	962
Galveston C	0.3	2.0	17.5	18.0	61.4	0.8	2,122
Grayson County C	1.1	0.6	4.3	1.7	92.2	0.0	3,146
Hardin-Simmons U	0.3	0.5	3.9	6.2	88.2	0.9	1,930
Hill C	0.8	0.5	4.9	7.2	86.6	0.1	1,634
Houston Baptist U	0.1	12.8	8.1	8.9	68.0	2.1	2,255
Houston CC Sys	0.3	8.0	21.3	14.6	55.2	0.7	36,437
Houston Graduate Sch of Theology	0.0	23.4	39.0	1.9	35.7	0.0	154
Howard County JC Dist	0.2	1.2	4.3	18.2	75.7	0.4	2,273
Howard Payne U	0.2	0.3	6.1	7.8	85.5	0.1	1,354
Huston-Tillotson C	0.0	2.2	83.2	3.8	2.0	8.8	714
Incarnate Word C	0.4	0.9	6.5	43.5	47.1	1.6	2,555
Inst for Christian Studies	0.0	0.0	10.3	5.2	77.6	6.9	58

TEXAS, cont.

	American Indian	Asian	Black	Hispanic	White	Foreign	Total
ITT Tech Inst Arlington	0.3%	2.2%	12.0%	29.1%	56.0%	0.3%	357
ITT Tech Inst Houston	0.3	5.3	16.2	31.0	45.2	2.0	606
Jacksonville C	0.4	1.5	10.7	1.5	73.9	11.9	261
Jarvis Christian C	0.0	0.0	98.0	0.3	1.7	0.0	598
Kilgore C	0.4	0.4	10.7	1.2	87.1	0.1	4,443
Lamar U							
Beaumont	0.3	1.9	16.9	3.0	75.4	2.5	11,489
Orange	0.7	0.2	8.1	1.8	88.7	0.5	1,282
Port Arthur	0.8	1.8	24.1	5.6	67.6	0.2	2,053
Laredo JC	0.0	0.3	0.1	91.1	5.4	3.0	5,123
Lee C	0.3	0.8	14.4	11.6	72.7	0.2	5,398
LeTourneau U	0.3	0.7	2.6	1.2	90.3	4.9	1,015
Lon Morris C	0.6	0.3	10.0	4.7	68.4	15.9	320
Lubbock Christian U	0.3	0.8	3.2	6.4	86.2	3.2	1,036
McLennan CC	0.2	0.9	12.7	6.8	79.1	0.4	5,614
McMurry U	0.2	0.8	8.0	8.4	81.2	1.4	1,631
Midland C	0.1	0.9	5.5	14.4	78.4	0.6	3,992
Midwestern State U	0.3	1.6	4.5	4.6	87.5	1.4	5,508
Miss Wades Fashion Merchandising C	0.9	2.5	29.6	10.9	54.5	1.6	321
Navarro C	0.0	3.0	16.6	5.8	73.6	1.0	2,827
North Harris Montgomery CC Dist	0.5	3.5	6.2	9.0	80.4	0.5	15,653
Northeast Texas CC	0.3	0.0	8.8	0.9	89.9	0.1	1,859
Northwood Inst	0.0	2.9	7.5	9.4	76.6	3.6	308
Oblate Sch of Theology	0.0	2.5	7.6	9.6	76.4	3.8	157
Odessa C	0.3	1.2	5.0	23.0	70.3	0.2	5,013
Our Lady of Lake U	0.3	0.8	6.4	50.4	41.5	0.7	2,689
Panola C	0.3	0.3	14.0	1.0	84.3	0.1	1,562
Paris JC	1.4	0.7	9.4	1.3	85.6	1.5	2,325
Parker C of Chiropractic	2.2	1.7	1.1	4.1	87.8	3.1	638
Ranger JC	0.4	0.3	28.1	9.0	62.3	0.0	726
Rice U	0.1	5.2	3.7	4.1	75.8	11.1	4,266
Saint Edward's U	0.4	1.7	4.8	22.2	65.9	5.1	3,081
Saint Mary's U	0.2	2.5	3.7	43.8	49.0	0.8	4,045
Sam Houston State U	0.2	0.6	10.0	5.9	82.0	1.3	12,753
San Jacinto C							
Central	0.2	2.9	4.6	12.2	76.5	3.6	9,424
North	0.5	1.9	14.3	16.1	66.2	1.0	3,778
South	0.3	5.4	6.7	11.5	75.2	1.0	5,273
Schreiner C	0.3	0.5	4.2	11.3	80.4	3.2	592
South Plains C	0.4	0.6	6.2	19.8	72.4	0.5	5,142
South Texas C of Law	0.2	2.7	2.5	3.9	90.7	0.0	1,363
Southern Methodist U	0.4	4.1	3.9	4.9	82.5	4.2	8,798
Southwest Inst of Merchandising and Design	0.0	0.4	2.2	68.5	24.0	5.0	279
Southwest Texas JC	0.4	2.6	10.0	19.9	66.3	0.7	2,653
Southwest Texas State U	0.3	1.1	5.2	14.3	78.1	1.0	20,940
Southwestern Adventist C	0.8	2.6	8.9	12.0	70.0	5.6	797
Southwestern Assemblies of God C	0.9	0.6	1.7	8.3	87.8	0.7	686
Southwestern Christian C	0.0	0.0	87.1	0.0	0.4	12.4	225
Southwestern U	0.3	3.4	3.0	8.6	84.0	0.7	1,208
Stephen F Austin State U	0.2	0.6	4.9	2.6	91.5	0.2	12,815
Sul Ross State U	0.2	0.2	3.1	38.7	56.9	0.9	2,265
Tarrant County JC Dist	0.4	2.4	8.1	7.2	81.5	0.4	28,161
Temple JC	0.2	0.8	9.4	9.7	79.4	0.4	2,269

	American Indian	Asian	Black	Hispanic	White	Foreign	Total
Texarkana C	0.0%	0.0%	10.3%	0.3%	89.3%	0.1%	3,894
Texas A&M U Sys							
Corpus Christi State U	0.4	1.1	1.9	32.3	63.9	0.3	3,801
Laredo State U	0.2	0.2	0.9	83.2	9.9	5.6	1,273
Prairie View A&M U	0.0	0.7	83.8	1.0	8.9	5.5	4,990
Tarleton State U	0.2	0.2	2.5	3.1	93.7	0.4	6,250
Texas A&I U	0.3	2.0	3.3	58.9	32.5	3.1	6,014
Texas A&M U	0.2	2.8	2.9	7.5	80.6	6.0	41,171
Texas A&M U Galveston	0.7	1.4	1.3	6.4	89.2	1.0	1,075
Texas Chiropractic C	0.3	5.1	3.9	4.8	83.2	2.7	334
Texas Christian U	0.3	1.3	3.7	3.7	88.1	2.8	6,458
Texas C	0.0	0.0	95.4	0.0	0.4	4.2	478
Texas C of Osteopathic Medicine	0.3	12.9	1.1	7.8	78.0	0.0	372
Texas Lutheran C	0.2	1.0	5.1	10.0	81.8	2.0	1,264
Texas Southern U	0.0	1.1	77.6	3.9	3.3	14.2	9,427
Texas Southmost C	0.2	0.3	0.2	87.5	10.8	1.0	5,635
Texas State Tech C Sys							
Amarillo	0.5	2.6	5.2	9.6	82.2	0.0	657
Harlingen	0.0	0.1	0.3	87.5	11.7	0.3	2,891
Sweetwater	0.0	0.2	4.1	20.0	75.7	0.0	806
Waco	0.1	0.7	8.1	9.6	81.0	0.6	3,803
Texas Tech U							
Main campus	0.2	1.3	2.8	7.6	84.8	3.2	25,363
Health Science Center	0.6	6.3	1.9	7.5	81.7	2.0	889
Texas Wesleyan U	0.3	0.1	8.2	5.3	81.1	5.0	1,429
Texas Woman's U	0.3	1.7	12.7	6.8	76.3	2.1	9,850
Trinity U	0.6	4.9	1.6	9.5	82.4	1.1	2,536
Trinity Valley CC	0.4	0.4	13.0	3.9	81.7	0.7	4,275
Tyler JC	0.4	0.4	15.1	1.7	81.0	1.4	7,950
U of Central Texas	0.9	3.5	22.8	7.1	62.5	3.2	539
U of Dallas	0.5	4.7	3.3	6.1	73.1	12.3	3,009
U of Houston							
U Park	0.5	8.9	8.0	9.3	67.2	6.2	33,115
Clear Lake	0.2	4.5	3.8	6.4	82.4	2.7	7,562
Downtown	0.2	11.9	23.4	23.5	37.8	3.2	7,621
Victoria	0.3	0.3	2.1	11.3	85.7	0.3	1,164
U of Mary Hardin-Baylor	0.5	1.4	6.8	10.0	77.2	4.1	1,808
U of North Texas	0.3	1.5	6.3	4.3	82.9	4.7	27,160
U of Saint Thomas	0.5	5.3	6.2	16.1	66.0	5.9	1,907
U of Texas Sys							
Arlington	0.5	7.7	7.1	5.8	74.1	4.9	24,782
Austin	0.2	6.3	3.7	10.8	71.2	7.8	49,617
Brownsville	0.1	0.4	1.0	77.0	21.1	0.3	1,448
Dallas	0.3	3.5	8.1	14.5	69.2	4.5	8,558
El Paso	0.3	1.3	3.0	57.5	30.4	7.4	16,524
San Antonio	0.2	2.7	3.3	30.3	62.6	1.0	15,489
Tyler	0.3	0.7	6.4	1.3	89.2	2.1	3,725
Health Science Center Houston	0.4	11.4	6.0	9.3	67.1	5.7	3,016
Health Science Center San Antonio	0.3	7.6	3.2	17.2	69.0	2.7	2,456
Medical Branch Galveston	0.6	9.3	6.8	8.3	70.9	4.0	1,800
Pan American	0.1	0.3	0.8	84.2	14.0	0.5	12,337
Permian Basin	0.1	0.6	2.5	13.0	82.0	1.8	2,041
Southwestern Medical Center Dallas	0.2	8.3	4.4	6.3	76.1	4.6	1,529

TEXAS, cont.

	American Indian	Asian	Black	Hispanic	White	Foreign	Total
Vernon Regional JC	1.0%	1.7%	9.0%	6.0%	82.3%	0.0%	1,823
Victoria C	0.4	0.8	4.1	21.4	73.1	0.2	3,328
Wayland Baptist U	0.5	1.5	8.6	14.7	74.7	0.0	2,081
Weatherford C	0.3	0.2	2.5	3.2	91.7	2.1	2,192
West Texas State U	0.4	1.1	3.0	7.6	85.2	2.6	6,193
Western Texas C	0.3	0.1	6.3	11.9	80.8	0.6	1,060
Wharton County JC	0.1	1.6	9.9	16.2	71.9	0.3	2,963
Wiley C	0.0	0.0	96.8	0.2	0.9	2.2	463

UTAH

Brigham Young U	0.4	0.6	0.1	0.4	93.8	4.7	31,662
ITT Tech Inst	1.3	3.6	1.3	7.4	86.6	0.0	476
Latter-Day Saints Business C	0.9	2.0	0.0	2.6	85.7	8.9	700
Stevens-Henager C of Business Ogden	0.5	1.1	5.4	7.0	86.0	0.0	186
Stevens-Henager C of Business Provo	1.4	2.7	0.0	4.1	91.8	0.0	146
Utah Higher Education Sys							
U of Utah	0.7	3.0	0.7	2.5	87.9	5.2	24,922
Southern Utah U	1.9	0.6	0.6	0.9	95.8	0.1	4,003
Utah State U	0.7	1.1	0.6	1.1	89.6	6.9	15,155
Weber State U	0.6	2.0	1.1	2.2	91.6	2.4	13,449
C of Eastern Utah	14.0	0.9	0.6	3.9	79.8	0.8	2,956
Dixie C	1.8	2.0	1.0	1.0	93.9	0.4	2,528
Salt Lake CC	1.1	4.2	0.6	3.6	90.5	0.1	13,344
Snow C	1.0	1.6	0.6	1.0	84.3	11.5	1,872
Utah Valley CC	1.2	1.3	0.2	2.4	92.3	2.6	7,879
Westminster C of Salt Lake City	0.6	1.9	1.2	4.0	90.7	1.5	2,025

VERMONT

Bennington C	0.2	2.6	1.5	1.7	89.2	4.8	581
Burlington C	1.2	0.0	3.5	1.7	93.6	0.0	173
Champlain C	0.2	0.6	0.6	0.3	98.3	0.1	1,916
C of Saint Joseph	0.5	0.0	1.2	0.7	94.5	3.1	419
Goddard C	2.4	2.9	3.6	6.9	84.1	0.1	1,317
Green Mountain C	0.0	0.0	0.5	0.2	95.8	3.5	597
Landmark C	0.0	0.0	0.0	0.0	100.0	0.0	27
Marlboro C	0.0	1.0	0.0	0.7	95.5	2.7	291
Middlebury C	0.0	4.5	3.0	2.7	87.8	1.9	2,039
Norwich U	0.9	1.7	1.9	2.6	90.8	2.2	2,626
Saint Michael's C	0.0	0.3	1.1	0.3	92.3	6.0	2,577
Sch for International Training	0.1	2.8	1.7	0.9	87.1	7.3	750
Southern Vermont C	0.1	0.6	2.4	1.3	95.1	0.4	676
Sterling C	1.2	0.0	0.0	0.0	96.4	2.4	83
Trinity C	0.2	0.4	0.3	0.7	98.1	0.3	1,118
U of Vermont	0.2	2.7	0.8	1.2	93.3	1.7	11,076
Vermont State C's Sys							
Castleton State C	0.1	0.4	0.3	0.3	98.8	0.2	1,975
CC of Vermont	0.6	0.2	0.2	0.2	96.4	2.5	3,895
Johnson State C	0.1	0.4	0.4	0.2	97.7	1.2	1,680
Lyndon State C	0.4	0.5	0.2	0.1	97.8	0.8	1,344
Vermont Tech C	0.1	0.3	0.4	0.0	98.7	0.4	940

VIRGINIA

	American Indian	Asian	Black	Hispanic	White	Foreign	Total
Averett C	0.1%	2.5%	9.7%	1.0%	85.0%	1.7%	1,446
Bluefield C	0.2	1.7	2.9	0.2	94.6	0.4	523
Bridgewater C	0.0	0.5	1.7	0.4	94.6	2.8	1,001
Christendom C	0.0	0.0	0.0	0.0	97.2	2.8	176
Christopher Newport C	0.4	1.9	11.5	1.6	84.0	0.7	4,861
C of William and Mary	0.2	3.1	6.3	1.1	85.9	3.3	7,672
Richard Bland C	0.4	1.7	16.1	1.4	80.2	0.2	1,205
Commonwealth C							
Norfolk	0.0	0.7	66.1	0.5	32.6	0.0	576
Richmond	0.1	1.2	53.5	2.5	42.7	0.0	944
Virginia Beach	1.4	3.9	26.3	5.0	63.4	0.0	722
Community Hospital of Roanoke Valley C of Health Sciences	0.0	1.2	6.4	0.0	90.4	2.0	250
Eastern Mennonite C and Seminary	0.1	0.8	1.7	1.6	91.2	4.6	1,089
Eastern Virginia Medical Sch	0.0	16.4	6.4	1.7	75.6	0.0	483
ECPI Computer Inst Main campus	0.3	3.4	34.5	2.1	59.6	0.0	614
ECPI Computer Inst Capital Center	1.1	3.1	40.7	0.0	55.1	0.0	356
ECPI Computer Inst Roanoke Center	0.4	0.4	33.8	0.2	65.0	0.0	452
Emory and Henry C	0.2	0.2	1.9	0.1	97.2	0.4	844
Ferrum C	0.1	0.7	7.6	1.7	89.2	0.7	1,208
George Mason U	0.4	7.9	5.0	3.0	80.2	3.4	20,308
Hampden-Sydney C	0.0	0.9	1.5	0.7	96.7	0.2	956
Hollins C	0.0	0.7	2.7	0.9	94.6	1.1	1,137
Inst of Textile Tech	0.0	0.0	0.0	0.0	100.0	0.0	30
James Madison U	0.2	1.9	8.4	1.3	87.6	0.6	11,251
Liberty U	0.1	0.4	1.8	0.4	96.1	1.3	18,533
Longwood C	0.2	1.1	7.6	0.5	90.4	0.3	3,329
Lynchburg C	0.2	0.7	6.1	0.4	90.5	2.3	2,446
Mary Baldwin C	0.1	1.0	4.1	0.8	91.2	2.8	1,157
Mary Washington C	0.2	1.4	4.7	0.8	91.7	1.0	3,744
Marymount U	0.3	7.6	7.7	5.4	76.9	2.1	3,177
National Business C	0.0	0.1	59.1	0.0	40.6	0.2	1,264
Norfolk State U	0.2	0.5	83.3	0.4	14.4	1.2	8,008
Old Dominion U	0.6	3.8	10.8	1.2	80.6	2.9	16,729
Presbyterian Sch of Christian Education	0.0	2.5	12.6	0.0	70.6	14.3	119
Radford U	0.3	1.2	3.6	1.0	91.8	2.1	8,990
Randolph-Macon C	0.1	1.5	2.8	0.7	93.5	1.4	1,139
Randolph-Macon Woman's C	0.1	1.9	2.2	1.2	90.6	4.1	691
Roanoke C	0.1	1.0	1.0	0.5	97.1	0.3	1,668
Saint Paul's C	0.0	0.2	94.1	0.3	4.9	0.5	574
Shenandoah U	0.0	0.9	5.6	0.3	89.6	3.5	1,158
Southern Seminary C	0.4	0.4	4.7	0.0	89.1	5.4	257
Sweet Briar C	0.0	0.9	3.7	0.9	89.4	5.0	538
Union Theological Seminary	0.0	4.3	4.3	0.5	85.9	4.9	185
U of Richmond	0.2	1.1	4.1	0.7	93.3	0.5	4,859
U of Virginia Main campus	0.0	4.7	8.5	0.8	82.9	3.1	21,110
Clinch Valley	0.1[a]	0.5	2.1	0.5	96.6	0.3	1,528
Virginia Commonwealth U	0.4	3.3	13.6	1.1	80.0	1.6	21,764

VIRGINIA, cont.

	American Indian	Asian	Black	Hispanic	White	Foreign	Total
Virginia CC Sys							
Blue Ridge CC	0.2%	0.5%	2.7%	0.3%	96.2%	0.0%	2,740
Central Virginia CC	0.1	0.5	11.8	0.4	87.2	0.0	3,913
Dabney S Lancaster CC	0.1	0.2	5.7	0.0	93.8	0.1	1,606
Danville CC	0.2	0.2	21.9	0.2	77.5	0.0	3,321
Eastern Shore CC	0.2	0.4	24.9	0.7	73.9	0.0	555
Germanna CC	0.3	0.9	7.9	0.6	90.2	0.1	2,328
J Sargeant Reynolds CC	0.5	1.4	24.1	0.5	73.3	0.2	11,542
John Tyler CC	0.1	1.1	20.1	1.3	77.1	0.3	5,492
Lord Fairfax CC	0.1	0.6	3.4	0.4	95.5	0.0	2,599
Mountain Empire CC	0.0	0.1	1.3	0.0	98.5	0.1	2,824
New River CC	0.1	0.5	3.8	0.3	95.0	0.3	3,703
Northern Virginia CC	0.3	8.5	9.1	4.6	75.8	1.7	35,194
Patrick Henry CC	0.1	0.2	11.6	0.1	88.0	0.0	2,223
Paul D Camp CC	0.1	0.3	30.3	0.3	68.8	0.2	1,441
Piedmont Virginia CC	0.1	1.1	10.1	0.5	87.9	0.3	4,203
Rappahannock CC	0.3	0.7	15.4	0.5	83.2	0.0	1,828
Southside Virginia CC	0.1	0.2	34.5	0.2	64.8	0.1	2,922
Southwest Virginia CC	0.1	0.1	0.8	0.1	98.9	0.1	4,782
Thomas Nelson CC	0.3	2.5	23.3	1.2	72.6	0.2	7,740
Tidewater CC	0.4	4.8	12.8	1.5	80.1	0.4	17,726
Virginia Highlands CC	0.1	0.4	3.0	0.3	96.1	0.1	2,236
Virginia Western CC	0.1	1.0	6.8	0.3	91.6	0.2	6,975
Wytheville CC	0.1	0.2	3.0	0.0	96.8	0.0	1,988
Virginia Intermont C	0.2	0.4	1.4	0.0	94.3	3.7	562
Virginia Military Inst	0.1	3.2	6.7	1.2	86.7	2.1	1,350
Va Polytechnic Inst and State U	0.1	5.0	4.2	1.0	84.1	5.5	25,568
Virginia State U	0.1	0.3	90.7	0.5	7.8	0.6	3,988
Virginia Union U	0.1	0.1	98.2	0.0	1.1	0.6	1,298
Virginia Wesleyan C	0.3	2.7	5.2	1.5	90.0	0.4	1,390
Washington and Lee U	0.1	1.4	3.9	0.7	93.5	0.3	2,010

WASHINGTON

Antioch U Seattle	0.6	0.6	3.5	1.8	92.1	1.3	2,444
Bastyr C	1.5	3.0	4.6	4.1	71.1	15.7	197
Bellevue CC	0.4	5.3	1.5	1.5	90.8	0.6	9,471
Big Bend CC	1.0	1.9	0.5	7.2	81.2	8.2	1,753
Central Washington U	1.2	3.0	1.2	2.8	90.9	1.0	7,696
Centralia C	2.1	0.4	2.8	1.5	92.9	0.2	3,412
City U	1.0	6.4	5.0	2.1	80.9	4.6	3,440
Clark C	1.0	2.7	1.0	1.5	93.4	0.4	7,554
Cogswell C North	0.0	8.6	0.0	1.1	90.3	0.0	186
Columbia Basin C	0.6	2.1	1.1	5.4	90.7	0.1	5,845
Cornish C of the Arts	1.1	3.4	2.0	1.6	87.5	4.3	440
Eastern Washington U	1.8	1.8	1.8	2.4	87.5	4.7	8,402
Edmonds CC	1.4	4.0	3.1	1.5	89.2	0.9	7,202
Everett CC	3.3	3.6	0.8	1.8	90.3	0.3	6,048
Evergreen State C	2.3	3.7	2.5	2.1	89.5	0.0	3,339
Gonzaga U	1.0	3.4	0.8	1.9	88.0	4.9	3,830
Grays Harbor C	3.5	0.8	0.3	0.8	94.5	0.1	2,400
Green River CC	1.1	2.6	1.2	1.1	94.0	0.1	5,894
Griffin C	1.0	8.9	16.8	2.1	65.5	5.7	1,456
Heritage C	12.8	5.5	1.1	14.9	65.6	0.0	966
Highline CC	1.2	6.9	3.2	1.7	86.8	0.1	7,734
Lower Columbia C	1.2	1.4	0.4	1.4	95.6	0.1	3,407
Lutheran Bible Inst Seattle	0.0	2.7	0.7	0.0	87.8	8.8	148

	American Indian	Asian	Black	Hispanic	White	Foreign	Total
Northwest C of the Assemblies of God	1.3%	3.4%	0.7%	1.6%	90.5%	2.5%	681
Northwest Inst of Acupuncture and Oriental Medicine	3.1	0.0	0.0	2.0	94.9	0.0	98
Olympic C	1.7	5.8	2.5	2.1	87.8	0.1	6,003
Pacific Lutheran U	0.9	3.8	1.4	1.3	89.9	2.7	3,649
Peninsula C	3.9	2.0	2.2	1.2	90.1	0.7	2,716
Pierce C	1.4	5.3	10.0	4.2	78.9	0.3	8,502
Puget Sound Christian C	0.0	1.4	2.9	0.0	95.7	0.0	70
Saint Martin's C	0.4	5.5	4.8	2.3	85.8	1.2	1,072
Seattle CC Dist							
North Seattle CC	1.2	11.4	3.1	1.9	82.2	0.2	6,720
Seattle Central CC	1.6	15.3	13.3	2.8	66.9	0.2	6,159
Seattle CC South	1.7	15.0	7.4	2.4	73.1	0.4	5,118
Seattle Pacific U	0.5	4.2	0.9	1.1	89.7	3.7	3,421
Seattle U	0.7	8.9	2.4	1.3	77.9	8.8	4,633
Shoreline CC	1.1	8.6	1.4	1.7	86.9	0.4	6,421
Skagit Valley C	1.5	2.5	1.0	3.4	91.4	0.2	5,144
South Puget Sound CC	1.6	5.4	1.2	2.0	89.7	0.1	3,980
Tacoma CC	1.7	6.2	7.8	2.6	81.6	0.0	4,612
U of Puget Sound	0.5	5.2	1.6	1.5	90.4	0.7	4,250
U of Washington	1.1	14.0	3.2	2.3	74.5	5.0	33,854
Walla Walla C	0.3	4.2	1.5	3.6	84.9	5.6	1,566
Walla Walla CC	2.1	1.1	6.5	5.5	84.1	0.8	4,115
Washington State CC Dist 17							
Spokane CC	2.5	1.9	1.0	1.4	93.1	0.2	6,318
Spokane Falls CC	2.6	2.3	1.7	1.5	91.9	0.1	10,404
Washington State U	0.8	4.0	1.5	1.5	86.2	6.0	18,412
Wenatchee Valley C	3.8	1.3	0.6	2.0	92.1	0.2	2,492
Western Washington U	1.4	3.9	1.3	1.5	90.3	1.5	9,730
Whatcom CC	1.8	2.0	0.8	2.0	92.6	0.8	2,700
Whitman C	0.5	5.5	1.2	1.1	89.2	2.5	1,300
Whitworth C	0.5	2.0	1.0	1.2	93.5	1.8	1,759
Yakima Valley CC	4.0	1.1	1.0	11.1	82.7	0.2	4,075

WEST VIRGINIA

Alderson-Broaddus C	0.1	1.7	4.2	1.1	90.3	2.6	744
Appalachian Bible C	0.5	3.8	1.4	0.5	92.0	1.9	212
Beckley C	0.2	0.4	5.5	0.2	93.8	0.1	1,942
Bethany C	0.1	0.7	2.4	0.9	91.2	4.7	859
Davis & Elkins C	1.3	1.6	3.3	1.1	90.8	1.9	892
Huntington JC of Business	0.0	1.9	11.2	0.0	87.0	0.0	483
National Education Center							
National Inst of Tech	0.0	0.0	6.1	0.0	93.9	0.0	377
Ohio Valley C	0.0	0.5	2.9	0.0	94.6	2.0	205
Salem-Teikyo U	0.0	0.2	8.4	3.1	49.7	38.6	523
State C Sys of West Virginia							
Bluefield State C	0.2	0.3	7.0	0.2	91.9	0.5	2,702
Concord C	0.1	0.4	3.7	0.2	94.9	0.7	2,651
Fairmont State C	0.2	0.2	2.3	0.4	96.0	0.8	6,305
Glenville State C	0.0	1.2	2.1	0.2	96.2	0.2	2,238
Shepherd C	0.4	0.4	2.2	0.6	96.5	0.0	3,694
West Liberty State C	0.0	0.2	1.5	0.3	97.3	0.8	2,386
West Virginia Inst of Tech	0.1	0.5	5.5	0.4	90.5	3.0	2,898
West Virginia State C	0.2	0.4	12.2	0.3	86.6	0.4	4,834
Southern West Virginia CC	0.1	0.3	1.8	0.1	97.6	0.0	2,911

W.VA., cont.	American Indian	Asian	Black	Hispanic	White	Foreign	Total
State C Sys of West Virginia, cont.							
West Virginia Northern CC	0.1%	0.6%	2.8%	0.3%	95.9%	0.2%	2,884
U of Charleston	0.2	0.3	2.9	0.5	93.8	2.3	1,420
U of West Virginia Sys							
Marshall U	0.1	0.6	3.3	0.3	94.9	0.8	12,407
C of Graduate Studies	0.3	0.9	3.9	0.4	94.2	0.3	2,153
West Virginia U	0.1	1.6	2.8	0.6	90.6	4.4	20,854
Potomac State C	0.7	0.1	9.1	0.6	89.2	0.3	1,348
WVa U Parkersburg	0.2	0.6	0.6	0.2	98.4	0.0	3,603
West Virginia Sch of Osteopathic Medicine	0.4	3.3	1.7	2.1	92.5	0.0	240
West Virginia Wesleyan C	0.1	1.2	4.7	0.4	90.5	3.1	1,629
Wheeling Jesuit C	0.0	0.7	1.1	0.4	94.7	3.0	1,396

WISCONSIN

	American Indian	Asian	Black	Hispanic	White	Foreign	Total
Alverno C	0.6	0.9	13.3	3.9	80.9	0.5	2,414
Beloit C	0.0	3.7	2.8	0.9	86.7	5.9	1,169
Blackhawk Tech C	0.3	0.2	1.7	0.3	97.6	0.0	2,151
Cardinal Stritch C	0.4	1.0	5.2	0.8	92.6	0.0	3,649
Carroll C	0.1	1.3	2.6	1.8	93.4	0.9	2,196
Carthage C	0.2	1.0	6.5	1.9	90.4	0.1	1,851
Chippewa Valley Tech C	0.4	0.9	0.1	0.1	98.5	0.0	3,362
Concordia U	0.7	0.9	3.8	0.3	90.4	3.8	1,758
Edgewood C	0.1	2.3	1.6	1.0	95.0	0.0	1,393
Fox Valley Tech C	0.5	0.7	0.5	0.5	97.4	0.4	3,909
Gateway Tech C	0.4	0.8	11.3	8.4	79.1	0.0	9,306
Lakeland C	0.3	1.0	4.5	1.3	92.4	0.5	1,994
Lakeshore Tech C	0.1	1.6	0.4	0.5	97.4	0.0	2,749
Lawrence U	0.2	1.7	2.6	1.1	87.7	6.7	1,237
Madison Area Tech C	0.5	1.2	2.4	1.3	94.6	0.1	12,410
Madison Business C	0.4	0.4	1.1	0.0	94.9	3.3	272
Maranatha Baptist Bible C	0.0	0.7	2.0	1.8	94.5	1.1	457
Marian C of Fond Du Lac	0.4	1.9	2.5	1.0	94.1	0.1	1,669
Marquette U	0.4	3.7	3.1	3.2	85.7	4.0	11,729
Medical C of Wisconsin	0.2	12.2	1.6	2.6	79.7	3.7	1,005
Mid-State Tech C	0.7	0.6	0.1	0.3	98.4	0.0	2,406
Milwaukee Area Tech C	0.9	2.0	18.0	3.1	75.9	0.1	21,600
Milwaukee Inst of Art and Design	0.6	1.7	3.5	3.9	89.4	0.9	462
Milwaukee Sch of Engineering	0.2	2.1	2.5	1.4	92.6	1.2	3,160
Moraine Park Tech C	0.5	0.9	0.3	0.5	97.8	0.0	5,553
Mount Mary C	0.2	1.0	3.7	1.8	92.2	1.1	1,451
Mount Senario C	9.5	4.0	3.4	1.1	80.1	1.9	1,059
Nicolet Area Tech C	7.4	0.7	0.1	0.5	91.3	0.0	1,342
Northcentral Tech C	1.5	5.1	0.0	0.1	92.1	1.2	4,553
Northeast Wisconsin Tech C	2.0	1.1	0.1	0.4	96.4	0.0	6,429
Northland C	6.0	1.3	0.8	1.9	88.2	1.9	756
Northwestern C	0.0	0.0	0.0	0.0	99.0	1.0	206
Ripon C	0.5	1.4	0.8	1.4	92.3	3.6	854
Sacred Heart Sch of Theology	0.0	0.6	0.6	2.8	90.5	5.6	179
Saint Norbert C	1.2	0.6	0.2	0.1	97.2	0.6	1,875
Silver Lake C	0.5	0.7	0.1	1.0	97.5	0.2	830
Southwest Wisconsin Tech C	0.7	1.3	5.6	1.9	90.4	0.2	1,701
Stratton C	0.2	0.3	1.0	0.2	95.7	2.6	580

	American Indian	Asian	Black	Hispanic	White	Foreign	Total
U of Wisconsin							
Madison	0.5%	3.0%	1.8%	1.6%	85.4%	7.7%	43,209
Eau Claire	0.4	0.8	0.5	0.4	96.3	1.5	10,941
Green Bay	2.5	0.8	0.9	0.6	93.9	1.3	5,137
La Crosse	0.4	0.8	0.9	0.5	96.5	0.9	9,118
Milwaukee	0.7	2.0	6.2	2.3	86.2	2.6	26,020
Oshkosh	0.6	1.2	1.2	0.6	95.7	0.7	11,740
Parkside	0.3	1.1	3.8	2.6	91.4	0.7	5,308
Platteville	0.4	1.2	0.8	0.4	96.2	1.0	5,465
River Falls	0.4	1.0	1.2	0.6	95.5	1.3	5,196
Stevens Point	1.0	0.6	0.5	0.5	94.9	2.4	9,433
Stout	0.5	1.9	0.8	0.5	94.7	1.7	7,629
Superior	1.7	0.9	0.8	0.4	95.1	1.2	2,675
Whitewater	0.2	0.9	3.0	1.2	93.3	1.4	10,820
Centers	0.4	0.8	1.1	0.8	96.0	0.8	11,654
Viterbo C	0.4	1.2	0.7	0.4	96.2	1.0	1,218
Waukesha County Tech C	0.3	0.4	0.3	1.6	97.4	0.0	4,975
Western Wisconsin Tech C	0.2	1.0	0.2	0.1	98.4	0.0	3,474
Wisconsin Indianhead Tech C	2.2	0.4	0.2	0.6	96.6	0.0	3,264
Wisconsin Lutheran C	0.0	0.0	3.2	0.4	95.8	0.7	283
Wisconsin Sch of Electronics	1.0	0.0	1.7	1.0	94.6	1.7	298

WYOMING

Casper C	0.5	0.2	0.6	0.9	97.3	0.5	4,023
Central Wyoming C	12.8	0.8	0.9	2.7	81.3	1.5	1,457
Eastern Wyoming C	0.7	0.3	0.5	4.6	93.7	0.2	1,353
Laramie County CC	0.6	0.8	2.1	4.6	91.8	0.0	4,362
Northern Wyoming CC Dist	1.2	0.3	0.3	1.9	95.8	0.4	2,418
Northwest C	0.8	0.2	0.2	2.0	95.7	1.0	2,001
Phillips C Tech Inst	1.7	0.6	1.3	3.0	92.9	0.6	703
U of Wyoming	1.1	0.7	0.8	2.7	90.9	3.7	12,517
Western Wyoming CC	0.4	0.9	0.9	4.6	92.8	0.4	2,492

The Chronicle of Higher Education

EDITOR Corbin Gwaltney

MANAGING EDITOR Malcolm G. Scully **ASSOCIATE EDITOR** Edward R. Weidlein

ALMANAC EDITOR Jean Evangelauf

ASSOCIATE MANAGING EDITORS Cheryl M. Fields (Point of View & Opinion), Paul Desruisseaux (International), Scott Jaschik (National)
NEWS EDITOR Robin Wilson
SENIOR EDITORS Goldie Blumenstyk (Business & Philanthropy), Mary Crystal Cage (Students), Thomas J. DeLoughry (Information Technology), Rose Engelland (Photography), Jean Evangelauf (Statistics), Catherine J. Hosley (Editorial Operations), Douglas Lederman (Athletics), Liz McMillen (Scholarship), Carolyn J. Mooney (Personal & Professional), Peter H. Stafford (Art Director), Edith U. Taylor (Gazette)
SENIOR WRITERS Lawrence Biemiller, Ellen K. Coughlin, Robert L. Jacobson, Kim A. McDonald, Beverly T. Watkins
ASSOCIATE SENIOR EDITOR Gail Lewin (Section 2)
COPY EDITOR Brian Manning
ASSISTANT EDITORS Nina C. Ayoub, Debra E. Blum, Stephen Burd, Michele N-K Collison, Colleen Cordes, Courtney Leatherman, Kit Lively, Denise K. Magner, Joye Mercer, Julie L. Nicklin, Frances H. Oxholm, Jean Rosenblatt, Christopher Shea, Lora Thompson, David L. Wheeler, David L. Wilson, Jim Zook
ASSISTANT ART DIRECTOR Ellen Verdon
EDITORIAL ASSISTANTS Michael R. Snyder, Esther S. Washington, Anne Millar Wiebe
ART ASSISTANTS Carl T. Benson, Scott Seymour
STUDENT ASSISTANTS Salma Abdelnour, Kristin Lieb, Tonya Whitfield

PRODUCTION AND COMPUTER DIRECTOR Gerard A. Lindgren
MANAGERS Cynthia J. Kennedy, Steve Smith
COMPUTER SYSTEMS MANAGER Timothy A. Steele
PRODUCTION ASSOCIATES Pamela Barton, Donna L. Edenhart, Brenda Hulme, Carol E. King, Pegeen McGlathery, David N. Miller, Charles E. Short

EDITORIAL AND BUSINESS OFFICES 1255 Twenty-Third Street, N.W., Washington, D.C. 20037, (202) 466-1000